5/04

Asian/Oceanian Historical Dictionaries
Edited by Jon Woronoff

Historical Dictionary of Cambodia

Justin Corfield and Laura Summers

Asian/Oceanian Historical Dictionaries,
No. 43

The Scarecrow Press, Inc.
Lanham, Maryland, and Oxford
2003

SCARECROW PRESS, INC.

Published in the United States of America
by Scarecrow Press, Inc.
A Member of the Rowman & Littlefield Publishing Group
4720 Boston Way, Lanham, Maryland 20706
www.scarecrowpress.com

PO Box 317
Oxford
OX2 9RU, UK

British Library Cataloguing in Publication Information Available

Library of Congress Cataloging-in-Publication Data

Corfield, Justin J.
  Historical dictionary of Cambodia / Justin Corfield and Laura Summers.
     p. cm. — (Asian/Oceanian historical dictionaries ; no. 43)
  Includes bibliographical references.
  ISBN 0-8108-4524-5 (hardcover : alk. paper)
  1. Cambodia—History—Dictionaries. I. Summers, Laura. II. Title. III. Series.
  DS554.25 .C67 2003
  959.6'003—dc21

                                                              2002012023

⊖™ The paper used in this publication meets the minimum requirements of
American National Standard for Information Sciences—Permanence of
Paper for Printed Library Materials, ANSI/NISO Z39.48-1992.
Manufactured in the United States of America.

Contents

CAMBODIA: Provinces and Muncipalities

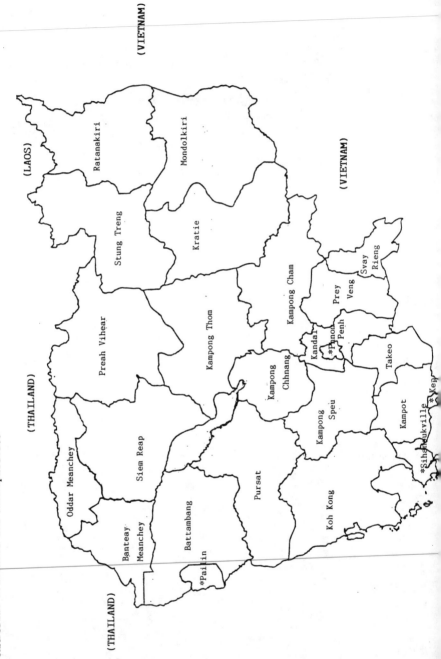

Editor's Foreword

Few people have endured more pain and hardship over past generations than the Cambodians. War, colonization, civil war, invasion, foreign domination, starvation, even genocide, they have seen it all. Worse, while some of the suffering was inflicted by outsiders, the worst resulted from policies ruthlessly imposed and pursued by their own leaders. It is hard to believe that this tragedy is over. Indeed, some fear the present democratic regime may just be an interlude. Whatever the future may bring, this is a better time than most to look back on Cambodia's history, recent and more ancient, in search of signposts as well as lessons.

This task, which can finally be undertaken with a modicum of hope and optimism, is greatly facilitated by the *Historical Dictionary of Cambodia*. It carefully surveys the facts and events, reaching far back into the past. It shows where the Cambodian people stand today, what their possible assets are (and what liabilities have been removed or at least reduced). It describes the political, economic and social situation, presents the cast of characters responsible for past successes and damage and, conceivably, a future recovery, and gives us a feel for what could be achieved now that the nightmare may be over. This is done in a wealth of concise but informative entries on persons, places, events and institutions, a helpful chronology, useful appendices and, for those who want to know more, a comprehensive bibliography.

This historical dictionary is one of the last in the Asian series, for fairly obvious reasons. Events have come fast and thick, political allegiances have frequently shifted, society has been in constant turmoil and even elementary data have been hard to find given the underground existence of many significant persons and the uncertain disappearance of countless others. Under such circumstances, readers should be very grateful for the sustained efforts of two dedicated authors, Justin Corfield and Laura Summers.

Jon Woronoff
Series Editor

Acknowledgments

This book would not have been possible without the timely assistance and support of many friends and colleagues around the world. We would like to record our personal thanks to David Ashley, David Chandler, Chhang Song, Chhlor Bounnie, Robin Corfield, Douc Rasy, Engly Piphâl, Tim Hall, Steve Heder, Heng Ham Kheng, In Thaddee, Kao Kim Hourn, Keo Ann, Khau Menghean, Kor Bun Heng, Lao Mong Hay, Jefferson Lee, Nhek Bun Chhay, Oeur Hunly, Ong Thong Hoeung, Oum Mannorine, Jan Ovesen, Grant Peck, Pok Nanda, Sam Rainsy, Sok Pirun, Eliza Rooney, Son Sann, Jay Scarborough, Jon Loren Summers, Suon Kaset, Tioulong Saumara, Ing-Britt Trankell, Truong Mealy and Ung Bun Ang. We would also like to thank Norman Horrocks, Debra Schepp, Marianne Stone and Jon Woronoff of Scarecrow Press for their patience and care in scrutinizing our long drafts and to acknowledge a general debt of gratitude to other scholars, including Khing Hoc Dy, Ben Kiernan, Raoul Marc Jennar, Phouk Chhay, Philippe Preschez and Michael Vickery for their studies of Cambodia's elites.

Justin Corfield and Laura Summers
August 2002

Reader's Note

Names of places have been standardized to those in common usage by recent Cambodian governments although the name "Kampong" has been used instead of "Kompong." Those of people prominent before 1975 follow the spellings used in the *Bulletin Administratif du Cambodge, Journal Officiel du Cambodge* and *Journal Officiel du République Khmère*. For others, that which is most commonly used in official documents has been preferred.

For readers seeking more information about a particular topic, bold type face has been used for cross references.

For many of the people included in this dictionary it has been hard to find exact dates of birth and death. Most Cambodians were not registered at birth with the French authorities, the issuing of birth certificates only becoming widespread after independence. Most of the dates cited come from published biographical information, family records or from my index of death notices in the Cambodian press from 1947-1975. Other dates have come from various school and university records, and overseas marriage and death certificates, where applicable.

List of Acronyms and Abbreviations

ACLEDA	Association of Cambodian Local Economic Development Agencies.
ADB	Asian Development Bank.
AGEK	Assemblée Générale des Étudiants Khmers.
AGKE	Association Générale des Khmers à l'étranger.
AKP	Agence Khmère de Presse.
ANKI	National Army for an Independent Kampuchea.
ANS	Armée Nationale Sihanoukienne.
ARVN	Army of the Republic of Vietnam.
ASEAN	Association of Southeast Asian Nations.
BGI	Brasseries et Glacière de l'Indochine.
BLDP	Buddhist Liberal Democratic Party.
BNC	Banque Nationale du Cambodge.
CC	Constitutional Council.
CCC	Cooperation Committee for Cambodia.
CDC	Cambodian Development Council.
CEDOREK	Centre de Documentation et de Recherche sur la Civilisation Khmère.
CFRC	Chemins de Fer Royaux du Cambodge.
CGDK	Coalition Government of Democratic Kampuchea.
CIA	U.S. Central Intelligence Agency.
COSVN	Central Office of South Vietnam.
CPAF	Cambodian People's Armed Forces.
CPK	Communist Party of Kampuchea.
CPP	Cambodian People's Party.
DK	Democratic Kampuchea.

EDC	Electricité du Cambodge.
EFEO	École Française d'Extrême-Orient (French Far Eastern School).
FANK	Forces Armées Nationales Khmères (Khmer National Armed Forces).
FAPLN	Forces Armées Populaires de Libération Nationale.
FARK	Forces Armées Royales Khmères (Royal Cambodian Armed Forces).
FTUWKC	Free Trade Union of Workers of the Kingdom of Cambodia.
FUNCINPEC	Front Uni National Pour Un Cambodge Indépendant, Neutre, Pacifique et Coopératif (National United Front for an Independent, Neutral, Peaceful and Cooperative Cambodia).
FUNK	National United Front of Kampuchea.
GRUNK	Gouvernement Royal d'Union Nationale du Kampuchea (Royal Government of National Union of Kampuchea).
ICORC	International Committee for the Reconstruction of Cambodia.
ICP	Indochina Communist Party.
ICSC	International Commission for Supervision and Control.
JSRK	Jeunesse Socialiste Royale Khmère (Royal Khmer Socialist Youth).
KKK	Khmer of Kampuchea Krom.
KNP	Khmer Nation Party.
KPNLAF	Khmer People's National Liberation Armed Forces.
KPNLF	Khmer People's National Liberation Front.
KPRP	Khmer People's Revolutionary Party (1951-1960).
LDP	Liberal Democratic Party.
MAC	Manufacture de Cigarettes du Cambodge.
MAGETAT	Magasin d'État.
MOLINAKA	Mouvement de Liberation Nationale du Kampuchea (National Movement for the Liberation of Kampuchea).
NADK	National Army of Democratic Kampuchea.
NBC	National Bank of Cambodia.
NCR	Non-Communist Resistance.

NFL	National Front for the Liberation of South Vietnam.
NGO	Non-Government Organization.
OFENET	Office des Entreprises d'État (State Enterprises Bureau).
OROC	Office Royal de Coopération.
PDK	Party of Democratic Kampuchea.
PERMICO	Permanent Military Co-ordinating Committee (of the KPNLAF).
PGUNUWBK	Provisional Government of National Union and Well-Being of Kampuchea.
PRK	People's Republic of Kampuchea.
PRPK	People's Revolutionary Party of Kampuchea (1981-1991).
PSR	Socio-Republican Party.
RAC	Royal Air Cambodge.
RCAF	Royal Cambodian Armed Forces.
RVN	Republic of Vietnam (South Vietnam).
SANGKUM	Sangkum Reastr Niyum (Popular Socialist Community).
SCM	Supreme Council of the Magistry.
SEATO	Southeast Asia Treaty Organization.
SKD	Société Khmère des Distilleries.
SNC	Supreme National Council.
SOC	State of Cambodia.
SONAPNEU	Société Nationale de Pneumatiques.
SONAPRIM	Société Nationale des Produits Importés.
SONATRAC	Société Nationale de Tracteurs.
SONEXIM	Société Nationale d'Exportation et d'Importation.
SRP	Sam Rainsy Party.
UFCDK	United Front for National Construction and Defense of Kampuchea.
UFNSK	United Front for the National Salvation of Kampuchea.
UIF	United Issarak Front.
UNDP	United Nations Development Program.
UNHCR	United Nations High Commissioner for Refugees.
UNTAC	United Nations Transitional Authority in Cambodia.
WFP	World Food Program.
WPK	Workers' Party of Kampuchea.

Chronology

1512-15	Tomé Pires writes *Suma Oriental*, first European visitor's account.
1528	Foundation of the future city of Phnom Penh.
1556	Gaspar da Cruz writes of his stay in the town of Lovek.
1623	King Chey Chettha II, whose queen is Vietnamese, allows the imperial court in Hué to establish a customs house in the small town of Prey Nokor (which later becomes Saigon).
1651-56	British East India Company maintains factory in Oudong.
1749	Khmer King cedes lower Mekong lands to the Vietnamese crown.
1772	Phnom Penh burned to the ground by an army from Siam.
1779	The King of Siam puts Ang Eng, aged seven, on the Khmer throne.
1811-12	War between competing Siamese and Vietnamese armies.
1835-40	Vietnam occupies the Kingdom.
1848	Coronation of Ang Duong who soon makes contact with France.
1860	King Ang Duong dies (19 October); accession of King Norodom.
1863	Norodom agrees to creation of a French Protectorate (11 August).
1865	King Norodom moves capital from Oudong to Phnom Penh.
1876	Prince Si Votha leads a series of revolts against the French.
1898	Thiounn becomes minister of the Palace, holding this position until 1941.
1900	Prince Yukanthor, son of King Norodom, criticizes French colonial rule; goes to France and later into exile.
1904	Death of King Norodom (24 April); accession of Sisowath.
1911	Foundation of Collège Sisowath.
1916	Peasants protest against high taxes imposed during World War I.
1920	Establishment of Albert Sarraut Museum which later becomes the National Museum of Cambodia.
1923	André Malraux visits and is arrested for stealing sculptures.
1925	Murder of French *résident*, Félix Bardez (18 April).
1927	Death of King Sisowath (9 August); accession of his son Sisowath Monivong.
1930	Creation of the Indochina Communist Party (3 February).
1936	Publication of *Nagaravatta*, the first Khmer-language newspaper; Collège Sisowath becomes Lycée Sisowath, the first school in

the protectorate to provide a full secondary education.

1937   Foundation of the Alumni Association of Lycée Sisowath.

1939   World War II begins. France declares war on Germany (3 September).

1940   Germany occupies France (June); Vichy agrees to Japanese occupation of Indochina (September); Thailand attacks Cambodia (December).

1941   Death of King Sisowath Monivong (23 April); Prince Sihanouk becomes King (25 April); coronation of Sihanouk (28 October). Japanese soldiers arrive in Phnom Penh.

1942   The Umbrella Revolt, demonstrations against the French (20 July); Son Ngoc Thanh flees to Japan, other organizers jailed.

1943   French reveal plan to romanize the Khmer alphabet; after protests from Buddhists and others, scheme abandoned two years later.

1945   Japanese *coup de force* (10 March); King Sihanouk proclaims an independent Kingdom of Kampuchea (12 March); Ung Hy becomes the first prime minister of Cambodia (18 March).
        Return of Son Ngoc Thanh from Japan; seizure of the Royal Palace by nine radicals (12 August); Son Ngoc Thanh becomes prime minister (14 August); Japanese surrender (15 August).
        British arrive in Phnom Penh and arrest Son Ngoc Thanh (16 October); French rule restored; Prince Sisowath Monireth becomes prime minister (17 October).

1946   In a *modus vivendi* agreement, France awards internal autonomy to Cambodia (7 January); formation of the Democrat Party by Chhean Vam, Sim Var and Ieu Koeus; Chhean becomes first secretary-general; Prince Sisowath Youtévong becomes leader.
        Elections held for the Constituent Assembly (1 September); Democrat Party wins 50 of the 69 seats.
        Thailand returns annexed provinces to Cambodia (October).
        Prince Youtévong becomes prime minister (15 December).

1947   The "Black Star" affair: French arrest Democrat deputies (March).
        Death of Prince Sisowath Youtévong (11 July); Prince Sisowath Watchayavong becomes prime minister (25 July).
        Elections for the first National Assembly (21 December); Democrat Party wins 54 of the 75 seats; Ieu Koeus elected president of the National Assembly.

1948   First elections for the High Council of the Kingdom (January).
        Chhean Vam becomes prime minister (20 February); cotton scandal;

fall of the Chhean Vam government; Penn Nouth becomes prime minister (15 August).

1949   Yèm Sambaur becomes prime minister (12 February); establishment of the Phnom Penh Casino; negotiations with France for limited independence.

King Sihanouk dissolves the National Assembly; Ieu Koeus forms an interim government (20 September).

Yèm Sambaur reappointed prime minister (29 September); *Khmer Issarak* commander, Dap Chhuon, surrenders to the government.

France grants semi-independence to Cambodia which becomes an Associated State of the French Union (8 November).

1950   Assassination of Ieu Koeus (14 January).

Khmer Issaraks, anti-French rebels, hold first congress (17 April).

King Sihanouk becomes prime minister (3 May); Prince Sisowath Monipong becomes prime minister (1 June).

1951   Prince Monipong reappointed as prime minister (1 January).

Oum Chheangsun becomes prime minister (3 March); Oum Chheangsun forms a new government (14 May).

National Assembly elections held (9 September); Democrats again win, with 54 seats; Formation of Khmer People's Revolutionary Party (30 September).

Huy Kanthoul becomes prime minister (13 October); Son Ngoc Thanh returns from exile in France (29 October).

1952   Son Ngoc Thanh flees to the Dangrek mountains (9 March) and forms his *Pracheacholana* ("Movement of the People").

Elections for the High Council of the Kingdom held (April).

Sihanouk launches his Royal Crusade for Independence (5 June); he sacks Huy Kanthoul government (15 June); Sihanouk becomes prime minister (16 June).

1953   National Assembly dissolved (13 January); Penn Nouth becomes prime minister (24 January); Penn Nouth forms a new government (29 July).

France grants Cambodia independence (9 November); Chan Nak becomes prime minister (23 November).

1954   King Sihanouk becomes prime minister (7 April); Penn Nouth becomes prime minister (18 April).

Geneva Accords signed with Cambodian independence recognized by international community (20 July).

Penn Nouth appointed prime minister (1 August); reappointed again (27 August).

King Sihanouk launches Operation *Samakki* against communists.

1955   Leng Ngeth becomes prime minister (26 January).

Referendum on King Sihanouk's popularity (7 February).

King Sihanouk abdicates in favor of his father (3 March); forms *Sangkum Reastr Niyum*; attends Bandung Conference (April).

Elections result in *Sangkum* winning every seat in the National Assembly (11 September); Cambodia admitted to the United Nations (14 September); Cambodia leaves the French Union (25 September); Prince Sihanouk becomes prime minister (3 October).

1956   Oum Chheangsun becomes prime minister (5 January); Prince Sihanouk becomes prime minister (1 March); Khim Tith becomes prime minister (3 April); Prince Sihanouk returns as prime minister (15 September); San Yun becomes prime minister (25 October).

1957   San Yun appointed prime minister (3 January); Prince Sihanouk becomes prime minister (9 April); Sim Var appointed prime minister (28 July).

Creation of Royal Khmer Socialist Youth (JSRK) (5 September).

1958   Ek Yioun becomes prime minister (11 January); Penn Nouth reappointed prime minister (21 January).

National Assembly elections, with women voting for the first time (23 March).

Sim Var reappointed prime minister (2 April); Prince Sihanouk becomes prime minister (10 July).

Cambodia establishes diplomatic relations with the People's Republic of China (17 July).

1959   Prince Sihanouk denounces "Bangkok Plot" (13 January); Sam Sary flees Phnom Penh.

Lon Nol arrives in Siem Reap to arrest Dap Chhuon (22 February); Dap Chhuon found dead (March).

Prince Sihanouk forms a new government (18 February); forms another government (13 June).

"Lacquer Box" assassination attempt on Royal Family.

1960   Death of King Norodom Suramarit (3 April); National Assembly elects Prince Sihanouk as head of state (14 April); Pho Proeung becomes prime minister (19 April).

Referendum to approve Sihanouk's rule (5 June).

Communists hold secret congress at Phnom Penh railway station (30 September).

1961   Penn Nouth forms a new government (28 January); Prince Sihanouk becomes prime minister (17 November).

1962   Nhiek Tioulong becomes prime minister (13 February).
First census of Cambodia (17 April).
National Assembly elections (10 June).
World Court awards Preah Vihear Temple to Cambodia (15 June).
Saloth Sar (Pol Pot) becomes acting secretary of the Khmer People's Revolutionary Party which takes the name Workers' Party of Kampuchea (20 July).
Chau Sen Cocsal becomes prime minister (6 August); Prince Norodom Kantol appointed prime minister (6 October).
Independence Monument inaugurated in Phnom Penh (9 November).

1963   Pol Pot confirmed as party secretary (February); the "34 Affair" (March); Chinese President Liu Shao-chi visits Phnom Penh (1 May); Saloth Sar (Pol Pot) and other leading communists flee to the countryside (May).
Prince Sihanouk names his son Prince Norodom Naradipo as his successor (12 November); National Congress of the *Sangkum Reastr Niyum* votes to reject U.S. aid.
Kitchpanich Songsakd flees to Bangkok with bank funds (December).

1964   Nationalization of banks (January); Execution of Preap In (20 January).
Cambodia threatens break in relations with United States if bombing in border areas continues (27 October).
Prince Kantol reappointed as prime minister (25 December).

1965   Indochinese Peoples Conference held in Phnom Penh (14 February).
U.S. bombing of Parrot's Beak region in eastern Cambodia (1 May); Cambodia breaks diplomatic relations with the United States (3 May); Prince Kantol forms a new government (7 May).

1966   French President Charles de Gaulle visits Phnom Penh (August/ September).
National Assembly elections (11 September); Lon Nol becomes prime minister (22 October); Sihanouk announces formation of an opposition Shadow Cabinet (4 November).

1967   Outbreak of Samlaut rebellion in Battambang (2 April); left-wing deputies Khieu Samphan, Hou Yuon flee Phnom Penh (25 April);

Lon Nol government collapses (30 April); Son Sann becomes prime minister (1 May).

National Front for the Liberation of South Vietnam establishes permanent office in Phnom Penh; left-wing deputy Hu Nim flees Phnom Penh (7 October). Hun Sen also leaves school to join guerrillas in jungle.

1968   Penn Nouth becomes prime minister (31 January).

Lon Nol appointed minister of defense (30 April).

Elections to the High Council of the Kingdom (13 October).

1969   U.S. secret bombing of Cambodia in Operation Menu (18 March).

Cambodia reestablishes diplomatic relations with the United States (11 June).

Lon Nol becomes prime minister (14 August); Prince Sihanouk leaves for Hanoi to attend funeral of Ho Chi Minh (3 September); Prince Sirik Matak becomes deputy prime minister.

1970   Prince Sihanouk goes to France (6 January); demonstrators sack the Vietnamese embassies (11 March); Sihanouk dismissed by National Assembly, Cheng Heng becomes head of state (18 March); Prince Sihanouk announces the formation of the National United Front of Kampuchea (23 March).

U.S.-South Vietnamese soldiers "invade" Cambodia (30 April); protests in the United States; four students shot dead at Kent State University (4 May); Prince Sihanouk, in Beijing, forms Royal Government of National Union (GRUNK) which is immediately recognized by China and North Vietnam (5 May).

Lon Nol forms a new government (2 July); Prince Sihanouk sentenced to death in absentia by Phnom Penh court (5 July).

Emory Swank, first U.S. ambassador since 1965, arrives in Phnom Penh (12 September); Proclamation of the Khmer Republic (9 October).

1971   Lon Nol leaves for Hawaii for treatment of stroke (13 February); returns (12 April); is proclaimed marshal (21 April); forms his fourth cabinet (5 May).

Operation Chenla II, last Republican military offensive, fails (1 December).

1972   Keo An denounces official corruption at press conference (25 February); student demonstrations begin.

Lon Nol appoints himself president (10 March); Son Ngoc Thanh becomes prime minister (20 March).

Koy Pech incident (23-28 April).

Referendum to approve new constitution (30 April); Presidential elections result in Lon Nol confirmed as president (4 June).

Elections held for the National Assembly (4 September) and Senate (17 September) won by Socio-Republican Party; Hang Thun Hak becomes prime minister (17 October).

1973   Lon Nol escapes assassination attempts (18 March); State of Siege proclaimed (21 March). Prince Sihanouk tours liberated areas near Phnom Kulen and Angkor Wat (23 March).

Creation of High Political Council to run Khmer Republic (23 April); In Tam appointed prime minister (15 May).

Accidental US bombing of Neak Luong (7 August); US bombing halt in Cambodia (15 August).

In Tam forms a new government (22 October); Long Boret appointed prime minister (26 December).

1974   Assassination of Keo Sangkim and Thach Chia at student demonstration (4 June); Long Boret forms a new government (16 June).

1975   Royal Government of National Union of Kampuchea (GRUNK) launches dry season offensive (1 January).

Long Boret forms a new government (21 March); Lon Nol leaves Phnom Penh (1 April); Saukham Khoy, acting president, leaves on Operation Eagle Pull, U.S. evacuation flights; Sak Suthsakhan becomes head of state (12 April).

GRUNK forces take control of Phnom Penh and evacuation begins (17 April); arrest of Son Ngoc Thanh in Vietnam (30 April); *Mayaguez* seized; U.S. loses 17 in retaliatory raid (12-15 May).

Prince Sihanouk returns to Cambodia (9 September).

1976   Promulgation of the Constitution of Democratic Kampuchea (January); elections for an Assembly of People's Representatives (March).

Prince Sihanouk resigns as head of state; Khieu Samphan named head of the state presidium; Pol Pot becomes prime minister in new government (2-14 April);

Pol Pot replaced as prime minister by Nuon Chea (27 September); Pol Pot becomes prime minister again (October).

1977   Democratic Kampuchea army initiates cross-border raids on Vietnamese border (January).

Death of Son Ngoc Thanh in Vietnam (8 July).

Following a deep penetration attack from Vietnam, Cambodia breaks diplomatic relations with Vietnam (31 December).

1978 Radio Hanoi broadcasts Khmer language appeals for an uprising against Pol Pot; border fighting intensifies (February-May); East zone is purged of suspected "enemy agents."

Creation of a United Front for the National Salvation of Kampuchea (UFNSK) backed by Vietnam (2 December); Malcolm Caldwell assassinated in Phnom Penh (23 December); Vietnam invades Cambodia (25 December).

1979 Vietnamese soldiers capture Phnom Penh (7 January); formation of People's Republic of Kampuchea (10 January).

Chinese invasion of Vietnam (17 February).

Tens of thousands of Cambodian refugees reach Thailand.

Formation of Khmer People's National Liberation Armed Forces (KPNLAF) (5 March).

Pol Pot and Ieng Sary put on trial in absentia in Phnom Penh (15 August); both sentenced to death (20 August).

Formation of Molinaka (31 August).

United Nations General Assembly adopts the first of many resolutions calling for the immediate withdrawal of all foreign forces from Cambodia (14 November). Democratic Kampuchea authorities permitted to retain Cambodia's seat.

Formation of Khmer People's National Liberation Front (KPNLF); and official creation of the KPNLAF (9 October).

Democratic Kampuchea cabinet reshuffled; Khieu Samphan replaces Pol Pot as prime minister (17 December).

1980 Decree provides for reintroduction of money into Cambodian economy (20 March).

Forced repatriation of some Cambodian refugees (17 June); border war begins in earnest.

1981 Prince Sihanouk forms National United Front for an Independent, Neutral, Peaceful and Cooperative Cambodia (FUNCINPEC) (February).

National Assembly elections held (1 May).

Pen Sovan, general secretary of the People's Revolutionary Party of Kampuchea, purged; replaced by Heng Samrin (4 December).

1982 Establishment of a Coalition Government of Democratic Kampuchea (CGDK) by the Party of Democratic Kampuchea (PDK), FUNCINPEC and KPNLF (22 June). Cambodia's seat in the United Nations General Assembly passed to the CGDK.

1984   Massive Vietnamese attack on Cambodian refugees in Thai-Cambodian border region.

1985   Hun Sen becomes prime minister (14 January).
Pol Pot announces "retirement" from public service (1 September).

1986   CGDK produces "eight-point proposal" to end war; plan rejected by Vietnam (17 March).

1987   Hun Sen meets Prince Sihanouk at Fère-en-Tardennois, France (2-4 December).

1988   Further talks between Hun Sen and Sihanouk (20-21 January).
First Jakarta Informal Meeting attended by Cambodian warring parties (25 July).

1989   Second Jakarta Informal Meeting (19 February).
National Assembly adopts new constitution, new flag and national anthem; restores the right to hold private property and declares Buddhism the state religion (29-30 April).
First Paris Peace Conference on Cambodia adjourned after one month of inconclusive talks on power sharing (30 August).
Unsupervised, unilateral withdrawal of remaining Vietnamese soldiers (end September).

1990   Third Jakarta Informal Meeting (26 February); creation of Supreme National Council to safeguard Cambodian sovereignty; Prince Sihanouk is appointed chair and 13th member.
Arrest and imprisonment of Ung Phan and others who attempted to launch a Liberal Democratic Socialist Party (May-August).
Hor Nam Hong appointed foreign minister (17 September).

1991   Supreme National Council accorded Cambodia's seat in the United Nations General Assembly.
People's Revolutionary Party congress abandons Marxism-Leninism; party renamed Cambodian People's Party (CPP).
Signing of Paris Agreements initiating a UN peacekeeping mission (23 October).
Khieu Samphan returns to Phnom Penh, but escapes near lynching, and returns to Bangkok (27 November).

1992   Yasushi Akashi arrives to head the UN Transitional Authority in Cambodia.
The Democratic Kampuchea army refuses to disarm (June); the Party of Democratic Kampuchea announces the formation of a National Union Party of Kampuchea but does not register the party for the United Nations-organized elections (November).

1993   Elections held (23-28 May); FUNCINPEC wins 46 percent of vote compared to 38 percent for the Cambodian People's Party. CPP refuse to accept defeat.

Prince Norodom Chakrapong and Sin Song, CPP defense minister, announce secession of eastern Cambodia, forcing FUNCINPEC to join a coalition with the CPP to prevent the breakup of the country.

Prince Norodom Ranariddh appointed first prime minister, with Hun Sen as second prime minister.

New constitution approved by Assembly (21 September); restores constitutional monarchy (24 September).

1994   Democratic Kampuchea forces continue armed struggle; Khieu Samphan announces the formation of a Provisional Government of National Unity and Well-Being of Kampuchea.

Prince Norodom Chakrapong and Sin Song attempt another coup (3 July); Chakrapong exiled and Sin Song jailed.

Sam Rainsy, finance minister, sacked following rift with CPP; Prince Sirivudh, foreign minister, resigns in protest.

1995   Amnesty International expresses concern about political intimidation by forces loyal to Hun Sen (May).

Sam Rainsy expelled from FUNCINPEC (August) and forms the Khmer Nation Party, a liberal democratic party seeking to oppose corruption in the government (November).

Prince Norodom Sirvudh hounded from Phnom Penh by Hun Sen who accuses the ex-minister of plotting to kill him (November).

1996   FUNCINPEC decides against forming an alliance with the CPP in the 1998 elections (March).

Ieng Sary and Democratic Kampuchea army divisions based in Pailin and Malai defect (August). Ieng Sary organizes non-electoral Democratic National Union Movement.

1997   FUNCINPEC forms a National United Front to fight elections against the CPP (January).

Hand grenade attack on Sam Rainsy; 16 people killed and a U.S. citizen injured (30 March). American FBI report blames the CPP.

Son Sen killed near Anlong Veng on Pol Pot's orders (10 June); Pol Pot arrested by Ta Mok.

Hun Sen accuses FUNCINPEC of illegal arms imports and launches coup against first prime minister, Prince Norodom Ranariddh (5 July); pro-Hun Sen forces murder interior minister Ho Sok and other FUNCINPEC officials; Ranariddh remains overseas and many royalists and NGO activists flee Cambodia. Hun Sen names foreign minister Ung Huot as the new first prime minister. Royalist General Nhek Bun Chhay leads armed resistance in O'Smach.

US journalist Nate Thayer witnesses the trial of Pol Pot in Anlong Veng. Pol Pot is found guilty of treason and murder and sentenced to "life imprisonment" (25 July).

1998   Prince Ranariddh returns to Phnom Penh (30 March).

Death of Pol Pot (15 April).

Elections held (26 July); CPP win 64 seats, FUNCINPEC win 43 and Sam Rainsy Party win 15 seats. Opposition supporters protest irregularities in voting and counting (28 July).

Grenade attacks at Hun Sen's Phnom Penh residence are blamed on opposition parties (7 September). FUNCINPEC enters into coalition government with Hun Sen (30 November).

Garrison at Anlong Veng surrenders (4 December); Khieu Samphan and Nuon Chea surrender (25 December); Khieu Samphan expresses sorrow over deaths during the Democratic Kampuchea period (29 December).

1999   Democratic Kampuchea soldiers are integrated into the Royal Cambodian Army (9 February).

National Assembly votes to establish the Senate (4 March); capture of Ta Mok (6 March); General Nhek Bun Chhay, amnestied, returns to Phnom Penh (7 March).

Far Eastern Economic Review locates the ex-Democratic Kampuchea security chief "Duch" (28 April), who is arrested; Cambodia formally joins the Association of Southeast Asian Nations (ASEAN) (30 April).

Murder of Piseth Pilika (July).

Ta Mok charged with genocide (7 September); Duch charged (10 September).

2000   Prime minister Keizo Obuchi visits Phnom Penh, the first Japanese prime minister to do so since 1957 (January).

Asian Development Bank dismisses government efforts to manage forests as "total system failure" (April).

Former Democratic Kampuchea army commander Chhouk Rin is acquitted of murder (July).

Greenpeace criticizes Cambodia for giving "flags of convenience" to ships illegally fishing for tuna in the Atlantic (August).

Severe flooding affects three million, destroying more than 500,000 hectares of paddy and 2,200 kilometers of roadbed (October).

President Jiang Zemin, president of the People's Republic of China, visits Phnom Penh; Chinese officials deny their advisors worked at S-21 (November).

2001   Constitutional Council approves law establishing a special tribunal for the prosecution of former Democratic Kampuchea leaders.
Khieu Samphan issues statement denying personal knowledge of or responsibility for killings in 1975-79 (August).

2002   Local government elections held (February).

Introduction

Many people around the world identify Cambodia with images from "The Killing Fields" of the late 1970s, from the 1984 film of the same name which came out at the height of the Cold War reemphasizing a Western view of fear of political extremism. The name "Khmer Rouge" and its leader Pol Pot became synonymous with barbarity and iconoclasm on a scale matched only by the Red Guards in China. Few newspaper or magazine articles, or news reports, on Cambodia failed to make some reference to the Killing Fields, the Khmer Rouge or Pol Pot. With the comparative stability of the country and the gradual clearing of minefields around Angkor Wat, the tourist industry has, in recent years, dramatically increased so much so that there is a problem accommodating the tourists as well as monitoring the general "wear and tear" on the temples themselves.

In sharp contrast to these vastly different images, news coverage of Cambodia of the late 1950s and 1960s was tied to Cambodia's leader Prince Norodom Sihanouk, and his policy of neutrality which journalists and commentators praised as preventing the country from becoming involved in the Vietnam War. Tourists who visited the Cambodian temples, mainly traveling in by land from Thailand, marveled at the peaceful nature of the countryside. Outside Cambodia the popular perception was also influenced by best-selling works of fiction by authors such as Hugh Clifford (*The Downfall of the Gods,* 1911); Somerset Maugham (*The Gentleman in the Parlour,* 1930); Edgar Rice Burroughs, creator of *Tarzan* (*Jungle Girl,* 1933) and Han Suyin (*The Four Faces*, 1963).

For Cambodians, the consciousness of the country is closely tied to the magnificent temple complex of Angkor Wat and this as an emblem has appeared on the flags of every government and major opposition group since the 1940s.

The origins of the country lie shrouded in mystery and the few written records which survive are either stone carvings or the work of visiting Chinese chroniclers. The former provide the official view—or at any rate the point of view that has been allowed to survive by later Kings. The latter include only scattered references which often leave many questions unanswered. The first "king" of the country is reputed to have been Kaundinya—an exile from India—who arrived in Cambodia in about AD 198. Marrying the daughter of a local chief, he founded what was to become the powerful trading kingdom of Funan, as it was known in China. Its capital was at Ba Phnom and artifacts from the Middle East and from Rome have been found there indicating that its connections reached as far as Europe. This kingdom began to lose its influence during the early sixth century and at about this time a new state, Chenla, arose. Chenla, which is recorded as sending tribute to China, existed from the early sixth century to AD 802 when it was supplanted by a new kingdom which was known as Angkor.

In AD 802 the great-nephew of one of the Kings of Chenla, who was probably a powerful general in the Chenla army, became King Jayavarman II. After a ceremony at Phnom Kulen, in the north of Cambodia, he became the "universal monarch" with "God-King" (Devaraja) status. Much of the information on the events at Phnom Kulen comes from a stone inscription of 1050 when the Angkor nobility honoured the occasion and linked their wealth and power to that event. This carving includes family histories which are genealogically impossible, but this should not detract from the obvious oral tradition concerning what happened in 802 and the effect it was to have on Cambodian history for the next six hundred years.

The descendants of Jayavarman II ruled what became the Kingdom of Angkor until the sacking of the capital in 1432 by the Thais. King Indravarman I (ruled 877-889), who succeeded Jayavarman II's son, began the temple building projects. The capital, Angkor, owes much to the pioneering work of King Yasovarman I (ruled 889-910), and the building projects reached a zenith with the construction of Angkor Wat by King Suryavarman II (ruled 1113-1150). During this period the Kingdom of Angkor prospered, obviously on the basis of agricultural wealth, trade and conquest. Recent infrared satellite photographs have revealed the vast spread of the city, some experts calculating that the capital could have been home to a million people when London and Paris had populations of 60,000 each.

The major enemies of Angkor in this period were the Cham peoples of what is now Central Vietnam. The Muslim Kingdom of Champa, with a strong navy and, apparently with the help of a Chinese guide, attacked the city of Angkor which they sacked in 1177. Angkor was, at that stage, ruled by a usurper, and it is possible that Cambodian rebels sided with the Chams.

With Angkor rendered seemingly powerless, King Jayavarman VII ascended the throne a year after the sacking of the capital. The massive bas relief stone carvings at the Bayon temple show a large sea battle and it appears that this is when Jayavarman VII managed to drive the Chams from Angkor and gain control of the capital. With his rule initially extending only over the wrecked city, he had to rebuild the empire which he did in a series of military expeditions. He waited until 1181 to be consecrated a "God-King." The temple of Angkor Thom was then built which included within it the Bayon, a richly decorated shrine with each side of its tower showing his face.

However, although Jayavarman VII was able to restore much of the glory of Angkor, the Empire was in decline. By the fourteenth century it was vulnerable to the Thais from Ayudhya in the west and the Vietnamese from the east—the Vietnamese having smashed the Kingdom of Champa and sent the surviving Chams as refugees into Cambodia where they remain to this day. In 1296-1297 a Chinese diplomat, Zhou Daguan, visited Angkor and his account, which survives, provides the most detailed description of daily life in the city which was at the beginning of its decline.

In 1432 the Thais sacked the city of Angkor, and rather than occupying it as the Chams had done, they burned the wooden buildings and enslaved the population sending tens of thousands of slaves to their capital of Ayudhya. For the next four hundred years the Cambodian lands shrank considerably with the Vietnamese taking land around the Mekong Delta, and rapidly outnumbering the local Cambodian population, some of whom remained in the region and others of whom moved westwards.

The kings of Cambodia established a new capital at Phnom Penh. Although Cambodian chronicles give the date of its foundation as 1432, it is more likely to have been in 1528 when surviving descendants of the Angkor Court finally decided to settle far from the site of their previous capital. The court was briefly moved to Lovek where the English East India Company established a trading factory in 1652. The Portuguese began some commercial dealings soon afterwards.

Both of Cambodia's neighbors were unable to make any further moves during the 18th century with the sacking, by the Burmese, of the Thai capital of Ayudya in 1767 and the Tay Son Rebellion in Vietnam. With the establishment of the Kingdom of Siam in Bangkok, and the defeat of the Tay Son rebels by the Nguyen dynasty of Vietnam, this meant that Cambodia was, once again, under threat.

The man who was to become King Rama I of Siam gained his reputation for military prowess in Cambodia, sacking Phnom Penh in 1772. He was, however, forced to cut short his invasion returning to Siam and being proclaimed king. In 1811-1812 the Siamese and the Vietnamese fought for control of Cambodia with Vietnam occupying the kingdom from 1835-1840.

Throwing off Vietnamese control, in 1848 Ang Duong became King of Cambodia and soon made contact with the French requesting their help. France had already established trading bases in southern Vietnam, and as one of the major naval powers in the region, it was thought that an alliance with France would guarantee Cambodia's borders. Ang Duong died in 1860, and his oldest surviving son became King Norodom I.

Norodom continued requesting the French to form an alliance and in 1863 agreed to the creation of a French Protectorate over Cambodia. This meant that, in theory, France controlled only the foreign affairs and defense matters of the kingdom, while Norodom administered the country. In practice the French "advised" him on appointments and regularly intrigued with officials to remove any members of the royal court who threatened their position. They also maintained Cambodia's borders and many Cambodians believe that without the French, Cambodia would have disappeared as an entity in the same way that the Kingdom of Champa had been destroyed in 1471.

Early French scholars, notably Henri Mouhot, became fascinated by stories of Cambodian temples in the jungles, and during their rule French archaeologists and scholars pored over each temple and every inscription around Angkor managing to establish a chronology of Cambodian kings and to detail the history of Angkor. Surviving records indicate that between 1550 and 1570 Portuguese "rediscovered" Angkor Wat for Europeans. Around this time the kings of Cambodia had sought help from the Portuguese in Malacca and the Spanish in Manila without success. Europeans were now aware that the temple complex existed. In the 1580s a Portuguese missionary wrote the best description thus far, but his work was not published until 1958 nearly 350 years after it had been written. Other missionaries, traders and adventurers mentioned the kingdom in letters or diaries but the man credited with "rediscovering" Angkor Wat was a French naturalist who had extensive writing and drawing skills. Henri Mouhot (1826-1861) with the moral support but no financial assistance from the Royal Geographical Society in London (Mouhot could get no support in France) set off in 1858 for Bangkok. From there he made four journeys of which the second, December 1858 to April 1860, was the most important as it was then that he came upon the Angkor complex at this stage mostly hidden by jungle. Henri Mouhot never returned to Europe, having died in Laos in November 1861. His brother ensured that his writings and some of his drawings were published in English in 1864, beginning an era of scholarship, artistic, photographic and religious examinations of Angkor and the gradual cutting back of the jungle from around the ruins enabling the temples to be restored as much as was practicable.

A number of revolts against French rule were ruthlessly suppressed. Two were led by men claiming to be members of the royal family: Assoa in 1862-1866; and Poukombo in 1865-1867. Prince Si Votha, a younger brother of King Norodom, led another rebellion in 1876. The French also took over Vietnam and Laos and these, along with Cambodia, were administered as French Indochina from Saigon.

French rule over Cambodia tightened in 1884 and in 1898 a pro-French court official, Thiounn, became minister of the palace, and used his position (which he held until 1941) to support the French and enrich himself. The violent crushing of the three revolts against the French during the 1860s and 1870s failed to stifle dissent. In the countryside the peasants felt a sense of hopelessness and there was no further uprising until the murder of the French official Félix-Louis Bardez in 1925. But there was constant court intrigue with Crown Prince Yukanthor, Norodom's eldest son, criticizing the French and going to France to protest against their excesses. He went into exile and two other princes who also intrigued against the French, Duong Chakr and Norodom Mayura, were also sidelined.

When King Norodom I died in 1904, the French chose a brother who became King Sisowath. Although Norodom had invited the French into the country, he had only done so to preserve Cambodia's borders. He never accepted the French in the way Sisowath did. Sisowath had led the Cambodian army against Poukombo and Si Votha during the 1860s and 1870s and had been seen as France's protégé. His appointment as king was not unexpected and many saw it as a reward for his collaboration with the colonial power.

Sisowath was keen on presiding over an increasingly prosperous country. After being crowned in 1906 Sisowath went on a state visit to France and traveled widely throughout Cambodia. In 1911 he founded Collège Sisowath, the first Western-style school in the country. It remained until 1975 the foremost secondary school in Cambodia. King Sisowath supported the French during World War I with thousands of Cambodians serving in the French forces on the Western Front. When he died in 1927 many of the public buildings in Phnom Penh had been constructed and rural banditry had been heavily reduced.

During the 1920s and 1930s when the "European" commercial empires were at their peak—the British in India, Burma, Malaya and China, the Dutch in the Indies, the Americans in the Philippines and the French in Indochina—Angkor assumed an identity which eclipsed the country of which it was a part. Angkor became an exotic destination for writers, painters, archaeologists, scholars and adventurers. Most notable of these was probably André Malraux, a left-wing French intellectual who went first to Saigon and edited a newspaper that often decried the French administration in Indochina. Then he went to Cambodia where he "souvenired" parts of a minor temple at Angkor. Arrested and tried, he was found guilty and sent back to France, eventually becoming a confidante of Charles de Gaulle. There were also other Frenchmen at the time, archaeologists, who were working on the Cambodian temples. The most famous of these were Georges Coedès and Georges Groslier. The preservation of many of the temples, and the recording of inscriptions on them, owe much to these two men.

King Sisowath was succeeded by his son, Sisowath Monivong. King Monivong was French-educated and had served in the French army in Algeria. A poet of some significance, and a patron of the arts, he helped with the foundation of the Buddhist Institute and the editing of the Cambodian Royal Chronicles. French rubber plantations and a road network, as well as a railway line connecting Phnom Penh with Thailand, led to an expansion of the Cambodian economy. Following the fall of France to Germany in June 1940, a pro-Vichy colonial administration was established in Saigon. Taking advantage of France's weakened position, Thailand invaded western Cambodia to retake areas which they had regarded as historically theirs. That the French so quickly lost the Franco-Siamese war of 1940-1941 and were forced to cede Battambang and much of Siem Reap (but not the Angkorean monuments) distressed King Monivong considerably. He died in April 1941, and the French overlooked his two sons, Monireth and Monipong, choosing his grandson, Prince Norodom Sihanouk as the new King.

Chosen because of his youth—he was 18 when he became King—the French hoped to dominate the country. However by this time the French colonial administration, loyal to the pro-German Vichy government, had allowed the Japanese to use Cambodia as a base for their attack on British Malaya in December 1941. With the Liberation of France in 1944 the Japanese became worried that the French, who had collaborated with them in Cambodia (and also Vietnam and Laos), might join the Allies and therefore decided to take control of Indochina for themselves.

In March 1945 the Japanese staged a *coup de force* and jailed the French, persuading King Sihanouk to proclaim independence which he did on 12 March 1945. Protests against French rule in 1942 had been harshly repressed but now the nascent nationalist movement began to make progress. The major nationalist figure during this period was Son Ngoc Thanh. A Khmer Krom, he had edited a Cambodian-language newspaper, *Nagaravatta*, during the late 1930s. After the 1942 protests he had fled Phnom Penh and spent three years in Tokyo. Returning to Cambodia, he became Prime Minister in August 1945. He gained support from the Khmer Issarak, an anti-French guerrilla group which had been established in Bangkok in 1940. The end of World War II on 15 August 1945 came as a surprise to the Cambodian nationalists. When British soldiers and Gurkhas arrived in Phnom Penh in October to take control and hand the country back to the French, Thanh was arrested and sent off to France where he was held in comfortable but secure house arrest.

King Sihanouk, with the advice of his uncle Prince Monireth, a former officer in the French Army, welcomed the French back to Cambodia. While the Vietnamese resisted the return of the French, the relatively low levels of political consciousness in Cambodia ensured that the transfer back to France was peaceful. Those Cambodians who refused to accept this went into the jungle and joined the Khmer Issarak. In 1946 the French agreed to allow internal autonomy to Cambodia and several political parties were formed. Thailand hastily returned the annexed provinces of Battambang and Siem Reap in October 1946 as the Thai government adapted to the political changes at the end of World War II.

The first political party established in Cambodia was the Constitutionalist Party, which was soon renamed the Liberal Party. Led by Prince Norodom Norindeth, it had considerable support from the French colonial administration, some palace officials and the Cham Muslim minority. It was rapidly overshadowed by the formation of the Democrat Party which was soon to be led by Prince Sisowath Youtévong. Youtévong, who had spent World War II in Paris studying astronomy, proved to be a dynamic leader. The Democrats formed party branches throughout the country and were assisted by some French colonial officials who were associated with the French Socialist Party. In the elections for the Constituent Assembly in September the Democrats won 50 of the 69 seats and Youtévong became Prime Minister in December 1946. The Constituent Assembly was dissolved and the new Constitution which it had established allowed for a National Assembly, the lower house elected by universal male franchise; and the High Council of the Kingdom, an upper house representing interest groups (palace, business, civil servants, judiciary, etc.).

The French were surprised and angered by the election victory of the Democrats and in March 1947 claimed that some of the Democrat politicians were involved in a plot to kill French officials. The claims—several Democrats were arrested and tortured to make confessions—were widely disbelieved. The death of Prince Youtévong in July 1947, of natural causes, was to prove more disastrous to the Democrats. While the Democrats were to win the next two elections, their percentage of votes declined and the inability of the party leadership to stop internal splits resulted in a lessening of their influence.

French and palace circles instigated the formation of two more political parties. One, the Khmer Renewal Party, was led by a powerful court figure Nhiek Tioulong, and the police chief Lon Nol. The other, the National Union, had much support from the elite (and none from the peasantry). The elections, in December 1947, to the first National Assembly, saw the Democrats winning 54 of the 75 seats. However in January 1948 they were severely defeated in the elections to the High Council of the Kingdom where, on a restricted franchise, the elite parties such as the National Union did well.

The new leader of the Democrats, Ieu Koeus, had been elected president of the National Assembly in December 1947; and Chhean Vam, another Democrat, became prime minister in February 1948. The two managed adroitly to divide their rivals in the High Council of the Kingdom but the Chhean Vam government fell in August.

The French had been unable to form or support any political force to defeat the Democrats at the polls. The royal palace was also nervous that the Socialist-leaning Democrats might erode their power. Both sought to exploit a division in the Democrat ranks and chose an ambitious Democrat politician, Yèm Sambaur, to become prime minister. To finance the government, he established the Phnom Penh Casino and began negotiating with France for some degree of limited independence. As Yèm Sambaur and his rebel Democrats, even with support from the smaller opposition parties, did not enjoy a majority in the National Assembly, King Sihanouk dissolved the assembly.

Although Yèm Sambaur has often been made out to be a French puppet, he did manage to make considerable political advances. His most important achievement was managing to get many of the Khmer Issarak rebels, who had maintained a low-level armed opposition to the French, to "rally"—he offered them money and positions in the army or the police. The rallying of Dap Chhuon, an Issarak leader and Siem Reap warlord, was a major triumph. This was followed by the Elysée Accord when France granted Cambodia "semi-independence." Locally Yèm Sambaur gained much support from the fishermen after he sent in soldiers to smash a weir that wealthy Chinese businessmen had erected in an effort to monopolize the fishing industry.

Yèm Sambaur's government did institute cutbacks in education leading to school protests and considerable alienation of the youth. Older students studying in France on government scholarships—Cambodia did not have its own university until 1956—decried the obvious undemocratic nature of the government and this anger intensified when the Democrat leader Ieu Koeus was assassinated in January 1950. Although a man was arrested soon afterward—and claimed initially to be, and later not to be, a member of the Liberal Party—many observers felt that Yèm Sambaur was guilty of organizing the killing, and Lon Nol, the police chief, responsible for the "non-capture" of the real offenders. Whether Yèm Sambaur was guilty or not was unproven but it was openly claimed to be the case at the alleged assassin's trial.

To avert public protests, King Sihanouk became prime minister in May

1950 and in September 1951 elections were held for a new National Assembly. The Democrats once again won the election but with less than half the votes—their right-wing opponents having their votes split between six parties. In the same month the Khmer People's Revolutionary Party, the forerunner of the Communist Party, was formed. In October former schoolteacher and longtime Democrat political activist Huy Kanthoul became prime minister, and Son Ngoc Thanh returned from exile in France to receive a hero's welcome as he was driven from the airport to Phnom Penh. Students spoke of watching, from their classroom windows, the plane coming in to land, this being the signal for them to rush out onto the street to cheer the motorcade.

Despite this rapturous welcome, Son Ngoc Thanh found the country in October 1951 very different from what he had left six years earlier. He was unhappy with the political setup and in March 1952 went into the jungle to form an armed resistance against the French. Leading his Khmer Serei movement, it was 18 years before he would be able to return to Phnom Penh. King Sihanouk, sensing that the French, losing the Indochina War in neighboring Vietnam, were anxious for support, launched his Royal Crusade for Independence, a series of peaceful staged political demonstrations and international diplomacy. At the same time Sihanouk promised to guarantee French assets and ensure French business predominance after independence. In June 1952 Sihanouk sacked Huy Kanthoul and made himself prime minister.

For some radical Cambodians, the sacking of the Democrat government signaled that there could be no compromise with Sihanouk. They realized that they could not hope to become an elected government if a mildly socialist one, such as that led by Huy Kanthoul, would be regarded as a threat. Some joined Son Ngoc Thanh and others started to plan a communist armed struggle.

Throughout 1953 Sihanouk kept up the pressure on the French and managed to get France to grant independence on November 9. France was in the final stages of the Indochina War and when the Geneva Conference was held in the following year, the Cambodian royal delegation was supportive of French moves. In July at Geneva the international community, ignoring the entreaties of the unseated delegation of the Khmer People's Party of Kampuchea, recognized Cambodian independence under the leadership of King Sihanouk. In a show of force at the end of the year the Royal Khmer Armed Forces was sent against the communists in Operation Samakki. This was largely for public relations purposes although a few communists were captured.

Unsure of his next move, Sihanouk held a referendum on his own popularity in February 1955 and getting a vote of confidence, on March 3 he abdicated in favor of his father, Prince Norodom Suramarit. Forming a political movement, *Sangkum Reastr Niyum,* he attended the Asian-African Conference at Bandung, Indonesia and became heavily influenced by the concept of non-alignment. This was to lead, during the 1960s, to leaders of "Nonaligned" countries visiting Cambodia—Haile Selassie of Ethiopia, Sukarno of Indonesia and Tito of Yugoslavia.

In the September 1955 elections *Sangkum* officially won every seat in the National Assembly—although there is evidence that some opposition parties did win some seats. From then until 1970 Sihanouk led the country unchallenged as its "leader," although his exact title varied. From 1955 until 1960 Sihanouk's father ruled as king (and hence was head of state). From 1960 until 1970 Sihanouk's widowed mother, Queen Kossomak, ruled in the name of the throne, but Sihanouk was officially head of state. During some of the late 1950s Sihanouk was prime minister—during the late 1950s and the 1960s most people knew him simply as "Prince Papa" or "Samdech Euv."

During the late 1950s Sihanouk oversaw a massive building program throughout the country. Schools, hospitals and other public buildings were constructed in cities and towns throughout Cambodia. Universities were created and Royal Khmer Socialist Youth, modeled on the Boy Scout movement was launched in 1957. On the political front, power was certainly in the hands of Prince Sihanouk who held National Congresses where anybody could come and ask questions of ministers. Peasants used this as an opportunity to air grievances and Sihanouk occasionally sacked ministers who were unable to answer their critics. As for the peasantry, who made up the vast majority of the population, they welcomed the return to royal power, rather than the creation of parliamentary democracy. Women were given the franchise and the *Sangkum* members were returned in the 1958 elections, all but one unopposed.

As far as Cambodia's foreign alliances stood, in 1958 the government extended diplomatic recognition to the People's Republic of China. At the same time Sihanouk was involved in friction with both Thailand and South Vietnam. The two neighbors had been sheltering Son Ngoc Thanh since 1952 and in January 1959 Sihanouk claimed that Thailand was behind a conspiracy to oust him. A close friend and political activist, Sam Sary, clearly involved in the plotting, fled the country and was assassinated in South Vietnam. In the following month Dap Chhuon, the governor of Siem Reap was implicated in a secession conspiracy, seemingly organized by the South Vietnamese with United States complicity. Soon afterward Dap Chhuon was found dead. Later the same year an assassination attempt on the royal family failed with a minor court official dying when he opened the parcel bomb.

In April 1960 King Norodom Suramarit died and Prince Sihanouk was elected head of state by the National Assembly with his mother "embodying" the throne. Sihanouk's ascension was confirmed in a referendum in June

1960. In 1962 Sihanouk achieved a major foreign policy success when he managed to get back Cambodian control of Preah Vihear Temple from Thailand. The case was sent for international arbitration and Cambodia's victory was seen by Cambodians as evidence of Sihanouk's international prestige and his ability to recover some of Cambodia's past glory without war or the threat of conflict. The visit of Jackie Kennedy to Phnom Penh and Angkor in 1967 attracted much international attention for the country.

Friction with South Vietnam, exacerbated by the "Buddhist Crisis" there, led Sihanouk to break relations in 1963. The assassination of President Ngo Dinh Diem in Saigon in November 1963, even though Diem was no friend of Sihanouk, worried the prince greatly. He named one of his sons, Prince Norodom Naradipo, as his successor, and he rejected any future U.S. aid.

While some Cambodian communists had welcomed Sihanouk's new foreign policy stance, especially with the visit of Chinese President Liu Shao-chi to Phnom Penh in 1963, others were wary of him. In 1960 they had held a secret congress in Phnom Penh and two years later a former schoolteacher, Saloth Sar (later known as Pol Pot) became acting secretary-general of the communists who changed their name to the Workers' Party of Kampuchea. They continued to distrust Sihanouk despite his moderate left-wing stance.

At this juncture Sihanouk started on a program of nationalization of the major industries to break the economic control by the Chinese community. This started badly with the banks—a banker fleeing Phnom Penh with the assets of one bank in December 1963. When control of these newly created public corporations was given to court officials and friends, some of whom were accused of syphoning off company funds, this began to seriously affect the economy of the country and led to economic stagnation.

By now the war in Vietnam had begun to impact on Cambodia with the Americans bombing Vietnamese communist bases along the Vietnamese-Cambodian border. Mainly over this, even though the cited cause was a magazine criticism of Queen Kossomak, in May 1965 Cambodia broke relations with the United States. It now seems evident that Sihanouk had struck a deal with the Vietnamese communists. In return for turning a "blind-eye" to the Ho Chi Minh Trail (through which they were funneling supplies along Cambodian jungle tracks into South Vietnam), if the communists were victorious, as Sihanouk had every belief that they would be, they would respect Cambodia's borders.

In the elections in September 1966, members of *Sangkum* freely competed with each other for seats—the first elections not controlled by Sihanouk since 1955. This democratic veneer saw a large number of right-wing candidates elected and when they took up their seats they voted for Lon Nol, the longtime defense minister, to become prime minister. He tried to "roll back" the nationalization plans and in April 1967 peasants in Battambang, in western Cambodia, revolted. Three left-wing members of National Assembly fled into the jungle to join the communist guerrillas as did a schoolboy, Hun Sen. Lon Nol was forced from office owing to injuries sustained in a car crash, but he returned as prime minister in August 1969. By now the Vietnamese communists were openly using the Cambodian border region for their supplies and the United States had begun bombing these bases.

Exhausted by the international situation and political intrigue, Prince Sihanouk went to France in January 1970 for a rest cure. After turmoil in Phnom Penh, the National Assembly voted to dismiss him on March 18. They appointed Cheng Heng, the President of the National Assembly, as Head of State, Lon Nol remaining prime minister. They issued orders to ban Sihanouk from returning to Cambodia—in July he was sentenced to death *in absentia*.

Sihanouk was in Moscow, departing for China, when he was told of his overthrow. In Beijing the Chinese government persuaded him to form the National United Front of Kampuchea and join with the Cambodian communists to wage a civil war against Lon Nol. Vietnamese communists rapidly captured much of eastern Cambodia resulting in the United States sending American and South Vietnamese soldiers into Cambodia. Five days later Prince Sihanouk, still in Beijing, proclaimed the formation of the Royal Government of National Union of Kampuchea (GRUNK), a government-in-exile, which was immediately recognized by China and North Vietnam.

Cambodia had reestablished diplomatic relations with the United States in 1969 but it was not until September 1970 that a U.S. Ambassador was once again accredited to the Cambodian government. A month later, on 9 October 1970, the Cambodian monarchy was abolished and the country was renamed the Khmer Republic. A new flag was introduced, with Lon Nol remaining as prime minister. Lon Nol's deputy and close friend, Sisowath Sirik Matak, also played a major role in the running of the country especially after Lon Nol suffered a stroke in February 1971.

The National United Front of Kampuchea (FUNK), with Sihanouk as its nominal leader, augmented by the prince's peasant supporters, and the Vietnamese communists, drove back the Republican armed forces and from early 1972 the Khmer Republic was only in control of urban areas. The Republic controled the majority of the population but the coalition of communists, royalists and nationalists working within the framework of the FUNK controled most of the countryside. With intense U.S. bombing of communist bases, there was essentially a military stalemate until early 1975.

Lon Nol appointed himself president in March 1972 and Son Ngoc Thanh, who had returned to Phnom Penh in 1970, became prime minister. Student demonstrations rocked Phnom Penh in mid-1972 as a new Republican Constitution was endorsed by referendum. Lon Nol won a presidential election in June 1972 and his Socio-Republican Party won every seat in the National Assembly and the Senate. Although by nature authoritarian, Lon Nol did make an attempt to run his government in a liberal democratic style, but this ended when he survived an assassination attempt in March 1973 and proclaimed a "State of Siege." The war became progressively more savage with atrocities on one side being matched by reprisals by their opponents. In April 1975 the Khmer Republic finally collapsed as the National United Front of Kampuchea forces seized Phnom Penh.

During the five years of war the Cambodian communists—which Sihanouk in the 1950s had called the Khmer Rouge—gradually came to dominate the National United Front. They managed to ease out of influence most of the Royalists and also many communists who had connections with the Vietnamese Communist movement. When they came to power on 17 April 1975 the Pol Pot communists, influenced by Chinese doctrines and practices, attempted their own "super Great Leap Forward" on top of radical policies of their devising.

The first move of the new government was to force all the population of the cities into the countryside. There were two important reasons for this. First within the overcrowded city there were pockets of soldiers of the Khmer Republic who were planning to "hold out." An otherwise empty city allowed these to be easily destroyed. Those who left could also be "screened." The second reason was that the cities were desperately short of food and the population could be immediately put to work in the fields planting a rice crop. Once in the countryside the "New People," as those evacuated from the cities were called, were used to do laboring tasks in the fields or on a small number of industrial projects. Some managed to escape to Thailand; others succeeded in reaching Vietnam.

Under this new government, called Democratic Kampuchea, led by Pol Pot, about a million Cambodians died. It is thought that a tenth of these were killed by the regime, the remainder succumbed to disease, exacerbated by malnutrition and overwork. The Khmer Rouge later acknowledged that the banning of medicine, the misapportionment of food and the heavy work regimen were "mistakes." Accounts of these horrors emerged from stories by refugees in Thailand. Few foreigners were allowed into Democratic Kampuchea, but those who were spoke well of the place. Consequently many of the refugee stories were initially discounted.

Though not immediately apparent, there were internal divisions within the ruling Communist Party of Kampuchea throughout its period in power from April 1975 until December 1978. At first disputes centered on whether there should be a currency of exchange or whether the rural cooperatives were correctly organized and managed. Disputes about economic and developmental policies extended to the question of strategic cooperation with Vietnam in the building of socialism. At the same time there was nationalist anxiety about the possibility that cooperation with Vietnam would lead to Vietnamese domination of Cambodia's revolution and territory. When border disputes broke out, Pol Pot attempted to resolve differences by closing the frontiers and refusing to attempt boundary adjustments in regions where territory was disputed to allow trade across the border. When production began to collapse, disputes within socialist ideology led to massive purges within the state, the party organization and local adminstrations, and the two communist countries went to war.

In late 1978 the Khmer Rouge seem to have launched an attack on the Vietnamese. Their army was allowed to enter deep into Vietnamese territory where it was annihilated. On 25 December 1978 the Vietnamese launched an attack on Cambodia. The 200,000 Vietnamese soldiers who went into Cambodia were there nominally to support the United Front for the National Salvation of Kampuchea (UFNSK) which had been formed just prior to the invasion. This consisted of Cambodian communists who supported Vietnam. When the Vietnamese captured Phnom Penh, this front appointed a temporary Revolutionary Council which quickly proclaimed the People's Republic of Kampuchea. For many years Cambodian governments had been hostile to Vietnam. Prince Sihanouk had feared the Vietnamese; Lon Nol had hated them; and the Khmer Rouge had invaded Vietnam. For the first time since the early 19th century there was a government in Cambodia that was not only openly pro-Vietnamese, but also quickly accused of being a puppet of Vietnam.

With the overthrow of the Khmer Rouge—they are defeated within a fortnight and took refuge along the border with Thailand—Cambodians from all over the country went in search of relatives or moved back to the cities. This massive dislocation in the population led to crops not being planted and a famine quickly resulted. Aid agencies from around the world became involved in helping the starving people of Cambodia and as the country gained a wider international profile, stories of life under the Khmer Rouge emerged.

Because of the sheer number of deaths, many Western commentators called these actions, or in many cases inactions, "genocide." For the most part the persecution of people was connected with their background (urban versus rural; middle class versus working class) rather than their racial origins, making potential trials for genocide impracticable. When evidence emerged that the Muslim Cham minority of Cambodia had been persecuted by the Khmer Rouge, this seemed to open up the possibility of a "genocide" trial.

However the debate on whether these people were killed because they were Chams or because they were Muslims may allow the Khmer Rouge to escape a trial for "genocide" over their deaths. That the leadership was guilty of war crimes and crimes against humanity is not in doubt—where to apportion the responsibility is still debated. Yet, with the exception of a trial in August 1979, when Pol Pot and Khmer Rouge Foreign Minister Ieng Sary were both sentenced to death *in absentia*, there has been little serious effort to bring any of the Khmer Rouge hierarchy to justice for events that happened under their rule.

Although the People's Republic of Kampuchea (PRK) faced the major task of rebuilding the country during its first years in power it seemed to focus on ideology and doctrine rather than on improving the conditions of many of the people. In December 1981 Pen Sovan, a rising politician in the PRK, was purged for speaking out against the continued Vietnamese presence in the country. In January 1985 Hun Sen became prime minister. After joining the Khmer Rouge in 1967, he had fought in the civil war (1970-1975) and spent the early years of Democratic Kampuchea close to the Vietnamese border. With the purges of pro-Vietnamese Cambodian communists in 1977, he fled to Vietnam returning to Cambodia with the Vietnamese forces in December 1978, becoming foreign minister in 1979. Hun Sen rapidly amassed power and a close circle of friends many of whom continue to dominate the Cambodian political scene.

Ranged against the PRK were a number of armed groups based along the Thai-Cambodian border. The remnants of the Khmer Rouge, resupplied with weapons and food from China, Sihanouk's Royalist National United Front for an Independent, Neutral, Peaceful and Cooperative Cambodia (FUNCINPEC) movement and the non communist Khmer People's National Liberation Front (KPNLF) together united, at a political level, to form the Coalition Government of Democratic Kampuchea (CGDK) which, from 1982 occupied the Cambodian seat at the United Nations. The UN General Assembly had already adopted many motions calling for the immediate withdrawal of all foreign forces from Cambodia but these were to no avail except that they did lead to the isolation on the world scene of both Vietnam and the PRK.

With a bitter guerrilla war being waged by the CGDK, often from sanctuaries in Thailand, on the one side, and Vietnamese soldiers backed by PRK militia on the other, initially peace talks were impossible. Following the meeting between Prince Norodom Sihanouk, head of the CGDK, and Hun Sen in France in December 1987, two meetings in Jakarta prepared the groundwork for what was to lead to the Paris Agreements in October 1991. To help prepare for this, Hun Sen's government reintroduced private ownership of land, and reestablished Buddhism as the state religion. They had also renamed the PRK the State of Cambodia. Just prior to the Peace Agreement, Hun Sen's People's Revolutionary Party abandoned Marxism-Leninism and renamed itself the Cambodian People's Party (CPP).

In late 1991, as United Nations officials began to arrive in Phnom Penh, King Sihanouk made a triumphal return amid rumors that a two-party alliance might be struck between the CPP and FUNCINPEC. Cambodian exiles, some who had not been to Phnom Penh since 1975 or earlier, returned to establish political parties. When Khieu Samphan, the nominal leader of the Khmer Rouge, arrived in Phnom Penh a large mob besieged the house which he was using as his office, and he narrowly escaped being lynched. Soon afterward the Party of Democratic Kampuchea left the peace process. Nevertheless preparations for elections continued with a Japanese technocrat, Yasushi Akashi, being appointed to head the UN Transitional Authority in Cambodia. With a massive budget and vast resources, the United Nations was particularly successful in getting the "displaced persons" along the Thai-Cambodian border to return to Cambodia.

In May 1993 elections were held for a Constituent Assembly to formalize a new Constitution. These were the first genuinely competitive elections in Cambodia since 1951. The Royalist FUNCINPEC led by Prince Norodom Ranariddh, son of Prince Sihanouk, won 46 percent of the vote, with Hun Sen's CPP coming second with 38 percent. Hun Sen refused to accept defeat and the United Nations was uncertain what to do next. With the CPP refusing to hand over power, a secession movement in the provinces along the Vietnamese border (which had generally supported the CPP) threatened to split the country. Eventually to end the secession and as the royalists needed a two-thirds majority to get motions through the Constituent Assembly, FUNCINPEC, the CPP and the smaller Buddhist Liberal Democratic Party formed a coalition government. Prince Norodom Ranariddh became First Prime Minister, with Hun Sen as second prime minister. A new constitution was approved and the monarchy was officially restored with Prince Sihanouk becoming King Sihanouk again.

Instability and disagreements between FUNCINPEC and the CPP, as well as a coup attempt, caused major friction. FUNCINPEC Finance Minister Sam Rainsy was sacked with Prince Sirivudh, the foreign minister resigning in protest. In 1995 Sam Rainsy was formally expelled from FUNCINPEC and formed his opposition Khmer Nation Party, which was soon renamed the Sam Rainsy Party. In the meantime the Khmer Rouge, who had remained outside the peace process, continued a low-level guerrilla campaign against the government. With national elections scheduled for 1998, in 1996 the Khmer Rouge split with one group (based at Pailin) forming an alliance with the CPP and the other (based at Anlong Veng) seeming about to form a pact with FUNCINPEC.

Political violence broke out on a massive scale in 1997. It began with an assassination attempt on Sam Rainsy in which 16 people were killed. Soon afterward there was a dispute between some of the Khmer Rouge at Anlong Veng. Pol Pot ordered the killing of his former Commander-in-Chief and Defence Minister Son Sen. In retaliation other military leaders led by Ta Mok arrested Pol Pot. When it looked as though the Khmer Rouge at Anlong Veng might join with FUNCINPEC, Hun Sen launched a coup against First Prime Minister Prince Norodom Ranariddh. Soldiers loyal to Hun Sen quickly took control of Phnom Penh after some brief fighting in which 80 people were killed including a number of senior FUNCINPEC officials.

The remaining members of FUNCINPEC within Cambodia chose Foreign Minister Ung Huot as first prime minister with soldiers loyal to Ranariddh making for the Thai border where they maintained an armed resistance at O'Smach. Soon afterward Pol Pot was put on trial by the Khmer Rouge at Anlong Veng with a U.S. journalist Nate Thayer as an observer. Pol Pot died nine months later by which time he had granted Thayer an interview. Pol Pot blamed the failures of his revolution on the Vietnamese and sabotage.

When elections were held in July 1998, the CPP won 64 seats with FUNCINPEC gaining 43 seats and the Sam Rainsy Party 15 seats. FUNCINPEC and Sam Rainsy Party supporters protested about the poll demanding a recount of the vote, which did not take place. Eventually, four months later, the CPP managed to form a coalition with FUNCINPEC. Hun Sen became prime minister with Prince Ranariddh becoming president of the Senate, a newly created upper house. By the end of the year the last remaining Khmer Rouge at Anlong Veng surrendered to the government, bringing to an end the civil war. These troops were then integrated into the Royal Armed Forces of Cambodia.

Greater stability had allowed Hun Sen to dominate his new coalition with FUNCINPEC leaving the Sam Rainsy Party the most viable opposition party and movement. In the February 2002 local government elections, amidst some polling irregularities and intimidation, the CPP polled well but the Sam Rainsy Party was able to make major inroads. The loser was FUNCINPEC many of whose voters had either joined the ranks of Hun Sen's supporters or supported the opposition.

The main problems facing Cambodia now are the nature of much of the wealth of the country coming from unsustainable logging and fishing "techniques." The long term economic future of the country is also threatened by the spread of AIDS. However, the tourist industry, frightened off by political conflict in 1997, has increased rapidly and now provides the country with much-needed foreign currency.

The Dictionary

-A-

"A-". A particle in the Khmer language indicating scorn or contempt. It is widely used in the expression *"a-Pot"* which means "the contemptible [**Pol**] **Pot**."

ABDUL GAFFAR PEANG METH (1944-). Educated in the United States, the **Cham** politician and academic Abdul Gaffar Peang Meth graduated from Hiram College with a B.A. in political science in 1967. After a failed bid for a seat in the **National Assembly** in a special election in **Kampong Cham** in December, he returned to the U.S. for graduate studies, earning an M.A. from Georgetown University in 1969. In March 1970, he was a doctoral student at the University of Michigan. From a family of **Democrat Party** activists, Peang Meth campaigned for the republican cause in the U.S. via *The Republic,* an English-language newsletter which he produced until the end of 1972. The family's tradition of democratic activism was upheld also by a brother in **Phnom Penh**, Abdul Gaffour Peang Meth, who became an aide to Brigadier General **Lon Non**.

After completing his doctoral thesis, "Cambodia and the United Nations" (University of Michigan, 1980), Peang Meth joined the **Khmer People's National Liberation Front (KPNLF)** then being organized from the Thai side of the Cambodian-Thai border. From 1981 until 1986 he was a member of its Executive Committee and from 1982, *Chef de Cabinet* to **Son Sann**, president of the KPNLF and prime minister in the **Coalition Government of Democratic Kampuchea**. His republican sympathies remained and in December 1985, he emerged as the spokesman for the Provisional Central Committee for the Salvation of the KPNLF formed by former senior **Khmer Republic** military officers who commanded the *Khmer Sereikar* and who sought the removal of Son Sann from the leadership of the front. On 15 February 1986 Son Sann expelled Peang Meth and other critics from his Executive Committee, in effect isolating the military and ardently republican wing of the KPNLF from the diplomatic arena. In November 1989 Peang Meth returned to the United States but lent support to the republican cause for a third time in 1992 when the civil-military split within the KPNLF was formalized by the creation of two separate parties: the **Liberal Democratic Party (LDP)** led by **Sak Suthsakhan** and the **Buddhist Liberal Democratic Party** led by Son Sann. Although he was a candidate for the LDP in the 1993 elections, it failed to win any seats. Finding no satisfactory role in the postwar, post-communist, neo-monarchical regime, Peang Meth returned to academic life. He teaches political science at the University of Guam.

ABDUL KOYOM (1943-). An ethnic **Cham** from **Kampong Cham** province, and the son of a teacher, Abdul Koyom studied medicine at the Faculty of Medicine in **Phnom Penh**, 1965-1975. Evacuated from the city in 1975, he survived the hard labor regime and purges of the **Pol Pot** era joining the Vietnamese-promoted **United Front for the National Salvation of Kampuchea** in January 1979, and soon after, the **People's Revolutionary Party of Kampuchea (PRPK)**. Acquiring some prominence after he served as a witness at the hastily organized People's Revolutionary Tribunal of 1979, which judged Pol Pot and **Ieng Sary** guilty of genocide, Abdul Koyom was elected to the PRPK-dominated **National Assembly** formed in May 1981. He served occasionally as acting secretary-general of the Assembly but his principal posts throughout the 1980s were in the health and public welfare branches of the Phnom Penh municipal administration.

ACHAR. The *achar* is a respected layman who acts as an intermediary between Buddhist temple communities and families served by the temple. An *achar* is often a former monk, and always a man respected for his knowledge and outstanding personal qualities and virtues (*neak meanbon*). In times of social or political crisis, local *achars* often assume mediating or leadership roles. Many were involved in the struggle for independence. For examples of *achars* who became prominent revolutionaries, see HEM CHIEU; SON NGOC MINH (*Achar* Mean); TOU SAMOUTH (*Achar* Sok).

ACLEDA. *See* ASSOCIATION OF CAMBODIAN LOCAL ECONOMIC DEVELOPMENT AGENCIES.

ACTION FOR DEMOCRACY AND DEVELOPMENT (ADD). An electoral party formed in July 1992 based on a development movement established near the Thai border in 1989. It was led by the prominent technocrat **Chak Saroeun**, and was the first political party to be registered for the 1993 elections by the **United Nations Transitional Authority in Cambodia (UNTAC)**. Required by the Paris agreements to promote multiparty democracy, the UNTAC election law of 1992 provided for the creation of multimember constituencies with **National Assembly** deputies being chosen from party lists in proportion to the votes received by the party. This ensured an end to the monopoly of power by one party and made a coalition government almost unavoidable. It also ensured that small parties, such as the ADD, would be excluded from the Assembly and the coalition cabinet. When the votes were counted, the bottom 16 parties, which included ADD, had a combined national total of 1.3 percent only of all votes cast.

ADMINISTRATIVE DIVISIONS. Excluding the **Pol Pot** years, 1975-1978, territorial divisions have remained constant through the centuries. The largest territorial units are *khet,* or provinces. These are subdivided into *srok,* or districts. Each *srok,* will have two or more *khum,* subdistricts or townships, which in turn have several *phum,* hamlets or villages. A provincial governor is known as a *chauvraykhet,* a district chief as a *chauvraysrok,* and a subdistrict headman as a *mékhum.* Under French colonial rule, Cambodia had 13 provinces: **Battambang** (after 1907), **Kampot, Kandal, Kampong Cham, Kampong Chhnang, Kampong Speu, Kampong Thom, Prey Veng, Pursat, Siem Reap, Stung Treng, Svay Rieng** and **Takeo**.

In the postcolonial era, 1953-1970, Cambodia retained these provinces, but some were divided to create five additional provinces: **Koh Kong** (western Kampot), **Mondolkiri** (eastern Kratié), **Oddar Meanchey** (northern Siem Reap), **Preah Vihear** (northern Kampong Thom), and **Ratanakiri** (northeastern Stung Treng). **Phnom Penh** became a municipality, enjoying the legal status of a province, and four smaller municipalities were subsequently established: **Bokor, Kep,** Tioulongville (**Kirirom**) and **Sihanoukville** (Kampong Som). The **Khmer Republic,** 1970-1975, retained these divisions, but for security reasons, and a desire to create more provincial administrative jobs, some provinces were further divided and four more were created: **Banteay Meanchey,** Sangkum Meanchey (**Pailin**), Phnom Dei and Prey Kbas.

National administrative divisions changed radically under the succeeding **Democratic Kampuchea** regime, 1975-1978. The country was divided into eight zones (*phumipheak*): North, Northeast, Northwest, Central, Western, Southwestern, Eastern and a special, autonomous zone centered on Kratié, each zone governed and administered by a revolutionary committee with territorially based divisions of the army. Local administration was entrusted to rural cooperatives with party-dominated management committees. In 1979, the **People's Republic of Kampuchea** restored traditional forms of local administration based on the 18 provinces originally organized under **Norodom Sihanouk,** 1954-1970. The Republican era province of Banteay Meanchey was also retained along with the municipalities of Phnom Penh and Kampong Som. These administrative divisions were retained by the **United Nations Transitional Authority in Cambodia (UNTAC)** and the Royal Government formed in 1993 which later awarded the status of municipality to Kep and to Pailin and changed the name of Kampong Som to *Krong Preah Sihanouk* or Sihanoukville. The March 1998 national **census** identifies 24 provinces (including four municipalities), 182 districts (*srok*), 1,623 subdistricts *(khum)*, and 13,408 villages *(phumi)*.

ADVISORS. Major Cambodian politicians today have personal advisory corps, a phenomenon with roots in the colonial experience but perpetuated as a result of the weakness of representational institutions and the absence of a professionally trained civil service. In the case of Prime Minister **Hun Sen**, advisors are an important element in the construction of a framework of personal control of policy areas and resources. The last published list of his private advisory corps contained 80 names. In addition to private advisors, there are a small number of advisors appointed by royal *kret* ("decree") who receive salaries corresponding to designated civil service ranks. Seven advisors were appointed to the government on 2 December 1998. These included **Ieng Mouly**, who has the rank of minister and responsibility for overseeing national mine clearance, and **Penn Thol**, also ranked as minister and given policy responsibility for public and foreign affairs. Ten others were appointed as advisors to the prime minister on 7 December 1998. Heading this list is **Kun Kim**, Hun Sen's long serving chief of staff, who holds the rank of minister. Another official advisor is Ho Sithy, his principal private secretary, who holds the rank (and salary) of a secretary of state. King **Norodom Sihanouk** also possesses a small corps of paid official advisors, chosen to represent major political orientations and military opinion. The principal royal advisors in 2001 included Samdech **Heng Samrin** and Sihanouk's oldest son, HRH Sdech Krom Luong **Norodom Yuvaneath**. *See also* FRENCH "RESIDENTS."

AGENCE KHMÈRE DE PRESSE (AKP). The official Cambodian news agency launched in 1951, it published daily bulletins in Khmer and French until April 1975. As well as selected articles from foreign news agencies, AKP carried official Cambodian government statements and press releases, some official correspondence of Prince **Norodom Sihanouk** (until 1970) and excerpts from articles appearing in the international press which mentioned Cambodia or reported on world events in ways favored by the government, or by Sihanouk. With other sources of information being controlled or difficult to access, AKP bulletins were the primary source of news for the national media, local journalists being few in number, and in the late Sihanouk period and throughout the **Lon Nol** period, freelance writers and the print medium in particular were subject to censorship and government-imposed suspensions of publication. Suppressed between April 1975 and January 1979, the dissident communists who met in Snuol on 2 December 1978 to create the **United Front for the National Salvation of Kampuchea** agreed to the creation of *Saporamean Kampuchea* (SPK), "News Agency of Kampuchea," which in January 1979 adopted the old formats and mimeographs of the AKP. SPK issued a three-part series of daily bulletins in Khmer: local news printed in red ink, international agency reports in blue, international press articles in green. Condensed versions carrying a selection of items from the three sections of the Khmer language bulletins were published in daily bulletins issued in French, English and, until 1991,Vietnamese. In August 1993, when it was clear that other elements of the prerevolutionary era were being restored, SPK renamed itself AKP. In 1997 it published three daily bulletins in Khmer, English and French with a total circulation of 4,000 only. Coalition government and lack of press freedom since 1993 have greatly undermined its historic dominance and influence.

AGRICULTURE. Agriculture, including **forestry** and fishing, is the most important sector in the Cambodian economy employing more than 70 percent of the economically active population and accounting for almost 50 percent of Gross Domestic Product in the mid-1990s. The agricultural sector is nevertheless seriously underdeveloped: political instability and wars have drained the sector of public investment and of male labor; national soils are mediocre, and in the absence of modern inputs annual fertilization depends heavily on alluvial deposits left by the receding flood waters of the **Mekong-Tonlé Sap** complex; only 10 percent of the cultivated land area is irrigated thereby restricting the area available for year-round cultivation; insect infestations and plant diseases reduce yields and output; monsoon rainfalls have become increasingly irregular in the 1990s, resulting in flash floods or drought; low returns from agriculture, arising from low average yields of between 1.1-1.4 tons of paddy per hectare in this decade, slow industrial growth in urban areas; the laying to fallow of approximately 300,000 hectares of farm land infested with landmines discourage household investment even though a postwar baby boom in the 1990s is creating demographic pressures on available land in many parts of the lowland plain. The agrarian cycle of many rural communities is moreover marred by disputes over land use rights and land boundaries, disputes arising as a result of the effort to promote large-scale agriculture and rapid growth during the **Pol Pot** period (1975-1978) and the attempt to restore small-scale managerial regimes in the 1980s, followed by the restoration of family economy after 1989 which led to many communist cadres awarding titles to the best plots to each other.

For most of the 20th century, until the outbreak of civil war in 1970, Cambodia was a net **rice** exporter with most government revenue being derived from the taxation of exports. Wartime conditions, including inflationary price rises for most essential goods and services, undermined commercial food and commodity production (e.g., coffee, tea, rubber latex). Free market exchange ceased altogether between 1975-1978 when all currencies of exchange were abolished. Even when markets and a new *riel* were gradually restored in the 1980s, most vegetable and food grain output was consumed on a subsistence basis or traded on a barter basis, often for fish or preserved fish products, the major source of protein in the national diet. Exports of rice resumed in the mid-1990s, on a very limited basis. Surveys of rural nutrition undertaken in 1998 revealed one in five children under six years of age is malnourished with many showing signs of stunted growth. Acute food shortages and the poor distribution of food within the economy indicate the grinding poverty of the rural poor in Cambodia, for those living away from the major towns and roads are often unable to secure supplementary, nonfarm employment and income, or the resources required to invest in supplementary food crops such as sweet potatoes, cassava, maize and beans. Because of the steadily rising demand for rice and land, the total land area given over to cultivation of secondary food crops and industrial crops such as sesame, sugar cane, soybeans and cotton has stabilized at around 180,000 hectares which is substantially less than in the 1960s. Average yields for most of these crops are also lower, an indication of the constraints on rural production in the absence of agricultural modernization. Political instability in **Phnom Penh** and corrupt practices at every level of public administration ensure that the negative trends in agriculture will not be easily reversed.

Agriculture in Cambodia requires substantial investment and reorganization in order to satisfy national cereal requirements and to produce surpluses. Although international assistance is greatly strengthening rural infrastructure, especially the road network, domestic markets for goods and labor are too small, weak and unstable to permit a rapid transformation in the life chances of the rural population. Deepening rural poverty is known to contribute to the trafficking of young women and boys into urban prostitution and to illegal migration to Thailand in search of work. *See also* RUBBER.

AHMAD YAHYA (1945-   ). Royalist politician of **Cham** Muslim origins, Ahmad was born in **Kampong Cham** and sought refuge in France during the 1970s and then the **United States**, where in the 1980s he became a supporter of the royalist **FUNCINPEC**. In February 1992, at the congress which transformed the Royalist front movement into an electoral party bearing the same name, he was elected to the party's executive, the Steering Committee, and was appointed to its Political Coordination Bureau. In the May 1993 elections Yahya won a seat in **Phnom Penh.** In October 1993, when the Constituent Assembly was transformed into the **National Assembly**, he was named chair of the Commission for Public Works, Transport, Communications, Industry, Energy and Trade and a member of the Commission for Parliamentary Procedures. In January 1995, together with other members of parliament, he created a nongovernmental organization, the Agency for National Development, which promotes rural development. He remained loyal to Prince **Norodom Ranariddh** after the *coup d'état* of July 1997, and briefly sought refuge in **Thailand**. He was reelected to the **National Assembly** in 1998 and was among the 21 incumbents reelected to the 36-strong Steering Committee of the FUNCINPEC party in 1999. He is now a Secretary of State for Public Works and Transportation.

AIDS (Acquired Immune Deficiency Syndrome). Statistics recently released by the National AIDS Authority confirm HIV infection has reached pandemic proportions with an estimated 100 new infections per day. In 2000, approximately 180,000 people were infected with the HIV virus and 20,000 of these were expected to succumb to full-blown AIDS. Very few AIDS sufferers have access to hospital treatment or other forms of professional care, public and private health services being limited to the capital city and major towns. The disease is spreading most rapidly among sexually active young men who visit prostitutes and who later infect their wives. In 1999, 2.7 percent of married housewives seeking medical attention were diagnosed as HIV positive or as AIDS sufferers while 38 percent of all HIV positive women were between 15-24 years of age. Annual reports from the country's two principal blood transfusion centers revealed 5.6 percent of blood donors in 1998 had HIV. Sample surveys carried out by NGOs indicate that more than 6 percent of the country's 60,000-80,000 policemen may be HIV positive, as are around 40 percent of prostitutes in **Phnom Penh**. The government's "100 percent condom use" campaign is far from effective but up to one million condoms a month are being distributed. Illiteracy and lack of understanding of human biology in rural areas obstruct public appreciation of the dangers posed to public health. Surveys of street children in 2001 and 2002 also revealed recent sharp increases in intravenous drug use in Cambodia.

AING BUN THA. A 1962 graduate of the Faculty of Law and Economic Sciences, Royal University of Phnom Penh, Aing Bun Tha worked for The Far East Life Assurance Company. He represented the Ministry of Justice in the **constitutional drafting committee** formed in 1971. In 1993 he ran for the **National Assembly** on the royalist slate in **Kampong Thom** province, but was too far down on the list to win a seat outright. Following **Cambodian People's Party**-**FUNCINPEC** agreements on power sharing, he was appointed third deputy governor of **Kampong Thom** in December 1993. Many top appointments by the ruling coalition parties led to resignations from the National Assembly seats, and Aing Bun Tha obtained a FUNCINPEC seat in the Assembly in 1994, taking his oath on 24 October 1994.

AKASHI, YASUSHI (1931-   ). Special representative of the UN secretary general in Cambodia, 1992-1993. Born in **Japan**, Akashi joined the United Nations in 1957. After the signing of the Cambodian peace agreement in Paris in 1991, Akashi, then under secretary-general for disarmament affairs, was chosen to head the **United Nations Transitional Authority in Cambodia (UNTAC),** which was responsible under the terms of the Paris Agreements on Cambodia for disarming and regrouping of the warring Cambodian armies, monitoring civilian administration, promoting and protecting **human rights**, restoring public order and organizing national **elections**. UN efforts were stymied, on the one hand, by the **Party of Democratic Kampuchea**, which refused to lay down its arms, and on the other by the State of Cambodia authorities who accepted international control and supervision only reluctantly, and who attempted to portray the UN presence as de facto recognition of their regime. In spite of the collapse of the cease-fire and the failure to demobilize the two principal party armies, more than 90 percent of the eligible electorate voted in the UNTAC-organized election of May 1993. A brief military rebellion by supporters of **Cambodian People's Party,** defeated by **FUNCINPEC** in the poll, was resolved by the formation of a two-party coalition and power sharing in key posts and ministries. Akashi was thereafter able to claim that UNTAC had achieved one of its major objectives: the restoration of legitimate government to the country. Akashi was subsequently chief UN envoy to the former Yugoslavia, but was replaced in October 1995 after the collapse of the UN safe haven at Srebrenica.

AM RONG (1929-1975). Born in **Battambang**, and one of four children from a modest farming family, he was a graduate of the Royal School of Administration and the Royal Military Academy who joined the Cambodian Army in 1953 and served as a paratrooper from 1956. In the late 1960s **Lon Nol**, then minister of defense, sponsored him on additional military training courses in **France** and in the **United States**. In 1970, and still Lon Nol's protégé, he was promoted to major and named spokesman for the **Khmer Republic** High Command, a post he held until 1975. He was arrested on 17 April 1975 after the fall of the Republic, being held and interrogated by them at the Monorom Hotel in downtown **Phnom Penh** until sometime in May. It is believed he was executed immediately after these interrogations.

AN MEANG. *See* KEO MEAS.

AN SUM. A colonel, he was head of the propaganda and education department of the Cambodian People's Armed Forces from September 1982, deputy-chairman of the Defense Ministry's emulation council from June 1983 and first deputy chief of the Defense Ministry's general political department from January 1989. An Sum was imprisoned in May 1990 along with **Ung Phan** and six others who were accused of subversion when they attempted to form a new, liberal democratic socialist party. He was released in October 1991 when a general amnesty for political prisoners was agreed upon in Paris.

ANG CHAN I (1510-1567). King of Cambodia 1556-1567. After a period of residence in the Siamese capital of Ayudhya, Ang Chan returned to the motherland, won a civil war and established a new capital at **Lovek**. During his long reign, he led armies to victory in several campaigns against the Siamese, visited and restored some of the temples at **Angkor** and opened trading relations with European powers. As he was the last powerful king of the Angkorean era, Ang Chan is honored as a national hero in many Cambodian legends and historical texts.

ANG CHAN II (1792-1834). King of Cambodia 1797-1834. He succeeded his father, King **Ang Eng** as a young boy and for the next 10 years was closely supervised by Siamese regents. After he began to rule in his own right in 1806, he tried to reduce his dependency on Siam (**Thailand**) by forging an alliance with **Vietnam**. Chan's attempts to play his neighbors off against each other prefigured the tactics of his great-grandnephew, **Norodom Sihanouk** in the 20th century. During the reign of Ang Chan II, the Khmer kingdom was battered and buffeted by invasions from Siam and Vietnam and suffered the humiliation of dual suzereignty. Chan emerges from contemporary accounts as a man unwilling or unable to exercise royal authority in response to the demands of stronger powers and anarchic local conditions.

Ang Chan married first *neak monéang* Tep, the daughter of **Baen**, and they had one daughter: Ang Baen (1809-1837), who was executed by the Vietnamese who judged her pro-Siamese. Ang Chan's second wife was *neak monéang* Krochap who bore him two children: Princess (later Queen) **Ang Mei** and Prince **Poukombo** (1818-1825). Ang Chan's third wife was Yos, and they had one daughter, Ang Peou (who married Ang Em, son of **Ang Eng**). A fourth wife, *neak monéang* Pen, was a younger sister of Krochap, and bore another daughter: Princess Ang Snguon (who married Ang Bhim, son of Prince **Ang Em**).

ANG DUANG (1796-1860). King of Cambodia 1848-1860. Succeeding his niece, **Ang Mei** (r 1835-1847), Duang was the youngest brother of King **Ang Chan II**. Following a Vietnamese invasion of Cambodia in 1811, Duang fled with two other brothers to Bangkok, where he sought the protection of the Siamese court and was in fact held hostage in Bangkok for the next 20 years. In 1835, following Chan's death and the defeat of a Siamese army at the hands of the Vietnamese, the Siamese placed Duang in charge of a formerly Cambodian province, **Siem Reap**, which had been under Siamese control since the 1790s. Three years later, in an obscure incident that may have followed a Vietnamese offer to Duang of the Cambodian throne, Duang was arrested by the Siamese, taken to Bangkok and forced to swear allegiance anew to King Rama III.

In 1841 he was allowed to return to Cambodia, accompanying a powerful Siamese military expedition that sought to dislodge the Vietnamese. Fighting between Siam (**Thailand**) and **Vietnam** sputtered along in Cambodia for several years, while Duang strove to kindle support among the country's decimated elite. When the Vietnamese withdrew in 1847, the Siamese placed Duang on the Cambodian throne. He settled in the former capital of Oudong, where he encouraged the restoration of Buddhist monasteries destroyed in warfare and reinstated royal patronage for local officials. Duang has been treated with respect by Cambodian historians, who see him as the founder of a modern, independent nation. An accomplished poet, a fervent Buddhist and a relatively popular ruler, he also successfully led Cambodian forces against **Cham** rebels and sought to lessen Siamese political influence by secretly appealing for British, and later French, protection. The Siamese court supported this initiative, but it was revived by Duang's eldest son, **Norodom**, who succeeded him in 1860, ushering in almost a century of French colonial rule.

Duang had many wives and 18 legitimate children. His 1st wife was Ong, with whom he had one daughter, Mom (1821-c1885). His 2nd wife was Ev (Eu), with whom he had two daughters: Tramol (1828-1872) and Ou (c1830-1866). His 3rd wife was Pen, daughter of *Okhna* Sauphea Tuphdey. She had three children: Chraloeng (King **Norodom**), born 1834; Changkoloney, born c1836 (married King **Sisowath**), and Kessaney, born 1840. With his 4th wife, Pou, Duang had one son, Sar, born 1840 (King **Sisowath**). Duang's 5th wife was *neak monéang* Kham; she bore a son, **Sivotha**, born 1841. With his 6th wife, Ieng, there was only one daughter, Daracar, born 1843. Duang's 7th wife was Meas, and they had one daughter, Ing. His 8th wife, Phaltep Savann, gave birth to a son, Serivong, in 1842. His 9th wife, *neak monéang* Monichot, had a daughter, Monthea Ti, born 1854. Duang's 10th wife was *neak monéang* Chanthou, and the mother of his son, Chantavong, born 1852. His 11th wife was *neak monéang* Lanter (who later married **Im**), and they had a daughter, Sra Ouk, born 1852. With his 12th wife, *neak néang* Nuong (sister of eighth wife Phal-tep-Savann), he had a son, Nupparot (the Court Chronicler for many years). Duang's 13th wife was *preah sucheat* Neari, and they had a son, Keo Monoha, born 1854. His 14th wife was Krapa Meas; and they had a daughter, Khandamali, born 1855. With his 15th wife, Khoun Cham Ev, he had a daughter, Chant Chhom, born 1856. His last wife was *neak néang* Im, daughter of a commoner, and they had a son, Nilawong, born 1859. Duang also had several concubines, one of whom gave birth to a daughter, *chaokhun preah* Yuravongs (whose daughter married Prince Norodom Hassakan).

ANG EM, Prince (1794-1844). The son of King **Ang Eng**, Ang Em served as co-regent of Cambodia 1811-1813 and governor of **Battambang** 1834-1844. He married Ang Peou, daughter of King **Ang Chan**, and they had a son, Ang Bhim (1824-1855), whose descent line includes Prince Sisowath Indravong and Prince **Sisowath Youtévong**. He died in Chaudoc, Vietnam.

ANG ENG (1773-1797). King of Cambodia 1794-1797. Founder of the dynasty that ruled from 1794, Eng spent much of his boyhood in exile in Siam (**Thailand**) under the protection of the Rama I. He was crowned king of Cambodia in Bangkok in 1794 and allowed back into his country under Siamese supervision. Soon afterward Siam assumed control of two Cambodian provinces, **Battambang** and **Siem Reap**, which were not returned to Cambodia until 1907. Eng's brief reign was uneventful, but because it came after a prolonged period in which Cambodia had no king, he is revered in Cambodian chronicle histories. He married *neak monéang* Ut and they had a son, King **Ang Chan II** (1792-1834). With his second wife, *neak monéang* Khe, he had two children: Prince Ang Bhim (1793-1798) and Princess Meatuccha. His third wife was *neak monéang* Rat, and they had a son, Prince **Ang Em**, born in 1794. His fourth wife was Ros, and they had a son, **Ang Duang**, who later became King of Cambodia.

ANG KIM KHOAN (1910-c1974). An ethnic Vietnamese who was naturalized in the 1950s, he was born on 10 February 1910 in **Siem Reap** town, the son of Ang Chhay and Mme (née) Tan Puy. He completed his secondary education in Cambodia and earned a fortune trading in jute and grain in **Battambang** and **Siem Reap** provinces. He was a member of the first *Conseil d'Administration* of the National Bank, established in 1954 and became a prominent member of the **Sangkum** after it was established in 1955. He was elected to the **National Assembly** in 1958 and again in 1962, representing Battambang. He was president of the economic affairs commission 1958-1959. He served as undersecretary of state for the Council of Ministers, and he directed the National Office of Tourism from December 1964 to 1965 and the national hotel network for tourism in the late 1960s. Overseas in March 1970 when Prince **Norodom Sihanouk** was deposed, he and wife rapidly declared their support for the prince and for the government in exile organized by Sihanouk with support and encouragement from **China** and the Democratic Republic of **Vietnam**. Ang Kim Khoan was sentenced to death *in absentia* for high treason in August 1970 after he was named a member of the Central Committee of the **National United Front of Kampuchea**. He was appointed **Royal Government of National Union** ambassador to the Democratic People's Republic of Korea in 1972, a post held until 1973.

ANG MEI (1815-1870). Queen of Cambodia 1835-1847. The daughter of King **Ang Chan** (r 1806-1834), she was named by Cambodia's Vietnamese protectors to succeed her father following his death. For the next six years, under close Vietnamese supervision, Mei performed such royal duties as she could, including the granting of seals of office to her officials. The Vietnamese arrested her in 1841. The move, which was associated with an attempt to annex the Khmer Kingdom and to oblige Khmer officials to serve the Vietnamese administration, sparked popular unrest. Over the next few years, in the war that ensued between Siam (**Thailand**) and **Vietnam**, Mei was often carried off to Vietnam. She was released by the Vietnamese when the fighting stopped in 1847 and thereafter lived in obscurity in Oudong, where her uncle **Ang Duang** and his son **Norodom**, her cousin, reigned as kings.

ANG SNUOL. A township just west of **Phnom Penh**, it was where, in January 1975, a particularly vicious massacre of civilians by the revolutionary communist army took place. As the killings occurred just prior to the seizure of Phnom Penh in April, they were seen, by some, in the anti-communist context of the Cold War, as prefiguring the evacuations and bloodbath to come.

ANG TASOM. This village, in **Takeo** province, was the site of some of the earliest public demonstrations against the overthrow of Prince **Norodom Sihanouk** in March 1970. In July 1972 the armies of the **Khmer Republic** and the **National United Front of Kampuchea** engaged in battle for control of Ang Tasom and surrounding regions. When the besieged republican forces were relieved on 12 July Colonel Hin Num was appointed governor of Takeo, replacing the civilian Kong Chhath.

ANGKAR or *ANGKAR PADEVAT*. *Angkar* is the Khmer language term for organization, and *padevat* the term for revolution. Both words were employed euphemistically by cadres of the highly secretive **Communist Party of Kampuchea** until 1997. Concealing the existence of the party behind references to the "revolutionary organization" or sometimes as *angkar loeu* ("upper echelon" or "senior ranks") also served to conceal the identity of the party's leadership. During the **Democratic Kampuchea** period, when "the organization" was in power, officials frequently claimed *Angkar* possessed superhuman, total power. *Angkar* had "as many eyes as a pineapple" and was both "mother and father" of the Cambodian people thereby replacing the family structure of prerevolutionary society. From 1977-1979 when the existence of the party was public and it was being heavily and secretly purged from "the party center," *angkar* or *angkar loeu* became eponymous references to **Pol Pot** or to the small group around him in the party's standing committee.

ANGKOR. Derived from the Sanskrit word *nagara* or "city," this designation was given (by European scholars) to the civilization that flourished in the land of the Khmer between AD 800-1432. From their capitals on the northeastern periphery of the **Tonlé Sap** basin, succeeding Khmer kings conquered and reigned over much of mainland southeast Asia including the southern part of contemporary **Vietnam**, eastern **Thailand** and southern Laos. With the rise of modern nationalism, Angkor has come to symbolize Cambodia's lost glory and uniqueness as a civilization, serving also as an emblem of power and national identity. Representations of Angkor Wat have appeared on all national **flags** since independence. *See also* ANGKOR THOM, ANGKOR WAT.

ANGKOR THOM ("big city"). The modern name for the capital city laid out by the Cambodian king **Jayavarman VII** (r 1178-c1220) near the present-day provincial capital of **Siem Reap**. The fortified part of the ancient city, about 3.3 square kilometers, was protected by a moat and contains the remains of the *Phimeanakas* (celestial palace) and its famous royal viewing stand, the Terrace of Elephants. Just outside the south wall lies the **Baphuon,** a monument dating from the mid-11th century reign of **Udayadityavarman II** (r 1050-1066) to represent the mythical Mount Meru. The **Bayon,** a Mahayana Buddhist shrine also built by Jayavarman VII lies just to the southeast. Its massive stone towers are capped on four sides with identical, carved faces thought to represent the compassionate bodhisatva Avalokiteshvara, although other possibilities have also been suggested. The Bayon is also richly decorated with bas-relief depicting ancient wars, everyday life, religious activity and mythical figures and animals.

ANGKOR WAT. The largest religious monument in the world and the centerpiece of a vast complex of approximately 1,000 ancient temples spread over 160 square kilometers. Although its original name is unknown, the temple was constructed in honor of the deity Vishnu by **Suryavarman II** (r 1115-1150) in the early 12th century AD. It is enclosed by an outer wall roughly one square kilometer (812 x 1000 meters) in length, the temple-mountain, which faces west, is built on three successive levels with towers at the four corners of its outer and inner sanctuaries, and with each of the outer walls pierced by a gate, aligned to the cardinal points of the compass. A central tower, signifying Mount Meru, brings the number of towers to nine. The inner walls of Angkor Wat are carved with bas-reliefs depicting scenes from the Ramayana and the life of Krishna, while columns and exterior walls are carved with floral designs and with hundreds of representations of celestial dancers or **apsaras**. The temple probably served as the tomb for Suryavarman II, and also as an astronomical observatory, for many structural aspects of Angkor Wat are reflections of complex astronomical calculations and astrological ideas. Recent remote sensing radar images also reveal the presence of circular mounds and hitherto unexcavated temple constructions to the northwest of Angkor Wat. The radar images of vegetation cover and water management constructions also indicate the region may have been occupied about 300 years earlier than is commonly believed.

Although Angkor Wat was abandoned in the 15th century, inscriptions found there reveal that the temple was partially restored from the 17th and 18th centuries. It is likely, in fact, that the region was always inhabited, and that Angkor played an important part in local rituals and beliefs. By the 1850s, when it was visited by French explorers, it was a Buddhist pilgrimage site much favored by local people and others who settled there. Under the French protectorate, the monument was carefully restored, as a national symbol of lost greatness and vitality. Angkor Wat remained a major national and international tourist attraction after independence, but French archaeological work on the temple ceased with the onset of war in the early 1970s. In the 1980s, when neglect of restoration work and thieving were taking a heavy toll, the **People's Republic of Kampuchea** invited conservationists from India to assist in efforts to protect the temples. Internationally financed restoration and preservation work resumed only in the 1990s after Angkor Wat became a UNESCO world heritage site. The new Apsara Authority whose first head was the architect **Vann Molyvann** regulates modern building. Its UNESCO partner organization is the International Coordinating Committee for the Safeguarding and Development of the Historic Site of Angkor chaired by Japan and France. *See also* BAPHUON.

ANINADIUTYAPURA. Pre-Angkorean city-state, probably located in the vicinity of present-day **Siem Reap**, and thought by some scholars to precede

Angkor as the preeminent city in the region until **Jayavarman II** established his seat of power in the area in 802 AD.

ANLONG VENG. This village which was the base camp and headquarters of the **Party of Democratic Kampuchea (PDK)** between 1993 and 1997, is in the northern province of **Oddar Meanchey** near the Thai frontier. It was to this region that **Pol Pot, Ta Mok** and **Nuon Chea** withdrew with their military forces after the PDK withdrawal from the United Nations-sponsored peacekeeping arrangements in 1992-1993. Anlong Veng was also the site of the trial of Pol Pot conducted by his comrades following the June 1997 assassination of his longtime comrade and former **Democratic Kampuchea (DK)** defense minister **Son Sen**. In June 1998, when Ta Mok was still attempting to consolidate his control, others in the senior leadership defected to the government or quietly slipped away to **Pailin,** joining **Ieng Sary** and others who had defected in 1996. Anlong Veng was then quickly occupied by the Royal Cambodian Armed Forces. Many former DK soldiers and their families have settled in the area, and are attempting to earn meager incomes from the land or cottage industries. Plans to transform the former residences of Pol Pot and Ta Mok into museums may generate tourism income especially as historic **Phnom Kulen** is not far away.

APRIL 17, 1975. The day communist forces took control of **Phnom Penh** ending the 1970-1975 civil war. Over the following days, residents of the city of approximately three million, of whom at least half were refugees, were forcibly evacuated to designated rural areas. Rural supporters of the revolution who viewed themselves as "base people" referred to the evacuees thrust upon them as "**new people**" or "**April 17 people**," the day they "joined" the revolution. April 17 was a national holiday in **Democratic Kampuchea** and in the **People's Republic of Kampuchea/State of Cambodia** until April 1993. Many of the ex-communist members of the **Cambodian People's Party** still commemorate what is seen as a day of victory. For others, it is a day of ignominy and dishonor.

APRIL 17 PEOPLE. *See* NEW PEOPLE.

APSARAS. Mythical, celestial dancers. *Apsaras* are prominent in bas-relief carvings on the courtyard walls at **Angkor Wat** and other temples of the Angkorean period. Their attire, especially their headdresses and jewelry, have inspired the costumes of the Royal Ballet over the past century. *Apsara* imagery is frequently employed in popular culture as a symbol of the Khmer nation and its culture. The **Cambodian People's Party** emblem features an apsara.

ARCHAEOLOGY. The travel diary of **Henri Mouhot**, first published in

1864, and reporting on visits to ancient sites between 1858 and 1860, ignited keen interest in archaeological research and restoration within the **École Française d'Extrême-Orient**. The professional and scholarly excitement of the many devoted French archaeologists who came to work in Cambodia nevertheless dovetailed perfectly with official French colonial perceptions of the Khmer people as a nation-race in terminal decline. **Georges Coedès** and **Georges Groslier** were among the distinguished scholars who worked on restoring **Angkor**, and the monuments and temples nearby, and who encouraged the study of archaeology by national scholars. Although restoration work was interrupted by the civil war, 1970-1975, and neglected during the turbulent **Democratic Kampuchea** period, 1975-1978, archaeological work resumed in the mid-1980s. By the 1990s the Faculty of Archaeology in the Royal University was among the more dynamic institutions in Cambodia.

ARCHITECTURE. Classical Cambodian architecture reached its apogée during the **Angkor** period (802-1432) when massive stone temples and sanctuary towers were built of brick, laterite and sandstone with *corveé*, enslaved, or prisoner of war labor. The most renown, **Angkor Wat** and **Angkor Thom**, display the three main characteristics of classical style: exceptional symmetry in design of complexes which were modeled after religiously inspired images of universal realms (e.g., temple-mountains, graduated levels of construction); stair-way approaches to sanctuary towers, known as *prasat*; wide galleries, grounds, walls and moats to set off the sacral spaces from temporal grounds. Most surfaces were ornately decorated, with floral motifs or basreliefs, as were faux columns, capitals, and doorways. Houses and palaces of the period were made of wood and have not survived.

Modern architecture is predictably influenced by French and classical forms. Until recently most Cambodian houses continued to be made of wood. In rural areas they are built on pilings with walls made of palm mats, floors of woven bamboo strips resting on bamboo joints and roofs of thatched material or tiled. Civic buildings and modern villas in **Phnom Penh** and provincial towns retain decoratif features of classical architecture such as tiered roofs, graduated levels and decorative sculptures and motifs. Some, such as the Chatomuk Theatre were originally designed by **Vann Molyvann**, widely regarded as the nation's leading, living architect.

ARMED FORCES. Prior to 1975 there were three services, the army, the navy and the air force with the latter two being subordinate to the army until 1970. The Royal Cambodian Army, *Forces Armées Royales Khmères* (FARK), was first formed in 1946 as a part of the French colonial forces. Initially all officers were French, but Cambodian officers were trained from 1949. In November 1953, when the army was formally transferred to Cambodian control, French advisors and technicians stayed on. Prince **Norodom Sihanouk** exercised command over the armed forces, with the commander-in-chief and the chief of the general staff responsible for operational control. From 1955-1966 the positions of minister of national defense, commander-in-chief of FARK and chief of the general staff were all held by **Lon Nol**. He returned to the cabinet as defense minister in 1968, after a year's absence following a car crash in 1967, when the **Communist Party of Kampuchea (CPK)** launched its armed struggle against the government.

In March 1970, following the overthrow of Norodom Sihanouk, the army was massively expanded for civil war, initially credibly disguised as a war against "Vietnamese invaders," for troops from northern **Vietnam** and the National Front for the Liberation of South Vietnam had been committed to Cambodian to support Sihanouk's appeal for an armed uprising. With the proclamation of the **Khmer Republic** in October 1970 the term "Royal" was expunged from the name of state institutions. FARK then became *Forces Armées Nationales Khmères* (FANK). While Sihanouk was in power, the army was awarded mostly ceremonial duties and lacked the training, experience and equipment required for most other military functions, including border control. The situation was abruptly transformed during the civil war of 1970-1975 when FANK fought to safeguard national territory and to compete with other armed forces for popular support. Once logistical support and supplies from the **United States** were reduced in 1974, and then, in 1975, cut off, defeat was inevitable.

In **Democratic Kampuchea (DK)**, the National Army of Democratic Kampuchea (NADK) was made up of territorially based divisions and local militia under CPK command. Regular army divisions existed at provincial or "center" levels and by 1978, most were committed to battle on the border with Vietnam where they took heavy losses. Some divisional and regimental commanders in the heavily affected east zone, including **Heng Samrin** and **Hun Sen,** also mutinied as the additional threat of purges appeared. The Vietnamese invasion of Cambodia in late December 1978 swept aside most remaining armed forces or sent them into rapid retreat to the west. In the second civil war or liberation struggle of the 1980s, the Vietnamese fielded by far the largest army, initially estimated at 180,000. The fledging **People's Republic of Kampuchea** slowly raised its own army and local militias, but these were noticeably reluctant to engage the opposition **Coalition Government of Democratic Kampuchea** armies. By 1989, when **Soviet Union** reductions in military assistance rendered its occupation untenable, Vietnam unilaterally withdrew its forces from Cambodia. Also affected by the loss of Soviet aid, notably oil supplies, the **Phnom Penh**-based Revolutionary People's Armed Forces, or the Cambodian People's Armed Forces (CPAF) (from 1990-1993), were unable to continue the war.

Following the formation of the Royal government in 1993, attempts were made to integrate royalist soldiers from the **National Army for an Independent Kampuchea**, the post-1990 name for the **Armée Nationale Sihanoukienne (ANS)**, republican troops from the **Khmer People's National Liberation Armed Forces (KPNLAF)** and ex-communist troops from the CPAF into a new Royal Cambodian Armed Forces. While a unified command structure was created, many units retained their wartime commanders. Mutinies of former ANS and KPNLAF units after the July 1997 **coup d'état** allowed **Nhek Bun Chhay** and **Khan Savoeun** to reestablish a resistance army in the northeast province of **Banteay Meanchey**. The submission of **Ke Pauk** and of the NADK garrison at **Anlong Veng** in 1998 combined with the resolution of the royalist mutiny also in 1998, brought an end to 30 consecutive years of political rebellion and conflict.

ARMÉE NATIONALE SIHANOUKIENNE (ANS) (Sihanoukian National Army). Established in 1981 by **In Tam** with a mandate from Prince **Norodom Sihanouk**, the initial military units came from many spontaneously formed *Khmer Sereikar* groups bearing nativist names such as *Praloeng Khmer* ("Khmer Soul") and *Khmer Angkor* ("Angkorean Khmer"). Disputes between In Tam and In Sakhân, commander of *Khmer Angkor*, and also with **Teap Baen** who was chief of staff of the ANS eventually forced In Tam to give up his command and to retire to America, clearing the way for Prince **Norodom Ranariddh to** become commander in 1986. The ANS changed its name to the *Armée Nationale pour un Kampuchea Independent* (ANKI), 1990-1992. The royalists fought against the combined forces of the **People's Republic of Kampuchea** and **Vietnam** until 1991. In compliance with the Paris Agreements of October 1991 most ANKI units were disarmed in 1992 and subsequently merged, as complete units, into the Cambodian People's Armed Forces. *See also* ARMED FORCES.

ARMY OF THE REPUBLIC OF VIETNAM (ARVN). The South Vietnamese Army, originally founded in 1950 by the **Bao Dai** administration as a national army, it had 38,000 troops by 1951. Steadily built up by the United States in the 1960s, by 1973 it had some 500,000 troops. ARVN's operations in Cambodia included action in the border zone in the 1960s, and the joint **United States**-ARVN incursion in May 1970. ARVN provided logistic support for the **Khmer Republic** from 1970 until the defeat of both regimes in 1975. *See also* VIETNAM.

ARUNA YUKANTHOR, Prince (1860-1934). Born in **Phnom Penh**, Prince Yukanthor was son and heir of King **Norodom;** he married Phaltep Soda Chand. As crown prince, he used his power and influence to oppose the extension of French power, in defense of the traditional aristocracy. An attempt to plead his case in **France** caused a major political furore known as the Yukanthor Affair. He was later exiled to **Thailand.** In 1913 he was living in Singapore, but later returned to Thailand where he died in 1934.

ASIAN DEVELOPMENT BANK (ADB). Established in 1966, it now has a membership of 32 Asia-Pacific countries, plus 15 from Europe and North America. Cambodia joined in 1968. Although the bank sent a mission to Cambodia in 1969, and approved a small loan in 1970 ($1.7m) and $80,000 in technical assistance for improvements to **Phnom Penh**'s electricity supply, major credits and grants have not been extended until recently.

ASSASSINATIONS. Political killings have occurred regularly in postwar Cambodia. The following list of assassinated politicians and activists is not complete and is supplied as an indication. Two recent, unsuccessful assassination attempts are equally noteworthy: the opposition leader **Sam Rainsy** was the intended victim of a grenade bombing on 30 March 1997 which killed at least 16 others; second prime minister **Hun Sen** was the target of sniper fire on 29 May 1997 but was not injured. No arrests or prosecutions have been made as a result of these assaults.

Ieu Koeus, cofounder of Democrat Party, **Phnom Penh**, 14 January 1950.

Jean de Raymond, French Résident, Phnom Penh, 29 October 1951.

Gen. **Dap Chhuon**, near **Siem Reap,** February 1959.

Nop Bophan, newspaper editor, outside police barracks, Phnom Penh, 10 October 1959 (died 12 October).

Tou Samouth, communist leader, Phnom Penh, May 1962.

Col. **Seng Sunthay**, Phnom Penh, 19 March 1970.

Kim Phon and Sos Saoun, deputies, Kampong Cham, 25 March 1970.

Lon Nil, brother of **Lon Nol**, Tonlé Bet, 25 March 1970.

Prince Norinractevong, former husband of Princess **Norodom Bopha Devi**, Phnom Penh, late 1970.

Mr. Rathasa (previously Prince **Sisowath** **Rathasa**), Phnom Penh, 21 December 1971.

Keo Sang Kim and **Thach Chia**, Phnom Penh, 4 June 1974.

Tou Chhom Mongkol, newspaper editor, 11 June 1994.

Nuon Chan, newspaper editor, 6 September 1994.

Chan Dara, journalist, 8 December 1994.

Thun Bun Ly, journalist, Phnom Penh, 18 May 1996.

Son Sen, former defense minister of **Democratic Kampuchea**, near Anlong Veng, 10 June 1997.

Ho Sok, interior minister, Phnom Penh, 6 July 1997.

Chau Sambath and **Krauch Yoeurm,** army generals, Kampong Speu, 8 July 1997.

Nou Kim Ei, newspaper editor, Phnom Penh, 11 Jan 1998.

ASSEMBLÉE GÉNÉRALE DES ÉTUDIANTS KHMERS (AGEK).
Formally established in 1964, AGEK was the vehicle of the politically conscious student generation of the 1960s. Its promoters came from the Faculties of Law, Pedagogy, Science and Medicine and included **Phouk Chhay**, **Van Piny**, **Tourn Sok Phallar**, Poc Kanell, **In Sopheap**, Mai Sokhan, Mai Lon, **Tiv Ol**, Yim Kim Tek and Kang Saran, together with Kang Boracheat and Kep Randy from the Royal School of Administration. Some activities centered on lycées, especially the prominent progressive Lycées **Chamroeun Vichea** and **Kambuboth** and Lycée Takhmau where three teachers, Thuch Rin, Sang Rin and Ké Kim Huot went underground when in 1967 Prince **Norodom Sihanouk** and the government banned the organization. Although it was not a Communist organization, or a front movement for the clandestine **Workers' Party of Kampuchea** or **Communist Party of Kampuchea**, as it was later known, the political positions taken by AGEK were greatly influenced by the anti-American, anti-imperialist trends of the decade. AGEK leaders identified with the antiwar and cultural revolution movements in the **United States** and **China** and insisted, in their turn, on the rights of *la jeunesse* ("the young generation") to play a prominent role in politics. The majority of activists came from affluent or well-informed civil servant families who were alienated by the incompetence, nepotism and corruption which was seen to be undermining national development. While the formal and public agenda of the Assembly stressed the importance of political education for young people and of contacts with like-minded youth movements overseas, the hidden agenda stressed struggle against the "suffocating" Sihanouk regime, judged the major obstacle to the nation's progress, happiness and prosperity. Public meetings of the movement were rare. Members met in three-person cell groups for political studies or for illegal distribution of leaflets denouncing United States policies in **Vietnam** or Cambodian government actions. The cells were responsible to and took instructions from a five-person presidium led by Phouk Chhay. By 1967 the movement had grown from about 200 members at the time of its formation to 2,000-3,000. It staged public demonstrations against the **Lon Nol** government formed in 1966 and was accused, erroneously some insist, of attacks on the casino at **Kep** in August-September 1966 and of instigating public protests leading up to the 1967 revolt in **Samlaut**. Because of close links to the Cambodian-Chinese Friendship Association—Phouk Chhay was a vice president—and to the **Phnom Penh** Embassy of the People's Republic of China, AGEK was banned by the government in September 1967 in an official crackdown against activities in support of the Chinese cultural revolution. Approximately 40 of the most active members of the movement,

including Phouk Chhay, were summarily arrested and imprisoned without charge or trial. Several hundred others went underground or sought refuge in the jungle base camps of the **Communist Party of Kampuchea**. Later reinspired by the May 1978 student uprising in France, some ex-AGEK members still at liberty in Phnom Penh briefly attempted to create a clandestine student organization under the name Union des Étudiants Patriotiques. Sihanouk's police succeeded within five months in locating and destroying the union's headquarters and more arrests followed. Most of those arrested in 1967 and 1968 remained in prison until 1970 when a general amnesty granted by the 18 March coup d'état government led to their release.

ASSOA. An anti-French nationalist leader, also known as Ang Phim, Assoa was a pretender to the throne and claimed to be the son of **Ang Em** in an uprising that began in 1862 and lasted until August 1866.

ASSOCIATED STATES OF INDOCHINA. The official name given to the 1949 French attempt to incorporate Annam, Cambodia, **Cochinchina**, Laos and Tonkin into a customs union within the French Union. Cambodia left the Associated States upon achieving independence in November 1953.

ASSOCIATION GÉNÉRALE DES KHMERS À L'ÉTRANGER (AGKE). Originally established as the Association des Cambodiens à l'Etranger in April 1975 by Cambodian intellectuals and neutralists in Paris. Its early membership included Nguon Pythoureth (secretary-general), **Truong Mealy**, Ea Chhor Kim Men, Buor Holl and Mme **Suon Kaset**. Reconstituted as the AGKE in 1976, its new membership included **Son Sann** as its president, with Truong Mealy remaining as secretary-general. The AGKE was the political foundation for the organization of the **Khmer People's National Liberation Front** following the Vietnamese invasion of 1979 and for the creation of **FUNCINPEC** in 1981.

ASSOCIATION OF CAMBODIAN LOCAL ECONOMIC DEVELOP-MENT AGENCIES (ACLEDA). A microfinance agency originally funded by the United Nations Development Program (UNDP) and the International Labor Organization (ILO), ACLEDA grants small, competitively priced loans to microenterprises and small businesses (maximum sums for each category are US$400 or US$4,000 respectively with interest fixed at 1.3 percent monthly). It was established to aid small, rural producers and home-based entrepreneurs who lacked access to credit or who become dependent upon local usurers or middlemen. In 1999 local private lenders charged about 2 percent per month for short term loans or 36-60 percent per annum on medium and long-term loans. At that time ACLEDA had 55,000 borrowers and held outstanding loans totaling $13.3m. In 2000, with assistance from United States Agency for International Development, the Association and its local branches were transformed into a development bank with the UNDP and ILO retaining majority (51 percent) control of the new institution. Shareholders reportedly include the World Bank and European Union financial institutions. By 2001 and with more than 86,000 customers, ACLEDA Bank was the largest of an estimated 72 agencies engaged in microfinance in Cambodia. While donor agencies perceive microfinance as essential for encouraging economic entrepreneurship and growth, rural credit schemes have been undermined by traditions of personal benevolence and dependence in the past. Acleda rates of interest will rise if defaults result in the need to draw on the government's Rural Development Bank for capital loans (costing 7 percent annual interest in mid-2001 compared to 3 percent for World Bank loans).

ASSOCIATION OF REVOLUTIONARY WOMEN OF KAMPUCHEA. One of the three mass organizations established by the communist authorities, 1979-1989. While the principal task of the ruling **People's Revolutionary Party of Kampuchea** was to organize and to control the state apparatus, the work of mobilizing and "educating" the people via diffusion of the party's propaganda was the responsibility of the Solidarity Front for the Construction and Defense of the Kampuchean Motherland, formerly the **United Front for the National Salvation of Kampuchea.** In practice most of its work was carried out by three mass organizations: the Association of Revolutionary Women, the Association of Revolutionary Youth and the Federation of Trade Unions of Kampuchea. In the mid-1980s, each of these claimed large memberships: 1.5 million; 700,000 and 90,000 respectively. Throughout the 1980s, the ARWK was chaired by **Mean Saman** and the deputy chairwoman was **Chhouk Chhim.** The director of the office of the Association was **Im Run.** Between 1989-1992, the term "revolutionary" was dropped from the name of the organization. Its leadership and activities focused on the newly created State Secretariat for Women from 1993.

ASSOCIATION OF CAMBODIAN WRITERS. Founded on 5 February 1956 in the office of the Alumni Association of **Lycée Sisowath**, its presidents included Rim Kin, Sam Tang, Hell Sumpha and **Trinh Hoanh**. Its aims were to promote literary expression principally in Khmer but also in foreign languages and in translation. The Association offered the Indradevi prize from 1960. Its library of titles authored by Cambodians and published mostly in Khmer or Pali held 925 volumes in 1969.

ASSOCIATION OF SOUTHEAST ASIAN NATIONS (ASEAN). Founded in Bangkok in 1967 by Indonesia, Malaysia, the Philippines, Singapore and **Thailand,** ASEAN sought to promote economic, social and cultural cooperation among the noncommunist states of Southeast Asia and to minimize great power intervention in regional affairs. By 1971, when the **United States** withdrawal from **Vietnam** was imminent, ASEAN leaders appealed for a zone of peace, freedom and neutrality. Attempts to normalize relations with Vietnam and to draw it into ASEAN after 1975 were disrupted by Vietnam's 1978 invasion of Cambodia. Brunei joined in 1984. **Laos,** Myanmar and Vietnam subsequently joined in 1997. Cambodia was refused membership in 1997 following the coup in **Phnom Penh** and social unrest after the 1998 elections, but was finally admitted on 30 April 1999. Although ASEAN received much credit in the diplomatic arena for its efforts in resolving "the Cambodian conflict," it was only when the five permanent members of the United Nations Security Council lent support to the stalled Paris Peace Conference on Cambodia (1989), and when Communist Party power collapsed in the **Soviet Union** (1991) that a regional accommodation of Vietnamese communism and military power and a settlement in Cambodia were attainable.

AT MAY. A civil servant, he won a seat in the **National Assembly** in 1947 in Taing Krassaing, **Kampong Chhnang** as a **Democrat.** Once in the Assembly, he established a private legal practice in Kampong Chhnang. He was among the 11 Democrat deputies who defected from the Democrat Party in 1948 to join the **Liberal Party.** In the 1951 elections, he was the Liberal candidate in Prey Kri, Kampong Chhnang, and narrowly lost to Pok Sem.

AU CHHEUN (1908-c1975). Born on 11 May 1908 at Vat Kandal, **Battambang,** the son of Au Sou and Mme (née Ouk Pel), Chheun was educated at **Collège Sisowath** and the School of Law, Hanoi. On his return to Cambodia he served in the administration as *Commis des Résidences* and by 1945 had attained the rank of *vorac montrey.* He was secretary-general, then director, of the École des Kromokars (School of Professional Arts). A delegate to the **Pau Conference,** Au Chheun was also a founding member of the **Progressive Democratic Party,** led by Prince **Norodom Montana,** and Chheun served as secretary of state for religion, religious work, and fine arts in the Prince **Sisowath Youtévong** government, December 1946 to July 1947, the only non-Democrat to serve in that government. Soon afterward, disillusioned by the outcome of the September 1946 elections, he left the Progressive Democratic Party to join the **National Union Party** of **Khim Tith.** Following the death of Youtévong, Au Chheun remained in the cabinet as minister for the interior from August 1947 to February 1948. In December 1947 he was created Chevalier of the Legion of Honour. At this time he married Auth Bophavann.

In January 1948, as a representative of the administrative branch of the civil service, Au Chheun was one of the seven successful National Union candidates to win in the elections to the High Council of the Kingdom. He left the cabinet when the **Democrat Party** leader **Chhean Vam** became prime minister, but returned to it following the assassination of **Ieu Koeus**. He was minister of finance in the cash-strapped second **Yèm Sambaur** government, September 1949 to May 1950; and in the Prince **Norodom Sihanouk** and Prince **Sisowath Monipong** governments, May to December 1950. In April 1950 Au Chheun helped Yèm Sambaur with the formation of the **National Recovery Party** and was named interior minister, January to March 1951; minister of interior and information, March to May 1951 and minister of finance, May to October 1951. In September 1951 Au Chheun was a candidate in Sauthnithon, Siem Reap for the **National Recovery Party**; and although his party was heavily defeated in the polling, he became an assistant to the prime minister, and also minister of foreign affairs and religion, January to July 1953. He subsequently became deputy prime minister, minister of religion, fine arts, of social action and labor from July to November 1953; minister of state for agriculture, trade, industry, public works and communications from 7-17 April 1954; minister of state for national economy from April-July 1954 and minister of state in charge of trade, finances and planning from April 1954 to January 1955.

Au Chheun was appointed to the **High Council of the Throne** on 24 November 1953; and in 1954 was named ambassador to the United Kingdom. He returned to London in 1959 following the **Sam Sary** scandal. He retired from the diplomatic service in 1965. In March 1972 he was appointed advisor to **Lon Nol**; and in March 1973 was promoted to special advisor to Lon Nol, a position he retained only briefly for the **United States** stopped financing the government "**advisors**" later that year.

AUSTRALIA. Australia has developed close diplomatic links with Cambodia since the 1960s. Its second ambassador, Noel Deschamps, became a close friend of Prince **Norodom Sihanouk** and dean of the diplomatic corps in **Phnom Penh**. In 1965, when Cambodia broke diplomatic relations with the **United States**, Australia represented U.S. interests in Phnom Penh; concurrently, Australia represented Cambodian interests in Saigon. In 1967 the Australian prime minister, Harold Holt, visited Phnom Penh. Nevertheless, in November of the same year Cambodia recalled its ambassador to Canberra, **Tim Nguon**, when the Australian government protested against Australian students who had sent contributions of cash to the Phnom Penh office of the **National Front for the Liberation of South Vietnam**. Australia's foreign minister, **Gareth Evans**, played a major role in the formulation and drafting of United Nations peace proposals, 1989-1990. Australian personnel were later prominent in the civilian and military components of the **United Nations Transitional Authority in Cambodia**.

Many Cambodian politicians hold dual Australian-Cambodian citizenship. These include **Ung Huot**, minister of education after 1993 and first prime minister in 1997; **Theam Bun Srun**, governor of Kampong Som until 1999; **Lay Prohas**, secretary of state in the Ministry of Planning; Poeu Savath, a CPP Senator from 1999-2001, and **Khau Meng Hean**, head of Phnom Penh investment bureau. **Lim Hong** is a member of the Victoria State legislature in Australia.

AUTOGENOCIDE. This is a term coined by French writers to describe events in Cambodia from 1975-1978. The aim was to compare, as well as to distinguish, the attempt made by the German Nazis to exterminate European Jews in the 1940s from the fratricidal killings in Cambodia. The term has no status in law. While a few scholars believe the **Pol Pot** regime to be guilty of statutory "genocide" against the **Cham** and **Chinese minorities** and have produced some evidence of racial discrimination, **human rights** lawyers are generally agreed that a *prima facie* case for prosecutions for the crime of "genocide" does not exist. There is, however, ample evidence of "crimes against humanity" and of war crimes during this period.

AYMONIER, ÉTIENNE FRANÇOIS (1844-1929). French naval officer and scholar-administrator. Aymonier was born in Savoy and joined the Marine Infantry. He was posted to the Inspectorate of Indigenous Affairs in November 1870 and appointed *Représentant* of the French Protectorate in Cambodia from January 1879 to May 1881. A fluent Khmer speaker, he traveled widely on foot and horseback, collecting inscriptions, locating archaeological sites and describing what he saw. His *Épigraphie Cambodgienne* was published in Saigon in 1885. His three-volume study *Le Cambodge* (Paris, 1901-1903), is an essential tool for historians, as is his collection of Khmer folk tales, *Textes khmers* (1876). The first director of the École Coloniale in Paris from 1888 to 1903, he wrote extensively in his retirement about precolonial Cambodia and about **Champa**.

-B-

BA PHNOM. A provincial center in **Prey Veng** province, it is believed to have been an important center of **Zhenla** (Chenla). In precolonial times, the region was one of the five *dei* or territorial fiefdoms entrusted to a *sdach tranh* ("regional monarch"). As late as 1870 criminals were ritually sacrificed at annual ceremonies honoring the goddess of the region, Uma Mahisasuramardini.

BAEN also **BEN.** An official of King **Ang Eng**, he was installed as *ta-la-ha* ("principal minister") by the court of **Thailand** in Udon, being named hereditary ruler of **Batttambang** by King Rama I, founder of the Chakri Dynastry in 1794. Battambang in that period included the modern province of **Siem Reap** and the **Angkor** complex. Under Governor Baen and his descendants, Battambang was semiautonomous, and the family's political influence endured after retrocession to Cambodia in 1907. Among the more prominent of Baen's descendants were **Nhiek Tioulong** and Khuang Aphaiwong, a cofounder of the Thai Democrat party and prime minister of **Thailand** in 1944-1945, 1946 and 1947-1948.

BAKONG. A temple-mountain in the Roluos (ninth century **Hariharalaya**) group, dedicated to Siva and built by King **Indravarman I** (r 877-889) between 881-889. Built on four levels, it displays the features of classical Khmer **architecture.** The central tower, in a contrasting style, was either replaced or renovated in the 12th century.

BAKU. *See* HINDUISM.

BALLET. *See* ROYAL BALLET.

BAM SUON (1925-   ). A native of **Battambang** and briefly ordained as a Buddhist monk, Suon farmed with his family from 1948 until 1979 when he joined the **People's Revolutionary Party of Kampuchea** and became a *mekhum*, a subdistrict headman, in the **People's Republic of Kampuchea (PRK)** administration. Elected to the PRK **National Assembly** in May 1981, he was a leading figure in the **United Front for National Construction and Defense of Kampuchea**. He was chairman of the Thmar Puok district People's Revolutionary Committee in **Banteay Meanchey** province until November 1989 when he was replaced by Soeng Phon.

BAN SOPHAL (1957-). Appointed third deputy governor of **Battambang** province by **FUNCINPEC** in December 1993, he joined the **Sam Rainsy Party (SRP)** in December 1997 following the ouster of Prince **Norodom Ranariddh** from the coalition government. He headed the SRP list in **Kampong Thom** in the 1998 elections but the SRP failed to win any seats in this province.

BANDUNG CONFERENCE. Convened in April 1955 in the Indonesian city of Bandung, this meeting of African and Asian nations prefigured the formation of the Non-Aligned Movement. It was here that the young Prince **Norodom Sihanouk** met and befriended Indonesia's Sukarno, India's Nehru and **China's Zhou Enlai**. These nationalist heroes and the "third world" outlook of the conference generally, encouraged Sihanouk to pursue a policy of "neutrality" in relations with the **United States** and the Soviet Union. Cambodia was surrounded by allies of the rival superpowers during the Cold War.

BANGKOK PLOT. This international conspiracy to topple Prince **Norodom Sihanouk** from power was initiated by **Sam Sary.** Recalled from his ambassadorial post in London in 1958, Sam Sary organized a **Party of the People** (*kanacpac reastrethipatay*) and campaigned for democratic constitutional change. Acting on the principle that "the enemy of my enemy is my friend," **Thailand**'s prime minister and dictator, Marshal Sarit Thanarat, lent his support to Sary's efforts to destabilize Sihanouk's state. But on 13 January 1959, Sihanouk publicly denounced a "Bangkok Plot" and ordered his army to round up those conspiring to stage a coup. Sam Sary immediately fled the country. In spite of official Thai denials, it became clear in the 1980s, when documentary evidence from Thai sources surfaced, that Sihanouk's fears and suspicions were well founded. **Dap Chhuon** also took flight but was caught and summarily executed by Colonel **Lon Nol** who thereby ensured he would divulge no names. Dap Chhuon's brother **Kem Srey** was put on trial and executed in 1960 for his role. *See also* CHAU BORY; NGO DINH DIEM.

BANKING. Modern banking was established during the final years of the colonial period, initially the unplanned result of French banks extending banking services to French residents and Chinese businessmen. Most colonial era bank branches remained in operation after independence but the money issue function held by the *Banque de l'Indochine* was transferred to the **National Bank of Cambodia (NBC)** organized in December 1954 by **Son Sann.** French domination of the sector was steadily diluted over the next 10 years as locally owned commercial banks were founded. All eight private banks received a jolt in November 1963 when Prince **Norodom Sihanouk** nationalized the sector and created two state commercial banks, the Inadana Jati Bank and the **Banque Khmère.** These failed in their basic aim which was to regulate and to enforce controls on domestic international commerce and inadvertently strengthened parallel (or black) markets for goods and services. Between 1975-1978 there were no banks and no national currency of exchange circulated in the country. From 1979, under the communist **People's Republic of Kampuchea**, there was a revitalized state bank with one foreign trading arm providing hard currency and other foreign exchange services.

Commercial and private banking institutions were fully restored only from 1992 operating under licenses issued by a resuscitated NBC which shed its commercial functions and reassumed its role as a central bank. In

December 2000 the NBC ordered the closure and liquidation of 11 of the existing 31 private banks as these had not satisfied recapitalization requirements of a 1999 banking law. The licenses of the remaining 20 banks were renewed but the renewals were conditional for 16 of the banks who were asked for additional details of restructuring and recapitalization. In 2002 several banks were experiencing difficulties with recapitalization which involves a deposit of 16 million dollars at the NBC. Banks also face difficulties in their lending operations. Currently only 20 percent of available rural capital is in the hands of banks and defaults on repayments are being recorded on one in five bank loans. There is also competition. NGO microfinancing projects and **ACLEDA** offer loans at cheaper rates.

BANQUE KHMÈRE. A private, commercial bank, the Banque Khmère was among those nationalized in November 1963. As it was the only one to be wholly Khmer-owned it held major state accounts (e.g., those of the National Distillery Company and the Royal Railways). In 1964 it was reorganized as a state bank being renamed Banque Khmère pour le Commerce (BKC). Until 1970 the BKC was restricted to financing import and export transactions for SONEXIM, the state trading company, and to controlling foreign exchange allocations made by the National Exchange Office. Informal market demand for dollars and francs greatly weakened the *riel* in currency exchanges, nearly exhausting currency reserves by 1970. *See also* CHAU SEN COCSAL; CHHEAN VAM.

BANTEAY CHHMAR. Translated as "Narrow Fortress," this temple complex 71 kilometers north of Sisophon dates from the early years of reign of **Jayavarman VII** (r 1178-c1220). Epigraphers believe it was constructed as a funerary monument to Jayavarman's deceased son Indravarman. Although the central sandstone sanctuary was damaged during T'ai invasions soon after its construction, the richly sculptured surrounding walls, comparable in quality to those at the **Bayon** and **Angkor Wat**, survived until 1998 when the site was plundered by art thieves. In 1999, Banteay Chhmar was placed on the UNESCO World Monument Fund's list of 100 most endangered landmarks.

BANTEAY MEANCHEY. A province bordering **Battambang, Siem Reap** and **Thailand** with a provincial capital bearing the same name. Created initially during the **Khmer Republic** and laid down under **Democratic Kampuchea,** it was recreated in 1987. Its capital was formerly known, and is still sometimes referred to, as Sisophon. According to the March 1998 census, the province has eight districts with a total population of 577,772. It has six deputies in the **National Assembly**, three from the **Cambodian People's Party,** two from FUNCINPEC and one from the **Sam Rainsy Party**.

BANTEAY SREI ("Women's citadel"). A small, beautifully proportioned and richly ornate Hindu temple, 19 kilometers north of the **Angkor** complex, it was built and dedicated by a prominent Brahmin family in 967. It was rediscovered by French explorers in 1914 and vandalized by the young **André Malraux** in 1923. Viewed by many as the jewel of classical **architecture**, it is made of rose colored sandstone, the soft color adding to its warmth and intimacy.

BAO DAI (1913-1997). Emperor of **Vietnam** 1926-1945, and head of state in the State of Vietnam 1949-1955, Bao Dai's reign spanned the late colonial years when most Khmers and Vietnamese struggled for independence. From 1954 until his death, he lived in splendid exile in **France**. Prince **Norodom Sihanouk**, who as a young king had sympathized with the nationalists of his generation, despised Bao Dai as a "French puppet." Having once overheard two Frenchmen remark that Bao Dai lived off French taxpayers, Sihanouk said in 1970 that he would fight his way back into power rather than endure such humiliation.

BAPHUON. A pyramidal temple in the **Angkor Thom** complex, the Baphuon was built in the mid-11th century under King **Udayadityavarman II** and dedicated to Siva. It was admired by the 13th century Chinese visitor **Zhou Daguan**, but, by the 15th century, it had been partially dismantled with hundreds of stones shifted for the purpose of constructing a reclining Buddha along one wall. French archaeologists were engaged in a long-term restoration program when civil war erupted in 1970, forcing them to abandon the site. In 1995 **France** agreed to resume restoration work at a cost of several million dollars. Work continued slowly in 2002.

BARAY. A district in **Kampong Thom** province, it was in this area in August 1971 that soldiers of the **National United Front of Kampuchea (FUNK)** under the command of **Ke Pauk** massacred Cambodian families who had earlier aided Vietnamese communist units assisting the FUNK during **Operation Chenla I and II**. Republican troops were shocked and startled by the internecine violence of "Khmer fighting Khmer" and also that there were Khmer on "the other side," not only North Vietnamese "aggressors" as the **Lon Nol** authorities insisted.

BARDEZ AFFAIR. While serving as the **French Résident** in **Kampong Chhnang**, Félix-Louis Bardez toured several villages in April 1925, collecting taxes. Arriving in Krang Leav on 18 April, his officiousness incited villagers who had assembled to celebrate *Chhoul Chnam*, the Khmer New Year. Bardez was set upon and killed. In the trial that followed, lawyers for the defense argued that the taxes had been excessive and the assassins provoked, but to no avail. Fifteen villagers were found guilty and sentenced, three of them to death. King **Sisowath** being devoted to

France, judged the villagers guilty of *lèse majesté* but in the 1970s and 1980s, communist propaganda claimed the murder was evidence of popular resistance to colonial rule.

BAROM REACHEA III. King of Cambodia, 1597-1598. After fleeing a T'ai invasion with his father, King **Satha**, Barom Reachea ascended the throne at **Longvaek** in his own right, having been encouraged by Spanish adventurers to do so. He was killed in the course of a Muslim rebellion in the year following his coronation.

BAROM REACHEA V. King of Cambodia 1601-1619. An uncle of King **Satha**, he was taken prisoner by a Siamese army in 1594 and held hostage for several years in Ayudhya. Released in 1601, he was placed on the Khmer throne only after agreeing that he would make regular tributary payments to the court in Ayudhya. His accession to the throne ended European merchant influence at the Khmer court and was the beginning of a long period of Siamese patronage. Barom Reachea tried to secure room to maneuver and to win favor from regional overlords in the lower **Mekong** Delta by arranging the marriage of one of his sons to a Vietnamese princess. This interdynastic liaison was viewed as a costly mistake in later centuries: the succeeding Khmer monarch was persuaded to relinquish sovereign control over the lower Mekong Delta, then thinly populated.

"BASE PEOPLE" (*neak mullatan*). Term used after 17 April 1975 in reference to those who actively supported the 1970-1975 revolutionary movement or who had lived under communist control prior to the "liberation" and evacuation of **Phnom Penh**. Base people received more favorable treatment in food rations and job assignments than those identified as "new people" (urban evacuees). Base people gradually lost their political primacy when crops failed and food shortages sapped revolutionary zeal and morale. **Communist Party of Kampuchea** cadres, unable to see or to admit to policy failures, suspected their revolution was being sabotaged.

BASSAC (Vietnamese: *Hau Giang***).** This is the Cambodian name for the lower branch of the **Mekong** which divides into two branches at **Phnom Penh** as it flows southwards toward **Vietnam**. During the 1970-1975 civil war, the Bassac was a major transport route for supplies shipped from Saigon to Phnom Penh. It was mined in 1975 during the final weeks of the siege of the capital.

BATTAMBANG. Northwestern province, bordering **Thailand**, and a major agricultural region since Angkorean times. In the 1790s, after placing King **Ang Eng** on the throne, the Siamese seized Battambang, administering it as a semiautonomous, tributary domain under the control of **Baen** and his descendents. In 1907 **France** negotiated its return to Cambodia. It then became the national rice-basket, producing most of the protectorate's rice for export.

In 1941, following the Franco-Siamese war, Bangkok again momentarily seized the province, being obliged to returned it in 1946. **Nhiek Tioulong** boasted at this time that his **Khmer Renewal Party** would sweep Battambang in the **National Assembly** elections, but it lent stunning support to the **Democrat Party** in 1947 and again in 1951. Battambang was the site of a major peasant rebellion at Samlaut in 1967. Compared to the rest of the country, it was little affected by the fighting of 1970-1975, although it was a center for cross-border smugglers servicing the war economy.

Between 1975-1978, it received over a million "April 17 people" or **"new people"** who were evacuated forcibly from **Phnom Penh**. **Pol Pot** expected the region to produce large agricultural surpluses with which to pay for his "super **great leap forward**" but these were vain, unrealistic aims which produced enormous hardships and hundreds of thousands of deaths from exhaustion and disease. The region's prosperity was only slowly restored during the 1980s and 1990s as its economy was greatly dislodged during the 1979-1991 civil war, being heavily constrained by the heavy mining of the Thai frontier, destructive smuggling of logs, gemstones and antiquities and increasingly effective controls on migrant labor. In the 1998 elections voters in the provinces elected three **FUNCINPEC** deputies, two **Sam Rainsy Party** deputies and three **Cambodian People's Party** deputies. It is the fifth largest province in population terms with 791,958 people according to the 1998 **census**.

BAYON. This is a Hindu-Buddhist Cambodian temple complex, built by **Jayavarman VII** at the end of the 12th century as the centerpiece, temple-mountain for his newly constructed capital city, now known as **Angkor Thom**. The temple is noted for its 54 towers, each bearing four massive carved faces. Although scholars do not all agree about the iconography, it is generally held that the faces there and on the gates of the city represent the *bodhisatva* Avalokitesvara and demonstrate the omnipotence and piety of Jayavarman VII. The temple rests on three levels. The first and second of these contain galleries that feature bas-relief depictions of war with **Champa** as well as scenes of ordinary 12th-century Cambodian life. The third level, associated with divinity, is dominated by a central sanctuary, which once housed a statue of the Buddha.

BEAUMONT, JEAN, COMTE DE (1904-2002). A colonial era deputy, repre-senting **Cochinchina**; postcolonial chairman and managing director of the *Compagnie du Cambodge*, part of the De Rivaud group and an intimate of Prince, later King, **Norodom Suramarit**. Originally established in 1921, the company owned half of the rubber plantations in Cambodia including the giant Chup plantation in **Kampong Cham**. It also invested in the coffee plantation in **Pailin**. A member of the French Parliament, repre-senting Cochinchina, Beaumont is best-known for his long service to the International Olympic Committee. In 1970 Prince **Norodom Sihanouk** accused Beaumont, who then lived in Paris, of conspiring with Prince **Sisowath Sirik Matak** to liberalize Cambodia's semisocialist economy. Indeed Beaumont, who usually invited the Prince to his residence, ignored Sihanouk's visit to Paris in March 1970. Beaumont is said to have anticipated a "restoration of capitalism" by April 1970 in time for celebrations of the 50th anniversary of the *Compagnie*'s operations in Cambodia. He died on 12 June 2002.

BEN KRAHOM (1906-?). Communist activist. A manual laborer employed at the electricity plant in **Phnom Penh**, Ben Krahom ("Red Ben") was likely the first **Khmer** in Cambodia to campaign for communism. He distributed leaflets in the street on 31 July 1930. Colonial reports of strikes by Chinese workers in the 1920s indicate the Cambodian Chinese knew about communist activities in **China**.

BENG REN (1951-   ). A supporter of the **National United Front of Kampuchea (FUNK)**, 1970-1975, she was arrested and imprisoned by the **Communist Party of Kampuchea** leadership in May 1975. She escaped from jail in August 1978 and joined communist dissidents already in rebellion against **Pol Pot**. After the expulsion of the **Democratic Kampuchea** government from **Phnom Penh** on 7 January 1979, Beng Ren returned to her native province of **Kratié** where she led the **Association of Revolutionary Women of Kampuchea**. In May 1981 she was elected to the **National Assembly**.

BIT SEANGLIM (1944-). Educationalist and politician. Born on 18 October 1944, he graduated from the Royal School of Administration in 1965 and worked in the Ministry of Finance until 1975. Fleeing to **Thailand**, he settled in the **United States**. He received a doctorate in education from the University of San Francisco in 1981. He visited Cambodia briefly in August 1988 and a second time in March 1989 when he was received by **Chea Sim**. He declined an invitation to join Chea Sim's party and chose to form his own Free Republican Party, in 1992. It was one of the many small parties failing to win any seats in elections of 1993 or the 1998 elections. His book, *The Warrior Heritage* (1991), provides a nationalist analysis of the sources of violence in Cambodian society.

"BLACK BOOK" or *LE DOSSIER NOIR*. An official policy document issued by the Foreign Ministry of **Democratic Kampuchea (DK)** in September 1978, the "Black Book" accuses **Vietnam** of military aggression for the purpose of creating a revolutionary federation of **Indochina**. The book was widely circulated by DK Foreign Minister **Ieng Sary** in the weeks preceding the 1978 Vietnamese invasion, being laid before the United Nations General Assembly in October. It relates, in highly emotive terms, a long history of conflict between the two neighboring nations and communist movements. Although the primary aim was to win international sympathy for Cambodia and the DK revolution in the approaching war, most foreign observers, including the Scottish political activist **Malcolm Caldwell**, were alarmed by the prospect of a new war in the region. **Pol Pot** is thought to be the principal author of this policy document.

BLACK STAR AFFAIR. An alleged conspiracy mounted by a nonexistent secret society which was supposedly uncovered and derailed by decisive French intervention in March-April 1947. The Black Star Affair is now recognized as a political imbroglio manufactured by the French security service (*Sûreté*) so as to discredit prominent leaders of the anticolonial **Democrat Party**. Using confessions extracted under torture, the French accused members of the 1946 **National Assembly** of belonging to a secret "Black Star" (*Étoile Noire*) association whose members were plotting to kill French officials. Members of the association were said to have links to Japanese secret societies and to the **Khmer Issarak** movement. It was claimed members tattooed black stars on themselves, a claim hotly denied by those arrested. The allegations provided a pretext for the jailing for several months of **Sim Var**, **Chhim Phonn** and 16 other Democrats at a time when the Assembly was attempting to draft a new constitution. No evidence has ever been found to support French allegations or conduct in this shameful episode.

BO RASI. See TY BORASY.

BOAT PEOPLE. Following the unification of **Vietnam** in 1976, and integration of economic zones there in 1978, many Vietnamese fled by boat to **China**, Hong Kong, Malaysia, the Philippines and Indonesia. Some made it to **Australia** or **Japan** while others perished at sea. By 1982 Vietnamese boat people numbered in the hundreds of thousands. Most Cambodian refugees in 1975 or 1979 escaped by foot to **Thailand** and were dubbed "Road People." A few Cambodian boat people landed in Australia in the early 1990s igniting debates on economic migrants *vs* asylum seekers. Most Cambodian boat people were eventually repatriated from Australia. Malaysia allowed Muslim **Cham** boat people from Cambodia to settle.

BOEUY KEUK (1939-   ). A highlander from **Mondolkiri**, he was a schoolteacher who in 1972 joined the **Socio-Republican Party** of **Lon Nol** and won a seat in the **National Assembly** of the **Khmer Republic**. In 1980 he agreed to support the **People's Republic of Kampuchea** and played a major role in reorganizing local administration in the northeast. He became chairman of the people's revolutionary committee of Mondolkiri province. In May 1993, heading the **Cambodian People's Party (CPP)** list, he won a seat in the Constituent Assembly which became the **National Assembly** in November. In 1999 he was among the CPP nominees appointed to the **Senate**.

BOKOR. A hill station in **Kampot** province, developed from 1922 by the French. Hundreds of workers, many prisoners from jails, died of malaria while building an access road to the summit. A cool retreat for members of the aristocracy as well as the French, King **Sisowath Monivong** (r 1927-1941) died there not long after receiving the distressing news of the loss of **Battambang** province to **Thailand**. By the late 1940s it was in the hands of the **Viet Minh** and **Khmer Issarak**. Reopened only in 1960, a **casino** began operations in the Bokor Palace Hotel in 1962. As Cambodians were forbidden by law to gamble, and few foreign visitors turned up, it closed within weeks of opening. It reopened in 1969 when gambling was legalized. Prince **Norodom Chantaraingsey** managed it until the **National United Front of Kampuchea** seized control of the region in 1972. The old hill station is now a major feature of Bokor National Park, with the shell of the hotel dominating the skyline. However the old road can be used only by hardy trekkers.

BOU THANG (1938-   ). Born on 15 August 1938 in Vèn Sai district, **Ratanakiri**, Bou Thang is from the Tampuon minority. He joined a **Khmer Issarak** group allied to the **Khmer People's Revolutionary Party (KPRP)** in 1953 and was among the Cambodians who "regrouped" in **Vietnam**, 1954-1970. In 1964 while still in Vietnam, he joined the **Communist Party of Kampuchea (CPK)**. In the civil war, 1970-1975, he led the CPK in Ratanakiri and was military commander of the **National United Front of Kampuchea** army in the Northeast Zone, 1972-1974. But when the CPK center began purging Vietnamese-trained cadres, he led a mutiny in Voeunsai with support from **Bun Mi** and **Seuy Keo**. Support from local hill tribe communities allowed the mutineers to establish a semiautonomous, revolutionary region straddling the Vietnamese border. Bou Thang nevertheless fled for his life to Vietnam at the beginning of 1975.

In 1978, at the behest of the Vietnamese party, he called for internal insurrections against the **Democratic Kampuchea** regime and was among the dissident communists who founded the **United Front for the National**

Salvation of Kampuchea in December 1978. From January 1979 when he became director of the state propaganda and political training commission, which he ran as a party training school, he was the principal ideologue of the fledgling **People's Republic of Kampuchea (PRK)**. In 1981 when the new **People's Revolutionary Party of Kampuchea** was officially launched, he was elected to the political bureau and ranked fifth in its hierarchy. He represented **Preah Vihear** province in the PRK **National Assembly** elected in May 1981. Allied from this date to **Chea Sim**, Thang survived the late 1981 purge of the PRPK Central Committee following the removal of secretary **Pen Sovan** from his post. With **Chan Si** as secretary Thang was promoted to deputy chairman of the Council of Ministers and became defense minister in February 1982.

Named deputy prime minister in 1985, he was replaced as defense minister in December 1986, returning to senior posts in the military, becoming head of the general political department of the army by April 1988. Elected to the 1993 Constituent Assembly in his native province, Ratanakiri, Bou Thang supported the June 1993 secessionist movement organized by Prince **Norodom Chakrapong**, a sabre-rattling bid for power on the part of his party in the face of its electoral defeat. Once the CPP and **FUNCINPEC** had agreed to share power, Bou Thang returned to **Phnom Penh** to take up his Assembly seat, joining the permanent committee of the Assembly chaired by Chea Sim. He was appointed to the King's Privy Council in December 1993, and reelected to the National Assembly in Ratanakiri in 1998.

BOUA CHANTOU (1952-   ). Born in **Kampong Cham** province, the daughter of Boua Kim Meua and Mme (née Chea Neat), she studied at Phnom Penh University and won a Colombo Plan Scholarship to study commerce at the University of New South Wales, graduating BComm in 1976. Unable to return to Cambodia, then in the throes of revolution, she took a teacher training course at Melbourne College of Advanced Education and from 1978 taught **Khmer** in high schools in **Australia**. In 1980 she married Ben Kiernan, and together they published *Peasants and Politics in Kampuchea 1942-1981* (1982). She returned to Cambodia in 1994 being employed as a consultant at the Secretariat of State for Women's Affairs then led by **Keat Sokun**. In this capacity she drafted Cambodia's statement to the 1995 Fourth World Conference on Women in Beijing. In recent years she has been director of Partnership for Development in Kampuchea (PADEK), a Non-Government Organization providing training for Cambodian aid personnel and professionals.

BOUN CHAN MOL. *See* BUNCHHAN MOL.

BOUR KRY. *Sangharaj* of the Thammayut Buddhist order. He was appointed by **Norodom Sihanouk** in 1992 to the **Throne Council**. *See also* BUDDHISM.

BOUN SAY. He was deputy general secretary of the **Khmer People's National Liberation Front (KPNLF)** participating in the organization of the movement on the Cambodian-Thai border from late 1979 together with other prominent Cambodians living in **France** such as **Son Sann, Dien Del**, Mme **Suon Kaset** and **Son Soubert**. Before 1975 he had been a leading member of the **Democratic Party** of **Chau Sau**. He remained loyal to Son Sann in the PCCS-Executive Committee split of 1985 and was minister for finance and economy in the **Coalition Government of Democratic Kampuchea** coordination committee for finance and economy formed in 1986.

BRAO. One of approximately 22 upland peoples in Cambodia, the Brao live along the Lao border in western **Ratanakiri** and **Stung Treng** provinces. Though they as well as the Krung and Kravet peoples share many customs and practices with the Loven groups of the Boloven plateau across the border in **Laos**, Brao (or Proh) have for many centuries viewed themselves as subjects of the King of Cambodia. Their communities are located in the tri-border region of Laos, **Vietnam** and Cambodia, near the Vietnamese revolutionary supply route known as the **Ho Chi Minh Trail**. As the American war in Vietnam widened in the 1960s, the authorities in Phnom Penh feared, not without reason, that highland minorities would support the revolutionary movement. This led to intense efforts to develop schools, youth projects and plantation industries in remote, upland regions.

The Brao rebelled in 1968 partly in opposition to the inward movement of lowland migrants and with the support from the **Communist Party of Kampuchea** and the Vietnamese communists. Brao also were prominent in the movement to oust the **Pol Pot** government in 1979, three being elected to the 117-member **National Assembly** of the **People's Republic of Kampuchea** in 1981. In 1986 a Brao delegate to the Fifth Congress of the United Front for the Construction and Defense of the Kampuchean Motherland (the former **UFNSK**) asked for development aid for Stung Treng province, more schools, roads and transport services in particular. Migration of lowland Khmer into upland regions and extensive logging by national and international forestry concessionaires today threaten the livelihoods of Brao, Krung, Kravet, Tampuon and Jarai peoples in the Northeast as most depend on shifting cultivation and on nontimber forest products for food, house materials, medicines and barter goods. The creation in 1993 of Virachey National Park has created a "buffer" zone straddling the Lao border that protects a total population of 11,700 (1999) hill tribespeople. About 3,000 of these would be ethnic Brao.

BREVIÉ LINE. This is the offshore line of demarcation between **Vietnam** and Cambodia drawn by French colonial official in 1939 and named after Jules Brevié, governor-general of Indochina from 1936-1939. It was accepted in the 1960s as the juridical sea boundary, or so Cambodian officials believed, but since 1975 when Vietnamese communist revolutionaries seized control of offshore islands well to the west of the Brevié line, the status of the line has been in dispute. The Paris Conference agreements on Cambodia in 1991 failed to settle the issue but a treaty on "historical waters" signed by the **People's Republic of Kampuchea** and the Socialist Republic of Vietnam in 1982 was reaffirmed by the Royal Government in 1999. Under this treaty much of the rectangular area between Poulo Wai Island, Tho Chu Island and the eastern coasts of Vietnam and Cambodia is jointly administered. Both **FUNCINPEC** and the opposition **Sam Rainsy Party** have rejected the agreement on the grounds that it ignores historical circumstances. Vietnam, a signatory to the UN Convention on the Law of the Sea, argues that its rules should apply and that the border should be equidistant from the coasts of Cambodia and Phu Quoc Island, an arrangement which would shift the frontier well to the west of the Brevië line. Joint administration of sea area on both sides of the line is officially viewed as a temporary compromise on both sides.

BROTHER NUMBER ONE *(Bang ti muoy)*. *See* POL POT.

BROTHER NUMBER TWO *(Bang ti pi)*. *See* NUON CHEA.

BU PHAT (1938-1978). Journalist and communist revolutionary. He was born in Romenh village, Khum Romenh, Koh Andet, **Takeo**, the youngest of seven children. His parents who died when he was young, were Bu Phok and Mme (née Nop Kouv). His oldest brother, Bu Tith, and a sister looked after him as he grew up. He went to Koh Andet primary school briefly between 1950-1953 and, at the age of 16, to the Buddhist school at Wat Prey Melong. In 1955 he moved to **Phnom Penh** to study in a school near Pochentong as Bu Tith, by then a paratrooper, was assigned to barracks there. By 1957 he was a student at the private Lycée **Kambuboth** where he was a classmate of **Nop Bophan**. A year later he was working for the newspaper, *Pracheachon (The People),* initially selling copies, then writing articles. When *L'Observateur* appeared in 1959, he left his brother's house in the middle of the night and moved into its premises. He was arrested and jailed along with **Khieu Samphan** when the police raided the paper and closed it down in 1960. Following his release, Bu Phat earned his living as a construction worker, sheltering in a Phnom Penh pagoda at night. When the *Pracheachon* reopened in 1961, Phat began writing for it again, but after one issue it was forced underground.

He became a full member of the **Communist Party of Kampuchea (CPK)** in April 1962 and was among those who fled with **Saloth Sar** and **Ieng Sary** into the jungle in 1963, spending some time in Vietnam assisting the National Front for the Liberation of South Vietnam with Khmer language radio programs and being assigned to propaganda and printing work at the CPK Central Committee offices in **Ratanakiri** province. During the civil war, he rose to second in command of Sector 103 in **Preah Vihear** province and while in this post was involved in executions of Cambodian communists who returned from Hanoi in 1974. When news of the killings reached the Western media, Phat's superior was blamed, purged and executed. Following the 17 April 1975 victory, Bu Phat fell under suspicion partly because a brother had been an officer in the enemy army. On 1 January 1978 he was summoned to **Siem Reap** and four days later taken to the CPK security office, S-21, now known as **Tuol Sleng**. He was forced to confess to long-term treachery and was executed, probably in February 1978.

BUDDHISM. Mahayana Buddhism existed alongside **Hinduism** in pre-**Angkor** and Angkorean Cambodia, assuming increasing importance in the 12th and 13th centuries. Also in the 13th century, and most notably during the reign of **Jayavarman VII**, Theravada Buddhism was widely embraced according to the Chinese visitor **Zhou Daguan.** Adopted as the official religion by all monarchs succeeding Jayavarman VII, Theravada beliefs gradually supplied the central moral beliefs for nearly all Khmer. Kings were patrons of Buddhist orders and communities, while those who formed the monastic hierarchy, or *sangha,* saw themselves and are seen to be guardians of Khmer culture and morality. Most young Khmer men, and occasionally, high-ranking politicians, abandon the demands of everyday existence to enter the ranks of the *Sangha* for short periods thereby earning merit and acquiring the rudiments of Pali canon knowledge. Cambodian art and literature since the 13th century has been heavily Buddhist in inspiration.

In 1864, in response to a reformist movement in Siam, the Thammayut order was formed under royal patronage. Little distinguishes the Thammayut from the much larger Mohanikay order. Both uphold the classic and fundamental doctrines of the Four Noble Truths relating to the trials of existence and the Eightfold Path which promises release and serenity (*nirvana*) and they organize their clerical hierarchies in nearly identical ways. Thammayut study and teaching of textual precepts claims to be and is judged more rigorous. During the colonial era, **France** retained Buddhist temple schools, imposing mild, secular reforms on the curriculum. In a related, equally successful move to undermine Thai cultural influence in their protectorate, the French established the prestigious **Buddhist Institute**. Buddhism was thereafter accorded prominence as an element of national identity, a nationalist trend encouraged by Prince **Norodom Sihanouk** and Marshal **Lon Nol**, but rejected by **Pol Pot**. Between 1975-1979 monks were disrobed and temple communities disbanded. With religious freedom partly restored under the administration of the **People's Republic of Kampuchea** and **State of Cambodia**, Buddhism was restored as the official religion in the Constitution of 1993. In 2002, Bou Kry was supreme patriarch of the Thammayut order and **Tep Vong**, supreme patriarch of the Mohanikay. There were 3,731 temples and 50,800 monks. *See also* KHIEU CHUM.

BUDDHIST INSTITUTE (*Institut Bouddhique*). This was founded in 1930 by **Suzanne Karpèles**, a French scholar and supporter of the Popular Front who was employed to catalogue manuscripts at the royal palace. It promoted the study of Khmer **Buddhism** in an effort to reduce T'ai cultural and political influence in the French protectorate. Under the direction of Karpèles, the Institute hired **Son Ngoc Thanh**, at the time a minor functionary in the Vietnamese colonial service, who founded the nationalist newspaper *Nagaravatta* ("Angkor Wat") in 1936. The Institute gradually became a major publisher of Khmer language **literature**, especially of morality texts known as *chhbab*. Though its work was disrupted from 1975-1988, the Institute was revived in the 1990s being relocated to the Wat Oualom. Its original headquarters now houses the Foreign Ministry.

BUDDHIST LIBERAL DEMOCRATIC PARTY (BLDP). Electoral political party founded in 1992 by **Son Sann** and superseding his **Khmer Peoples' National Liberation Front**, the military resistance movement organized to overthrow the Vietnamese-imposed government. In the May 1993 elections its candidates, including Son Sann, won 10 seats in the constituent assembly. As the third largest party, it became a junior partner in the coalition government of Prince **Norodom Ranariddh** and **Hun Sen**. However, in 1996 leadership of the party was disputed by Son Sann (and his son, **Son Soubert**) and **Ieng Mouly** who led a breakaway group. The claims of Mouly's splinter were encouraged for opportunistic reasons by **Hun Sen** and the **Cambodian People's Party**. He convened a party congress on 9 July 1995 which elected him leader. Son Sann's attempt to hold a rival congress in October 1995 was disrupted by grenade attacks. The dispute over ownership of the party, or more precisely, its name, came to a head when parties sought to register for the 1998 elections. With BLDP-Ieng Mouly registered as BLDP, Son Sann was obliged to register under the name Son Sann Party. Greatly weakened by their rivalry, neither the BLDP nor the Son Sann Party was able to win any seats in the 1998 **National Assembly**.

BUDDHIST SOCIALISM. Name given by Prince **Norodom Sihanouk** to describe the eclectic, state ideology promoted under his rule from 1955-1970. The appeal of Buddhist socialism resided in the linkage Sihanouk made between the traditional moral order of **Buddhism**, kingship, nation and modern progress. Socialism represented the ideals of modernity and material progress, not an alternative social or economic system or an ideology which marginalizes both royalty and tradition. Sihanouk was not advocating radical change, and certainly opposed socialist revolution, but he lent great prestige and importance to his leadership by uniting traditional and modern moral orders in this communitarian manner.

"BUILD AND DEFEND THE COUNTRY" (*kosang nung kapea prateah*). This slogan, stressing love of country, was used in the early days of **Democratic Kampuchea** to mobilize popular support for massive works projects and collectivization of the economy.

BUN MI. Deputy party secretary of sector three in the northeast region (**Ratanakiri**) in the early 1970s. Along with **Bou Thang** and other communists in Ratanakiri, he was involved in the mutiny in Voeunsai district in 1974. After this, and fearing retribution from the **Communist Party of Kampuchea** leadership, he retired to **Vietnam**. He reemerged as a member of the Central Committee of the **United Front for the National Salvation of Kampuchea** formed with Vietnamese support in 1978.

BUN PAN THAN CHHOEUR (1962-). A member of the **Sam Rainsy Party** he was elected in the 1998 elections for **Pailin**. His election was especially remarkable as he won an absolute majority of the votes, his constituency being the only one where counting of the ballot papers was not controlled by the ruling **Cambodian People's Party**. The local Democratic National Union Movement led by **Ieng Sary** did not field candidates in the elections.

BUN RANY (née **BUN SAM HEANG**). A native of Rokarkhnau, Kroch Chhmar district, **Kampong Cham**, she is the wife of prime minister **Hun Sen.** She joined a medical training program in the **National United Front of Kampuchea (FUNK)** in 1970 and was a nurse in a revolutionary hospital in 1975 in which Hun Sen was treated for battlefield injuries. They were married in January 1976 in a group ceremony together with 13 other couples and then separated until 1979. A capable businesswoman, Bun Rany is believed to have accumulated a small fortune since the removal of state controls on the economy in 1989. She is also president of the national Red Cross society, a post once held by *neak monéang* Monique Sihanouk (now **Queen Monineath**). In 1999 she was accused of using her influence unlawfully when a private company, allegedly acting at her behest, bypassed normal bidding procedures to secure a profitable fishing lot for the Red Cross. Later the same year she was accused of complicity in the murder of **Piseth Pilica** whose diaries, published in **France** by her family, revealed an affair with the prime minister. Hun Sen dismissed the reports as an "invention" manufactured by his opponents. No arrests or charges have been made in the case and a law suit against *L'Express* and other French papers has not materialized.

BUNCHHAN MOL or **Boun Chan Mul (1914-)**. A son of Bunchhan Mongkhun (1880-1949) and Mme (née Poc Loun), he grew up in **Phnom Penh** and was one of the organizers of public protests against the French in 1942. For this, he was arrested by the colonial authorities and sentenced to five years in prison with hard labor by a court in Saigon. After the Japanese *coup de force* in 1945, he was freed from the notorious prison on **Poulo Condore** and returned to Phnom Penh, where he served as a bodyguard to **Son Ngoc Thanh**. When Thanh was arrested on 15 October 1945, Bunchhan Mol went to **Thailand** taking money provided by Huot Sam Oeun of the Foreign Ministry, which was to be used to purchase supplies for the **Khmer Issarak** in **Battambang**. He stayed in Battambang until it was returned to Cambodia in December 1946 and then moved to Bangkok to live with his uncle **Poc Khun** and the Issaraks there. He returned to Poipet on 26 July 1949, and although still serving as a "letterbox" for Thanh, he entered mainstream politics by joining the **Democrat Party**. In 1951 he was elected to the **National Assembly** for Kandal: Prek Tameak.

When King **Norodom Sihanouk** decided to seize power from the Democrat Party, Bunchhan Mol's political career ended. He was arrested on the night of 13 January 1953, and held in jail as the Democrat Party crumbled. After independence, he retired from active politics, but with the overthrow of Sihanouk he enlisted in the **armed forces** and became an advisor to **Lon Nol**. In 1971, he represented the Buddhist Association of Cambodia on the **constitutional drafting committee**. He also campaigned for Lon Nol in the June 1972 presidential elections. Bunchhan Mol joined the **Socio-Republican Party** and was elected to the National Assembly for the **Khmer Republic**, September 1972 for Daun Penh, Phnom Penh. He published two *Khmer*-language books on Cambodian politics during the Khmer Republic: *Kuk Niyobay ("Political Prisoner")* in 1971 and *Charit Khmer ("Khmer Mores")* in 1973.

BUNCHHAN PLANG (1911-1966). Born on 11 December 1911 at **Phnom Penh**, the second son of Bunchhan Mongkhun (1880-1949) and Mme (née Poc Loun), he went to school in Phnom Penh. Plang took part in the July 1942 demonstrations against the French along with his younger brother **Bunchhan Mol**. In December 1942 he was sentenced to five years hard labor at a court martial in Saigon, and spent the next two years at **Poulo Condore**. In March 1945 he was freed by the Japanese and returned to Phnom Penh where he became secretary to Prince **Sisowath Monireth**. He was district headman of Chhleng, Kratié; then Thbaung Khmum, Kampong Cham. On 9 March 1947 he married So Sivorne and they had three children. Bunchhan Plang favored Franco-Cambodian cooperation and, possibly influenced by the conservative Prince **Sisowath Monireth**, he joined the **Khmer Renewal Party**. He was governor of **Kampong Speu**, **Kratié** and then **Kampot**; becoming secretary-general at the Ministry of Foreign Affairs and then ambassador to Cairo in 1963. Living in Phnom Penh, next to Wat Langka, he died from a heart attack.

BUOR HELL (1935-   ). Son of Buor Horng, Buor Hell's family was long connected to the royal family. Buor Hell was Prince **Norodom Sihanouk**'s aide-de-camp and was appointed a commander of the Royal Guard in 1968. His half-brother, Buor Horl, was commissioner of police in March 1970 and prevented the first attempt to overthrow Sihanouk on 16 March. They were both arrested on 18 March 1970 and Buor Hell left Cambodia to live overseas c1973, establishing himself as a successful businessman. In 1983 he was appointed the Sihanoukist representative on the Finance Committee of the **Coalition Government of Democratic Kampuchea**. A general in the **Armée Nationale Sihanoukienne** in 1984, he broke with the Sihanoukists and tried to establish his own army, but this move, ridiculed by Sihanouk, was unsuccessful. In February 1997 his political party, the Khmer Neutral Party, entered a four party alliance with **Sam Rainsy**'s Khmer Nation Party, **Son Sann**'s **Buddhist Liberal Demo-cratic Party** and Prince **Norodom Ranariddh**'s FUNCINPEC.

BUOY SRENG (c1945-1976). A journalist, born in **Prey Veng**, he was a teacher and joined the **Sangkum** during the 1960s. Buoy Sreng unsuccessfully contested the 1966 **National Assembly** elections for Rocar, Prey Veng, and moved to **Phnom Penh** where he worked as a journalist. In 1972 he published a story about the rigging of the presidential elections by **Lon Non** in the Chinese language daily *Sroch Srang Cheat*. Lon Non threatened him and then offered him a position in the army to suppress the story. On 18 March 1973 he was arrested on the charge of organizing protests against **Lon Nol**, and sent before a military tribunal. By 1974 and still working as a journalist in Phnom Penh, he had edited and published two volumes of the speeches and editorials of **Douc Rasy**. Although in Phnom Penh on 17 April 1975, he evaded arrest by the communists until 22 February 1976. He was sent to **Tuol Sleng** where he was executed on 27 May 1976.

BUTT CHUON (1914-1975). Born on 7 October 1914 at Prek Kak, **Kampong Cham**, son of Butt, he was employed in the Custom's Office, but was transferred to the Land Registry Office after exposing corrupt practices. He then moved to the Ministry of Agriculture in the late 1940s and worked under **Lon Nol** clearing deeds for people buying or selling land. After the realignment of the political parties in 1955 he joined **Sangkum Reastr Niyum** and was elected unopposed to the 1958 **National Assembly** for Prek Po.

Butt Chuon was reelected to the National Assembly in 1962, but in 1966 was defeated in a bid for the seat of Prek Dambauk, Kampong Cham. From 1968-1975 he returned to the Land Registry Office, at its central office in **Phnom Penh**. At the defeat of the **Khmer Republic**, he joined the evacuation of the city with his wife, Ean Bun, and four daughters. In June 1975 he was recognized by a communist soldier, arrested and presumably killed soon afterward. His widow died in the following year at Kampong Speu. Teeda, the youngest daughter, married Vitou Mam and wrote about the family's travails in two books, *To Destroy You Is No Loss* (1987) and *Bamboo and Butterflies: From Refugee to Citizen* (1992).

-C-

CADASTRAL OFFICE. The Land Registry had its headquarters in **Phnom Penh**, but there were regional offices in each of the provincial capitals. They ceased functioning in 1975 when the victorious **Royal Government of National Union of Kampuchea** and the succeeding **Democratic Kampuchea** government appropriated and nationalized all property including land. Land and housing remained nationalized during the People's Republic of Kampuchea until the liberalization of the economy in 1989. Sitting tenants in urban areas then began to receive property titles thus dispossessing pre-1975 owners. Similarly collectively owned farmland was officially allocated to families who received usufruct titles. The new system of land allocation and registration often ignored pre-revolutionary claims to ownership. Local cadre also frequently allocated the best land to themselves generating even more disputes and grievances. Land disputes originating from this period, and from more recent development projects, give rise to many problems of social order today.

CALDWELL, (JAMES ALEXANDER) MALCOLM (1931-1978). A Scottish Labour Party activist and a lecturer at the School of Oriental and African Studies, London University, from 1960, Caldwell specialized in the economic history of east and southeast Asia. As the **United States** war in **Vietnam** expanded, he became a prominent spokesman for the antiwar movement. Together with Lek Hor Tan, he wrote *Cambodia in the Southeast Asian War* (1973) which was sympathetic to the **National United Front of Kampuchea**. Caldwell arranged a visit to **Democratic Kampuchea (DK)** in December 1978 with Elizabeth Becker, then with the *Washington Post*, and Richard Dudman, then with the *St. Louis Post Dispatch*. They arrived in Cambodia on 3 December 1978, and after a tour, which included visits to rural collectives, they met and interviewed **Pol Pot** on 22 December. At 1 a.m. on 23 December, a group of armed Cambodians broke into the guest house and shot Caldwell. The DK foreign minister **Ieng Sary** issued a statement attributing the murder to "enemies" of the DK revolution but the identity and motives of the killers have yet be clearly established. Guards at the guest house were arrested and interrogated and forced to implicate leading cadres close to **Son Sen,** the DK Defense Minister, in a conspiracy. Some have speculated that **Pol Pot** may have ordered the killing in response to critical questioning from Caldwell but both Becker and Dudman cast doubt on this theory. The possibility of Vietnamese involvement cannot be ruled out as Caldwell had already taken sides in the Cambodian-Vietnamese border war, arguing that social democrats had a special obligation to attempt to understand the position of the smaller, weaker state when fraternal parties resorted to violence. It was also known that he planned to visit the Chinese-Vietnamese border, as a guest of the Chinese, after leaving Cambodia.

CAMBODIAN PEOPLE'S PARTY (CPP). This is the name taken by the ruling **People's Revolutionary Party of Kampuchea (PRPK)** at its special congress in 1991. The change parallels and follows the systematic suppression of revolutionary terminology from the name of the state, the army and other national institutions from 1989. The party retained the same leaders but it abjured Marxism-Leninism as its ideology, laid down its secretariat and declared its willingness to promote a multiparty, democracy. Fully expecting to win in 1993, the CPP threatened to invalidate the elections with a *coup d'état* after the royalist **FUNCINPEC** narrowly defeated them at the polls. The party soon accepted a power-sharing deal with two prime ministers that left effective control of central, provincial and local administration, the army and the state security apparatus in its hands.

In a July 1997 *coup d'état,* triggered by an internecine split among top **PDK** leaders in **Anlong Veng,** the CPP prime minister **Hun Sen** seized full power. Prince **Norodom Ranariddh** narrowly escaped assassination as CPP armed forces, reinforced by former **NADK** soldiers, rioted in the streets of **Phnom Penh.** Several dozen prominent royalists were murdered while others fled the country. The deposed "first prime minister," Prince Norodom Ranariddh, supported by the **United States** government, appealed for economic sanctions to be applied. While donors suspended aid programs, the **Association of Southeast Asian Nations (ASEAN)** countries postponed Cambodia's admission to ASEAN (agreed upon finally only in late 1998 with the formation of a new coalition government). Troops loyal to Ranariddh quickly returned to old resistance bases in the northwest with the intention of launching another civil war. But following Japanese and American mediation, Prince Ranariddh, and other prominent politicians, officiously described as "self-exiled," returned to Cambodia under United Nations protection to compete in the July 1998 elections. These were decisively won by the CPP amid allegations of massive vote-rigging and intimidation. The party's hegemony nonetheless certified, an expanded coalition government, led by **Hun Sen**, was formed in late 1998.

CAO DAI. This is a syncretic religious movement founded in **Vietnam** in 1927 in the **Mekong** Delta province of Tay Ninh. The movement incorporated Buddhist, Hindu, Christian and Confucian beliefs and saints, and gained so many Khmer adherents that an alarmed King **Sisowath Monivong** declared that Cambodians who frequented Cao Dai temples were apostates from state-sponsored Theravada **Buddhism**. Popular enthusiasm for the movement rapidly faded in the 1930s.

CARDAMOM MOUNTAINS (*chuor phnom kravanh*). Straddling the southwest land and sea frontiers with **Thailand**, these mountains and adjacent forests covering approximately 1.5 million hectares in southern **Battambang** and central **Pursat** provinces are the most biodiverse in the country. An internationally supported survey conducted in early 2000 found evidence of the existence of more than 200 species of birds, 65 mammals and many, possibly new, species of insects and reptiles. The mountain slopes facing seaward are covered with virgin rainforest while pine forests are found at higher elevations where broadleaf evergreens also flourish among a rich flora that includes a wide variety of herbaceous plants. The highest mountain areas, Mt. Aural (1,771 meters) and Mt. Samkos (1,717 meters), both in Pursat province, were declared national heritage sites in October 2000. The move is an attempt to protect forest reserves, wildlife and entire ecosystems established there.

The Cardamoms are home to a wild elephant herd which has been partly destroyed by poaching and may now count no more than 200. Wild tiger conservation groups and international forestry and environ-mental protection agencies also protest against the award of timber concessions in the mountains. Illegal logging is also a problem. The United Nations Development Program, through its Cambodian Area Rehabilitation and Regeneration Project (CARERE) program, is overseeing the resettlement of several thousand former National Army of Democratic Kampuchea (NADK) soldiers and their families in their former base area of Veal Veng district which is inside the Phnom Samkos wildlife sanctuary area. The officially protected area around Mt. Aural now has some 20 illegal sawmills with much of the processed timber being marketed openly in the old royal capital of **Oudong**. Most of the sawmills are operated by the former NADK soldiers who say they are unable to earn a living any other way. Meanwhile the Cambodian Timber Association, representing corporate logging interests, is pressuring the government to honor logging contracts issued before 2000 or to pay compensation to five companies holding suspended 25- to 30-year logging concessions in the mountains.

CATHOLICISM. The first recorded contact with Catholic missionaries was in the 16th century when **Portuguese** and Spanish missionaries, based in the Philippines and Malacca, fanned out into southeast Asia in search of converts. Missionaries worked without much success in Cambodia throughout the 16th century, and some of them visited **Angkor** and wrote valuable reports about it. Most converts during the colonial era and afterward were ethnic Vietnamese. In the **Democratic Kampuchea** era, the practice of Catholicism, like all established religions, was prohibited, and the historic central Cathedral of **Phnom Penh** was dismantled. François Ponchaud's *La Cathédrale de la Rizière* (1990) notes that the community of believers numbered 65,000 in March 1970, with barely 7,000 surviving **Lon Nol**'s 1970-1971 deportation of Vietnamese residents.

CEMETERIES. As most Cambodians are Buddhists, and cremate their dead, the small cemeteries outside many cities and towns contain graves of the local **Chinese**. There were also three major Christian cemeteries in **Phnom Penh**. The two in central Phnom Penh were for French residents and French citizens which included some Cambodians and many Vietnamese. The older cemetery was in the grounds of the Cathedral of Phnom Penh. It appears to have been destroyed when the Cathedral was razed to the ground in 1975. The other cemetery was off Boulevard Achar Mean, close to the building that became the French Embassy. It was in the grounds of the French Convent which also housed the École Providence. This cemetery once possessed a Memorial to the French and Cambodians who died in World War I. However, the memorial also was destroyed by the communists in 1975, and the cemetery was bulldozed, probably in the early 1990s. The National Cemetery, the largest of the three, was situated at Chakrey Ting, and was managed by **Chak Saroeun** in the late 1960s and early 1970s. *See also* CATHOLICISM.

CENSUS. The first rigorous estimate of the population of Cambodia was in 1909, and estimates were subsequently produced for the French minister of the colonies on an annual basis. However the first genuine census was conducted in 1921; later "censuses" in 1926, 1931 and 1936 were all basically compilations and tabulations of local estimates. Some useful data can be found in French censuses for 1906, 1931, 1936 and 1946. The first postcolonial estimates of the population commenced in April 1958. Under the auspices of the Direction de la Statistique et des Études Économiques, a partial census was conducted in a third of the villages, with information collected on household composition, occupation, housing, and mortality and migration. A follow-up demographic survey carried out in April 1959 involved 10 percent of the villages in the 1958 count. Between 1958-1960 censuses were carried out in **Phnom Penh** and the following cities: **Kampot, Kampong Speu, Siem Reap** (twice), **Battambang, Kratié, Prey Veng, Pursat, Stung Treng, Takeo, Svay Rieng** and **Kampong Chhnang**. In January 1960 it was announced that a full national census would be conducted by December 1961; but it took place finally on 18 April 1962, under the direction of **Laau Bounpa**. This census excluded the diplomatic corps and others not at home on the night and employed the following categories for nationality: Khmer, Chinese, Vietnamese, Laotian, other Asian, French, others or stateless. Ignoring administrative counts in 1972 and 1980, the next, and last, full census was conducted in March 1998. The long gap between the two censuses, the result of political turmoil between 1970-1991, has made it difficult to work out meaningful rates of change but the current average annual rate of growth since 1996 is officially estimated at 2.44 percent. Cambodia's population in 2000 is estimated at 12.2 million.

CENTRAL OFFICE OF SOUTH VIETNAM (COSVN). Created in 1951 COSVN was the mobile military command headquarters of the **Viet Minh**, and, later, for the Front for the National Liberation of South Vietnam and the People's Army of Vietnam operating in southern **Vietnam**. By the mid-1960s, it was based in Mimot district of Cambodia's **Kampong Cham** province. It was to this "Parrot's Beak" region that Saloth Sar (**Pol Pot**) fled in 1963-1965. The joint **United States**-South Vietnamese invasion of 1970 sought to locate and destroy COSVN, but it had been moved northwards into **Kratié** province before the invasion. Tense relations between COSVN and **Pol Pot**'s office 870, and especially with "Muoi Cuc," the *nom de guerre* of Nguyen Van Linh, are described in the infamous **Black Book**. Following the 1973 evacuation and expulsion of Vietnamese troops from the Cambodian battlefield COSVN was disbanded.

CENTRE DE DOCUMENTATION ET DE RECHERCHE SUR LA CIVILISATION KHMÈRE (CEDOREK). A cultural association organized and promoted by **Nhiek Tioulong, Nouth Narang** and other Cambodians in **France**, it was based in Paris during the late 1970s and 1980s. It published *Seksa Khmer* ("Khmer Studies"), a scientific journal, scholarly books, notably *Les êtres surnaturels dans la religion populaire khmères* by Ang Chouléan and reissues of works by modern Khmer-language authors including Rim Kin and **Nuon Khoeun**. In 1993 it moved to **Phnom Penh**.

CERCLE SPORTIF. The sports club established by the French on the periphery of **Phnom Penh** was a favored place of rendezvous and gossip under the postcolonial **Norodom Sihanouk** and **Lon Nol** regimes. Seized by the communists on 17 April 1975, both **Long Boret** and Prince **Sisowath Sirik Matak** were executed there.

CHA RIENG (1927-   ). A communist politician of Thai nationality, Cha Rieng was born in **Koh Kong** province, joining the "Khmer **Viet Minh**" movement in 1948. Among those "regrouped" in **Vietnam** in 1954, he returned to Cambodia during the civil war in 1971, escaping to Vietnam a second time in 1974 when purges of Vietnamese-trained cadres commenced. In the wake of Vietnam's 1978 invasion, he was appointed to a leading role in Koh Kong district and named an **advisor** to the **People's Republic of Kampuchea** government with responsibility for finance, in 1980. He represented Kandal province in the 1981 **National Assembly**. Also in 1981 he was appointed deputy director of the National Bank, in charge of the Foreign Trade Bank; and in July was appointed managing director of the National Bank, with the rank of minister. From January 1986 until June 1993 he was managing director of the National Bank with the rank of minister in the Council of Ministers.

CHAI THOUL (1916-   ). Born on 8 January 1916 in **Kratié** son of Chai Pech and Mme (née Sin Von), he studied at two elite institutions, the **Collège Sisowath** and the Royal School of Administration and worked in colonial administration. He was among the first senior administrators to secure a senior executive post after independence. He was appointed governor of **Takeo** from September 1954 to 2 July 1955, and then of **Battambang** until 29 September 1956. He was subsequently secretary-general of the **National Assembly** and then of the Council of Ministers. From 1963 he was associated with the National Bank and was its deputy governor from 1963-1969, and was acting governor for a period after the retirement of **Son Sann** in 1968. Like Son Sann he retired to **France** during the **Khmer Republic** years. In the 1980s Chai Thoul was a member of the Council of Elders of the **Khmer People's National Liberation Front.**

CHAK BORY (c1935-   ). Educated at **Lycée Sisowath**, he joined the Royal Cambodian Army and, fighting in support of the **Khmer Republic,** he rose to the rank of lieutenant colonel. He lived with his family in the

United States after 1975 but returned to the Cambodian-Thai border region in 1982 where he took charge of logistics for the **Khmer People's National Liberation Front Armed Forces**. He was a member of the Permanent Military Co-ordinating Committee (PERMICO) established in 1984 for the purpose of coordinating field operations with the **Armée Nationale Sihanoukienne** and one of the eight officers who broke with **Son Sann** in December 1985, joining **Sak Suthsakhan**'s Provisional Central Committee for the Salvation.

CHAK SARIK (1936-). Born in **Svay Rieng**, the son of Chak Vong, he went to Lycée Descartes, studied finance and graduated in the fourth promotion from the Royal School of Administration. He became an Inspector in the Finance Ministry in 1965. When his older brother, Vong Saren, left his post as chief of protocol to Prince **Norodom Sihanouk**, Chak Sarik was offered and took the post, overseeing the visit to Cambodia of major foreign visitors, including Charles de Gaulle. In 1967-1969 he studied management in France, receiving a degree from the École d'Organization Scientifique du Travail. After his return, he worked once again in the Finance Ministry. Because of his past connection to the royal palace, he was judged a Sihanoukist after March 1970 and was sidelined into journalism. He worked briefly on the weekly, French-language news magazine *Réalités Cambodgiennes* and then at the Information Ministry. In Bangkok in April 1975, he succeeded in obtaining refugee status in the **United States**. Chak Sarik met **Kong Sileah** in January 1979 and assisted in the formation, in August 1979, of **Molinaka**. He was a political advisor to **Nhem Sophon** and later became President of Molinaka. In June 1987 he rallied to **FUNCINPEC**. He was briefly minister of finance in the **Coalition Government of Democratic Kampuchea** and on 18 December 1993 was appointed governor of **Kandal** province, being removed in 1995.

CHAK SAROEUN (1934-). Born in **Svay Rieng**, and brother of Vong Saren and **Chak Sarik**, Saroeun graduated with a diploma from *the Institut d'études Supérieures des Techniques d'Organization* in Paris. From 1957-1960 he was the managing director of **Royal Air Cambodge**. In May 1960 he contested the by-election for Koki, **Kandal**. In 1965 he was appointed chairman and managing director of the National Cemetery at Chakrey Ting; and from 1973-1975, he was chairman of the *Banque de Secours et de Crédit*. From 1975 until 1992 he lived in **France** becoming a founder-member of **FUNCINPEC** and briefly its secretary-general. In 1982 he was the second member of the Education and Culture Committee in the **Coalition Government of Democratic Kampuchea** but in 1989 he created and assumed leadership of **Action for Democracy and Development**, a movement registered as a political party in July 1992. He was a candidate for the **National Assembly** in the 1993 UN-supervised poll but was not elected.

CHAM. A largely Muslim ethnic community in Cambodia, descended in part from refugees from the coastal kingdom of **Champa** overrun by **Vietnam** in the 17th century. In the 1990s there were an estimated 200,000 Chams living in Cambodia. This is fewer than in the early 1970s, as the group suffered severely from forced assimilation under **Democratic Kampuchea**. Thousands of survivors also emigrated to Malaysia in the 1980s, where they were welcomed as Muslims. The Cham possess their own Malayo-polynesian language and literature and religious hierarchies and traditionally benefited from the protection of the Khmer Royal Court. Since precolonial times they have been prominent in fishing, silk weaving and cattle raising, particularly in the eastern part of Cambodia surrounding **Kampong Cham** and along the coast near **Kampot**.

CHAM PRASIDH, né **Ung You Teckhor (1951-   ).** Born on 15 May 1951 in **Phnom Penh**, and nephew of Pak Boramy, Cham Prasidh studied at Lycée Descartes and then studied business at the University of Phnom Penh, graduating in 1973. From September 1973 until April 1975 he worked as a mortgage agent for *Crédit Foncier*. At the fall of the Republic, he was evacuated to **Battambang** where he remained until January 1979. In August 1979 he was a witness at the People's Revolutionary Tribunal of 1979 convened in Phnom Penh by the Vietnamese-supported, communist government. Later he explained that he changed his name in response to the intense, official anti-Chinese sentiment of the time and the request that he act as a representative of the persecuted **Chinese minority** during the trial. In March 1980 Cham Prasidh was employed as an interpreter to the Ministry of Foreign Affairs and received a five-month intensive training course in diplomacy. In November 1981 he was assistant to the chief of the press office of the Ministry and in February 1982 personal secretary to the minister of foreign affairs, then **Hun Sen**. From July 1984 he was briefly director of the General Policy Department but in January 1985 he was transferred to the Prime Minister's Office and fluent in several languages, served as Hun Sen's translator at many overseas meetings. Cham Prasidh became a deputy-minister attached to the Council of Ministers with responsibility for economic and financial matters as well as foreign affairs from June 1987 to June 1993. In rapid succession he was named deputy-minister of economics and finance then secretary of state for economics and finance, being finally appointed minister for trade on 20 October 1994. Although he resigned this post briefly in 1998, in a bid for another post, he was reappointed trade minister in the 1998 Hun

Sen government. He was elected to the Cambodian People's Party Central Committee in February 1997.

CHAMKAR MON ("silkworm fields"). The residence of Prince **Norodom Sihanouk** after his abdication in 1955. It was built on a site where Chinese entrepreneurs had once cultivated silkworms. He remained there until his overthrow in 1970 when it became the presidential palace of **Lon Nol**. Bombed twice in 1973, it is today used as a reception center and guest house for visiting foreign dignitaries.

CHAMPA. An ancient **Hindu-Buddhist** kingdom, it flourished in what is now south-central **Vietnam** between the second century and 1471 when its capital was overrun by Vietnamese forces. The relations between Champa and **Angkor** have not been sufficiently studied, particularly in the 12th century AD, when the two kingdoms were often at war and when the Khmer prince who later became the Cambodian monarch **Jayavarman VII** lived in exile in Champa, and likely acquired his Mahayana Buddhist faith. Equally, very little is known about Cambodian-**Cham** relations after Jayavarman VII's reign and the abandonment of Angkor, but thousands of Chams fled to Cambodia in the 17th and 18th centuries in the aftermath of their defeats by Vietnamese forces. By then, most Chams had converted to **Islam**, and the immigrants remained Muslims, finding economic niches for themselves in cattle raising, slaughtering and fishing. The Cham were singled out for mistreatment under **Democratic Kampuchea**, their religious practices and dietary requirements being forcibly suppressed but allegations of "genocide" are not supported by known documentary evidence and do not mesh with the large number of Chams who survived the regime. Many survivors left the country in the 1980s.

CHAMROEUN VICHEA ("progressive knowledge"). A private secondary school in the southern part of **Phnom Penh**, where Saloth Sar **(Pol Pot)** taught civics, geography and French literature between 1956 and 1963, earning a reputation as a good teacher. Other progressive intellectuals associated with the school who later joined the communist movement include **Uch Ven, Phouk Chhay** and **Van Piny**. One aim of the association promoting the school was to prepare students from disadvantaged backgrounds for the examinations required for admission to public high schools, or lycées.

CHAN CHAKREY (1943-1976). Born Prom Sombat, he was a former monk who joined the communist movement in the 1950s. He was a member of the standing committee of the **Communist Party of Kampuchea**, and later senior deputy head of the general staff and commander of the Phnom Penh Special Region. In September 1976 he was arrested after having been implicated in an alleged coup attempt against **Pol Pot** in May 1976. He was executed soon afterward.

CHAN NAK (1892-1954). Prime minister 1953-1954. Born on 27 May 1892 in **Phnom Penh**, he studied in the Cambodian School of Administration, the École Coloniale in **France** and worked in the French colonial judiciary. In 1923 he became a magistrate, and by 1927, he was a member of the Consultative Assembly. Two years later, he was assistant to the minister of justice, and in 1931 was elected president of the Consultative Assembly. In 1941 he was a member of the Federal Council of Indochina, and then minister of justice in 1942.

Chan Nak was reappointed minister of justice in the first government of the independent Kingdom of Kampuchea when it was formed on 18 March 1945 with Japanese sponsorship. He remained in the cabinet until 13 August when **Son Ngoc Thanh** formed his government. Chan Nak was clearly trusted by the French because he returned to the cabinet on 17 October as minister of justice, after Thanh was arrested and Prince **Sisowath Monireth** became prime minister. He remained in office until 14 December 1946, and worked with **Khim Tith** in the formation of the **National Union Party**. In 1948 he was elected to the High Council of the Kingdom representing the judicial branches of the civil service, and awarded the Legion of Honour. He was minister of justice, May to December 1950. A delegate to the **Pau Conference** which agreed conventions on financial arrangements, Chan Nak next became a member of the Royal Council and one of the two private advisors (privy councillors) to King **Norodom Sihanouk** in 1951. He became president of the Council of Ministers, 23 November 1953 to 6 April 1954, as well as holding the portfolios of interior and information from 23 November 1953 until 6 April 1954. He died in November 1954 in Paris, survived by three children: Chottana, Thouk (Mme Tan Kim Tek), and Suon. Suon, an airline pilot, contested the 1966 **National Assembly** elections. He was killed in a rocket attack on **Kampong Speu** in the early 1970s.

CHAN NATH (1911-). Born at Kirivong, Takeo, he worked in the Land Registry office before becoming a merchant in Kirivong dealing in dry goods and salt. In 1947 he was elected a **Democrat Party** member of the **National Assembly** for Reani Andoeur, Takeo. He left this party in 1948. In February 1951 he joined the **Victorious Northeastern Khmer Party**, and in the 1951 elections, ran for an Assembly seat in **Siem Reap**; and in the 1952 High Council of the Kingdom elections for **Battambang** and Siem Reap again without success. Chan Nath was elected to the High Council of the Kingdom in 1955 to represent the Chamber of Commerce. In 1959 he ran once again for the High Council elections for **Kampong**

Speu, **Kampong Chhnang** and **Pursat**, but lost.

CHAN PHIN also **Chan Phing (1930-)**. A native of **Svay Rieng** province, he joined the revolutionary section of the **Khmer Issarak** movement in 1949 and was evacuated to Hanoi in 1955. While in **Vietnam**, he earned a degree in economics and taught economics there until 1978. Reemerging as a member of the **United Front for the National Salvation of Kampuchea** in 1978, he was minister for finance and national banking from 1979 until 1981, elected to the **National Assembly** for **Takeo** in May 1981 and was then appointed minister of finance from June 1981 to March 1986. In May 1981 he was elected to the newly reestablished **People's Revolutionary Party of Kampuchea** Central Committee (ninth in order of rank), and to the Party's seven-man Secretariat. In the mid-1980s, as minister for trade within the centrally planned economy, he was in charge of the National Committee for Rice Procurement. Later, as industry minister in the renamed State of Cambodia government, he sparked public controversies for promoting joint venture agreements with foreign investors, resulting in the loss of jobs, and was the focus of demonstrations against government corruption in April 1992 when sitting tenants were evicted from housing owned by the ministry. A senior advisor to **Hun Sen** on finance, banking and trade throughout the 1990s, he was appointed to the **Senate** in 1999.

CHAN RATTANA. See YIM SOKHA.

CHAN SAMAY (né **Lam Phay**). A **Khmer Krom** revolutionary, born in Travinh, **Vietnam**, and brother-in-law of **Son Ngoc Thanh**, he studied in **France** for nearly 10 years in the 1930s. On his return from Europe, Samay continued to live in French **Cochinchina** where he joined the **Viet Minh** in the 1940s and became an aide to **Son Ngoc Minh**, leader of the revolutionary **Khmer Issarak**. Samay was deputy chairman of the National Central Executive Committee of the Issarak, and vice-president of the United Issarak Front formed in 1950. He moved to Hanoi in the post-Geneva Conference regroupment period, and became director of ethnic minorities in North Vietnam. He is presumed to have died in Vietnam.

CHAN SENG (1935-1989). Born in **Kampong Cham**, Chan Seng supported **Issarak** activities after 1948 but was not among those regrouped in Hanoi after 1954. Resuming political activities in 1970, he supported the **Democratic Kampuchea** regime until the crisis in the East Zone in May 1978. Later in the year, he helped to organize the **United Front for the National Salvation of Kampuchea**. By 1981 he was a party chief as well as chair of the provincial People's Committee (effectively governor) in **Siem Reap** province and member of the Control Commission of the Central

Committee of the **People's Revolutionary Party of Kampuchea**. He was elected to the Party political bureau in September 1985 with policy-making responsibilities for local administration as well as party control work. Elected to the **National Assembly** in May 1981, he represented Siem Reap until his death in February 1989.

CHAN SI (1932-1984). Prime minister 1982-1984. Born on 7 May 1932, in **Kampong Chhnang**, he joined the Communist movement in 1949 and by 1950 was active in the 545th Khmer **Viet Minh** Army Unit in the Krakor district of **Pursat**, fighting the French. In 1952 he returned to his native province of Kampong Chhnang where he was a member of the 305th Military Central Mobile Unit. Following the Geneva Agreement, he sought refuge in Hanoi, joining the **Khmer People's Revolutionary Party** in 1960. It is possible that he remained in Hanoi after 1970, but more likely that he returned to Cambodia briefly in 1970-1972. An official biography states he was alienated from the communists by 1972 and was in **Vietnam** in 1978 when he became one of the founding members of the **United Front for the National Salvation of Kampuchea**, together with **Heng Samrin**. This front, officially formed on 2 December 1978 and aided by 200,000 Vietnamese "volunteers" invaded Cambodia on 25 December, seizing power in **Phnom Penh** on 7 January 1979.

Chan Si was president of the Political Commission of the new People's Revolutionary Armed Forces, becoming deputy minister of defense. Appointed to the politburo of the newly formed **People's Revolutionary Party of Kampuchea (PRPK)** in May 1981, he became deputy prime minister and defense minister in June. He became prime minister of the **People's Republic of Kampuchea**, following the purging of **Pen Sovan** in February 1982. He died on 24 December 1984 of a heart attack, in a Moscow hospital. Official reports issuing from Phnom Penh date his death a week later.

CHAN SOURATH. An officer in the first company of the 2nd Battalion of the Royal Army, he was stationed in Sisophon, **Battambang** in March 1953 when he was ordered to establish an outpost at Kralanh. On 16 March, telling his soldiers that he had a secret order from the king, he persuaded 120 men to load ordnance into trucks and drove into the jungle. While resting, they were surprised by supporters of **Son Ngoc Thanh**. Sourath then proclaimed that King **Norodom Sihanouk** was a traitor and that he was joining Thanh. Thirty of his men remained with him, while the remaining 90 returned to Sisophon.

CHAN TITH (1939-c1976). A historian, he was born on 29 January 1939 in Romduol, **Svay Rieng**, earning his *licence-ès-lettres* from the Royal University in 1965. In 1967 he was principal of Lycée Santepheap in

Kampong Speu. The curator at the National Museum, in June 1971 he was a member of the **constitutional drafting committee** representing the Association of Khmer Historians. A member of the **Socio-Republican Party**, he was elected to the **National Assembly** of the **Khmer Republic** in September 1972, representing Rokakong, **Oddar Meanchey**. He was killed in the early months of the **Democratic Kampuchea** period.

CHAN VÈN (1937-   ). A politician, born in Svay Rieng, the son of peasant farmers, he graduated from the Faculty of Pedagogy in **Phnom Penh** in 1965 and became a mathematics teacher. He was principal of Collège Svay Rieng during the **Khmer Republic** and imprisoned for part of the **Democratic Kampuchea (DK)** period, fleeing to **Vietnam** in August 1978. Well-known and respected, his voice was regularly heard on Radio Hanoi in December 1978 urging an uprising against the DK regime. Chan Vèn was one of the few promoters of the **People's Republic of Kampuchea** who was not from a communist background and one of the 14 founding members of the Central Committee of the **United Front for the National Salvation of Kampuchea (UFNSK)** formed in December 1978. In January 1979 he was named minister of education and chairman of the People's Revolutionary Committee of the **Phnom Penh** municipality. From September 1979 until September 1986 he was president of the Kampuchea-Vietnam Friendship Association. In 1981 he was elected to the **National Assembly** representing Phnom Penh, and was a member, then secretary-general to the Council of State from 1981 to 1993. In May 1993 he campaigned for a seat in **Sihanoukville** on behalf of the **Cambodian People's Party**, but was not elected. Assistant secretary-general of the National Assembly, from November 1993, he has been on several Cambodian delegations overseas.

CHAN YOURAN (1934-). A prominent diplomat, he was born on 7 January 1934, the son of Chan Duch and Mme (née Op Lmon). At **Lycée Sisowath** he met **Hu Nim** and both were caught up in student politics. An excellent student, he graduated 11th in the annual baccalaureate examinations of July 1953. He then taught at **Kambuboth** while studying for his *Licence* in Law at the Royal University, finishing in May 1956. He next completed a diploma in diplomacy at the Royal School of Administration and worked in senior administrative posts and several overseas embassies, before returning to Cambodia as director of *Agence Khmère de Presse*, the government press agency, by August 1969. In the following month he was appointed ambassador to Senegal, a posting which he held until March 1970 when he declared his support for the **Royal Government of National Union of Kampuchea (GRUNK)**.

Chan Youran was GRUNK minister of popular education and youth from May 1970, and a member of the Political Bureau of the Central Committee of **National United Front of Kampuchea (FUNK)**. For this he was among those sentenced to death in absentia for high treason in August 1970. Following the victory of GRUNK in April 1975, he returned to **Phnom Penh**. In late August 1975 he accompanied **Ieng Sary**, **Sarin Chhak** and **Thiounn Prasith** to Lima, Peru; and by 1978 was the **Democratic Kampuchea** (DK) ambassador at large. In the late 1980s, he was ambassador for the **Coalition Government for Democratic Kampuchea** to Beijing and prominent among representatives of the **Party of Democratic Kampuchea** (PDK) at international meetings, including the Paris Conferences of 1989 and 1991. He returned to Cambodia in November 1991 with **Khieu Samphan** when the latter was nearly lynched by crowds organized by **Hun Sen**. After talks in Pattaya, the Democratic Kampuchea party delegation to the **Supreme National Council** received a safe house in the grounds of the royal palace. Chan Youran supported the late 1992 PDK decision to boycott the United Nations-sponsored elections and slipped away from the capital in early 1993. In mid-1998 he surrendered to the Royal Government along with other intellectuals and diplomats associated with the defeated DK government and revolution. He now lives quietly in Phnom Penh.

CHANTO TRES (1919-). The son of Chanto, a **Phnom Penh** doctor, Chanto Tres was a supporter of **Son Ngoc Thanh** who fled to Thailand in October 1945 after his mentor was arrested by the British and handed over to the French. He then became active in the **Khmer Issarak** in **Battambang** and was one of the group which attacked **Siem Reap** on 7 August 1945. Soon afterward he was a member of the Issarak band of Prince **Norodom Chantaraingsey** and was put in charge of foreign affairs in the Cambodian National Liberation Committee in 1949. Chantaraingsey's Issaraks surrendered to the government soon afterward, giving rise to suspicions, probably false, that he had been working for the French all along. Suffering no apparent sanction from the colonial power, Chanto Tres pursued technical studies in **France**. On his return to Phnom Penh he worked in the Ministry of Industry and joined the **Sangkum**. He ran unsuccessfully for the 1966 **National Assembly**, in Trapeang, **Koh Kong**.

CHAP NHALIVUTH (1952-). The son of Chap Huot, a onetime member of the **Victorious Northeastern Khmer Party**, and *neak monéang* Phat Kanhol (**Norodom Sihanouk**'s first wife), Nhalivuth served on the Steering Committee of **FUNCINPEC** until March 1999. He was elected to the **National Assembly** in 1998 on the party list for **Phnom Penh** but gave up his seat to become governor of **Siem Reap** province.

CHAU BAN (1930-). Born on 15 January 1930 in Triton, Chaudoc, **Cochinchina**, he studied political science at the Royal University graduating in April 1960. He then worked in the research section of the National Bank while teaching part time at the Faculty of Law and Economics. Active in the **Khmer Krom** diaspora, Chau Ban was chairman of the Khmers of Kampuchea Krom (KKK) association in the early 1960s. As a **Sangkum** candidate, he was elected to the **National Assembly** in 1962 in Treal, **Kampong Thom**. Defeated in his bid for re-election in 1966, he became managing director of Sonaprim (National Company for distribution of Imported Goods) by the end of the decade when he supported moves toward liberalization of the economy. In June 1971 he was appointed to the **constitutional drafting committee** representing the KKK.

CHAU BORY (?-1960). A former civil servant, and a supporter of **Son Ngoc Thanh**, he fled from Cambodia to South **Vietnam**, and then to **Thailand** in the 1950s. He returned to public view as vice president of the Democratic People's Party created by **Sam Sary** in 1959. Sentenced to death in absentia in December 1959, for complicity in the **Bangkok Plot**, he and his brother Chau Mathura were later captured and executed with the approval of Prince **Norodom Sihanouk**. In another sign of the absence of democratic civil liberties, Chau Bory's wife, a French citizen, was put on trial in 1960, for corresponding by letter with her husband. She received twenty years hard labor.

CHAU SAMBATH (né NGOV) (1946-1997). A Sino-Khmer businessman who resided on the Thai-Cambodian border in the 1980s, he was an officer in the **Armée Nationale Sihanoukienne**, and after 1992, in the Royal Armed Forces of Cambodia. As a close collaborator and confidante of First Prime Minister Prince **Norodom Ranariddh**, he was a target in the 1997 coup. Soldiers loyal to **Hun Sen** captured him together with **Kruoch Yoeurm** on 8 July 1997 in **Kampong Speu** province. The two were tortured and then murdered. *See also* ASSASSINATIONS.

CHAU SAU (1924-1975). A liberal democrat, he was born on 3 June 1924 in Triton, Chaudoc, **Cochinchina**, son of Chau Si, farmer, and Mme (née Miech). He earned his baccalaureate II from **Lycée Sisowath** in 1948 leaving soon afterward for **France** where he earned his *licence* and a doctorate in law from the University of Paris in 1954. He was briefly governor of **Svay Rieng** province and then under-secretary of state for finance, with responsibility for the budget in the Prince **Norodom Kantol** government of 1962-1964, secretary of state for finance from 1964 to 1965, secretary of state for planning from May to October 1966. Following the election of the **Lon Nol** government in 1966, he held the portfolio for planning, finance, trade and the economy in the shadow cabinet established by Prince **Norodom Sihanouk**. By 1968 he was chairman and managing director of the Inadana Jati (National Credit) Bank in which **Khmer Krom** personnel were prominent. During the **Khmer Republic** years, he helped to revitalize the old **Democrat Party** and was judged by some observers as a possible compromise leader in the final stages of the civil war. He disappeared from view and is presumed to have been executed soon after 17 April 1975.

CHAU SEN CHUMNOR (1944-   ). Born on 15 September 1944 at Chrey, **Battambang**, he studied at the Faculty of Medicine in **Phnom Penh** and spent the period of **Democratic Kampuchea** working in the countryside. In 1979 Sen Chumnor, then in the Nong Chan refugee camp, joined **Molinaka**, becoming political advisor for the movement's armed forces. Later a brigadier general of the **Armée Nationale Sihanoukienne**, Chau Sen Chumnor joined **FUNCINPEC** in 1991 and chaired its election committee for **Kampot** province. He was elected to the **National Assembly** in Kampot in the 1993 elections, and in October 1993 was appointed as a member of the Commission for Finance and Banking.

CHAU SEN COCSAL "CHHUM" (1905-   ). Prime minister 1962. Born on 1 December 1905 in Triton, Chaudoc, **Cochinchina**, he was the son of Khun Kim and brother of the anti-French activist Kim Vong Kuon. Chau Sen Cocsal was educated in **Phnom Penh** and at Lycée Chasseloup Laubat in Saigon. He was awarded a baccalaureate in philosophy in 1927 and entered colonial service later the same year. On 9 March 1945, and already governor of **Kampong Cham**, Chau Sen Cocsal actively supported the declaration of independence but after the arrest of his brother Kim Vong Kuon and **Son Ngoc Thanh** on 15 October 1945, he resigned from his post, and with several supporters, left **Kampong Cham** on 26 October to join **Pach Chhoeun** and about 100 other Cambodians in Triton. They organized a Free Cambodia Party seeking to restore the independence the monarchy had just lost, but after the French reoccupied Chaudoc and Triton, the majority fled back to Cambodia. Chau Sen Cocsal surrendered to the authorities on 20 February 1946 in **Kampot** and was appointed governor of **Kandal** the following year. Also in 1947, he served as an advisor to **Nhiek Tioulong** and **Lon Nol** in founding the **Khmer Renewal Party**. Until 1951 he collaborated with the French, by way of supporting monarchy and royal administration, and in 1950 was appointed director of national monopolies.

After the **Pau Conference** which was viewed as a diplomatic success, he was appointed chargé d'affaires in Bangkok on 6 April 1951. In view of the deepening conflicts between the French and the **Viet Minh** and between King **Norodom Sihanouk** and the **Democrat Party,** this was a sensitive posting. In January 1953 it came to the attention of King Sihanouk that many in the legation in Bangkok were in contact with Son Ngoc Thanh, and while he, personally, was not, Chau Sen Cocsal was, nonetheless, recalled for failing to control his staff. Joining the **Sangkum,** he was elected in 1958 to the **National Assembly** to represent Kampong Cham town. Reelected in 1962, and also president of the Sangkum for these elections, he was briefly prime minister from 6 August to 5 October 1962. In 1963 the **Banque Khmère,** which he had founded only a few years earlier, was nationalized. In 1966 Chau Sen Cocsal, who was among those sceptical of national economic policy and favoring liberalization, was reelected to the National Assembly with a large majority. He was initially first vice-president of the Assembly, but withdrew from active politics after the coup in 1970. He went to **Vietnam** in 1975 or 1976 where he lived for a few years in a refugee camp. Vietnamese officials sought him out seeking his support for the **United Front for the National Salvation of Kampuchea** effort to overthrow the **Pol Pot** regime but he refused to take part. After 1981 he lent his support to **FUNCINPEC,** the royalist resistance movement and was appointed as one of the two Sihanoukist representatives on the **Supreme National Council (SNC)** formed in 1990. He quickly relinquished his seat to permit Prince Sihanouk to chair meetings. A privy counselor to the king throughout the 1990s, in 1998 he was a royal appointee to the **Constitutional Council.**

CHAU SENG (1929-1978). A Socialist politician, he was born on 15 March 1929 at Triton, **Cochinchina,** a son of Chau Sam and Mme (née Kam). Chau Seng studied at École Normale, **Phnom Penh,** and from 1949 at the École Normale in Montpellier, **France.** Remaining in France he received a *licence* from the University of Montpellier and a diploma in educational psychology at the Sorbonne in 1956. He joined the **Sangkum** in 1957, won a seat in the 1958 Assembly elections (for Phnom Penh: 3rd district) holding portfolios in most of the succeeding Sangkum cabinets. His dynamism and intelligence ensured that even when his progressive views irritated ruling elites, he continued to received government appointments. He was secretary of state for commerce in the first **Lon Nol** government from 14 November 1966 to 30 April 1967 and minister of state for national economy in the Son Sann government from 1 May to 11 September 1967. Chau Seng was dismissed from this post and forced to flee to France because of his support for the Khmer-Chinese Friendship Association, suppressed and banned in September 1967. He was pardoned in January 1970 and joined Prince **Norodom Sihanouk** in Beijing in April. He was among the Sihanoukists sentenced to death in absentia for high treason by the Lon Nol coup regime in August 1970.

In addition to his government posts, Chau Seng made a very substantial contribution to the development of the national press working successively as editor-in-chief of the official *Néak Cheat Niyum* ("The Nationalist"), *La Dépêche du Cambodge* ("The Dispatch of Cambodia") and the succeeding *La Nouvelle Dépêche du Cambodge* ("The New Dispatch of Cambodia"). He was also general secretary of the **Royal Khmer Socialist Youth** movement and rector of the Buddhist University from the mid-1960s. In 1970 Sihanouk appointed him minister for special missions in his **Royal Government of National Union of Kampuchea (GRUNK)** 1970-1975. Most of his work as a spokesman and representative of the GRUNK was in Europe and Francophone Africa. Recalled to Cambodia in December 1975, along with other foreign-based GRUNK personnel, he was detained, sent to a special political camp and later arrested and sent to **Tuol Sleng** in late 1977.

CHAU XENG UA (1927-). Born on 5 August 1927 at Chaudoc, **Cochin-china**, the son of Sam Mem and Mme (née Lean), Chau Xeng Ua earned his *licence* in social sciences from the University of Paris (1956) and then studied part-time at the Faculty of Law and Economic Sciences at the Royal University, earning a doctorate in economics in May 1965. In 1962 he was elected to the **National Assembly** representing **Kampong Thom**. In August 1969 Chau Xeng Ua was appointed assistant secretary of state for labor and employment. Among his civic activities, he was a member of the Board of Directors of the Red Cross. A supporter of Lon Nol, Chau Xeng Ua continued to serve as assistant secretary of state for labor and employment from March 18-July 1970 when he became minister of social welfare, labor and employment. In May 1971 he was made minister of state for social action, labor and employment and in March 1972, minister of labor and social welfare in the second **Son Ngoc Thanh** government, which fell in October 1972. In June 1971 he was chosen to represent the Cabinet on the **constitutional drafting committee**.

CHAU YAN PHOU (1937-). Born on 10 December 1937 at Khum Svaypor, **Battambang**, son of Chau Yao (1903-1973) and Mme (née Suy Sung), he was an official in the Ministry of Public Works and assistant to the chief of the water and electricity supply center for **Phnom Penh**. Currently residing in Belgium, he was an official representative of the **Khmer People's National Liberation Front (KPNLF)** in the joint KPNLF-FUNCINPEC office established in Brussels in 1983.

CHAY SAING YUN (1953-). Born in Thala Bariwat, **Stung Treng**, he studied in Collège Stung Treng and supported the **National United Front of Kampuchea** in the 1970s and very likely served in the **Democratic Kampuchea** army. In March 1980 he was appointed deputy head of the intelligence services of the new **People's Republic of Kampuchea (PRK)** then being created. Between September 1982 and January 1990 he headed the planning department of the army. In June 1984 Saing Yun was appointed deputy head of the chiefs of staff, and in December 1985, commander of the 3rd Military Region, holding that post until January 1990 when he was appointed first assistant to the head of the army's political department. Throughout the 1980s, he rose through the ranks of the party, the state and the army. In October 1985 he was elected to the Central Committee of the **People's Revolutionary Party of Kampuchea (PRPK)** and he continues to be a member of the Central Committee of the postcommunist **Cambodian People's Party (CPP)**. From December 1990 until March 1992 he was president of the PRPK/CPP committee in **Kampot** and was elected to the **National Assembly** in this province in 1993. Still holding a military commission, he was promoted to major general in January 1989 and to colonel general in March 1992. From this year Chay Saing Yun was deputy minister of defense. He was implicated in the July 1994 coup attempt mounted by **Sin Sen** and **Sin Song** but exposed the conspiracy to **Hun Sen** and testified in court against the others when the finger of suspicion pointed toward him. Reelected to the Assembly in 1998, he was reappointed as CPP secretary of state in the Ministry of Defense.

CHEA CHANTO (1951-). Born on 9 October 1951 at **Kampong Thom**, he studied economics at the University of Phnom Penh. He was evacuated from **Phnom Penh** in 1975 and later escaped to or was deported to **Vietnam**, where he earned a doctorate in economics. Employed mostly in the banking sector, he was named director of the hastily assembled People's Bank in 1980 and helped to oversee the reintroduction of a currency of exchange. Two years later he was appointed deputy director of the National Bank and by 1983 he was vice-president of Foreign Trade Bank. In 1986 he was promoted to deputy minister of planning in the **People's Republic of Kampuchea**, becoming minister in 1989 as **Chea Soth** gradually reduced his duties. A member of the Central Committee of the **People's Revolutionary Party of Kampuchea** and of the successor **Cambodian People's Party**, he was minister of planning in the Royal Governments formed in 1993. He was elected to the **National Assembly** in 1993 in Kampong Thom province and represented the province in the Assembly until 1998.

CHEA CHHUT (1933-1997). A lieutenant in the Republican Armed Forces, he escaped to **Thailand** during the **Democratic Kampuchea** period and became active in a renewed **Khmer Serei** resistance organized from the Thai side of the Thai-Khmer frontier. In 1980, after malaria had claimed the life of **Kong Sileah**, he was elected leader of the royalist **Molinaka**. By 1983 his allegiance had shifted to the **Khmer People's National Liberation Front (KPNLF)**. By the mid-1980s, Chea Chhut was commander at Prey Chan and the Nong Chan refugee camp. He remained loyal to the **Son Sann** group in the KPNLF after the December 1985 split between the military and political wings of the movement. Remaining politically active after 1993, he was among the former border resistance officers to be murdered in the wake of the 1997 **coup d'état**.

CHEA CHINKOC (1904-1975). A senior civil servant by the late colonial period, Chea Chinkoc was born on 29 June 1904 in **Kandal** province, the son of Chea El and Mme (née Nhiep). He entered public service in 1924 when 20 years old. In the anti colonial struggles of 1946, he helped Prince **Norodom Montana** to form the **Progressive Democratic Party** becoming secretary-general of the party from May 1946. In 1947 he was Chief Clerk in the Ministry of National Economy and briefly, governor of **Takeo** province before becoming minister of industry and trade, June 1950 to May 1951. He then worked at the Ministry of the Interior, resigning to run in the 1951 **National Assembly** elections for a seat in **Phnom Penh** which he did not win. Joining the **Sangkum** in 1955, he was named secretary of state for foreign affairs and the interior, minister of the interior and surface defense, April to July 1956, minister delegate for the chairman of the Council of Ministers, for coordination of research and reforms from January to April 1957, and under secretary of state for the interior and national security from July 1957 to January 1958. Elected to the 1958 National Assembly for Cham, **Prey Veng**, he was attached once again to the Council of Ministers as a secretary of state for the chairman from January to April 1958 and as a minister delegate for the chairman of the Council for Reform from April to June 1958, and for coordination of research and reform from July 1958 to February 1959. Chea Chinkoc was next appointed minister of state for the Departments of National Education and Fine Arts from February to June 1959; and minister of state for the President of the Council, for the Interior Ministry from June 1959 to April 1960; minister of state for the President of the Council for the Ministry of National Education from April 1960 to January 1961; and minister of national education and fine arts from January to August 1962. He was elected to the High Council in 1966 as a representative of the civil service. He married Yim Saron in 1929 and they had three children, including **Chea San** and **Chea Thay Seng**. He refused to take part in the evacuation on Phnom Penh and was killed on 17 April 1975.

CHEA KEO alias **Muth (1924-1975).** He owned a general store in **Phnom Penh** and supported the **Viet Minh**-backed **Khmer Issarak** from at least

1949. After the **Geneva Conference** he was evacuated to **Vietnam** along with the regrouping guerrilla forces and remained in Hanoi from 1955-1970. Already fluent in Thai, Lao, French and Vietnamese, while living in Vietnam he learned Chinese, English and Russian. In 1970 he was sent back to Cambodia to organize the revolution in **Stung Treng** and by February 1971 was secretary of the provincial branch of the **Communist Party of Kampuchea**. He was among the Vietnamese-trained cadres who was purged and executed in 1974-1975.

CHEA KIV (1899-1983). A self-made businessman, Chea Kiv was born in Voar Sar, Samrong Thom, **Kampong Speu**. He had some legal training as a young man and was briefly an interpreter for the **French Résident** in Kampong Speu. He then moved to **Phnom Penh** where he operated a lumber business and served as a juror in the Criminal Court. In 1947 he was one of the founding members of the **Khmer Renewal Party**. Three times he was *mékhum* (headman) of Chbar Ampeou, and in 1951 he was a candidate for the **National Assembly** seat in Voar Sar, Kampong Speu. Following the realignment of political parties in 1955, he gave up politics but continued to run his lumber business throughout the 1960s. In 1979, with his wife and his nephew, **Khau Meng Hean**, he fled to **Thailand**. The family was resettled in **France** in 1982 where he died in February 1983.

CHEA OUM (1913-   ). Born in **Battambang** on 2 July 1913, the son of Chea Om and Mme (née Ou Or), Oum was an inspector of primary education from 1944. After serving initially in **Kampong Chhnang**, he was appointed director of Collège Sihanouk, **Kampong Cham**, in 1945. A supporter of **Son Ngoc Thanh**, he was among those who went to **Vietnam** with **Chau Sen Cocsal**, after Thanh's arrest in October. He surrendered to the French in March 1946 and then in May helped to form the **Liberal Party** which favored gradual decolonization in collaboration with **France**. From 1947 he was once again an inspector of schools. In the **Sangkum** period, he was briefly secretary of state for education in early 1956 and a Sangkum deputy in the **National Assembly** 1958-1962 representing Kampong Popil, **Prey Veng**, and again in 1962-1966 representing **Battambang**. He was president of the Religious and Cultural Commission in 1958-1959. In the **Black Book** published by the Foreign Ministry of **Democratic Kampuchea** in 1978, it is alleged that Oum had been recruited by Vietnamese interests in the 1940s, an allusion to the **Khmer Krom** and **Cham** intellectuals associated with the Liberal Party who sought independence within the framework of continuing association with France and monarchy.

CHEA SAN (1930-1978). A career diplomat, Chea San was born on 19 September 1930 in **Phnom Penh**. The son of **Chea Chinkoc** and Mme (née Yim Saron), he studied international relations at the Institut d'Études Politiques de Paris and diplomacy in the Royal School of Administration. He was then appointed first secretary at the Cambodian embassy in London. Following this tour, he was briefly secretary of state for information, May-October 1966. During the election campaign, he lent support to several left of center candidates which cost him his job when the **Lon Nol** government was formed. Prince **Norodom Sihanouk** invited him to join his opposition shadow cabinet formally announced on 1 May 1967, and he was publisher and managing editor of its daily *Bulletin du Contre-Gouvernement*. It published many investigative reports on crises within nationalized companies among other developmental problems. In May 1969 he was named ambassador to Moscow, from where, in March 1970 he declared his continuing loyalty to the deposed Prince Sihanouk. He was in rapid succession brought into the political bureau of the **National United Front of Kampuchea (FUNK)** and given the portfolio for justice and judicial reform in the **Royal Government of National Union of Kampuchea**. He held this post until December 1973. Chea San was meanwhile sentenced to death in absentia for high treason by the **Lon Nol** authorities in August 1970. Recalled to Phnom Penh in 1975 he was detained and confined to special camps with other noncommunist diplomats and intellectuals undergoing political reeducation. Never "rehabilitated," he was sent to **Tuol Sleng** in March 1978 and executed on 27 May 1978.

CHEA SIM (1932-   ). President of the **Senate** and chairman of the **Cambodian People's Party (CPP)**. Born on 15 November 1932 in Romeas Hek, **Svay Rieng**, Chea Sim went to school for five years only studying ethics and Pali in a Buddhist temple school. In 1952 he joined the clandestine **Khmer Issarak** movement led by *Achar* Mean who was later known as **Son Ngoc Minh.** He was attached to an armed propaganda team responsible for recruiting among Buddhist monks. He joined the **Khmer People's Revolutionary Party (KPRP)** only in 1959 becoming party secretary in several eastern districts in the 1960s. He remained in the eastern border region during the civil war and **Democratic Kampuchea** periods, becoming secretary and military commander in *tambon* ("sector") 20 in mid-1978. He was among the east zone cadres who attempted to mount a rebellion against the party center as purges of top cadre progressed. He then fled to **Vietnam** and was one of the communist dissidents who founded the **United Front for the National Salvation of Kampuchea** on 2 December 1978, being its vice-president. In the period immediately following the 7 January occupation of **Phnom Penh,** he held the interior portfolio in the people's revolutionary council as the government was then known. After the May 1981 elections in which he won a seat in **Prey Veng,** he was named chairman of the **National Assembly.** In July, he was revealed to be the fourth ranking member of the Political Bureau of the new **People's Revolutionary Party of Kampuchea (PRPK).** In December 1981 he became chairman of the National Council of the **United Front for Construction and Defense of the Kampuchean Motherland.** This restructuring mirrors the peacetime transmogrification of the wartime **Viet Minh** front into the Fatherland Front in **Vietnam.**

Officially ranked number two in the party after the fifth Congress in 1985, he emerged as top leader in 1991 when he was elected chairman of the restructured **Cambodian People's Party (CPP),** easing **Heng Samrin** into an honorary post. Frequently described as the *eminence grise* as well as the principal power broker in the CPP, he devotes most of his time to party affairs and to maintaining links of patronage with party officials in provincial administration. Elected to the National Assembly in **Prey Veng** in 1993, he was elected president of the National Assembly. In that role he served as acting Head of State when King **Norodom Sihanouk** was abroad. The holder of this post is also a member of the small **Throne Council** which chooses a new king in case of the king's death. Chea Sim was reelected in the 1998 National Assembly elections but the formation of a second FUNCINPEC-CPP coalition government was stalled by FUNCINPEC insistence that Prince **Norodom Ranariddh,** a claimant to the throne, be awarded the presidency of the Assembly. He is now president of the new 60-member **Senate** established in 1999. An amendment to the Constitution adds the president of the Senate to the list of members of the Throne Council. Although not a member of the cabinet, Chea Sim is arguably the best-connected and the single most powerful individual in the country.

CHEA SOPHARA. A member of the Central Committee of the **Cambodian People's Party (CPP)** since 1997, Sophara was appointed governor of **Phnom Penh** in November 1999 with the agreement of Prince **Norodom Ranariddh,** leader of **FUNCINPEC** who could identify no candidate for the post. Following the formation of the new **Hun Sen** government in November 1998, most governors and their deputies were appointed in March 1999 with each FUNCINPEC governor backed by a first deputy from the CPP, or *vice versa.* Unable to find a suitable candidate, FUNCINPEC agreed at that moment to allow Sophara, who was appointed first deputy in 1995 and who became acting governor in July 1997 when the FUNCINPEC appointee, **Chhim Seak Leng,** abandoned his post, to carry on as acting governor. His promotion to the post was agreed upon only after further attempts to identify a suitable FUNCINPEC functionary failed. **Than Sina**, previously a FUNCINPEC secretary of state in the Ministry of Interior, has been appointed first deputy governor.

Chea Sophara's aggressive and hands-on approach to his job draws admiration from some and criticism from others. It was he who ordered the deportation of several hundred illegal Chinese immigrants in 1999 and 2000 and the suspension of two municipal judges whom he regarded as inefficient and dishonest (and who were later reassigned to other posts by the Supreme Council of the Magistry which accepted the wholly unconstitutional dismissals). Sophara wants Phnom Penh to become once again a clean, well ordered city with parks and recreational areas, well-controlled traffic and less crime. His worthy aspirations are paired with ruthless means. The city has been systematically evicting squatters. In 1999 a community of Vietnamese **boat people** moored near Monivong Bridge were simply cut loose and towed down the **Bassac**, the city declaring them "illegal immigrants." A fire in a squatter settlement near the city center in May 2001 led city planners to accelerate plans to construct a park. The governor has also quareled with powerful business groups and individuals over zoning matters, refusing for example to allow Ariston Sdn Bhd to build a casino in his city even though the government has entered into a contract. Regarded as one of the three "strong men" in Hun Sen's immediate entourage, he possesses personal power and backing which no FUNCINPEC appointee could hope to match or challenge. *See also* HOK LUNDY, KUN KIM.

CHEA SOTH (1928-). A veteran communist revolutionary, Chea Soth was born on 15 August 1928 in **Prey Veng** city. He joined the **Khmer Issarak** in 1949 and the **Indochinese Communist Party** in 1950. In 1951 he become secretary to **Tou Samouth** and headed the Office of the Committee for the Liberation of the East of Cambodia. Regrouped in 1954 he lived in Hanoi serving as a liaison officer with the clandestine party in Cambodia. He also worked briefly for the Radio Beijing foreign broadcasting service. In 1970 he joined the **National United Front of Kampuchea** and worked in **Hu Nim**'s Ministry ʊf Information in the **Royal Government of National Union of Kampuchea**. While still in **China** in 1974, he learned of the purges of Vietnamese-trained cadre and defected, seeking asylum in **Vietnam** and joining **Heng Samrin**.

Chea Soth was appointed ambassador of the **People's Republic of Kampuchea** to Vietnam from January 1979 until November 1980. He then joined the **People's Revolutionary Council** with responsibility for planning and economics in 1980-1981; was named deputy chairman of the Council of Ministers and minister of planning in 1981-1986; deputy chairman of the Council of Ministers in 1986-1992 and was from May 1981 a member of the Political Bureau and the Central Committee of the **People's Revolutionary Party of Kampuchea,** later the **Cambodian People's Party (CPP).** In May 1993 he was elected to the **National Assembly** in **Kandal.** No longer in the cabinet, he became a member of the King's Privy Council on 25 December 1993. In 1998 he was reelected to the National Assembly as a deputy from **Prey Veng.**

CHEA THAY SENG (1933-1976). The son of **Chea Chinkoc** and a brother of **Chea San,** Thay Seng received his *licence-ès-lettres* at the Sorbonne and had also studied museum work in the École du Louvre. Back from **France** in 1964, he was dean of the faculty of archaeology at the Royal University and a curator of the National Museum. During the final years of the **Khmer Republic,** he worked at the Ministry of Information. He was arrested by the **Democratic Kampuchea** security police sometime after April 1975 and executed at **Tuol Sleng** on 27 May 1976.

CHEA VANNATH. A prominent NGO activist, she is director of the Center for Social Development (CSD) which encourages public debate and state-society cooperation on issues of wide public concern. CSD aims to promote the growth of civil society in Cambodia and also to encourage democratization of the state by encouraging greater transparency and accountability in public policy. CSD sponsored a major conference on corruption in 1996 and more recently, has developed a National Issues Forum, which has taken up the issues of prostitution and national reconciliation. The forums have been broadcast on national television. A frequent commentator on breaking social news, Vannath became director in 1997, succeeding Pok Than, secretary of state in the Ministry of Education since 1998.

CHEAM YEAP (1946-). Deputy. Born in Peam Ro, **Prey Veng** province, Yeap is a graduate of the Faculty of Pedagogy and worked as a high school teacher, 1967-1975. Until April 1977, he was submitted to the **Democratic Kampuchea** labor regime but then sought refuge in **Vietnam.** He returned in January 1979 to take charge of propaganda and information work in his native province on behalf of the new revolutionary authorities. Among the "new people" to join the new **People's Revolutionary Party of Kampuchea,** he chaired the People's Committee of **Prey Veng** from 1981-1986 and represented the province in the **National Assembly** from 1981-1993. In 1989 Cheam Yeap was appointed deputy-minister in the office of the Council of Ministers with responsibility for tourism. In 1993 and 1998 he was reelected to the National Assembly in **Prey Veng** on the **Cambodian**

People's Party list. He was elected to the CPP Central Committee in the early 1990s.

CHEANG AM. A senior **Cambodian People's Party** politician, he rose through the ranks of the party via the army. He was deputy director of the General Political Department of the People's Revolutionary Armed Forces in December 1984 and a prominent spokesman for the **People's Revolutionary Party of Kampuchea** committee in the army by the late 1980s. He was promoted to major general in June 1990 and in August of the same year became party secretary of **Kampong Thom** province and a member of the Central Committee of the party. In 1992 he was named governor of the province and won a seat in the **National Assembly** in the United Nations-supervised 1993 election. He resigned his seat in support of the secessionist movement mounted by Prince **Norodom Chakrapong**. He was reappointed governor of Kampong Thom by the new government on 18 December 1993 and in March 1999 he succeeded **Hun Neng** as governor of **Kampong Cham**.

CHEAV SEAN LEANG (1940-). A native of **Kampong Cham**, he studied pharmacology, specializing in gynecology, at the University of Toulouse. He was then appointed dean of the Faculty of Pharmacology in **Phnom Penh** from 1969-1975. In March 1973, after the marriage of his brother, Cheav Sean Lân, to **Lon Nol**'s adopted daughter Andet, Cheav Sean Leang was appointed as advisor to Lon Nol for public relations. In the following year he became minister of industry, fishing and maritime resources in the second **Long Boret** government, 16 June 1974 to 21 March 1975, and took on the tourism portfolio until 12 April 1975 when he left the country. He worked with the French government in Beirut between 1978-1984 and since 1984 has taught at the Faculty of Pharmacology in Tours.

CHEM SINGATH (1931-1976). Born in **Phnom Penh**, the daughter of Chem Nau and Mme (née Tin), she studied at the École Normale, **Phnom Penh** and then in **France**. On her return she married **Chine Reine**. Among the few women of her generation to obtain a high post in the government, she was Headmistress of Collège Preah Norodom and was secretary of state for information in the **Son Sann** government, May 1967-January 1968. She then worked for the United Nations International Children's Emergency Fund. Her husband was among the senior civil servants who disappeared soon after the communists seized Phnom Penh in 1975. She was arrested and taken to **Tuol Sleng** in March 1976 and executed on 27 May 1976.

CHEM SNGUON (1926-1999). Born in **Phnom Penh**, Snguon studied law in **France** and diplomacy at the Royal School of Administration. In 1967

Chem Snguon worked briefly in the Office of **Norodom Sihanouk** securing an appointment the following year as director of the Political Affairs Department in the Foreign Ministry. Remaining loyal to Sihanouk in 1970, he joined the Central Committee of the **National United Front of Kampuchea** for which he was sentenced to death in absentia for high treason in August 1970. From 1970-1975 he was ambassador for the **Royal Government of National Union of Kampuchea** and the **Democratic Kampuchea (DK)** government in Algeria and Egypt. Returning to Cambodia in 1975 he was briefly detained and then sent to the special political camp for returnees established in **Kampong Cham** province where he remained until 1978. In the confusion surrounding the Vietnamese invasion in December 1978, he was apprehended by or surrendered to the advancing Vietnamese forces.

Chem Snguon renounced all association with the DK authorities and agreed to work for the new revolutionary council. In September 1979 he was appointed secretary-general of the **United Front for the National Salvation of Kampuchea**; and in May 1981 he became an assistant to the secretary of its permanent standing committee, **Heng Samrin**. Beginning in December 1983 he worked at the Justice Ministry, initially as deputy-minister (1983-1993), and then as minister (1993-1998). Viewed by the ruling party as a figure who had the capacity to draw Sihanouk and other "old society" personalities back into the framework of the **State of Cambodia (SOC)**, he was appointed to the SOC council of state in its final years, 1990-1993. In 1993, Snguon won a seat in the **National Assembly** in **Svay Rieng**. He was deputy chairman of the Commission for Drafting the Constitution—he presented the constitution to the public on 24 September 1993. As minister of justice in the 1990s, he endured much criticism for his tolerance of the "culture of impunity" and resistance to judicial reforms. In 1998 he was reelected to the National Assembly but his health failing, he lost his ministerial portfolio. He died of cancer in New York on 14 June 1999.

CHEM WIDHYA. The son of **Chem Snguon**, Widhya studied at Lycée Descartes but completed his university education in the German Democratic Republic in the 1980s. Returning to Cambodia around 1989 he worked in the private secretariat of **Hun Sen.** In 1991-1993 he was a **Cambodian People's Party (CPP)** representative in the secretariat of the Supreme National Council. From June until September 1993 he was assistant secretary-general to the Constituent Assembly while his father played a leading role in the drafting of the constitution. Following the promulgation of the constitution in October 1993, he was appointed permanent secretary of the Ministry of Foreign Affairs, a post he continued to hold in 2002.

CHENG AN (?-1978). Cheng An joined the Communist Party in 1959 and by 1963 was a member of the **Phnom Penh** city party committee. By 1971 he was secretary of *tambon* ("sector") 15, a strategically important region to the west of Phnom and in 1972 he was among the first to speak out against Vietnamese involvement in Cambodia's revolution. After 1975 he was chairman of the Committee for Industry. Although a member of the Permanent Standing Committee of the **Communist Party of Kampuchea (CPK)**, he was among the senior cadres executed in late 1978. As he was being driven past the D-3 factory to his place of execution, he is said to have shouted out, "I am Cheng An. Rebel, everyone! Don't follow **Pol Pot** . . . he is a murderer"!

CHENG HENG (1910-1996). Head of state, 1970-1972. A Sino-Khmer, he was born on 10 January 1910 in Samlong, **Takeo**, studied at **Lycée Sisowath** and the Royal School of Administration and then worked in provincial administration before earning a degree in law. In 1957 he became head of the National Penitentiary Services and director of the Central Prison, **Phnom Penh**. Deciding after this to enter politics, he joined the **Sangkum** and was elected to the **National Assembly** in 1958, and again in 1962 in Takhmau, **Kandal**. A large landowner who promoted commercial agriculture, he was secretary of state for agriculture in four successive governments from April 1960 to August 1962. He was also a manager of SONEXIM, the state import-export agency established after Prince **Norodom Sihanouk**'s nationalization of banking and commerce. Although he was not reelected to the Assembly in 1966, he won a by-election in 1967. He then succeeded **Chau Sen Cocsal** as president of the Assembly on 23 October 1968.

Cheng Heng became acting head of state by constitutional fiat on 18 March 1970 following the vote to depose Sihanouk. Confirmed in this post in his own right after the proclamation of the republic, Cheng Heng was elbowed aside on 10 March 1972 when **Lon Nol** assumed the position of president. By that time Cheng Heng had acquired public respect as a head of state who managed to avoid day-to-day political machinations. Briefly retiring to private life, he lived comfortably in Phnom Penh in his urban villa surrounded by animals from his private zoo, until he was brought back into the government as a member of the Supreme High Council in 1973. He left Phnom Penh on 29 March 1975, in an attempt to assist **Long Boret** to reach a compromise with Prince Sihanouk, one that never eventuated.

Relocating to the United States, Cheng Heng became a real estate agent in Milwaukee and then moved to Dallas, Texas. He returned to Phnom Penh on a "secret" visit in 1989 and in 1991 established his own political party, the Republican Coalition Party. He ran in the 1993 elections, but did not win a seat in the new Constituent Assembly. He died on 15 March 1996. He was married to a daughter of **Ung Hy**, minister of finance in the Japanese-backed government of March 1945.

CHENLA, KINGDOM OF. *See* ZHENLA.

CHEY CHETTA II. King of Cambodia 1607-1627. In 1594 as a young prince, he was taken into exile in **Thailand** with his father. He completed his studies in Ayudhya and returned in 1604 to Cambodia with his father, who was regarded by Ayudhya as the reigning king. Chey Chetta married a Vietnamese princess, was himself crowned in 1620 and built a new capital at **Oudong**. Over the next few years, he resisted several Thai attacks, and also welcomed European traders to Cambodia. Because the Vietnamese had helped him against the Thai, Chey Chetta ceded to them the unimportant **Khmer** fishing village on the coast that later became Saigon-Ho Chi Minh City.

CHEY CHETTA III (So). King of Cambodia 1661-1707. He ascended the throne in 1677 at the age of 16 but the first years of his reign were disrupted by the need to prevent his uncle, aided by the Vietnamese, from gaining power. He was driven from **Oudong** briefly, but the uncle eventually died in 1690. King Chey Chetta III abdicated the throne briefly on five occasions, finally allowing his son Srey Thommarechea to reign in his place. He lived for another 17 years.

CHEY CHUM (1921-1977). Born on 30 November 1921 in **Takeo**, and educated at **Lycée Sisowath** and a class of 1941 graduate of the Royal School of Administration, he was a member of the **Democrat Party** and among those arrested on 13 January 1953 in a police crackdown. A left-wing member of the executive of the party in 1954-1955 when Saloth Sar **(Pol Pot)** and **Norodom Phurissara** promoted it, he was a candidate in the 1955 elections in the plantation district of Chup, **Kampong Cham**. After his defeat, and the victory of the **Sangkum**, he gave up on politics. On 30 May 1972 he joined the **National United Front of Kampuchea (FUNK)**. He was named president of the FUNK committee for **Phnom Penh** on 14 December 1973 and deputy chairman of the Kampuchea-**Vietnam** Friendship Association committee on 27 January 1975. Neither committee was functional. Likely detained in a special camp after 1975, he was taken to **Tuol Sleng** on 16 March 1977.

CHEY KANH NHA. A medical doctor, she escaped to **Vietnam** between 1975-1978 after her husband had been executed during **Democratic Kampuchea**. Recruited from a refugee camp, she agreed to support the Vietnamese-promoted **United Front for the National Salvation of**

Kampuchea formed in December 1978 and was a member of the National Council of the succeeding **United Front for the National Construction and Defense of the Kampuchean Motherland** until 1989. She was secretary of state and often acting minister of health in the **People's Republic of Kampuchea** throughout the 1980s.

CHEY SAPHON (1930-). He fought with the **Khmer Issarak** from 1947, was evacuated to **Vietnam** in 1954. Returning in 1970 to support the **National United Front of Kampuchea,** he fled the country in 1974 when the purging of Vietnamese-trained cadre intensified. A journalist, he was named director-general of the official Sarpordamean Press Agency (SPK) in March 1979, the most important propaganda arm of the emerging **People's Republic of Kampuchea (PRK)**. In October 1980 he became editor-in-chief of the official magazine *Kampuchea,* later edited by **Khieu Kanahrith.** In May 1981, as one of the few communists in the regime with links to the 1940s, he played a central role in the creation of the **People's Revolutionary Party of Kampuchea (PRPK)** and was elected to its Central Committee. However, his generation was being slowly eclipsed and he was not reelected to the Central Committee in October 1985 and was thereafter sidelined as head of the party's History Commission. Elected to the PRK **National Assembly** in May 1981, he represented **Prey Veng** until May 1993. In the May 1993 elections, his was the eighth name on the **Cambodian People's Party (CPP)** list for Prey Veng but he was not elected.

CHHAK SARIN. *See* SARIN CHHAK.

CHHANG SONG (1939-). Ex-senator. Born in **Takeo**, he completed a degree in agriculture at Louisiana State University and briefly taught French literature in the **United States** before returning to **Phnom Penh** in the late 1960s. Capitalizing on his excellent command of the English language, he worked in journalism and became an information officer in the army in 1970 rising to become official spokesman for the High Command. On 16 June 1974 he was appointed minister of information in the second **Long Boret** government partly because of a strong working relationship with foreign war correspondents. He relinquished this post on 21 March 1975 when he became press secretary to **Lon Nol.** He left **Phnom Penh** with Lon Nol on 1 April 1975 and settled after some months in Washington, D.C. After 1979 he founded Save Cambodia Inc., a nongovernmental organization based in Arlington, Virginia, which assisted the settlement of Cambodian refugees in the United States. In 1987 Chhang Song became a U.S. citizen. He returned to Phnom Penh in 1995, and in the following year became a personal assistant and advisor to **Chea Sim.**

He was appointed to the **Senate** in 1999 by the **Cambodian People's Party (CPP)** but was expelled from the Senate and the CPP on 6 December 2001, together with two others, when they spoke in opposition to a CPP-proposed revision of the penal code. *See also* KEO SANN, LAO MONG HAY.

CHHANN SOKHOM (1924-1975). Politician. Born on 22 December 1924 in **Phnom Penh**, the son of Pal Chhan and Mme (née Ouk Samreth), he was a longtime supporter of **Lon Nol** and friend of **Lon Non**. An official in the Phnom Penh municipal government, he was a deputy in the **National Assembly** from 1962-1966, but failed to hold his seat, in Phnom Penh, in 1966. In August 1969 he was appointed assistant secretary of state for special missions, attached to the cabinet, and in January 1970 was appointed secretary of state for national education. In this position, it was he who had primary responsibility for organizing the demonstrations against the Vietnamese presence in March 1970 and the student protests against the allegedly pro-Vietnamese policies of Prince **Norodom Sihanouk** that followed. On the morning of 18 March 1970 he was one of the small group of advisors who urged Lon Nol to continue with the plans to overthrow Sihanouk. Appointed minister of education, he decided to place more emphasis on English language instruction and to drop French language instruction in primary schools, one of the major legacies of the **Khmer Republic**. Holding the education portfolio until 5 May 1971, he was minister of industry, mineral resources and fisheries from March to October 1972, minister of state in charge of justice from October 1972 to April 1973, minister of state in the prime minister's office from May to December 1973 and minister of the interior, religion, general mobilization, pacification and reconciliation from December 1973 to June 1974. He is believed to have been executed on 17 April 1975 or soon afterward.

CHHAY THAN (1947-). Appointed head of the Taxation Department at the Ministry of Finance in August 1981, he was promoted in rapid succession to the post of advisor to the Ministry of Finance in January 1983, deputy minister of finance in 1984 and then minister of finance 1986-1993. Within the party, Chhay Than was elected as an alternate member of the Central Committee of the **People's Revolutionary Party of Kampuchea** at its congress in 1985 and was a full member by 1989. He was elected in **Takeo** on the **Cambodian People's Party (CPP)** list in the May 1993 elections but resigned his seat to become assistant secretary of state, and later secretary of state, in the Ministry of Economy and Finance headed by **Keat Chhon**. He is currently minister of planning in the **Hun Sen** government formed on 30 November 1998.

CHHAY YAT (1936-). Educated at Collège Sihanouk, he was a supporter of **Son Ngoc Thanh** who campaigned for the **Democrat** Party in 1955. In 1972 he joined the **Socio-Republican Party** of **Lon Nol**, and was elected to the Assembly of the **Khmer Republic**. In California since 1975, he has been active in émigré politics, and is a supporter of the World Anti-Communist League, based in Taiwan.

CHHBAB **(literally "law").** A **Khmer** literary genre, originating in the post-Angkorean era. *Chhbab* are aphoristic poems setting out ethical or morally desirable standards of conduct. These also often mirror Buddhist teachings. Some are addressed to men, others to women, and still others to children, or children of high officials. *Chhbab* were widely used in monastic schools and in the home during the precolonial and colonial eras and are still an important aspect of Khmer identity for many, especially for older people.

CHHEA SONG (1944-2001). One of the organizers of the **People's Revolutionary Party of Kampuchea (PRPK)** in **Pursat** province in 1981, he was deputy minister of agriculture in the **People's Republic of Kampuchea** and in the **State of Cambodia**, 1986-1993. Appointed assistant-secretary of state for agriculture, forests and fishery in the coalition government of November 1993, he was promoted to secretary of state on 20 October 1994. In 1998 he was elected to the **National Assembly** in **Banteay Meanchey** and named minister of agriculture, forestry and fisheries in the **Hun Sen** government formed on 30 November 1998. He died of liver disease in 2001.

CHHEA THANG (1935-). Born in Sangke, **Battambang**, he studied medicine and public heath at the University of Rennes. He then worked in the Faculty of Medicine and at the Khmero-Soviet Hospital. Between 1970-1975 he was the administrative officer for the minister of health. Evacuated from the capital in 1975, he survived the **Democratic Kampuchea** period. In September 1979 he joined the Central Committee of the **United Front for the National Salvation of Kampuchea** and was deputy minister of health, 1980-1993. In the May 1993 **National Assembly** elections he was elected on the **Cambodian People's Party (CPP)** list in **Kratié** province. He was minister of health in the Royal Government of November 1993. In 1999 he was one of the former CPP ministers appointed to the **Senate**.

CHHEAN VAM (1916-2000). Prime minister 1948. Born on 16 April 1916 in **Battambang**, Chhean Vam graduated from **Collège Sisowath**, in 1938 and the University of Paris in 1941. His *licence* was in philosophy. Upon his return to **Phnom Penh**, he taught at the upgraded Lycée Sisowath and was named its principal in 1946. In April 1946, he, together with **Ieu Koeus** and **Sim Var**, formed the **Democrat Party** and Chhean Vam was its first secretary-general. Prince **Sisowath Youtévong**, who returned from **France** some months later, became its leader. Chhean Vam resigned from his teaching post to become minister for national education in the Youtévong government from December 1946 to July 1947. He remained minister for national education after Youtévong's death and until February 1948 when he became prime minister from 20 February to 14 August 1948. He felt obliged to resign the premiership on 14 August 1948 after the Democrat-controlled **National Assembly** refused a request to lift the immunity from prosecution of named deputies who were implicated in illegal sales of public relief goods to unsuspecting rural people. He was then briefly minister for national defense from August 1948 to February 1949 when his party splintered and **Viet Minh** partisans began in earnest to challenge French power. He retired completely from political life thereafter, until 1978.

Between 1950 to 1975, and beginning with a small jewelry business, Chhean Vam became one of the country's top businessmen and company directors. He was at different times and sometimes concurrently the chairman and managing director of Tridara company, a privately owned import-export business; the Huileries du Cambodge, and chairman of the **Banque Khmère,** 1962-1964, as it was purchased and nationalized; and then head of SONEXIM, the state-owned export-import agency, **Royal Air Cambodge** and other state-owned firms, notably the state tire plant. Although regularly asked, he refused, as a matter of principle, to participate in any of the governments formed in the **Sangkum** and **Khmer Republic** eras. In the **Democratic Kampuchea** period, he and his wife, Thiounn Thieum, sister of **Thiounn Thoeun, Thiounn Mumm** and **Thiounn Prasith** were in **Svay Rieng** and by 1978 in detention but they escaped and secured asylum in France in 1979. Chhean Vam was vice-president of the **Khmer People's National Liberation Front** formed on 12 October 1979 by **Son Sann** and others. He was among the members of the council of elders who traveled to Bangkok in December 1985 in a futile effort to mediate civil-military disputes within the KPNLF. His death in Paris on 19 January 2000 was widely viewed as the end of the first stage of Cambodia's struggle for democracy.

CHHEAN VUN (1951-). A diplomat, born on 20 January 1951 in Srey Santhor, **Kampong Cham**, and the son of a Sino-Khmer businessman, he moved to **France** where in 1975 he earned a *licence* in economic sciences. Having acquired French citizenship, he worked as chief accountant at Nouvelles Galleries Réunies Paris in 1976, and then in Mexico City on a French-funded rapid transit project 1977-1979, returning to France to work in financial institutions, notably GEFCO-Peugeot. Chhean Vun returned to Cambodia in 1991 at the invitation of **Chea Sim**, and was appointed deputy minister of finance from 1991-1993. In 1993, before the elections, his bodyguards held six United Nations soldiers at gunpoint after they attempted to search his compound for a stolen UN vehicle. On 10 June 1993 he was elected to the Constituent Assembly on the **Cambodia People's Party (CPP)** list in **Battambang**, becoming president of the **National Assembly** Commission for Finance and Banking, in October 1993. Within the CPP he disagreed with **Hun Sen**, arguing unsuccessfully for a large increase in salaries for members of the National Assembly. In 1994 he resigned his seat to take up an appointment as ambassador to Australia and New Zealand in 7 March 1994, remaining until 1998. He is now the Cambodian ambassador to the Republic of Korea.

CHHENG PHON (1934-). From **Kampong Cham**, and the son of a teacher, Chheng Phon studied at the École Normale in **Phnom Penh** until 1956. He then joined a theatrical troupe from which he was expelled for political indiscretions, but he continued his studies in the Faculty of Fine Arts in 1958, specializing in lighting. He was a professor of dramatic arts at the University of Fine Arts in 1975 when Phnom Penh was evacuated. It is not known if he remained in **Democratic Kampuchea (DK)** through 1978 but he claimed to have been "a marked man" and to have eluded DK security personnel who searched for him. He was one of few non-communist, old society intellectuals openly to support the **People's Republic of Kampuchea (PRK)** in 1979 and the first to secure ministerial level employment. He no doubt benefited from the political policy of hiring people who were both highly alienated from and unable to cross over to "the enemy" side but unlike other non-communists, he also had revolutionary associations, having lived and studied the arts in **China** with other anti-Sihanoukists between 1961-1964. In 1980 he was appointed director of the National Conservatory of the Arts and president of the Association of Artists. In May 1981 he was elected to the PRK **National Assembly** and represented Kampong Thom until May 1993. He was named minister of culture and information in May 1981 and held this portfolio until August 1990 when he fell from favor and was removed from his post. An alternate member of the Central Committee of the **People's Revolutionary Party of Kampuchea (PRPK)** in 1984, he became a full member November 1985, but was not reelected at the PRPK Congress in July 1990. He was then eased from the chairmanship of the Cambodian-Cuban Friendship Association and his ministerial position. The strategic thinking behind his marginalization is clear: a lifelong anti-Sihanoukist was an impediment to a settlement with the prince and the other side. In 1994 he was director of the private Khmer Institute for Culture and Meditation.

CHHIM CHHUON (c1925-1975). Army officer. He graduated from the Military School in 1947 and married a niece of **Lon Nol**. Promoted to lieutenant colonel in the 1960s, by 1968 he was governor of **Stung Treng**. The following year he headed the military office of the president of the Council of Ministers, Lon Nol. It was he who met and secretly transported South Vietnamese Vice-President Nguyen Cao Ky from Pochentong airport on 12 March 1970 to, presumably, a meeting with Lon Nol. Promoted to colonel soon after the 18 March 1970 coup against Prince **Norodom Sihanouk**, and promoted again to brigadier general a few months later, and as commander of the military police Chhim Chhuon acted as Lon Nol's "right hand" in many affairs. He represented the Ministry of Defense on the **constitutional drafting committee** in June 1971, was a member of the Armed Forces Council created in September 1972 and was deemed "one of the most corrupt officers of the Republic" by François Ponchaud. The **United States** demanded his dismissal from the army high command in May 1974. He was among the personalities who visited the *Sangaraja* **Huot Tat** on 17 April 1975 and left saying he would discuss surrender with **Lon Non**. He was captured outside the Ministry of Information and executed later that day.

CHHIM KHET (1935-1976). Born on 10 March 1935 in Samlong, **Takeo**, the son of Khut Khet and Mme (née Ev), he graduated from the Faculty of Law and Economic in October 1958. He then joined the **Sangkum** and was elected to the **National Assembly** in **Kampong Speu** in 1962. Gradually specializing in economic matters, he worked steadily in ministries, undertaking some overseas missions, and was assistant secretary of state for finance, with responsibility for the national budget from September 1969 until 5 May 1971. He then moved to **France** where he submitted a diploma dissertation on *Les Khmers Rouges et le développement au Cambodia* ("The Red Khmer and development in Cambodia") in February 1975. Approaching the subject from a strongly anti-imperialist and nationalist standpoint, the study casts doubt on the socialist character of the economic policy reforms promised by the **National United Front of Kampuchea (FUNK)**. A supporter of the FUNK, he returned to Cambodia in 1976 and, unable to endure the punishing conditions, died in the special camp in **Kampong Cham** where he was detained.

CHHIM PHONN (1915-). Born on 15 April 1915 in **Phnom Penh**, the son of Chhim and Mme (née Chea), he worked for the railways from 1933. A supporter of **Son Ngoc Thanh**, Chhim Phonn was promoted to section head in the railways after 10 March 1945, but was not confirmed in the post when the French returned later in the year. Judged one of the "extremist" nationalists in the **Democrat** party he was jailed in 1946, being sent to Saigon along with **Sim Var**, **Pach Chhoeun** and **Hem Chiam Roeun** and others implicated in the **Black Star Affair**. Released from jail in 1947 he secured temporary work as an inspector for the national police, in the section devoted to economic policing, but was implicated in 1951 in the trafficking of arms for the benefit of the **Khmer Issarak** led by **Puth Chhay**. His activities, and those of dozens of other Democrats discussed in colonial intelligence reports, indicate that the administration of the protectorate was riddled with functionaries who had no loyalty to **France**.

CHHIM SEAK LENG (1940-). Born on 12 April 1940 in **Kampong Cham**, he earned a diploma in electrical studies in 1964 and managed the thermal division of the Kampot Cement Works 1964-1975. He was evacuated to the countryside in 1975 but moved to the Thai-Cambodian border after 1979. In 1984 he was **FUNCINPEC** administrator of Ta Tum camp, and of Site B, the principal royalist holding center the following year. In 1991 he directed community development projects in royalist controlled zones of Cambodia. These were funded in part by "non-lethal" assistance from the **United States**. In February 1992, at the first congress of FUNCINPEC convened on national territory, he was elected to the party's National Council, today referred to as the Steering Committee. He was one of the party's principal organizers during the electoral campaign in 1993 and was himself elected to the Constituent Assembly on the FUNCINPEC list in Kampong Cham. Designated minister of cults and religion in the provisional royal government formed immediately after the election, he was instead appointed governor of **Phnom Penh** municipality in December 1993 and relinquished his seat in the **National Assembly** in mid-1994. Remaining loyal to Prince **Norodom Sihanouk** during the July 1997 coup, he abandoned his post in the municipality effectively ceding the job to **Chea Sophara**. In November 1998 he was appointed senior minister and minister of rural development in the new coalition government led by **Hun Sen**. He defended the staff in his ministry when it faced criticism from the Japanese Embassy for mistakenly or fraudulently attempting to secure $570,000 in reimbursements for road project costs already charged to other donors. Hun Sen resumed his criticisms in 2001.

CHHIM TIP (1931-). Born on 1 January 1931 in Pro Phnum, Angkor Chey, **Kampot**, he was a teacher in **Takeo** and from 1970-1975, inspector of schools in **Phnom Penh**. After enduring the hardships of 1975-1979 under the **Democratic Kampuchea** regime, he was a member of the people's revolutionary committee established in Tram Kah district, **Takeo**, and president of the Education Office in Tram Kah from 1979-1981. He retired in 1991, at the age of 60, and joined **FUNCINPEC**, becoming secretary-general of the party in Takeo. He was elected to the **National**

Assembly on the FUNCINPEC list in Takeo in June 1993 and was a member of the Commission for Education, Religion, Culture and Tourism. He was also first deputy governor of Takeo province.

CHHIM TOUN (1914-). Born on 7 October 1914 at Peamchilang, **Kampong Cham,** he was a teacher who in October 1945 traveled with **Chau Sen Cocsal,** the just resigned governor of Kampong Cham, to **Cochinchina** in order to raise support for the **Khmer Issarak.** Cocsal sent him back to Cambodia to arrange a surrender but he decided instead to go to Bangkok to work with **Poc Khun,** becoming leader of a band of 250 Issaraks. He surrendered to the colonial authorities with all his well-armed troops on 19 May 1947 shortly after the new constitution was promulgated on 6 May and was reappointed as a teacher. He then joined and campaigned for the **Khmer Renewal Party** formed in September, and in 1949-1950 he took a leave of absence to work with the army high command as the Issarak insurgency expanded. He resigned his teaching post in order to run in the 1951 **National Assembly** elections in Koh Mith, Kampong Cham. He was beaten by a **Democrat.** He was a **Sangkum** deputy in the National Assembly from 1962-1966.

CHHIT CHHOEUN. *See* TA MOK.

CHHORN EAM. A functionary in the **People's Republic of Kampuchea** in the late 1980s, he was elected to the National Council of the **United Front for the National Construction and Defense of Kampuchea** at its fourth congress in January 1989. A deputy minister of religious affairs in the **State of Cambodia,** he retained his post, retitled as assistant secretary of state for Cults and Religious Affairs in the Royal Government of 1993-1998. He was promoted to Secretary of State for Religions and Cults in the **Hun Sen** government of November1998.

CHHORN HAY (1936-). A prominent student activist in the 1960s, he graduated from **Lycée Sisowath** in 1958 then studied engineering at the École Nationale Supérieure des Télécommunications in Paris. While in **France** he was active in the left-wing Khmer Students' Union (UEK) and its secretary-general in 1963 when his scholarship was withdrawn. In 1971 he attended the congress of "patriotic intellectuals" supporting the **National United Front of Kampuchea (FUNK)** and appears to have been assigned to propaganda work during the 1970-1975 war. He was chief of staff for Prince **Norodom Sihanouk** from September 1975 when he returned to **Phnom Penh** until 30 March 1977 when he was transferred to the heavily purged Ministry of Information of **Democratic Kampuchea (DK),** 1977-1979. He was among the senior DK officials who made a hasty exit from the capital to western border regions in January 1979.

He was named minister of telecommunications in the **Khieu Samphan** government announced on 15 December 1979, but was assigned to work in **China** being in charge of daily DK radio transmission broadcasts on Chinese transmitters, once again heading the Office of the President of the **Coalition Government of Democratic Kampuchea** in 1982-1993 established by Sihanouk. He also edited the prince's *Bulletin Mensuel de Documentation*, issued from Beijing. On 12 June 1994 he was named secretary-general of the Royal Palace Office, but as his party had withdrawn from the United Nations-sponsored peace settlement and continued its armed struggle against the new coalition government, the government refused to allow him to return. He is believed to have left **Anlong Veng** for **Pailin** in 1997-1998.

CHHOUK CHHIM (1952-). She was deputy chair of the Cambodia-Vietnam Friendship Association established in 1979, an indication that her support for the **People's Republic of Kampuchea** was obtained while she was a refugee in **Vietnam**. She was elected to the National Council of the **United Front for the National Construction and Defense of Kampuchea** in May 1981 and vice-president of the **Association of Revolutionary Women** in 1985, becoming president in 1990 succeeding **Men Saman**. A member of the **Cambodian People's Party**, she was an unsuccessful candidate in the 1998 **National Assembly** elections but, in 1999, was appointed to the **Senate**.

CHHOUK MENG MAO (1920-1977). Born on 29 October 1920 at Kanthar, **Kampot**, son of Chhuk Meng and Mme (née Ouk Hun), he was a "normalien," trained in the colonial system before the pedagogical institute was created, who had a distinguished career as an inspector for primary education, an author of primary school reading books, an editor of teaching magazines and as director of pedagogical services in the Ministry of Education. An activist in the **Democrat Party** between 1946 and 1955, he withdrew from politics in the **Sangkum** era devoting himself to his educational work. He remained in the Ministry of National Education and Fine Arts until 1971 when he was appointed advisor to **Lon Nol** and commissioner general for youth. In 1971 he represented teachers on the **constitutional drafting committee**. He left Cambodia in 1975 but decided, along with his friend **Phung Ton**, to return to **Democratic Kampuchea** to assist in national reconstruction. They were detained on arrival. Chhouk Meng Mao was taken to **Tuol Sleng** on 8 December 1976 and executed in February or March 1977.

CHHOUK RIN (1956-). A former National Army of Democratic Kampuchea (NADK) commander, Chhouk Rin led the 26 July 1994 train robbery that resulted in the deaths of 13 Cambodians and the kidnapping of three foreigners (David Wilson, 29, from Australia; Jean-Michel Braquet, 29, from France and Mark Slater, 28, from the United Kingdom). On 15 September, long before the fate of the three foreigners was known, Rin surrendered to Royal Army commanders laying siege to his Phnom Vour stronghold in **Kampot**. He claimed the hostages had been handed over to **Nuon Paet**, his immediate superior. Although Australia, France and Britain repeatedly demanded his prosecution for kidnapping and murder, he was not brought to trial. In July 1999 he testified at the trial of his former commander, Nuon Paet who was convicted of murder. Renewed demands for Rin's arrest and prosecution were once again, or at least, initially ignored in official circles but on 17 January 2000 he was arrested and placed in custody without bail. Brought to trial in midyear after an alleged but secret investigation, he was acquitted of murder on 18 July 2000 on the grounds that he qualified for an amnesty extended to surrendering **Party of Democratic Kampuchea (PDK)** cadres under the terms of a 7 July 1994 law proscribing the party. There was much criticism of the court ruling. Lawyers claimed the alleged crimes had nothing to do with membership of the PDK and that the government should have prosecuted Rin under ordinary criminal codes.

CHHOUR LEANG HUOT (1941-   ). Born on 8 January 1941 in Baray, **Kampong Cham**, the son of businessman Chhour Pech, he graduated from the Faculty of Law in 1965 and was presiding judge at the Phnom Penh Municipal Court during the **Khmer Republic** years, 1970-1975. Evacuated to the countryside in April 1975, he was among the 10 jurors ("people's assessors") chosen to hear the case of the People's Revolutionary Tribunal against **Pol Pot** and **Ieng Sary**, on 15-19 August 1979. From 1979 until 1989, he was attached to the Ministry of Justice of the **People's Republic of Kampuchea** and vice-president of the Supreme Court. In 1997 he was elected to the Central Committee of the **People's Revolutionary Party of Kampuchea.** Elected to the Constituent Assembly on the **Cambodian People's Party** list in his native province in June 1993, he was named chair of the **National Assembly** Commission for legislation in October 1993. Reelected to the 1998 Assembly, he is a member of its Standing Committee.

CHHUM CHHEANG (1948-   ). From 1983-1986 Chheang was military commander of the Phnom Dangrek base of the **Khmer People's National Liberation Armed Forces (KPNLAF)**. He was among the field commanders who indicated his allegiance to **Son Sann** during the civil-military split of the KPNLF by attending a service of remembrance with the president in honor of **Penn Nouth** at Nong Chan Camp in January 1986. On 28 January 1986, he was elected secretary-general of a provisional military committee of base commanders established with the quiet urging and support of the Thai army which attempted to mediate intra-KPNLF disputes and took direct delivery of foreign aid goods and cash handled by the Thai thereby bypassing both Son Sann and General **Sak Suthsakhan**. He was promoted to major general on 24 Feb 1987. He later joined Son Sann's **Buddhist Liberal Democratic Party** and was appointed governor of **Mondolkiri** in July 1994.

CHHUN, ALEXIS LOUIS. A member of the Catholic minority in Cambodia, he was closely associated to the royal court and became the favorite of **Ernest Doudart de Lagrée**. As a child he charmed Doudart de Lagrée with his interest in French affairs, and when he was 13, he began working as an interpreter for the French. He rose through various grades as interpreter and by 1878 had become the principal interpreter. In 1886 he was appointed to the judicial service, and after a short period in retirement, by 1900 the French had appointed him an official at the royal treasury. By the end of 1900 he was head of the royal treasury, but in the following year he was accused of misappropriating large sums of money from the treasury for his own use. Chhun claimed King **Norodom** had approved his use of the money for a private business venture, producing a letter to that effect. However **French Résident** Léon Boulloche maintained the letter was forged. To avoid a scandal he revoked Chhun's appointment. Chhun was thereafter closely supervised. In 1905 he was appointed supervisor of the King's civil list, which suggests that his claims of earlier innocence may have been true. In 1911 he was appointed minister of justice.

CHHUON MUCHULPICH. *See* DAP CHHUON.

CHHUT CHHOEUR (1932-). Born on 10 October 1932 at Svaypor, **Battambang**, the son of Kim Chhut and Mme (née Tui Om), he graduated from **Lycée Sisowath** and was awarded a Fulbright scholarship to the **United States**. He majored in mathematics at Purdue University and obtained a master's degree in civil engineering from the Massachusetts Institute of Technology. Back in **Phnom Penh** in the late 1950s, he worked in the Ministry of Public Works. On 6 October 1962 he received the portfolio for industry in a cabinet which contained some young, foreign-trained intellectuals. He lost his post in the reshuffle triggered by the flight of **Kitchpanich Songsakd** and the nationalization of banking and trade.

Returning to the public administration, he then became general manager of mixed public-private enterprise, *Electricité du Cambodge*.

Following the overthrow of Prince **Norodom Sihanouk**, he was part of a delegation sent to the United States and the Caribbean to promote the **Lon Nol** government. In September 1970 he was made a colonel in the army. In 1973 he was appointed ambassador to **Australia** and New Zealand, resident in Canberra and in 1974, permanent representative to the United Nations. The General Assembly, divided by a bid from the **Royal Government of National Union** led by Sihanouk for Cambodia's seat, voted by a majority of two to allow the **Khmer Republic** to retain it. Securing asylum in April 1975, he joined the consulting firm of Louis Berger International, working on several missions overseas. Between 1979-1981 he worked for the United Nations in Rwanda. He resided in Silver Spring, Maryland, before settling in Texas.

CHI KIM AN (1926-1972). Born on 6 June 1926 at Anlong Thuot, **Pursat**, he was the son of Chy Soun and Mme (née Pu Ngourn). Orphaned as a teenager, he lived with Koch Bin who worked in the Land Registry office for **Kandal**. From 1948-1953 he studied engineering in **France** on a government scholarship and participated in the Marxist study circle with Saloth Sar **(Pol Pot), Ieng Sary, Son Sen, Hou Youn, Mey Mann, Phung Ton, Thiounn Mumm, Ea Sichau,** Rat Samoeurn, **Keng Vannsak** and other future Democrats and communists. While many of the young Paris-educated intellectuals returning in 1953 supported the **Democrat Party** after visits to **Khmer Issarak** or **Viet Minh** bases, Chi Kim An openly supported the **Pracheachon** group, this being the electoral arm of the underground **Khmer People's Revolutionary Party.** He was editor of *Pracheachon* ("The People") newspaper when in July 1955 it denounced the **United States**-Cambodian military agreement. After a brief period in jail and a short period in **Vietnam** where he likely attended a party school, he became a director in a land registry office.

His name was on the list of 34 suspected communists prepared by **Lon Nol** in response to Prince **Norodom Sihanouk**'s request for the names of all those who "knew how China worked"! The prince summoned all of them to a meeting offering them cabinet posts if they would use their knowledge to develop the Cambodian state and economy. All refused and fearing the worst many fled the capital, sensing for the first time from this bizarre episode and the imprisonment of **Non Suon** and the disappearance and possible capture of **Tou Samouth** the year before, that their lives were in danger. Chi Kim An joined the **National United Front of Kampuchea** in 1970, and signed the 1971 **Declaration of Patriotic Intellectuals**, a public appeal to other intellectuals to join the anti-imperialist FUNK. For reasons that remain obscure, he is said to have committed suicide in Sre Andaung village, near Anleang, in April 1972 while attached to the information and propaganda unit led by **Hu Nim** in the special administrative and military region led by **Ke Pauk.**

CHIEM OUM (1938-   ). Born on 25 May 1938 at Po Damnak, Bakan, **Pursat**, he completed primary school and nurse's training at the École de Médecine in Pursat town. His first job was in the provincial clinic of Pursat and he stayed with it for two year before enlisting in the Royal Cambodian Armed Forces in 1960 at the age of 22. In 1972 he was commissioned a lieutenant in the Republican Army but his unit was the security detail for the Red Cross team working in Pursat from 1972 until 1975. During the **Democratic Kampuchea** year, he was forced to relocate but returned to Pursat where he supported the establishment of a rural pagoda in his village from 1979-1990. At the first opportunity, in 1991, he joined **FUNCINPEC** and at its first national congress in February 1992 was elected to its National Council, now known as its Steering Committee. He was elected to the Constituent Assembly in the 1993 elections, on the FUNCINPEC list in Pursat and was named a member of the Assembly Commission for Public Health, Social Affairs and Women's Affairs in October 1993. In 1998 Oum was reelected to the **National Assembly** in Pursat.

CHINA. Relations between mainland China and Cambodia can be traced to prehistoric ages. Chinese accounts of visits to a coastal kingdom known to them as **Funan** are the earliest texts describing ancient Cambodia. These contain valuable ethnographic information about **Khmer** society prior to its extensive interaction with Indian culture. A few centuries later Chinese texts no longer referred to Funan but rather to the Kingdom of Chenla **(Zhenla)**, assuming, probably wrongly, that Chenla held sway over a vast domain. In the next period, Chinese traders settled at **Angkor**, often marrying local women, a pattern repeated through the centuries until after World War II and thereby gradually building the modern Sino-Khmer elite stratum of modern times. Over the centuries Chinese emperors received tribute from **Khmer** kings on an irregular basis, but did not accord any particular status or importance to the Khmer kingdom.

This would change under the People's Republic of China (PRC) and after Cambodia gained full independence from **France.** Prince **Norodom Sihanouk**'s friendship with **Zhou Enlai**, initiated at the **Bandung Conference** of 1955, was one of the cornerstones of his foreign policy of "neutrality" in the Cold War. Cambodia was one of the first noncommunist countries of Asia, and the world, to extend diplomatic recognition to China, and Beijing granted recognition and economic assistance in gratitude. Warm relations gelled only briefly when the Cultural Revolution sent waves through Chinese schools and student circles in **Phnom Penh**, and when the Communist Party of China began, surreptitiously, to support the **Communist Party of Kampuchea (CPK)** led by Saloth Sar **(Pol Pot)**. China graciously granted political asylum to Prince Sihanouk after the 18 March 1970 coup, and encouraged a military alliance between the prince and the clandestine **Communist Party of Kampuchea.** In 1970 Lon Nol established relations with the Republic of China (Taiwan) with their representative, Michael Tung, taking up residence in Phnom Penh.

After the victory of the **National United Front of Kampuchea (FUNK)** of 1975, China became the most important ally of **Democratic Kampuchea (DK)**. Over 1,000 Chinese technicians and experts worked in Cambodia during the **Pol Pot** era. When armed conflicts with **Vietnam** erupted in 1977, China immediately tried to mediate and to protect the much smaller state of **Democratic Kampuchea (DK)** but failing in this, eventually backed DK. After Vietnam's invasion, China once again protected Prince Sihanouk with a political base in exile, and the prince also decided to accept support provided by President Kim Il Sung. Beijing was motivated not simply by opposition to Vietnam's actions, or any lingering respect for Pol Pot's revolutionary methods but a concern to limit the influence of the **Soviet Union** in Vietnam and Asia. The strategic relationship changed again with the resolution of the Sino-Soviet dispute in 1989. Acting on pledges exchanged with the Soviets in that year and agreements struck among the five permanent members of the United Nations Security Council in 1990-1991, China withdrew its military support from all of the Cambodian resistance armies in 1991, on the eve of the Paris Peace Conference.

Since 1992 China's relations with Cambodia have been subordinated to new strategic aims linked to China's economic development. The People's Republic continues to provide regular medical treatment for the aging King Sihanouk and also backs Prime Minister **Hun Sen** in his reluctance to bring former leaders of DK to trial for crimes against humanity. By insisting that other world powers should not interfere in Cambodia's affairs, China reinforces the nationalist aspirations of all ruling groups in Cambodia quietly playing the role of compradore and go-between. *See also* CHINESE MINORITY.

CHINE REINE (c1930-1975). A graduate of **Lycée Sisowath** and of the Faculty of Law, Reine studied finance at the Royal School of Administration. He was secretary of state for finance from 22 October 1973 until the fall of the **Khmer Republic** in April 1975. Because of his senior administrative role, he is believed to have been among the "class enemies" executed soon after the communists seized power on 17 April 1975. He was married to **Chem Singath**.

CHINESE MINORITY. Explorers, immigrants and traders arrived from China as early as the third century BC and a sizeable community of émigrés was established by the 13th century. Most settlers came from the southern provinces of Kwantung and Fukien or from Hainan Island often via overland routes through Vietnam. In the 1850s the first French explorers noticed trading throughout the Khmer kingdom was in Chinese hands. Equally the commercial quarter of **Phnom Penh**, along the Tonlé Sap, was inhabited by Chinese, who controlled the export trade in rice and most trade in other commodities, apart from **rubber**, controlled largely by the French and their European business partners. Many of the skilled craftsmen producing silver objects, jewelry and fine silk cloth were Chinese. Intermarriage with Khmer was frequent such that in modern times, the small stratum of ruling families, including those leading the Communist movement, were of mixed Chinese-Khmer descent. Chinese language newspapers and privately run Chinese-language schools were permitted throughout the **Norodom Sihanouk** era, becoming centers of unrest during the Cultural Revolution. The Chinese business community was nonetheless widely disgruntled by Sihanouk's imposition of state controls on the economy in 1963, a policy shift producing the abrupt departure of the Cambodian Chinese banker **Kitchpanich Songsakd**.

Prominent Sino-Khmer and Chinese businessmen broadly welcomed Sihanouk's overthrow in 1970 and in some instances, also, his resistance to the U.S.-supported **Lon Nol** regime. At least one, **Kuch An**, made a bold attempt to avert a rupture of relations with **China**. The 1970-1975 war economy disrupted small Chinese family-based shop businesses, especially in rural areas, and under the wholly collectivized **Democratic Kampuchea** economy, Chinese traders and workers were persecuted as class enemies. Hundreds of thousands are believed to have perished. After 1979 a reformed socialist regime both restored and restricted family commercial freedom, Chinese entrepreneurship and international connections contributed to the revitalization of the economy in the 1990s and stimulated the growth of Chinese language schools, about 70 in 2001.

The size of the Chinese minority in Cambodia is disputed. A colonial estimate from 1947 was 104,300. The 1962 **census** identified 163,115 native speakers of Chinese dialects. The demographer Jacques Migozzi later reassessed the data, producing a revised estimate of 208,700 for 1962 and c450,000 for 1970. Large numbers of Chinese-Cambodians sought exile abroad or died in the 1970s. A March 1995 Ministry of Interior report claimed only 47,180 ethnic Chinese. Data from the 1998 census relating to mother tongue or place of birth has not been released. Annual statistics on visitors, immigrants plus tourists, suggest a new wave of immigration. Several hundred illegal workers were deported by Phnom Penh municipal authorities in 2000 and 2001.

CHOEUNG EK. A memorial and tourist site, this is the camp about 14 kilometers from central **Phnom Penh** where men, women and children who had been detained at **Tuol Sleng**, between 1975-1978, were taken to be executed and buried. It is believed that 15,000-17,000 people may have died there; there are 129 mass graves. The remains of 8,985 people were exhumed in 1980, some of the skulls and other bones being mounted for display in glass cupboards. Forty-three graves have been left undisturbed.

CHOU CHET (1926/7-1978). A veteran communist of rural origin, he was born and grew up in Samrong, **Kampong Cham** and went to Buddhist schools from the age of seven. In 1940 he went to **Phnom Penh** where he studied Pali at Wat Keo Preah Phleung but his classes were suspended in 1941 by bombing and he moved to a wat in Baray district, **Kampong Thom**. Although he later took the advanced Pali examinations, he failed to pass them, and by 1949 he was studying and teaching in a monastery in **Takeo** province. In April 1950 he was persuaded by **Khmer Issarak-Viet Minh** under the command of Chau Yin to go with them to **Vietnam** where they attended the **Hem Cheav** political school. Chou Chet joined the **Indochinese Communist Party** there on 20 April 1951 before returning to Cambodia in 1952. In 1954 he was a Khmer Issarak delegate to the Geneva Conference which refused to recognize or to seat the delegation. Back in Phnom Penh, he edited left-wing newspapers including the **Pracheachon** group's official newspaper, *Pracheachon*, suppressed in 1960, and then *Panchasila*, mostly with ex-Pracheachon staffers, and *SmarDey Khmer*.

Chou Chet was arrested and jailed in January 1962, together with his friend and ally **Non Suon**, and like him, tried, convicted and sentenced to death for treason, a charge arising from an article on corruption. His sentence was later commuted to life imprisonment, but he was released from prison after one year. Although he was among those who attended the March 1963 meeting of the "34" alleged communists summoned by Prince **Norodom Sihanouk**, the meeting which triggered the flight of Saloth Sar (**Pol Pot**), **Ieng Sary** and **Son Sen** to the countryside, Chou Chet remained in Phnom Penh working underground for the party. He was named deputy minister of health, religious and social affairs in Sihanouk's **Royal Government of National Union of Kampuchea (GRUNK)**, later becoming minister of religious and social affairs in 1973. During the civil war he led the West Zone and was known by his revolutionary name "Si." Although a member of the party's Central Committee since the 1960s, Chou Chet was accused of conspiring against

Pol Pot after the **Communist Party of Kampuchea**'s postwar policies began to fail. He was arrested in 1977, forced to "answer" to the Party at **Tuol Sleng** and then executed in April 1978.

CHRONICLE HISTORIES (*bangsavatar*). Cambodian literary genre, either in verse or prose, relating the activities of kings. In ancient and medieval times the *bangsavatar* formed part of a monarch's regalia. The chronicles maintained at **Angkor**, although mentioned in inscriptions, have not survived, and those written later, on events in the 15th and 16th centuries, were to a large extent concocted from Thai chronicles and have been dismissed by modern scholars as spurious. Those dealing with 17th and 18th century events, sometimes corroborated by other sources, are more reliable, and chronicles are a major historical resource for 19th century history. The chronicles kept by the last three kings, **Sisowath Monivong**, **Norodom Sihanouk** and **Norodom Suramarit**, have not been published, and are of only antiquarian interest. National historians embraced Western forms of historiography from the 1930s.

CHROUI CHANGWAR BRIDGE. This bridge over the **Tonlé Sap** links **Phnom Penh** to Chroui Changwar, a market town and spiritual center for the **Cham** community. A naval base was located there in the 1960s and early 1970s. The bridge was destroyed by Vietnamese allies of the **National United Front of Kampuchea (FUNK)** on the night of 6-7 October 1972 but rebuilt soon afterward. On 17 April 1975 Sydney Schanberg and his four companions were held there, as shown in the film *The Killing Fields*. Destroyed again in 1975, the bridge is also known as the Japanese bridge because the Japanese, who first built it in the 1940s, financed its reconstruction in 1993.

CHUM HORL (1931-   ). A native of Kampong Som, Chum Horl joined the **Viet Minh** supported **Khmer Issarak** in 1949 and apparently remained in Cambodia after 1955. Imprisoned on 5 May 1978 in Prey Sar by the **Democratic Kampuchea (DK)** authorities, he was released after the Vietnamese invasion. The political line employed in the building of a new anti-**Pol Pot** administration awarded priority in appointments to those who had suffered or lost most under DK. He was named chairman of the People's Committee of Kampong Som city in 1979. He was later elected to the **National Assembly** of the **People's Republic of Kampuchea** in May 1981, holding a seat for Kampong Som.

CHUON BUNTHOL (1937-1999). Born in Ponhea Leau, **Kandal**, Bunthol studied nursing. Evacuated to the countryside in 1975, he went to **Battambang** in 1979 and under the administration of the **People's Republic of Kampuchea** he worked as a nurse and then an administrator in Battambang Hospital. He was elected to the Constituent Assembly on the **Cambodian People's Party** list in Battambang in June 1993 and from October, he served as member of the **National Assembly** Commission for Public Health, Social Affairs and Women's Affairs. Reelected to the Assembly in 1998, he failed to attend many sessions in 1999 and died of lung cancer in December.

CHUON NATH, *Samdech* **(1883-1969).** Buddhist patriarch. Born into a peasant family on 6 March 1883 at Kamrieng, **Kampong Speu** the elder son of Chuon (1851-1930) and Mme (née Youk; 1851-1926), he was a novice from 1898, *bhikkhu* from 1904, and from 1915 onward. A highly respected religious scholar, he worked on the editorial committee for the first printed **Khmer** dictionary. In 1921-1922, when he was a teacher in the Pali school in **Phnom Penh,** he and **Huot Tat** were sent to Hanoi to study sanskrit and ancient inscriptions with Louis Finot, who was then director of the **École Française d'Extrême-Orient.** In the next two decades, he traveled widely in **Indochina.** In 1931 he represented Cambodia at the opening ceremonies for the **Buddhist Institute** in Luang Prabang, an institute modeled upon Phnom Penh's. In 1933 he toured **Khmer Krom** temples in order to encourage pagoda schools in step with French policy and in 1939 he returned to **Laos** to assist with difficulties in the Institute and to promote pagoda schools there. From 1935 he taught languages (Khmer, Lao, Pali and Sanskrit) to the *classe terminale* ("final year") at the newly created **Lycée Sisowath** and, from 1936, he and Huot Tat were associated with **Nagaravatta, Pach Chhoeun** and **Son Ngoc Thanh.** As colonialism waned Chuon Nath became director of the Pali Higher School in 1942 and *chauatticar* ("abbot") of **Wat Ounalom,** Phnom Penh in 1944. He was elevated to the dignity of *sangaraja* of the Mahanikay sect, in 1963, receiving the title "Samdech" from Prince **Norodom Sihanouk** at the same time. He wrote 19 books in Khmer and Pali, including a two-volume Khmer-Pali dictionary which was published by the Buddhist Institute in 1929. Samdech Chuon Nath died on 26 September 1969, but his funerary cremation was delayed more than 15 months, until January 1971 because the civil war made it dangerous for monks to travel to the capital from the provinces in order to pay their respects.

CHUON SAODI (1928-c1977). Born on 16 April 1928 at Prek Ropeau, Mongkolborey, **Battambang,** he was the son of Chuon Ou and Mme (née Diep). After studies at **Lycée Sisowath,** he studied agronomy and forestry in Belgium from 1949-1957 and joined the Ministry of Agriculture upon his return. In 1962 he was principal inspector for waters and forests. Appointed secretary of state for agriculture under **Norodom Kantol** from

May to October 1966, he was governor of Tioulongville (**Kirirom**) from 1967-1968, and minister of agriculture under **Penn Nouth** and **Lon Nol**, from 31 January 1968 until his resignation 27 December 1969. He was one of four ministers to object to the reversal of the economic policies of Prince **Norodom Sihanouk**. Chuon Saodi was married to Sum Nipha.

CHUOP HELL (1909-c1975). Born in November 1909 in **Phnom Penh**, he studied agriculture in the colonial college in Hanoi and became a clerk in the Waters and Forests Service in 1929 rising to the position of chief by 1955. A founding member of the **Khmer Renewal Party**, he was minister of agriculture and animal husbandry in the second interim **Oum Chheang Sun** cabinet in 1951 established for the purpose of arranging fresh elections. He was a candidate for the **National Assembly** in **Kampong Cham** town in September 1951 but failed to win, returning to the Ministry of Agriculture. He joined the **Sangkum** in 1955 and with its endorsement won a seat in the 1958 National Assembly in Baray, **Takeo**. Chuop Hell was elected president of the Assembly from 10 April 1959 until 9 April 1961 and was therefore interim head of state upon the death of King **Norodom Suramarit** in April 1960. It was the Assembly he led which in June presided over the creation of a special new role as constitutional head of state for Prince **Norodom Sihanouk** who declined to reascend the throne he had abdicated in 1955. The creation of a nonreigning head of state imposed a distinctly "presidential" focus on the representational order. Chuop Hell later entered the diplomatic service and was consul-general in Hong Kong and ambassador to Singapore in 1968.

CHUOP SAMLOTH (1908-1967/9). Son of Kvann Chuop and Mme (née Kham Phong), he was born on 11 January 1908 in **Phnom Penh** and studied in France, entering the judicial service in 1936. In February 1946 he was appointed chief of the National Police, and was a delegate to the **Pau Conference**. A member of the **Sangkum**, he served as minister of justice from January to September 1955 and was elected to the 1955 **National Assembly** in Trakor, **Prey Veng**. He was minister of justice and religion from October 1955 to January 1956 and from March to September 1956. He was reelected to the 1958 and 1962 Assemblies. He was a judge briefly before his death. Chuop Samloth married Douc Pok, sister of **Douc Rasy**.

CIVIL REGISTRATION. Introduced by the French from 1910, the registration of births, marriages and deaths was haphazard in the protectorate. Very few peasants registered births or deaths unless they had contact with the French. Residents of towns, and especially Chinese foreigners were subjected to an annual *droit d'immatriculation* ("registration fee") until

1929 when the French *Résident Supérieur* decided it would be replaced by a tax on commerce or a graduated residence fee. As modern primary schooling expanded, civil registration became more common. During the final years of the French protectorate and until 1975 civil servants were given salary increments or child supplements upon the birth each new child, which encouraged registration. Records of French citizens born in Cambodia are held at Nantes.

COALITION GOVERNMENT OF DEMOCRATIC KAMPUCHEA (CGDK). Formed in 1982, this government in exile was put together by nationalist forces and was based on the **Democratic Kampuchea (DK)** government organized under **Pol Pot** in April 1976 and reshuffled under **Khieu Samphan** December 1979. The coalition was formed by three parties: **Party of Democratic Kampuchea (PDK)** led by Samphan, **FUNCINPEC** led by Prince **Norodom Sihanouk** and the **Khmer People's National Liberation Front (KPNLF)** led by **Son Sann**. The CGDK was recognized by the United Nations (UN) and awarded the seat reserved for Cambodia in the UN General Assembly. On the battlefield, the CGDK was dominated by the PDK because it had the largest and most effective army. While Sihanouk was president of the coalition, and Son Sann was its prime minister, the PDK leader **Khieu Samphan** its foreign minister. The nationalist parties agreed to form the coalition government to strengthen Cambodia's legal case for sovereign independence and to prevent the UN from voting to accept the credentials of the **Peoples' Republic of Kampuchea**, sponsored by **Vietnam** and created in the wake of an invasion that violated the UN charter. In 1990 in the run-up to the **Paris Peace Agreement** of October 1991, the CGDK was renamed the National Government of Cambodia, thereby discarding its connection to the discredited DK regime. The PDK, KPNLF, FUNCINPEC and the **Cambodian People's Party** government in Phnom Penh then formed the **Supreme National Council**, to represent and embody national sovereignty during the interim period of supervision and control by the **United Nations Transitional Authority in Cambodia (UNTAC)**. The national elections for the Constituent Assembly in May 1993, organized and supervised by UNTAC, laid the basis for renewed, internationally recognized, constitutional government.

COCHINCHINA. This is the name originally given by Portuguese explorers in the early 17th century to the provinces of southern **Vietnam** which **France** seized between 1863 and 1867. Centered around Saigon, the colony was to become the most prosperous element of the five-part colonial federation of **Indochina**. It was the basis for the Republic of Vietnam proclaimed in 1955, and the name "Cochinchina," never favored by the Vietnamese, was rejected.

COEDÈS, GEORGES (1886-1969). A distinguished historian, Coedès was affiliated with the **École Française d'Extrême-Orient**, and was its director from 1930-1946. After his first work, a translation of a text of Bhavavarman II, published in 1904 when he was only 15, he devoted much of his life to epigraphy, the ordering and translating of the early inscriptions of the **Khmer** so as to expose the course of pre-Angkorean and Angkorean history. In addition to an eight-volume collection of inscriptions, with French translations, published between 1937 and 1966, he also produced a seminal scholarly study of the Indianization of Southeast Asia. He died on 2 October 1969.

COLLÈGE TECHNIQUE. A vocational school run by the government, it was established in the 1930s. Its alumni include **Pol Pot**, and also **Preap In,** and it had a record for radicalism. On 19 November 1952 there was a strike at the school when students complained that the administration was serving bad food and profiteering. In part generated by nationalists supporting the **National Assembly** in struggles with the king, this protest precipitated sympathy strikes at the École Normale, in **Lycée Sisowath**, the Upper Pali School, the officer training school and in France. King Sihanouk responded by dissolving the **Democrat Party**-controlled Assembly on 13 January 1953, declaring the "national in danger" and assuming emergency powers.

COLONIAL EXPOSITION (1931). Held in Vincennes, to celebrate the triumphant progress of **France**'s overseas empire, a model to scale of a portion of **Angkor Wat** was one of the most popular and most effective exhibits. The expo, the last of its kind, was a burden on the budget of **Indochina.** Even before the depression, **French Résidents** had faced criticism for their extravagant spending on public works projects.

COMMUNIST PARTY OF FRANCE (CPF). After World War II, and until 1956, the CPF was one of the largest, most dynamic communist parties in Europe. Under the leadership of Maurice Thorez, it was loyal to Moscow, and idolized Joseph Stalin. Despite or perhaps because of its radical orthodoxy, and the Cold War polarization of the times, it attracted into its ranks many students from French colonies. Many Cambodians, including **Chau Seng, Son Sen, Ok Sakun, Thiounn Mumm, Ieng Sary, Ieng Thirith, Khieu Samphan** and Saloth Sar **(Pol Pot)** learned about Marxism-Leninism and joined the party while in France, only to return to Cambodia to find the revolutionary movement facing extinction. The failure of the CPF to support anti-imperialist struggles in Algeria and discord arising from "de-Stalinization" and Soviet repression of revolts in Poland and Hungary gradually undermined its appeal.

COMMUNIST PARTY OF KAMPUCHEA (CPK). The name adopted by the Cambodian party in 1966, following the visit of Saloth Sar (**Pol Pot**), **Son Sen, Nuon Chea, Ieng Sary, Ieng Thirith** and others to **Vietnam** and **China**. Between 1960 and 1966, the party was known underground as the Workers' Party of Kampuchea, and from 1951-1960, as the **Khmer People's Revolutionary Party**. The change of name in 1966, which was not communicated to the Vietnamese party, reflected a strategic alliance with the Communist Party of China in the Sino-Soviet conflict. The CPK remained a secret, underground vanguard until 1977, when Pol Pot announced its existence, probably with Chinese urging, and just before making a second visit to Beijing. The CPK was heavily purged under Pol Pot and was formally disbanded in 1981. Ex-CPK members then identified themselves as the **Party of Democratic Kampuchea**.

COMMUNIST PARTY OF THAILAND (CPT). Founded in 1942, the CPT was never as influential in Cambodia as the **Indochina Communist Party**, but **Nuon Chea**, brother-No. 2 in the **Communist Party of Kampuchea** joined the CPT before joining the Indochinese party. Between 1975-1978, CPT cadres came to Cambodia for training, remarking later that the intellectual level of most Cambodian cadres was low. The Chinese-backed Thai communist insurgency was effectively derailed in 1979 when the People's Republic of **China** formed a united front with the Thai authorities in opposition to the invasion of Cambodia by **Vietnam**. This led to termination of Chinese support for the CPT in exchange for Thai assistance in transferring aid supplies to the three Cambodian resistance parties in the Coalition Government of Democratic Kampuchea.

COMMUNIST YOUTH LEAGUE OF KAMPUCHEA *(sampoan yuva-chun kommunis kampuchea).* This clandestine, vanguard organization complemented the **Democratic Youth League of Kampuchea**, a mass organization of the clandestine **Workers' Party of Kampuchea/Communist Party of Kampuchea**. It was created in October 1972 as a vehicle for ensuring more careful recruitment of militant younger people from the mass organization and the national liberation armed forces into the candidate ranks of the party. Distinguishing between democratic and genuinely revolutionary radicalism was deemed especially important in areas where party organization was weak.

CONSTITUTIONAL COUNCIL. Chapter 10 of the Constitution of the Kingdom of Cambodia (1993) establishes this body entrusting it with "the duty to safeguard respect for the Constitution, to interpret the

Constitution, and the laws passed by the Assembly." (Article 117.) It has nine members, each with a nine year term, one third being replaced every three years. Three are appointed by the king; three, by the **National Assembly**; and three by the Supreme Council of the Magistracy. The Constitution awards the Council "the right to examine and decide on contested cases involving the election of Assembly members" (Article 117) but this appeals body had not been created in 1995 when the Steering Committee of **FUNCINPEC** voted to expel **Sam Rainsy** from the party and to award his seat in the Assembly to another member of the party on the 1993 electoral list in **Siem Reap** province. While the Council had been formed in 1998 when there were many election complaints, it was not functioning. Later in the year, **Say Bory**, one of the king's appointees, issued a report protesting the political partisanship of the six **Cambodian People's Party** members. Another of the king's appointees affirmed that in practice, there were two councils: the Council of Six and the legal Council to which the king's appointees were invited along. In early 2001 the Council rejected a draft law establishing a special tribunal to try the former leaders of the **Democratic Kampuchea** regime because it contained a provision allowing for the death penalty. This contradicted Article 32 of the constitution which affirms, "There shall be no capital punishment." The Council approved an amended draft in August 2001.

CONSTITUTIONAL DRAFTING COMMITTEE (1971). Created by the **Khmer Republic** government in June, this "committee" was in reality a constitutional convention. There were 231 members, including many of the country's leading intellectuals, representing 57 civil associations and government departments. The Committee had been asked to prepare a draft republican constitution for the **National Assembly** but, when disagreements blocked its progress and the mandate of the 1966 Assembly also ran out, **Cheng Heng** declared the defunct Assembly to be a Constituent Assembly and transferred the task of preparing a **constitution** to this smaller and more docile group.

CONSTITUTIONS. There have been six constitutional regimes since 1946. The first was prepared by a mixed French-Khmer commission in 1946, passed to an elected 67-member consultative assembly dominated by the Democrat Party and promulgated by King **Sihanouk** on 6 May 1947. It envisaged a strong National Assembly, but had the flaw of allowing governments to be formed by unelected figures. The result, as in France, was a series of "revolving door" cabinets prior to independence. Although the 1947 text remained in force until 1970, it was several times overtaken by Prince **Norodom Sihanouk**'s absolutist impulses and amended many times. The **Khmer Republic** constitution, promulgated in 1972, was modeled on a blend of the **United States** and South Vietnamese constitutions, with a strong presidency, and accepted in a referendum. The communist text that replaced it in 1976 was formally awarded "to the people" and abolished private ownership. The 1982 **People's Republic of Kampuchea** constitution, drafted with Vietnamese guidance, was modeled on the postwar Vietnamese constitution. In 1989 the **State of Cambodia** issued a new constitution, reinstating **Buddhism** as the national religion and liberalizing the economy to allow the holding of land and private property. A new constitution prepared by the Constituent Assembly elected in May 1993, was promulgated on 24 September 1993. It restored the constitutional monarchy and introduced new clauses on human rights and civil liberties. It was heavily amended in 1998 when a second legislative chamber, the **Senate,** was created. The role of foreign powers in crafting succeeding Cambodian regimes has restricted the development of a fully constitutional basis for sovereign power.

COOPER-CHURCH AMENDMENT. This amendment to the **United States** Foreign Military Sales Act was named after U.S. Senators Frank Church and Sherman Cooper. It was adopted in May 1970 in opposition to the U.S.-South Vietnamese invasion of 30 April, outlawed the introduction of any U.S. troops to the Cambodian battlefield after 30 June 1970, forbade the introduction of U.S. military advisors and prohibited all U.S. air support operations over Cambodia. It was regularly violated. U.S. bombing of Cambodia did not end until 15 August 1973.

COUNCIL OF STATE. The highest executive body in the communist **People's Republic of Kampuchea (PRK)**, it was composed of seven members elected by the **National Assembly** from among its members. **Heng Samrin**, who chaired the council throughout the 1980s, served as head of state. The council had the formal power to appoint and remove cabinet ministers, ambassadors and envoys accredited to foreign governments.

COUP D'ÉTAT. Only two events are regularly described as coups. References to *the* coup, as if there were one only, refer to the 18 March 1970 decision of the **National Assembly** to remove Prince **Norodom Sihanouk** from his post as *Chef d'état (*"head of state"). This vote was engineered by a coup group led by Prince **Sisowath Sirik Matak** and the army commander and prime minister, **Lon Nol**. References to the coup of July 1997 refer to the violent events surrounding the 5 July ousting of first prime minister Prince **Norodom Ranariddh** from the coalition government by (then) second prime minister **Hun Sen**. More than 100 people died and several hundred others sought temporary exile overseas.

-D-

DAMBAN. Cambodian (and Thai) administrative term, usually translated as "sector," and widely used during the civil war and **Democratic Kampuchea** periods, when the country was divided into numbered *damban*. Sector boundaries were often coterminous with those of pre-revolutionary administrative districts, or *srok.*

DANGREK RANGE (Chuor Phnom Dangrek). Sometimes described as a mountain range, the Dangrek range of cliffs and hilltops in northern Cambodia is formed by the sharp drop of the Koret plateau along much of the norther frontier with **Thailand**. During the 1950s Phnom Dangrek, a mountain (756 meters above sea level) which is not far from Phnom **Preah Vihear** (625 meters high) was the base area of **Son Ngoc Thanh**'s **Khmer Serei** group. As a result the faction of the **Socio-Republican Party** which supported **Son Ngoc Thanh** was known as "Dangrek."

DAP CHHUON (né **KHEM PHET**) **(1912-1959).** Born in **Siem Reap**, he grew up in Prey Veng and then served as a member of the Cambodian colonial militia. During the **Franco-Thai** war of 1940-1941 he was captured by (or defected to) the Thai army, in whose forces he served. When **Battambang** and Siem Reap were annexed by **Thailand** in 1942, he joined the Cambodian National Guard and was a sergeant of local levies in 1943 when he deserted his post at Bang Mealas, reportedly taking his men's pay with him. Dap Chhuon then became a leader in the **Khmer Issarak** movement in the Siem Reap area, being elected in 1948 as president of the Liberation Committee of the Khmer People, founded in Thailand. He rallied to the king in October 1949 with his 300 men, a move which aided **Norodom Sihanouk** just at the time he had dissolved the **Democrat Party**-controlled national assembly and when the **Yèm Sambaur** government had thrown its support to the French army in Siem Reap in opposition to royal forces there. At the time he was the chief of the Free Khmer Corps (established from his Issarak group) with responsibility for maintaining order in Siem Reap. He then became military governor of Siem Reap, and cofounder of the **Victorious Northeastern Khmer Party** which he led in the 1951 elections, being promoted to colonel in 1954 after **Operation Sammaki**.

With the foundation of the **Sangkum**, he became closely identified with the leading right-wing opponents of the Democrats and served as minister for national security and religion from September 1956 to July 1957. In 1959 Sihanouk feared that Dap Chhuon, in league with the Central Intelligence Agency, was planning to secede from Cambodia with **Khmer Serei** support, and eventually topple him replacing him with a prowestern republic. Alerted by several informants, Prince Sihanouk despatched **Lon Nol** and some troops to Siem Reap supposedly to bargain with Chhuon but in fact to kill him and collect the gold which he had gathered to bankroll his plot. Dap Chhuon escaped from Lon Nol's soldiers, but was later captured and killed in late February 1959 near Phnom Kulen. His body was found on 3 March 1959. The incident featured in Sihanouk's film *Shadow over Angkor* which was completed in 1968. It has been alleged by Prince Sihanouk that Lon Nol killed Dap Chhuon to hide his own involvement in the plot.

Dap Chhuon married many times, but his principal wife, Tang Neang Im, died in Phnom Penh on 29 March 1959. Dap Chhuon's brother, **Kem Srey**, assisted him in many intrigues and worked for **Puth Chhay** in the early 1950s. Their younger brother, Kem Penh, was an international arms dealer during the nationalist period. Dap Chhuon also had a half-brother, **Slat Peou** and a secondary wife, Monisa "Tim," who were charged with involvement in the 1959 plotting.

DAY OF HATE. This was a national holiday, established during the Vietnamese occupation in the 1980s, to recall to peoples' minds the evils of the **Democratic Kampuchea** regime. The date chosen, 20 May, was the date in 1973 when the **Communist Party of Kampuchea** had inaugurated the collectivization of agriculture in the zones under its control.

DE RAYMOND, JEAN (1907-1951). De Raymond's appointment as **French Résident** in Phnom Penh came soon after the dismissal of the **Democrat**-controlled **National Assembly** in September 1949 by King **Norodom Sihanouk**. He supported the king's move, working well with the dissident Democrat Prime Minister **Yèm Sambaur**. He was assassinated on 29 October 1951 by a Vietnamese houseboy, probably as a result of a domestic dispute. The servant escaped and was later honored by the **Viet Minh** as a hero of the anticolonial struggle.

DECLARATION OF PATRIOTIC INTELLECTUALS. This declaration in support of the **National United Front of Kampuchea**, was issued on 30 September 1971 and was signed by 91 "Patriotic Intellectuals" with the "**three ghosts,**" the missing parliamentarians **Khieu Samphan, Hou Youn, Hu Nim**, heading the list. Prefiguring the political division of society into "**base people**" and "**new people**," the declaration urges all those who feel they cannot join the liberated zones "to think hard and to make a clear distinction between friend and foe" and to avoid being led astray by "the psychological warfare and the subversive activities of American imperialism and the treacherous Lon Nol clique."

DECOUX, JEAN (1884-1963). Governor-general of French Indochina 1940-1945 and a career naval officer, Decoux was appointed governor-general by the Vichy government when **France** was under German occupation and without allies in the Far East. Lacking the forces to resist the invading Japanese, Decoux agreed to the presence of Japanese troops in French Indochina, in exchange for being allowed to maintain the semblance of French administrative control. In 1941 Decoux recommended to the French government in Vichy that **Norodom Sihanouk** be crowned king of Cambodia on the death of King **Sisowath Monivong**. Over the next four years, Decoux encouraged the young Sihanouk to travel around his kingdom, thereby allowing him to acquire self-confidence and popularity. Decoux was detained by the Japanese in March 1945, and Sihanouk declared Cambodia's independence. When the French returned in force at the end of the year, Decoux was held in disgrace as a collaborator and placed in preventive detention in France, without trial, until 1949.

DEMOCRAT PARTY *(kanapac pracheathipatay)*. It was organized in January 1946 by **Ieu Koeus**, **Chhean Vam** and **Sim Var**. Following the return to Cambodia of Prince **Youtévong** in March, it was constituted as a political party in April with support from some French lawyers with Socialist leanings in **Phnom Penh**. The party was run by a committee located at party headquarters (66 rue Picquet) and a provincial committee in the capital of each province, as well as organizing committees in each *srok*. Membership of the party was open to males above the age of 21 who had not been convicted of a criminal offense (not always enforced); but monks and soldiers were not eligible. The party symbol was an elephant (representing power) carrying three lotus flowers (signifying king, religion and people).

The party supported the establishment of a constitutional monarchy under the formula "The king reigns but does not govern"; establishment of a single legislative chamber, with a government responsible to it; regulation of "democratic freedoms"; amnesty for political prisoners; development of the economy; nationalization of water and electricity (and possibly transport); development of social works, public health and public education (with scholarships for study in French universities); replacement of the poll tax with a graduated income tax; creation of a state bank; a unified system of justice with French and Cambodian judges; obligatory national service and establishment of a Cambodian army. The foreign policy program called for continued membership of the French Union, but withdrawal from the Indochinese Federation; a greatly reduced, advisory role for the **French Résident**; support from all Republican and anticolonial French; the return to Cambodia of the western provinces ceded to **Thailand** and eastern provinces ceded to **Cochinchina**; and unrestricted use of the **Mekong** with Cambodia sharing in the customs revenue.

On 22 April 1946 the first executive committee of the party was constituted consisting of Chhean Vam (secretary-general); Thong Saphron, **Huy Kanthoul** (assistant secretary-general); **Sim Var**, Saing Sophon, Tea Chhay, Kim Kouy (commissioners); **Ieu Koeus** (treasurer); **Ouk Thoutch** and **Huy Mong** (assistant treasurers). Prince **Sisowath Youtévong** was elected as party president. Party members present at that first general meeting included: **Chuop Hell**, Duong Sam An, Prince **Sisowath Essaro**, **Hem Chiam Roeun**, **Hak Mong Sheng**, Hum Sarath, Ith Sean, **Ith Seap**, Ko Hoc Chang, Meach Konn, Nhek Suong, **Penn Nouth**, Sarin Tong, Prince **Sisowath Sirik Matak**, **Son Sann**, **Sonn Voeunsai**, Tan Nau and Yim Saman. The party then bought its own printing press and established two newspapers. *Le Démocrate*, in French, was published weekly with **Im Phon** as director and Sonn Voeunsai as chief editor. The first issue (free) was published on 24 June 1946, and the paper gained a circulation of 1500 copies. *Pracheathipatay* (The Democrat) was published weekly in Khmer, being directed and edited by **Menh Nakry** and managed by Dith Chhoeung. Its circulation was 2,500 copies.

The Democrat Party was the first political party to be organized on a national scale, and it campaigned vigorously for the 1946 Constitutional Assembly elections by distributing many leaflets and giving theatrical/ satirical shows criticizing the **Liberal Party**, their main opponents. In the elections on 1 September 1946, the Democrats won 70 percent of the vote and 50 of the 62 seats they contested, gaining an overwhelming majority of the Assembly. They then elected Ieu Koeus president of the assembly and filled most of the civil service positions with party members. Prince Youtévong died in July 1947, and Ieu Koeus took over leadership of the party. In the elections for the first **National Assembly** on 21 December 1947, most of the party campaign had concentrated on criticizing the **Franco-Cambodian Treaty**, suggesting that only the Democrats could look after the national interest. It took credit for the return of the western provinces from Thailand; and also urged the return of Cambodian soldiers serving in **Cochinchina**. The Democrats once again won the election, receiving 63.1 percent of the votes and winning 55 of the 75 seats. Ieu Koeus was reelected as president of the National Assembly, but the Democrats won only 5 of the 18 seats in the High Council. In spite of this, they managed to get their candidate, **Khuon Nay**, elected as president.

In February 1948 Chhean Vam became president of the Council of Ministers and in May named four Democrats (**Pann Yung**, Sim Var, **Sok Chhong** and **Thonn Ouk**) as his country's representatives in the Assembly of the French Union. However, in July 1948 a serious split appeared in the party, with **Sam Nhean** and **Yèm Sambaur** breaking away to found the **Party of the People** and the **National Recovery Party** respectively. This caused Chhean Vam's government to fall, but the party managed to get Penn Nouth elected as president of the Council of Ministers in August 1948. In January 1949 Yèm Sambaur brought down the government and had himself appointed president of the Council of Ministers. Throughout 1949 hostility between Yèm Sambaur and the Democrats divided the political nation, and Yèm Sambaur managed to get the National Assembly dissolved in September 1949. In January 1950 Ieu Koeus, leader of the Democrats, was assassinated. Soon afterward more Democrats defected to the National Recovery Party. In June, King **Norodom Sihanouk** appointed Monipong as president of the Council of Ministers with three Democrats (Khuon Nay, Son Sann and Sonn Voeunsai) as ministers. On 8 April 1951 an extraordinary General Assembly of the Democrats met and urged the recall of the Assembly. In September 1951 the Democrats won the elections for the Second National Assembly, after a campaign directed by Huy Kanthoul attacking first the National Recovery Party then the **Khmer Renewal Party**. The Democrats won 54 of 78 seats, with 44.6 percent of the vote. Huy Kanthoul became president of the Council of Ministers in 1951, when party membership stood at 10,000. The executive committee of the party then included: Huy Kanthoul (secretary-general), Sonn Voeunsai and Menh Nakry (assistant secretaries), **Svay So** (general treasurer), Yim Ngan and Yok Ho (assistant treasurers), Hak Monsheng, Hem Chiamreun, Im Phon, Khuon Chuop, Khuon Nay and Nhek Suong (commissioners). On 15 June 1952, King Sihanouk sacked the Huy Kanthoul government, the last Democrat government to run Cambodia.

The Democrats' control of the National Assembly (1947-1951) coincided with Sihanouk's increasing popularity, independent-mindedness, and political skill. Throughout 1952 and 1953 the Democrat Party found itself on the defensive, and party members were uneasy with the flight of **Son Ngoc Thanh** into the jungles in March 1951. Most of all the party was demoralized by its lack of power, and when Sihanouk managed to get the French to grant independence to him in 1953, the major platform of Democrat Party policy had been removed. In February 1955, Prince **Norodom Phurissara**, who had been secretary-general since 1953, along with **Keng Vannsak** and some party radicals, took over the Party Executive Committee and stacked it with a younger generation of activists. The new committee favored repudiation of foreign military aid, rejecting **United States** "assistance," and a foreign policy of nonalignment. Sim Var and many of original leaders of the party opposed policies and either resigned or were excluded from the party.

The Democrats went into the 1955 National Assembly elections unprepared and with a new management team. They faltered in the face of opposition from the palace and police repression. Sihanouk used his police, under **Dap Chhuon** to harass party leaders. In rapid succession, closure of the party newspapers, the arrest of candidates, including Keng Vannsak and the shooting of campaign workers, contributed to the massive defeat of the Democrats by the new **Sangkum**. In March 1956 *Le Démocrate* was allowed to reappear, but collapsed after several issues. In March 1957 Huy Kanthoul and Phurissara said that they probably would not contest the next elections. In June of the same year two party committee members were arrested and charged with treason; and on 11 August 1957 Sihanouk invited leading Democrats to visit him for a debate. Five who turned up were set upon and beaten by palace guards at the end of the meeting. By the end of 1957 the Democrat Party was laid to rest. It was later "re-founded" as the **Democratic Party** in 1972.

DEMOCRATIC KAMPUCHEA (*Kampuchea pracheathipatay*). The name taken by the Marxist-Leninist regime which governed Cambodia between April 1976 and January 1979, when it was overthrown by a Vietnamese invasion. In exile, the DK government, led by **Pol Pot** until December 1979 and by **Khieu Samphan** from 1979, retained its name and its seat in the United Nations (UN) until 1982, when it was amalgamated with two anti-Communist factions to form the **Coalition Government of Democratic Kampuchea**. Democratic Kampuchea diplomats remained at the United Nations. The three-party coalition joined the **State of Cambodia** to form the **Supreme National Council** envisaged by the Paris Peace Agreement of October 1991. In June 1992, however, the Democratic Kampuchea party gradually withdrew from the peace process, forbidding UN troops access to its zones and refusing to register people in the zones as voters or to regroup and disarm its forces. It announced in October 1992 that it would not compete in United Nations-sponsored elections.

DEMOCRATIC PARTY. Founded by **In Tam** in 1972, the party drew support from people who had supported the **Democrat Party** of the late 1940s and 1950s, although many allied to **Son Ngoc Thanh** joined the **Socio-Republican Party**. The Democratic Party was funded largely by Tan Kim Chhieng, and its members included **Douc Rasy**, **Ieng Mouly** and **Tan Bun Suor**. The party newspaper was *Khmer Angkor*, although it relied on support from other newspapers such as *Sangros Chiet* and *Sangkorh Khmer*. The Democratic Party Congress on 2 July 1972 elected a 21-member National Committee with In Tam as president and **Chau Sau** as secretary-general. It was prepared to stand in the September 1972 Legislative elections nominating 118 candidates to contest the 126 seats, but withdrew on 5 August when Chau Sau's faction defeated In Tam's supporters and voted to boycott the election. The party, led by Chau Sau, refused to participate in the establishment of the Supreme Committee on 11 April 1975, and was preparing to negotiate for forming a coalition government at the fall of the Republic.

DEMOCRATIC YOUTH LEAGUE OF KAMPUCHEA *(sampoan yuva-chun kampuchea pracheathipatay)*. A mass organization created by the underground **Workers' Party of Kampuchea** in 1962 for recruiting young people to the cause of democratizing the "neocolonial and feudalist" **Norodom Sihanouk** regime. It prepared the way for the creation of the **Communist Youth League of Kampuchea** in 1972 once the party's armed struggle for power was well underway.

DENG XIAOPING (1904-1997). Paramount leader of People's Republic of **China** after the death of Mao Zedong, he was minister of finance from 1953, joining the Politburo two years later. Purged in 1967, he reemerged in April 1973 as deputy premier, only to be purged again in April 1976. The death of Mao in 1976 and the eclipse of the Gang of Four in 1978, marked, in hindsight, a massive shift in China's role in Southeast Asia. Deng's more even-handed approach to the **Vietnam-Democratic Kampuchea** conflicts was seen by some as encouraging Vietnam to invade in December 1978. Deng nevertheless ordered China's largely retaliatory attack on Vietnam in 1979 in order "to teach Vietnam a lesson" (in balance of power politics), and he remained a supporter of Cambodian independence, persuading all Cambodian nationalists—the royalists, republicans and communists—to form the **Coalition Government of Democratic Kampuchea (CGDK)** in 1982. Deng's policy of openness to "the outside world" and his entente with the West also created the basis for international support for the CGDK, and for promotion of the **Paris Peace Agreement** in 1989-1991.

DEUCH, BROTHER. *See* KANG KEK IEU.

DEVARAJA. A Sanskrit term, usually translated as "king of the gods," a *devaraja* cult was established in 802 AD and maintained by successive Cambodian kings. The Sdok Kak Thom inscription relates that the cult was first consecrated on Phnom Kulen by **Jayavarman II**, founder of the Angkorean line. Some scholars have argued that the cult assured or declared the divinity of the ruler. Others believe the cult was one honoring the Hindu god Shiva on behalf of royalty. Although the cult disappeared after the 14th century, the idea of "god-king" is part of the political culture and may help to account for why peasants both supported and revered Prince **Norodom Sihanouk** in the 1950s and 1960s.

DIEN DEL (1932-). Born on 15 May 1932 at Soc Trang, South Vietnam, and from a Khmer Krom family, he attended the Royal Military School from 1952 to 1956. He then studied at the Royal Military Academy and the School of Military Administration at Montpellier in 1959. He returned to Cambodia and was commissioned commander of a company of light infantry. Rapidly promoted, Dien Del was a captain in 1960 and remained at this rank when two years later he was appointed assistant to the general staff in charge of logistics, but he was a major in 1965 and commander of a battalion of special forces 1965-1970; a lieutenant-colonel in 1970; full colonel in 1971; and brigadier general in 1972. He was a member of the Armed Forces Council created in September 1972. In the last months of the civil war, Dien Del saw his 2nd Division gradually whittled away. He managed to escape from **Phnom Penh** on 17 April 1975.

In May 1975 Dien Del went to live in the **United States**; but determined to organize an anticommunist resistance movement, he moved, in May 1977, to France. There he had a long series of meetings with **Son Sann** and **Sak Suthsakhan** laying the groundwork for what eventually became the **Khmer People's National Liberation Front** (KPNLF). Dien Del was offered the leadership of the army of the KPNLF, much to the consternation of **In Tam**; and from early in 1978 Dien Del visited **Thailand**. The Vietnamese invasion of Cambodia took Dien Del and others by surprise, but on 1 February 1979 he flew to Thailand, and the KPNLF was inaugurated on 5 March on Cambodian territory. Chief of staff of the **Khmer People's National Liberation Armed Front (KPNLAF)** until 1986, Dien Del was involved in the dispute with Son Sann which saw several generals, including Dien Del, taking control of the Provisional Central Committee for Salvation on 7 December 1985. On 15 February 1986 he was expelled from the KPNLF Executive Committee by Son Sann, and became, albeit briefly, a Buddhist monk. Assistant chief of staff of the KPNLF Armed Forces from 1987-1993, he was vice-president of the KPNLF. However the divisions of 1985 ran deep, and in 1990 Dien Del joined with Sak Suthsakhan in forming the **Liberal Democratic Party**. He was a candidate in the 1993 elections, but was not elected. Later Dien Del joined **FUNCINPEC**. In 1998 he was elected to the **National Assembly** in **Kandal**. He chairs the Assembly's Commission on Interior, National Defense, Investigation and Anti-Corruption.

DIEP DINAR (1934-1975). Politician. Born on 12 March 1935 at Chhoe Kach, **Prey Veng**, she married Ngin Chhoeun and was active in the **Sangkum** movement and was a candidate in the by-election in Koki, **Kandal**, in 1960. Finally elected to the **National Assembly** in 1962 in Prey Veng and reelected in 1966, she became a good friend and ally of

Long Boret. Appointed secretary of state for national education in the first **Lon Nol** government, October 1966 to April 1967, she represented the Cambodian Women's Association in the **constitutional drafting committee** of 1971. On 17 April 1975 she tried to escape from Phnom Penh. **Sak Suthsakhan**, Long Boret and **Thach Reng** were ready to take off in the first helicopter provided by the Special Forces. When Mme Diep Dinar appeared, Long Boret climbed out of that helicopter so that he could escort her to the second helicopter. Sak Suthsakhan and Thach Reng's helicopter took off, and flew to **Thailand**. However neither of the other two helicopters worked. It is presumed Mme Diep Dinar was captured soon afterward and executed.

DITH MUNTY (1941-). Born in **Kampot**, and grandson of Nouth Oum (1879-1974), he studied law at the Royal School of Administration and was a magistrate in the municipal court of **Phnom Penh** before 1970. During the **Democratic Kampuchea** years he lived in exile. A supporter of the **People's Republic of Kampuchea (PRK)**, Dith Munty was the court-appointed lawyer for the defense at the trial in absentia of **Pol Pot** and **Ieng Sary**, 15-19 August 1979. After that he worked for the official PRK press agency. In 1984 Dith Munty was appointed ambassador of the PRK to India being recalled to Phnom Penh in August 1986 when he was appointed vice-president of the Supreme Court. From December 1986 until September 1990 he was deputy minister for foreign affairs; and from 1989 president of the commission for propaganda and education of the Central Committee of the **People's Revolutionary Party of Kampuchea**, and its successor, the **Cambodian People's Party (CPP)**. Appointed to one of the six CPP seats in the **Supreme National Council** from 13 February 1991, he was minister of information in the State of Cambodia administration, 1992-1993. In June 1993 he was elected deputy for **Kampong Cham** in the Constituent Assembly and was reelected in 1998, but promoted to president of the Supreme Court, he relinquished his seat. Also a member of the small Standing Committee of the ex-communist CPP, negotiations with the United Nations concerning a possible international tribunal to try former officials of the **Democratic Kampuchea** regime faltered in 2002 partly because UN negotiators viewed the likely inclusion of Dith Munty in the tribunal as unacceptable.

DITH PRAN (1942-). Born on 23 September 1942, son of Dith Proeung and Mme (née Meak Ep), he attended Lycée Siem Reap. He first worked as interpreter for the **United States** Military Assistance Group 1960-1965 and for the British Film crew of *Lord Jim*. He also worked as a receptionist at Auberge Royale des Temples until 1970 when he then became a guide and interpreter for journalists in **Phnom Penh**. His work and friendship with Sydney Scharnberg of *The New York Times* provided the storyline for the award winning film *The Killing Fields*. He worked at Dam Dek during the **Democratic Kampuchea** period and until the toppling of their regime by the Vietnamese forces, with whom he worked for several months. He then escaped to Thailand in 1979, and settled in Brooklyn, U.S.A. He has worked for *The New York Times* since 1980.

DOUC RASY (1925-). Politician and diplomat. Born on 8 March 1925 in **Phnom Penh**, he was the youngest son among the 10 children of the magistrate Kvann Douc and brother-in-law of prominent nationalist **Pach Chhoeun** who married his sister Douc Ok. Educated at **Lycée Sisowath**, he was a keen observer of political developments in Phnom Penh during the Japanese period and was present at the 1943 demonstration against the French. Douc Rasy completed his high school education in 1946 and then studied law in France from August 1946 to September 1957 earning a *Doctorate d'état* from the University of Paris in 1957. Returning to Phnom Penh in 1957, he joined the diplomatic corps and was posted to the Cambodian Mission to the United Nations as first secretary at the end of 1958 and in December 1960 became first secretary of the Cambodian Embassy in **Thailand**, a post held only until December 1961 when relations between the two countries were broken. He then worked in the Ministry of Foreign Affairs in Phnom Penh, resigning his post in September 1962 when he stood for and won the seat for Kampong Chhnang, Kampong Tralach, in the **National Assembly**.

While a deputy, he also taught law at the Faculty of Law in Phnom Penh and in December 1962 founded and edited *Phnom Penh Presse* which was supported by 18 deputies, including **Chuop Samloth**, another brother-in-law. The newspaper was banned by **Norodom Sihanouk** in September 1967, along with all other private newspapers in the country. Douc Rasy had concurrently acted as dean of the Law Faculty 1963-1965. In September 1966 he was reelected to the National Assembly representing Peani, Kampong Chhnang, in spite of Sihanouk's efforts to ensure he would be defeated. This achievement was due in no small measure to the fact that Douc Rasy was among the few critics and opponents who was not afraid publicly to criticize Sihanouk.

After the overthrow of Sihanouk in 1970, Douc Rasy was appointed editor of *Réalités Cambodgiennes* and remained in the National Assembly until its dissolution. He represented the Khmer Press Association on the **constitutional drafting committee** of June 1971, being one of only three government advisors in it. However in October he was sacked as editor of *Réalités Cambodgiennes* for having reported sympathetically some complaints of bad treatment from soldiers and in the 1972 presidential elections he backed **In Tam**, speaking out against the rigging of the election and corruption in the government. In 1973 he was appointed ambassador to the United Kingdom, also holding the posts of ambassador to Denmark, Bulgaria and Ireland. He moved to France after the defeat of the **Khmer Republic** and taught law at the Unversity of Amiens, retiring in 1991. He married Meas Sétha and they have five children.

DOUDART DE LAGRÉE, ERNEST (1823-1868). French naval officer and colonial administrator. He arrived in Cambodia in 1863, when he facilitated negotiations of the protectorate treaty with King **Norodom**. Doudart de Lagrée became fascinated with the country, learned the language, visited **Angkor Wat** and collected valuable manuscripts. In 1866, with **Francis Garnier**, he led an expedition to the headwaters of the **Mekong**, hoping to discover a gateway to China. He died two years later in Yunnan. One of the major streets in **Phnom Penh** was named after him in the colonial era then renamed Boulevard Norodom after independence.

DOUMER, PAUL (1857-1932). Governor general of **French Indochina** 1897-1902. Under Doumer, the administrative framework of the five-part federation of Indochina was established ensuring his permanent place in history as the architect of French Indochina. He became president of France in 1931 but was assassinated in Paris in the following year.

DUONG KHEM (1933-). Born in **Prey Veng**, he completed elementary school and became a forestry agent in 1947. In 1948 he joined the provincial police and, in the following year, the newly created paratrooper regiment as an orderly. He was commissioned lieutenant in 1970 and in 1972 was given the position of chief of the 11th Paratrooper Battalion. During the **Democratic Kampuchea** years, he was held in a camp in **Battambang** but escaped in 1978 reaching **Thailand** with a force of 180 men in 1979. In the refugee camps along the Thai-Cambodian border, he was vice-president of **Molinaka** from August 1980; and he helped to arrange the integration of Molinaka into the **Armée Nationale Sihanoukienne (ANS)** in 1983. Succeeding **Nhem Sophon** as president of Molinaka, Duong Khem commanded the 1st Brigade of the ANS. He was also appointed personal advisor to Prince Ranariddh on political matters in 1988. Promoted to major general in the renamed ANS, the **National Army for an Independent Kampuchea**, he was a member of the steering committee as well as a member of the National Council of **FUNCINPEC** in February 1992. In the May 1993 elections, he was elected to the **National Assembly** on the FUNCINPEC list in Phnom Penh and became vice president of the

Assembly Commission for Finance and Banking. He gave up parliamentary duties on 5 July 1994, having been appointed governor of **Banteay Meanchey** province, 18 December 1993. By January 1997 he and another ex-general **Toan Chhay** were among the ex-resistance fighters who had joined **Ung Phan** and others in making public criticisms of Prince **Norodom Ranariddh**'s leadership of FUNCINPEC. He was politically marginalized after the July 1997 coup against his former leader and no longer a provincial governor by 1999.

DUONG SAM OL (1919-). Born on 15 March 1919 in Lolok Sar, **Pursat**, the son of Duong Un and Mme (née Om), he studied at the Royal School of Administration in 1938-1939 and then joined the army. A lieutenant based in **Phnom Penh** in November 1947, he became a strong supporter of **Norodom Sihanouk**. Rising rapidly through the ranks of the officer corps, he was a full colonel and deputy chief of staff of the **armed forces** by 1963; a brigadier general from August 1965 and major general from November 1966, serving as minister of national defense from May 1967 until April 1968. Duong Sam Ol and his wife were overseas in March 1970 and banned from returning to Cambodia. Rallying to the newly formed **Royal Government of National Union of Kampuchea (GRUNK)**, Duong Sam Ol was named GRUNK minister of military development and general armaments in May 1970, a member of the political bureau of the Central Committee of **National United Front of Kampuchea (FUNK)** and of the Central Committee of the FUNK. While a GRUNK minister he accompanied Sihanouk on an 11-nation tour, May to July 1973. By February 1974 he had become chairman of the FUNK Committee in Beijing where Sihanouk resided and returned to Phnom Penh soon after the 17 April 1975 victory. He was present at a banquet in September 1978 in Phnom Penh (described as being "very old, sick"), one of the few non-communist Sihanoukists to have survived the purges of this group in 1977-1978. After 7 January 1979, he made his way to holding centers on the Thai-Cambodian border and has since resided in the United States and France.

DY BELLON (c1929-1975). The son of a primary school teacher, he married a daughter of Moshine Mahamedbhay, and they had several children. Bellon was a policeman and served as under-secretary of state for territorial defense from January to February 1956; under-secretary of state for planning, production and equipment from February 1959 to April 1960; and under-secretary of state for planning from April 1960 to August 1962. He was elected to the 1966 **National Assembly** for Chrak Motes, **Svay Rieng**, and was under-secretary of state for the interior in charge of national security and surface defense in the first **Lon Nol** government from October 1966 to April 1967. A supporter of the overthrow of Prince **Norodom Sihanouk** in March 1970, he was appointed director of general mobilization in 1970 and advisor to Lon Nol on 21 March 1973. He and his brother, Dy Balen, a magistrate, took refuge in the French Embassy at the fall of the Khmer Republic, and they were expelled from the embassy on 20 April 1975. Both are presumed to have been killed later that day.

DY PHON (1932-). A dental surgeon, he studied medicine at the Faculty of Medicine in Paris and married Tan Pauline, who graduated at the same time in Natural Sciences from the Faculty of Science in Paris, both returning to Cambodia in 1959. He became head of the dental surgery section of the Khmero-Soviet Hospital. In 1970 Dy Phon slipped out of **Phnom Penh**, rallied to the **National United Front of Kampuchea** and signed the 1971 **Declaration of Patriotic Intellectuals**. After April 1975 he worked once again at the April 17th Hospital (the renamed Khmero-Soviet Hospital), but as purges of the administration widened, he fell under suspicion of counter-revolutionary activities, and was arrested on 10 December 1978 and taken to **Tuol Sleng**. He was still there on 7 January 1979 when the Vietnamese freed him. His wife, born in 1933 at Krav, **Kampong Speu**, taught at the Faculty of Sciences, Phnom Penh in the 1960s and received a doctorate from the University of Toulouse in May 1969. She moved to France in 1980.

DY POK (1920-1998). Mother of **Hun Sen.** Her death after long illness is said by some in government circles to have been triggered by the violence and damage experienced in Phnom Penh after the collapse of the Hun Sen-**Norodom Ranariddh** coalition in July 1997. Cash gifts totaling US$100,000 were collected during her funeral ceremonies. The money was given to 10 provincial governors for the construction of wells which bear plaques stating "Gift of Madam Dy Pok, mother of Hun Sen." After restrictions on religious practice were lifted in 1988, Dy Pok contributed large sums in support of Buddhist temple renovations in **Phnom Penh**.

-E-

EA MENG TRY (1938-). After completing his studies in the École Normale, he studied at the Faculty of Law and Economic Sciences in **Phnom Penh** from 1960-1964 and then taught geography in Phnom Penh secondary schools, including Lycée **Kambuboth** from 1965-1971, before being commissioned to the army. In 1972 Meng Try joined the **Socio-Republican Party** and was elected to the **National Assembly** of the **Khmer Republic**

in September 1972 in Kampong Som Loeu, Kampong Seila. In 1973 he left Phnom Penh for France for doctoral studies in demography at the University of Paris. In 1981-1982 he was a visiting fellow in the Department of Demography at the Australian National University and after five more years in France, he settled, in 1988-1989, in Adelaide. In 1998 he was the third candidate on the **Sam Rainsy Party (SRP)** list in **Banteay Meanchey** but the SRP won only one seat in the province.

EA SICHAU (1920-1959). Independence activist. Born on 3 January 1920 at Chihé, **Kampong Cham**, the son of Ea Bun Seng, from a Khmer-Chinese family, Ea Sichau studied in **Phnom Penh** and then at the Faculty of Sciences in Hanoi. A protégé of **Son Ngoc Thanh,** he was sent, as Cambodia's "ambassador" to China in 1945, on an abortive mission to seek support and recognition for Cambodian independence. He then went to study at École des Hautes Études Commerciales, Paris, from May 1946 to December 1950, returning in April 1951. While in **France,** he had been president of the Cambodian Students' Association and a participant in the Marxist study group but he alongside **Phung Ton** and **Keng Vannsak** were not among those who proceeded to join the **Communist Party of France (PCF).**

Back in Phnom Penh, he assisted Thanh in producing *Khmer Krauk* (Khmers Awake) while working in the Foreign Ministry as an economics expert. On 9 January 1952 he was appointed director of customs; and on 6 March 1952, was briefly interim secretary-general to **Huy Kanthoul**, president of the Council of Ministers. He joined Thanh in his flight to the jungle in March 1952 where with assistance from Thai intelligence they established the **Khmer Serei**. During his time in the jungle, he was said to have been involved in the execution of eight students and teachers who wanted to rally to the government. He broke with **Keo Tak** who was rapidly acquiring a reputation for resorting to violence, and Thanh in 1954, returning to Phnom Penh to join the newly rejuvenated, left of center, **Democrat Party** led by **Norodom Phurissara.**

Sichau was admired in intellectual circles for his personal integrity, his austere style and his intellect. Although he associated with radicals on the left and the right, and viewed state management of the economy as the key to social progress, he viewed corruption and violence as the most serious constraints on Cambodia's development. His repudiation of armed struggle and of Son Ngo Thanh was irreversible from 1955, when Thanh sought asylum in neighboring countries, and was seen to ally himself with the "Free World." Sichau was a Democrat candidate in the 1955 elections in Phnom Penh (3rd district), losing to the **Sangkum** candidate. He died suddenly in 1959, reportedly of cerebral hemorrhaging.

EAO CHIN CHAY. He was a member of the **Democrat Party** who ran without success for the **National Assembly** in the 1947 elections in Prey Kri, **Kampong Chhnang**. Elected in a by-election the following year, he was one of the 11 Democrat deputies who resigned from the party in 1949 in order to support the break-away **National Recovery Party** led by prime minister **Yèm Sambaur** and its coalition partner, the **Victorious Northeastern Khmer Party** formed by **Mao Chay**.

EAP KIM CHORN (1930-1973). Born and educated in Phnom Penh, he graduated from **Lycée Sisowath** and studied law at the Faculty of Law and Economic Sciences, receiving his degree in October 1953. He then studied briefly in France earning a diploma in Public Law. Upon his return, he was attached to the Permanent Military Tribunal which tried captured **Khmer Serei** rebels. A member of the **Sangkum**, Eap Kim Chorn was elected to the **National Assembly** in 1958 representing Samrong Thom, Kandal. He was assistant secretary of state for finance, April 1960-January 1961. In 1970 he was chairman and managing director of the Cambodian Development Bank. He died of natural causes in July 1973.

EAP LEAN HOAT (1919-). Born on 5 February 1919 at Svaypor, **Battambang**, the son of Eap Khut, Lean Hoat was a prominent businessman in **Phnom Penh** who was a subscriber to the military cemetery near Phnom Penh, and a patron of **Lycée Sisowath**. As a member of the **Sangkum**, he stood for election in the 1959 High Council elections for **Kandal** province without success. He then won an October 1960 by-election for a seat in the **National Assembly** and won a full term in 1962 in **Prey Veng** and was then reelected there in 1966. Lean Hoat was defeated by **In Tam** for the presidency of the National Assembly in November 1970; but was chairman of the Economic Planning Committee in 1971. He married Tan Vat Tho, daughter of **Tan Pa**.

ÉCOLE FRANÇAISE D'EXTRÊME-ORIENT (EFEO). This prominent research institute was established in 1900 as construction of the colonial administrative framework for French Indochina neared completion. Much of its scholarly work focused on the arts and civilization of ancient Cambodia. The school also took charge of preservation and restoration work at **Angkor Wat**. Distinguished scholars attached at different times to the EFEO include Louis Finot, **Georges Coedès**, **Bernard Groslier** and Jean Filliozat. French conservationists were forced out of Cambodia immediately after April 1975, but the EFEO opened a new office in **Phnom Penh** in 1992.

ECONOMY. One of the poorest countries in Asia, Cambodia has a predominately agrarian economy. **Agriculture**, including forestry and fishing enterprises, employs between 75-80 percent of the economically active population but as much production is subsistence production, the contribution made by agriculture to the Gross Domestic Product (GDP) was estimated by the International Monetary Fund (IMF) as 43 percent in 1998. In the same year, **industry** with about six percent of the labor force, accounted for just 20 percent of GDP and services produced 37 percent. Growth and development of the economy has been highly uneven in recent years. On the one hand this is a legacy of political and economic instability inside Cambodia since the mid-1960s while on the other hand, and more recently, setbacks and stagnation may be blamed on the impact of the regional currency crises of 1997-1998. Because of high international donor support of the economy, that is, less reliance on short-term capital, and the widespread use of the U.S. dollar as a second currency of exchange (and for domestic saving), the Cambodian *Riel* had depreciated by 25 percent by the end of 1998. Rates of real growth were greatly affected: from 6.5 percent in 1996, they fell to 1 percent in 1997 and to zero in 1998 before rebounding to about 4 percent in 1999. Since then, growth in GDP has stalled at around 5 percent per annum while GDP per capita continues to hover around $300 per capita.

As of 2002 there is much pessimism as well as anxiety about the medium term outlook for developmental change and progress. Concerns focus on long-term budgetary problems and the seemingly irreversible decline in **foreign investment**. Domestic investors and manufacturers also face price competition for their products as the same goods imported from Thailand or Vietnam are often less expensive. Meanwhile international assistance programs, heavily focused on the development of the country's infrastructure, are plagued by problems of organization and corruption. "Informal payments" add at least 7 percent to total production costs, according to garment manufacturers, and these costs are likely higher for rural development projects. As for the budgetary problems, payments on outstanding debts and arrears might cost as much as 15 percent of total budget revenue in 2003. International financial institutions also continue to press for greater fiscal rationality, specifically for decreased defense spending, improved controls on illegal timber operations, as well as the trafficking of logs, labor and drugs and increased taxes on gasoline, alcohol and casinos. Effective revenue collection is next to impossible however, because of the poor salaries of public workers, including teachers and civil servants. Economic development including, especially, any further industrialization of the economy, is highly unlikely in the near term. National budget and currency stability are meanwhile assured by joint World Bank and IMF support for restructuring linked to poverty reduction and by Asian Development Bank and United Nations Development Program support for the current five-year Socio-Economic Development Plan process.

EDUCATION. Education was from medieval times available from Buddhist pagoda schools which were available only to boys. Instruction was primarily moral and didactic and focused on Buddhist texts written in either Pali or Khmer. During the colonial era, 1863-1953, secular education was promoted but limited to a very small elite of mostly aristocratic Khmer children and even larger numbers of Vietnamese and Chinese pupils, the children of colonial civil servants or businessmen. The *École Sisowath* was established in 1873, primarily to promote the study of French language and culture, and by 1893 it had been upgraded to **Collège Sisowath**. By 1911 it had acquired the first cycle of the secondary curriculum and with the addition of the second in 1935, it became **Lycée Sisowath**. The *École Normale*, after independence, the Institute or Faculty of Pedagogy, was also developed in this period. The Royal School of Administration opened its doors in 1917. In the interwar years as provincial capitals each acquired a modern primary school, French educators arranged the "*renovation*" (renewal) of the pagoda school curriculum, in effect giving them the same secular, three-year primary school program of reading, writing and arithmetic as the modern schools but with no French language. A few other schools such as the École Miche (mainly for French), École Malika (for girls) and École (later Lycée) Descartes operated in Phnom Penh but Lycée Sisowath remained the only secondary school in the country until the opening of Collège Battambang in c1938. However when during World War II, Battambang was seized by the Thais, the need for another secondary school led to the creation of Collège Preah Sihanouk in Kampong Cham in 1942. At this time Lycée Sisowath had 744 students of whom 76 only were women. There were 908 pagoda schools with 38,853 boys and no girls and 393 other schools, including a School of Arts and a Technical School as well as secular elementary schools with 19,965 pupils of whom 3,350 were girls. Most teachers were untrained in their craft and did not possess primary school leaving certificates. French neglect of public education is a central theme in the history of colonialism in Cambodia (and in **Laos**).

During the Prince **Norodom Sihanouk** years education was free and compulsory for both boys and girls. Primary and secondary schools were opened throughout the countryside; and, for those who qualified, scholarships were provided for University study overseas. French was the language of instruction in all lycées and courses continued to be validated in accordance with French standards which ensured a high rate of failure in the annual examinations. A large number of private schools were established for commercial and other reasons. **Chamroeun Vichea** and **Kambuboth** are examples of these and provided instruction for bright students who had not performed well enough on French-language examinations to gain free places in the public secondary system. The **Chinese** community ran their own schools until 1967 when these were proscribed. In the school year 1964-1965, there were 215 privately owned and managed Chinese schools, 16 Vietnamese schools, 19 French schools and 171 Khmer schools (of which 53 were primary and 118 were secondary). Though school provision appeared sufficient, the 1962 **census** revealed that more than half of the population above the age of 10 years could neither read nor write. Illiteracy among females over the age of 10 was just over 80 percent while only about 30 percent of males were illiterate. The census also revealed that only 16,100 Cambodians possessed the equivalent of a high school diploma and only 300 held higher degrees in a total population (then) of 5,729,000.

Sihanouk's educational system also included several "universities." The first university was the Royal University of Phnom Penh, founded in 1956 as the National Institute of Legal and Economic Studies. The other universities were the Royal University of Fine Arts, the Royal Technical University, the Buddhist University, the Royal University of Agricultural Sciences, the University of Agronomic Science and the University of Takeo-Kampot all created by law in January 1965. These were based on earlier faculties and specialized schools of engineering (Royale University of Kampong Cham) or dance (Royale University of Fine Arts) and were not upgraded from their previous status as schools or faculties in the usual manner or properly funded as universities.

Under the **Lon Nol** government, from 1971 Khmer replaced French as the language of instruction. However these reforms were short-lived. During the **Pol Pot** years, there were few schools, emphasis in formal study was on Khmer language and elementary science and the use of all foreign languages was proscribed.

Schools were reopened or reorganized from 1979 but often without sufficient books, desks, blackboards or paper. New schoolbooks were rapidly prepared, and a state curriculum, this time emphasizing the historic solidarity with **Vietnam** was prepared. Debates over the content of history books and the omission of reference, often, to the 1975-1979 years persist. Surveys and estimates of literacy continue to show that education of women, especially of women in the poorest strata of society, continues to be inadequate. About 55 percent of women above the age of 15 continue to be illiterate; 42 percent of women above the age of 15 have never attended school. Even though primary school registers show that girls make up over 40 percent of first graders, they are less likely to stay in school than boys, often because their labor is required in the household. Surveys also reveal that parents often believe education is more important for boys and that they are anxious about the personal security of their daughters especially as they approach the age of 12. Because teachers are poorly paid and obliged to take outside work to survive or are seen regularly to accept bribes in relation to examination supervision, there is a wide consensus that national education is failing to meet developmental needs and requirements.

Some universities and university-level faculties have been revived or established. The current institutions are as follows: University of Phnom Penh; Institute of Technology of Cambodia, Institute of Business, Faculty of Law and Economic Sciences, the private Maharishi Vedic University, Royal University of Agriculture, University of Fine Arts and Faculty of Medicine.

870. Security code number used by the **Communist Party of Kampuchea (CPK)** in the 1970s as a way to designate the Standing Committee of the Central Committee and especially in field radio communications. Also known as the "organization" *(angkar)*, the Standing Committee was led by **Brother Number One**, the party rank of comrade **Pol Pot** and included **Brother Number Two** who was known also as **Nuon Chea**. Documents emanating from "870" can be assumed to have been written by Pol Pot or, when he was ill, by Nuon Chea. In the 1980s, after **Democratic Kampuchea (DK)** had been overthrown and the **Communist Party of Kampuchea** had been disbanded, 870 continued to be used to designate the headquarters of the DK army and exparty leadership. In this era, and especially after his official retirement, Pol Pot was respectfully referred to as "Grandfather 87" *(Ta 87)*.

EK PROEUNG (1933-). Career Soldier. Born in **Svay Rieng**, and a former student at **Lycée Sisowath**, he was an emissary between **Lon Nol** and President Richard Nixon in 1972. As a brigadier general he was a member of the Armed Forces Council created in September 1972. By 1974 Proeung was a major-general and minister of the interior, general mobilization, pacification, security and religion in the second **Long Boret** government (June 1974 to March 1975). He also headed President Lon Nol's national security council. His wife, Meas Konth, a teacher since 1951, was active in the Cambodian Red Cross.

EK SAM OL (1944-). Born in **Ba Phnom**, Prey Veng, he has a *licence* in Khmer literature, and was secretary general of the Faculty of Arts, Phnom

Penh, 1970-1975. During the **Democratic Kampuchea** period, he was evacuated to the countryside. In 1980, Sam Ol founded the Association of Cambodian Intellectuals and headed the training department of the Ministry of Education. From March 1985 until June 1993 he was deputy-minister of education in the **People's Republic of Kampuchea** (and **State of Cambodia**) and promoted the Khmerization of higher education. In 1993, he was elected to the **National Assembly** on the **Cambodian People's Party (CPP)** list in the former Eastern Zone province of Prey Veng. He was elected to the CPP Central Committee at its congress in 1997 and reelected to the National Assembly in 1998.

EK SEREYWATH. The son of **Ek Yi Oun** and Mme (née In Sauth), Sereywath studied political science at the *Institut d'Études Politiques de Paris* and at the University of Paris I. He then became a journalist for *Le Figaro* and the Cambodian Association's *Centre Cambodgien*. In the late 1980s he moved to Bangkok to work with **FUNCINPEC**, and by 1989 headed the information department of **Armée Nationale Sihanoukienne/** FUNCINPEC-Kampuchea. In the 1993 elections, he was elected to the **National Assembly** on the royalist list for **Phnom Penh**. He was subsequently appointed deputy-minister of information in the provisional government, and then secretary of state for national defense. Failing narrowly to be reelected to the Assembly in 1998, he received the FUNCINPEC seat vacated by Pok Than upon the latter's appointment as secretary of state in the Ministry of Education. In 1999 Sereywath gave up the seat, having been appointed ambassador to the Philippines.

EK YI OUN (1910-). Prime minister 1958. Son of Ek and Mme (née Van), he was brother of Ek Nath, a concubine of King **Sisowath Monivong**. Born in **Phnom Penh** and educated at the Royal School of Administration, Yi Oun was appointed a judge to the court in **Kampong Cham** in 1942 and in **Kratié** in 1947. He served briefly in the army and joined the **Liberal Party** of Prince **Norodom Norindeth**. In 1950 he was appointed assistant prosecutor in Phnom Penh and won a by-election for the **National Assembly** in Tram Kak, **Takeo**. Although he failed to be reelected in the general elections of 1951, he was appointed to a seat in the High Council of the Kingdom, of which he was briefly president.

In 1952 Ek Yi Oun was *chef de cabinet* of the Ministry of Justice and then vice-president of the National Consultative Council in 1953. In 1955 he joined the **Sangkum** and was elected to the 1955 National Assembly, becoming vice-president of the National Assembly and president in 1956. From 11-16 January 1958 he was interim president of the Council of Ministers as the Assembly had been dissolved and elections were pending.

Sim Var, then president of the Council of the Kingdom, and others, who had resigned from the cabinet, ensured Ek Yi Oun was not a candidate in the 1958 or 1962 elections; but he ran in the 1959 High Council elections for **Kampot** and Takeo and was finally elected in 1966 to represent Nheang Nhang, Takeo. During the **Khmer Republic** years, he was advisor to **Lon Nol** for cultural affairs, until the Americans persuaded Lon Nol to cease appointing so many of his friends to paid advisory positions. Ek Yi Oun married In Sauth and they had two children: Ek Samboll and **Ek Sereywath**.

ELECTIONS. The first general elections to be held in Cambodia were organized by the French colonial administration in 1946 and were for a Constituent Assembly. These elections, won by the proindependence **Democrat Party**, were followed by fresh elections for a **National Assembly** in 1947 and a successor Assembly elected in 1951. On both occasions the Democrats won large pluralities although in 1951 they won less than half of the votes cast. Alarmed by growing popular support for the more radical **Khmer Issarak**, on the one hand, and the failing French war on the **Viet Minh** regime, on the other, King **Norodom Sihanouk** launched his **Royal Crusade for Independence** in late 1953 after dissolving the divided, Democrat-dominated National Assembly. For the next two years the King governed by decree. When elections resumed, in 1955, more than a year after independence had been secured, every seat was won by the **Sangkum Reastr Niyum**, the political movement formed by Sihanouk upon his abdication from the throne earlier in the year.

The Sangkum extended its monopoly grip on the National Assembly in the succeeding elections of 1958 and 1962, for which Sihanouk hand-picked a single slate of candidates. Only one opposition candidate, Keo Meas, a member of the Pracheachon group, contested the 1958 election. In 1966, when all other parties had been suppressed, Sihanouk allowed Sangkum candidates to run against each other. In the resultant campaign, those elected owed more to local interests and to their constituents than to the Prince. In 1970, when Sihanouk was abroad, it was this Assembly, backed by the army, which dismissed him from his role as chief of state. Several months later Cambodia was declared a republic. In June 1972 **Lon Nol**'s promotion to president was confirmed in an election marred by fraud. In September, elections to the **National Assembly** and the **Senate** were dominated by Lon Nol's **Socio-Republican Party**. The only opposition came from two "puppet" parties, both controlled by **Lon Non**.

The **Communist Party of Kampuchea** waited a year after coming to power before conducting an election in April 1976 for a People's Representative Assembly. There was no campaigning, and in some regions only "full-rights" members of the rural cooperatives were allowed to vote. The election was intended to legitimize the new regime in the eyes of its supporters, national and international. No tallies were published, and following communist practice, the candidates were chosen by local party committees.

Elections in the **People's Republic of Kampuchea (PRK)**, proclaimed in 1979, were held in May 1981. Once again all candidates were chosen by the ruling **People's Revolutionary Party of Kampuchea**, and while some were not communist, most of those elected were party members. Further elections should have been held at least every five years, according to the PRK constitution, but from 1986 onward they were regularly postponed. The holding of "free and fair" elections under the supervision of the United Nations (UN), thereby upholding the rights to political self-determination of the Cambodian people, were a condition of the political settlement negotiated in Paris in 1991. Under UN protection new political parties were allowed to form and to campaign. Twenty competed in the elections held 23-28 May 1993. Because a proportional representation system was employed in each of the provinces, no clear winner emerged from the polling. The royalist party, **FUNCINPEC** topped the poll winning 45.5 percent of the votes and 58 seats in the new Constituent Assembly while the **Cambodian People's Party (CPP)** won 38.2 percent and 51 seats. The **Buddhist Liberal Democrat Party** finished third, winning 3.8 percent of the votes and 10 seats and **Molinaka**, which won 1.4 percent of the nationwide poll, qualified for one seat in **Kampong Cham** province. Though beaten into second place, the CPP, capitalizing on the fact that FUNCINPEC lacked the two-thirds majority required to govern on its own, threatened to split the country into two zones. This forced the royalists into a coalition government with two prime ministers and two coministers of defense. The CPP also retained effective control over the ministries and all provincial and local government posts, as well as the army high command and the police. Provincial governorships were divided between the two parties only in 1995.

According to the 1993 **constitution**, new elections for the National Assembly were required no later than five years after those conducted in 1993, and following local elections. (The latter were once scheduled for 1996, and then postponed, and finally held in 2002.) The 1997 CPP *coup d'état* against First Prime Minister **Norodom Ranariddh** threatened to derail the constitutional process entirely, but after international mediation, Ranariddh was persuaded to return to the country and the July 1998 elections were held with a view to restoring political stability. Although there was much intimidation of opposition candidates, the polling resulted in a clear CPP plurality (41.4 percent) with FUNCINPEC finishing second (31.7 percent) and **Sam Rainsy Party (SRP)** third (14.3 percent). Formation of the Hun Sen government, also a coalition with FUNCINPEC, was delayed until November 1998 due to opposition protest against many irregularities in vote-counting procedures. Local elections in February 2002 for commune (*khum*) heads and councils confirmed the near monopoly grip of the CPP on administrative power: the CPP won 7,721 of the available 11,259 local council seats (68.6 percent) and 1,597 of the 1,621 headships (98.5 percent). FUNCINPEC won 2,182 seats (19.4 percent) and only 10 headships topped by the SRP which won 13 headships and 1,354 seats (12 percent). All of the parties promised to reduce violence in society, to improve education and health services, to deal with land occupancy and water use problems, to promote the role of women in society and political life and to address problems of illiteracy and drug trafficking.

ELYSÉE ACCORDS. *See* FRANCO-CAMBODIAN TREATY (1949).

EM SAM AN (1947-   ). Originally from **Kampong Cham** province, Em Sam An briefly attended a local primary school and was still living with his parents when in 1970 he became an active supporter of the **National United Front of Kampuchea.** Still living or working in the Eastern Zone of **Democratic Kampuchea (DK)** after the war, he fled to **Vietnam** on 25 May 1978 when DK army forces led by **Ke Pauk** turned against regional army forces loyal to **So Phim.** After the Vietnamese invasion of December, he was appointed deputy to the director of the official press agency of the **People's Republic of Kampuchea (PRK).** By 1984 he had been promoted to director, a post held until 1993. He also represented **Kandal** in the **National Assembly** of the PRK from May 1981-May 1993. In 1993 he was appointed advisor to Second Prime Minister **Hun Sen** on security matters. In July 1994 he was appointed cosecretary of state in the interior ministry. In the Hun Sen government formed in November 1998, he was promoted to principal secretary of state in the interior ministry and given responsibility for the National Authority for Combating Drugs, an agency of the ministry, officially headed by Minister of Interior **Sar Kheng**. Following a lacklustre attempt to disrupt marijuana cultivation in remote regions of southern **Kampot** province in early 2000, the national press questioned the government's determination and effectiveness in curbing drug production or trafficking. In October 2001 he was fired when his personal assistant and three others were arrested for smuggling drugs from **Laos** into **Phnom Penh** and onward to **Vietnam**.

ENG HUN (1924-   ). Born on 8 April 1924 at Kampong Thmar, Kampong Thom, Eng Hun was the son of Khean Eng and Mme (née Sanh Chhit).

He was the first director of the national exchange bureau in the National Bank, December 1954-February 1959, when he was named minister of Trade and Industry, February-July 1959, and then minister of Trade and Finance, July 1959-April 1960. Eng Hun next worked for SONEXIM, the state-owned export-import enterprise, becoming chairman and managing director in the late 1960s. In 1970 he published an article in the magazine *New Cambodge* sharply critical of Prince **Norodom Sihanouk**'s incompetence in managing the economy after independence and especially between 1963-1970.

ENG MARIE (Princess Norodom Marie Ranariddh) (1948-). Born on 21 December 1948 in **Phnom Penh**, her father was **Eng Meas** and **Eng Roland** is her older brother. She married Prince **Norodom Ranariddh** in September 1968. After the prince became first prime minister, she became president of the Cambodian Red Cross, a post once held by Queen **Monineath** and customarily reserved for the "first lady" of government. Following the 1997 *coup d'état* against her husband mounted by **Hun Sen**, his wife, **Bun Rany**, took Marie's role as president of the Red Cross. In 1999 Princess Marie was reelected to the Steering Committee of **FUNCINPEC** while her brother, Roland, was excluded from it.

ENG MEAS (c1917-1976). The son of Eng Lean and Mme (née Ton), and from a **Cham** background, he was an inspector in the National Police and a friend of **Lon Nol**. He was a member the **Khmer Renewal Party** and was a candidate for the party in the 1951 **National Assembly** elections in Phnom Kong, Kampot. Later, as a member of the **Sangkum** he was elected to the 1955 National Assembly in which he became vice-president. In November 1956 he was cochair (with **Sam Sary**) of Cambodia's delegation to the second conference of Asian Socialists in Bombay. He married and had 10 children: **Eng Roland**, **Eng Marie**, Eng Rosenthal, and seven other children who lost their lives during the **Democratic Kampuchea** period. Eng Meas was arrested in 1976 and sent for execution from Tuol Sleng prison on 27 May 1976.

ENG ROLAND. Born in **Phnom Penh**, son of **Eng Meas** and brother of Princess Norodom Marie Ranariddh, née **Eng Marie**, Roland was a student in France for most of the 1970-1975 war. In exile in Aix-en-Provence between 1975-1987, Roland became head of the Bangkok-based information and public relations department of **FUNCINPEC** from 1988-1992. Returning to Phnom Penh with Prince **Norodom Sihanouk**, he was initially coordinator of humanitarian affairs for FUNCINPEC then elected to the **National Assembly** for **Kampot** in May 1993, but he resigned from the Assembly in 1994 in order to become ambassador to Malaysia,

Singapore and Thailand, residing again in Bangkok. He was concurrently Cambodia's representative to the Economic and Social Commission for Asia and the Pacific (ESCAP). In July 1997 he proclaimed his support for **Hun Sen**'s coup against his brother-in-law, Prince **Norodom Ranariddh**, thereby retaining his ambassadorial post. In 1999, he was appointed ambassador to the **United States** upon nomination by **FUNCINPEC** in spite of being voted out of the party Steering Committee.

ENGLY PIPHÂL (1944-   ). Born on 28 January 1944 in Kampong Cham, the daughter of diplomat Engly Honglay and Mme née Vann Bophan, the daughter of Sung Vann, a member of the High Council of the Kingdom, she married Thann Hin, *chef de bureau* of the export section of SONEXIM. He was on a Colombo Plan scholarship to Australia in April 1975 when the communists seized **Phnom Penh**. Piphâl, a qualified librarian, worked in Melbourne before being appointed minister-counsellor at the Cambodian Embassy in Canberra in 1994. General-Secretary of **FUNCINPEC**-Australia from 1983, she continued to support Prince **Norodom Ranariddh** after July 1997 and was removed from her embassy post in March 1998. She subsequently catalogued the Khmer collection at the National Library of Australia.

EVANS, GARETH JOHN (1944-   ). As minister for foreign affairs and trade in Australia, 1988-1996, he played a prominent and perhaps decisive role in promoting a settlement to the **Third Indochina War**. The reconvening of the stalled Paris Conference in October 1991 owed much to Australian success in persuading Hanoi and Phnom Penh of the need for a United Nations role in a settlement, an idea first elaborated in a "red" book entitled *Cambodia: An Australian Peace Proposal* prepared for the Jakarta Informal Meeting on Cambodia, 26-28 February 1990.

-F-

FERNANDEZ, JEAN (c1925-   ). The son of **Samson Fernandez**, and brother of **Sosthene Fernandez**, Jean was a career soldier, promoted to lieutenant colonel in 1971. In the final year of the civil war, he was appointed governor of **Kampot** on 9 April 1974, but in early 1975 when the siege of Phnom Penh was underway and river haulage to the city cut off, he secured exile in the United States. He lives in Bellflower, California, where he heads the Cambodian Veterans' Association.

FERNANDEZ, SAMSON (1891-1971). Born in **Phnom Penh**, the son of a Filipino father and Vietnamese mother and a Catholic, Samson was naturalized as a Cambodian citizen in 1915. He was an instructor in a school in Pursat, but taking advantage of a colonial reform of the judiciary, he become a judge serving in courts in Kampong Speu and Svay Rieng and then a senior magistrate in Kampong Cham by 1928. A promoter and political advisor to the **Liberal Party**, Samson Fernandez was an editor of the party newspaper *Sereipheap* (Liberty) as well as business agent for Princess Pindara, Prince **Norodom Norindeth**'s mother. The assassination of **Ieu Koeus** in 1950 was blamed on Norindeth, and Khuorn Luth, a Liberal member of the **National Assembly**. Fernandez defended Chau Sun, the bodyguard (of Norindeth) who was charged with the murder, arguing successfully that the accused had been framed. He also implicated **Yèm Sambaur** in the murder and, in return, was subject to personal attacks that he was attempting to arrange the murder of Sambaur and the National Police Chief Tan Kim Tik. Elected to the 1951 National Assembly in Kandol Chrum, Kampong Cham, he served briefly as minister of public health, social action and labor in the Second **Penn Nouth** government, January to July 1953, but played no active part in politics during the **Sangkum** period. He died 10 March 1971 survived by his wife, Maria Ken, of Franco-Vietnamese origin, and five children including **Sosthene** and **Jean**.

FERNANDEZ, SOSTHENE (1923-). Born on 28 November 1923 in Pursat, and son of **Samson Fernandez**, he taught in the national Military School and was commissioned lieutenant in 1947. From then until 1949 he participated in French operations against the **Khmer Issarak**, but in 1949-1950 he was in France, at the *École d'Application d'Infanterie in Coetquidan*, proceeding to the *École d'État Major*, France. Returning in 1953, he worked in the secretariat of the Ministry of National Defense. He took command of the 3rd military region in Battambang, 1956-1958, before returning to France to study at the *École Supérieure de Guerre* 1958-1960. On his return in 1961, he was promoted to lieutenant colonel and commander of the 1st military region, Kampong Cham. Promoted to full colonel, Sosthene returned to civil life to become secretary of state for national security from January 1968 to August 1969 and then became secretary of state for the interior, charged with national security until 17 March 1970. He participated in the suppression of the **Samlaut Uprising** in Battambang in 1967 and was loosely involved in events surrounding the overthrow of Prince **Norodom Sihanouk**, his sacking in March, perhaps was orchestrated with Fernandez's consent so as to allow the anti-Sihanouk members of the **National Assembly** to test their strength. This led to his recommisioning in April 1970 as brigadier general and appointment as commander of the Second Military Region, Kampong Speu. He was rapidly promoted to major general, then lieutenant general and, in September 1972, chief of staff and commander-in-chief of the army of the **Khmer Republic**.

Fernandez was well known to reporters to whom he regularly explained the Republic's predicaments but was criticized for using the navy to collect protection money for guarding river transport services in which his family had investments. He was awarded the Grand Cross of the Khmer Republic on 12 March 1975, being relieved of his office on the same day. He left for France less than a week later, on 18 March 1975, with his wife and their seven children. He became president of the Cambodian Mutual Aid Association in 1976. Renewing contact with Prince **Norodom Sihanouk** in 1979, he accompanied Prince Sihanouk on a visit to the **United States** in 1980 but refused to participate in a coalition with the **Party of Democratic Kampuchea**, his former enemies.

FILMS. The first commercial movie producers in Cambodia were Films Meanchey, a company formed on 11 April 1960. Its principal investors included Prince **Sisowath Sirik Matak**, Bou Thol of the Bank of Phnom Penh and Som Sam Al, who managed the company. The leading independent film producer is **Norodom Sihanouk** who has approximately 50 films to his credit. His passion for film making emerged at a young age when as a child he saw French and Hollywood films with his parents. His first films, produced as a young King, already displayed his preoccupation with Cambodia's place in the world: *Tarzan among the Kuoy* and *Double Crime on the Maginot Line*.

Although most of Sihanouk's films were made to entertain Khmer audiences, he has also produced 12 documentaries. As a genre these state publicity films might be compared to **chronicle histories** providing as they do an official record of Cambodia under his leadership. *Cambodian Women in the Time of the Sangkum Reastr Niyum, An Army for Construction, Cambodia 1965* and *The GANEFO of Royal Cambodia* (GANEFO being the "Games of the New Emerging Forces") all depict the changing social and architectural landscapes of modernizing Cambodia in the 1960s, and other documentaries such as *Tourism in Royal Cambodia, Four Smiles but One Soul, Royal Palace, The Pagoda of the Emerald Buddha,* and *The Visit of General De Gaulle to the Kingdom of Cambodia* attempt to demonstrate that sovereign power in modern times arises from past achievements and glories.

No less historically and culturally significant for being fictional, his romantic films represent a more complex mixture of nationalist imaginings and ambition. These are very often set at **Angkor** or in the idealized countryside and sometimes showcase historical events. There are dances invoking celestial intervention, panoramic landscapes dwarfing humanity and studies of social situations contributing to dilemmas in the 1960s, 1980s or 1990s. For example *Shadow over Angkor* (1967) envisages the possibility of American (and South Vietnamese) intervention, *Divine Sanctuary* (1966) recounts the Thai occupation of **Preah Vihear** temple in 1958, and *The Joy of Life* (1968) explores the level of corruption and the problems of social modernization. In the 1980s *I Will Never See You Again, Oh My Beloved Kampuchea* (1990) highlights the Vietnamese occupation of Cambodia and *Farewell, My Love!* (1989) the March 1970 coup d'état against Sihanouk. In the 1990s *Peasants in Distress* (1994) attacks **Democratic Kampuchea** for disrupting the UN-directed process of national reconciliation, *Heir of a Vanquished Secessionist* (1995) considers the 1993 attempted secession by Prince **Norodom Chakrapong** and other leaders of the **Cambodian People's Party**. The themes of political betrayal, corruption, greed, selfishness and jealousy in the face of national calamity also feature in *The Last Days of Colonel Savath* (1996), *My Village at Sunset* (1996) and *An Ambition Reduced to Ashes* (1996), an allegorical tale acknowledging the manipulation as well as the demise of royal power. Most of these films are romantic tragedies, but a few, including *The Ghost of My Beloved Wife* (1993) and *The Joy of Life* (1968) are satirical comedies.

For most of these films, Sihanouk has been producer, director, writer, editor and, in the 1960s, a principal actor. Together with his principal consort, Princess Monique Sihanouk (who became Queen in 1993 taking the reign name **Monineath**), he starred in *The Enchanted Forest* (1966), *Shadow over Angkor, Twilight* (1968) and *Rose of Bokor* (1969). In most of his other films Sihanouk has selected his cast almost exclusively from amateurs drawn from his entourage, and he has employed professional actors only for the more difficult roles. Amateur actors in his films have included Prince **Norodom Sihamoni** in *The Little Prince* (1967) and *My Village at Sunset* (1992), Princess **Norodom Bopha Devi** in *The Enchanted Forest* and *Heavenly Dancers* (1965), General **Nhiek Tioulong** in *The Joy of Life* and *Heavenly Dancers*, **Chhorn Hay** in *The Mysterious City* (1988), **Oum Mannorine** in *The Flower of the Champa of Battambang* (1992), and **Roland Eng** and **Truong Mealy** in *To See Angkor Again . . . and Die* (1993). Several films produced during the 1980s while he resided in North Korea also employed North Korean cameramen, technicians and extras.

Since his return to Phnom Penh, some of the king's old films have been shown on Cambodian television (on TVK, Channel **FUNCINPEC**, and Channel FARK) or at open-air festivals attended by several thousand and before a Special Film Panel (1993). A 10-day film festival held in October 2000 featured *Shadows Over Angkor* alongside other "fantasy flicks" produced in the late 1960s, including two by Ly Bun Yim: *Sappseth*

(1965), the tragic tale of two birds who suffered a terrifying loss and who plead to the gods for aid, and *Khmers After Angkor* (1971), an examination of Cambodian marriage traditions. The new generation of film makers featured at the festival included Yvon Hem, *Shadow of Darkness* (1988), starring the late **Piseth Pilica**, Panh Rithy, *The Rice People* (1994) and Som Khemara, *Women and Labor* (1999), a fictional account of the trials of an impoverished country woman seeking employment in Phnom Penh. The festival was organized by the cinema department of the Ministry of Culture and Fine Arts to encourage public support of the reemerging national film industry.

FLAGS. The national flag of the Kingdom of Cambodia has a wide, red horizontal field, with a white, three-towered image of **Angkor Wat** in the center, framed by solid blue horizontal bands on the top and bottom. This flag, initially introduced during the colonial era, was used until 1970. All Cambodian flags since the 1940s have carried an image of Angkor Wat. Overlooking the **Khmer Issarak** flag (Angkor Wat in gold, emblazoned on a solid field of red), there have been five state flags: the Kingdom of Cambodia (1953-1970, 1992-the present), the **Khmer Republic** (1970-1975), **Democratic Kampuchea** (1975-1979), the **People's Republic of Kampuchea (PRK)** (1979-1989) and the **State of Cambodia (SOC)** (1989-1992). The **Coalition Government of Democratic Kampuchea,** nominally headed by the deposed Prince **Norodom Sihanouk**, used the same flag as the Kingdom of Cambodia. The Khmer Republic shifted the image of Angkor Wat to the top left hand corner, also adding three stars representing upper, lower and central Khmer populations *(Khmer Leu, Khmer Krom, Khmer Kandal* respectively). The Democratic Kampuchea flag restored the Sihanouk era flag, but without the blue borders and with Angkor Wat in yellow. Under the PRK, the flag carried a revised image of Angkor with five towers, in gold on a red field. Republican opponents of the regime attacked the image as a representation of renewed "Indochinese" unity, the five towers allegedly symbolizing the former territorial components of the French federation. In 1989-1991, as Vietnam withdrew and peace initiatives gathered pace, the new SOC flag restored a three-towered image of Angkor, in white, on background fields of red and blue. This was replaced in 1993 by the royal flag upon royal insistence, the restoration of peace being associated with restoration of monarchy.

FOREIGN INVESTMENT. A law on foreign investment adopted in August 1994 and offering generous concessions and incentives to investors yielded real benefits from 1994 through 1998. In these years total investment averaged $650 million per annum. However, total capital investment fell in 1999 to $480 million, and to $269 million in 2000 while only $56 million dollars was secured in the first half of 2001. In addition to the 1997 currency crisis which has weakened investor confidence everywhere in the Southeast Asian region and in the Cambodian **economy**, all investors, foreign as well as domestic, have been discouraged by the inadequate legal infrastructure, by corruption and by a requirement to deposit a sum equal to 1.2 to 2 percent of the proposed capital investment upon receipt of notification of project approval. It is also the case that Cambodia's once strong competitive advantage in wage costs is being eroded by the falling costs of labor elsewhere in Asian. The largest shares of foreign investment have been attracted by the garment sector, which employs about 150,000 workers in approximately 200 plants, and by tourism. Continuing investment in the increasingly competitive garment sector is assured in large measure by a special Bilateral Textile Agreement signed with the **United States** in December 1998 and renewed in December 2001. It provides for annual increases of from 9 to 18 percent in the U.S. garment import quotas if Cambodia demonstrates compliance with international labor laws, especially "core" norms in relation to workers' rights. While the **ASEAN** countries supplied the largest shares of foreign investment up to 1998, China and other Asian investors are currently the leading foreign investors. In April 2002 a new investment law was approved by the government in draft form. The new law modifies tax incentives for new investors while guaranteeing those already negotiate. The proposed changes are cushioned by a "trigger period" of up to three years or the first year of profit, if earlier, before the reduced tax holiday kicks in. This will be followed by a flat-rate, 20 percent tax on corporate profit. Companies will also be required to obtain annual certification of compliance with national labor laws. The Asian Development Bank estimates that Cambodia needs to secure and to absorb around $250 million in private investment, in addition to current levels of official development assistance, if its economy is to continue to industrialize. Tourism industries and services display steady growth. There were 640,919 visitors in 2001 compared to 466,365 in 2000.

FORESTRY. As recently as 1969, 73 percent of the surface area of Cambodia (13.2 million hectares) was covered with forests but by the early 1990s, when aerial surveying resumed, forested areas amounted to around 35 percent (7.5 million hectares). Rapid, illegal cutting of valuable reserves of teak and other hardwoods began in the 1970s when Thai entrepreneurs took advantage of insecurity in border areas to encroach on Cambodian forests. The closing of the frontiers by the **Democratic Kampuchea** government in 1975 brought timber smuggling to an abrupt halt. Forests continued to receive some protection under the succeeding **People's Republic of Kampuchea** regime, but as Soviet aid faltered and when in 1989 the departure of Vietnamese force followed an agreement between China and the USSR to end their military assistance to their allies, the three Cambodian resistance armies as well as the State of Cambodia army immediately turned to logging activities as a quick source of revenues. Exports of round logs in 1991 and 1992 were estimated at 200,000-400,000 cubic meters per annum. The maximum sustainable level of exports is estimated at 100,000 cubic meters per annum.

Warned by United Nations experts of the dangers to **agriculture** and fishing as a result of deforestation, the government imposed the first of several bans on round log exports in 1992. This and subsequent bans have been ignored with impunity. Regional **Royal Cambodian Armed Forces** commanders, provincial governors and local customs or police officials in areas astride rivers or international frontiers are engaged in the illegal cutting and trafficking of logs as are an estimated 37 timber companies, most based in **Thailand**, Malaysia, Indonesia and Japan. Government revenues from timber totaled around $20 million in 1995 and again in 1996 when the total value of legal and illegal timber exports was estimated at $300 million. Meanwhile the loss of forest cover is blamed for the steady loss of topsoil in hilly regions, falling water levels, the silting of fisheries in the **Tonlé Sap** and fluctuations in seasonal rainfalls compounding problems of water control in agriculture.

FOUR-YEAR PLAN, 1977-1980. A far-reaching economic development document drafted by leading members of the **Communist Party of Kampuchea (CPK)** during secret meetings in August and September 1976. The plan, which was never published, called for a doubling of rice output on a national scale and earmarked income from the sale of surpluses abroad for the purchase of agricultural machinery and fertilizer with which to accelerate agricultural development even further. The aims of the plan were to hasten industrialization and to achieve socialism more quickly than it had been achieved elsewhere. The means for doing so consisted of harvesting three metric tons of paddy from each cultivated hectare, roughly tripling the prerevolutionary national average. Unsurprisingly, this target proved impossible to attain. The plan was poorly conceived and inadequately researched. Its ideas were drawn loosely from Vietnamese and Chinese communist practice, including the disastrous **Great Leap Forward** of 1958-1959. Once conceived the plan fueled excessive expectations and disappointments and then fears and suspicions of betrayal. Shortfalls in planned production meant reductions in supplies of food set aside for consumption, and this led gradually to the deaths of hundreds of thousands from malnutrition, exhaustion and starvation. And while the plan was quietly shelved, thousands of party officials deemed responsible for its implementation, and by extension, its failure, were systematically and violently purged. Those who conceived the plan, foremost Saloth Sar (**Pol Pot**) and **Nuon Chea**, have never publicly acknowledged its glaring defects nor accepted responsibility for the loss of human life, instead attributing failure to the schemes of others who they denounce as "traitors." *See also* AGRICULTURE.

FRANCE. France intervened in Cambodia in the mid-19th century as it sought to protect its imperial interests in Vietnam and to expand them via the **Mekong** River, thought for a time to offer navigable passage to China. Having endured the steady humiliation of dual vassalage and loss of land to succeeding Siamese and Vietnamese rulers, the Khmer Kings **Ang Duang** (r 1848-1860) and his son **Norodom** (r 1860-1904) sought French "protection," initially in exchange for rights of free trade, residence and extraterritoriality. The Siamese court protested but accepted **Battambang** and **Siem Reap** provinces in exchange for abandoning its claims to suzerainty over the entire kingdom. The "lost" provinces were later "returned" in 1907 as a result of French pressure and consolidation of its Union of Indochina. Relying heavily on the institution of monarchy as the moral and administrative focus of colonial administration, France imposed a system of regional *résidents* to oversee trade, to collect taxes and to monitor local developments. Relations with the Khmer court waxed and waned as Norodom, in his later years, grew to resent his loss of sovereign power. Upon his death, France crowned **Sisowath** (r 1904-1927) and **Sisowath Monivong** (r 1927-1941) thereby promoting a schism within the Khmer royal family. King **Norodom Sihanouk** (r 1941-1955), born of a Norodom father and a Sisowath mother was crowned during the Japanese occupation in the bid to ensure that the Khmer nation would remain loyal to France. Deprived of an important symbol of ethnic solidarity and nationhood, the independence struggles launched by **Khmer Issarak** were quickly divided into groups favoring abolition of monarchy, limited monarchy or communist revolution and all of these faced resistance from Francophone elite families who remained staunchly royalist.

The postcolonial Sihanouk regime (1954-1970) was proudly neocolonial. French remained an official language in independent Cambodia. French advisors and *cooperants* (volunteers) held posts in many public services, including the army and national ministries. Refusing to extend full diplomatic recognition either to Sihanouk's **Royal Government of National Union of Kampuchea (GRUNK)** or to **Lon Nol's Khmer Republic**, France gradually saw its political, economic and cultural influence eroded by an expanding **United States** involvement in Cambodia. Although France exploited its historic links with the Khmer monarchy to assist the countries in the **Association of Southeast Asian Nations** and the United Nations to promote a peaceful settlement of the conflict with Vietnam, and has reestablished a large cultural presence since 1991, and enjoys cordial relations with the postcommunist Hun Sen government, its once unchallenged cultural hegemony and political influence in Cambodia has been eclipsed by other powers. *See also* BARDEZ AFFAIR; FRANCO-SIAMESE WAR; FRENCH INDOCHINA; FRENCH "RESIDENTS."

FRANCO-CAMBODIAN TREATY (1949). This treaty negotiated by Prime Minister **Yèm Sambaur** on behalf of King **Norodom Sihanouk** brought an end to the protectorate and awarded Cambodia the status of an "associated state" within the French Union. Phnom Penh received full control of most internal affairs of state, including control of the army, subject to some conditions, and French citizens retained rights of extraterritoriality in criminal matters. The army was to be placed under Union (French) command in times of war, then prevailing, and foreign diplomatic relations with other states were subject to approval by France. The treaty divided the nationalist movement. On the one hand, it helped Yèm Sambaur to persuade some **Khmer Issarak** to lay down their arms, thereby earning him increased favor in the royal court. On the other hand, the **Democrat Party**-dominated **National Assembly** refused to ratify the treaty because it failed to grant full independence and strengthened the alliance between royal and colonial power. In an attempt to assert the principle of democratic accountability to parliament, the Assembly passed a motion of censure against the government. When in response, Sambaur asked the Assembly to withdraw their motion, and the Assembly refused, the king dissolved the Assembly. These developments radicalized many Democrats and deepened opposition to colonialism and monarchy among some Issarak who looked increasingly to **Son Ngoc Thanh** and the **Viet Minh** for support and leadership. *See also* FIRST INDOCHINA WAR; PAU CONFERENCE.

FRANCO-SIAMESE WAR (1940-41). Following the fall of **France** to Germany in June 1940, the nationalist military regime of Field Marshal Phibun in Bangkok made irredentist claims to territory in Cambodia and Laos ceded to France at the turn of the 20th century. Overland military assaults on French positions were successful (Kriangsak, later Prime Minister of Thailand, served in this campaign), but French aircraft scored devastating hits on the Thai navy, prompting the Japanese to mediate the conflict in support of **Thailand**. Thai administrators installed in the reoccupied territories promoted assimilationist policies, introducing Thai language and textbooks in all schools and integrating Buddhist monks into the relevant Thai *sangha*. Although Battambang and Siem Reap were handed back to the French *Protectorat du Cambodge* in 1946, Thailand's actions dealt a serious blow to French power. A victory monument was erected in northern Bangkok.

FRENCH INDOCHINA. The colloquial term for the Union of Indochina formed by **France** in 1887 for the administration of the five colonial territories now known as **Vietnam** (and under the French divided into Tonkin, Annam and **Cochinchina**), Laos and Cambodia. The colonial enterprise obscured and sought to bridge the cultural watershed which separates Indianized Cambodia and Laos from Sinicized Vietnam. The attempt to forge an integrated colonial economy and administration was understandably more popular in Vietnam, than in Cambodia or Laos, because the French governor-general was based in Hanoi and Saigon and his administration became the hub of commercial life and international trade for all five territories. In the 1970s **Pol Pot** and the revolutionary government of **Democratic Kampuchea** viewed Vietnamese revolutionary appeals for eternal solidarity among the three revolutionary peoples of Indochina and proposals for economic cooperation among the three countries with extreme suspicion, fearing the subordination of Cambodia's revolution in a new union. *See also* FRENCH RÉSIDENTS.

FRENCH "RÉSIDENTS." The position of *résident supérieur* in the colonial administration was held by French officials who lived in **Phnom Penh** and "advised" the kings of Cambodia, advice that had to be accepted. While some had little impact on political life, a few had a major impact— either through reforms or through the playing of "court politics." There were also *résidents* in each province who reported to the *résident supérieur*. Among the most prominent were Philippe Hahn, Albert de Verneville, Alexandre Ducos, Paul Luce, Félix Bardez, Jean Risterucci and **Jean de Raymond.** The legacy of the colonial advisory system extends to the present. There are seven official **advisors** appointed to the government and ten appointed to serve the prime minister. *See also* BARDEZ AFFAIR.

FRONT UNI POUR LA LUTTE DES RACES OPPRIMÉES (FULRO). Formed in 1964 in Darlac, Republic of **Vietnam**, to fight for the rights of national minorities in opposition to the communists as well as to the government in Saigon, this movement launched an uprising in the province of **Mondolkiri** in the late 1960s. Allied for a time with paramilitary forces linked to the Khmers du **Kampuchea Krom** and the **Khmer Serei**, FULRO forces fought communist and royalist troops in alliance with the army of the **Khmer Republic**. One FULRO unit believed to have been under the command of General **Les Kosem** was involved in the defense of Phnom Penh. Some 150 of them, with their **Cham** leader Y Bam Enuol and Colonel Y Bun Suor sought refuge in the French Embassy on 17 April 1975, but they were expelled on 20 April and killed later the same day.

FUNAN. Chinese histories dating from the early centuries of the Christian era use this name when refering to a powerful trading kingdom located somewhere on the contemporary Cambodian-Vietnamese coast of the Gulf of Siam. No written records from Funan have survived, but Chinese accounts reveal that it was a prosperous, Indianized kingdom (or group of kingdoms), consisting of several port cities. Excavations in the 1940s at Oc Eo in **Vietnam** indicated the extent of one of these cities and yielded artifacts from as far away as Rome and the Middle East. Some scholars believe "Funan" may be a Chinese transliteration of **Ba Phnom**.

FUNCINPEC. Political party founded at a national congress in 1992 and based on the wartime, royalist resistance movement of the same name (see next entry). From its creation the party has been led by Prince **Norodom Ranariddh**, eldest son of King **Norodom Sihanouk**, honorary head of the party. Officially embracing "Sihanoukism" as an ideology, FUNCINPEC has emphasized classical paternalist themes in all of its campaigns but the attempt to link king, people, safety and well-being has been undermined in recent years by the party's huge shortage of qualified technocrats and administrators to fill high positions. There is also much tension between the royalist veterans of the military struggle and the many overseas supporters of the movement who financed it and who were rewarded by appointments to many senior posts in the government from 1993. FUNCINPEC won the 1993 election, winning 46 percent of the votes and 58 seats in the Constituent Assembly, but this failed to impress alarmed elements in the defeated **Cambodian People's Party (CPP)** who had governed in the former **State of Cambodia**. Led by **Norodom Chakrapong**, they mounted a secessionist rebellion in the eastern region of Cambodia forcing King Sihanouk to propose a power-sharing arrangement involving two prime ministers, two coministers of defense and two coministers of interior. From the beginning the coalition was an uneasy and competitive one. The July 1997 *coup de force* mounted by the Second Prime Minister **Hun Sen** against First Prime Minister Ranariddh forced him and many other leaders of FUNCINPEC to seek temporary refuge abroad. **Ung Huot** was appointed first prime minister in his place and in the run-up to the 1998 elections after which the constitution mandated there should be only one prime minister. Deprived of much military power and patronage FUNCINPEC finished second in the 1998 elections, winning

31.7 percent of votes and 43 Assembly seats (compared to 41.4 percent and 64 for the CPP). Reluctantly, Ranariddh agreed to the formation of a second coalition government, led by **Hun Sen**, in exchange for the post of President of the National Assembly. FUNCINPEC also received 13 ministerial portfolios, one being given to **Norodom Bopha Devi**, the King's oldest daughter and Ranariddh's full sister. The Steering Committee of the party elected at the Congress in March 1999 contained several new members, including **Sisowath Sirirath, Mu Sokhua** and **Khek Vandy**, all longtime royalists who remained loyal to Ranariddh during the 1997 crisis, and some new recruits to the party, notably, **Kem Sokha** and **Pok Than**. The results of the local commune committee elections in 2002 suggest that FUNCINPEC has yet to recover from the effects of defeat and division stemming from the 1997 coup. It ran a weak second to the CPP, winning only 2,182 seats (19 percent) of the available 11,259, compared to 7,721 (69 percent) for Hun Sen's party. It finished third in the competition for commune headships winning only 10 of them, compared to 13 for the **Sam Rainsy Party** and 1,597 for the CPP (with one undecided).

FUNCINPEC: FRONT UNI NATIONAL POUR UN CAMBODGE INDÉPENDENT, NEUTRE, PACIFIQUE ET COOPÉRATIF (NATIONAL UNITED FRONT FOR AN INDEPENDENCE, NEUTRAL, PEACEFUL AND COOPERATIVE CAMBODIA). This was formed in March 1981 in Paris, as a political vehicle for Prince **Norodom Sihanouk** who was president of the movement until 1989. **Nhiek Tioulong** was first vice president; **In Tam** was second vice president and **Chak Saroeun** was secretary-general. In Tam was the movement's first commander-in-chief and with support from leaders of **Molinaka** created the Sihanoukian National Army, in French, *Armée Nationale Sihanoukienne* (ANS). (In 1985 In Tam was replaced as second vice president by the Princess Sihanouk Monique, now Queen **Sihanouk Monineath** and as Commander by Prince **Norodom Ranariddh**.) The front joined the three-part **Coalition Government of Democratic Kampuchea (CGDK)** formed in 1982 with Prince Sihanouk being restored as the nominal head of state in this government-in-exile. The "front" or movement was dissolved in 1992 when the FUNCINPEC was re-established as the FUNCINPEC Party, the acronym becoming a neologism. Throughout the period of temporary United Nations authority, FUNCINPEC was one of the four political groups represented in the **Supreme National Council**, a body designed to embody and to represent Cambodia's national sovereignty during the transition from cease-fire in 1991 to the investiture of the new government in November 1993.

-G-

GARNIER, FRANCIS (1839-1873). A French naval officer, administrator, author and explorer, his dramatic life and death encapsulated the adventure-seeking, romantic phase of French colonialism in Asia. He traveled widely in Cambodia in the early years of the protectorate, and with **Ernest Doudart de Lagrée** led the ill-fated **Mekong** Expedition of 1866, recording his observations in an elegantly written, sumptuously illustrated book. He returned to France and took part in the defense of Paris during the Franco-Prussian war. Back in Indochina, he was killed in 1873 during a flamboyant attempt to recapture the Vietnamese city of Hanoi from irregular Chinese troops.

GENEVA CONFERENCE AND ACCORDS (1954). Convened soon after the French defeat at Dien Bien Phu to arrange a political settlement of the **First Indochina War**, the Cambodian delegation, led by its foreign minister, **Tep Phan**, skillfully resisted pressures to reduce royal sovereignty in the wake of the French withdrawal. Neither the "Khmer-Viet Minh" nor the noncommunist **Khmer Issarak** insurgents were permitted to have temporary regroupment zones (i.e. bases) inside Cambodia, as in Laos and Vietnam. Cambodia agreed to conduct national elections, under international supervision, but these were won by the specially created **Sangkum Reastr Niyum** set up by Prince **Norodom Sihanouk** immediately following his abdication of the throne on 2 March 1955. Away from public view and in violation of the agreements, **Lon Nol** and the army engaged in a campaign against former communist guerrillas.

GENOCIDE IN CAMBODIA. Genocide became an issue in Cambodia when the scale of killings and loss of life in **Democratic Kampuchea (DK)** became known. Estimates of the toll varied between the regime's own admission of "several thousand" mostly unintentional deaths and figures exceeding three million, offered by the Vietnamese-supported **People's Republic of Kampuchea (PRK)** after 1979. It was the PRK which took the lead in accusing the DK leaders of "genocide" and which hastily conducted a show trial in August 1979. In the same period **Vietnam** attempted to link the violence of the **Pol Pot** revolution to "fascist" and "Maoist" ideological impulses rather than implicate Stalinism or socialism. Even so, evidence that specific groups were singled out for elimination, aside from "traitors" allegedly in the hire of foreign enemies or other nonethnic "enemies of the revolution," is both inconclusive and contradictory.

In the 1980s, considerable international pressure was brought to bear on members of the United Nations to bring Pol Pot to trial for genocide, but because Pol Pot had targeted his *political* opponents he was not liable to prosecution under the UN's genocide convention. Independent assessors have further concluded that criminal proceedings for crimes against humanity and for war crimes would produce successful prosecutions. In so far as these investigations focused on a possible prosecution of Pol Pot, DK prime minister and secretary of the ruling **Communist Party of Kampuchea**, they proved fruitless. He eluded those seeking to arrest and indict. Disagreements about what happened in the DK period currently focus less on the death toll arising from the regime policies of collectivization, war and purging, but on the intentions driving the regime so clearly responsible for the policies and the resort to violence. *See also* AUTOGENOCIDE.

GHANTI, ISOUP (1929-1976). From an Indian family long-established in Phnom Penh, Ghanti married Princess Norodom Siddharangsy and joined the Foreign Ministry in the late 1960s being posted to Prague in the spring of 1969. In August 1970 he led a group who "captured" the embassy and proclaimed its support for Prince **Norodom Sihanouk**. Three years later Ghanti was appointed chargé d'affaires for the **Royal Government of National Union of Kampuchea** in Albania, and was their resident representative in Stockholm, Sweden, in 1975. Recalled to Cambodia in September 1976 by the **Democratic Kampuchea** government, he was taken to **Tuol Sleng** upon arrival and executed on 6 December 1976.

GHOSANANDA BHIKKHU (1924-). A native of **Takeo** and the founder of the national walks for peace and reconciliation known as the *Dhammayietra*, he was ordained in the last years of the colonial regime in 1943. His preceptor was *Sangharaja* (Sangha head) **Chuon Nath**. Between 1953 and 1978, he pursued his studies of **Buddhism** with many international teachers and in prestigious institutions and conferences, staying for extended periods in India, Burma, Japan and Thailand. Following the Vietnamese invasion of Cambodia in 1978, he helped refugees seeking sanctuary along the Thai frontier to establish Buddhist temple communities in their holding centers or camps. A cofounder of the interfaith "Mission for Peace" in 1980, he next traveled worldwide, living for a time in the United States promoting ecumenical activities in support of peace in Cambodia and the world. Pope John Paul invited him to attend the first day of prayer for peace in Assisi in 1986. The holder of many honorary titles and awards, Ghosananda Bhikkhu received an honorary doctorate from Providence College in Rhode Island in 1989 and the royal title of *Samdech Preah* (His Holiness) from Prince **Norodom Sihanouk** in 1992. From 1995, recognizing that most casualties in the ongoing, low-intensity war were caused by landmines, he called for a total ban on their production, use and sale. He was nominated by U.S. Senator Claiborne Pell for the Nobel Peace Prize in 1994 (and by others in succeeding years). Should he win the prize, Ghosananda would be the first Cambodian to be so honored by the Nobel Committee.

GOVERNORS (*chauvraykhet*). The governors of provinces and municipalities have traditionally possessed considerable power and autonomy. This localization of power arose from historical practices in relation to royal revenue collection and policing and was reinforced by indirect colonial control of administration outside of the towns in which **French Residents** resided. Most governors were recruited from families with connections either to the Khmer or Thai courts or to the colonial regime. An elite comprised of families with access to both colonial and royal privileges had emerged by the mid-20th century. Many former (and a few current) governors have entries in this dictionary. The established modes of rural powerholdering were radically disrupted in the years from 1975 to the present as governors are now chosen by ruling parties and are increasingly accountable to central ministries. *See also* BAEN.

GREAT LAKE. *See* TONLÉ SAP.

GREAT LEAP FORWARD AND "SUPER GREAT LEAP FORWARD" (*Maha Lout Ploh*). The latter slogan, borrowed from the Maoist canon and associated with economic development policies pursued in the People's Republic of China in 1958-1959, was used by the **Communist Party of Kampuchea (CPK)** leadership to describe its drive for development in 1975-1976. The aims were to achieve a large-scale, modernized agriculture within 20 years for the purpose of promoting industrialization. The Chinese "Great Leap" was a response to severe problems arising from the First Five-Year Plan which concentrated most resources in the industrial sector and inadvertently promoted rapid urbanization and intense pressure on urban food supplies and industrial raw materials. Accelerating the pace of agricultural development was thus essential for multiple reasons, but capital resources, other than labor, were lacking. Labor-intensive strategies involving the mobilization of massive production teams for the construction of huge fields, irrigation networks, dams and roads ensured increases in cereal grain output in some regions, but resistance to the development of communes, and other organizational problems linked to the management of activities on such a large-scale, ensured that the desired windfall harvests remained elusive. Between 20-30 million Chinese died, largely of starvation, as an indirect result of the campaign, which was abandoned without fanfare in 1960. This Chinese example of forced draft collectivization and specialization nevertheless served as a model for Pol Pot's revolution and not in the least because Pol Pot and other CPK leaders were unaware that "the Leap" in China had failed so catastrophically. Indeed, it was only in the 1980s, well after the defeat of the Gang of Four and the toppling of the Pol Pot regime that Chinese and western scholars were able to determine the extent of the disaster in China. *See also* GENOCIDE IN CAMBODIA.

GREENSHIRTS. Organized by **Thiounn Mumm** in 1945, this paramilitary youth movement sought to block French reoccupation of Cambodia following the surrender of the Japanese. It mobilized some 500 students, many drawn from **Lycée Sisowath** and Collège Sihanouk including Prince **Norodom Chantaraingsey, Mey Pho, Oum Mannorine**, Pok Saman, **Sak Suthsakhan** and Savang Vong who later joined the **Khmer Issarak**. Their uniform was made of green fabric, given by **Khim Tith** who purchased a large supply of the cloth from a Kampot merchant. The emergence of the movement, and its rapid demise after the king decided to resume relations with the French, exposed the fragility of the emerging *jeune élite* consensus against colonial rule.

GROSLIER, BERNARD PHILIPPE (1926-1986). French archaeologist and son of **Georges Groslier**. Born in Cambodia, he was educated in France, returning to Cambodia in 1950 with the *École Française d'Extrême-Orient*. In 1959 he was named conservator of the Angkor region. In this role and until 1970, he worked energetically to restore the historic sites and monuments there. By 1970, he directed a thousand laborers and technicians. In the same period, he produced scholarly studies of Angkor in the 16th and 17th centuries, drawing on Spanish and Portuguese archives which had been made available in 1957. In January 1972 soldiers from the **National United Front of Kampuchea** (FUNK) ejected Groslier from Angkor. Moving to Phnom Penh, in 1973 he returned to France where his research focus shifted to Angkorean agriculture. He also published a study of the inscriptions from the 12th-century temple, the Bayon.

GROSLIER, GEORGES (1887-1945). A French archaeologist, he was born in Cambodia, where his father was a colonial civil servant. Groslier studied art in Paris before returning to **French Indochina** in 1912. In 1920 he supervised the construction of the National Museum in Phnom Penh and later organized an affiliated national art school where traditional Cambodian arts were revived and taught. Groslier published widely on classical Khmer art and archaeology and wrote two novels about life in Indochina. For his work in the anti-Japanese resistance in World War II, he was arrested and tortured by the Japanese, dying in captivity in June 1945.

GUIMET MUSEUM (MUSÉE GUIMET). Established at 6 Place d'Iena in Paris in 1889 by the industrialist Emile Guimet (1836-1918), the Guimet specializes in Asian art. Its collection of classical **Khmer** sculpture, including a seventh century **Harihara,** is the largest outside of Cambodia. Closed in 1997 for renovation, French President Jacques Chirac presided at its reopening on 15 January 2001.

-H-

HAK MONG SHENG (1915-1969). A Sino-Khmer politician, he was born at Kampong Trabek, **Prey Veng,** the son of Lim Hak and Mme (née Suon). After completing his baccalaureate, he studied law for two years before entering public service. Among his earliest posts, in the 1940s, he was a district (*srok*) headman in Kampong Cham and a chief clerk in the Ministry of Finance before becoming governor of Stung Treng in 1946. Hak Mong Sheng joined the **Democrat Party** and was secretary of state for finance in the December 1946 to July 1947 Youtévong government. He was elected to the 1947 **National Assembly** in **Kampong Cham** where he acquired a sawmill business and became leader of the Democrat parliamentary group as well as a secretary to the **National Assembly.** Outspoken in his anti-colonial views, Hak Mong Sheng was also deemed to be among the most ardent republicans of his generation. By 1949 French intelligence had identified him as one of the prominent Democrats in touch with **Khmer Issarak** "rebels." Though elected to the Democrat Party Steering Committee in 1950, he was defeated in the 1951 **National Assembly** elections by the Liberal Party candidate in Kampong Trabek, his native village. In 1955, with independence obtained, he left the Democrats to join the royalist **Sangkum.** In common with many other republican activists of late colonial era, however, he devoted himself to business activities. He was president of the economic commission of the Council of the Kingdom, and president of the Timber Exporters' Association. He died on 15 December 1969 at the Calmette Hospital, Phnom Penh.

HANG CHUON. From 1979 until October 1981, he was the administrative officer to **Chan Vèn** who was minister of education in the People's Revolutionary Council (1979-1981) established on 8 January 1979. An advisor to the Ministry of Education by late 1981, he was named deputy-minister of education in the **Chan Si** government in May 1982. In October 1988 he was appointed deputy-minister of culture and information and succeeded **Chheng Phon** as minister in August 1990. On 10 July 1993 he was appointed personal advisor to **Hun Sen** for culture and education and was elected to the **Cambodian People's Party (CPP)** Central Committee. In reward for his long service to the party and its leader, he was appointed to the **Senate** in 1999, being the third-ranked nominee on the CPP list.

HANG PHANN (1909-1972). The son of Hang and Mme (née Puy), Phann was born at Skous, **Kampong Speu**, and studied at the Royal School of Administration. He then worked as a magistrate at the Sala Outor. A councillor of the Sala Outor in **Phnom Penh**, he joined the **Sangkum** and was invited to and ran in the 1958 **National Assembly** elections in **Kratié**. Once in the Assembly, he was vice-president of the Committee for Judicial and Constitutional Affairs. Although reelected in 1962, his bid for a third term in 1966 resulted in a tough contest with two other candidates, both of whom beat him in the polling. He died on 25 September 1972 and was cremated at Wat Langka, Phnom Penh.

HANG SARUN (1914-). A teacher and politician, the son of Keo Hang, he studied at **Lycée Sisowath** (later serving as assistant treasurer of the Alumni Association). He joined the **Khmer Renewal Party** and ran in the 1947 **National Assembly** elections for a seat in Peam Okhna Ong, **Kandal** as well as the seat of Preah Nippean, **Kampong Speu** in 1951. In 1955, after joining the **Sangkum**, he was elected to represent Kok Lak, **Ratanakiri**. From 1958 until 1966 he returned to teaching physical education. In 1966 he was once again elected to the National Assembly in Kok Lak. By 1972 he was a lieutenant colonel in the Republican army and was elected by the Council of the Armed Forces to the **Senate** of the **Khmer Republic** in 1972.

HANG THUN HAK (1926-1975). Prime minister 1972-1973. Born on 2 August 1926 at Prek Kak, **Kampong Cham**, he was the second of six children of Hang Chhin (1898-1970), a farmer, and Mme (née Chheang Chim Say). He studied at **Lycée Sisowath**, being taught and greatly influenced by **Ea Sichau** and making his literary mark at 21 when in 1947 his essay "Koki Komar" was runner-up in a literary competition. Later that year, he went to France to study drama at the Sarah Bernhard École des Comédiens, returning in 1951. He was among the many in his generation to be attracted by the politically dynamic **Son Ngoc Thanh** and accompanied Thanh and Ea Sichau when they slipped into the jungle in March 1952. For the next year, Hang Thun Hak assisted Thanh with information and propaganda work but returned to Phnom Penh in 1954 when other young "progressives," including **Keng Vannsak** and Prince **Norodom Phurissara**, took control of the faltering **Democrat Party**. In the elections in March 1955, dominated by the **Sangkum**, he lost his bid for the **National Assembly** seat of Prek Tameak, **Kandal** province.

Embarking on an academic career, Hang Thun Hak was named dean of Faculty of Fine Arts of the Royal University. He nevertheless continued to support the underground and illegal **Khmer Serei** movement throughout the 1960s and was one of the organizers of the student groups responsible for the sacking of the Vietnamese Embassies in Phnom Penh on 11 March 1970. He also was one of those who persuaded the hesitating **Lon Nol** to throw in his lot with the anti-Sihanoukists on the morning of 18 March 1970. On 2 July 1970 he became minister of community development, a position he held until 5 May 1971 when he was promoted to minister of state for the chair of the Council of Ministers, who was Prince **Sisowath Sirik Matak** then acting prime minister. Hang Thun Hak next accepted a sinecure appointment as assistant to the president for cultural affairs. As a former Democrat, a leading Buddhist and somebody who had retained links with some socialist Cambodians, he was drawn into a scheme to introduce a Soviet-backed peace settlement involving the organization of a pro-Moscow Communist Party (the "**Third Force**"), ultimately controlled by **Lon Non**. This party failed to materialize, possibly because it had no hope of success.

Desiring access to power, Hang Thun Hak and his supporters joined the new **Socio-Republican Party** of Lon Nol, forming its Dangrek faction. At the first Party Congress on 9 July 1972 he was elected to the 20-man Central Committee receiving more votes than any other candidate. With backing from Keng Vannsak and Son Ngoc Thanh, he became secretary-general of the party and led the Socio-Republican Party to victory in the September 1972 National Assembly elections against a token opposition. After Thanh tendered his resignation, Hang Thun Hak assumed the prime ministership on 17 October 1972.

As prime minister, Hang Thun Hak's primary, and somewhat ironic, mission was to reach a compromise with Sihanouk and the **Royal Government of National Union of Kampuchea (GRUNK)**. His faction of the Socio-Republican party still hoped, out of step with the realities of the Sino-Soviet split, that the Soviet Union, acting in concert with a moderate prime minister, might cut short the civil war with other communists. Although the GRUNK never included Hang Thun Hak among the "super-traitors" in the Republic, they nevertheless responded contemptuously to his attempts to arrange a political settlement as the **Khmer Republic** was clearly losing the war. It was in other ways also a difficult moment to be prime minister. Violent clashes among Cambodian students in Paris and continuing student protests in Phnom Penh resulted in strong-arm tactics by Lon Non and retaliation in the form of the **So Photra** incident on 18 March 1973. With his government also scandalized by mounting allegations of corruption, Hak finally, at the behest of the **United States**, sacked or retired most of the advisors to Lon Nol, over a hundred of whom were drawing cabinet salaries. A month later, on 17 April 1973 Hang Thun Hak himself resigned his premiership, handing over to **In Tam**.

For the next two years Hang Thun Hak remained outside the cabinet and attempted to regain his position in the Socio-Republican Party which had slowly fallen under the domination of Lon Non. Promoted initially in the expectation that his progressive background would facilitate a peace settlement, Hang Thun Hak failed in the end to broker a settlement. He faded from mainstream political life, reappearing only briefly as acting prime minister during **Long Boret**'s absence from Phnom Penh in early 1975 and as deputy prime minister in charge of political affairs and special missions on 21 March 1975, an appointment which terminated with the establishment of the Supreme Committee by **Sak Suthsakhan** on 12 April. He was the Socio-Republican Party representative in the committee. Remaining in Phnom Penh, he was seized at Vat Katt on 17 April 1975. He is presumed to have been killed later the same day.

HARIHARA. An Indian divinity, popular in pre-Angkorean and Angkorean Cambodia, who was believed to be the offspring of Shiva from a marriage with a female incarnation of Vishnu. Representations of this deity blended iconographic characteristics of Shiva and Vishnu.

HARIHARALAYA. In honor of the deity **Harihara,** this name was given by the first Angkorean kings to their capital, located near present-day Roluos in **Siem Reap**. The capital was moved to the vicinity of Phnom Bakheng under King **Yasovarman I** (r 889-910).

HARSHAVARMAN I. King of Cambodia 910-c923 and a close relative of **Yasovarman I**. He left no inscriptions, but the small temple of Baksei Chamkrong, near **Phnom Bakheng**, has been dated to his reign. It was likely the funerary temple for his parents.

HARSHAVARMAN II. King of Cambodia 942-945 and a son of **Jayavarman IV**. His short, apparently turbulent, reign at Koh Ker is poorly documented. He was succeeded by his cousin, **Rajendravarman II**.

HARSHAVARMAN III. King of Cambodia 1066-c1080. Brother and successor of **Udayadityavarman II**, his reign was marked by warfare with the neighboring kingdom of **Champa** and ended with a revolt. He was succeeded by **Jayavarman VI**.

HELL SUMPHA (1921-1971). Born on 23 April 1921 at Phsar Krom, **Pursat**, he taught at **Lycée Sisowath** and then worked in the Ministry of

Education. In 1962 he was elected as the **Sangkum** candidate to the **National Assembly** to represent **Siem Reap**, briefly serving as secretary of state in the Ministry of Social Action and Labor. In 1966, when the Sangkum did not endorse candidates, he was not reelected but was appointed as a judge at the Court of Appeals (*Sala Vinichhay)* and editor of the official weekly *Neak Cheat Niyum.* The author of seven books, and a former president of the Khmer Writers' Association, he was among the more prominent members of the **constitutional drafting committee** established in June 1971, but he died prematurely on 4 September 1971, a death perhaps hastened by the deadlock in debate over the constitution.

HEM CHIAM ROEUN (1910-1975). Born on 10 June 1910 in **Phnom Penh**, the son of Hem Som and Mme (née Suos Im), Hem Chiam Roeun studied agricultural and forestry sciences at the University of Hanoi and was an inspector of forests and waterways in the service of the French protectorate. In 1936, he assisted **Son Ngoc Thanh** with the publication of *Nagaravatta.* Partly because of his nationalist standpoint, he was appointed head of the National Forests and Waterways Service following the Japanese coup of 9 March 1945. Between July and September, and upon instruction from Son Ngoc Thanh, he quietly secured arms from the Japanese for a militia — some 30 pistols and 10,000 cartridges. Following the return of the French, he joined the **Democrat Party** and worked as director of the office of Prince **Sisowath Youtévong,** leader of the party. He was accordingly among the prominent Democrats implicated in the **Black Star Affair** and was imprisoned in Saigon for eight months from February 1947. Once back in Phnom Penh, in 1948, he was appointed chief clerk to the president of the Council of Ministers. Although French intelligence reports from this period accuse him of engaging in black market sales of cotton yarns diverted from state warehouses, he was once again named head of the Department of Waterways and Forests in 1949. By 1951 he had left active politics to become a prominent businessman in Phnom Penh.

In 1955 Hem Chiam Roeun was commissioner-general of the International Exhibition of Phnom Penh (being sentenced, in December 1959, to a suspended sentence of one year for being implicated in the disappearance of 18 million riels) and in 1963 was the president of the committee for the study of watercourses and bridge construction on the road over the **Cardamom Mountains**, which reported to the secretary of state for agriculture. He was director of political and economic affairs at the Ministry of Foreign Affairs and director of the National Tourism Office. He married Ouk Dakpeav (sister of Mme **Huy Mong**) and they had nine children including Tong who married Prince Sisowath Kossorak, son of

King **Monivong** and Khun Meak, first cousin of **Pol Pot**). During the Lon Nol period, Hem Chiam Roeun plunged into politics again. He joined the **Socio-Republican Party** and won a seat in the **Senate** in October 1972. He is believed to have died soon after April 1975.

HEM CHIEU, *Achar* (1898-1943). Born in Ponhea Lu, Kandal, he was a Buddhist monk, at Wat Onalom, and a teacher of Pali at the School of Pali in **Phnom Penh** as well as a leading opponent of French colonialism. A close associate of **Son Ngoc Thanh** and **Pach Chhoeun**, he helped organize demonstrations in Phnom Penh in July 1942. These led to his arrest and evacuation to Saigon where he was charged with preaching treasonous sermons to the Cambodian militia. The French arrest, indeed, snatching of a serving monk, who was seen by the Sangha and the lay Buddhist community as immune from secular prosecution, sparked the 20 July 1942 anti-French demonstration in Phnom Penh. By the late 1940s this event was identified as the beginning of Khmer militancy in the struggle for independence. Imprisoned on the island of **Poulo Condore**, Chieu died there on 2 October 1943. In commemoration of their first martyr, underground communist revolutionaries celebrated *Achar* Hem Chieu's birthday from 1949 onward and, on 11 June 1950, a **Viet Minh** cadre training camp in the southeastern region near Hatien was given the name Achar Hem Chieu School. In the **People's Republic of Kampuchea** period, his name was given to the downtown portion of the wide and gracious street known in the 1960s as Boulevard Charles de Gaulle.

HEM KETH SANA (1924-1975). The man who tried, in 1972-1973, to persuade the **National United Front of Kampuchea (FUNK)** to compromise with **Lon Nol**, Hem Keth Sana was born on 19 March 1924 in **Phnom Penh**. He studied at the Royal School of Administration in 1946 and afterward worked in the provincial administration, starting as Commissioner of Police in Siem Reap. In 1952 while district headman of Kampong Trabek, he withstood a blistering verbal attack from **Hoeur Lay Inn** who accused him of corruption in the **National Assembly**. He joined the **Sangkum** only in 1958, before gaining a law degree from the Royal University in 1964. Briefly director-general in the Ministry of the Interior in 1962, he was first deputy to the Royal Delegate to Phnom Penh in 1963, chief of the public relations bureau of the head of state in 1965, and under-secretary of state for the interior in 1966. Governor of Svay Rieng 1968 until July 1970, Keth Sana was named in the National Assembly several times for failing to curtail smuggling in the province. He was ambushed by the **Viet Cong** in early 1970 and helped organize the initial demonstrations on 10 March which cleared the way for those that led to the overthrow of Prince **Norodom Sihanouk** on the 18th. Commissioned as a general by the Lon Nol government, he was director-general in the Ministry of Trade which he represented on the 1971 **constitutional drafting committee**; minister attached to the prime minister's office in the **Hang Thun Hak** government, October 1972 to April 1973; minister of the interior and religion in 1973 and then minister of state for negotiations and peace, the post in which he was seen to fail. As the Republic neared defeat, Keth Sana returned to the cabinet as minister of state in Prime Minister **Long Boret**'s cabinet, March to April 1975.

His son, Hem Keth Dara (c1950-1975), a student activist and associate of **Lon Non**, seized the political initiative on 17 April 1975 when he and some friends dressed in militia gear resembling that worn by the FUNK forces. Proclaiming themselves to be leaders of an unknown national movement, Monatio, they attempted to take power before the communists. Keth Dara was captured and both he and Keth Sana are believed to have been summarily executed.

HEM KHAN (1951-   ). Born at Ang Snuol, Kandal. he studied medicine 1970-1975 and spent the period of **Democratic Kampuchea** in the countryside. After the collapse of the Democratic Kampuchea administration in 1979, he became district chief in Kong Pisey and was secretary of the **People's Revolutionary Party of Kampuchea (PRPK)** in **Kampong Speu** by June 1986, chairman of the People's Committee of the province and a member of the Central Committee of the PRPK and then the **Cambodian People's Party (CPP)**. In May 1993 he was elected to the Constituent Assembly on the CPP list in Kampong Speu and in October joined the Commission for Finance and Banking. He was reelected to the **National Assembly** in 1998.

HEM SAVANG. The son of Hing Hem, Hem Savang was a clerk in the postal service in 1945. A promoter of the attempted coup on 9 August, Savang was one of the seven officials who stormed into the royal palace to force the ministers to resign and the King to impose a fully independent government under **Son Ngoc Thanh**'s leadership. Arrested two days later by Prince **Sisowath Monireth**, he was sentenced to 15 years hard labor, but in December 1945 escaped from jail, fled to Vietnam and received military training from **Viet Minh** forces in **Cochinchina**. Returning to Cambodia via Bangkok where he stayed with **Poc Khun**, Savang was a member and a military instructor with the first **Khmer Issarak** Committee in **Battambang**, formed in March 1946 and by December 1946, commander of 180 Issaraks at Sisophon. On 14 September 1947 he attended a meeting of the Southeast Asia League promoted by Pridi Banomyong at which he was chosen to head the Cambodian section of the League. From 1948 he was a member of the National Liberation Committee of the Issarak movement with responsibility for foreign relations. Meanwhile, he replaced **Dap Chhuon** as commander of Issarak forces in Surin. As his liaison work with Bangkok grew, so did his pro-Viet Minh sympathies by some accounts. For this reason, as well as personal rivalry, he was likely assassinated by Dap Chhuon in July 1949. A conflicting account alleges he sought refuge in Thailand. For whatever reason, his revolutionary career ended abruptly without a trace.

HENG PICH (?-1977). A Sino-Khmer and career soldier who studied for a period in Moscow, he was a general in the Royal Armed Forces who remained loyal to **Norodom Sihanouk** after the *coup d'état* of 18 March 1970. Initially attached to Sihanouk's staff in Beijing, Pich was a member of the Central Committee of the **National United Front of Kampuchea** formed in May 1970 and deputy minister of military supplies in the **Royal Government of National Union of Kampuchea**. Having joined the secret **Communist Party of Kampuchea (CPK)** under the tutelage of **Ieng Sary**, Pich returned secretly to the liberated areas of Cambodia in 1974. After 17 April 1975, he was assigned to B1, the Foreign Ministry of **Democratic Kampuchea (DK)** headed by Ieng Sary where he was known by his party name, Chhân. Concerned from the first that CPK policies were not effective, he criticized leading cadres in the ministry for relying on organizational rather than ideological methods in responding to problems. In late 1976, when cadres with past connections to Moscow fell under suspicion of working for the KGB, he was accused of economic sabotage, arrested on 18 December 1976 and taken to **Tuol Sleng**. In a statement he made under duress in January 1977, shortly before his execution, Heng Pich confessed to not believing party assurances that the DK system of agricultural cooperatives was "evolving well." The reality as he saw it was that ordinary people suffered greatly from food shortages and poor health while authoritarian cadres turned a blind eye and ate too well.

HENG SAMKAI né **Heng Samheum (1930-).** Born in Svay Rieng province according to an official election poster from 1981 but in a family from Ponhea Krek district of **Kampong Cham**, he is the oldest brother of **Heng Samrin**. While a small boy "in a large family of poor peasants" in Kampong Cham, he studied in a Buddhist wat school and later became a monk. He joined the underground communist movement in 1955, the year his father died and assisted the **Khmer People's Revolutionary Party** in their "revolutionary struggles against American imperialist aggressors and their valets." His village, Anlung Krek, was one of the two eastern zone underground base areas of the party after 1954 and throughout the postcolonial Sihanouk and republican periods. It is likely that he, together with **Chea Sim**, recruited his younger brothers into the communist movement first as couriers for the party and then as members. He appears to have defected from **Pol Pot**'s party center in the course of the Eastern Zone crisis of May 1978.

After 7 January 1979 Samkai was appointed chairman of the People's Revolutionary Committee of **Svay Rieng** province, a post equivalent to the governorship in the **People's Republic of Kampuchea (PRK)**. He also won a seat in the PRK **National Assembly** for Svay Rieng province in May 1981, participated in the December 1981 founding congress of the **People's Revolutionary Party of Kampuchea (PRPK)** and was PRPK party secretary in Svay Rieng province and a member of the Central Committee of the Party from 1986. He appears to have given up his Assembly seat in 1989, and though he was officially designated governor of Svay Rieng province in 1992, he was replaced in this role in 1994 and thereafter politically marginalized.

HENG SAMRIN (1934-). Head of state 1979-1991. Born on 25 May 1934 in Anlung Krek, Ponhea Krek district, **Kampong Cham**, Heng Samrin gradually engaged in revolutionary activities as he grew up, following the lead of his older brother **Heng Samkai**, finally becoming a full member of the **Khmer People's Revolutionary Party (KPRP)** in 1959. When his clandestine activities were exposed in the aftermath of the 1967 **Samlaut Uprising**, Samrin went into hiding in the forest together with **Chea Sim**. The following year, he was made commander of a battalion of **Communist Party of Kampuchea** troops. He received a regimental command in 1970 when he fought in southeastern Cambodia and was commander of the Fourth Division of the People's National Liberation Armed Forces, Commander of the Eastern Zone military region and a member of the Eastern Zone party committee headed by So Phim.

By 1978 Heng Samrin was the fifth highest ranking CPK cadre in the Eastern Zone of **Democratic Kampuchea (DK)**. Under threat as a result of Pol Pot's purges and the resulting suicide of Phim, Samrin defected to Vietnam on 25 May 1978 where together with 14 others, he worked with the Vietnamese Communist Party to organize a **United Front for the National Salvation of Kampuchea (UFNSK)**. As the senior defector Heng Samrin was named chairman of the Front at its foundation meeting on 2 December 1978. Just over one month later, he was named chairman of the interim People's Revolutionary Council, the government established by the UFNSK on 8 January 1979 and which administered the country until 2 July 1981. In December 1981 he was elected general-secretary of the new **People's Revolutionary Party of Kampuchea (PRPK)**, replacing the ousted **Pen Sovan,** and his leading role was confirmed by his appointment as chairman of the Council of State of the **People's Republic of Kampuchea** from 1981-1993. His role and influence in the party-state waned after 1986 by which time the more reform-oriented **Hun Sen** had left the foreign ministry to become prime minister and a key player in international negotiations. In October 1991, when the PRPK officially abandoned Marxism-Leninism, laid down the party secretariat and changed its name to the **Cambodian People's Party,** Heng Samrin was eased to the sidelines as honorary party president while Chea Sim and Hun Sen were elected party chairman and deputy party chairman respectively. Following King **Norodom Sihanouk**'s reascension to the throne, Heng Samrin was awarded the royal title of Samdech and joined the multiparty privy council of the king. In both 1993 and 1998 Heng Samrin was elected to the **National Assembly** in his native province of Kampong Cham. He continues to play an active role in public life as a royal **advisor** and as first vice-president of the 11-person, Standing Committee of the Assembly which is chaired by **Norodom Ranariddh.**

HENG VONG BUNCHHAT. Son of Tan Chin Hoc, Bunchhat studied law and political science in Paris, completing a thesis on the institution of the national congresses in 1970. He was dean of the Law Faculty in Phnom Penh until 1975, when he returned to France and acquired French nationality, essential for employment in French universities. He was an associate professor in the Law Faculty at Toulouse when he became vice-president of the **Liberal Democratic Party (LDP)** of **Sak Suthsakhan** and agreed to direct the party's election campaign 1992-1993. However when the LDP failed to win any seats in the 1993 elections, he joined the **Cambodian People's Party** and was appointed deputy minister of higher education and technical training and served as an **advisor** to the committee selected by the Constituent Assembly to draft the **Constitution of Cambodia**, from June to August 1993. Although named secretary of state for justice and a legal advisor to Hun Sen on 19 July 1993, he resigned these posts in February 1994 and joined the royalist **FUNCINPEC** party becoming a legal advisor to Prince **Norodom Ranariddh.** He was reappointed secretary of state for justice in 1995 and worked in the ministry throughout 1996. Bunchhat's brother, Heng Vong Boun Chhoeut, married Princess Norodom Soriya Roeungsey, a daughter of King **Norodom Sihanouk.**

HIGH COUNCIL OF THE KINGDOM. This was the upper, consultative house in Cambodia from 1948 until the promulgation of the Republican constitution by President **Lon Nol** in 1972. Two members were appointed by the king from among members of the royal family and the rest were elected by restricted or direct suffrage to represent other designated constituencies. The **National Assembly** was permitted to elect two members, with the municipality of **Phnom Penh**, the civil service and the chamber of commerce were permitted to elect others. Those representing provincial administrators were elected by **governors** and their councils. The High Council of the Kingdom met in annual session in tandem with the National Assembly, being given the chance to express its opinion on all bills and on the budget following their introduction and first reading in the lower house. If the Council sought to amend something, it would be sent back to the Assembly which was obliged to look at it again and to decide on the proposed changes. If the Council had no opinion, or was in agreement, the bill adopted by the National Assembly became law. If the Council rejected a bill from the Assembly, the **constitution** stipulated that the National Assembly could not debate the matter again for two months (or one month for the budget). In practice, this rarely happened.

HIGH COUNCIL OF THE THRONE. Although not mentioned in the 1947 and 1953 **constitutions** which departed from the traditions of absolute monarchy, the throne council was a traditional advisory body to the king. During the 1950s and 1960s it was headed by a trusted member of the royal family, and its four other members, who were usually former government officials, were appointed by Prince **Norodom Sihanouk**. Its main role was to advise Sihanouk on ministerial decrees and regulations. The High Council of the Throne went into abeyance on 18 March 1970 and was abolished in October 1970. Sihanouk revived it on an unconstitutional basis, in 1993, initially restoring four former **advisors** to their positions of favor: **Nhiek Tioulong** (now deceased), **Son Sann** (deceased), **Ngo Hou, Chau Sen Cocsal**. He also appointed a Military Council initially comprised of **Oum Mannorine, Buor Hell, Teap Baen** (deceased), **Sak Suthsakhan** (deceased). With due regard for the **FUNCINPEC-Cambodian People's Party (CPP)** coalition, several CPP dignitaries, including **Heng Samrin, Say Phuthang, Chea Soth, Bou Thang, Mat Ly, Pung Peng Cheng** and his son, Prince **Norodom Yuvaneath** were included among the high privy counselors of the king.

HIGH COURT OF JUSTICE. Established by the 1947 **constitution**, this court functioned as the supreme court until 1972. It had five judges: two chief magistrates, an additional one elected by the **National Assembly** and two further members elected by the **High Council of the Kingdom**. As the highest court in the land, it had primary jurisdiction in cases involving treason and constitutional rights and heard appeals from lower courts on all other matters.

HIGH POLITICAL COUNCIL. This political body was organized at American urging on 23 April 1973 in a vain attempt to promote greater unity of purpose among the four major politicians in the fractious **Khmer Republic**: **Cheng Heng**, **In Tam**, **Sisowath Sirik Matak** and **Lon Nol**. It failed to promote policy consensus or to reduce political infighting.

HIM CHHEM (1939-   ). Born in Romeas Hek, **Svay Rieng**, he was a teacher who after surviving **Democratic Kampuchea** worked in the culture and information office of the **People's Republic of Kampuchea (PRK)** from 1979. He was PRK deputy minister of culture 1980-1993. In June 1993 he was elected to the Constituent Assembly for Svay Rieng on the **Cambodian People's Party** list. In October of that year Chhem was appointed to the Commission for Education, Religion, Culture and Tourism. In 1998 he was reelected to the **National Assembly** in Svay Rieng.

HINDUISM/HINDUIZATION. Hindu religious and political traditions arrived in the land of the Khmer in pre-Angkorean times, and by the sixth century AD were firmly established. There was much creative blending with local transitions and syncretism. The Hindu deity Siva was associated closely with local ancestor spirits, and for several centuries Vishnu and Siva were merged into the unique, very popular divinity **Harihara**. The caste system of ancient India possessed substantially less appeal than its gods. Brahmans in Angkorean courts often married women from non-Brahmanic backgrounds, and while there were distinctive social levels of unequal social and moral worth, there were no untouchables and no genuine *varna* developed. Arguably, the most enduring impact of Hinduism was its indelible imprint on Khmer conceptions of kingship, the state and administration as well as epic literature, architecture, and agrarian technologies. Sanskrit writing was adapted for the writing of Khmer, originally an exclusively oral vernacular. When Theravada **Buddhism** spread into Cambodia in the 14th and 15th centuries, Hinduism rapidly lost much of its moral and practical centrality, largely because royal patronage was withdrawn and concentrated elsewhere. Elements of Shivaism survived in Khmer court rituals as late as the 1950s.

HING KUNTHEL (1927-). Born on 28 November 1927 at Suong, Thbaung Khrun, **Kampong Cham**, son of Hing Duong, *mékhum* of Suong, and Mme (née Sim Kim Heng), Kunthel graduated from **Lycée Sisowath**. Awarded a government scholarship he then studied in France where he was a student in the Faculty of Law, University of Paris, 1949-1955 and in the Institute of Juridical Sciences and Applied Finance, 1955-1956. Once back in Cambodia he taught history and geography at Lycée Sisowath and worked in the general directorate of the **National Bank of Cambodia**. A member of the **Sangkum**, he was elected to the 1958 **National Assembly** in Chup, Kampong Cham, and was reelected in 1962. He was appointed secretary of state for national defense under **Sim Var**, April to June 1958, before being named minister of finance in the first **Lon Nol** government 1966-1967. From 1970 he served as governor of the National Bank. In 1980 he was living in Paris.

HING KUNTHUON (1932-). A statistical engineer and a prominent early supporter of the **Khmer People's National Liberation Front (KPNLF)**, Kunthuon was born in **Kampong Cham** and graduated from the Royal University with a degree in law in March 1963. By 1975 he was chairman of the board of directors of the *Banque Khmère pour le Commerce*. He lived in the countryside during the **Democratic Kampuchea** period but fled to Thailand in 1979 where he joined the general staff of the **Khmer People's National Liberation Armed Forces** being given responsibility for civilian affairs inside Cambodia. Among the grassroots, frontline critics of the KPNLF president, **Son Sann**, Kunthuon was a member and promoter of the Provisional Central Committee for the Salvation of the KPNLF formed in Bangkok in December 1985. He was subsequently expelled from the KPNLF by Son Sann in February 1986 and now lives in France.

HING SOKHOM (1935-1976). An American-educated academic, he was teaching economics at the State University of New York at Stony Brook, when he chose to return to **Democratic Kampuchea** in September 1976. Upon arrival at Pochentong Airport, he was taken to Talay reeducation camp where he was arrested and sent to S-21, today known as **Tuol Sleng**. He was executed on 6 December 1976 after being forced to write multiple reports on his allegedly subversive activities in the **United States** in collaboration with alleged U.S. CIA agents who included Don Luce and Cora Weiss, two well-known critics of the U.S. foreign policies and intelligence operations as well as **Son Ngoc Thanh**. In October 1970 Sokhom joined the **National United Front of Kampuchea (FUNK)** via **Ok Sakun** who headed the FUNK office in Paris and **Thiounn Mumm** who then worked in Beijing. From then and until his departure in 1976 Sokhom was the principal spokesman for the Group of Khmer Residents in America (GKRAM), a group created to lend support to the deposed Prince **Norodom Sihanouk**, his **Royal Government of National Union of Kampuchea (GRUNK)** in exile and its military wing, the FUNK which was supported by liberal intellectuals of the 1950s and 1960s. With support from Reverend Luce, many early GKRAM meetings were held in New York's Washington Square Methodist Church. Sokhom Hing's activism stemmed from his student activism in **Phnom Penh**. He met **Ieng Sary** in

1949-1950 during his first year at **Lycée Sisowath** and from 1952 became friends with **Chhorn Hay**, also at Sisowath. In 1957-1958, while waiting for his scholarship from the **United States**, he taught briefly at **Kambuboth** high school. After finishing his BA in 1962 he planned to return to Cambodia, in 1963, but Sihanouk's repression of progressive movements in that year, and Ieng Sary's disappearance in particular, frightened him off. Deeply engaged in the study of Cambodia's developmental problems in spite of his long absence from the country, he did not see much of his homeland before his death.

HING UN (1927-). After graduating from the Faculty of Agronomy at Gembloux, Belgium, he worked as an engineer in the Ministry of Agriculture from 1965 and represented this Ministry on the **constitutional drafting committee** of 1971 by which time he was Dean of the Faculty of Agriculture. In October 1973 he and his wife, Chheang Neang Touch, a teacher of literature at the Faculty of Pedagogy, announced their support for the **National United Front of Kampuchea (FUNK)**. Hing Un then succeeded **In Sokan** as chair of the FUNK Committee in Paris. In 1977 he was among those who welcomed returnees to **Democratic Kampuchea (DK)** and who worked at the Boeung Trabek indoctrination and rehabilitation center. In April 1979 he attended a conference in Stockholm along with Sam San, a former DK ambassador to **Laos**. He was briefly minister-advisor at the Mission of Democratic Kampuchea at the United Nations in New York but on 23 July 1980 he was appointed ambassador of the **Coalition Government of Democratic Kampuchea (CGDK)** to Senegal and Mauritania, to Togo in 1982, the Gambia in 1983, Gabon and Liberia in 1985 and later Sierra Leone, Nigeria and Cameroon. He continued to represent the CGDK abroad throughout the 1980s and in November 1992 was among the founding members of the National Unity Party which was formed by **Khieu Samphan** just weeks before the **Party of Democratic Kampuchea** withdrew from the United Nations-sponsored election process.

HO CHI MINH TRAIL. This was a network of paths and roads through Laos and northeastern Cambodia which were built by the armed forces of the Democratic Republic of **Vietnam** to infiltrate men and military equipment into southern Vietnamese battle zones. In use from 1960-1975, initial construction on a north-south supply route was authorized by the Central Committee of the Vietnamese Workers' Party in May 1959. Work on what was initially only a footpath was underway by the end of the year. Passage into Laos occurred at three points, the Mu Gia Pass, the Ban Karai Pass and the Ban Raying Pass, all just north of the demilitarized zone at the 17th parallel. Exits south of the parallel through Cambodia into Vietnam led to depots and safe areas in all regions of the U.S.-supported Republic of Vietnam.

Aerial interdiction of these supply lines began in 1964 when truck convoys were bombed occasionally by the Royal Laotian Air Force. U.S. air raids began in 1965, rising from an average of 25 per day in that year to more than 200 sorties per day in 1967 and 1968. By 1970-1971, anti-aircraft weapons installed along "the trail" and its side routes greatly limited the impact of U.S. air strikes, some mounted by B-52s but most by fixed wing aircraft and helicopter gunships. Between January 1970 and April 1971, self-declared U.S. Air Force losses came to 65 aircraft. In this same period, U.S. military sources claimed less than one half of the supplies shipped via the trail were being delivered and that the volume of supplies reaching the south was inadequate for a successful war effort. This was a misjudgment, most fundamentally of the character of the war.

Because of the heavy Vietnamese use of the Ho Chi Minh Trail and Cambodian sanctuaries associated with it, border disputes erupted between the **Democratic Kampuchea** government and Vietnam from as early as 1973, intensifying after 1975 and resulting in military conflict along the border from early 1977. The intense nationalism of the **Pol Pot** generation of revolutionaries associated with Vietnamese wartime use of Cambodian territory and postwar land-grabbing along the border by Vietnamese peasants were viewed as manifestations of a long historical process of "annexing" Cambodia as well as a desire by the Vietnamese communists to create a new Indochina Federation. Moreover, the Vietnamese intervention in Laos in 1977 was facilitated by the existence of the Ho Chi Minh Trail network. Cambodian perceptions of the Vietnamese as "historic" actors were matched by Vietnamese perceptions of the Cambodians as agents of the Chinese. Knowledge of the terrain in eastern Cambodian greatly facilitated Vietnam's invasion and occupation from December 1978.

HO NON also **Ho Naun (1947-   ).** A leading politician, she once was a textile engineer, receiving her professional training during the **Democratic Kampuchea (DK)** period. In 1979-1983, she was deputy director of finance and deputy director of the textile plant in **Battambang**. In 1984-1985 she was deputy governor of the province, or in the terminology of the **People's Republic of Kampuchea,** deputy chair of the province's People's Revolutionary Committee. Elected to the Central Committee of the **People's Revolutionary Party of Kampuchea (PRPK)** at its 5th Congress in 1985, she held a number of cabinet posts under Hun Sen. Ho Naun was a deputy minister attached to the Council of Ministers in 1985-1986 and minister of trade from September 1986 until August 1988 when she received the portfolio for industry. After 1993 Ho Naun worked as an **advisor** to second Prime Minister **Hun Sen**. In this capacity she was elected to the CPP Central Committee in 1997. Her absence from the Central Committee after the restructuring of the PRPK in 1991, plus her high appointments from 1979, indicate close family or historical connections to Vietnamese trained communists. In 1998 she was elected to the **National Assembly** on the CPP list in **Kandal** province.

HO SOK (1958-1997). A colonel in the royalist **National Army for an Independent Kampuchea (ANKI)**, he was appointed secretary of state in the Ministry of Interior in 1995. He gained some prominence as an opponent of **Hun Sen** partly for his criticism of official corruption and drug-trafficking. In July 1997 he was one of the principal targets of Hun Sen's *coup de force* against First Prime Minister **Norodom Ranariddh**. Captured early on the morning of 6 July while trying to escape from Phnom Penh, he was taken to the Interior Ministry where he was shot at point blank range allegedly while under interrogation. His is the only murder of an opponent that Hun Sen acknowledges to have occurred during the weeks of violence surrounding Ranariddh's flight into temporary exile. Nobody has been arrested for this murder, presumably witnessed by many. Estimates of the total number of high-ranking opposition personalities assassinated between July-September 1997 range from 80 to more than 100.

HO TONG HO (1918-1977). Born on 2 August 1918 at Ponlei, **Battambang**, he was the son of Ho Bun Dos and Mme (née Thap Prang). **Ho Tong Lip** is his brother. Tong Ho completed a teacher training course in St. Cloud, France, in 1948-1949 and became inspector of primary teaching in Battambang. In 1951 he was a member of Prince **Sisowath Monipong**'s delegation which met **Keo Tak**. In 1971 Tong Ho was appointed to the **constitutional drafting committee** to represent teachers. He remained in Battambang after 17 April 1975 but was arrested on 3 October 1977 and executed at **Tuol Sleng** soon after.

HO TONG LIP (1920-1978). The second son of Ho Bun Dos and Mme (née Thap Prang), and brother of **Ho Tong Ho**, Tong Lip studied in **France** 1946-1952, earning his *Licence-ès-Sciences* and a diploma in agronomy at Nancy University. On his return he was an agricultural engineer in the Ministry of Agriculture and taught in the Faculty (later University) of Agricultural Sciences. A supporter of the 18 March 1970 overthrow of Prince **Norodom Sihanouk**, he criticized the prince for his inadequate grasp of rural development problems and his superficial attempts to promote agricultural development via slogans and campaigns. In June

1971 Ho Tong Lip represented the Agriculture Ministry in the **constitutional drafting committee.** He became an **advisor** to **Lon Nol** in the following year. After 1975, his private library was among the primary resources of the Institute of Technology established by the **Democratic Kampuchea** government under the direction of **Thiounn Mumm.** For part of the 1975-1978 period, Tong Lip was in charge of rice seed development and selection at an experimental station near Phnom Penh. He died of illness in 1978.

HOEUR LAY INN (1922-   ). One of the more outgoing politicians during the **Khmer Republic,** Hoeur Lay Inn was the son of Hoeur Chay Eng and Mme (née Tin Sabath). He was born in Chhlong, **Kratié,** and studied at Lycée Chasseloup Laubat, Saigon together with Prince **Norodom Sihanouk** with whom he talked politics and developed a long friendship. A forester, with Chinese ancestry, Hoeur Lay Inn owned land in **Kampong Cham,** as well as in the northeast where he had established business connections with *Khmer Loeu* (highland) peoples. He supported the **Khmer Renewal Party,** running for the party in the 1947 **National Assembly** elections in Kratié and trying again in 1951. By 1955 Hoeur Lay Inn had diversified his business activities from forestry to trading in foodgrains. On 3 October 1955 Hoeur Lay Inn, now a member of the **Sangkum,** was named secretary of state for labor, social action and sanitation problems in the Council of Ministers, a portfolio he held until January 1956. In March he was appointed secretary of state for agriculture, peasant affairs, social action and investment and in the following month became secretary of state for agriculture, social action and labor, a post he held until September. Making heavy use of his personal wealth and connections in Kratié, he was elected to the 1966 National Assembly. He was among the top businessmen who used their positions in the Assembly to pressure the government for economic liberalization and renewed contact with capitalist economies. He gained national notoriety in 1972 when, in a debate on the draft **constitution** in the Assembly, he violently assaulted **Ung Mung,** a personal rival. An **advisor** to **Lon Nol** for cultural affairs for the duration of the Republic, he went into exile overseas, probably in early 1975 until 1991 when he returned to Cambodia to be on hand for Sihanouk's triumphal return.

HOK LUNDY (c1950-   ). One of the three "strong men" behind Prime Minister **Hun Sen,** Hok Lundy is a native of **Svay Rieng** province and of Vietnamese ancestry. Following the 1977-1978 border war between Cambodia and **Vietnam** which engulfed his province and Vietnam's full-scale invasion, he rose steadily through the ranks of the Vietnamese promoted **People's Revolutionary Party of Kampuchea (PRPK)** but only after former East Zone cadres led by **Chan Si**, elected party secretary in December 1981, were firmly in control. In March 1982 he was named chairman of the Organization and Inspection Bureau of the PRPK in Svay Rieng. He became deputy secretary of the province's Provisional Party Committee in April 1985 and was secretary of the provincial party briefly from November 1988 before his dual appointment, in August 1990, as secretary of the PRPK in **Phnom Penh** municipality, and he was chairman of the city's People's Committee (effectively governor of Phnom Penh). He was a candidate in the May 1993 elections on the Phnom Penh list of the **Cambodian People's Party (CPP)**, but was not elected. On 18 December 1993 he was appointed governor of Svay Rieng province, but in November 1994 he was promoted to director-general of the national police at the Ministry of the Interior, a post he continues to hold. He was among those alleged to be responsible for detaining the interior ministry secretary of state **Ho Sok**, subsequently murdered, triggering a wave of violence at the time of the 5 July 1997 coup and among the senior officials implicated in alleged cover-ups after the 6 July 1999 murder of **Piseth Pilica**. His administrative and personal power, which stems from his close friendship with the prime minister, was consolidated by his election to the CPP Central Committee in February 1997 and to the party's 21-person Standing Committee in July 2001.

HOLLAND. Holland began trading with Cambodia in the early 17th century, and trade grew rapidly after the Dutch East India Company established a post. In July 1639, the company recorded the purchase of some 125,000 deerskins for export to Japan but trade was disrupted due to intrigues in the royal palace. Dutch ships were attacked on the Mekong River in two separate incidents in 1643-44. A thousand Cambodians were killed, 156 Dutch were killed and two Dutch ships were seized, with 50 sailors taken prisoner. Dutch trade continued but turnover never again reached pre-1643 volumes. Dutch sources, like other European ones, testify to the prosperity of the Khmer Kingdom at the time. Yet, civil wars, foreign invasions and chronic feuding at court forced Holland to close its trading stations by the end of the century.

HONG HOEUNG DOEUNG (1927-). Born on 19 May 1927 at Kiensvay, **Kandal**, the son of Oum Hong and Mme (née Tim Oul), he taught at **Lycée Sisowath** and was arrested on 13 January 1953 in a police crackdown on supporters of the **Democrat Party**. In 1955 he was a member of the party executive committee led by Prince **Norodom Phurissara**. After a short period in the political wilderness, Hoeung Doeung worked for the

United Nations Educational, Scientific and Cultural Organization and then joined the Ministry of Foreign Affairs, becoming secretary at the Cambodian Embassy in Cairo and serving in Cambodian missions to the United Nations in New York and Bangkok.

HONG SUN HUOT (1947-). A medical doctor, he served in the **Armée Nationale Sihanoukienne** at Site B, on the border with **Thailand**. He briefly represented the **Coalition Government of Democratic Kampuchea** at the World Health Organization. He was a candidate on the **FUNCINPEC** list for **Kandal**, in May 1993 emerging from the elections as an alternate or reserve member of the Constituent Assembly. Briefly named minister of health in the provisional government formed in July 1993, this portfolio passed to **Chhea Thang**, a **Cambodian People's Party** member, when the new government was later confirmed. He gained a seat in the **National Assembly** in July 1994, however, as a result of vacancies arising from resignations, and in October he was reappointed minister of development and health. He was minister for rural development in 1995 when the ministry was split but lost his job in September 1997 as he was among the Royalist ministers and intellectuals who fled the country temporarily and who remained loyal to the prince in the July 1997 coup crisis. In 1998 he was elected to the National Assembly in **Kandal** and reappointed minister of health.

HOR NAM HONG (1935-). Minister of Foreign Affairs, Hor Nam Hong was born in **Phnom Penh** and studied at the Royal School of Administration. In 1967 he was posted to Paris as the first secretary of the royal embassy there. In 1970, and while still in Paris, he announced his support for the deposed chief of state **Norodom Sihanouk** and for the **National United Front of Kampuchea**. In 1973, after completing a diploma course in international law, he was appointed ambassador to Cuba, representing Sihanouk's **Royal Government of National Union of Kampuchea (GRUNK),** and in this capacity, accompanied **Ieng Sary** to Lima in August 1975. Recalled to Phnom Penh in December 1975 along with all other serving GRUNK diplomats, he was interned in section B-32 of the Boeung Trabek reeducation center. By the end of 1977, after the arrest and removal of **Van Piny**, Hor Nam Hong became chairman of the committee in charge of the group and was among the intellectuals deemed "rehabilitated" by mid-1978. But in January 1979 he was separated from the groups evacuated from Phnom Penh and rapidly joined the Vietnamese promoted **United Front for the National Salvation of Kampuchea**. In May 1981 he was named deputy minister for Foreign Affairs and was elected to the **National Assembly** of the **People's Republic of Kampuchea (PRK)** representing

Kampong Cham province. From 1982 until 1990 he was PRK ambassador to Moscow.

Upon his return, and in view of the rapid changes in relations with the **Soviet Union**, Hor Nam Hong was attached to the office of the prime minister with the rank of minister and with responsibility for advising the prime minister on foreign and legal affairs. On 7 November 1990 he was appointed minister for foreign affairs. In 1990-1993 he served as a State of Cambodia member of the **Supreme National Council (SNC)**, the body which enshrined and protected Cambodia's sovereignty during the 1991-1993 transition period. With the post of Minister of Foreign Affairs being given to **FUNCINPEC** in the coalition government of 1993, and especially as Sihanouk's nephew, **Norodom Sirivudh** was appointed minister. There was no senior role for Hor Nam Hong who in 1990-1991 had pursued Sihanouk for libel in relation to accusations that he headed a "**Khmer Rouge** concentration camp" in which many, including specifically Prince **Sisowath Methavi**, died. On 28 September 1994 he was named ambassador to Paris, with accreditation to the European Union, Austria, Belgium and to the United Nations in Geneva. Political developments in Phnom Penh commanded his attention, however, and he spent little time in Europe. Elected to the CPP Central Committee in February 1997 and to the National Assembly in 1998 Hor Nam Hong was reappointed minister of foreign affairs in the **Hun Sen** government of 1998. His son, Hor Nam Bora, was appointed ambassador to Australia in 1999.

HOU HONG (1925-1975). A graduate of the Royal School of Administration, Hou Hong was one of the zealous antiroyalists and anticommunists who attempted to supply determination and inspiration to several republican governments in the early 1970s. Rising steadily through administrative ranks from 1945, he had been governor of **Siem Reap** province, a director at Customs and Monopolies, director-general of the Royal Office for Cooperation before entering the cabinet in February 1970 as secretary of state for health and in July 1970 as minister of trade, supply and transport. In the March-October 1972 government of **Son Ngoc Thanh** he was minister of health and served concurrently as assistant secretary of state for national defense. From June 1974 until March 1975 he was a minister attached to the Prime Minister's Office responsible for "national concord." During the last month of the ill-fated **Khmer Republic**, with Phnom Penh under siege and relying upon supplies delivered by U.S. airlift, he was minister in charge of the interior, general mobilization and religion.

HOU YOUN (1930-1975). Born on 14 January 1930 in Angkar Ban, **Kampong Cham**, Hou Youn distinguished himself in his studies at the local

Lycée Preah Sihanouk where he befriended **Khieu Samphan** and at **Lycée Sisowath** in Phnom Penh where he earned his baccalaureate II (Philosophy) in 1949. Among the student activists who received scholarships from the **Democrat Party** government, he went to France in September 1949 where, in 1952, he joined the Marxist study circle organized by **Ieng Sary** and **Keng Vannsak**. Although his government scholarship was suspended on two occasions for political reasons, he completed a *Doctorat ès Sciences Economiques* at the University of Paris in December 1955.

Back in Cambodia in January 1956, he taught in the progressive, private lycées organized by his student friends and other progressives. In 1958 he was elected to the **National Assembly** on the **Sangkum** slate and was subsequently named minister of trade and industry in the government. The "opening to the left" encouraged by Prince **Norodom Sihanouk** at this time was a means of co-opting talented young technocrats, the maneuver failing to dilute Hou Youn's profound opposition to monarchy. By 1960, he was nudged out of the cabinet but nevertheless easily secured reelection to the National Assembly in 1962 and 1966. He was among those summoned by Sihanouk in 1963 during the "Affair of the 34," those considered by Sihanouk and **Lon Nol**, his **advisor** on the matter, to be communists and in the vain hope that they could be publicly shamed into helping to resolve the government's economic problems. Fearing mass arrest and worse, several clandestine communist leaders including **Ieng Sary**, **Son Sen** and Saloth Sar (**Pol Pot**) abruptly fled to rural redoubts. Though a Marxist, Hou Youn was not a member of the party at this time (or perhaps ever).

His turn to flee, together with Khieu Samphan, came in April 1967 in the aftermath of the **Samlaut Uprising** when Sihanouk suggested the two would be stripped of their parliamentary immunity and sent before the military tribunal. A third prominent National Assembly deputy, **Hu Nim**, chairman of the Cambodia-China Friendship Association joined them later in the year when Sihanouk, alarmed by the cultural revolution in **China** and an enthusiastic student response in Cambodia, decided to shut down Chinese schools, the free press and several allegedly subversive organizations. When after 18 March 1970 communiques appeared under the names of the missing parliamentarians, military spokesmen and representatives of the **Lon Nol** coup group dubbed them the "**three ghosts**," a calculated play on public fears that they had been secretly assassinated years earlier by Sihanouk's security police. Each one held a portfolio in Sihanouk's **Royal Government of National Union of Kampuchea**, Hou Youn being named minister of the interior, communal reforms and cooperatives. From 1973 he was excluded from decision making because of his opposition to wartime collectivization and, later, in 1975, the abolition of a currency of exchange and wage incentives. He disappeared soon after the 1975 evacuation of Phnom Penh, likely the victim of an assassination ordered by leaders of the **Communist Party of Kampuchea** who refused to tolerate dissent from admired intellectuals.

HOUR TROUK. In 1970 he was the colonel in the Royal Armed Forces to whom Prince **Norodom Sihanouk** had awarded the strategically important command of Tioulongville **(Kirirom)**. Being the main tank base near **Phnom Penh**, Trouk's forces would have provided the key military muscle in any attempt to prevent Lon Nol from staging a coup. However Trouk was arrested on the morning of 17 March 1970 and detained on a boat in the **Mekong** with **Oum Mannorine**, **Tim Dong** and **Pheng Phan Y**. He appears to have been released in 1973.

HU NIM (1932-1977). A prominent, "progressive" politician from the late 1950s, Hu Nim was born on 25 July 1932 in Mien, Prey Chhor district, **Kampong Cham**. Like his friends and near contemporaries, **Hou Youn** and **Khieu Samphan**, Hu Nim was educated at Lycée Preah Sihanouk in Kampong Cham and **Lycée Sisowath** in Phnom Penh. His *Licence* in law was earned in France in 1957, and a doctorate in law, from the University of Phnom Penh in 1966. He was elected to the National Assembly in 1958 winning 86 percent of the votes cast in his Kampong Cham constituency and was reelected in both 1962 and 1966. After joining the **Sangkum** in December 1957, and while a member of the Assembly, he worked as an editor for several pro-Sihanouk French-language publications including *Réalités Cambodgiennes* ("Cambodian News") and *Neak Cheat Niyum* ("The Nationalist").

By 1963, when he reported favorably on visits to China and North Korea as a member of a national delegation, he drew fire from Sihanouk for his pro-Chinese views and was included on the "list of 34" alleged "reds" published in that year. From its formation in October 1966 until May 1967, Hu Nim was a member of the shadow cabinet formed in opposition to the first **Lon Nol** government of 1966. He was also vice-president of the Cambodia-China Friendship Association at the time of the Cultural Revolution in China. When Sihanouk banned the organization and raided its offices for evidence of treachery, Hu Nim fled for his life becoming in October 1967 the third parliamentarian to disappear and later one of the **"three ghosts"** together with **Hou Youn** and **Khieu Samphan**. In 1970, Hu Nim was named minister of information in the **Royal Government of National Union of Kampuchea (GRUNK)**. In the **Democratic Kampuchea** government formed in 1976, he was minister of information but was purged in a campaign against intellectuals from urban, middle class backgrounds which swept through the ranks of the party and state apparatus in early 1977. His "confessions" while undergoing courses of torture at **Tuol Sleng** reveal that he likely disagreed with the party's attempts to revise its official history of struggle in the 1960s, its abolition of a currency of exchange and its reliance on manual labor as the principal means of production. Some poetry composed by him while he was there also survives.

HUMAN RIGHTS ASSOCIATION OF CAMBODIA (Association des Droits de l'Homme du Cambodge/ADHOC). Established in 1992 by **Thun Saray**, Khan Matoury, Ang Eng Thong and others, ADHOC monitors and campaigns against human rights abuses. In recent years, it has focused on the issue of impunity: human rights offenders abuse others and the law but are rarely arrested by the police or taken to court, the **judiciary** or system of justice being far from impartial or effective.

HUN LONG SENG "NENG" (1949-). A brother of **Hun Sen**, Neng was born in Peam Koh Snar, **Kampong Cham**. In December 1983 he was appointed chairman of the People's Revolutionary Committee in Kroch Chhmar district, Kampong Cham, becoming chairman of the People's Committee (i.e., governor) of the province in June 1985. An alternate member of the Central Committee of the **People's Revolutionary Party of Kampuchea (PRPK)** from 1985, he became a full member in April 1989 and continues to be a member of the successor **Cambodian People's Party** Central Committee. As chairman of the committee of Provincial Governors, he gave a speech in December 1991 in support of Prince **Norodom Sihanouk** which helped thaw relations between the prince and Hun Sen. From the time of the **United Nations Transitional Authority in Cambodia,** his name has figured in investigations of murders, intimidation of opposition politicians and dubious business activities including illegal logging. Between 10-17 June 1993 he participated in the secessionist movement of Prince **Norodom Chakrapong**. On 18 December 1993, the new Kingdom of Cambodia having been launched, he was reappointed governor of Kampong Cham. On 12 March 1999, he was appointed governor of **Svay Rieng** province.

HUN SEN (1952-). Prime minister 1985-1991, 1998-. Born on 4 April 1952 in Peam Koh Snar, Stung Trang district, **Kampong Cham**, the third son of Hun Neang and Dy Pok, Hun Sen went to Lycée Indra Devi in **Phnom Penh** until 1968. He then left school and joined the communist guerrillas in the countryside when his revolutionary mentor, a monk at Tuol Kork, was arrested in the wave of killings and arrests following the **Samlaut uprising**. Hun Sen later sought to shift the moment of his departure to 1970, he could link his support for the communists to their decision to form an alliance with **Norodom Sihanouk**. Fortunately, there is sufficient evidence available to distinguish real history from the revised.

For the period 1968-1970, Hun Sen was assigned to agitprop work among rubber plantation workers whose support was desired for the communist uprising against the government. In this work he succeeded as soon as and only when Sihanouk was overthrown and when many peasants also engaged in militant protests. A combat soldier in the 1970-1975 civil war, Hun Sen lost his left eye in battle near Kampong Cham on 16 April 1975, the day before the communist revolutionaries seized power in Phnom Penh. From April 1975 until January 1976 he was in hospital recovering from his injuries. On 5 January 1976, in a large group ceremony involving 14 couples, he married Sam Hieng, who later changed her name to **Bun Rany**.

In the **Democratic Kampuchea** period, Hun Sen was deputy regimental commander in region (*tambon*) 21 of the Eastern Zone. A wave of arbitrary executions and fear of imminent arrest led him to flee to Vietnam on 20 June 1977, along with some of the soldiers under his command. His haste was such that he left his family behind. At the end of the following year, with Vietnamese support, he helped to organize the **United Front for the National Salvation of Kampuchea (UFNSK)** on 2 December 1978. Hun Sen became a member of the Central Committee with responsibility for creating the movement's youth wing.

When less than three weeks later the Vietnamese army invaded Cambodia, the UFNSK formed a temporary, revolutionary people's council on 7 January 1979 and proclaimed a **People's Republic of Kampuchea (PRK)** on 12 January 1979. From 7 January, Hun Sen was in charge of foreign affairs in the Revolutionary Council. In the national elections of May 1981, in which he won a seat in the **National Assembly**, he became minister of foreign affairs in the government formed and led by **Pen Sovan** (July-December 1981) and the succeeding **Chan Si** government (December 1981-December 1984). Also in May 1981 he was elected to the Central Committee of the **People's Revolutionary Party of Kampuchea (PRPK)** and to its top policy making body, the Political Bureau. The new PRPK laid claim to the historical legacy of the old **Khmer People's Revolutionary Party** founded in 1951, principally by claiming the May 1981 Congress as its Fourth (not the First).

Following the death of Chan Si in December 1984, Hun Sen became chairman of the Council of Ministers (on 14 January 1985). Preferring to conduct his own foreign policy especially after informal talks linked the withdrawal of Vietnamese occupation troops to a possible political settlement with the forces of the **Coalition Government of Democratic**

Kampuchea (CGDK). Without abandoning the premiership, he resumed control of the Ministry of Foreign Affairs from December 1986 until December 1987 and once again in September 1990. He was among those in the PRPK who were reluctant to embrace the Soviet reform movement mounted by Mikhail Gorbachev, especially his idea that regional conflicts should yield to all-party "national reconciliation" government. When it was realized that Soviet aid would end and that the Vietnamese army of occupation would leave, Hun Sen's government called upon Prince **Norodom Sihanouk** to return to Cambodia and, from April 1989, promoted limited political and economic reforms. The term "revolutionary" or "people's revolutionary" was removed from the names of state bodies and provincial committees. The PRK was renamed, **State of Cambodia (SOC)**.

Constitutional amendments saw the reintroduction of **Buddhism** as the state religion and legalized the reliance upon family management in agriculture by promising to issue land-use title deeds. These changes cleared the way for a settlement with Prince **Norodom Sihanouk** and his **Coalition Government of Democratic Kampuchea (CGDK)** in exile. Just before the signing of the Paris Peace agreements, a special congress of the PRPK formally abandoned Marxism-Leninism, laid down the party's secretariat, declared itself a membership party (abandoning the cadre party structures) and took the name, **Cambodian People's Party (CPP)**. The leading post, that of chairman, was taken by **Chea Sim**. Hun Sen was named deputy chairman and leader of the party's election campaign.

He remained prime minister of the SOC until June 1993 when this governmental framework was laid down. In the United Nations-organized elections of May, he promoted himself as the only leader with the will and determination to fight the "Polpotists," The Royalist opposition rejected war as a way forward and promised the integration of all parties into the national family under the leadership of Sihanouk. Though the CPP came second in the elections, Hun Sen emerged as cochairman of the Council of Ministers and cominister of defense and the interior in a coalition CPP-FUNCINPEC coalition. In November 1993 when the government was reshuffled, he was appointed second prime minister with Prince **Norodom Ranariddh** named as the first prime minister.

Although Prince Ranariddh was the nominal leader of the government, and was able to insert some functionaries into the former SOC administration, Hun Sen retained most state power for himself and most public posts for CPP members. In spite of intense dislike of monarchy, Hun Sen was conscious of the substantial popular affection enjoyed by King **Norodom Sihanouk**, a political fact which led him to treat the king with great deference when in the public eye and with wariness otherwise. However Hun Sen became increasingly anxious to remove Prince

Ranariddh and his supporters from the coalition government after 1995 when the royalist finance minister **Sam Rainsy** was sacked and from 1996, following the arrest and deportation of the foreign minister Prince **Norodom Sirivudh** and the defection of **Ieng Sary** and other top cadres from the remnants of **Pol Pot**'s movement.

By early 1997 with both prime ministers seriously implicated in massive illegal logging operations and engaged in mutually exclusive, secret negotiations to win over the last of the **Democratic Kampuchea (DK)** armed forces in **Anlong Veng**, an attempt was made on the life of Sam Rainsy in March 1997 resulting in the deaths of at least 16 bystanders. This was followed in July by an armed *coup de force* triggered by the murder of **Ho Sok**, the FUNCINPEC secretary of state in the interior ministry and the flight into exile of Prince Ranariddh and dozens of other royalists and NGO activists who feared for their lives. Ranariddh's home and offices were ransacked; top FUNCINPEC military commanders and security officials were captured, tortured and killed. Soldiers, including some ex-DK forces loyal to Hun Sen, went on a rampage in downtown Phnom Penh terrifying the civilian population and prompting the leading tycoon **Teng Bunma** to offer Hun Sen huge cash resources for restoring order. **Ung Huot**, then FUNCINPEC minister of education was appointed acting first prime minister and several absent Ranariddh loyalists in the government were replaced. Lending a gloss of constitutionality to the elbowing and violence, the CPP won the majority of seats in the National Assembly elections of 1998, Hun Sen winning a seat in Kandal province. Though the 1997 coup, the 1999 **Piseth Pilica** affair and corrupt practices all around him cast long shadows, his strongman status is now undisputed.

Hun Sen's oldest son, Hun Manet, born 1978, graduated from West Point Military Academy in 1999. His other children are: Hun Mana, a daughter, born in 1980; Hun Monet, born 1981; Hun Manit, born 1982; and Hun Maly, a daughter, born 1983. He and Bun Rany have two other adopted children. Hun Sen's oldest brother, Hun Sam, an entrepreneur in transport, formerly worked at the Ministry of Transport. Another, **Hun Neng**, is the governor of **Svay Rieng**. Two younger sisters married generals in the police (killed in November 1996) and the army respectively. A younger brother, Hun Bunthoeun, is not active in politics.

HUOT SAM ATH (1912-). Born on 17 October 1912 in Phnom Penh, he attended the Agricultural High School of Indochina, in Hanoi, and was a secretary to the **French Résident** in 1936. During the war years, he was head of the Tuol Samrong agriculture station and provincial agent for **Kampong Cham**. In 1945 he was appointed to the Ministry of National Economy as director of the *Office of Crédit Populaire*, the colonial, agricultural credit agency. He was a member of the Cambodian delegation to the Economic Conference in Dalat, the Economic Commission for Asia and the Far East Conference in Australia 1945-1950, the **Pau Conference** in 1950, and was director of the Foreign Trade Office by 1951. An efficient bureaucrat, he was a member of the commission established in 1953 to plan the transfer of the administration of Cambodia from France, general secretary of the Cambodian delegation to the Franco-Khmer conference in Paris in June 1955 and then, in recognition of his service and loyalty to the **Sangkum,** he held a series of ministerial posts between 1955-1957: minister of public health and information; minister of planning, telecommunications and public works; minister of telecommunications and public works; minister of finance, planning and industrialization and minister of education, socialist youth and clean government (i.e., anti-corruption).

Instrumental in the establishment of diplomatic and economic relations with China, he headed the April 1956 Cambodian Economic Mission to the People's Republic of China which negotiated a $22.4 million assistance package. In 1957 he was appointed president of **Royal Air Cambodge**, and later served as ambassador to Yugoslavia. Though not especially an active party member, Huot Sam Ath joined and was, for a time, general treasurer of the Sangkum as well as managing director of the Royal Office for Cooperation, the Sihanouk era agricultural marketing and credit organization.

HUOT SAMBATH (1928-1976). A diplomat who proved himself a loyal Sihanoukist in 1970, he was born in **Phnom Penh**, the son of Nay Huot and Mme (née Tan Vuoch Keao). While a student in Paris, he befriended several French socialists, married Marie Kan, a Spanish Republican refugee. Joining the **Sangkum** on 11 May 1955, he was appointed secretary of state for foreign affairs that November, receiving a portfolio then held by Prince **Norodom Sihanouk**. In later cabinets spanning 1956-1964, he was secretary of state for national education, fine arts, youth and sports; secretary of state for public instruction, education and fine arts; secretary of state for labor and information; president of the Assembly's foreign affairs commission and secretary of state for foreign affairs, gaining a reputation for "anti-Western" views in the latter posts.

In 1968 Huot Sambath was appointed permanent representative to the United Nations, a post from which he was dismissed by the new Lon Nol government in March 1970. On 1 April 1970 he went to Beijing being among those who attended the Summit Conference of the Indochinese Peoples on 24-25 April 1970 held in southern China close to the Lao-Vietnamese border. He was appointed minister of public works, telecommunications and reconstruction in Sihanouk's **Royal Government** of National Union (GRUNK) and became a member of the Political Bureau and the Central Committee of the **National United Front of Kampuchea (FUNK)** founded on 4 May 1970 at a meeting in Beijing.

Although he was among the Sihanoukists sentenced to death *in absentia* for high treason in August 1970, he was seen, by 1971, to be a possible intermediary by **"The Third Force,"** a group centering on Prince **Norodom Kantol, Cheng Heng** who were seeking to mediate a peace settlement through **Hang Thun Hak, Lon Non** and possibly the Soviet Union. **Huot Sambath** was responsible for negotiating with the Polish Embassy officials based in Beijing, a task that was to earn him the enmity of the underground **Communist Party of Kampuchea**. Once back in Cambodia in December 1975, he was sent to a series of base camps for re-education. According to an eye witness account, he and **Isoup Ghanti**, another GRUNK diplomat, were accused of fraud and received harsher treatment than others in their group of returned diplomats. Huot Sambath was taken to **Tuol Sleng** on 9 September and executed on 17 November.

HUOT TAT, *Samdech* **(1891-1975).** Buddhist patriarch. One of the foremost Buddhist scholars of the 20th century, Huot Tath was born in a village near **Oudong** and placed in the care of monks in Prang monastery at the age of seven. When 20 years old, he was ordained as *bhikkhu.* Within a few years, in 1919, he joined the editorial committee of the Khmer dictionary, the origins of the authoritative text now known as the **Buddhist Institute** dictionary. Having attracted the notice of French scholars, he was sent to Hanoi together with **Chuon Nath**, to study Sanskrit, the history of Buddhism and premodern Khmer history. Upon his return in 1925, he taught Sanskrit in the Upper Pali School. Thereafter he was a spokesman for Cambodian Buddhism at major world conferences and promoted Buddhist education and morality in national society by means of diverse writing and speaking activities, including support for *Nagaravatta*. He translated numerous religious texts from Pali into **Khmer** and wrote on monastic discipline, alcoholism, the study of Buddhism and ways properly to serve the throne and the nation. Many of these studies were informed by his studies of other languages and cultures: he was a fluent speaker, reader and writer of Thai, Lao and French. Honored as Chevalier of the Legion of Honor in 1948, he became *sangharaja* of the Mohanikay order in 1969, upon the death of Samdech Preah Sanghareach Chuon Nath. A friend and supporter of **Son Ngoc Thanh** and other nationalists, Huot Tath was close to many politicians who promoted the **Khmer Republic** but deeply regretted the national civil war. He broadcast an appeal for calm on 17 April 1975 but was then led away by communist soldiers and executed. *See also* KHIEU CHUM.

HUY KANTHOUL (1909-1991). The last **Democrat Party** prime minister of Cambodia, his sacking in June 1952 combined with the resumption of direct rule by the king generated intellectual disquiet. Huy Kanthoul was born in Phnom Penh on 1 February 1909, the son of Huy Plok and Mme (née Lé). He attended **Collège Sisowath** and the Faculty of Pedagogy, University of Hanoi, earning his teaching diploma in 1931. He then taught at Lycée Sisowath from 1931-1937. In 1937 he won a scholarship to France where he lived and studied for five years. In 1943-1944 he was delegate for information, propaganda and press in the Ministry of National Education. In 1946 he was among the first to join the Democrat Party, initially serving as an assistant secretary and then as secretary-general. He was also vice-president of the Friends of the Lycée Sisowath Alumni Association. Between 1946-1951 he held ministerial posts in five different governments, specifically those led **Chhean Vam**, **Penn Nouth**, **Sisowath Monipong** and **Oum Chheangsun** in addition to his own all-Democrat cabinet formed on 13 October 1951. The return of **Son Ngoc Thanh** from exile nevertheless divided and paralyzed the democracy movement. In an ill-considered response to demands for his resignation, Huy Kanthoul arrested **Yèm Sambaur**, a strong ally of the royal family. Thus provoked, and with French backing, King **Norodom Sihanouk** dissolved the Assembly and government on 15 June 1952 and assumed emergency powers for three years. Fearing personal reprisals, Kanthoul fled abroad, receiving temporary exile in France.

In 1955, after refusing to join the **Sangkum**, he was the unsuccessful Democrat candidate in Talam, **Battambang**. His interest in politics on the wane, Kanthoul gave up party politics in order to work in business, mostly as a company manager. For many years in the 1960s he was ambassador to the **Soviet Union**. Following the republican coup against Prince Sihanouk, Huy Kanthoul lent his support to the revitalized **Democratic Party** led by **In Tam**. From 1979 both he and his son Vora were active promoters of the **Khmer People's National Liberation Front (KPNLF)**, Kanthoul serving as a member of its Council of Elders. He was among the elders who in 1985 joined the Provisional Central Committee for the Salvation of the KPNLF in opposition to the leadership of KPNLF President **Son Sann.** He died on 13 September 1991, just before the reconvening of the Paris Conference, but not without leaving unpublished memoirs which are sharply critical of Sihanouk's conduct in 1952-1955 and of monarchy as a form of government.

HUY MONG (c1902-1975). Huy Mong worked as a secretary in the French Administration from 1926 until 1945, and by 1947 he was director of the Royal Printing Company as well as an officer in the **Democrat Party**. In the late 1940s he was closely associated with **Yèm Sambaur** and served as secretary of state for national defense in the Democrat cabinet led by **Chhean Vam**, and he was minister for national defense in Sambaur's 1949 government. As governor of Kampot in the following year, he was an early supporter of the **National Recovery Party**, the splinter party formed in May 1950 by Sambaur after his breakaway from the Democrat Party. The party hoped to secure power in the elections due in 1951 but when one of its leading personalities, **Mao Chay**, broke away in the course of a dispute with Yèm Sambaur and established the **Victorious Northeast Khmer Party**, Huy Mong then found himself in an exposed position. His party, and its leader, were out of power, though both were in league with conservative elite opinion on the question of independence, but he was Royal Delegate to **Siem Reap**, heartland of a new movement attempting to oppose the king and the French as well as the Democrat-dominated government and Sambaur's splinter.

Huy Mong was forced to abandon his post by **Dap Chhuon**, who had decided to support Mao Chhay's party and who was a personal enemy. His post in Siem Reap no longer tenable, he returned to Phnom Penh to become administrative director of the Ministry of Information, taking up his appointment on 11 July 1952. Adopting a pragmatic view of the Democrat Party split of 1952, Mong held a succession of posts in national administration, fading into political obscurity after being charged, in August 1956, with insulting members of the royal family. He reappeared on the political stage in 1972 when he declared his intention to stand against Lon Nol in the presidential elections. Little was known of his views, but he was regarded as a candidate out of touch and to the right of Lon Nol, and when he decided not to contest the elections, most of his supporters voted for Lon Nol. He was still in Phnom Penh in April 1975 and is believed to have been executed soon thereafter.

-I-

IENG MOULY (1950-   ). A prominent Republican politician, born on 2 November 1950 at Snaypol village, Peareang, **Prey Veng**, Mouly was the son of Ieng Muth, an active member of the pre-1955 **Democrat Party** and younger brother of Ieng Sinuon, who in the 1960s was critical of Prince **Norodom Sihanouk**. Mouly attended Lycée Peareang and the University of Phnom Penh earning diplomas in commerce (1968) and accountancy (1970). He worked in the accountancy section of the state-owned brewery enterprise *Société Khmère des Distilleries* (SKD), 1968-1970 and then as a financial controller at *Société Khmère pour l'Industrie Laitière* (Sokilait), the mixed state-private milk enterprise and for Comin Khmer, a private import-export firm, 1970-1973. In exile in France from 1973, he worked as an accountant and financial controller for French firms.

In 1982 he moved to **Thailand** so as to work on the Cambodian border with **Son Sann**, and the **Khmer People's National Liberation Front (KPNLF)** and as general secretary of the KPNLF Red Cross founded on 17 July 1982. He was loyal to Son Sann throughout the schismatic debates dividing the military and civilian wings of the KPNLF from 1985, and in March 1988 he was appointed secretary-general of the KPNLF. In 1990, he and Son Sann represented the KPNLF in the eight-member **Supreme National Council**. He was, predictably, first vice-president of the **Buddhist Liberal Democratic Party (BLDP),** the electoral party established by Son Sann in 1991, in anticipation of the United Nations-sponsored elections of 1993.

In May 1993 he was among the 10 BLDP deputies to be elected to the **National Assembly**, but was not among the party members appointed to the provisional government, the first sign of a rift. Following the creation of a "Khmer New Generation" caucus within the BLDP, he was named minister of information in the coalition government formally invested in November when most other BLDP politicians joined Son Sann in opposing the formation of the **FUNCINPEC-Cambodian People's Party** coalition. Mouly was also appointed president of the Cambodian Centre for Action against Mines (CMAC). He was elected president of a rump faction of the BLDP at a party congress in July 1995 securing government recognition of his ownership of the party name in 1998. Failing in his bid to be returned to the Assembly in 1998, he was made **advisor** to the government with responsibility for mine clearance.

IENG SARY né **Kim Trang (1929-).** Ex-**Democratic Kampuchea** foreign minister. Born into a poor **Khmer Krom** family in southern Vietnam, Ieng Sary won a scholarship to **Lycée Sisowath** and moved to Phnom Penh. Once there, he befriended many nationalist radicals including **Keng Vannsak** and read Marxist-Leninist texts for the first time. He met Saloth Sar (**Pol Pot**), in 1947, and the two campaigned for Democrat candidates for the **National Assembly**. Sary organized the anticolonial student strike at Lycée Sisowath in 1949, an event that radicalized his generation. Not unrelated to his activism, he received a scholarship to study in France, an award granted by Democrats and approved by French officials as a means of isolating him in the metropole. In Paris he renewed his acquaintance with Saloth Sar and Keng Vannsak. Sary and Vannsak sponsored a Marxist study group that met in Vannsak's apartment in the 15th arondissement. By 1952 Sary, and others, had joined the French Communist Party. In

1953 he married **Khieu Thirith**, a student of English language and literature.

Returning to Phnom Penh in 1957 Sary taught history at Lycée Sisowath until 1959, and then at **Kambuboth**, all the while secretly engaged in underground Communist Party work. In 1963, after Sar had become secretary of the **Workers' Party of Kampuchea**, the name adopted in 1960 by the **Khmer People's Revolutionary Party**, they fled together into the *maquis*, their political careers united for the next 30 years. In 1971 Ieng Sary moved to Beijing, where he was "special representative of the interior." He kept a watchful eye on **Norodom Sihanouk**, titular leader of the communist-backed **National United Front of Kampuchea**, and Head of State in the **Royal Government of National Union of Kampuchea**. After 1975, as foreign minister for **Democratic Kampuchea,** he traveled overseas or received foreign visitors making him the regime's most visible spokesman. In recent years, he has denied detailed knowledge of internal developments or of the purges carried out by other senior party officials. By his account, purges were secretly authorized and carried out under the guidance of only four people, named as Pol Pot, **Nuon Chea, Son Sen** and **Yun Yat.**

After the Vietnamese invasion of 1978-1979, Ieng Sary faded from public view, but from his border redoubt in Phnom Malai, he was the official conduit for Chinese military and political assistance to the **Party of Democratic (PDK)**. In 1991, when this assistance ended, he was said to be in poor health, and following disputes with a younger generation of party leaders, to have been removed from positions of responsibility. In 1996, in the course of more fractiousness, dividing PDK leaders in **Pailin** from Pol Pot's group in **Anlong Veng,** he defected, with the Pailin group, to the Cambodian government. Although nominal leader of the non-electoral **Democratic National Union Movement** formed in Pailin, he has resided in seclusion in Phnom Penh since 1999. Under sentence of death in absentia from a 1979 **People's Republic of Kampuchea** Court, he received a royal pardon from King **Norodom Sihanouk** following his defection in 1996. *See also* Y CHHIEN.

IENG THIRITH (1932-). A prominent teacher and wife of **Ieng Sary**, she was a daughter of Khieu, a **Battambang** judge and a sister of **Khieu Ponnary** and Khieu Tham. Khieu Thirith met Ieng Sary when both were students at **Lycée Sisowath.** They married later on 19 May 1953 when both were studying in Paris. While in France they devoted much of their time to political activities to which his degree was sacrificed, but Thirith earned the distinction of being the first Cambodian to receive a *licence* in English language and literature (in 1958). Partly as a means to earn money for underground party activities, she then taught at state and private schools in Phnom Penh, including the Khmer-American High School, before joining her husband in the *maquis* in 1965. For most of the civil war period, she was in charge of the principal **National United Front of Kampuchea** radio station in Hanoi, a role linked to her position as deputy-minister of education and youth in the **Royal Government of National Union of Kampuchea**. In **Democratic Kampuchea (DK)**, she was minister of social action, and in this capacity, responsible for supporting schools, clinics and vulnerable groups having few of the usual resources. Ieng Thirith fled **Phnom Penh** to "rear-base" areas along the Thai frontier in 1979, traveling occasionally in the 1980s to international meetings such as the United Nations Conference on trade and development in May 1979. She was renamed minister of social affairs in the reshuffled DK government formed by **Khieu Samphan** in December 1979 but failed to receive a ministerial portfolio in the succeeding, noncommunist tri-party **Coalition Government of Democratic Kampuchea (CGDK)** formed in 1982. Since the early 1990s, she has cared for her sister, Ponnary, who never recovered from a mental breakdown in the 1970s. Her son, Ieng Vuth, is first deputy governor of **Pailin** and acts as spokesman for the Democratic National Union Movement led by his aging father.

IEU KOEUS (1905-1950). One of Prince **Sisowath Youtévong**'s closest collaborators in April 1946, and a politician respected in his time and across the political spectrum, Ieu Koeus was briefly prime minister in September 1949. Born in **Battambang**, he was the son of Ieu Heng and a graduate of the *École Supérieure d'Hanoi* where he studied in 1925-1927. He then worked for several rubber plantation enterprises before branching out on his own, establishing a construction business and a soap factory among others. In the 1930s he was associated with **Son Ngoc Thanh** and other nationalists working for the **Buddhist Institute** in Phnom Penh. In 1940 he was appointed to the colonial Chamber of Representatives of the People. Ieu Koeus was a member of the first executive committee of the **Democrat Party** and the party's treasurer. He and **Chhean Vam**, the first general-secretary of the party, did much to ensure the Democrat Party victories in the Constituent Assembly elections of 1946 and in the 1947 **National Assembly** elections. Ieu Koeus held a seat in each election, the second time in Phnom Penh. When Prince Youtévong died on 17 July 1947 he became party leader and in January 1948, president of the National Assembly at a time when his party fell under the influence of the *Khmer Issarak*, arousing the anger of both the government and king with the result that the Assembly was dissolved. Ieu Koeus was appointed interim president of the Council of Ministers and minister of the interior from 20-

28 September 1949, reporting only to the king, but was dismissed after eight days to make way for the return of **Yèm Sambaur**.

It was in the context of royal manipulation of disputes among Democrats that Ieu Kroeus was assassinated on 14 January by a peasant who rolled a handgrenade under his desk while he worked on a speech. Responsibility for the assassination has never been clearly established, **Lon Nol** bungling the investigation. However, suspicion fell upon Prince **Norodom Norindeth** who fled the country and upon Yèm Sambaur. To the chagrin of King Sihanouk and the French, his funeral drew a massive crowd of 50,000 mourners. He is still much-admired as one of the great nationalist leaders of his generation. He left a large family. One son, Ieu Pannakar, married Oum Sophanith, sister of **Oum Mannorine**. Ieu Pannakar collaborated with Prince **Norodom Sihanouk** on some films and was one of the two Royal appointees to the **Senate** in 1999.

IEU YANG (1926-). A Republican politician, Ieu Yang was born on 12 November 1926 in Trapeang Preng, **Kampong Cham**, the son of Ieu Neang and Mme (née Keam). Yang attended **Lycée Sisowath** and was active in the **Democrat Party**. Following their first election victory, he was sent on a government scholarship to France in October 1947. He studied at the *École d'Électricité Industrielle* in Chartleat, and the *École Violet*. On his return to Cambodia in 1950, he became a supporter of **Son Ngoc Thanh**'s wing of the nationalist movement joining Thanh, **Ea Sichau** and others in the *maquis* after 9 March 1952. He returned to **Phnom Penh** in 1954 and was the Democrat candidate for Saukong, **Kampong Cham**, in the 1955 **National Assembly** elections. Following the **Sangkum** victory in the elections, he studied law at the Royal University of Phnom Penh, receiving his degree in September 1964. He then worked for the **National Bank of Cambodia** whose governor **Son Sann** was also a prominent former Democrat Party leader. In 1972 he joined the **Socio-Republican Party** and was elected to the National Assembly of the **Khmer Republic** in September 1972, representing Kauk Morn, **Oddar Meanchey**. He was elected to head the Legislative committee for interior and security. From June 1974 until March 1975 Yang was minister of trade and development under **Long Boret**, becoming minister of public works, transport and trade in the last month of the Republic.

IM CHHUN LIM (1942-). Born at Kratié, he studied history at the *École Normale Supérieure* and the Royal School of Administration and was a schoolteacher when he was evacuated to the countryside in 1975. Among the many **"New people"** who rallied to the support of the **People's Republic of Kampuchea** government in the early 1980s, he initially worked at the Ministry of Health and the Ministry of Foreign Affairs. By

April 1985 he was attached to the Central Committee of the **People's Revolutionary Party of Kampuchea (PRPK)** where he served in several departments, becoming deputy director of the Central Committee Office in April 1989. Elected as a member of the Central Committee in July 1990, he was one of the six representatives of the **State of Cambodia** on the **Supreme National Council** from February 1991 until 1993; he served briefly director-general of the state-controlled Radio-Television service, December 1991 until March 1992 and was minister of education, 1992-1993. In the May 1993 elections, Im Chhun Lim was elected on the **Cambodian People's Party** list for Phnom Penh. He was secretary of state for the interior and public security in the 1993 Royal Government. In the **Hun Sen** government of November 1998, he was named minister of regional planning and construction.

IM PHON (1912-1993). A brother of **Mey Pho**, and a brother-in-law of **Khuon Nay**, Im Phon was principal secretary to the governor of **Kampong Cham** and then a lawyer, practising in the town of Kampong Cham by 1944. A founding member of the **Democrat Party** in April 1946, he was elected to the Constituent Assembly in 1946 in his native district of Kandal Stung, **Kandal**, and then to the 1947 National Assembly for Kuk Trap, Kandal. He was reelected in 1951 to represent Kandok, Kandal. Within the Assembly, he played a key role as parliamentary secretary to **Ieu Koeus**, and by 1951 he also had a law practice in Phnom Penh. He was among those arrested on 13 January 1953 in a police crackdown on supporters of the Democrat Party. He lent his support to the radical takeover of the Democrat Party in 1954 and became a director of the Party Executive Committee in February 1955. Although he was the candidate for the Democrats in the 1955 National Assembly elections in his former constituency of Kandok, he lost to the **Sangkum** candidate and retired from politics. When, in 1966 Prince **Norodom Sihanouk,** decided against designating official Sangkum candidates for the National Assembly elections, allowed antiroyalists once again freely to compete, Im Phon ran again, in Phong, **Kampong Speu**, and was elected. It was this Assembly, dominated by wealthy businessmen and affluent republican personalities from the 1940s which chose **Lon Nol** to form the government, putting him in position for the 1970 deposition of Sihanouk, a move the Assembly promptly ratified.

IM RUN (1941-). A teacher between 1963-1975 and a **Socio-Republican Party** member of the National Assembly, 1972-1975, Im Run was among the surviving **"new people"** who returned to **Phnom Penh** in 1979. Initially she worked in the **People's Republic of Kampuchea** Ministry of Education but from 1981-1986, she managed the office of the **Association of Revolutionary Women of Kampuchea**, the official mass organization for women. From 1987-1993 she was the only woman judge in the Supreme Court, the highest court in the poorly functioning judicial system. In 1993 she was a **Cambodian People's Party (CPP)** candidate in **Kampong Cham** province, but did not win a seat in the Constituent Assembly. She was then appointed assistant secretary of state for Women's Affairs in the State Secretariat for Women's Affairs in the Royal Government of 1993-1998, informally serving as the liaison of the Secretariat with the CPP-dominated government. Elected to the expanded CPP Central Committee in 1997, Im Run's second run for the **National Assembly**, in 1998, and again in Kampong Cham, was successful. *See also* CHHOUK CHHIM; MEAN SAMAN.

IM SAROEUN (1933-). An electrical engineer who studied in Grenoble in the late 1950s, he returned to **Phnom Penh** in 1961 becoming director of National Radiodiffusion-Television in the Ministry of Information and rector of the Technical University. In the early years of the **Khmer Republic**, he was involved in the Khmer-Mon Institute promoted by **Lon Nol** and other prominent military personalities. He assisted in the preparation of the revised, published version of Lon Nol's radically nationalist essay, *Neo-Khmerism* (Phnom Penh, 1971) but quickly thereafter lost confidence in the effectiveness of the republican leadership. He moved to France before 1975 and was among the large number of Francophone technocrats residing in France who for a time looked to the **National United Front of Kampuchea** as a possible alternative to the Lon Nol government.

During the Vietnamese invasion crisis of 1979, when the United Nations-recognized **Democratic Kampuchea (DK)** delegate **Ok Sakun** was attempting to rally nationalist support among overseas Cambodians to oppose the Vietnamese occupation, Im Saroeun accepted an appointment as deputy permanent representative of Cambodia to the United Nations Educational, Scientific and Cultural Organisation (UNESCO) in Paris. He was a member of the delegation from France that met with the new DK Prime Minister **Khieu Samphan** in August 1980 and argued effectively for armed resistance against the Vietnamese, advocating support for all nationalist armies, including the remnants of the discredited DK regime army and the insipient royalist and republican resistance movements taking shape along the border with **Thailand**. He left the UNESCO mission quietly in 1982, once the all-nationalist **Coalition Government of Democratic Kampuchea (CGDK)** had been established. Subsequently, he was a member of the Collectif Soutien Cambodge (Cambodian Support Collective), coeditor with Prom Thuch of the Collective's newsletter *Aramn Khmae* ("Khmer Essence") and promoter in recent years of the **Kram**

Ngoy Center, formed by technocrats in the diaspora who are sponsoring technical and professional training programs in Cambodia. He retired from his post as *Maître de conférence*, Faculty of Sciences, University of Montpellier, in the late 1990s.

IM SETHY (1947-). Born in Phnom Penh, he was a high school teacher in **Svay Rieng** until 1970 who worked in the Ministry of Education until the end of the 1970-1975 war. Returning to Phnom Penh from the countryside in 1979, he joined the **People's Republic of Kampuchea** administration as director of the office of the minister of education, later being attached to the office of the Council of Ministers where he rose in administrative rank to deputy minister. In 1993 he was attached to the secretariat of the **Supreme National Council** and was elected to the **National Assembly** on the **Cambodian People's Party** list in **Kampong Cham**. In October he became a member of the Assembly's Commission for Foreign Affairs, International Cooperation, Information and the Media. In 1998 he was reelected to the National Assembly in Kampong Cham and appointed secretary of state in the Ministry of Education, Youth and Sports.

IM YOU HAY (1943-1975). A student activist, he helped to organize the demonstrations culminating in the overthrow of Prince **Norodom Sihanouk** on 18 March 1970. He represented Cambodian students on the **constitutional drafting committee** in June 1971 and promoted student protests against the corruption, bad government and lack of competence of several named ministers in 1972. **Lon Nol** noticing that he was not personally criticized by the protestors, took this opportunity to recruit allies from the ranks of the antigovernment critics. Im You Hay was persuaded to shift his support to **Lon Nol** and persuaded others to follow him. His reward was nomination by Lon Nol's **Socio-Republican Party** for the **National Assembly** seat in Lomphat, **Ratanakiri**. He disappeared from view not long after the evacuation of **Phnom Penh** in 1975.

IN SOKAN (1929-1979). Born on 28 June 1929 in **Phnom Penh**, the first son of five born to In Chân, a provincial governor, and Mme In Chhieun Kim. He received his baccalaureate II in mathematics from **Lycée Sisowath** in June 1947 and then a government scholarship for higher education in France where he lived and studied from 1950-1959. He graduated in December 1958 from the Faculty of Medicine, with a specialization in gynecology and obstetrics. While in France he was an active participant in student campaigns against colonial rule and monarchy and was among those who formed the progressive Union of Khmer Students on 30 August 1955, an act which led to the loss of his scholarship. He nevertheless succeeded his friend and fellow communist **Ieng Sary** as president of the movement while at the same earning his medical degree.

In Sokan returned to Phnom Penh in 1959 entering practice at the Khmero-Soviet Friendship Hospital and teaching in the Faculty of Medicine, University of Phnom Penh. He was also the medical head of the national antituberculosis service. Identified as one of the country's leading "leftists" in the 1963 "affair of the 34" (which forced Ieng Sary, **Son Sen** and Saloth Sar **(Pol Pot)** to run for their lives) he decided to seek foreign refuge and with his French wife returned to France. **Ok Sakun,** a friend, also a member of the secret Communist movement and also married to a Frenchwoman did the same. In Sokan was among the first prominent intellectuals in France to lend support to the **Royal Government of National Union of Kampuchea (GRUNK)** in April 1970 and the **National United Front of Kampuchea (FUNK)** when it was created in May 1970. In Sokan was the first chairman of the FUNK committee formed in Paris in 1970-1971 and occasionally stood in for Ok Sakun as acting Head of Mission, GRUNK, between 1970-1975.

He returned to Phnom Penh in December 1975, along with all other GRUNK diplomatic personnel. Following a brief period of reeducation in a "base camp" together with Ok Sakun, the two of them were assigned to B1, the **Democratic Kampuchea** foreign ministry led by Ieng Sary. Sokan is said to have fallen ill and to have died during the hasty evacuation of B1 personnel from Phnom Penh in early January 1979.

IN SOPHANN (1938-1977). The third son of In Chân and a brother of **In Sokan**, he studied engineering at the *École Centrale des Arts et Manufactures* in Paris, graduating in 1963 and returning to Cambodia in 1964. He worked at the Ministry of Industry, 1964-1968, and taught at the Khmer-Soviet Higher Technical Institute. He then began a detailed study of the economy and in 1971-1972 was appointed director of studies and documentation at the Ministry of Industry. In October 1973, while still chairman and managing director of SONATRAC, the national tractor enterprise, In Sophann joined the **National United Front of Kampuchea.** He served in the diplomatic service of the **Royal Government of National Union of Kampuchea** as chargé d'affaires at the Cambodian Embassy in Albania until 1976 when he was recalled. He was arrested in 1977 and executed after interrogation at **Tuol Sleng.**

IN SOPHEAP (1943-). The fourth son of In Chân, Sopheap completed his *Licence-ès-maths* at the Faculty of Sciences, Phnom Penh, in 1969 and his degree in engineering at the *École Centrale des Arts et Manufactures* in Paris in 1972. In these years, he was a member of the executive committee of the Union of Khmer Students and leader of the pro-Chinese tendency within the organization which eventually broke away to form a National Union of Khmer Students. Together with his oldest brother **In**

Sokan, Sopheap supported the **National United Front of Kampuchea** from the time of its establishment. From 1972-1974 he worked as a secretary and aide to **Ieng Sary** and then left Beijing for the "liberated zone" spending several months in Hanoi en route. While there, he was formally inducted into the **Communist Party of Kampuchea** under the sponsorship of **Ieng Thirith**. After 17 April 1975 he was attached to the Foreign Ministry of **Democratic Kampuchea (DK)**, working again with Ieng Sary. In early January 1979, he was among those sent to Beijing in order to set up a Chinese-based, Radio DK broadcasting unit. From 1981-1984, he worked in the United Nations Mission in New York, and then served as counselor, and from 1986, ambassador of the **Coalition Government of Democratic Kampuchea** to Egypt, Somalia and Sudan until 1991. Reassigned to Phnom Penh, he was attached to the **Party of Democratic Kampuchea (PDK)** delegation of the **Supreme National Council** until its withdrawal in 1993. He was a member of the Party of National Unity founded by the PDK in 1992 and of its Provisional Government of National Unity and Well-being announced in 1994. In 1997 he was among the intellectuals who left **Anlong Veng** and abandoned the DK movement in the disorder resulting from **Pol Pot**'s assassination of **Son Sen**.

IN TAM (1922-). Prime minister, 1973. Born on 23 September 1922 at Prek Kak, Stung Trang district, **Kampong Cham** province, the son of In Iv and Mme (née Mam), In Tam studied at the Pagoda School in Stung Trang 1928-1929, **Lycée Sisowath** and the Royal School of Administration, finishing in 1942. Entering the Cambodian Administration on 1 July 1943 after a year's further study of physical education in Annam, he held various administrative posts in **Prey Veng**, **Siem Reap**, Kampong Cham and in the northeast plateau region. From 1953, he began to specialize in police work, joining the provincial police in Kampong Cham, tracking down **Khmer Issarak** and directing the training school for the provincial guard at **Kampong Chhnang** in 1956-1958.

In Tam was governor of **Takeo** from 1958-1964 and was acting in this capacity when he arranged the 1963 arrest and execution of **Preap In**, who had joined **Son Ngoc Thanh**'s Vietnamese-based **Khmer Serei** movement. That In Tam had recently served as director of the Royal Police Academy 1959-1962, may account for the political zeal on display in this brutal and widely publicized episode, for **Preap In** was not only a nephew of In Tam's but well-known and well-connected in **Khmer Krom** circles. His loyalty to Prince **Norodom Sihanouk** solidly established, in 1965-1966 he was named minister of the interior, capitalizing even more on his new prominence, he ran for the **National Assembly** in 1966. He was elected to represent Krach Chhmar, Kampong Cham province, his wife,

In Tat, being elected in a constituency nearby. He resigned his seat several months later and in response to the **Samlaut uprising**, he was appointed governor of **Battambang** on an emergency basis. In 1968 he returned to the cabinet as minister of agriculture and was reelected to the Assembly in a by-election in Prey Chhor, Kampong Cham province in 1969.

In 1970 In Tam was one of the main parliamentary players in the overthrow of Prince **Norodom Sihanouk**. In recognition of this, he succeeded **Cheng Heng** as president of the National Assembly which meant that it was he who issued the formal proclamation of the **Khmer Republic** in October 1970. Widening civil unrest, much of it centered on his native province, led to his appointment as governor of Kampong Cham and commander of the Kampong Cham military subregion, 1970-1971. Never popular with the Phnom Penh elite, In Tam's activist, populist political style was a valuable political resource, earning him the affection of most peasants, and soldiers also held him in esteem. However, many professional officers regarded him with hostility, judging him an incompetent field commander and blaming him for some of the losses incurred in the 1971 **Operation Chenla I** campaign. His political star barely tarnished by battlefield blunders, on 5 May 1971 he was appointed first deputy president of the Council of Ministers, responsible for the interior, security, religious affairs, and many aspects of rural development and counter-insurgency.

Opting to run for president of the republic in the heavily rigged June 1972 presidential elections, In Tam officially finished second to **Lon Nol**, but he was convinced that he had won, a view shared by many observers at the time. He formed the **Democratic Party** later the same year to contest the elections for the National Assembly, the lower house of the Khmer Republic parliamentary structure, but withdrew his candidates when he saw that the elections would be a farce. He then withdrew from politics. The American Embassy, which was overseeing the round-the-clock B-52 bombing campaign of the countryside at that time, broadly and rather naively favored In Tam as the most democratic of national politicians. As the United States also sought to extend the cease-fire agreements struck with the Vietnamese communists in January, they appealed for an end to the increasingly bitter, high-level in-fighting among leading republican politicians. Fearing suspension of aid, the response from the Republican elites was rapid. On 23 April 1973 the National Assembly approved Tam's appointment to the **High Political Council**. His most bitter foe, **Lon Non**, was forced to leave the country on 30 April and on 15 May 1973 In Tam was appointed prime minister. Effective power remained with Lon Nol, in spite of the gestures, and In Tam, although reappointed prime minister on 22 October, was relieved of his portfolio and all other duties on 26 December, when **Long Boret** was appointed prime minister.

Announcing his retirement for the second time in eight months, In Tam moved to Poipet. He fled from his farm there into Thailand on the morning of 18 April 1975 in the company of two of his sons, In Suchadee and In Boondarm. His several attempts to establish a counter-revolution force along the Thai-Cambodian border quickly proved futile, and not least because the vast majority of Cambodians were tired of war as well as inclined to welcome the new regime. Meanwhile, Thai authorities, not at all desirous of being seen to sponsor a new insurgency, deported In Tam to France in December 1975. By October 1976 he had secured permanent asylum in the United States. In 1979 In Tam was briefly in touch with **Son Sann, Sak Suthsakhan** and **Dien Del** who were establishing the **Khmer People's National Liberation Armed Forces (KPNLAF)** and the **Khmer People's National Liberation Front.** With the sought-after command of the KPNLAF going to Sak Suthsakhan, In Tam rallied once again to Sihanouk's cause, becoming first of all, an official representative of Prince Sihanouk in Southeast Asia and then commander-in-chief of the **Armée Nationale Sihanoukienne (ANS),** until May 1986 when Prince **Norodom Ranariddh** took charge. Also relieved of his role in the Defence Committee of the **Coalition Government of Democratic Kampuchea**, In Tam returned to the United States in December 1986. He returned to Cambodia for two private visits in January and April 1989, clearly attempting to find a new role as interlocutor between the **Hun Sen** government and Khmers in exile. In 1990 he became an **advisor** to the **State of Cambodia**. Unable to suppress rumors that he was intent upon forming a new political movement, and more fortunate than the incarcerated **Thun Seray** and **Ung Phan,** he was forced to return to the United States in 1991. His new **Democratic Party**, inspired in part by the U.S. party, was founded in 1992, but it failed to win any seats in the United Nations-organized 1993 elections. In Tam retired once again to the United States.

IN THADDÉE (1960-2001). A graduate of the *École Nationale Supérieure des Industries Agroalimentaires* and a resident in France, he published *Cambodge Politique,* a newsletter helping to galvanize resistance to the Vietnamese occupation of Cambodia in the 1980s. After 1993 he was a dynamic critic of the **Cambodian People's Party** dominance of government and politics and an effective advocate of press freedom in postwar Cambodia. It was he who arranged the February 1996 visit to France of the opposition journalists Hen Vipheak (*Sereipheap Thmei,* "New Liberty" News), **Chan Rattana** (*Samleng Yuvachon Khmae,* "Voice of Khmer Youth") and **Thun Bunly** *(Uddam Katec Khmae,* "Khmer Ideal"). In 1995, he created the *Comité de Soutien aux Patriotes et Démocrates* *du Cambodge* (Support Committee for Patriots and Democrats in Cambodia). This committee campaigned in support of the resistance to **Hun Sen**'s July 1997 coup against **Norodom Ranariddh**. In 1998 In Thaddée returned to Cambodia as press officer for the **Sam Rainsy Party (SRP)** election campaign. A member of the executive committee of the SRP, his life and political activism ended abruptly in a fatal car crash in France on 11 January 2001. He was a son of **In Sokan**.

INDOCHINA. *See* FRENCH INDOCHINA.

INDOCHINA WAR, FIRST, SECOND and **THIRD**. This term is used to indicate successive international conflicts engulfing Cambodia, Laos and Vietnam. The First Indochina War is dated 1946 to 1954. It began when postwar talks between the **Viet Minh** regime in Hanoi and the French government collapsed in conflict and was concluded at the **Geneva Conference and Accords** of 1954 when all three countries were formally granted their independence from France. The **Geneva Accords** called for the temporary division of **Vietnam** and the regrouping of the warring armies. The conference also confirmed *de jure* the independence of Cambodia, granted by France in November 1953 following the **Royal Crusade for Independence** mounted by King **Norodom Sihanouk**. Confronted with a formidable electoral challenge from the **Democrat Party**, Sihanouk abdicated the throne in 1955 to mobilize the peasantry anew in support of continuing, neomonarchal leadership and rule. He succeeded also in capturing support from prominent elite families whose political parties merged with the **Sangkum**. French military failures in Cambodia, combined with the **Khmer Issarak** failure to present a unified, nationalist resistance to colonialism, plus the willingness of Sihanouk to remain neutral in the Vietnam conflict ensured for a time his leading role.

The Second Indochina War is conventionally dated as 1960-1975, and refers mostly to the second major conflict in Vietnam. The first date represents the year in which the Vietnamese communist party officially launched an armed struggle against the U.S.-supported Ngo Dinh Diem regime. Supply routes through Laos and Cambodia, including the **Ho Chi Minh Trail**, were opened by the mid 1960s but it was **Lon Nol**'s coup in 1970 that triggered an expansion of war into Cambodia. The coup led to a joint U.S.-South Vietnamese "incursion" into Cambodia, the formation of the **National United Front of Kampuchea (FUNK)** and the 1970-1975 civil war. Following hasty evacuations of American diplomatic personnel from two capitals, the Second Indochina War ended with the "liberation" of Phnom Penh on 17 April 1975 and of Saigon on 30 April 1975.

The Third Indochina War, the first between two communist states, began in December 1978 when the People's Army of Vietnam invaded **Democratic Kampuchea,** toppling the **Pol Pot** government and installing **Heng Samrin, Pen Sovan** and other defectors from the **Communist Party of Kampuchea** in his place. Vietnam's occupation and the war of resistance against it came to an end because of the gradual withdrawal of foreign military support to the fighting parties and armies and with the signing of cease-fire and political agreements at the **Paris International Conference on Cambodia** in October 1991.

INDOCHINESE COMMUNIST PARTY (ICP). Founded in Hong Kong in 1930 with assistance from the Comintern agent Nguyen Ai Quoc (Ho Chi Minh), the party consisted exclusively of ethnic Vietnamese. Perceiving Indochina as a single economic unit historically forged by French capital, Moscow instructed the party to organize in Cambodia as well as in Laos. The first members recruited in Laos or Cambodia were mostly ethnic Vietnamese, those working on French-owned plantations or as tradesmen in towns or ethnic Chinese. Ethnic Khmer were not recruited in any substantial numbers before 1949 when the anticolonial struggle, propelled by nationalist rejection of limited autonomy within the French Union, gathered momentum. By 1951, as the war against the French expanded, the underground ICP was superseded by the formation of three national parties, namely the Workers' Party of Vietnam, the **Khmer People's Revolutionary Party (KPRP)** and the Laotian People's Party. As a people's party, the KPRP was not a Marxist-Leninist organization, as was the Vietnamese Party. The KPRP was expected to recruit and to stimulate revolutionary momentum within the Khmer population only, while the ethnic Chinese and ethnic Vietnamese communists residing in Cambodia retained membership in the Vietnamese Party. Restrictions on the KPRP's independence and autonomy were rectified at the party's Second Congress in 1960 when, with Vietnamese approval, the party was reorganized and renamed as the **Workers' Party of Kampuchea.**

INDRAVARMAN I. The King of Cambodia 877-889, he succeeded **Jayvarman III** at Hariharalaya (Roluos) after a series of military campaigns that expanded the Cambodian empire into what is now northeastern Thailand. In 879 he supervised the construction of the Sivaite temple of Preah Ko in the Roluos group. Two years later, also in Roluos, Indravarman built Ba Kong, the first of a series of temple mountains constructed by Cambodian kings over the next 400 years.

INDRAVARMAN II. King of Cambodia 1219-1243, he succeeded his father, the renowned **Jayavarman VII**, but no documentation survives from what seems to have been a 25-year reign.

INDRAVARMAN III. King of Cambodia c1295-1308, it was during his rule that Angkor, his capital, was visited by the Chinese emissary **Zhou Daguan**. According to Zhou's report, Indravarman, a Buddhist, presided over a kingdom which remained orderly, rich and powerful in spite of a recent invasion.

INDUSTRY. Industrial activity was limited to home-based enterprise until the arrival of the French colonialists who established a few dozen major plants (e.g. ice, carbonated drinks, alcohol distilleries, chemicals, tobacco, soap, power plants, rubber latex and food processing plants) but who concentrated most investment in the neighboring colony of **Cochinchina**. From 1954, the statutory end of colonial rule, national statistical accounts reveal the most important industries were jewelry manufacturing (345), rice mills (277), brick and tile plants (c200), charcoal plants (178) and sawmills (124), including mechanized and hand-operated. Sihanouk also accepted gifts of turn-key glass, cement, plywood and jute factories from foreign powers but these and older industries were operated as state-owned enterprises after 1963. Total output was undermined by a devastating combination of poor management, corruption and competition. A strong demand for liberalization of the economy from private sector traders and entrepreneurs underlay the wide elite consensus in support of the 1970 *coup d'état.* Under communist rule, some emphasis was placed on industry linked to agriculture such as farm machinery, household goods, transport (e.g. boats), latex processing and textiles but workers were often demobilized soldiers who lacked training and experience as well as raw materials, spare parts for aging equipment, electricity and fuel. Apart from encouragement of craft industries, Cambodia made little industrial progress under Vietnamese occupation and protection, 1979-1989, though a less than fully successful attempt was made to revitalize rubber plantations. From the beginning of the United Nations interregnum in 1991, foreign donors have financed postwar reconstruction of national infrastructure in an effort to encourage both national and international private capital investment. By 1999 the buoyant garment industry was the largest employer of waged labor (413,651) followed by agriculture (32,000), services (17,188) and tourism (11,634). Industry has steadily attracted the largest number of investment projects with agri-industries, food processing, household goods, garment and textile manufacturing, wood processing and cement being the most attractive sectors. Industry makes up 15 percent only of national GDP while industrial workers represent about 6.4 percent of the natonal work force. *See also* FOREIGN INVESTMENT.

ING KIETH (1926-). The son of Ing Say and Mme (née Kim Boy) and a brother of Ung Pech, one of the few to survive imprisonment at **Tuol Sleng**, Kieth studied civil engineering in France first at the École Spéciale des Travaux Publics du Bâtiment et des Mines, until 1954, and École Nationale des Ponts et Chaussées, Paris until 1959. Once back in Phnom Penh he was, in rapid succession, director of the School of Public Works and Mines; executive director of the office of mechanical engineering; governor of Kirirom; secretary of state for labor and social affairs, October 1962 to December 1964; secretary of state for public works, December 1964 to May 1965 and again in May to October 1966. An advisor to the Royal Cambodian Armed Forces in the late 1960s, he was on the board of *Société Nationale de Pneumatiques* (SONAPNEU) by 1969.

In September 1970 Ing Kieth was among many top technicians who received a commission in the army, in his case, as a colonel. It is perhaps as a result of his somewhat privileged view of disastrous military developments in 1971 that his support for the Republic ebbed rapidly. In 1973 he moved to Algeria where he joined the management team in charge of the construction of Bethiowa El Djedid port. While still there, he announced his support for the **National United Front of Kampuchea** and for Sihanouk's **Royal Government of National Union of Kampuchea.** Returning to France in 1975, he worked in the French Ministry of Development and Transport. In 1991 he joined the **FUNCINPEC** office in Bangkok, serving as a liaison officer in talks surrounding the revival of **Mekong** committee activities, and returned to Cambodia as a member of committees planning rehabilitation, natural resources strategy and the protection and restoration of the monuments of **Angkor.** Following the May 1993 elections, in which he won a seat, he was named second vice-president of the Constituent Assembly, a member of the **Throne Council** and, in October, a minister of state as well as minister of public works and transport. Concurrently, he was chairman of the Council of the Mekong River Commission and president of the National Mekong Committee of Cambodia. Within FUNCINPEC, he was member of the National Council and Steering Committee (until March 1999). In 1998 he was elected to the **National Assembly** for Kandal but resigned his seat when he was appointed ambassador to Japan. His daughter, Ing Kuntha Thavy, was named secretary of state in the Ministry of Women and Veteran's Affairs in December 1998.

INSCRIPTIONS. Over a thousand of these, incised onto stone in Sanskrit and Khmer, have so far been recovered. They are the main source for the history of pre-Angkorean and Angkorean Cambodia, and provide much data, only some of which can be verified from other sources. Inscriptions in poetic form are often in Sanskrit and tend to glorify the activities, often religious, of the kings or high ranking figures who sponsored the inscriptions and the ceremonies which they recollect. Inscriptions in prose are more often composed in Khmer and deal prosaically with everyday matters related to land ownership, slaves and legal disputes.

INTERNATIONAL COMMISSION OF SUPERVISION AND CONTROL (ICSC). This was a monitoring body set up by the **Geneva Conference** in 1954 to oversee the implementation of decolonization agreements relating to Vietnam, Laos and Cambodia. The ICSC consisted of a Communist member (Poland), a Western member (Canada) and a neutral member (India). The three were seldom able to agree, although they certified that the 1955 elections, which were marred by much violence and fraud, had been "free and fair." The ICSC lingered on in Cambodia until the mid 1960s, partly because similar postcolonial elections were never held in Vietnam.

ISANAPURA. An important pre-Angkorean city, it is mentioned in inscriptions relating to **Chenla**. On the strength of this evidence, it was probably located near the seventh century ruins of Sambor Prey Kuk in **Kampong Thom**.

ISANAVARMAN II. The King of Cambodia 923-928, and son of **Yasovarman I**, he succeeded his brother **Harshavarman I**. Isanavarman left no inscriptions, although Prasat Kravanh at **Angkor** and Neang Khmau in Takeo were constructed during his brief reign.

ISLAM IN CAMBODIA. Although Arab traders were very likely active at **Angkor** as they were throughout medieval Southeast Asia, evidence for their presence is sparse. Islam did not become important in Cambodia until the collapse of Champa in the 17th century an event that saw thousands of **Cham**, including many Muslims, seeking refuge in the kingdom of the Khmer. With the approval of the Khmer court, they settled in the eastern region of the country which acquired the Malay derived name of **Kampong Cham** ("Cham town"). The Chams practiced their religion openly, and received some government subsidies for the Haj until 1975. All religious activity was suppressed by the **Pol Pot** revolutionaries. Iman Haji Res Los, the Grand Mufti of Cambodian Islam, was executed on 8 October 1975 at Konhom, Peam Chisor, **Prey Veng**, and a few scholars have argued the Cham community was subjected to a genocidal assault. Ministry of Interior population estimates for the 1990s consistently show Kampong Cham to have the largest population of any in the country: 1,608,914 (or 14 percent of the country's total) according to the 1998 census and a March 1995 estimate put the total Cham population at 203,881.

ITH SARIN. He was an inspector of schools in the late 1960s who was critical of Prince **Norodom Sihanouk** for his repression of civil liberties. After the 1970 coup, of which he approved, he next became disillusioned with the corruption of the Lon Nol government, left the capital, and spent nine months with communists based in **Kampong Speu**. Sarin's book, *Regrets of a Khmer Soul*, published in Khmer in 1973, displays much scepticism about the new collective life being introduced in 1972. He survived the **Democratic Kampuchea** period, as one of the **"new people,"** but emigrated to the United States in 1981.

ITH SEAM (1910-). A prominent Sino-Khmer businessman, brother of **Ith Seap**, and cousin of **Hak Mong Sheng**, Ith Seam was educated at the École Doudart de Lagrée and **Collège Sisowath**. He entered colonial service as a secretary for the **French Résident** of Kandal and then Kampong Cham from 1928-1936. He then established logging and transport enterprises earning a small fortune from public orders. A **Democrat Party** militant, he was elected to the 1947 National Assembly in Speu, **Kampong Cham**, and was secretary of state for trade, industry and development in the **Chhean Vam** cabinet of February to August 1948. Giving open support to the **Khmer Issarak** and **Viet Minh** armed struggles, he did not run in the 1951 elections and withdrew from political life after losing a by-election in Sampong Chey, Kampong Cham, in 1952.

ITH SEAP (1910-). Ith Seap accompanied his brother **Ith Seam** through school and also worked in the colonial administration from 1928-1945. In March 1945, he was appointed director of the Plantation of Prek Kak, taking over from a Frenchman dislodged by the Japanese coup. A member of the **Democrat Party**, he was elected in 1947 to the National Assembly, representing Stung Trang, **Kampong Cham**. French intelligence reports from this time say it was Seap who organized student demonstrations against **Yèm Sambaur** in 1949, in opposition to the **Franco-Cambodian Treaty**. Like many other ardent nationalists and republicans, he became demoralized by late-colonial politics, did not run in the 1951 elections and devoted himself to business pursuits. In the mid-1960s, with profits from his big bus company hit by the closure of the lucrative **Phnom Penh**-Saigon route, Seap shifted most of his capital into new rubber plantation developments in **Ratanakiri**. The plantations were later sprayed with chemical defoliants by the U.S. Air Force causing him to lose his fortune. A daughter, Ith Nary, who has degrees in both finance and law, was briefly national treasurer of Cambodia. Many in the Ith family have lived in France since 1975.

IV TUOT (1893-c1969). A highly respected Buddhist leader in **Battambang**, he was born at Phsar Svaypor, Sangker, becoming a novice at age 13 and *chau athicar* (abbot) of Wat Pothiveal in 1921. Elected mekon of Battambang in 1945, he received the dignity of *Preah Vannarath Reachea Kanak* in 1953; the title of *Samdech* was conferred in 1964. A dynamic teacher, Wat Pothiveal became a national center of Buddhist learning under his guidance.

IZZI, MONIQUE. *See* MONINEATH SIHANOUK, QUEEN.

-J-

JAKARTA INFORMAL MEETINGS (JIM). These discussions, initially chaired by Indonesia on behalf of the member countries of the Association of Southeast Asian Nations, were held in Jakarta on 25-28 July 1988, and were attended by representatives of each of the warring Cambodian parties as well as delegations from Laos, Vietnam and the ASEAN countries. A second round of talks, jointly chaired by France, took place on 19 February 1990 and included Australia. An "Australian Plan" called for a political settlement involving a transitional, United Nations administration working with a **Supreme National Council (SNC)**. The Cambodian parties agreed to form the SNC, having failed in August 1989 to agree on a coalition government. The political settlement agreed in Paris in October 1991 was devised by the permanent members of the United Nations Security Council.

JAPAN. Buddhist pilgrims from Japan visited Angkor in the 17th century, and Japanese traders lived in Lopburi and Phnom Penh at this time. Japan and Cambodia were cut off from each other for the 18th and 19th centuries, and Japanese commercial interest revived only with the economic drive into Southeast Asia in the 1930s. The Japanese military occupation of Cambodia in **World War II** had less enduring effects then Japan's diplomatic intervention in the Franco-Thai war, in favor of Thailand, an act which is believed to have hastened the death of King **Sisowath Monivong** and led to the enthronement of the young King **Norodom Sihanouk**. In the 1951 peace conference held in San Francisco, Cambodia protested against the conditions imposed on Japan and waived its own right to reparations and trade resumed immediately after independence.

After an exchange of visits between heads of state in 1955 and 1956, economic relations expanded rapidly. Between 1959 and 1966 Japan extended some $4.2 million in economic aid to Cambodia. Two prominent conservative politicians served as Cambodian Ambassadors to Tokyo: Prince **Sisowath Sirik Matak** 1965-1968 and **Sim Var** from 1968 (who married a Japanese woman during his tour). In 1979 Japan joined the United States and European Union embargo on aid, trade and investment with Vietnam and Cambodia but throughout the 1980s, either via the

United Nations or on a bilateral basis, Japan was active on the diplomatic front in an attempt to secure a resolution of the "Cambodian problem." A Japanese diplomat, **Yasushi Akashi**, was appointed to head the **United Nations Transitional Authority in Cambodia** 1991-1993. Japan is now Cambodia's most important aid donor, pledging $100 million at the June 1999 international donor's meeting which it hosted in Tokyo.

The Paris International Conference on Cambodia resulted in the Cambodian Embassy in Tokyo being returned to the new Cambodian government. The original building had been demolished to make way for building developments for the 1960 Olympic Games. In return the Japanese government had given Cambodia a new site, on a city bloc, adjoining the Imperial Palace. Details of its sale for a rumored US$440 million abound despite official denials.

JATAKAS. These are noncanonical Buddhist narrative tales which in Cambodian **Buddhism** are linked to the *samsara* or cycle of births and reincarnation. (The term *jataka* denotes the previous existences of the Buddha.) Bhikkhu Meas Yang provides several examples of national Jataka tales in his study, *Le Bouddhisme au Cambodge* (Bruxelles, 1978). The telling and retelling of the tales formed part of traditional moral education in the family, alongside the secular, poetic recitation of *chhbab.*

JAYAVARMAN I. King of Cambodia c657-700, he is mentioned in inscriptions found as far apart as **Battambang** and **Prey Veng**. He is believed to take his name from "Java," an ancient kingdom, almost certainly not the modern island known by that name, as historians once believed. His capital, not yet located precisely by historians was called Purandarapura.

JAYAVARMAN II (c770-c834). The first king to reign at Angkor, 790-c834, his is an important but poorly documented reign. An inscription carved long after his death asserted that he had returned home to Cambodia toward the end of the eighth century after being held prisoner or hostage by rulers of "Java," probably a kingdom in present-day Malaysia. In 802 he participated in a ceremony on **Phnom Kulen**, north of Angkor, whereby he became a "universal monarch." These ceremonies also consecrated the *devaraja* ("god king") cult, the full significance and content of which has vexed scholars. Clearly Sivaite, debate centers on whether it honors Siva as the king of all gods, or the Khmer king as the supreme king, or god, among kings. Jayavarman's activities between 770 and 802 probably consisted in carrying on military campaigns and forging alliances among local chiefs in what is now northwestern Cambodia to gain recognition as their overlord.

JAYAVARMAN III. King of Cambodia c834-877. Son of **Jayavarman II**, with his capital in the Roluos region, who has left very slight traces in inscriptions (one refers to him as having ruled 'wisely'). His reign may have been more brief than indicated and the territorial reach of the empire may have diminished under his control. Restoration was achieved by **Indravarman I**, his successor.

JAYAVARMAN IV. King of Cambodia 928-942, he seized power following the death of his nephew, **Isanavarman II**. While claiming to be "king of kings," his capital was **Koh Ker**, some 100 kilometers north of **Angkor**. His attachment to that area where he had lived prior to his accession is preserved in the form of several impressive, apparently unfinished monuments. His kingdom included parts of modern **Battambang, Siem Reap, Kampong Thom, Kampong Cham** and **Takeo** provinces.

JAYAVARMAN V. King of Cambodia 968-1001, and son of King **Rajendra-varman II**. During his reign, which began in warfare, construction of the temple of Ta Keo commenced and that of **Banteay Srei**, begun earlier, was completed, the latter under the patronage of Jayavarman's Sanskrit teacher, Yajnavaraha. Once established, his long reign was unusually peaceful.

JAYAVARMAN VI. King of Cambodia 1080-1107. Few inscriptions survive from his long, apparently peaceful reign, which may have commenced with an act of violence. He was a patron of widespread temple communities, including one in **Preah Vihear,** another in **Phimai,** established toward the end of his reign and now in northeast Thailand, and another in Wat Phu in southern Laos.

JAYAVARMAN VII. King of Cambodia 1178-c1220. The most celebrated of the Angkorean kings in modern nationalist thought, his early life is obscure but his accession in 1178 is a subject of controversy and so is his relationship with the kingdom of **Champa**, where he spent many years as a hostage or in exile. While there he probably embraced Mahayana ("Greater Vehicle") **Buddhism**. He came to the throne in 1178, in the aftermath of a Cham invasion of **Angkor**. His role in this invasion is unclear but his rule was consecrated in 1181.

Owing to the sheer scale and grandeur of **Angkor Thom**, and the large number of other temples and sites constructed during his reign, archaeologists, led by **Georges Coedès**, viewed Jayavarman VII as the most creative of Cambodia's kings, a perception visibly reinforced by the powerful, larger than life size, statue portraits depicting the monarch deep in meditation. In fact, the extant evidence tells us remarkably little about his intelligence, personality or reign, aside from the chronology of his building program, the art he patronised and the fact that he was a devout Buddhist.

JAYAVARMAN VIII. King of Cambodia 1243-1296 and a grandson of **Jayavarman VII.** During his long reign, **Angkor** defeated an expeditionary force dispatched from China but lost control over Thai tributary states such as Sukothai and Louvo, which in this period declared their independence. A Hindu, Jayavarman VIII may be responsible for the defacing of some of the Buddhist statuary in the **Bayon** where, in addition, the central Buddha image was replaced with one of the Hindu deity **Harihara.** *See also* HINDUISM.

JELDRES, JULIO A. Official biographer of King **Norodom Sihanouk.** Jeldres wrote to Prince Sihanouk in 1967 when he was a high school student in his native Chile. The two pursued a correspondence which continued for many years, including Sihanouk's years of exile in **China** from 1970-1975. Julio immigrated to Australia in 1972, but lost contact with Sihanouk in September 1975, reestablishing it six years later, in 1982, when he visited the Prince in Pyongyang, North Korea. In 1983 he moved to **Thailand** to work in the Bangkok office of **FUNCINPEC,** later being appointed private secretary to Sihanouk and moving to Beijing. He returned to Phnom Penh with the Prince in 1991 when he was instrumental in founding one of the first Cambodian NGOs, the **Khmer Institute of Democracy.** He was appointed roving ambassador for the king in late 1993, and in 1995, after his return to Australia, official biographer.

JUDICIARY. Fully reorganized in the 1980s and 1990s with lower courts, an appeals court and a Supreme Court, the national judicial system is widely criticized for ineffectiveness, on the one hand, and for the corruption among judges on the other. The legacy of history is part of the problem. In the 19th century there was no separation of judicial and administrative power. Governors and local headmen adjudicated all forms of disputes and they, as well as the king, extended patronage and protection in the process. The Treaty of Protection signed with **France** in 1863 provided for the creation of a mixed Franco-Khmer tribunal and succeeding royal ordinances awarded competent French administrators the right to organize all judicial proceedings involving foreign nationals. Meanwhile "indigenous" justice remain unchanged. For legal purposes "Annamite" (Vietnamese) citizens from Cochinchina residing or working in the Cambodian protectorate were allowed to register on an annual basis for the status of "French subject" giving them restricted rights of extraterritoriality and, as Khmer saw it, privilege. From as early as 1912, the colonial consultative assembly expressed a desire for a national system of justice which was separate from "executive" (i.e., French) power, and not least because immigrant Chinese increasingly benefited from special treatment and the **French Résidents** were intervening in local justice.

In 1922, a major reform of the "indigenous" justice system formally laid the basis for a European-style system of civil and penal courts, creating many new posts in the administration of the protectorate. Court clerks, secretaries, magistrates, investigative judges and heads of tribunals were employed, paid and promoted in accordance with grades and length of service comparable to those in civil administration. There is little evidence that the reform yielded improved legal outcomes: training, professional esteem and rewards were all seriously overlooked in the scramble for appointments. Those hoping for rule of law, then or since 1993, lamented the failure to respect extant law, the absence of suitable laws, the bribe-taking of underpaid court officials and judges and their alleged political biases. In these discourses, judges were blamed too much for everyday politics. Their verdicts depended less on the merits of a case than on the social status of the plaintiff or defendant, whether well-connected or "strong" in the sense of commanding resources or otherwise deserving of a reciprocally rewarding accommodation within the repressive system.

By constitutional design, liberal due process should be protected by two institutional safeguards. A **Constitutional Council** exists to review the constitutionality of laws or of their application and a Supreme Council of the Magistracy possesses the power to discipline judges. Neither body is active or is able to function satisfactorily in a context where neglect and abuse of the law is widespread. Moreover, the judiciary in some jurisdictions remains under the thumb of executive power. On his own initiative Phnom Penh governor **Chea Sophara** "suspended" two municipal judges for alleged misconduct, a move ratified with no comment from the Supreme Council of the Magistracy, a body established by the constitution for overseeing appointments to the bench, disciplining judges and assuring judicial independence. A few weeks after the event, the suspended pair were quietly assigned to other posts. Adding to the institutional mix, an extra-constitutional seven-member Judicial Reform Council was created by the government in April 2000. Civil rights NGOs protested against the clear violation of the democratic separation of executive and judicial powers but to no avail.

-K-

KAMBUBOTH. Also known by its full expansion, Kampuchea Both, this was a privately organized secondary school, established in 1962 by former **Democrat Party** activists. The principal of the school, Chan Oul, was believed to be procommunist. He hired many "progressive" intellectuals, including **Ieng Sary, Hou Youn, So Nem, Khieu Samphan**, Ros Sarin and **Mey Mann**, who had no sympathy for the elitism of the **Sangkum** era. Some staff were definitely anticommunist as well as antielitist, for example, Ea Chhong, who became a brigadier general in the Republican Air Force in the early 1970s. **Bu Phat** and **Nop Bophan** were among the former students who eventually joined the Communist movement. **Uch Ven** was a teacher associated with both Kambuboth and **Chamroeun Vichea** where Saloth Sar (**Pol Pot**) taught full time. Staff and students at both schools lent support to the university-based **Assemblée Générale des Étudiants Khmers**.

KAMBUJA. A glossy magazine published in French and English editions by the state, 1965-1970, under the direction of Prince **Norodom Sihanouk**. The hands-on work fell to Mme **Suon Kaset** who was editor in chief of the publication as well as director for the (original) French-language edition. **Measketh Caimirane** and **Khek Lerang** were the chief administrators. Produced primarily for foreign consumption, *Kambuja* tried to convey a modernizing, stable image of Cambodia. Sihanouk used the editorial pages to comment on foreign or other topical issues.

KAMPEXIM. This was the state-owned, import-export trading agency established by the **People's Republic of Kampuchea (PRK)** in the 1980s. Until 1987, when the private sector was permitted to resume some exporting, KAMPEXIM had a monopoly on all foreign trade. It received imported goods supplied by other socialist states either on credit or as grant aid and exported Cambodian goods in exchange, that is, payment. Comparatively little trade was conducted with hard-currency areas. In 1990 around 70 percent of foreign trade remained state-controlled with the annual deficit reaching an estimated $111 million. The total volume of trade for the same year was $230 million. KAMPEXIM's role diminished rapidly after 1991 as private trading and trade with dollar zones grew.

KAMPONG CHAM. The most populous province in Cambodia, it covers 10,498 square kilometers and borders **Vietnam** as well as the provinces of **Kratié, Prey Veng, Kampong Thom** and **Kampong Chhnang**. Its capital town, of the same name, is near the center of the province. The *General Population Census of Cambodia 1998* surveyed 16 districts, 173 communes and 1,748 villages with a total of 1,608,914 people. Of these, only 2.8 percent were classified as urban, the lowest of all provinces. The high density of the population on the available land, 164 per square kilometer compared to the national average of 64, is a reflection of the extent and intensity of agricultural activities and rural commerce. Its prosperity attracted Malay, Cham and Chinese immigrants to the region, and commercial activity encouraged intensive garden farming and commercial plantation industries. The French established the first rubber plantation in Kampong Cham in 1921 and from the 1950s the tobacco industry was there. The province figures prominently in modern politics, not only because of its size and the complexity of its social structure but because of its interchange with Vietnam. During the first **Indochina War** both the *Khmer Issarak* and the communists recruited successfully in the province. Saloth Sar **(Pol Pot)** went into hiding there in 1963-1965 and **Hun Sen**, a native of the province, went underground there in 1967.

KAMPONG CHHNANG. Another central plains province with a capital town of the same name, Kampong Chhnang borders the provinces of **Kampong Speu, Pursat, Kampong Thom** and **Kampong Cham** and the **Tonlé Sap.** It covers an area of 5,520 square kilometers and has 417,693 people. The province has been noted since Angkorean times for its giant earthenware water jars, the *chhnang.*

KAMPONG SOM. *See* SIHANOUKVILLE.

KAMPONG SPEU. This mountainous province is just south of **Kampong Chhnang** and also borders the provinces of **Koh Kong, Kandal, Kampot, Takeo** and **Pursat**. It has an area of 7,016 square kilometers and the March 1998 **census** recorded its population as 598,882. In the 1950s and 1960s **agriculture** in the province was constrained by poor soils, drought and shortages of arable land. The average density of population is 85 per square kilometer, above the national average of 64. Kampong Speu town and its environs were badly damaged by artillery and air bombardments in the 1970-1975 war.

KAMPONG THOM. A province and provincial capital, notable for its archaeological sites, for its **Kuy** minority community, its iron deposits, and as the birthplace of Saloth Sar **(Pol Pot)**. It is one of the provinces ringing the **Tonlé Sap**. It is surrounded by **Siem Reap, Preah Vihear, Stung Treng** and **Kratié** to the north and east and by **Kampong Cham** and **Kampong Chhnang** to the south. The province covers an area of 12,251 square kilometers and the final report of the March 1998 **census** records its population at 569,060 people. The census also reveals a high percentage of female-headed households (28.8 percent). During the early 1990s, Kampong Thom was fiercely contested between troops loyal to the authorities in Phnom Penh and to **Democratic Kampuchea**. The conflict generated tens of thousands of refugees.

KAMPOT. This province, the 11th largest in population, borders **Vietnam, Takeo, Kampong Speu** and **Koh Kong,** covering an area of 9,862 square kilometers. In the March 1998 **census** its population was recorded as 528,408 people (4.6 percent of the nation's total). Life in this delta province is deeply influenced by developments in Vietnam with which there is much communication, and by the presence of a large Chinese population, the result of 19th and 20th century immigrations from southern China. The old colonial hill station of **Bokor** is now a central feature of Bokor National Park and the province also boasts the favored seaside retreat of the leisured colonial elites, **Kep**. A cultural crossroads with, in most periods, a high population density for the available, arable land, Kampot was a hot-bed of resistance to the French in the First **Indochina War**, and a "red zone" once again in the 1970s, providing base areas and cadres for the revolution. Large parts of the province remained insecure in the 1990s while landowning families lucky enough to have reclaimed the land they owned in the 1960s frequently say they must produce or find enough food for twice as many people as they supported then.

KANDAL. The central or capital city province, Kandal is nestled around the lowland **Mekong-Tonlé-Bassac** River plain, roughly the central portion of the Mekong Delta south of the **Tonlé Sap** and north of the Vietnamese delta. "Kandal" means "central" in the Khmer language. The second largest province in population terms, it had 1,075,125 people in 1998, 9.4 percent of the nation's total, and 52 percent were female. Covering an area of 33,813 square kilometers, Kandal has 11 *srok* (districts), 147 *khum* (subdistricts) and 1,087 *phum* (villages). It currently possesses 11 seats in the **National Assembly**, of which 4 are held by the **Cambodian People's Party**; 5 by **FUNCINPEC** and 2 by the **Sam Rainsy Party**. A singularly distinctive feature of the economy of the province is the highly intensive garden farming on the silt-enriched riverbanks. Fruit and vegetables of high quality and wide variety are grown and sold in **Phnom Penh** municipal markets or via river or overland routes, in Ho Chi Minh City. The town of Takhmau, population 58,264 (1998), originally created in the early 1950s as an industrial and market center serving the capital is the only urban part of the province.

KANG KECH IEU alias **Duch (1943-).** Born in Kampong Chen, Staung, **Kampong Thom**, the son of a Chinese father and a Khmer mother (née Kang Siew), the young Kech Ieu was an outstanding pupil who received his *baccalauréat* in mathematics in 1959 after studies at **Lycée Sisowath**. For most of the 1960s, he taught at Lycée Balaing in Kampong Thom town but in 1964, he accepted a post at the National Institute of Pedagogy where Chinese exchange students reportedly won him over to Marxism-Leninism. He taught briefly at Lycée Chhoeung Prey in **Kampong Cham** town in 1967-1968 where he was involved in demonstrations in which a bus was burnt outside the local police station. Although he was arrested and jailed, in relation to this incident and as part of a crackdown on pro-Chinese activists and suspected communists, his family and friends quietly secured his release sometime in 1968 when he returned to Kampong Thom. In 1970 Kang Kech Iev joined the **National United Front of Kampuchea** and worked in **Kampong Chhnang** (*Tambon* 33) taking the underground, revolutionary name "Duch." By late 1971 Duch had responsibilities for security affairs and by 1973 he worked in what was known as the "Special Zone" with two leading communists: **Vorn Vet** and **Son Sen**, who are known to have been involved in secret purging from 1973 onwards.

Following the 17 April 1975 "liberation" of Phnom Penh, Duch directed the **Communist Party of Kampuchea** security center, known only by its party code, S-21 ("S" for *sala* or meeting hall, and "21," the numerical designation for party-state security police, *santebal*). Known since 1979 as, **Tuol Sleng**, about 14,000 people, most purged from their posts in the state apparatus, the army and cooperative management committees were imprisoned, tortured and sent to their deaths by Duch and his staff, believed to have numbered around 45 people. Duch reported directly to Son Sen who as chief of staff of the armed forces and standing committee member responsible for security affairs had overall charge and some files were passed directly to **Nuon Chea** who was responsible for internal party affairs. Duch disappeared from view in January 1979 when the Vietnamese army occupied Phnom Penh. He remained with the **Democratic Kampuchea (DK)** movement until 1992, when, under a new name, he secured jobs with **United Nations** and private relief groups working along the border with **Thailand**. In 1999 a few year after he had become a Christian, he was recognized by journalists and freely confessed to his past criminal actions. He was arrested and imprisoned, partly for his own protection. He has not been charged nor tried for crimes against humanity or genocide as of 2002 because Cambodia lacks the necessary legislation or an appropriate court.

KANN MAN (1947-). Born in **Prey Veng**, he was secretary to **Hun Sen** 1981-1985, and permanent secretary of the **People's Republic of Kampuchea** Ministry of Foreign Affairs 1986-1990. In 1990, together with **Ung Phan** and **Thun Seray**, he founded a Liberal Democratic Socialist Party. All three were jailed without trial from May 1990 to October 1991 when they were released under the terms of a general amnesty for political prisoners in the **Paris International Conference on Cambodia**. Joining **FUNCINPEC** in July 1992, Kann Man was elected to the Constituent Assembly for **Kandal**, and from 1993-1998 headed the Assembly's Commission for Public Health, Social and Women's Affairs.

KEO TAK (1906-1955). A native of **Siem Reap** born of a Chinese father and Khmer mother, he married a Khmer-Thai woman from Surin and was a small shopkeeper in Chong Kal district (today part of **Oddar Meanchey** province) until 1946. During the Thai occupation, 1941-1946, he was a subdistrict headman (*mesrok*) in Samrong but remained loyal to **Son Ngoc Thanh** and other nationalists associated with the *Nagaravatta* group. He took part in the administration of the Kingdom of Kampuchea after March 1945, but had to flee from Phnom Penh in December 1945 and was thereafter active in the **Khmer Issarak**. In a test of his local power, he tried to run as an independent in the **National Assembly** elections in 1951 without success. In 1952, he lent renewed support to Son Ngoc Thanh and his republican guerrilla movement based in the **Dangrek Range**. His antimonarchal sentiments by then firmly established, he was among the former Issarak militants killed in 1955 in advance of the September elections. The execution was reliably reported to have been arranged by **Dap Chhuon**, a one-time ally turned rival local power broker, as a sign of Chhuon's postcolonial willingness to work with **Norodom Sihanouk**. After the assassination, **Hang Thun Hak** married Tak's daughter and looked after the family. *See also* BANGKOK PLOT; KEM SREY.

KARPÈLES, SUZANNE (c1890-1969). A French Buddhist scholar, she was the founding secretary of the Buddhist Institute established in 1930. Her work brought her into close collaboration with many early nationalists, including **Son Ngoc Thanh**, **Pach Chhoeun** and **Sim Var**, founders of the Khmer-language newspaper, *Nagaravatta* ("Angkor Wat"), 1936-1942. Conceived as a device for reducing international, especially Thai, influence on Cambodian Buddhism, the Institute heightened national identity and pride beyond expectations. Although sometimes accused of "radical" views, it was Karpelès's dedicated pursuit and encouragement of national knowledge that ensured her contribution to the nationalist movement was both fundamental and enduring.

KE KIM SE. An interpreter at the **Democratic Kampuchea (DK)** Ministry of Foreign Affairs from 1975-1979 and brother of Kê So Sê (Mme Pech Bun Ret), he may have lived in Canada, 1984-1991. In 1992 he joined the staff of Prince **Norodom Sihanouk** with the rank of ambassador. On 12 June 1994 he was appointed head of the royal secretariat and became editor in chief of Sihanouk's *Bulletin Mensuel de Documentation*.

KE KIM YAN (1955-). Chief of Staff of the Royal Cambodian Armed Forces. Born in Bakau, Pursat, and educated to lycée level in **Battambang** province, Ke Kim Yan lived in the countryside during the **Democratic**

Kampuchea (DK) period and lent active support to the **People's Republic of Kampuchea** administration from 1979. In October 1985, he was elected to the Central Committee of the **People's Revolutionary Party of Kampuchea (PRPK)** being already Secretary of the Battambang province provisional party committee and chairman of the province's People's Revolutionary Committee. In December 1986 he became deputy defense minister and chief of staff of the armed forces, appointments that reflected the importance of the regional army in Battambang. **Ung Samy**, a nephew of party secretary **Chea Sim**, replaced him as provisional party committee secretary of the province. Promoted to two-star lieutenant general in January 1989, Ke Kim Yan actively defended Chea Sim's leading role in the period immediately before the special congress of October 1991 at which Marxism-Leninism was officially abandoned and the PRPK was reorganized as the **Cambodian People's Party (CPP)**. In 1993 he was elected to the 1993 Constituent Assembly on the CPP list in **Banteay Meanchey** province, giving up his seat to accept renewed appointment as chief of staff. Not always on the best of terms with **Hun Sen,** reports of his death among the first killings reported at the time of the July 1997 coup sent his wife and children fleeing to Thailand on a Thai government evacuation flight. Although these reports proved erroneous, it later emerged that Ke Kim Yan disputed an order to deploy the army on the streets of **Phnom Penh**. Hun Sen's 1999 appointment of **Kun Kim** to the general staff led to speculation that the prime minister was seeking to tighten his grip on the army, using his top personal advisor to ease out Ke Kim Yan. All parties concerned dismissed the speculation and Ke Kim Yan retains his post as of early 2002.

KE PAUK alias **Ke Vin (1934-2002).** Born in Baray, Kampong Thom, he was the son of Keo Ke, a farmer. After receiving some education in Buddhist pagoda schools, the young Vin joined a **Khmer Issarak** band in 1950. Arrested in 1954 he was sentenced to six years in jail but was released after serving half of his sentence. Returning to his native village, he married and had at least six children when in 1964 he found himself in trouble with the police. He vanished into the forest where he joined forces with the underground **Communist Party of Kampuchea (CPK)** becoming a military commander in the northwest by the late 1960s. In 1970-1975 he was deputy secretary of the northern zone as well as secretary of the **Siem Reap** sector where he was associated with some of the more violent and racialist policies introduced by the party during the wartime period. Having won the trust and support of **Pol Pot**, he replaced **Koy Thuon** as acting secretary of the northern zone in January 1977 following violent purges and then restructured the zone, becoming commander of its army by midyear. In the final months of **Democratic Kampuchea (DK)**, using the military forces under his command, he assisted the party center in the purging of the northern half of the East Zone party leadership under **So Phim**. In the course of the mutiny, popular rebellion and massacres arising from the purging, over 100,000 people are believed to have died.

In December 1979, after the Vietnamese occupation, Pauk was identified as deputy secretary general of the National Army of Democratic Kampuchea High Command or fourth in command after Pol Pot, commander in chief; **Ta Mok**, chief of staff and **Son Sen,** secretary-general and deputy prime minister for national defense. By 1986, however, he was purged and sidelined by the CPK hierarchy having been found guilty of smuggling along the Thai border. Although he continued to have administrative responsibilities, notably, in civilian and rear base camps, his duties in **Anlong Veng** appear to have been restricted to agricultural and forestry administration by the mid-1990s. He defected to the Royal Government with some military forces at the end of March 1998. Immediately appointed as an advisor to the Ministry of Defense, in January 1999 he was made brigadier general in the **Royal Cambodian Armed Forces**. Several **human rights** groups objected in view of his role in some of the worst violence of the 1970s but government spokesmen insisted his appointment as well as those of other senior DK politicians were a means of ensuring their loyalty to the state. Pauk himself disappeared from public view in mid-1999 after the trial and sentencing of another former DK official, **Nuon Paet,** to life imprisonment for the kidnapping and murder of three western hostages. Living quietly in Siem Reap he died on 15 February 2002.

KEAT CHHON (1934-). Born in Chhlong, **Kratié** province, he studied civil engineering at the École Nationale Supérieure du Génie Maritime in Paris, then served as an intern at the nuclear center in Saclay, France. On his return to Cambodia he was befriended by Toch Phoeun among others, supported their "progressive" activities and was identified as a possible communist subversive in the "Affair of the 34" in March 1963, the event that put **Pol Pot** and others on the run into clandestinity. Rector of the Royal University of **Kampong Cham** 1965-1968, he did not join the revolutionary movement until 1967 when he served briefly as secretary of state for the national economy, in charge of Industry. He was minister for industry and trade, 1967-1969, when pressures from the business community in favor of liberalization began to fuel coup conspiracies.

Firmly opposed to **Lon Nol** and the March 1970 coup, Keat Chhon rallied to the **Royal Government of National Union of Kampuchea (GRUNK)** on 10 July 1970 and was appointed to a ministerial rank to

Prime Minister **Penn Nouth's** office in Beijing. For this gesture, he among many others was sentenced to death *in absentia* for high treason by a court sitting in Phnom Penh in August 1970. Chhon remained in China throughout the "liberation" war but lost his ministerial post in a reshuffle of the GRUNK in January 1975, one aimed at weakening the hands of those connected to Prince **Norodom Sihanouk**. In September 1975 he returned to Phnom Penh with Prince Sihanouk; became minister-delegate to the prime minister's office and worked in this capacity as interpreter and aid to Prime Minister **Pol Pot** and Deputy Prime Minister **Ieng Sary**. In 1977 he joined the **Democratic Kampuchea (DK)** delegation to the United Nations. On 11 January 1979 he accompanied Prince Sihanouk to a meeting of the United Nations Security Council which was discussing the situation in Cambodia. He was still minister-delegate in the prime minister's office when in December 1979, **Khieu Samphan** replaced Pol Pot. In 1981, he was appointed roving ambassador for DK and toured several Francophone states including Senegal, Mauritania, Togo, Gabon, Upper Volta (now Burkina Faso), the Central African Republic and, in 1982, Niger. But after the formation of the **Coalition Government of Democratic Kampuchea** later that year, he quietly slipped away from the DK movement, accepting a post with the United Nations Development Program in Zaire in 1983. He acquired French nationality in 1986.

In 1992, in the wake of the **Paris International Conference on Cambodia,** he returned to Phnom Penh and became an economic advisor to Hun Sen. In January 1993 he was chairman of the National Investment Committee, renamed after 1994 as the Cambodian Investment Board. In June 1993 he was elected to the **National Assembly** on the **Cambodian People's Party** list in **Kampong Cham**. Initially identified as a possible vice-president in the Council of Ministers office in the provisional national government of 1993, he emerged as minister of state for Planning and Development in the November 1993 cabinet, and secretary-general of the Rehabilitation and Development Board of Cambodia. In October 1994 he became Minister of Finance and the Economy, taking over from the sacked **Sam Rainsy**. Reelected to the National Assembly in 1998, he was reappointed Minister of Finance and promoted in the civil service to minister of state. One of the most experienced technocrats in the government, he has succeeded in imposing greater budgetary controls on spending in recent years.

KEAT SOKUN. The adopted son of Prince **Sisowath Sovannareth**, Sokun was born in **Kampong Cham**, received his *baccalauréat* in Phnom Penh in 1966, a diploma in administration in 1970 and was a law student at the University of Phnom Penh in 1975. During the early years of **Democratic**

Kampuchea and while enduring the hardships of dislocation and hunger, he nursed his adopted father who had been badly injured in an assassination attempt in 1972. Fleeing the country in 1979, by October 1980 he was resettled in Sydney. From 1981-1986 he worked on the railways in New South Wales, before returning to the Thai-Cambodian border in 1986 where he was an economic advisor to the president of the **Khmer People's National Liberation Front (KPNLF)** at Site 2. Back in Sydney he established and ran *Smaradey Khmer*, the first Cambodian newspaper in Australia.

He returned to **Phnom Penh** in 1992 and was attached to the KPNLF section of the secretariat of the Supreme National Council. In the 1993 elections he was the second candidate on the **Buddhist Liberal Democratic Party (BLDP)** list for **Siem Reap** but failed by a narrow margin to win a seat. He was named as minister for women, youth and sport in the provisional government of 1993 but this provisional portfolio disappeared in succeeding months and he became secretary of state for women's affairs in the Royal Government formed in October, a post held until 1998.

KEM SOKHA (1953-). Human rights activist and politician. Born in Tram Chan, **Takeo** province, Kem Sokha was a law student in **Phnom Penh** in 1975 when he was evacuated to Takeo and then in a second evacuation, to **Kandal** 1978-1979. By December 1979 he had found work in the municipal office of Phnom Penh and other offices and bureaus being opened by the new **People's Republic of Kampuchea (PRK)**. From 1981-1986, having obtained a Czechoslovak government scholarship, he studied industrial chemistry in Prague, receiving a Master of Sciences degree in 1986. Returning to Cambodia and under attachment to the Ministry of Industry, he worked in Kampong Som where he helped with the restoration of the distillery. A promoter of chemistry, mathematics and physics in schools during late 1980s, in 1991 he with other teachers and professionals founded Vigilance, an organization for promoting awareness and education on human rights; he was the first secretary-general.

Kem Sokha joined the **Buddhist Liberal Democratic Party (BLDP)** led by **Sak Suthsakhan** in May 1992 becoming a member of the Steering Committee of the party and one of the party's candidates in the 1993 elections. He was elected in his native province, Takeo, and named chair of the Commission on the Protection of Human Rights and Reception of Complaints in the National Assembly from 1993-1998. In 1997 following the **Hun Sen** Coup, he fled to Bangkok on one of the emergency Thai evacuation flights. He returned to Phnom Penh for the 1998 elections only after some United Nations protection had been secured. With the **Ieng Mouly** faction in control of the BLDP name and logo, Sokha ran for the Assembly on the hastily renamed Son Sann party list, but as a result of changes in the election procedures, only the leading two parties won seats in the Assembly. When the Son Sann party was laid down, he rallied to **FUNCINPEC**. Nominated by FUNCINPEC to the **Senate** in 1999, he leads a human rights caucus within the Senate.

KEM SREY (?-1960). Brother of **Dap Chhuon** and Kem Penh, he worked with **Puth Chhay**, whom he is said to have "controlled" for his brothers. French colonial intelligence officials believed him to be responsible for many murders in Chhay's zone of operations in **Kandal** province during the **Khmer Issarak** rebellion. Though regarded by French colonial officials as a "bandit" of seriously incorrigible proportions, he nevertheless worked in local administration in the Samrong and Chongkal districts, near the **Dangrek Mountains** close to the base established by **Son Ngoc Thanh, Ea Sichau** and **Hang Thun Hak**. He was likely involved in the 1955 murder of **Kao Tak**, an Issarak leader and republican power broker in the region who was reportedly "eliminated" as a sign of Dap Chhuon's postwar loyalty to Prince **Norodom Sihanouk**. Caught on the run in March 1959, Kem Srey was executed in February 1960 for his involvement in the **Bangkok Plot**, a conspiracy led by **Sam Sary** from the Thai capital and orchestrated by Dap Chhuon from **Siem Reap**.

KENG VANNSAK (1925-). Political activist. Born on 19 September 1925 in Kampong Beng, **Kampong Chhnang**, the son of Keng Siphan, a local subdistrict headman, and Mme (née Cheas Hân), he attended **Lycée Sisowath** observing the August 1945 "coup" while there. After receiving his *baccalauréat (2ème partie)* in philosophy, in 1946, he continued his studies in France, living in Paris, and briefly in London, from August 1946 until October 1952. He earned his *licence-ès-lettres* from the Sorbonne in 1951. (A subsequent *doctorat de 3ème cycle* in philology was completed much later in 1971.) While in Europe he organized anticolonial meetings at the *Maison de l'Indochine*, the residence used by Cambodian students in Paris before Cambodia House (*Maison du Cambodia*) opened in 1957. He took some time out from his studies to teach Khmer at the School of Oriental and African Studies, University of London, 1948-1950 working with Judith Henderson (later Judith Jacobs). In this fruitful period, he devised the typewriter keyboard for the Khmer alphabet which is still in use today, and, in 1952, he convened a Marxist reading group in Paris to discuss texts such as the *Communist Manifesto* and Stalin's *History of the Communist Party of the Soviet Union.* Many future communist leaders including Saloth Sar (**Pol Pot**), **Son Sen, Hou Youn, Mey Mann, Phung Ton, Thiounn Mum**, Rat Samoeurn and **Ieng Sary** participated.

On his return to Phnom Penh in 1952, Keng Vannsak taught at Lycée Sisowath and joined the **Democrat Party** which he had supported while in France. He was part of the younger, "radical" faction in the party which seized control of the party leadership in early 1955 forcing **Sim Var** and many others of the founding generation to leave. As secretary-general of the Democrats, his role in the 1955 elections was so central that it prompted Prince **Norodom Sihanouk** to refer to him as "King Vannsak" in private conversation. He was arrested by **Sam Sary** on 11 September 1955, just before polling day, being falsely accused of conspiring to murder Sam Sary and **Sim Var**.

Chastened, and believing the electoral route to power was permanently blocked by the **Sangkum**, he bowed out of party politics. Throughout the Sihanouk years, he worked as a teacher or a functionary in the Ministry of Education, where he was not always out of trouble. In January 1961 he was sacked as director of the Teacher Training Institute (*Institut de Pedagogie*). He was dean of the Faculty of Arts at Phnom Penh University for only one additional year. In the "Affair of the 34" in March 1963 he was identified as a "subversive," and accused of promoting student protests in **Siem Reap**. He was jailed in August 1968, again for alleged conspiracies against the state, but released soon afterward. After the 1970 coup, Vannsak found new favor as a nationalist theoretician. He was named director of the extremist Khmer-Mon Institute, July-August 1971, a think tank devoted to popularizing **Lon Nol**'s ideas about a superior "Khmer-Mon" civilization giving rise to the modern Khmer nation.

Keng Vannsak also helped to launch the **Socio-Republican Party** of Lon Nol, drafting the party statute and joining the first Central Committee formed in July 1972. Dispatched to Paris in 1973 as a member of the delegation to the United Nations Educational, Scientific and Cultural Organization which was controlled by Sihanouk's **GRUNK** and as a *chargé d'affairs* attached to the mission of the **Khmer Republic** in France, he remained there after April 1975. He was a strong critic of **Democratic Kampuchea**, of the **People's Republic of Kampuchea** and of Cambodian émigré groups.

KEO ANN (1931-1991). Republican maverick. Born on 10 December 1931 in Svay Rieng, eldest son of Keo Long (c1910-1978) and Mme (née Som Chum), Ann was the older brother of **Keo Sann**. He attended a local school from 1937-1939, was a boarder at Svay Rieng Primary School 1939-1942 and was then admitted to **Lycée Sisowath** in 1942. While still in Phnom Penh in 1952, his mother was murdered by the **Viet Minh**, forcing Keo Ann to return home—her brother Hun Khurth, a local policeman had contested the **National Assembly** seat of Cham, Prey Veng in the 1951 elections. In July 1953 he finished eighth in the national baccalaureate examination at the Juridical Studies Institute and in 1954 left for France to study law and economic sciences at the University of Paris. He completed his studies with a thesis on the Cambodian Customs Service while working part-time for the *Banque de l'Indochine.*

Returning to Phnom Penh in 1963, Keo Ann became an inspector with the National Cash Register Company and taught law at the Higher School of Commerce and later the National Police Academy. It was as a founding member of the Khmer-Chinese Friendship Association formed in 1963, following the visit of Chinese leader Liu Shaochi to Cambodia, that he first began to engage in politics. The Association campaigned for improved links and relations with the People's Republic, playing a leading role in a national tilt toward China as the war in Vietnam intensified. Keo Ann was among the up and coming activists invited by Prince **Norodom Sihanouk** into the shadow cabinet after the 1966 elections. He was appointed assistant secretary of state for posts and telecommunications the following year, his first government post.

A republican, he took part in the protests that led to Sihanouk's overthrow. From 1970 he was reappointed dean of the Law Faculty exploiting this position of high visibility to influence legal developments in the fledgling **Khmer Republic**, including preparation of the Constitution, 1971-1972. After openly criticizing the government, and **Sisowath Sirik Matak** in particular, for authoritarianism, he was fired as dean in February 1972. Student protests in the form of sit-ins and mass meetings spread throughout Phnom Penh ensuring his celebrity.

Firmly identified with populist politics Keo Ann stood in the June 1972 presidential elections in opposition both to Lon Nol and **In Tam** promising that, if he were elected, he would allow Sihanouk to return as a private citizen. He received, by official tally, just under 21 percent of the vote. He may have won more than this, in view of the rigging involved, and certainly believed he had won, a claim discounted by most informed observers. (Remarkably his rival In Tam was equally convinced that Lon Nol had robbed him, In Tam, of victory.) Ann continued to be a thorn in the side of successive Lon Nol cabinets and ministers and was one of the first arrested in a crackdown on dissidents on 18 March 1973 when another wave of intellectuals fled the capital to join the revolutionaries. Keo Ann was accused of taking part in a Royalist plot and jailed for 14 months until May 1974. He was permitted to leave Phnom Penh on 25 March 1975 to work overseas as a roving ambassador taking advantage of this opportunity to secure political asylum in France. On 11 November 1978 he declared himself president of a Free Cambodian Government. He mounted his campaign for recognition during the early 1980s when the international community was sharply divided over the competing claims for recognition advanced by the **Coalition Government of Democratic Kampuchea** and the **People's Republic of Kampuchea**. He did not live to see this contest resolved, losing his life in a car accident in May 1991.

KEO BUN THUOK (1930-). She was one of King **Norodom Sihanouk's** two royal appointees to the **Senate** in 1999 and one of only eight women original chosen (for 61 seats). Her connection to the king or his family is unknown but she distinguished herself in diplomatic service in the United States, first as minister-counselor in the Permanent Mission of Cambodia at the United Nations and then as deputy chief of mission in the royal embassy in Washington until 1998. She was educated to university level in France.

KEO CHANDA (1934-1989). Born in Kampong Speu, and from a farming family, he joined the **Khmer Issarak** movement in March 1951 and three years later was one of about 1,500 Khmer **Viet Minh** who left the country, with withdrawing Viet Minh forces, who then received further education or military training in Hanoi. He was among the first, in 1970, to lend support to the **National United Front of Kampuchea (FUNK)**, but withdrew for a second time to Vietnam in 1973 when the **Communist Party of Kampuchea (CPK)** purges of Vietnamese-trained cadres began. In January 1979 he returned to Phnom Penh as minister of propaganda, culture and information in the Revolutionary Council. He represented the **People's Republic of Kampuchea (PRK)** at the second conference of Indochinese foreign ministers in Vientiane in July 1980. Later that year he was appointed chief justice of the People's Revolutionary Court of Phnom Penh, being already party secretary and *de facto* governor of the capital. In June 1981 following the **National Assembly** elections in May, the propaganda, culture and information portfolio was passed to **Chheng Phon** and Chanda became minister of industry. Though he lost this portfolio and received no other cabinet post after the fall of **Pen Sovan** in December 1981, he remained secretary of the Provisional Party Committee of Phnom Penh until June 1985 when, soon after **Hun Sen** became prime minister, he was ousted for corruption. He died of a stroke in 1989.

KEO MEAS (1928-1976). Born in Svay Yea, Svay Chrum, Svay Rieng, he was educated at the Teachers' Training College, Phnom Penh, becoming involved in the communist branch of the anticolonial struggle during his fourth year in 1947. By 1951 he was in the United Issarak Front, and a founding member of the **Khmer People's Revolutionary Party (KPRP)**. Among the **Khmer Issaraks** who chose not to go to Hanoi, he worked with **Non Suon** and others to establish the **Pracheachon** party, the electoral arm of the underground KPRP which fielded communist and former Issarak candidates in the 1955 National Assembly elections. Working as a teacher in **Phnom Penh**, Meas did some work for the **International Commission of Supervision and Control** and was therefore able to tour the countryside to reassure the beleaguered Pracheachon and **Democrat Party** candidates. He is believed to have been chairman of the underground KPRP committee for Phnom Penh at this time. Running himself in a Phnom Penh constituency, Keo Meas was defeated by the **Sangkum** candidate. By 1958 when the **Democrat Party** decided not to compete, and indeed dissolved their party, Keo Meas and four other Pracheachon candidates bravely decided to run alone against the Sangkum. Making full use of his privileged access to the media, Prince **Norodom Sihanouk** published a series of articles on communism in Cambodia critical of the patriotic credentials and ethnic purity of all candidates on the left. Frightened for their lives, all but Keo Meas were intimidated from campaigning. Running again in Phnom Penh, he received 396 votes; the **Sangkum** candidate, 13,542.

Elected to the Central Committee at the secret party congress of the **Workers' Party of Kampuchea** of 1960, Meas was among those who accompanied Saloth Sar (**Pol Pot**), **Son Sen**, and other party leaders to Vietnam and China in 1965-1966. He was then assigned to propaganda and information work in Hanoi in 1969 under the direction of **Ieng Sary** and **Ieng Thirith**. Remaining in Hanoi and Beijing throughout the 1970-1975 liberation struggle, as the CPK termed it, he returned to Cambodia after the 17 April 1975 victory. In September 1976, following the death of Mao Zédong, he was accused of treason alongside other party members supposedly "tainted" by contact with or training under the auspices of the Vietnamese communists. His forced statements of confession protested not only his innocence but also his deep admiration for comrade "Pouk" (**Pol Pot**). Though in great danger, he attempted to tell to Pouk about Soviet revisionism, expressing the fear that it may have completely surrounded the party likening this invisible, blinding process to the enveloping of the pure, sweet core of a sticky rice cake by a banana leaf. He was sent to his death at the end of 1976.

KEO PRASAT (1947-   ). The son of Leav Keomoni, a businessman who joined the **Khmer Issarak**, and nephew of **Keo Meas**, he commanded one of the victorious divisions entering Phnom Penh on 17 April 1975 but was arrested within hours under suspicion of being a Vietnamese agent. He escaped from jail in August 1975 and joined a group already in rebellion against the new regime before making his way back to Vietnam. Upon his return to Phnom Penh in early 1979, he was named head of the political department of the Foreign Ministry, and in October he became the ambassador of the **People's Republic of Kampuchea** to the **Soviet Union**.

He was appointed secretary-general of the Foreign Affairs Ministry in January 1989. In June 1990 he replaced **Khieu Kanharith** the long-term editor of the weekly newspaper *Kampuchea*, the organ of the Central Committee of the Solidarity Front for Construction and Defense of the Motherland, the post-1981 name for the **United Front for the National Salvation of Kampuchea.** At the time *Kampuchea* was the most successful newspaper in the country with a print run of 55,000. Readers were clearly attracted by the professional reporting of local news encouraged by Kanharith during the late 1980s but under Prasat and exposed to competition from a free press after 1991, the paper's appeal and circulation sank.

KEO PUTH RASMEY. A relative of **Nhiek Tioulong**, Peou, as he is known, was a member of the office of Prince **Norodom Sihanouk**. In 1990 in Bangkok he married Princess **Norodom Arun Rasmey**, daughter of Sihanouk, and they had several children including Keo Put Pinita, born in 1991. For a few years he was in charge of the international politics section of the **FUNCINPEC** office in Bangkok and in 1994 was appointed head of the king's secretariat. On 11 June 1994 he was appointed ambassador to Indonesia, the Philippines and Brunei. In 1999 he received royal appointment as ambassador to Malaysia.

KEO SANG KIM (c1937-1974). A Khmer Krom, he studied medicine in Paris where he completed a thesis on precancerous conditions of the larnyx in 1959. Returning to Phnom Penh he was physician to **Lon Nol**. Sang Kim was appointed minister of education by **In Tam** in May 1973. Still in possession of this portfolio he was caught up in a student protest on 5 June 1974, along with his deputy **Thach Chia**. They were taken to 18 March Lycée (formerly **Lycée Sisowath**) where they were both killed by an unknown gunman who escaped in the ensuing panic and alarm. Although (unidentified) student militants were blamed at the time, responsibility for the killings and the identity of the gunman were not firmly established. In the early 1980s, a defector from the **Communist Party of Kampuchea** claimed that a special assassination team was responsible. He said they had decided to intervene in the situation so as to radicalize the student movement and to stir up hatred against the government.

KEO SANN. The second son of Keo Long, and younger brother of **Keo Ann**, he was a medical doctor. In 1966 he was elected to the National Assembly for Takhmau, **Kandal**, easily defeating the other candidates who included **Cheng Heng**. He was elected vice-president of the National Assembly in 1969, but was ousted by **In Tam** in early 1970 just prior to the overthrow of Prince **Norodom Sihanouk**. Before the defeat of the

Khmer Republic in April 1975, he moved with his wife, Chuop Sisovann, to France where he practised medicine. Returning to Phnom Penh in the early 1990s Keo Sann joined the **Cambodian People's Party (CPP)** and was appointed an advisor to **Hun Sen**. In 1999 he was appointed to the **Senate** by the CPP. He was expelled from the party and from the Senate in January 2002 for having raised questions about the budget proposed for the royal palace in the annual budget law.

KEOUM KUN (1933-). A native of Takeo province, Kun joined the **Khmer Issarak** in 1949 and fought in Regiment 160 against the French in **Kampong Chhnang, Kampong Speu, Kampot** and **Pursat**. With the end of hostilities, he was evacuated to Vietnam on a Polish ship and settled in Thanh Hoa province where he married a Vietnamese woman and had two children. After joining the **Khmer People's Revolutionary Party** in 1957, he received extensive military training and was at Son Tay military training center in November 1970 when he was infiltrated back into Cambodia. It is not clear if he was among the Khmer who worked for the special "P-36" unit established by the Vietnamese Communist Party in 1966. Members of this unit are known to have returned in 1970 and to have reported on the military situation to the Vietnamese political bureau via Le Duc Tho. Arriving in **Kratié** in February 1971, Kun fought in Kampong Speu and then in **Takeo** becoming rapidly disillusioned by the fact that the Vietnamese allies seemed to be in full charge of local resistance efforts and the Cambodian battlefield. He defected to the **Lon Nol** side in late 1971 just before **National United Front of Kampuchea** forces took the offensive in **Baray**.

KEP. Similar to **Bokor**, the seaside resort of Kep was originally developed in 1908 by French colonialists as a holiday retreat for themselves and local elite families who worked in or served the colonial administration. Today it is a city of 28,660 according to the 1998 **census** and is legally established as a province, the second smallest in population, being just larger than *Krong* **Pailin**. It has one deputy in the **National Assembly**. During the 1960s and early 1970s the nearby island of Antay was the second largest prison in the country. In June 1970 the town was momentarily occupied by the Vietnamese People's Army whose officers arrived with lists of every house and their owners. They searched those belonging to officials of the **Lon Nol** government but left everything intact. Afterward the houses were plundered by South Vietnamese troops, ostensibly in close pursuit, and by opportunistic local residents. Located on a small headland, the area is now too populated for Kep to be the peaceful retreat it once was but its economy remains centered on the beach and weekend tourism.

KEP CHUTEMA. A member of the **Cambodian People's Party (CPP)**, he was governor of highland **Ratanakiri** province from 1993 until 1999. He was also one of the "up and coming" party members elected to the party's greatly expanded Central Committee in early 1997. On 12 March 1999 he was appointed governor of the lowland province of **Takeo** being replaced in Ratanakiri by Kham Khoeun, also a member of the CPP Central Committee. Both governors are of non-Khmer ethnic origin.

KER MEAS (c1905-1977). He was the grand master of ceremonies in the Royal Palace Service from 1968-1970 and was abroad on 18 March 1970 when Prince **Norodom Sihanouk** was deposed and among the royal servants barred from returning. Sihanouk appointed him **Royal Government of National Union** ambassador first in Pyongyang and then in Beijing where he was replaced on 10 February 1973 by Toch Kham Doeun. He returned to **Phnom Penh** from France in 1976 but was detained upon arrival and later taken to **Tuol Sleng** on 2 January 1977. Although his date of death is not indicated on available records, it is assumed he was executed some weeks later.

KETYA VOLEAK (1958-). A civil servant, she is prominent in the women's wing of the **Sam Rainsy Party (SRP)** and was elected deputy secretary-general of the party at the national congress held 13-14 February 2000. She holds the portfolio for civil service reform in the SRP shadow cabinet formed in May 2001.

KEUK KYHEANG (1921-). Born in **Siem Reap** to Keuk Neth (1894-1970), a fishing entrepreneur, and Mme (née Lim Lek Kieng), he was an older brother of **Keuky Lim** and a member of the Steering Committee of the **Khmer Renewal Party**. In 1948 he had, with legal authorization, constructed a weir at Kampong Tralach which destroyed fish habitats in the **Tonlé Sap** producing protests from other fishermen. **Yèm Sambaur**, then prime minister, finally ordered the army to destroy the dam. Kyheang sued Sambaur for 6 million riels in damages. He won the case, but the damages were never paid.

　　The scandal resonated through the years ensuring that Kyheang failed to win election to the **National Assembly** in 1951 or in 1960 when he ran twice in by-elections. He was later elected to the High Council of the Kingdom and became president of that body in 1968 just as the career of **Lon Nol**, another former Khmer Renewal Party leader was on the rise. In December 1970 Kyheang was appointed to Lon Nol's executive cabinet and was a member of the **Khmer Republic** delegation to the Asian Parliamentary Union in Saigon. In 1973 he was a patron and a vice-president of the **Chuon Nath** Association.

KEUKY LIM (1937-). Born on 7 March 1937 in Kampong Khleang, **Siem Reap**, a son of Keuk Neth, and brother of **Keuk Kyheang**, Keuky Lim earned a baccalereate II in experimental sciences at **Lycée Sisowath** before undertaking pharmaceutical studies in Texas, and the faculty of pharmacy in Paris, from which he graduated in 1964. He was elected to the National Assembly in 1966, in Sang Voeung, Siem Reap. From July 1970 until May 1971 he was minister of information in the **Khmer Republic**, partly because of his connections to the **United States** and his command of the English language. He joined the **Socio-Republican Party** and won reelection to the Assembly in September 1972, this time representing a constituency in Phnom Penh. Appointed minister of state in charge of foreign affairs by **Long Boret** in December 1973, he worked in the republican government until 21 March 1975 when he quietly left for Siem Reap. In April 1975 he sought refuge in Thailand and now resides in Paris.

KHAN SAVOEUN (1943-). Born on 13 May 1943 in Prey Chhor, **Kampong Cham**, he was a soldier in the **Khmer Republic** army, 1970-1975, who survived the **Democratic Kampuchea** years in the countryside. In 1979-1980 he joined the **People's Republic of Kampuchea** police but as a secret agent for the royalist **Molinaka**. After helping to free some political prisoners in 1980, he moved to Nong Chan and was among those who participated in the merging of the armed forces of Molinaka into the **Armée Nationale Sihanoukienne** at Tatum in 1984. He was appointed major general of the 4th Division in 1990. During the 1993 election campaigns, he was attached to the FUNCINPEC police and was a member of the FUNCINPEC electoral committee for **Kampong Thom**. Elected in that province, he became secretary of state for the interior and public security but resigned to command the 4th Division of the Royal Army. He survived attempts on his life in July 1997 and with **Nhek Bun Chhay** recreated a royalist resistance movement in support of the deposed Prince **Norodom Ranariddh**. In 1998, following Ranariddh's return to the country, he was elected to the National Assembly on the FUNCINPEC list in his native Kampong Cham but resigned his seat in 1999, when he was appointed deputy chief of staff (one of the four) in the **Royal Cambodian Armed Forces**. In August 2002 the National Assembly rejected his nomination as FUNCINPEC cominister of defense to replace **You Hockry**.

KHANG SARIN (1935-). A native of **Kampot**, he joined the anticolonial struggle in 1954 and was among the "regroupees" who went to **Vietnam** after the Geneva Conference. He returned to Cambodia in 1970 but was rapidly disillusioned and alarmed by "devious" developments within the

Communist Party of Kampuchea. Unlike **Keoum Kum**, he returned to Hanoi in 1972 resurfacing in 1979 as commander of the **Phnom Penh** garrison and deputy chairman of the general staff of the newly created **People's Republic of Kampuchea (PRK)** army. He was PRK minister of the interior from June 1981 through February 1986 when he was removed from the Central Committee of the **People's Revolutionary Party of Kampuchea (PRPK)**, allegedly for selling public goods on the black market on October 1985. In a "poacher turned gamekeeper" gesture, he was appointed chairman of the Supreme Court in March 1986 and briefly returned to political life when he was appointed to a vacant seat in the PRK Assembly in 1989 to represent his native province of Takeo. Since 1991, when the ruling PRPK communists abandoned Marxism-Leninism, Khang Sarin, **Heng Samrin** and most other communists once regrouped in Vietnam, have been sidelined.

KHAO-I-DANG. A holding center in eastern **Thailand** established by the **United Nations** in 1979 and administered by UN agencies until it closed in 1993. Hundreds of thousands of Cambodians who fled to the Thai frontier in the wake of the collapse of the **Pol Pot** regime in fear of renewed repression under the Vietnamese-imposed **Heng Samrin** administration went there to seek resettlement in third countries. There were almost 200,000 Cambodians there in 1980 but only about 40,000 residents in 1983. It was the only center for "displaced persons" in Thailand under international control and administration. Up to eight other border camps and settlements were affiliated with and administered by one of the three Cambodian political parties resisting the Vietnamese occupation. Cambodians confined in the "holding centers" and under national administration were denied the rights normally accorded to international refugees and asylum seekers, but Bangkok allowed international governments and multilateral agencies to provide humanitarian assistance. Long-term residents of the camps were repatriated to Cambodia in 1992-1993 by the United Nations High Commissioner for Refugees.

KHAO PHRA VIHARN. *See* PREAH VIHEAR.

KHAOU CHULY (1931-   ). The owner of Khaou Chuly Company, one of the largest building contractors of the 1960s and early 1970s. A native of Phnom Penh, Khaou Chuly favored large civil engineering projects such as the Olympic Stadium but also designed and constructed family villas, often with **Vann Molyvann**, his favorite architect. Among the Teochew businessmen to whom **Lon Nol** awarded lucrative contracts, Khaou Chuly restored the governmental palace in **Chamkar Mon** after it was damaged by air attacks in 1973. Nominated by Lon Nol's **Socio-Republican Party**, he was elected to the **Senate** of the Khmer Republic in September 1972.

He remained in besieged Phnom Penh until early April 1975 before seeking exile in Paris where he established the *Association des Résidents d'origine Indochinoise en France*. In 1996 he returned to Cambodia hoping to invest in a new business venture, but was accosted and robbed, barely escaping with his life, and returned to France. Later in Cambodia he formed the Khaou Chuly Group which merged with Korean-owned Tong Yang Major Corporation to build a cement plant in southeastern Cambodia. One son, Khaou Vibobrith, is active in French politics. Another son, Khaou Phallaboth, married the daughter of **Chea Sim**.

KHAU MENG HEAN. Son of Khau and Chea Heng Ky (sister of **Chea Kiv**), he was born in **Kampong Speu**, attended **Lycée Sisowath** in 1959-1964 and then studied in France, in Montpellier and Toulouse. He returned in 1969 and worked for SONAPNEU, the state tire company, completing a masters degree at the Faculty of Law and Economic Sciences, University of Phnom Penh at the same time. He was among the students who defused the **Koy Pech Affair** in April 1972. Meng Hean worked in the **Khmer Republic**'s Foreign Ministry in 1974-1975 and remained in the country throughout the **Democratic Kampuchea** years, but left for the Thai-Cambodian border with his uncle, Chea Kiv, immediately afterward. The extended family was resettled in France in 1982, but following Chea Kiv's death in 1983, Meng Hean moved to Australia. In 1990 he became editor of Victoria's first Khmer language newspaper *Angkor*. Returning to **Phnom Penh** in 1991 he took charge of the Cambodian Investment Bureau. A member of **FUNCINPEC** and a loyal associate of Prince **Norodom Ranariddh**, Khau Meng Hean fled Phnom Penh for a short time after the July 1997 coup. His wife Tina was a candidate for FUNCINPEC in the 1998 elections, running in Phnom Penh. His importance in Royalist circles was confirmed when he was named secretary of state in the Ministry of Parliamentary Affairs and Inspection in the November 1998 **Hun Sen** government and by his election to the FUNCINPEC Steering Committee at the party's congress in March 1999.

KHEANG KAON (1934-). A native of **Kampong Cham**, he studied in France from 1953 where he joined the Union des Étudiants Khmères, then led by **Ieng Sary, Khieu Samphan** and other progressives. He returned to Cambodia in 1965 with a *Licence* in mathematics from the University of Paris. From 1967 to 1970, he taught science and was dean of the Faculty of Physical Sciences and Mathematics, Royal University of Kampong Cham, abandoning this post to join the underground, communist resistance shortly after the 18 March 1970 coup. He was among the intellectuals working with Dr. **Thiounn Thioeun** when **Ith Sarin** visited the special zone base area in **Kampong Speu** in 1972. Between 1976-

1979, he was attached to the Ministry of Culture and Education of **Democratic Kampuchea (DK)** headed by **Yun Yat**, wife of DK Defense Minister **Son Sen**. Separated from others during the hasty DK exit from **Phnom Penh** in January 1979, he lived as a peasant in the Leach region of **Pursat** until 1981 when he rejoined the **Pol Pot** forces along the Thai frontier. Assisting **Mey Mann** and others to establish schools in the areas and camps controlled and administered by the **Party of Democratic Kampuchea (PDK)** straddling the frontier, he wrote textbooks for elementary math. From 1984-1991 he worked with the PDK delegation attached to the Economic and Social Commission for Asia and the Pacific, an agency of the **United Nations** also known as ESCAP. He was transferred to the PDK stronghold in **Pailin** in 1991 and from there to **Anlong Veng** in 1994. Named as a minister in the short-lived provisional government of the National Unity and Well-Being of Kampuchea Party formed by Khieu Samphan in 1994, Kheang Kaon was among the last of the DK intellectuals to quit the movement in 1997-1998.

KHEK LERANG (1939-   ). Born on 11 November 1939, a younger brother of **Khek Penn, Khek Sysoda** and **Khek Vandy**, in 1969 Khek Lerang married Princess Virivinn, daughter of Princess **Norodom Viriya**, and they had two daughters. Lerang managed the Office of Prince **Norodom Sihanouk**, head of state in post-revolutionary Cambodia 1975-1976 but left for France when in 1976 Sihanouk refused the presidency in the newly proclaimed **Democratic Kampuchea** and was replaced by **Khieu Samphan**. On 23 December 1993 he was appointed ambassador of the Royal Government to **Laos** and, in 1999, ambassador to Germany. His appointment is the result of nomination by **FUNCINPEC**. He was subsequently appointed ambassador to China.

KHEK PENN (c1933-1977). Older brother of **Khek Sysoda, Khek Lerang** and **Khek Vandy**, he studied at the National Institute for Pedagogy in the 1950s along with **Koy Thuon, Ke Kim Huot** and other revolutionaries, and worked with the **Hou Youn** teaching group at Lycée **Kambuboth**. He joined the underground **Workers' Party of Kampuchea** (later renamed **Communist Party of Kampuchea**) in the early 1960s and, by 1975, was deputy secretary of the northwest zone. He is said to have treated "**new people**" compassionately. After **Ieng Sary**'s October 1975 visit to Bangkok, Khek Penn was asked to chair the **Thailand** liaison committee based in Poipet, a group responsible for controlling official **Democratic Kampuchea** trade with Thailand. When other north and northwest zone leaders were arrested for alleged coup attempts in 1976, Penn fell under suspicion partly because of his urban middle-class origins and education. Being among the many teachers associated with Koy Thuon who was forced to implicate him in subversion under torture. Penn was taken to **Tuol Sleng** in early 1977 and executed.

KHEK SYSODA (1938-). Born on 21 August 1938 in **Kampot** and a brother of **Khek Penn, Khek Vandy** and **Khek Lerang**, Sysoda studied at Lycée Descartes and received a diploma in commerce from the University of Lyon. Back in **Phnom Penh** from 1961 he was an assistant director of external trade 1963-1965, head of the office of the Ministry of Economics 1965-1966 and director of internal trade 1966-1968. From then until 1973 he was director-general of SONEXIM, the state-owned import-export enterprise established as a result of the nationalization of commerce and banking in 1963. He left the country for France in 1974, declaring his support for the **National United Front of Kampuchea** on 12 March 1974. From July 1982 until November 1993 he worked steadily for the Royalist cause as a personal aide to Prince **Norodom Sihanouk** holding several protocol posts and serving the **Coalition Government of Democratic Kampuchea** as ambassador to Pyongyong from December 1983 until 1991. In November 1993 he was appointed ambassador of the Royal Government to **China** and continues to serve there as of 2002. Mrs. Khek Sysoda, known as Nanou, was director of Protocol for Sihanouk, 1983-1991, and also holds the rank of ambassador.

KHEK VANDY (1935-). Brother of **Khek Penn, Khek Lerang** and **Khek Sysoda**, he studied commerce in Lyon returning to **Phnom Penh** where he went into business. Among his business associates in the late 1960s was Monique Sihanouk (now Queen **Monineath**). In the late 1960s, he was director of the Magasin d'État, the state-owned store system known as MAGETAT which, alongside other state enterprises, was slowly undermined by graft and corrupt practice. Indeed in August 1969 Prince **Norodom Sihanouk** lodged a suit for libel against a newspaper owned by **Sim Var** in which Vandy was accused of corruption. **Lon Nol, Cheng Heng** and Queen **Kossamak** successfully persuaded Sim Var to avoid a confrontation that the prince was determined to have. In 1970, at the time of the overthrow of Prince **Norodom Sihanouk**, he was in Japan, in charge of the Cambodian Exhibition at the EXPO in Osaka. Flying immediately to Beijing, he was among the first of many courtiers to extend support to the **National United Front of Kampuchea**. He also firmly declined to return to revolutionary Cambodia with the Prince and Monique in 1975 choosing to settle in France instead.

In March 1985 he was the FUNCINPEC member of the Health and Social Affairs Committee of the **Coalition Government of Democratic Kampuchea** replacing Prince **Norodom Chakrapong** who had abandoned the resistance in favor of the Phnom Penh side. He was, by this time, the consort of, Princess **Norodom Bopha Devi**, Sihanouk's eldest daughter and only sister of Prince **Norodom Ranariddh**. Together he and Bopha Devi returned to Phnom Penh quietly in 1991 or 1992. Though not on good terms with Prince Ranariddh in the 1980s and for most of the 1990s, Khek Vandy (and his brothers) remained loyal to the king and to **FUNCINPEC** during the July 1997 coup crisis. Running for public office for the first time in the 1998 **National Assembly** elections, he was elected on the FUNCINPEC list in **Takeo**. Princess Bopha Devi became minister of culture in the new cabinet. Her consort's increasing importance in the Royalist movement was confirmed by his election to the FUNCINPEC Steering Committee in 1999.

KHIEU CHUM (c1915-1975). Buddhist dignitary and activist. The son of a **Kandal** farmer, Khieu Chum was *chauathikar* ("abbot" or "chief") of Wat Langka in Phnom Penh between 1970-1975. As a young cleric, he took part in the 20 July 1942 anticolonial demonstration against the French, a protest organized by **Son Ngoc Thanh** after the colonial authorities had arrested two Buddhist monks. A lifelong supporter of Thanh's, and close to many of the most fervently republican **Democrat Party** activists of the 1950s, including **Keng Vannsak**, he discreetly supported the abolition of monarchy after March 1970 and advocated formation of a republic.

In October 1971, he organized a silent demonstration of monks who opposed the dissolution of the **National Assembly**. A manifesto issued by the monks called for the creation of a presidency, urged Lon Nol to take this post and to choose "men of unquestionable Republican credentials" as vice-president and as advisors. The reference to unquestionable republicanism was intended as a signal that **Sisowath Sirik Matak** was not acceptable. The demonstration was intended to obstruct a Sirik Matak maneuver to replace **Lon Nol** as premier while at the same time a means to beckon the return of Son Ngoc Thanh to power. Thanh who was still living in Saigon at the time not only inspired but partly orchestrated the events. In the following week, **Huot Tat**, head of the **Mohanikay** order, brought the demonstrations to a halt by issuing a statement calling on monks to respect monastic discipline and to withdraw from political life. The demonstrators nevertheless achieved many of their aims including the return and promotion of Thanh to the premiership.

Though a "political" monk of immense historical importance, his conservative doctrinal outlook was out of step with Lon Nol's more radical and mythical sense of Buddhism as a moral force in politics. He opposed the president's use of Buddhism in official republican ideology. Widely regarded as "Thanhist," Chum was among the many intellectuals executed in April 1975 for alleged "CIA" sympathies and "enemy" activities.

KHIEU KANHARITH (1951-). Born on 13 September 1951 in Koh Sautin, **Kampong Cham**, he completed his *baccalauréat* in 1969 and was a student of law and diplomacy when the **Khmer Republic** collapsed in 1975. Living as a peasant in **Kampong Cham** in 1975-1979, he returned to **Phnom Penh** in February 1979 to seek a job. By September he was named second assistant secretary-general of the Central Committee of the **United Front for the National Salvation of Kampuchea (UFNSK)** and a teacher in the Front's political training school. By 1981 he was a deputy editor of *Kampuchea*, the newspaper of the Front and became editor in chief in August 1982. By January 1989, when *Kampuchea* was the most widely circulated and influential paper in the county, he was elected to the National Council of the Solidarity Front for Development and Defense of Kampuchea, the former UFNSK. Developing his skills in the English language, he also translated many English language books into Khmer in this period, including Ben Kiernan's *How Pol Pot Came to Power* and James Clavell's novel, *Shogun*.

In June 1990 Khieu Kanharith lost his editorial post, being among those arrested with **Kann Man, Ung Phan** and **Thun Sarey** for allegedly planning to establish an opposition Liberal Democratic Socialist Party. Released in 1991 under the terms of an amnesty for political prisoners contained in the **Paris Peace Agreements**, he became a personal advisor to **Hun Sen**. Elected in 1981 to the National Assembly of the **People's Republic of Kampuchea** (the **State of Cambodia** after 1989), he was elected to the Constituent Assembly in May 1993 on the **Cambodian People's Party** list in Phnom Penh. Appointed secretary of state for information in the Royal Government of 1993, he was reelected to the National Assembly in 1998, standing in his native province of Kampong Cham and reappointed to his post in the Ministry of Information in the Hun Sen cabinet of 1998.

KHIEU LUNG. He was a court official and later a judge in **Kampong Cham**. He married Por Kong and they had five children: **Khieu Samphan**; Khieu Sok, a daughter who married a tax collector; Khieu Sokun, who worked with SONATRAC; Khieu Seng Kim; and Khieu Seng Thy, who died in 1971. The family was well-liked and active in the community. After Lung's death in about 1950, Kung supported her family by working as a street vendor. In 1967 following the **Samlaut Uprising** and the disappearance of her oldest son Samphan, she became a nun. In December 1972 she disappeared from the *wat* in Kampong Cham where she had been living. While searching for her in January 1973, her remaining children were told she had gone away with two men. Her exact fate is unknown.

KHIEU PONNARY (1920-). The first wife of **Pol Pot**. From an elite family with connections to the royal family, Khieu Ponnary was one of the first women to obtain a *baccalauréat* from **Lycée Sisowath**. She accompanied her sister, Thirith to Paris in 1951 partly in anticipation of her marriage to another student there, **Ieng Sary**, and for training at the École Normal Supérieure 1952-1953. While in France she befriended Saloth Sar (**Pol Pot**), a close friend of Sary's and seven years her junior. They later married in Phnom Penh on Bastille Day in 1956. Ponnary remained at her post at Lycée Sisowath in 1963 when Saloth Sar, then secretary of the clandestine **Workers' Party of Kampuchea**, slipped away from the capital along with **Ieng Sary** and **Son Sen**. She and **Ieng Thirith** slipped away to join them only in 1965. While working in Phnom Penh, Khieu Ponnary like many other "progressives" of the 1960s acquired an enviable reputation for her intelligence, activism, probity and patriotism. She was a known feminist and encouraged solidarity among women by publishing a women's magazine. Once underground in rural base areas, she was prominent in the grassroots promotion of the official women's wing of the **Workers' Party of Kampuchea** (later the **Communist Party of Kampuchea**) then known as the Democratic Women's League (or Association).

During the war period, 1970-1975, Ponnary worked with Yun, the wife of **Koy Thuon** in **Kampong Thom** province, and other party intellectuals, mostly in the northeast, north and northwest zones and she was among those who played host to Prince **Norodom Sihanouk** and Princess Monique (now Queen **Monineath**) on their secret visit to liberated zones in 1973. From mid-1975, she began suffering bouts of mental illness and rarely appeared in public in the **Democratic Kampuchea (DK)** period even though she was nominally president of the Women's Association of Democratic Kampuchea. Her health deteriorated further in the 1980s after the DK government was overturned. Under constant care in rear base camps on the Thai border, and estranged from her husband, she survived at least one assassination attempt by an unknown assailant. In 1984 Pol Pot married **Mea Som**, reportedly with Ponnary's consent. Periodic medical treatment in hospitals in Thailand and China failed to restore her to sound mental health. She has lived with her sister, Thirith, since 1996.

KHIEU SAMPHAN (1931-). President of the State Presidium, **Democratic Kampuchea**, 1976-1979. The eldest child of **Khieu Lung** and Kung, Khieu Samphan was born on 27 July 1931 in Svay Rieng. Most of his elementary schooling was at Collège Preah Sihanouk followed by studies for the baccalaureate at **Lycée Sisowath** from 1948-1954—briefly attending Lycée Descartes. Having won a scholarship to France, he then studied economics and third world development at the University of

Montpellier and the Faculty of Law, University of Paris. His unpublished thesis, submitted in 1959, assesses the impact of colonial rule on economic development in Cambodia. Embracing technocratic and reformist positions, Samphan recommended the imposition of corrective fiscal controls on import-export trade, greater state support and protection of domestic **agriculture** and **industry** and improved self-government through a widening of political participation. The work is available in an English translation under the title, *Cambodia's Economy and Industrial Development.* (See bibliography.) While in France, he was active in the Union des Étudiants Khmers (UEK) and alongside **Ieng Sary, Son Sen, Saloth Sar** and **Thiounn Mumm** likely joined the Communist Party of France.

On his return to Cambodia, he taught mathematics at the "progressive" **Lycée Chamroeun Vichea** rapidly acquiring a good reputation for his professional integrity among students and intellectuals. He also founded and was managing editor of *L'Observateur,* a French-language newspaper focusing primarily on politics and problems of economic development. The paper sought to raise the nationalist consciousness of the country's neocolonial, francophone elite and to expose the inadequacies of the national development policies promoted by Prince **Norodom Sihanouk.** On 13 July 1960 **Kou Roun**'s security police accosted him in the street, beat him up and stripped him naked to humiliate him. A month later Samphan and his staff were among some several dozen journalists arrested and held without charge for about five weeks. *L'Observateur* ceased to appear.

By 1962, with Sihanouk alarmed by growing U.S. military intervention in Saigon and grateful for new economic assistance from Beijing and Eastern European states, Khieu Samphan was among the progressives nominated by the **Sangkum** and elected to the **National Assembly.** He turned up for Assembly meetings riding on either a bicycle or motorcycle, having declined the gift of a car offered as a bribe for turning a blind eye to shady business activities. He was concurrently secretary of state at the Ministry of Trade where he attempted to promote fiscal propriety in state accounts. He was obliged to resign from this government post after parliamentary censure tantamount to dismissal in July 1963. Although he was one of four deputies—the others being **Hou Youn, Hu Nim** and an articulate right-wing campaigner for probity in high places, **Douc Rasy**—whom Sihanouk wanted defeated in the 1966 National Assembly elections, Samphan was reelected with a comfortable majority (as were all the others). However, fearing for his life after public accusations of complicity in the **Samlaut Uprising**, he and Hou Youn fled Phnom Penh on 24 April 1967 joining the communist underground on Mt. Aural. Since the government was engaged in a violent crackdown again dissent, especially against members and associates of the Association des Étudiants Khmères, the general public believed they had been assassinated while some senior officials, **Khim Tith** for one, obligingly insisted they had inside knowledge of the deed and of the secret burials. Between 1970-1976, the **"three ghosts"** including Khieu Samphan reappeared, Samphan as deputy prime minister and minister of national defense in the **Royal Government of National Union** and commander-in-chief of armed forces of the **National United Front of Kampuchea**.

In 1976, after the promulgation of the new constitution and the refusal of Prince Sihanouk to continue to work with the revolutionaries, Khieu Samphan was named president of **Democratic Kampuchea**. Of greater political significance, he was attached to the Central Committee of the **Communist Party of Kampuchea (CPK)** from 1971 and chaired its central headquarters management committee from February 1977. His duties included taking the minutes at meetings of the Standing Committee (or political bureau) of the CPK. In this role, he likely gained some idea of the scale of the party's crackdown against its "enemies" even if reports from S-21, the special state security office today known as **Tuol Sleng** museum, were kept secret from the party's leading body. Briefly prime minister in a reshuffled DK government formed in December 1979 on the Thai-Cambodian border, Khieu Samphan became foreign minister in the superseding **Coalition Government of Democratic Kampuchea (CGDK)** organized in 1982.

The senior CGDK negotiator, alongside Prince Sihanouk, once the Vietnamese-installed government of **Hun Sen** came to the negotiating table in 1987, Khieu Samphan was one of the two DK delegates in the 12-man **Supreme National Council (SNC)** formed in 1991. However when, on 27 November 1991, he returned to Phnom Penh, supporters of the **Cambodian People's Party** staged a violent demonstration at his house, eventually breaking in and attempting to lynch him and **Son Sen,** the other **Party of Democratic Kampuchea (PDK)** member of the SNC. The PDK withdrew its delegation, temporarily in this instance, but while more secure offices were eventually supplied on the grounds of the royal palace, the party refused in 1992 to participate in the United Nations-monitored disarmament of party armies or the UN-supervised elections of 1993. In July 1994 Khieu Samphan announced the formation of a new National Unity Party and a Provisional Government of National Unity and Well-Being of Kampuchea in which he was prime minister. He continued to be recognized as the nominal state leader within the DK movement after the 1997 murder of **Son Sen** and during the people's trial of **Pol Pot** in **Anlong Veng**. Meanwhile many of his aides, including several who held portfolios in the inconsequential provisional government of National Unity, slipped away from Anlong Veng to **Pailin**. Khieu Samphan officially surrendered to the government along with **Nuon Chea** in December 1998. He has retired to a secluded compound in Pailin city together with his wife and their two youngest children. While denying personal culpability for the crimes committed during the DK era, he has indicated to Prime Minister **Hun Sen** his willingness to give evidence to an international tribunal when one is established.

KHIEU THIRATH (c1930-1977). A sister of **Khieu Ponnary** (first wife of **Pol Pot**) and **Khieu Thirith** (married to **Ieng Sary**), she was a teacher at the elite Lycée Déscartes. She married Tep and her son, **Tep Khunnal**, was among the intellectuals who left **Anlong Veng** in 1997. Evacuated from Phnom Penh in 1975, she died of illness and exhaustion in early 1977.

KHIEU THIRITH. *See* IENG THIRITH.

KHIEU VANN (1914-). Born on 7 March 1914 in Phnom Penh, the son of Khieu Prak and Mme (née Ker Sophi), he completed his primary education and a diploma in forestry studies. While a civil servant in the colonial era Department of Waters and Forests, he helped to establish the **Khmer Renewal Party** becoming a member of its Steering Committee in charge of financial matters. Following the abdication of the young King **Norodom Sihanouk** in 1955 and the realignment of the political parties, he joined the **Sangkum**. Vann was elected to the **High Council of the Kingdom** in 1955 to represent civil servants in technical services and was assistant secretary of state for agriculture and head of forestry and fisheries from January 1958 but lost this position in 1960 because of conflicts with Yim Dith, also in agriculture at this time. In a major career shift, he became political director of *Réalités Cambodgiennes* and a technical advisor attached to the head of state's private secretariat. In the 1962 elections, running as the officially endorsed Sangkum candidate, he won a seat in the **National Assembly** in **Svay Rieng** province. In 1966 when there was no official list of Sangkum nominees and more rivalry among Sangkum members at the polls, he failed to get elected. A supporter of **Lon Nol**, one of the original leaders of the Khmer Renewal Party, Khieu Vann joined the **Socio-Republican Party** and was elected to the **Senate** of the Khmer Republic in 1972.

KHIM TITH (1896-c1975). Prime minister in 1956. Born in Phnom Penh, he was a soldier with the French Colonial Forces in Flanders during World War I, returning in 1920. Graduating from the École d'administration in 1924, he worked in the colonial administration until 1945. He was minister of national defense, public works and health in the **Son Ngoc Thanh** government from 14 August 1945 but opposed the efforts of Thanh and **Ea Sichau** to gain diplomatic and military support from the **Viet Minh** government in Hanoi. Although he has denied it, it is widely believed that Khim Tith contacted the British occupation authorities in Saigon to arrange the arrest of Thanh and the restoration of French colonial power. British officials gained the impression that he acted at the behest of the Queen Mother **Kossamak**.

In 1946 he founded the **National Union**, a political party dedicated to defending the role of the elite and their civil service. **Democrat Party** militants challenged this orientation by their preoccupation with *la jeune élite* or the rising generation. Predictably, the National Union failed to capture much support at the polls, the Democrats sweeping the 1947 elections. The party nevertheless succeeded in winning a large share of the seats in the **High Council of the Kingdom** thus acquiring a platform in public affairs. Khim Tith worked in the Ministry of Public Works until May 1951 when he was appointed governor of **Kandal** province. A succession of Royal appointments followed the king's dismissal of the Democrat government in 1952 and the assumption of "full" power: minister for national defense, November 1953 to April 1954; of the interior and surface defense, April to July 1954; president of the Council of Ministers and minister of planning and sanitation, April to September 1956. The collapse of this government due to corruption scandals involving his own family brought an end to his ministerial career.

After a period out of public service, he was named High Commissioner to France on the death of Prince **Sisowath Monipong**. He served as Cambodian ambassador to the **Soviet Union** and Poland from October 1960; and to Czechoslovakia in 1963. In 1967 Khim Tith published his version of the events in 1945 in the official weekly *Réalités Cambodgiennes*. Later that year he claimed he had seen conclusive evidence that **Hou Youn**, **Hu Nim** and **Khieu Samphan** had been murdered by Prince **Norodom Sihanouk**. He was appointed Cambodia's permanent representative to the **United Nations** from 1970-1972 and remained in the United States after 1975.

KHIN CHHE (1911/18-). Born in Peam Chikang, **Kampong Cham**, he attended **Lycée Sisowath** and was a deputy governor of **Kandal** province in 1947 and a **Democrat Party** deputy in the **National Assembly** representing Prek Ambel, Kandal, when he decided to resign from public life and concentrate on his businesses, a bookshop and a jewelry store. A nationalist associated with the **Son Ngoc Thanh** "tendency," as French colonial reports put it, Khin Chhe provided support for anticolonial protests in November 1947, and, in May 1952, the latter being organized by **Hu Nim** and other young progressives in the Democrat Party. On 13 January 1953, the day King **Norodom Sihanouk** issued a declaration of a state of emergency and dissolved the Democrat-controlled National Assembly, he was among the Democrats arrested for their alleged support of **Khmer Issaraks** engaged in armed struggle or for being pro-**Viet Minh**. Khin Chhe remained in the Democrat Party after the creation of the **Sangkum** in 1955 and, in spite of the violence and harassment involved, ran for the National Assembly in Rocarkong, Kandal. He was arrested during the campaign and held in prison for several years after the poll. He practised law in Phnom Penh after his release, avoiding party politics. Khin Chhe, who was among the first to experience persecution under the Sangkum regime, was the court-appointed attorney for the defense at the trial *in absentia* of Prince **Norodom Sihanouk** in July 1970. Sihanouk was judged guilty of high treason.

KHIN SOK (1942-). Born on 6 April 1942, he is one of Cambodia's most prominent historians. He studied at the Royal University, Phnom Penh, and worked with **Bernard Philippe Groslier** after he retired to France in 1973. Many of research articles on Angkor and post-Angkor inscriptions can be found in the bulletin of the **École Française d'Extrême-Orient**. His important study of Cambodia's history of troubled relations with Siam and Vietnam, *Le Cambodge entre le Siam et le Viêtnam (de 1775 à 1860)*, was published in 1991. In April 2001 he gave testimony before the **Senate** on the "brutalization of the Khmer language" by the national mass media. His was a protest against the massive intrusion of foreign loanwords into everyday life and a plea for regulatory oversight of language development.

KHMER. The principal language of Cambodia is sometimes referred to as "Cambodian" but it is *Khmer*. The Khmer people who take their national identity from their common language are the dominant ethnic group in Cambodia. Nearly all Khmer are practicing or nominal Buddhists belonging to the lesser or Theravada school of **Buddhism**. Non-Khmer, male or female, who marry into the community are expected to embrace Buddhism and to assimilate to the national language and customs. Khmer was the language of power and administration in mainland Southeast Asia during the **Angkor** Empire and is among the most widely used, living languages in the Mon-Khmer language family. In ancient times, Khmer speakers adopted and elaborated a Sanskrit writing in the first centuries AD, with both speech and writing being subsequently enriched and transformed by loanwords or roots borrowed from Pali, Thai and French. Linguists stress the comparative absence of borrowing from Vietnamese or Chinese languages. Spoken by over 90 percent of the country's population, Khmer language and religious studies were not promoted during the colonial era until the creation of the **Buddhist Institute** and the appearance of **Nagaravatta**, the first Khmer-language newspaper, in 1936. French and Teochew remained the key languages of government and commerce until well into the 1960s. Khmer only surpassed French as the language of postprimary instruction in the years of the **Khmer Republic** when the lifting of state controls on the press also triggered a burst in modern literary output. Since 1975 and especially since 1979, Khmer language and cultural studies have been promoted within the Cambodian diaspora as a means of ethnic boundary maintenance and solidarity among Khmer who are separated from the "Motherland." Scholarly discussions of Khmer linguistics, grammar, literature, drama and family life may be found in the works of **Saveros Pou**, Judith Jacob, Franklin E.Huffman, Khing Hoc Dy, Toni Samantha Phim (née Shapiro) and May Ebihara cited in the bibliography.

***KHMER DAOM* (literally "original Khmer").** A pseudonym used by Saloth Sar (**Pol Pot**) at the end of a handwritten essay entitled "Monarchy or Democracy?". It appeared in the Paris-based Khmer language magazine, *Khemareak Nisut*, ("Khmer Student") in August 1952 in an issue devoted to King Sihanouk's dissolution of the **Democrat Party**-controlled National Assembly in June. Judging the king's actions as a royal coup d'état against democracy, the young Saloth Sar argues that the monarchy is the enemy of the people, religion and knowledge and both the ally of French colonialism and a creation of French colonial power. Like many of Saloth Sar's later writings and speeches, the article displays a tendency to impose firm interpretations on selected events from Cambodian and world history and to weld these interpretations to a nationalist conviction that all "genuine" Khmers will surely see things in exactly the same way.

***KHMER EKAREACH* PARTY ("Party of Independent Khmers").** This party competed in the 1955 **National Assembly** elections. Its party symbol was five lotus buds. Prominent members were Som Chheng, Chap Sum, Ouch Chhim, Kong Seng, Say Tatak, Sam Lang, Chap Ven, Chap Var, Prak Chauchan and Kep Pach. It competed for 13 seats only (of the 91) winning a total of 794 votes (of 761,958 cast nationwide) and disappeared from the political scene. Capitalizing on the populist, each-his-own-sovereign notion of "independence" to convey his anti-Sihanoukism, **Sim Var** founded a newspaper named *Khmer Ekareach* in the mid-1960s.

KHMER INSTITUTE OF DEMOCRACY. A nongovernmental organization, established by **Julio Jeldres**, it was headed until 2002 by **Lao Mong Hay**. Founded during the United Nations period in October 1992, it provides training and education on democracy and human rights issues. Devoting most resources to reforming the political culture at a national level and through projects involving opinion leaders, for example, government officials, military officers, teachers, policemen and civil servants, the Institute has also been involved in the production of television programs promoting democratic values.

KHMER ISSARAK (**"Khmer Freedom Fighters"**). This term designates individuals or groups who took up arms against the French during the struggle for independence from 1945-1953. The Issaraks displayed diverse political and ideological tendencies. Some bands were formed or crystallized with the arrest of **Son Ngoc Thanh** in 1945, often with support from the anticolonial Pridi government in **Thailand**. Thanh formally created a *Issarak Pracheacholana* ("People's Freedom Movement") in March 1952. The *Khmer Viet-Minh Issarak* were guerrillas trained and armed by the Vietnamese communists from 1948. Following the French grant of limited autonomy within the French Union in 1949, some Issaraks, notably **Dap Chhuon**, rallied to the king, thus isolating the Thanhist republicans and Viet Minh-backed Issaraks. **Norodom Sihanouk** seized the political initiative from both and broke his colonial partnership with France by abruptly demanding full independence during his 1953 **Royal Crusade for Independence**.

KHMER KRAHOM (**"Red Khmers"**). *See KHMERS ROUGES.*

KHMER KROM and *KAMPUCHEA KROM* (**"Lower Khmer"** and **"Lower Kampuchea/Cambodia"**). These Khmer language terms referred to the ethnic Khmer people living in areas of the lower **Mekong** Delta which are today part of Vietnam but which were historically part of the Khmer Kingdom (Kampuchea Krom). Many prominent Cambodian nationalist politicians were Khmer Krom, or born in Kampuchea Krom, including **Son Ngoc Thanh, Son Sann** and **Ieng Sary**. While young Khmer Krom benefited from the existence of a modern school system in **Cochinchina**, they were disadvantaged as they progressed to secondary school by having to study in the Vietnamese language medium. The best and the brightest, including those named above, moved to Phnom Penh to attend Lycée and to acquire positions of power, influence and wealth. The resumption of armed struggle in southern Vietnam from 1960 heightened anti-Vietnamese nationalism among Khmer Krom who could expect to gain little from either side in the Vietnamese conflict. Thanh, in Saigon in this decade, recruited among the Khmer Krom for the Civilian Defense Irregulars Group, a U.S. Army paramilitary force, and for his *Khmer Serei* movement. In Phnom Penh, the situation exacerbated irredentist sentiments in relation to the "lost provinces" of Kampuchea Krom. Khmer Krom refugees uprooted by the fighting, and often led by Buddhist monks, appeared regularly on the border requesting aid and sanctuary. Generals **Lon Nol** and **Les Kosem** were among the senior officers in the Royal Armed Forces of the period who quietly established paramilitary forces to carry out raids along the frontier in retaliation. In spite of some fantastical thinking about the recreation of a Khmer-led alliance of all non-Vietnamese ethnics, there was great fear of Vietnam's power and seemingly inexorable "march to the west" as **Nuon Khoeun** put it. In spite of the grassroots suffering and agitation of the Khmer Krom and meddling by the Cambodian military in interethnic conflicts in Vietnam, the diplomatic position of the **Norodom Sihanouk** and **Pol Pot** governments was to insist strenuously that Vietnam, having snatched Kampuchea Krom, could expect *no more* Khmer territory. Thus, while Lon Nol's expulsion of most Vietnamese residents from Cambodia in 1970-1971 and Pol Pot's deportation of the rest in 1975-1976 were misguided, intensely racist maneuvers, they may also be seen as desperate, shortsighted attempts by weak and violent leaders to defend what was left of the Motherland within the existing borders.

KHMER LOEU ("Upper Khmer"). A term that is historically twinned with **Khmer Krom** ("lower Khmer") in so far as it refers to Khmers resided in the upper **Mekong** River valley, that is, the stretch that extends from the town of **Kratié** northward to the Laotian capital of Vientiane. The Khmer people living in **Thailand** in districts north of **Preah Vihear, Anlong Veng** and Phnom Malai refer to themselves as *Khmer Loeu*. However, and since the 1950s, the term has been used in reference to the non-Khmer communities inhabiting mountainous plateau areas of **Stung Treng, Ranatankiri** and **Mondolkiri** provinces. In the late 1960s, they were estimated to number no more than 200,000 (which compares to a 2002 population for these three provinces of 211,851). While most of the Khmer-Thai are rice growers, most highland *Khmer Loeu* engage in slash and burn agriculture or rely on nontimber forestry products for their livelihoods. Some are migratory and most retain communalist social arrangements and uphold animist beliefs. Many do not speak or understand Khmer. Saloth Sar (**Pol Pot**) established the office of the Central Committee of the **Communist Party of Kampuchea** in highland Ratanakiri in 1966 and launched his armed struggle there in 1968 with support from *Khmer Loeu* long alienated from the authorities in **Phnom Penh** (and Saigon). Since the 1990s, use of the designation *Khmer Loeu* has declined. Highlanders are now usually identified individually, the larger groups being the **Brao,** Krung, Kravet, Tampuon and Jarai. **Norodom Sihanouk,** inspired by Pathet Lao attempts to group multiethnic citizens into lowland, highland and mountain Lao, is the person most responsible for modifying the classical meanings of *Khmer Loeu, Khmer Kandal* ("central plains

Khmer") and *Khmer Krom* whose ethnic claims for citizenship were reinforced by this linguistic and cultural revision.

KHMER MON INSTITUTE. *See* KENG VANNSAK.

KHMER NATION PARTY (KNP). An opposition party founded in November 1995 by **Sam Rainsy** but never registered or recognized by the authorities as a legal organization. Attempts to open regional offices met with harassment from local officials, soldiers and police loyal to the **Cambodian People's Party (CPP)**. Party signs were pulled down, the neo-monarchical political culture associating these with lordly power (over the terrain and its population), and party meetings were disrupted or obstructed. Both the palace and the government insisted the KNP party symbol, a bust of the revered **Jayavarman VII**, be replaced, and it was, with a bust of a less distinctive "Angkorean man." By 1998 when a new election law laying down procedures for party registration came into effect, a 1997 splinter faction, patronized by the CPP authorities as the genuine KNP, was awarded the party name. Rainsy's KNP was registered as the **Sam Rainsy Party**.

KHMER PEOPLE'S NATIONAL LIBERATION ARMED FORCES (KPNLAF). *See* KHMER PEOPLE'S NATIONAL LIBERATION FRONT.

KHMER PEOPLE'S NATIONAL LIBERATION FRONT (KPNLF). Initially conceived in Paris in 1978 as the organizational instrument for a counterrevolutionary armed struggle against the **Pol Pot** regime, efforts to organize and launch military operations in the Thai-Cambodian frontier failed. Efforts resumed in March 1979 as the Vietnamese army of occupation and hundreds of thousands of Cambodian refugees marched to the border of **Thailand**. Formally established on 9 October 1979 under the leadership of **Son Sann**, **Dien Del** and **Sak Suthsakhan**, the armed forces were assembled from disparate *Khmer sar* ("white Khmer") groups whose leaders had diverging political agendas but who gradually agreed to work within a unified command structure. Much of the movement's organizational capacity was focused on assuming control of the many conglomerations of displaced Cambodians seeking asylum or sanctuary, trading opportunities or work. Thus the armed wing of the KPNLF, the Khmer People's National Liberation Armed Forces (KPNLAF) took control of the settlements of Non Mak Mun, Nong Samet and Nong Chan in 1980.

In 1982 the KPNLF entered the tripartite **Coalition Government of Democratic Kampuchea (CGDK)**. The new coalition included the **Party of Democratic Kampuchea** led by **Khieu Samphan** and the royalist resistance movement known as **FUNCINPEC** and was duly accorded the seat reserved for **Democratic Kampuchea** in the **United Nations** General Assembly. The KPNLF and KPNLAF recruited heavily in the holding centers in Thailand, or the informal market towns straddling the border, and financed its military and diplomatic operations with support from émigrés and "nonlethal," including developmental assistance from the **United States** and the European Union. The weapons and food supplies required for the troops came almost exclusively from **China**. The **ASEAN** accorded much international diplomatic support to the CGDK but especially to the KPNLF component whose leaders were judged reliably anticommunist, republican and pro-western, if not always democratic.

The movement was riven by factionalism, often of a civil-military character, and by personality disputes. Only the strong nationalist consensus on the need to roll back the Vietnamese army held it together. Under the Paris Peace Agreements of 1991, the KPNLF received two seats in the 12-man **Supreme National Council** (SNC), the all-party, quasi-state council which represented Cambodian sovereignty during the interim administration of the **United Nations Transitional Authority in Cambodia (UNTAC)**. In March 1992 as UNTAC operations got underway, the civilian wing of the Front under the leadership of President Son Sann, convened a Congress in Phnom Penh and formed the **Buddhist Liberal Democratic Party**. The military wing of the Front, led by its commander-in-chief, General Sak Suthsakhan, later formed the **Liberal Democratic Party**. *See also* ABDUL GAFFAR PEANG METH.

KHMER PEOPLE'S REVOLUTIONARY PARTY (KPRP), 1951-1960.

This "people's" party for the Khmer nation was established in Cambodia following the disbanding of the clandestine **Indochinese Communist Party** (ICP) in February 1951. Its 15-man provisional Central Committee was formed on 30 September 1951 and by year's end, the party claimed to have 1,000 members. At the time of the Geneva Conference of 1954, membership may have reached 3,000, between 1,000-1,500 of these being "regrouped" with Vietnamese troops evacuated to northern Vietnam. The rest went underground. The Krom **Pracheachon** ("people's group") was the party's electoral front in the 1955 elections, which were dominated by the abdicated king's **Sangkum** movement. With many of its cadres abroad, others demoralized by the suspension of armed and class struggles and some terrorized by the anticommunist suppression campaign of the army, the KPRP lost about 90 percent of its members in the 1955-1960 period and the party secretary defected in 1959. Mobilizing the Khmer people (and non-Khmers residing in Cambodia) for socialist revolution was complicated by the fact that Chinese and Vietnamese residents of Cambodia remained in the Vietnamese branch of the revolutionary movement, which was not an ethnic party but a more advanced class-based, "workers" party. In September 1960 following a secret congress, the KPRP reorganized itself as a Marxist-Leninist organization. Led by **Tou Samouth**, the new party took the name **Workers' Party of Kampuchea**.

KHMER RENEWAL PARTY (*kanapac khemara ponnakar*). Founded with quiet support from the royal court by **Lon Nol** and **Nhiek Tioulong** in September 1947, this party was known in French as the *parti de rénovation Khmère*. The "Renos" as they were dubbed, were determined to challenge and to defeat the antiroyalist **Democrat Party**. The party had a vision of the historical place of Cambodia in world history, and of the ruling dynasty, in the emerging postcolonial order, a vision partly communicated by the party's emblem, an image of the Earth Goddess superimposed on a map of the protectorate. In brief, the Renos favored independence within the framework of the French Union, membership in the **United Nations**, a resolution of problems relating to the **Khmer Krom** living in **Cochinchina** and continuing involvement of France in national administration, national security and defense. In this quasi- feudalist perspective, the Khmer people were seen to be entitled to have all posts in the colonial administration, and to have the use of French "technicians" secured on a contractual basis, and the French army was obliged to remain in the protectorate to "avoid the costs of maintaining a national army." The party was less interested in winning the political loyalty of the **Khmer Issarak** or of other citizens and appreciated that no national army could be relied upon to suppress those rebelling against the French, the king and the established hierarchies of elites in the countryside, the Buddhist *Sangha* and national administration. **Nhiek Tioulong** was president of the first Steering Committee of the party. Other prominent officers were: **Chau Sen Cocsal, Chuop Hell, Lon Nol, Seng Tho** and **Tim Nguon**. There were six provincial committees established before the 1947 election. Its weekly newspaper, *Khmera* ("*Rénovation*" or "Renewal"), was published in both French and Khmer. Lon Nol was the publisher of the paper, and **Nginn Nippha** was editor in chief. Circulation was about 1,500.

The party won no seats in either the 1947 **National Assembly** elections nor the 1948 High Council elections. Divisions and splits within the Democrat majority allowed it to survive. In June 1950 **Tim Kenn** received a ministerial portfolio, becoming the first party leader to hold high office. In August 1950 Lon Nol became head of the police. In September 1950 the party backed the Democrats in their battle with **Yèm Sambaur**'s breakaway **National Recovery Party**, and in the 1951 elections, Khmer Renewal won 9.1 percent of the vote, but only two seats. Tioulong boasted he would win all the seats in Battambang (for he and Lon Nol had worked there in the 1940s) but they won not one. Ridiculed by the Democrats for having no program and disillusioned by its electoral performance, the party issued a joint statement with the **Victorious Northeastern Khmer Party** in October 1954 announcing they were "rightist, monarchist, traditionalist and in principle opposed to party politics." In May 1955, in the wake of the king's abdication, the Renewal Party dissolved itself and urged its members to join the **Sangkum** which most did.

KHMER REPUBLIC, 1970-1975. The proclamation of a republic on 9 October 1970 was a bold attempt to bring an end to more than 11 centuries of monarchal rule, both absolute and constitutional. The honor of reading the proclamation fell to **In Tam**, a key actor in the March 1970 overthrow of **Norodom Sihanouk**, a former member of the postwar **Democrat Party** and president of the National Assembly after **Cheng Heng** became head of state. The republic endured just over four and a half years, until the occupation of Phnom Penh by communist forces on 17 April 1975. After much debate and delay, a Constitution was promulgated on 10 May 1972. While its provisions revealed democratic aspirations, political power was monopolized by **Lon Nol** who proclaimed himself president of the republic in March 1972 and by the army already sensing defeat in the war following the failure of its **Chenla II** operation. As early as 1971 it was derided as "the Sihanouk regime without Sihanouk." Its democratic promise evaporated in the destruction of lives and livelihoods which came with civil war. Its high officials, with only rare exceptions, were notorious for corruption. Arguably, the most positive legacy of the short-lived Republic was its bold rejection of Francophone, neocolonial culture. Khmer displaced French as the language of government and as the language of instruction in the modern secondary schools for the first time ever, and the even more radical transformations attempted under the successor **Democratic Kampuchea** regime ensured that Francophonie would not be restored.

***KHMERS ROUGES* (literally "Red Khmer," colloquially, "Reds" or "Commies,"** *Khmae Krahom* **in Khmer). Norodom Sihanouk** used this pejorative in all three languages in the 1950s to discredit his many critics on the liberal democratic or extreme left. With even more disdain, right-wing politicians who dared to criticize the authoritarian style of the prince, or his hostility to the "Free World," and his nationalization policies were sometimes dismissed as *Khmer Bleu* ("*Khmer Khieu*" *or* "Blue Stocking" Khmer). In the 1970s the English language media, picking up on the official rhetoric of the **Khmer Republic,** began to use Khmer Rouge for Cambodian Communist and to distinguish the coalition of *Cambodian* guerrillas then fighting under the nominal leadership of Prince **Norodom**

Sihanouk from the "**Viet Cong**," definitely "Reds" in the outlook of most journalists of the day but denounced by **Lon Nol** in more racialist terms as communist "atheists" and "barbarian aggressors" from the north (meaning North Vietnam). In post-Cold War Cambodia, *Khmer Rouge* signifies "Polpotism" a particular brand of communism dismissed by Vietnamese and other Marxist-Leninists as left-wing chauvinism and not genuinely "red" at all. Scholars avoid the term. Former members of the defunct **Communist Party of Kampuchea** are referred to as ex-Khmer Rouge.

KHMER SEREI ("Free Khmers"). A Thai and U.S.-supported, anti-communist and anti-Sihanouk rebel movement led by exiled, dissident nationalist **Son Ngoc Thanh** after 1955. It was implicated in the **Bangkok Plot**. In the former Republic of Vietnam, its members were recruited from the ranks of the **Khmer Krom** minority. Because Thanh also recruited for the U.S. Army Civilian Irregular Defense Group (CGDG), *Khmer Serei* units often had access to U.S.-issue weapons and training. Some 800 *Khmer Serei* "defected" to the Royal Government at the end of 1969, after Thanh had been informed of the plans to overthrow **Norodom Sihanouk**. At different moments **Lon Non, Les Kosem** and **Kim Nguon Trach** provided liaison. The movement was disbanded in 1970, its troops being incorporated into the new, rapidly mobilized republican army.

KHMER SEREIKAR ("Liberation Khmers"). This was the shorthand designation for the guerrilla fighters of the **Khmer People's National Liberation Front** under the overall command of **Sak Suthsakhan** and **Dien Del**.

KHUON NAY (1891-c1988). Born in Kampong Cham, the son of Kong Khuon and Mme (née Chak Heng), Khuon Nay entered the judicial services in 1923 and rose to the rank of magistrate. He and his brother-in-law **Im Phon** were founding members of the **Democrat Party**. With strong support from his own party, he was elected to the **High Council of the Kingdom** to represent civil servants (technical branch), and, benefiting from the discord among the minor parties, he was elected president of the Council serving from January 1948 to January 1950. He survived an assassination attempt toward the end of his presidency and served as vice-president of the Council of Ministers. Khuon Nay was minister of the national economy in May 1950, minister of agriculture from June 1950 to 1951 and elected to the 1951 National Assembly for Phniet, **Battambang**. He then served as president of the National Assembly until 2 January 1953. He served in the National Consultative Assembly in 1953 and contested Sambuor Meas, **Kampong Cham** province in 1955. By his many wives, one of whom was Princess Sisowath Sovet (Thavet), daughter of King **Sisowath Monivong**, Khuon Nay had a large family. His eldest son was **Nay Valentin**. Another son, Khuon Phlayveth, is a member of **FUNCINPEC** and was appointed to the **Senate** in 1999.

KHUON SODARY (1951-). A leading member of the **Cambodian People's Party (CPP),** she represents **Kandal** province in the National Assembly of 1998. She finished college just before 1975 and was a high school English teacher before being evacuated to the countryside. In 1979 she decided to support the **People's Republic of Kampuchea** and from 1985 she worked on the twice-weekly official Communist Party newspaper, *Pracheachon* ("The People"), edited by another woman, **Som Kim Suor.** In 1991 when the **People's Revolutionary Party of Kampuchea** abandoned Marxism-Leninism and reorganized itself as the CPP, the paper became a noncommunist daily and the official organ of the postcommunist CPP. By 1998 Khuon Sodary had succeeded Som Kin Suor as its editor in chief.

KHVAN SIPHANN (1917/8-1976). He was a schoolteacher at Collège Norodom Sihanouk in **Kampong Cham** and briefly taught the young Saloth Sar (**Pol Pot**). Later, after completing further training in France in 1955, he taught in schools in the capital and in the Institute of Pedagogy in the early 1960s. A republican, he was elected to the **Senate** of the **Khmer Republic** in 1972 and for this reason was among high, "old regime" office holders "extracted" from the "ranks" of the "revolutionary" people for execution in 1976.

KHY TANG LIM (1936-). A civil engineer who trained at the École Polytechnique in Montréal, Canada, and a supporter of the *Khmer Serei* in the 1960s, he was commissioned a colonel in the republican army in September 1970. He held ministerial posts in every new government formed during the **Khmer Republic**. In 1971 he was named minister of public works. He boasted in this year of finding some way to mount another coup which would bring **Son Ngoc Thanh** to power. His were among the unseen hands behind the Buddhist protests organized by **Khieu Chum** in October. Thanh was named prime minister of the succeeding cabinet in which Khy Tang Lim was minister of housing, public works, posts, telecommunications and transport (March to October 1972). In successive cabinets, he was minister of public works and telecommunications (October 1972 to April 1973); minister of planning (May to October 1973); minister of state for planning, and coordination of the Ministries of Finance, Agriculture, Trade, Development, Industry and Handicrafts (October to December 1973); minister of finance, planning and economy (December 1973 until 21 March 1975), and minister of state in charge of finance, planning and production until 12 April 1975. He left the country just as the capital was about to be seized by the communists. During the 1980s, his fervent anticommunism and nationalism moved him to lend support to **FUNCINPEC**. In 1998 he won a seat for this party in the National Assembly elections in **Kampong Cham** and was named minister of public works and transport in the **Hun Sen** cabinet. His route to power in the 1970s and his return to it in the 1990s indicate that elite networks still matter and that elite visions of power and order continue to obstruct democracy.

KIENG VANG (1947-). Khmer Krom. Recruited into the **United States**-trained civilian defense irregulars group operating in South Vietnam in the late 1960s, he was assigned to the Cambodian battlefield in 1970 as part of the "Mike Force." He joined **FUNCINPEC** in the 1980s and joined the **Armée Nationale Sihanoukienne** rising to the rank of division commander. He was elected to the National Assembly in **Siem Reap** in June 1993 and appointed assistant secretary of state for the interior in November 1993. He remained loyal to Prince **Norodom** in 1997 and was reelected to the National Assembly in 1998 in **Kampot** but gave up his seat when he was promoted to secretary of state in the Ministry of Interior.

"THE KILLING FIELDS." This award winning film, directed by Roland Joffé and produced by David Puttnam, tells the story of *New York Times* war correspondent Sydney Schanberg in the **Khmer Republic**, and that of his assistant and interpreter, **Dith Pran**, portrayed by **Ngor Haing**, who was left behind in **Democratic Kampuchea**. Released in 1984, the film had a forceful impact on Western popular images of the human suffering and violence in **Pol Pot**'s Cambodia.

KIM NGUON TRACH (1923-1975). A lifelong activist and prominent **Khmer Krom** administrator, Kim Nguon Trach attended primary school in **Cochinchina** then earned his baccalaureate from a lycée in Paris in 1939. He received a post in the colonial administration of the Protectorate of Cambodia soon afterward. In 1946 he was a founding member of the pro-French **Liberal Party** which was established in response to the nationalist struggles of the **Democrat Party** and of the **Khmer Issarak**. As the **Viet Minh** war intensified, Trach returned to France or to Vietnam in 1949-1953 (and possibly both) where he acquired professional training in accountancy and finance. By the late 1950s and early 1960s he was an inspector of finance attached at different times to the Treasury and the Ministry of Finance. He was also director of the *Caisse Nationale d'Equipement* ("National Development Fund"). By the mid-1960s, he was prominent in Khmer Krom support groups and a commander in some of the shadowy paramilitary operations mounted by **Lon Nol** and the *Khmers du Kampuchea Krom* (KKK). Prince **Norodom Sihanouk** also criticized him publicly for looking after the family of **Son Ngoc Thanh** while Thanh, from the safety of Saigon, directed illegal **Khmer Serei** activities. In the months preceding and following the 18 March 1970 coup, Kim Nguon Trach was among those who transported Khmer Serei "defectors" from the Vietnamese frontier to Phnom Penh. An accomplished technocrat with limited tolerance for the cut and thrust constitutional politics, he was nevertheless deputy governor and then governor of the National Bank in the final days of the **Khmer Republic**. He refused a U.S. offer of evacuation by helicopter in the final days of the siege of Phnom Penh and was executed by the communists on or very soon after 17 April 1975.

KIM PHON (?-1970). Briefly a member of the **National Recovery Party** in the early 1950s and, after 1955, the **Sangkum**, he failed on several occasions to win a seat in the National Assembly. He ran against **In Tam** for the seat of Poes, **Kampong Cham**, in the 1966 Assembly elections and In Tam won. A few months later, in the wake of the **Samlaut Uprising**, In Tam was named governor of **Battambang** province and resigned from the Assembly. Kim Phon won the vacated seat in a by-election held in December 1967. On 18 March 1970, he walked out of the National Assembly chamber, refusing to take part in the vote to depose Prince **Norodom Sihanouk**. In spite of this, when street protests erupted in Kampong Cham city one week later, he and **Sos Saoun**, also a deputy, drove to the scene in an attempt to reason with the demonstrators and to persuade them to support the **Lon Nol-Cheng Heng** government. Angered by this gesture, the demonstrators dragged the two parliamentarians to a textile factory and killed them both. *See also* TONG SIV ENG.

KING MEN (c1932-1985). Soldier and deputy chief of staff of the **Armée Nationale Sihanoukienne (ANS)**. King Men first joined the army at the age 13 and fought on the republican side from 1970-1975, settling afterward in the United States. While in the ANS he was promoted to major general and distinguished himself in the defense of Tatum, a hill fort on the cliffs overlooking northern Cambodia. King Men was killed when his bunker took a direct hit from Vietnamese artillery fire on 8 March 1985. Prince **Norodom Sihanouk**, Princess **Monique** and also his brother, King Sam Nang, from San José, California, attended his service of cremation in Surin province, Thailand. His replacement as deputy chief of staff was Prince **Norodom Chakrapong**.

KINGDOM OF KAMPUCHEA, 1945. This was the official English language name of the Cambodian state between March and October 1945, following a grant of "independence" from France awarded by the occupying Japanese. The nationalist preference for use of "Kampuchea," a transcription which more clearly approximates the Khmer pronunciation of the word pronounced in English as "Cambodia" and in French as

Cambodge, resurfaced 31 years later when in 1976 the communists led by
Pol Pot renamed the state **Democratic Kampuchea**.

KIRIROM. A hill station 100 kilometers southwest of Phnom Penh, Kirirom
was the site of a military base during the 1960s and Prince **Norodom
Chantaraignsey**'s military stronghold in the early 1970s. In peaceful times
it was a pleasant rural retreat for public employees (e.g., the National
Bank) and members of the **Sangkum**. From 1967-1970 it was renamed
Tioulongville after its first governor, **Nhiek Tioulong**. Still known today
as Kirirom, its official name is Preah Suramarit Kossamak National Park.

KITCHPANICH SONGSAKD (1932-). Born on 10 November 1932 in
Battambang, the son of Gau Yong King and Mme (née You Kitchpanich),
he was appointed honorary mandarin at the court and was a prominent
businessman and banker in **Phnom Penh**. Among his many business
interests, he was president of the Bank of Phnom Penh and of the Far East
Life Assurance Co. (Cambodia). He also invested in insurance, fishing,
phosphate, gas and cotton plantations via his private holding company
Etats Songsakd Kitchpanich. A man with powerful contacts at court
reportedly stemming from an introduction to **Norodom Suramarit** at a
young age, his financial empire crumbled in late 1963 when Prince
Norodom Sihanouk nationalized the banking and insurance sector.
Songsakd was forced to flee Phnom Penh on 22 December, taking up to
$4 million in bank funds with him. Settling in Bangkok, he bought a
hotel and reestablished himself in business circles there. In the 1980s he
is rumored to have invested in gem-mining in **Pailin**.

KOH KER. This barely accessible and neglected ancient site is 80 kilometers
from **Siem Reap** town. It was the capital of the usurper King **Jayavarman
IV** between c928 until his death in 942. The archaeological evidence
indicates it once had 68 monuments centered on the *Prasat Thom* ("big
temple") which was built on seven levels to a maximum height of 35
meters. An inscription asserts Jayavarman "founded by his own power a
city which was the seat . . . of the universe." If a Council for Development
project proves successful, the site will be restored and developed as a
major tourist attraction.

KOH KONG. A coastal province, bordering **Pursat, Kampot** and **Kampong
Speu**, it covers 11,140 square kilometers. The **census** of 3 March 1998
recorded a population of 132,106. Its population density is 12 per square
kilometer, much lower than the national average of 64, but much of the
inland terrain is mountainous, heavily forested and uninhabitable. Its
capital town, of the same name, is a bustling center for international trade
with **Thailand** and the rest of the region. In October 2001 the government

chose an area of 225 ha just inside the border from Thailand's Klong Yai district, Trat province, as the site for the first export processing zone in Cambodia. It is being developed jointly by the Council for Development of Cambodia (CDC) and the National Economic and Social Development board of Thailand.

KOH SANTEPHEAP ("Island of Peace"). A daily newspaper during the Lon Nol period, it closed its doors on 15 April 1975. Resurrected in January 1993 by its former editors, with an initial investment of US$7,000, it had a print-run of 20,000. The first issue took advantage of historically unprecedented (in Cambodia) guarantees of press freedoms under the **United Nations Transitional Authority in Cambodia (UNTAC)** by attacking corruption in high places. One of its reporters, Chan Dara, was murdered in 1994 possibly for naming too many wrongdoers. Originally criticized for its nonpartisan muckraking, it has been regarded as pro-**Hun Sen** since 1995 and among the four papers must sympathetic to the government.

KOL TOUCH (1914-2002). Born in **Svay Rieng**, Kol Touch studied agriculture and farmed in his native province, also working as a controller of the waters and forests department. **Son Sann** appointed him secretary of state for the national economy, in charge of industry in May 1967, a portfolio he held until January 1968. He refrained from politics in the **Khmer Republic**, apart from agreeing to be a member of the Central Committee of **Sisowath Sirik Matak**'s **Republican Party**, and continued to live in Svay Rieng throughout the **Democratic Kampuchea (DK)** period. Because he was widely respected, he along with **Chhean Vam** survived. He refused to become a minister in the **People's Republic of Kampuchea** in 1979 and moved to Paris. In the 1980s he was associated with the **Khmer People's National Liberation Front** and often traveled to the Thai-Cambodian border, at his own expense, to teach French and history to schoolchildren. Kol Touch died in Paris on 18 February 2002. One of his sons, Kol Dorathy, a textile engineer trained in France and a supporter of the **National United Front of Kampuchea (FUNK)** returned to DK with other FUNK militants in 1976. He was arrested and sent to **Tuol Sleng** but courageously refused to admit to any treachery or to denounce any friends before being executed.

KONG KORM (1941-). Senator. A native of **Kampong Cham** province and a graduate of the University of Phnom Penh, he was a schoolteacher in **Prey Veng** province in the mid-1960s and in his native province from 1968 until 1973. He then worked on the land in a liberated area controlled by the communists, remaining in the East Zone after 1975. He was likely among the East Zone militants who fled to **Vietnam** in 1978. In 1979 he was appointed advisor to **Hun Sen**, foreign minister in the **People's Republic of Kampuchea (PRK)** and from late 1980 to April 1982 he was PRK ambassador to Vietnam. Recalled to Phnom Penh, he was first deputy minister of foreign affairs, 1982-1986, until Hun Sen's promotion to the presidency of the Council of Ministers, then succeeded his mentor as minister of foreign affairs, December 1986-December 1987. As peace talks got underway, he was shifted to the Council of Ministers' office as an advisor to the president on social and cultural questions and then entered the government as minister responsible for the state affairs inspectorate, replacing **Sin Song**. In this post his professional integrity, party and personal loyalties were put to the test. A full member of the Central Committee of the Marxist-Leninist **People's Revolutionary Party of Kampuchea**, he appears to have been marginalized in 1991. He had no post in the government formed in 1993 and joined the **Khmer Nation Party (KNP)** becoming vice-president and deputy to **Sam Rainsy**. He remained loyal to Rainsy in 1996-1997 when Hun Sen encouraged two breakaway movements and awarded the party's name to one of these. He was appointed to the **Senate** in 1999, a **Sam Rainsy Party** nominee.

KONG SAM OL (1936-). Born in Kangkor, **Kandal** province, he graduated from Phnom Penh University in 1963 with a degree in agronomy and was briefly a foreign exchange student at the University of Georgia. He then worked in the Ministry of Agriculture. On 17 April 1975 he and his family joined the evacuation from the city, many of his family being "sorted out" for execution. In 1979 he was one of the prominent noncommunist supporters of the People's Revolutionary Council and its successor **People's Republic of Kampuchea (PRK)** and was attached to the Council of Ministers with duties relating to agriculture, planning and technology. In October 1980 he became a member of the Central Committee of the **United Front for the National Salvation of Kampuchea (UFNSK)**.

President of the **Mekong** Committee of the PRK from November 1980 to October 1986, he was concurrently minister of agriculture from June 1981 until March 1985. After a brief attachment to the Council of Ministers where he was responsible for agricultural matters and rubber plantations, he was named deputy prime minister from November 1987 until June 1993. By this time he had joined the **People's Revolutionary Party of Kampuchea (PRPK)** and became a member of its Central Committee by 1989. In May 1991 he was one of the six PRPK members appointed to the all-party **Supreme National Council**, the temporary repository of Cambodia's national sovereignty for the duration of the **United Nations Transitional Authority in Cambodia**. In June 1993 he was elected to the National Assembly on the **Cambodian People's Party (CPP)** list in **Kampong Chhnang**. He was appointed director-general to the royal palace and residences and in charge of relations between and among the royal palace, the government and the Assembly during the unstable weeks following the elections. He was appointed minister of agriculture, forests and fishing in the CPP-**FUNCINPEC** government of November 1993 but he lost this post to Tao Seng Hour in the cabinet reshuffle approved by the Assembly on 20 October 1994. In 1998 he was reelected to the Assembly in **Kampong Chhnang**.

KONG SILEAH (c1935-1980). Leader and founder of the *Mouvement de Libération Nationale du Kampuchea*, known by the acronym **Molinaka**. He graduated from a naval academy in France in 1958 and served in the royal navy, rising to the rank of captain. After the defeat of the republican armed forces in 1975, Kong Sileah eluded capture by the revolutionaries and settled briefly on the Thai-Cambodian border before returning to France in 1976-1978. In June 1979 he met **Nhem Sophon** and together, on 31 August 1979 they formed Molinaka, a force of several hundred men based in 1980 near the Nong Chan land bridge. He died on 16 August 1980, officially from cerebral malaria, but rumors of foul play abound. He reportedly signed an oath of allegiance to the **Khmer People's National Liberation Front (KPNLF)** in 1979, earning the enmity of KPNLAF chief **Dien Del** when he failed to honor it. He also disapproved of black market trading along the border and had conflicts with Thai soldiers after the rape of a young Khmer woman in one of the camps.

KOSAL (1904-   ). Born in **Cochinchina** and from a prominent **Khmer Krom** family, he received a privileged education proceeding from **Collège Sisowath** to Collège Chasseloup Laubat and graduating from the École Supérieure de Pédagogie in Hanoi in 1928. He taught upper primary school from 1929-1933 then accepted an appointment as a magistrate. He was named minister of justice in 1949 and was in this post on 14 January 1950 when **Ieu Koeus** was assassinated. As minister it was Kosal who decided that suspects in the killing would be interrogated by the National Police not the investigating magistrate. The defense lawyer in the trial protested this violation of the law but to no avail. (By some accounts, Kosal was a counselor in the court of review at the time.) An anti-**Democrat Party** establishment figure, he helped **Yèm Sambaur** organize the **National Recovery Party** and was the party's secretary-general. He was a Recovery Party candidate in the 1951 National Assembly elections but lost.

KOSSAMAK. *See* SISOWATH KOSSAMAK, Princess/Queen.

KOU ROUN (1911-c1990). Although he entered the **judiciary** in 1938, he was a senior personal assistant or secretary to Prince **Norodom Sihanouk** by the early 1950s and gradually acquired responsibility for running the secret police. He strongly opposed the **Democrat Party** and joined the **Khmer Renewal Party** quietly promoted by the royal court as soon as it was established. In October 1955 he was appointed minister of public works and telecommunications in the first **Sangkum** government and, in the third, minister of public health (April to September 1956). In the eighth government formed April 1957 he became minister of national economy, and in the 10th, formed in January 1958, he was appointed minister of public works, posts and telecommunications. Also in 1958 Kou Roun received a royal appointment to the **High Council of the Kingdom** and in January 1959 was named chief of police. A month later he became minister of state for national security and surface defense. While holding both of these posts, he organized the street attack on **Khieu Samphan** in July 1960. Kou Roun was appointed minister of state for national security and territorial defense from May 1965 until October 1966, and was a member of Sihanouk's shadow cabinet from 1966-1970. The brother-in-law of **Kim Nguon Trach**, he worked closely with **Lon Nol** as the latter edged steadily closer to power. Some informants state he was widely feared. The newspaper *Souvannaphum* ("Golden Land") was fined heavily in 1969 for libeling him. He was likened to an "asura," a mythical demon.

KOUN WICK (1919-1999). From a **Khmer Krom** family, and cousin of **Chau Sen Cocsal**, Koun Wick was a career diplomat throughout the **Sangkum** era. Prominent in colonial administration he was appointed governor of **Kampong Chhnang** province in 1952 then attached to the Cambodian embassy in the **United Kingdom** from 1954-1957. He then worked in the Ministry of Foreign Affairs, assisting with the preparation of Cambodia's case for the World Court hearing on the temple at **Preah Vihear**. After resolution of the case in mid-1962, he was named chargé d'affaires then ambassador to Indonesia in 1963 and in May 1965 he became minister of foreign affairs for the first time, but only for three months. He was ambassador to Yugoslavia in March 1970 and deported by the Yugoslav government for his support of **Lon Nol**. Back in Phnom Penh, Koun Wick was foreign minister in the *Gouvernement de Sauvetage* formed in July 1970 and retained this portfolio until he was replaced by **Son Ngoc Thanh** in March 1972. In December 1972, was appointed ambassador to the Ivory Coast. After 1975 Koun Wick lived in the United States, dying in London on 27 December 1999.

KOY PECH AFFAIR. Koy Pech, an ex-school teacher, was a student in the Faculty of Law at the University of Phnom Penh in 1971 where he was taught by **Keo Ann**, dean of the faculty, among others, but the two formed a friendship based on mutual regard. Pech was elected president of the law students' association in 1971. By April 1972 students in the faculty were demonstrating against the government and denouncing Prince **Sisowath Sirik Matak,** in particular for obstructing approval of the new democratic constitution. On 23 April 1972, during a television interview, Koy Pech referred to **Lon Nol** as a *"Sdach arul mech"* ("King of monsters"). When **Thappana Nginn**, minister of the interior, ordered his arrest, he fled to the law faculty. Students supporting Koy Pech surrounded and guarded the building, but in clashes with the police, a schoolboy was killed. Pech finally gave himself up on 28 April, after the government agreed not to prosecute him. Media coverage of the standoff propelled Keo Ann to national prominence preparing the way for his run for the presidency later in the year.

KOY THUON (1933-1977). A native of **Kampong Cham**, his earliest studies were in temple schools at a time when many monks were deeply engaged in the nationalist movement led by **Son Ngoc Thanh, Hem Chieu** and **Pach Chhoeun.** At **Lycée Sisowath** in 1949 he was caught up in the anti-colonial and anti-royalist student movement led by **Ieng Sary** and **Hu Nim.** He graduated from the Institute of Pedagogy in 1954 and was assigned to a post in **Kratié**. He joined the **Democrat Party** in 1955 reestablishing contacts with some Thanhists of his school years, but when in 1958 he returned to the Institute of Pedagogy for further studies, he met **Tiv Ol** who slowly recruited him into the Communist movement. He was inducted into the **Workers' Party of Kampuchea** in 1960 by **Son Sen**. Koy Thuon next recruited other friends, notably **Khek Penn**, and while he was principal at Lycée Preah Sihanouk in **Kampong Thom** from 1960-1964, he was known as a progressive and recruited **Tourn Sok Phallar** and **Pech Cheang** among others. He was already a candidate member of the party Central Committee when in March 1963 his name appeared along with those of **Son Sen, Ieng Sary,** Saloth Sar (**Pol Pot**) and others on a list of 34 "reds" summoned to meet Prince **Norodom Sihanouk**. He joined them underground in July 1964. Among some of his secret party assignments in the years up to 1970, he helped Hu Nim to win reelection to the National Assembly in 1966.

In 1970 Koy Thoun was appointed to the Central Committee of the **National United Front of Kampuchea** and to the **Royal Government of National Union** as deputy minister of finance from 1970-1974. As the liberation war progressed and royalists were marginalized, he was minister of economy and finance (November 1974-April 1976). In the military and party structure, he was in charge of the north zone which embraced the provinces of **Oddar Meanchey, Siem Reap** and **Preah Vihear** and parts of **Stung Treng.** In the **Democratic Kampuchea** state structure, he was chairman of the state trading committee to which Khek Penn was attached. Koy Thuon was secretary of the northern zone when, in January 1977, he was arrested by **Ke Pauk**, his deputy and successor.

"Thuch" as he was known displayed sympathy for "**new people**" and intellectuals and gave important roles to former teachers and those with knowledge and skills. His outlook and approach were judged too "liberal" by Pol Pot and other leading cadres in the **Communist Party of Kampuchea (CPK)**. Thus when his zone failed to reach plan targets, he was purged for concealing too many class "enemies" who ought to have been "swept away," which meant, executed. While under torture at **Tuol Sleng**, he was forced to confess to conspiring against the party leadership with "Thanist" elements (i.e., middle-class people or intellectuals with republican and pro-American leanings) and to identify a large number of alleged coconspirators in the 1960s student movement. He was sent to his death in April or May 1977.

KRAM NGOY né **Ngoy Ouk Ou (1865-1936)**. A renowned poet, musician (sitar) and singer of verse, Ngoy studied in temple schools as a boy and was ordained *bhikkhu*, a Buddhist monk, at 21. Later in life he left the monkhood, married and had children. It was in this period that he became well-known as a talented musician, and he also received the honorific title of *kram* to indicate his role as intermediary between the village and the state. His performances attracted the attention of **Georges Coedès** who introduced him to **Suzanne Karpèles** of the **Buddhist Institute**. She then arranged performances in the presence of a scribe and publication of the verses by the Institute. Before the wars and the revolution, Kram Ngoy's verses were used in schools and in the home for moral and practical instruction. They offer shrewd advice and commentary on the vicissitudes of everyday life, especially for the rural poor, and warned **Khmer** people to be on guard against mischievous others who will exploit their shortcomings. The mischief makers are sometimes clearly identified as Chinese merchants or Vietnamese "enemies."

KRATIÉ. A province in the northeast divided on its north-south axis by the **Mekong** River, it is located between **Kampong Thom** and **Kampong Cham** provinces to the west and **Mondolkiri** province to the east. It covers an area of 11,094 square kilometers much of the terrain being on a plateau and mountainous. Its population was recorded at 263,175 in the March 1998 **census** but put at 253,454 only at the time of the February 2002 *khum* (commune) elections. The census also reports the presence of more than 500 households of no fixed location, those of transient *Khmer loeu* ("upper" or "highland" people). According to the census these households together with homeless people and some Mekong houseboat families, numbered 4,185. There is a high dependency ratio on the economically active population, heavily concentrated in primary sector activities (78.3 percent) along the banks of the Mekong. Poor infrastructure, including river transport and the lack of electricity, constrain the province's economic development.

***KROM SAMMAKI* ("solidarity groups").** These were small production groups organized on a family and village or subvillage basis after 1979. Their main aim was to restore rice production as rapidly as possible. A full and immediate return to family farming was impossible in the wake of the collapse of much of the **Democratic Kampuchea** irrigation system and because of shortages of work animals, tools, seeds and, in some regions, labor. Rice production thus remained partly collectivized with female heads of households, disabled war veterans and nonagricultural workers (e.g., schoolteachers) being assured of some community support. In theory group leaders made annual allocations of *krom sammaki* land to households for their temporary use. In practice many families reclaimed ancestral properties or treated allocated plots as family-owned with the complicity of local *krom sammaki* leaders which meant the annual allocation and planning was mostly a paper exercise. Private rights to the use of land were restored in 1989 but the customary land-use permits were issued region by region at a snail's pace. Land disputes of many kinds—land grabbling by officials, contested claims, boundary disputes, access or water rights—divided local communities with many local **People's Revolutionary Party of Kampuchea** (or, after 1991, **Cambodian People's Party**) cadres being seen to manage the process corruptly.

KROUCH YOEURM (c1935-1997). A member of **FUNCINPEC** and a former royalist army officer close to Prince **Norodom Ranariddh**, he was assistant secretary of state in the Ministry of National Defense in the Royal Government from 1993. As violence erupted in the streets in July 1997, he escaped from the capital, together with **Chau Sambath**, but the two were captured on 8 July 1997, tortured and murdered, presumably by troops or bodyguards loyal to **Hun Sen**. The two royalist officials were among 83 people murdered or assassinated during and after the July 1997 coup.

KRUOCH SAVANG (SAVANG VONG). A clerk in the colonial administration in the office of the **French Résident** of **Kampong Speu** province, he joined the Royal Khmer Army immediately after the 9 March 1945 coup against France. By 1947, after officer training, he was commissioned a second lieutenant and received a field command. He next deserted with all of his men and joined a **Viet Minh**-supported band of **Khmer Issarak** on 3 March 1949. Some French intelligence reports claim he helped the Issarak form a coalition with the Viet Minh while others say he was hostile to the Vietnamese. King **Norodom Sihanouk** believed the French secretly slipped arms to him and that he was a French-backed "fake" Issarak. All of these claims may be true, or true in some measure. Savang Vong and Prince **Norodom Chantaraingsey** were among the last of the Issarak leaders to lay down arms on 20 February 1954.

KUCH AN. Born in Chhlong, **Kratié** province, and initially a timber entrepreneur and publisher of the Chinese-language newspaper *Mekong Yat Pao*, Kuch An was the principal intermediary in the transport of food, arms and other supplies to the **National Front for the Liberation of South Vietnam**. After making a fortune, he became entangled in a smuggling operation which the authorities refused to settle in the usual manner. Prince **Norodom Sihanouk** exiled him to Canton in 1967. General **Lon Nol** arranged and agreed to his return in 1968 after a gift of 10 bulldozers. By 1969 Kuch An was the principal compradore and go-between in all matters financial and economic for the general. He was also the person to whom the Chinese government turned when they sought to strike a bargain with General Lon Nol between 18 March 1970 and 5 May 1970. The Chinese initially proposed to extend diplomatic recognition to the coup government if Cambodia was prepared to continue to lend maximum material assistance to the communist revolutionary forces fighting in South Vietnam, to allow the Vietnamese to have border sanctuaries and to support the anti-American struggle in Vietnam in official statements and broadcasts. Lon Nol refused, without further consultations. When the general also announced the details of the Chinese approach on national radio, to demonstrate his intentions of entering into an anti-communist alliance, Kuch An fled into exile.

KUN KIM (1956-). Senior advisor to **Hun Sen** and one of the three "strong men" in the prime minister's personal entourage. (The other two are **Chea Sophari** and **Hok Lundi**.) He fought for the **National United Front of Kampuchea** in the civil war, 1970-1975 and subsequently worked in the **Democratic Kampuchea** administration in **Kampong Cham**, being among the East Zone cadres who fled to **Vietnam.** In 1979, he was a "people's assessor," one of the 11 on the jury at the trial of **Pol Pot** and **Ieng Sary** conducted by the **People's Republic of Kampuchea**. Between 1983-1986, he was deputy governor of Kampong Cham and from 1990-1997, deputy governor of **Kandal** province. Although he was on the candidate list of the **Cambodian People's Party (CPP)** for Kandal province in the United Nations-sponsored elections of 1993, he did not win a seat in the **National Assembly**. He is widely believed to have had a hand in the violence surrounding his party's election campaign. His reputation was no doubt a factor in his failed bid for a seat in the CPP Central

Committee in January 1977. During the July coup, it was he who initiated armed combat by ordering Hun Sen's bodyguards to attack FUNCINPEC forces. This action was taken after Chief of Staff **Ke Kim Yan** refused to obey an order to deploy regular army forces on the streets of the capital. In 1998 Kun Kim was active in the violent suppression of post-election protests and in 1999 he was identified as a facilitator of the prime minister's secret liaisons with **Piseth Pilica**. His appointment as one of the four deputy commanders-in-chief of the Royal Cambodian Armed Forces in November 1999 surprised unnamed senior military officers who complained to the press that Kun Kim had not seen active service for more than 20 years. The appointment, made by Prime Minister Hun Sen, gave rise to speculation about Ke Kim Yan's future. *See also* ADVISORS.

KUY or **KUOY**. This highland, minority nation speaks a language belonging to the Mon-Khmer linguistic family but the vocabulary and pronunciation are quite distinct from the national *Khmer* language. The Kuy were historically dispersed throughout the northeast highland plateau region though the largest concentrations were likely in **Preah Vihear**, **Stung Treng**, **Kampong Thom** and **Kratié** provinces. Traditionally engaged in iron ore mining and smelting, the Kuy were thought to number 14,186 in March 1995. As Ministry of Interior estimates are based on village registration books they are almost certainly low. No figures from the 1998 **census** have been made available. Many Kuy were dislodged from or for other reasons left their villages during the wars in the 1970s. A not inconsiderable number appear to have intermarried with **Khmer** and to have assimilated to Khmer society. The **Communist Party of Kampuchea** recruited successfully in Kuy villages in the late 1960s when **Pol Pot** established his Central Committee in their region. Laurence Picq, commenting on the ethnic origins of the staff of the Foreign Ministry in **Democratic Kampuchea**, reported that ethnic Kuy were favored, and likely the largest single group. In 1994 ethnic Kuy fought in the National Army of Democratic Kampuchea battalion which seized **Anlong Veng** permitting Pol Pot to establish his last base there.

KY LUM ANG (1949-). One of the most prominent women politicians in Cambodia, Ky Lum Ang was a secret agent working behind the lines for FUNCINPEC during the resistance war in the 1980s. She was elected to the **National Assembly** in 1993 on the FUNCINPEC list in **Battambang**. In that Assembly, she chaired the Commission on the Economy, Planning, Investments, Agriculture, Rural Development and the Environment. Reelected in 1998, she continues to chair this body, one of the nine standing committees of the National Assembly. She was reelected to the Steering Committee of FUNCINPEC in 1999.

-L-

LAM KEN (1921-1971). Born on 7 October 1921 at Soctrang, Cochinchina, the son of Lam Bun and Mme (née Thi Xum), he studied in France. He worked as a veterinarian and in 1950 was delegate to the **Pau Conference**. Although suspected by the **United States** Embassy of being a secret sympathiser with the communists, in 1950 he cofounded, with **Yèm Sambaur**, the National Recovery Party which hoped to outpoll the **Democrat Party** in the September 1951 elections. It failed to win any seats in the **National Assembly**, and Lam Ken gave up politics. He married first Mme Josephe Gilles, a cousin of a prominent French veterinary doctor, who died on 3 January 1970 and then Mme **Nou Neou**. He was director of the veterinary services and a brigadier general in the army of the **Khmer Republic** at the time of his death on 5 September 1971.

LAO MONG HAY. A British-educated, democracy activist, he was concurrently Director of the Institute of Public Administration and Head of the Human Rights Unit of the **Khmer People's National Liberation Front (KPNLF)** and an aide to KPNLF President **Son Sann** from 1988-1992. In 1993-1994 he was Acting Director of the Cambodian Mine Action Center and then Executive Director of the **Khmer Institute of Democracy**, 1995-2002. He assessed the expulsion of **Chhang Song**, Pou Savath, Phay Siphan and **Keo San** from the **Cambodian People's Party (CPP)** and the **Senate** as the triumph of party discipline over democracy suggesting also that CPP attempts to discipline their Senators have placed constitutional guarantees of parliamentary immunity in jeopardy.

LAOS. In the Angkorean era, much of southern Laos was under intermittent Cambodian control. An important pre-Angkorean temple is located at Wat Phu in southern Laos. However, because dense forests separated the two countries, and because the **Mekong** is not navigable much above the Cambodian-Lao border, the two countries, while sharing the same religious and other cultural traditions, developed as separate kingdoms. Contacts were revived at least at elite levels when Laos, like Cambodia, became part of the federation of territories known as **French Indochina**. In the 1940s the royal families of the two countries exchanged visits, but during the 1960s Prince **Norodom Sihanouk** was alienated from the pro-American neutrality of the Vientiane government and monarchy and aligned his foreign policy with that of the antiimperialist Prince Souphanouvong, a leader of the Pathet Lao. Their alliance deepened when Sihanouk was overthrown. After the communist People's Revolutionary Party of Laos entered a coalition government in Vientiane, relations with the **Khmer Republic** chilled, and because of the withdrawal of the **Democratic Kampuchea** from international or regional relations, intergovernmental contacts were not fully renewed or revived until Vietnam established the **People's Republic of Kampuchea** in 1979.

LAY PRAHOAS né **Lim Prohas (1965-).** Born in Phnom Penh, son of Lim Polai, engineer with SONAPNEU, he and his family settled in Melbourne, Australia in c1981. After earning a degree in commerce from the University of Melbourne, he worked for Bourne Griffiths Boyd, chartered accountants, Melbourne, and was president of the Cambodian Youth Association of Victoria. In 1990-1991 he campaigned on behalf of the Cambodian boat people who arrived in northern Australia, arguing they should be allowed to settle in Australia. In 1991 he returned to Cambodia to work for **FUNCINPEC** and was appointed deputy minister of planning in the provisional government of 1993 before being confirmed as an assistant secretary of state in the Royal Government formed in November. In 1998 he was on the **FUNCINPEC** reserve list in the elections and appointed secretary of state in the Ministry of Planning.

LECLÈRE, ADHÉMAR (1853-1917). French scholar and administrator. An early sympathizer with socialist thinking, Leclere was appointed vice-résident of Cambodia in 1886. He served as an administrator for 25 years, becoming fluent in Khmer and intellectually engrossed in Khmer cultural and historical studies before retiring to France in 1913. He produced a wide range of original and edited works, including collections of folk-stories, studies of private and public laws, Khmer Buddhism and customs and his *Histoire du Cambodge* (1914), the first European text to use the **chronicle histories** as a framework for the study of the past.

LEGAL NORMS. Certain **Khmer** language terms relating to **administrative divisions** and to legal actions are often not translated into foreign languages. The principal terms are *Kram* ("law"), *Kret* ("decree" or "enabling act"), *Anukret* ("regulation"), *Prakas* ("Procedure") and *Sarachor* ("Circular" or "Guidance"). *Kram* are acts or bills adopted by the **National Assembly** and then approved by King **Norodom Sihanouk**. When he is abroad, these are signed on his behalf by the president of the **Senate** who becomes acting head of state and countersigned by the prime minister and the relevant minister. *Kret* are issued by the Council of Ministers within the constitutional framework of its executive and regulatory powers. The King also approves and signs these. Any supplementary *anukret* is issued by the prime minister, countersigned by the minister concerned. *Prakas* are issued by ministers or by the governor of the National Bank (who is a member of the Council of Ministers), and these set out regulations, while *sarachor*, circulars and guidance documents, instruct administrators on the ways to implement laws and regulations.

LENG NGETH (1900-c1975). Prime minister in 1955. Born in **Phnom Penh**, he studied at **Lycée Sisowath**, Lycée Albert Sarraut, Hanoi and the Cambodian School of Administration. He then studied law, specializing in it during his studies at the École Coloniale in Paris. On his return to Cambodia, he was a magistrate, and eventually, a judge of the Court of Appeals. Because of his legal background, he accompanied King **Norodom Sihanouk** to Paris in 1953, having been made a Royal Councilor in February. Soon after this he began to act as a family lawyer to Sihanouk. Leng Ngeth became president of the Council of Ministers from 26 January to 30 September 1955, after which he resumed his post as Royal Councilor, with special responsibility for foreign affairs and legal questions. He was appointed ambassador to the Soviet Union and minister to Poland and Czechoslovakia in August 1956. Returning to Cambodia in July 1957, Ngeth was appointed ambassador to China in 1958. By 1963 he was Cambodian ambassador to Laos. He married Ung Thip and they had two children, Sorang, who later served in Prince Sihanouk's private secretariat, and Vanny who married Ly Chinly, a diplomat. An older brother, **Leng Saem**, was cofounder of the **National Union Party**.

LENG SARIN (1917-). A member of the **Khmer Renewal Party**, he was elected to the **National Assembly** in 1951 to represent Kong Pisei, **Kampong Speu**. He was one of only two successful candidates running for the Renewals to be elected to this Assembly. In 1953 he served in the National Consultative Assembly but then he joined the **Democrat Party** and appears to have competed in the 1955 National Assembly elections on their behalf. He later joined **Sangkum**. In 1966 he lost a race for a seat in the National Assembly elections in Phong, **Kampong Speu**. He seems nevertheless to have been a keen observer of party politics because a **United States** Embassy memo from 1970 described him as a "useful and friendly contact." Joining the **Socio-Republican Party** of **Lon Nol** in September 1972 he was elected to the **National Assembly** of the **Khmer Republic**.

LES KOSEM. A **Cham** officer in the Royal Cambodian Army deeply and secretly engaged in the **Front Uni pour la Lutte des Races Opprimées (FULRO)**, he and irregular military forces under his command were active in events surrounding the 1970 coup against **Norodom Sihanouk**. Promoted to colonel by **Lon Nol** after 18 March 1970, he received command of a mostly Cham battalion in the Republican Army. Well-known for his ferocity, as well as corruption and some generosity, he fled to Malaysia in 1975 where he died of natural causes within a few years.

LIBERAL DEMOCRATIC PARTY. Founded in Bangkok in 1990 by a large, essentially republican faction of the **Khmer People's National Liberation Front (KPNLF)** then in dispute with the KPNLF President

Son Sann, it held its first national congress in **Phnom Penh** in September 1992. Its leader and president was **Sak Suthsakhan,** the last commander-in-chief of the defeated **Khmer Republic** army and commander of the KPNLAF. The party was supported by prominent "border" officers, activists and highly skilled technocrats including **Dien Del, Pin Yathay, Abdul Gaffar Peang Meth,** Ok Serei Sopheak and **Tan Bun Suor.** Broadly in step with the more liberal and democratic traditions of the old Republican movement, the LDP was strongly anticommunist and pro-United States and pro-ASEAN; and it favored free enterprise and "honest, good government." Inspiring rural Khmer voters about these ideals was difficult, however, the party had few grassroots, peasant networks and therefore limited appeal or credibility. In the elections in May 1993, it received 62,698 votes only (1.56 percent) and won no seats in the Consultative Assembly.

LIBERAL PARTY (*kanapac sereipheap*). A party founded on 14 May 1946 by Prince **Norodom Norindeth** and supported by many French, notably **Louis Manipoud,** the Liberals advocated "gradual" independence within the framework of the French Union in a riposte to the sometimes strident demands of the leading **Democrat Party** for immediate independence. The party drew its support from prominent court mandarins and courtiers, high-ranking functionaries in the administration of the Protectorate, prosperous landowners, Chinese businessmen and moneylenders and the **Cham** community. Although it favored maintaining and strengthening the administrative and social hierarchies of the day, including constitutional monarchy, the party also favored expansion of modern individual rights and freedoms, especially property rights and civil rights. Its emphasis on legal reform and modernism was not so apparent in the party emblem which was a representation of Angkor Wat. The party program acknowledged the king as the head of the Khmer nation but emphasized that he must rule in consultation with the **National Assembly.** The party also called for the franchise to be extended to all Cambodians over the age of 21, including women and monks, who were able to read and write in the Khmer language.

The first Steering Committee established in May 1946 was led by **Meas Hell** (president), Khouth Khoeun (vice-president), Kong Maing (secretary-general), **Chea Oum** (assistant secretary), and Thong Yim (treasurer). Other members included: Sok Tith, **Kim Nguon Trach, Van Molyvann,** Khout Khoeun, Koch San, Vann No, Tep Thansay, Tes Phnieth, Saone Chheangsun. Their newspaper *Flambeau Khmer* appeared from May 1946, but in the elections of September 1946 they won only 14 seats of the 66 they contested. This was mostly because the Democrats were easily able to portray the party as pro-French.

In 1947 the Liberals hoped to do much better and not least because of the repression of the Democrats in the **Black Star Affair** and other incidents in which they may have planed a role. However, Norindeth ran a bad campaign, underestimating the anti-colonial sentiment of the era, and the Liberals again lost badly. Norindeth himself retired to France in July 1948 leaving Meas Hell in charge of the party. Although he returned briefly in 1948, and again in mid 1949, party morale was hit badly by the defection of **Neal Phleng** and also by **Samson Fernandez** threatening many times to run as an independent candidate.

Norindeth fled to France in 1951 after being implicated in the assassination of the Democrat Party leader **Ieu Koeus**. In June 1951 a new Steering Committee for the party was elected with Meas Hell (president), **Neth Senn** (vice-president), and Seng Nguon (secretary). During the 1951 election campaign, the Democrats devoted most of their energy to fighting other parties, enabling the Liberals to capture 23.5 percent of the vote, their best showing. The dissolution of parliament by King **Norodom Sihanouk** in 1952 and his **Royal Crusade for Indepen-dence** next produced a significant realignment of conservatives interests in the party, and in 1955 the Liberal leadership resigned en masse party to join the **Sangkum**. A rump of members ran 43 candidates in the September 1955 elections, all of them being beaten heavily. The party was formally dissolved on 24 June 1956.

LIM HONG né **Lim Muy Hong.** Born in Saang, Kandal, he studied at Lycée Khmero-Anglais and was awarded a Colombo Plan scholarship to study at the University of Tasmania, Australia. In mid-1985 while serving as the official representative of the **Khmer People's National Liberation Front** representative in Victoria, he hosted the visit of the movement's president, **Son Sann**. With support from the Cambodian Association of the state, he was elected to the Legislative Assembly of the State of Victoria in 1995, the first Cambodian to hold major elected office outside Cambodia. He is married to Bopha, daughter of Nuon Sarun, and first cousin of **Eng Marie**. He was reelected to the Victoria state legislature in 1999.

LITERATURE. Until recently the Khmer language was an oral vernacular. Inscriptions at **Angkor** confirm that literary works from other parts of Asia, notably the Ramayana, the Mahabharata and other Indian epic tales and poems were enjoyed but they were read and studied in Sanskrit. The earliest extant text of the Khmer Ramayana is probably no older than the 17th century. This century also fostered the emergence of a genre of Buddhist-inspired morality poems known as *chhbab*. By the 19th century, narrative poems became popular and circulated in manuscript form. Many of the authors were monks, former monks or members of the royal family whose writings often conveyed supernatural influences. Among the most well-known were *Kakei*, written by Prince Duang in the 1840s before he became King **Ang Duang** and *Tum Taev,* a story in verse relating an ill-fated romance. Although printing was introduced by the French in 1900, most literary output remained oral and much of it was also religious. Historical or chronicle writing was done by hand and most of the precious texts or copies were kept in Buddhist temples.

The first prose novel in Khmer did not appear in print until the 1930s. By that time, the **Buddhist Institute** had begun to act as a clearing house for national literary output. In the 1940s and 1950s, after independence, the Institute collected and printed valuable collections of Cambodian folk tales and *chhbab*. Several hundred good novels were published in the 1960s and early 1970s. Most of these were short, romantic works written for light entertainment but a few writers, for example Nou Hach and **Soth Polin**, wrote more ambitiously, adapting European genres. In total some 60 writers appear in Khing Hoc Dy's important survey of writers and their works (see bibliography). A significant number of authors published in the 1970-1973 which they saw as a period of relative optimism and freedom. In the new millennium Cambodians are reading more newspapers and magazines than ever before but poverty and illiteracy greatly restrict production and consumption of fiction. Compared to 30-40 new novels per month before the **Pol Pot** era, only 10 novels a year appear now, according to the Khmer Writer's Association which is responsible for awarding an annual prize for fiction.

LITTAYE-SUON, PAUL (1916-1975). A soldier turned journalist, Paul Littaye-Suon was born on 29 July 1916 in **Phnom Penh**, son of Jean Baptiste Tep Suon and Mme (née Adele Littaye). Educated in France he earned a *docteur-ès-lettres* from the University of Montpellier. He then rejoined the Ministry of Defense, holding several administrative posts before being appointed as chef de cabinet in the ministry. In 1963 he was a commander, attached to the Council of Ministers office, in charge of special operations. Between 1963-1967, he regularly contributed editorial comments to the conservative French-language newspaper *Phnom Penh Presse* using the pen name "Le Huron." Although he retired from the army in 1966, at the age of 50 and with the rank of colonel, he became a fierce advocate for the establishment of a Republic following the overthrow of **Norodom Sihanouk**. By 1970, he was editor of the official state paper *Le Cambodge*, promptly renamed *Le Republicain*. He became an advisor to Lon Nol as director of veterans' affairs and the disabled. During the June 1972 elections he urged voters to support **Lon Nol**, and when, in

March 1973, all but 10 of the 93 advisors, who had been drawing cabinet salaries, were relieved of their appointments, Paul Littaye-Suon was among those who kept his position.

Aimé, Paul's older brother, was a brigadier general in the **Khmer Republic** army and was appointed recording secretary of the Armed Forces Council created in September 1972. On 17 April 1975, as the troops of the **National United Front of Kampuchea (FUNK)** occupied **Phnom Penh**, the two brothers donned their best dress uniforms and presented themselves to the Red Khmer soldiers who had seized the Ministry of Information. They were led away and executed soon afterward.

LOEUNG NAL (c1922-1975). A teacher in **Kompong Cham**, he began his political career as an aide and interpreter to **Dap Chhuon** who spoke little French. Loeung Nal then worked for **Lon Nol** and served as minister for social affairs and refugees in the **In Tam** governments in 1973; minister for tourism in the **Long Boret** government which followed; and minister of public health in the last Long Boret government, March to April 1975. He sought refuge in the French Embassy on 17 April 1975. The French were obliged to evict all Cambodian nationals four days later. He was handed over and executed soon afterward.

LOEUNG SINAK alias **Ta Maing (1939-1988).** Born on 5 February 1939, he had hardly completed his primary schooling before his formal education was cut short by the death of his father. Forced by these circumstances to take charge of the family farm, he retained a keen interest in the martial arts and coached many boys in the district. In April 1975 Sinak was appointed, by the victorious **Communist Party of Kampuchea** cadres in the region, to head his local village, but in July 1975 he fled to Thailand with 20 others intending to form a guerrilla resistance. By 1979 he had some 850 men under his command. In October 1979 they joined the **Khmer People's National Liberation Front (KPNLF)** under the leadership of **Son Sann**. In the **Khmer People's National Liberation Armed Forces (KPNLAF)** he took the *nom de guerre* Ta Maing and personally led many of his soldiers into combat. On 24 February 1987 he was to promoted major general of the KPNLAF. Afflicted from time to time by recurrent bouts of malaria, he died suddenly in rural **Siem Reap** province on 5 February 1988.

LON NOL (1913-1985). Prime minister 1966-1967, 1969-1972; president 1972-1975. Born on 13 November 1913 at Prey Chraing, Kanchai Mea, **Prey Veng**, the son of Lon Hin, a minor government official, and Mme (née Mam Nuon), daughter of the governor of Prey Veng, Lon Nol began his education in a primary school in **Phnom Penh** and then went to Lycée

Chasseloup Laubat in Saigon. There he befriended Prince **Sisowath Sirik Matak**, later to be one of his strong political allies. Lon Nol spent six years in Saigon where he enjoyed a reputation in sports, especially boxing and soccer. He also took part in a few anti-French demonstrations.

On completing his schooling in 1934, he returned to Cambodia and took up a post as a magistrate in **Siem Reap**. He transferred from the judiciary into the civil administration of the Protectorate in 1937 serving for a few years as a policeman in **Kampong Cham** before becoming a district headman in Koh Soutin. He entered national politics only in 1945 when under the Japanese collaborationist cabinet he was appointed governor of **Kratié** province by **Son Ngoc Thanh** and, a few months later, head of the national police. Reassigned to police and pacification work in the provinces after the arrest of Thanh and the return of the French, he was appointed governor of **Battambang** province in 1947.

In September 1947 Lon Nol along with **Nhiek Tioulong**, formed the **Khmer Renewal Party (*Parti de la Renovation Khmère*)**, whose members were known as "Renos". It was supported by two Sisowath Princes: **Sisowath Monireth** and **Sisowath Monipong**, the first having been bypassed for the throne in 1941. Tioulong was the party leader while Lon Nol was the general secretary and principal spokesman. As a conservative party, it shared many policy positions with the **Liberal Party** but the "Renos" were almost exclusively high civil servants in the administration of the Protectorate. In December 1947 it won no seats in the National Assembly. Lon Nol himself ran in Suong, Kampong Cham, and lost.

Recalled to Phnom Penh in 1949 Lon Nol was asked in January 1950 to take charge of investigations into the assassination of the **Democrat Party** leader **Ieu Koeus** but managed to bungle the entire police effort. In the September 1951 elections, he ran again for the Renos, in Mohaleap, **Kampong Cham**, and again without any success, although the Renewal Party did pick up two Assembly seats in this election. The subsequent Democrat government of **Huy Kanthoul** placed him under arrest very briefly. The four hours he was held in detention rankled and this was one of the causes which led to the dismissal of the government in June 1952.

In another career shift Lon Nol abandoned civilian administration for the army in 1952 accepting a field command as a lieutenant colonel; he is promoted to full colonel on 3 December 1953 after collaborating with the King during Sihanouk's "Operation Samakki" ("Solidarity Offensive"). In 1955 Lon Nol's Renewal Party was one of the first to disband and merge into the **Sangkum**.

Lon Nol became a brigadier general on 27 March 1957, major general on 11 April 1958 and lieutenant general on November 1961. He was appointed commander-in-chief of the Royal Khmer Armed Forces, also known as FARK; *Forces Armées Royales Khmères*, in June 1960 and held command throughout the difficult period which followed Sihanouk's rejection of United States military aid in 1963 and again after the break with America two years later.

In the 1966 elections, supporters of Lon Nol, including some former Renos, won control of the National Assembly and the general was chosen as Prime Minister. However controversy surrounding his heavy-handed manner of dealing with dissent led to an uprising in the Samlaut district of Battambang. Sihanouk requested that Lon Nol, as Prime Minister, and Oum Mannorine as Minister for Territorial Defense, crack down on the rebels. Accused of conspiring with the rebels, and fearing for their lives, **Khieu Samphan** and **Hou Youn** fled to the jungles, later joined by **Hu Nim**. The rebellions and disappearances plus an untimely car crash in which he endured serious injury caused Lon Nol to resign, citing ill-health.

Lon Nol's participation in the **coup d'état** of March 1970 has generated much debate over whether he, or Sirik Matak, was the first to initiate the conspiracy. The evidence points to Lon Non being one of the early movers, and certainly to having active knowledge of plots during the late 1960s. It is probable that the planning leading up to the overthrow of Sihanouk in March 1970 was initiated by Sirik Matak, although Lon Nol was kept fully informed. In fact in January 1970 when preparations were well under way, Lon Nol was still in Europe. He met Sihanouk on 7 January in Rome, and again some days later in Paris. During the Rome meeting Sihanouk may have instructed Lon Nol to organize anti-Vietnamese demonstrations to enable the prince to negotiate with the Russians and the Chinese with a stronger hand.

Lon Nol, on his return, appears to have established lines of communication with **Son Ngoc Thanh**, then still under sentence of death for treason in Cambodia. On 11 March 1970 street demonstrations against the Vietnamese led to the sacking of the embassy of the **Provisional Revolutionary Government of South Vietnam**, followed by that of the Democratic Republic of Vietnam. The attacks were led by special forces in mufti supplied by General **Les Kosem**. The conspirators lost control of some demonstrations, however, and it was only on 18 March, after a failed attempt two days earlier, that Lon Nol was persuaded to back a motion to be placed before the National Assembly to remove Prince **Norodom Sihanouk** from his post as head of state.

After a meeting in joint closed session, the National Assembly and the High Council of the Kingdom voted unanimously to depose Sihanouk. A devout Buddhist, Lon Nol declared war on the Vietnamese "unbelievers" (*thmil*) claiming that they were annexing Cambodia's sacred soil. With divine, and American, help, he assumed an aroused Khmer nation would triumph over the "aggressors."

Lon Nol took personal command of the disastrous 1970 military offensive known as **Operation Chenla I**, aimed at restoring communications between Phnom Penh and Kampong Thom. The offensive, encouraged by the United States, was poorly planned and Lon Nol's troops were defeated by superior Vietnamese forces. In 1971 a similar offensive, Chenla II, also failed. Between the two campaigns, Lon Nol suffered a disabling stroke and for the remainder of his time in office functioned at a reduced capacity, refusing to delegate authority. Lon Nol welcomed the American bombing campaign of 1973 as a quasi-miraculous *deus ex machina* intervention and struggled to retain a monopoly on political patronage in the Khmer Republic, convinced that whatever happened he would eventually be "bailed out" by his "personal friend" and patron U.S. President Richard Nixon.

As the war went badly and the economy collapsed, Lon Nol fell increasingly out of touch with reality. In March 1975 he was declared a national hero and sent into exile by his cabinet colleagues, who then tried in desperation to negotiate a peace settlement with the **Royal Government of National Union of Kampuchea (GRUNK)** who had by then encircled the capital. After suffering the indignity involved in being forced to leave the country, the American government offered the ailing president $500,000 to aid his retirement.

In exile, Lon Nol lived in Hawaii, before moving to Fullerton, California. There he bought a large house; but in February 1981 Lon Nol's eldest son, Lon Rithidara, was arrested on felony charges. After accusations of abuse by the mother against two other children, four of Lon Nol's children were then taken into protective custody. A broken and unhappy man, he died in a local hospital on 17 November 1985.

LON NON (1930-1975). Born on 18 April 1930 at Taing Krassaing, Santuk, **Kampong Thom**, the fourth son of Lon Hin, and younger brother of **Lon Nol,** Non was educated at Collège Sihanouk in **Kampong Cham**, where his older brother, Lon Nol, was in the administration. After leaving school, he joined the police force and rose gradually to the rank of captain. In early 1970 he helped to stage manage the events leading up to the overthrow of Sihanouk. He was present at the attacks on the Vietnamese embassies on 11 March 1970. In fact he was the major force in persuading Lon Nol to agree to support Sihanouk's dismissal. Lon Non then actively canvased support for declaring a republic, anxious as he was to declare one soon after Sihanouk had gone. However Lon Non was unable to persuade the government to agree to such a move and had to be content with the eventual declaration in October. Often cast in the shadow of his older brother, whom he greatly respected and served loyally, Lon Non was the more decisive of the two, and the one who often persuaded Lon Nol to act, or to decide. Lon Non also wanted to establish a political vehicle of his own, and the Socio-Republican Association founded in late 1971 was his first major move in that direction.

Lon Non rapidly rose from captain to brigadier general, and his brother's influence was no doubt important here. Lon Non, however, generally preferred to pull the strings, or pretend he was, from a discreet distance. With modest military successes in Operation Akineth Moha Padevuth in May 1971, a military campaign widely reported in Cambodian and some foreign media, Lon Non, now "The Boss," began to establish his own powerbase. He took credit for padding the voters' rolls in the 1972 presidential elections by saying that he padded the payrolls of his 15th Infantry Brigade in much the same way. The **Socio-Republican Party** was also very much his creation and he pinned his hopes on it for a smooth transition to power in case of Lon Nol's death. For these and many other reasons, the American Embassy and not a few Cambodians despised him. Some thought he was forming a paramilitary fascist grouping, and others saw him as leaning too heavily toward Moscow. By sheer coincidence he had been in high school with many of the leading leftists on "the other side," including Saloth Sar (**Pol Pot**) and **Khieu Samphan**. At one point he tried negotiating with Moscow in the hope of forming an alliance between the Republicans and the moderate wing of the **Royal Government of National Union of Kampuchea (GRUNK)**. Nothing came of this but while still hoping for a deal he set up a new **Pracheachon** ("People's Party") to provide token opposition to the Socio-Republicans in the September 1972 National Assembly elections.

On 17 October 1972 Lon Non was forced to give up his positions within the Socio-Republican Party in order to assume the portfolio of minister in charge of liberation and construction (community development), general mobilization and rallying. In this public role he regularly displayed his personal arrogance. He proclaimed in January 1973 that "corruption is as old as the land." By March 1973 following a nationwide teachers' strike which resulted in several deaths and the defections of many of its leaders, including **Nuon Khoeun**, to the **National United Front of Kampuchea (FUNK)**, the American Embassy lobbied the cabinet to remove Lon Non from any position of influence. Lon Non who was backed by a Special Committee of Coordination, whose members included **Pin Yathay**, could not be eased from office but he was eased into exile.

On the pretext of seeking medical treatment and visiting **United States** military bases, he left Phnom Penh on 30 April 1973 for Paris and then settled in Silver Spring, Maryland, United States, where he lived until early 1974. His wife, Sla Peou, and their children appear to have remained in the United States.

Returning to Phnom Penh on 21 September 1974 Lon Non was determined to retake organizational control of the Socio-Republican Party. The Americans lobbied heavily against his election to the secretary-generalship which he won easily. He resigned from the army on 25 March 1975 to become "acting" secretary-general of the party. Early in the morning of 17 April he may have been involved in an attempt to seize power. It failed. He was captured by the communists and disappeared, presumably executed.

LONG BORET (1933-1975). Prime minister, 1973-1975. The son of Long Meas and Mme (née Ieng Buth), he was born on 3 January 1933 at Chbar Ampeou, Kiensvay, **Kandal**, and grew up in **Stung Treng** and **Phnom Penh.** In his twenties, he wrote several romance novels, directed a few movies, and was one of the nation's top champion runners and swimmers. He worked as inspector of labor, joined **Sangkum,** and was elected to the National Assembly in 1958 in Lomphat, Stung Treng. In 1960 he was the political director of *Echos de Phnom Penh*, the managing editor being Georges Boyer, a Swiss citizen. Long Boret was reelected (unopposed) in 1962, and again in 1966, campaigning on elephant back in a tough election race. His reward was the portfolio of industry in the first **Lon Nol** government from October 1966 until April 1967. He was seen to be a protégé of Lon Nol.

In 1968 Long Boret, an opponent of Sihanouk's 1963 economic reforms, led the campaign for Cambodia to rejoin the **Asian Development Bank (ADB)**. He lived in the Philippines at the time, the homebase of the ADB and was working in international banking circles. He returned to Cambodia in 1969 with Prince **Sisowath Sirik Matak**, who had completed his tour as ambassador to Japan and the Philippines, and the two planned a greater role for the free enterprise system in Cambodia's economy. Long Boret was involved in the preparation of the ousting of **Norodom Sihanouk**, although he was careful to keep a low profile. In May 1971 he was appointed minister of information, retaining the portfolio under **Son Ngoc Thanh**. It was in this position that he used his influence to support Lon Nol in the 1972 presidential elections. Following Thanh's resignation in October 1972, Long Boret was appointed foreign minister, one of his major tasks being to defend the claim of the **Khmer Republic** for Cambodia's seat in the General Assembly of the **United Nations**. Gradually he established a powerful political base in the **Socio-Republican Party**, and when **In Tam** was appointed prime minister, Long Boret remained as minister of state for foreign affairs and was named prime minister on 26 December 1973.

By this time Long Boret was seen by the Americans as the republican leader best able and best placed for negotiating with Prince Sihanouk and the **Kampuchean Royal Government of National Union**. His first term as prime minister gave rise to hopes, ultimately unmet, for the revitalization of the Khmer Republic, which had lost public momentum and support as corruption deepened. Succeeding nevertheless, with American support, in keeping **Lon Non** out of sight until January 1975, Long Boret was reconfirmed as prime minister on 21 March 1975. He flew to Bangkok with President Lon Nol on 1 April 1975, where he tried to strike a deal with Prince **Norodom Yuvaneath**, Sihanouk's eldest son. It failed, and Long Boret returned to Phnom Penh.

On the night of 11 April Long Boret refused to flee in **Operation Eagle Pull** which took place the following day. He asked his commander-in-chief **Sak Suthsakhan** to try to achieve an orderly surrender on 17 April and was at his desk in the prime minister's residence when some Red Khmer soldiers entered the house. Hoping for a dignified surrender in accordance with conventional protocol, Long Boret was instead forced to flee since those who burst into his room extended no recognition. He and his wife then surrendered to the communist commanders at the Ministry of Information. They were taken away and killed at the **Cercle Sportif** later the same day.

LONG BOTTA (1942-). A teacher educated at the École Normale Supérieure and the University of Phnom Penh, he earned a doctorate in nuclear physics from the University of Toulouse in 1967. Returning to Cambodia, he was secretary of state in the Ministry of Education from March 1970 to July 1971 and director of the École Normale Supérieure in 1970. Although he was rapidly disappointed by and disenchanted with the coup regime in 1970, by 1972 Botta was appointed director of religious affairs, youth and tourism and had joined the **Socio-Republican Party**, became one of its deputy secretary-generals, and eventually party president. In October 1972 he was appointed secretary of state for youth and sports in the **Hang Thun Hak** government. In the last cabinet of the Republic, he was minister of culture, from 21 March to 12 April 1975 only, and was the only cabinet minister apart from **Saukham Khoy** who agreed to be evacuated by the Americans in **Operation Eagle Pull**. He went into exile in France.

LONG TOUTCH (1902-1974). Born in **Phnom Penh**, he was a member of the **Democrat Party** and a candidate in the 1951 **National Assembly** elections in Sauthnikon, **Siem Reap**. In April 1952 he was elected to the

Assembly in a by-election for the seat of Taing Krassaing, **Kampong Chhnang**. An opponent of French colonialism, he was arrested on 13 January 1953 in a crackdown on supporters of the Democrat Party. He was among the brave democrats who ran against **Sangkum** candidates in the 1955 National Assembly elections, but after failing to be elected, he retired from politics and became a civil servant. At his death on 2 April 1974, he was vice-president of the association of retired civil servants.

LOVEK (LONGVAEK). A town and military base on the **Tonlé Sap** River some 45 kilometers north of **Phnom Penh.** King **Ang Chan** established his court there in the 16th century surrounding it with stone fortifications. He and his successors regularly fought the Siamese who attacked and finally occupied Lovek in 1592-1594 installing a military governor, the first alien overlord in the kingdom. The town is today known as Peam Lovek.

LU LAYSRENG (1940-). A member of the **Socio-Republican Party** of **Lon Nol,** he was elected to the **National Assembly** of the **Khmer Republic** in September 1972 in Pailin. In the late 1980s, after Prince **Norodom Ranariddh** had become commander, Lu Laysreng was an official spokesman for the **Armée Nationale Sihanoukienne**. An unsuccessful candidate on the **FUNCINPEC** list in the May 1993 elections, Ranariddh initially appointed him as deputy trade minister in the provisional government and he was confirmed as the senior secretary of state for trade in the Royal Government formed in November 1993. A Ranariddh loyalist throughout the coup crisis in 1997 he was elected to the 1998 National Assembly in **Kampong Speu** province and appointed Minister of Information in the **Hun Sen** cabinet of November 1998.

LY THOUCH (1963-). Another prominent **FUNCINPEC** politician and Ranariddh loyalist, Ly Thouch directed the office of First Prime Minister **Norodom Ranariddh** in 1993 and was appointed assistant secretary of state for the environment in 1995. In 1998 he was elected to the **National Assembly** in **Pursat** province and appointed secretary of state in the Ministry of Rural Development. The new minister was **Chhim Seak Leng** also a veteran of the resistance struggle in the 1980s. The latter was forced out by **Hun Sen** in 2001 as a result of corrupt practices involving foreign donors and personal appropriation of Phnom Penh municipality land. The abuses are credited to senior officials from the prime minister's own party. Upon his promotion to minister on 21 August 2001, and without acknowledging that the situation was beyond his control, Ly Thouch indicated that he expected the Ministry of Finance, the Ministry of Inspection and the prime minister to rein in the wrongdoers.

LYCÉE SISOWATH *See* SISOWATH, COLLÈGE/LYCÉE

-M-

MACHHWA, TAYEBBHAY HIPTOOLA (1889-1964). Born in **Phnom Penh**, of an Indian father and Cambodian mother he was the owner of *Le Petit Paris*, a shop in central Phnom Penh selling expensive French imports. He married Pouk Proeung and they had two daughters: Fatemed (who married Moshine Mahamedbhay, a prominent Afghan-Indian trader in Phnom Penh) and Nema (who married **Son Sann**). In 1947 Tayebbhay became a crucially important supporter of the **National Union** established by **Khim Tith**. He was a candidate in the 1947 **National Assembly** elections, though not elected, but was elected to the **High Council of the Kingdom** in January 1948 to represent business interests. He ran for the National Assembly again in 1951, in which year he was appointed to the Royal Council. He died on 20 February 1964.

MALAY CAMBODIANS. Cambodians who speak languages of Malay origin include immigrants from peninsular Malaya or Malay-speaking areas of Indonesia. These together with the Malayo-Polynesian speaking and Muslim Chams, are commonly referred to as *"khmae islam"* or Islamic Cambodians. The Muslim community of Cambodia also includes a very small number of descendants of immigrants from the south Asian sub-continent who are not of Malayo-Polynesian stock but who are Muslim.

MALRAUX, ANDRÉ (1901-1976). French author, art historian and political figure who visited Cambodia in 1923 with a view to stealing bas-reliefs from the recently discovered Angkorean temple of **Banteay Srei**. Apprehended after the theft and while awaiting his own day in court, Malraux attended the trial of the peasants accused of assassinating Félix-Louis Bardez and wrote satirically on the trial and the **Bardez Affair** for the local press. After losing in his own trial, Malraux had his conviction overturned on appeal. A fictional account of his adventures in Cambodia can be found in his novel, *The Royal Way*.

MAM PROM MONY (1931-). Born in the northwest, then under Siamese occupation, and a monk from the age of 12, Prom Mony was a soothsayer who claimed to have foreseen the overthrow of Prince **Norodom Sihanouk** in 1970. A lifelong supporter of **Son Ngoc Thanh**, he returned to Cambodia after March 1970, accepting a commission in the 54th Infantry Brigade, and becoming an advisor to **Lon Nol**, one of those who tried to harness supernatural powers to the **Khmer Republic**.

MAM SONN. *See* SONN MAM.

MANIPOUD, LOUIS JEAN FRANÇOIS (1887-1977). Born in Savoy, Manipoud went to Phnom Penh in 1912 to take up a position in the colonial education services. During World War I he served in Saigon, Sisophon and then **Kampong Cham**. Working in **Takeo** from 1921-1923 and at **Kampot** from 1924-1929, he was inspector of primary schools and responsible for the modernization of the pagoda schools. In Phnom Penh from 1930-1946, he was in charge of the local education system, teaching at **Lycée Sisowath**. He also participated in the formation of the **Liberal Party**. He left Cambodia in 1954, retiring to Lyon. He died 6 November 1977 in Cannes.

MAO CHAY (1901-c1975). Born in **Battambang**, Mao Chay was a nurse in the health service for over 20 years before joining the **Democrat Party** in 1946 and winning a seat for the party in Pranet Preah, **Battambang**, in the 1947 **National Assembly** elections. He soon grew close to **Dap Chhuon** and left the Democrats in 1949 to form the **Victorious Northeastern Khmer Party** with **Oum Sam** on 21 June 1951. An electoral pact calculated to prevent the Democrats from returning to power was arranged with the **National Recovery Party** of **Yèm Sambaur** during the 1951 election, but this failed even though Mao Chay managed to win his race in Snuol, **Siem Reap**. In January 1953 King **Norodom Sihanouk**, then concurrently prime minister, appointed him assistant secretary of state for health and social action, in charge of peasant affairs, a position he held until November. In 1953 he served in the National Consultative Assembly. Among those who assisted the King in creating the **Sangkum,** in January 1955 he was appointed minister of information, social action and labor, a portfolio he held until 30 September 1955. In March 1955 Mao Chay was elected once again in Pranet Preah.

The leader of the "deputies revolt" of December 1956 which overthrew the **San Yun** government, he also destabilized the next government. His supporters in the National Assembly were connected to private business and trading firms, and less openly, he was loyal retainer of (the now abdicated) Prince **Norodom Sihanouk**, in charge of security operations, and reporting to **Kou Roun**, which means he likely held a semi-secret position in the National Police. Retired since the 1960s, he lived in Prek Enh and is presumed to have been killed in 1975.

MARCHAL, HENRI (1876-1970). French archaeologist who spent over half a century in Cambodia (1905-1937, 1947-1970), most of it working for the conservation of **Angkor**. He supervised the restoration of many Angkorean temples, notably **Banteay Srei** and the **Baphuon**, and wrote extensively about Angkorean art. In the 1950s he also advised the newly independent Laotian government on the restoration of historic buildings. He retired to Siem Reap in 1957, and died peacefully there.

MARXISM. *See* COMMUNIST PARTY OF KAMPUCHEA.

MAT LY (1930-). Born in Tbong Khmum, **Kampong Cham**, the son of Cham leader **Sos Man**, he joined the **Viet Minh**-backed, anticolonial **Khmer Issarak** in 1948, joined the **Khmer People's Revolutionary Party (KPRP)** and was KPRP secretary of a cell in Tbong Khmum when he was arrested and jailed in 1957. Released from prison in 1970, he rallied to the **National United Front of Kampuchea** and resumed his revolutionary activities within the **Communist Party of Kampuchea (CPK)**. In 1976 he was appointed to the standing committee of the People's Representative Assembly of **Democratic Kampuchea (DK)**. But by mid-1978 as the CPK began to purge the eastern region and quashed the rebellion mounted by supporters of Sos Phim, the regional secretary, Mat Ly fled to **Vietnam**. Among the 14 founding members of the **United Front for the National Salvation of Kampuchea (UFNSK)** formed in December, he was appointed deputy minister of agriculture in the **People's Republic of Kampuchea (PRK)**, a post held from January 1979 until March 1982. In May 1981 Mat Ly was elected to the PRK **National Assembly** in his native province and became vice-president of the Assembly. Elected to the political bureau of the **People's Revolutionary Party of Kampuchea (PRPK)** in October 1985, and already president of the party's mass organization for workers, he replaced **Vandy Kaon** as secretary-general of the PRPK front organization, the National Council of the United Front for the Construction and Defense of the Motherland, the former UFNSK, in January 1986. He was still an active campaigner when in June 1993 he was elected on the **Cambodian People's Party** list to the **National Assembly** in Kampong Cham. On 25 December 1993, he was among the senior members of the CPP appointed to the King's Privy Council. He was reelected to the National Assembly in 1998.

MAU SAY (1926-). Born on 1 June 1926 at Kbal Romeas, **Kampot**, the son of Mau and Mme (née Neang Ke), he was educated in **Phnom Penh** and in Paris 1946-1954 where he studied economics. Upon his returned, he was appointed to a post in the Ministry of Finance. In January 1955 he was appointed secretary-general of the King's High Council and was a member of the Cambodian delegation to the **Bandung Conference** later the same year. Thereafter he held several portfolios in successive **Sangkum** governments. He was minister of finance, political and economic affairs, March to April 1956; minister of national education, sports and youth, July 1957 to January 1958; minister of information and planning, July 1958 to February 1959 and secretary of state for planning from 1964 until December 1965, taking up the latter post after the resignation of **Hou Youn**. Mau Say was also prominent in the **Royal Khmer Socialist Youth (JSRK)**, the management of state enterprises, notably the *Société Khmère* *d'Oxygène et d'Acétyléne,* and in 1965 was elected to the **High Council of the Throne**. An editor of the official **newspaper** *Neak Cheat Niyum* ("The Nationalist"), by the mid-1960s, he was appointed vice-president of the Council of Ministers in October 1966 and minister responsible for the coordination of economic affairs, finance, planning, public works and production in the first **Lon Nol** government. He retained the post until Lon Nol resigned in April 1967. In March 1972 **Son Ngoc Thanh** appointed Mau Say as minister of state, attached to the Prime Minister's office, a post he retained in the **Hang Thun Hak** and **In Tam** governments until December 1973. A prominent francophone in a pro-American regime, he played no public role from 1974.

MAYAGUEZ. This U.S. registered cargo ship strayed into Cambodian waters near Kampong Som in May 1975, shortly after the 17 April 1975 defeat of the **Khmer Republic**. Impounded briefly by the triumphant communists, the ship and crew were quickly released but not before U.S. military retaliation, including a bombing raid on the oil refinery at Kampong Som and an amphibious landing on Koh Tang ("Tang Island") by 21 U.S. Marines. Eighteen U.S. servicemen are still listed as MIA's from the incident. The U.S. Congress, urged by the Ford administration, imposed a complete ban on aid, trade and investment with Cambodia *and* **Vietnam** whose forces were not involved in the incident.

MEA SOM (1954-). From sometime in 1984 until his death in April 1998, she was married to **Pol Pot**. Their daughter, Mea Set, was born in 1985. She was with Pol Pot on 14 April 1998 when in response to reports that he was to be handed over to international authorities he planned to escape into **Thailand** where he hoped he might be able to live out his life incognito as a Thai citizen. Frightened by artillery fire (from Cambodian forces) during an aborted crossing, he became short of breath and died on 15 April. Mea Som is now married to **Tep Khunnal** and lives in Malai, Banteay Meanchey. *See also* **Khieu Ponnary.**

MEAN SAMAN (1956-). A native of **Prey Veng** province, and a high school graduate, she was a soldier in the armed forces of the **FUNK** who lived in **Vietnam** from 1975, ostensibly for training but likely because of disputes and purging within the **Communist Party of Kampuchea** in that year. Back in Phnom Penh in 1979 Mean Saman headed the **Association of Revolutionary Women of Kampuchea**, the official mass organization for women in the **People's Republic of Kampuchea (PRK)**. She was elected to the PRK **National Assembly** in May 1981 representing **Takeo** and to the United Front for Construction and Defense of the Motherland in December 1981 and became a member of the **People's Revolutionary Party of Kampuchea (PRPK)** central committee in

October 1985. Although not elected to the 1993 Assembly, she worked as an advisor to **Chea Sim**, president of this Assembly, and in 1998 was appointed to the **Senate**.

MEAS CHANLEAP (1940-1995). One of the ten **Buddhist Liberal Democratic Party (BLDP)** members elected to the **National Assembly** in May 1993, he committed suicide on 8 August 1995 in the Assembly building. A professional militaryman who had been on active duty from 1967-1975, and who had served as the appointed representative of the **Khmer People's National Liberation Front** in Tokyo throughout the 1980s, he left a note saying that he was distraught as a result of the internal BLDP strife. He was replaced by Lay Y Pisith who was next on the BLDP electoral list for **Kandal** province in 1993 and who was a supporter of **Ieng Mouly**.

MEAS HELL (1899-). Born in April 1889 in **Phnom Penh**, Meas Hell had a long career as a provincial governor and was among the conservative elite personalities who founded the **Liberal Party** in 1946. Elected to the 1947 **National Assembly** in Ngaun, **Kampong Thom**, he became vice-president of the Assembly, later serving as minister of religion and fine arts, June to December 1950, and of information, January to March 1951. While in the National Assembly he was caught up in a scandal involving the hiring of government employees. He ran again in the 1951 National Assembly elections for Prey Puoch, Kandal, but was defeated.

MEAS SAMNANG (1929-). Born in rural **Kampot** province, he joined the *Khmer Issarak* movement in 1949 then the **Viet Minh**-sponsored **Khmer People's Revolutionary Party**. He was among the Cambodians who were "regrouped" to North Vietnam with the Vietnamese communist forces in 1954 and studied engineering, returning to Cambodian only in the 1970s. Defecting from the **Communist Party of Kampuchea** in 1978, in February 1979 he was chairman of the Trade Union for National Salvation and minister of industry in the **People's Republic of Kampuchea (PRK)** from November 1979. Elected to the PRK **National Assembly** in 1981, he gave up his seat when he was named ambassador to the Soviet Union in 1982. He was then replaced in Moscow by **Hor Nam Hong** and returning to **Phnom Penh** he was once again given the industry portfolio and was a member of the National Assembly representing his native **Kampot**. He retired in August 1988.

MEAS YANG (1921-). Born on 17 June 1921 in Phnom Penh, the son of Meas and Mme (née Koum), he married Soc Sarinn in 1942 and they had eight children. A civil engineer, he was secretary of state for public health in 1956 and under secretary of state for religion in 1957-1958. A member of the **Khmer Renewal Party**, he was a candidate in the 1951 **National**

Assembly elections in Kampong Chhnang town. Joining the **Sangkum** as soon as it was created in 1955, he was elected to the Assembly in Phnom Penh (4th quarter). In 1966 he was elected again, this time in Talo, **Pursat**. Lon Nol, who had led the Renewal Party in the 1940s, appointed him as minister of agriculture in October 1966, a portfolio he held until Lon Nol's resignation in April 1967. He became an advisor to Lon Nol from July 1970 until May 1971 and died in exile in France.

MEASKETH CAIMERON (1916-). The son of Meas Nal and Mme (née Keth Sane) and brother of **Measketh Caimirane**, he was born on 15 December 1916 in **Phnom Penh**. He married Oung Hammaly and they had five children. He was a founding member of the **Khmer Renewal Party** in 1947. A career diplomat, Caimeron was appointed to Mission of Cambodia at the United Nations by 1953, and was ambassador to Czechoslovakia in 1970-1971.

MEASKETH CAIMIRANE (1932-). The brother of **Measketh Caimeron**, he was born on 31 December 1932 in **Kampot**. A graduate of the National School of Civil Aviation in Paris and of the Royal School of Administration, **Phnom Penh**, he was appointed director of civil aviation at Pochentong International Airport in 1957 and was director general of the national post office by 1967. Following the overthrow of Sihanouk in 1970, he was appointed administrator of *New Cambodge*, the glossy magazine promoting **Lon Nol**'s government in 1970-1972.

MEBON. This was the name given to two Angkorean temples erected on man-made islands in the eastern and western *baray* (reservoirs) respectively. The East Mebon, which is now accessible on foot, was built under **Rajendravarman II** and dedicated in 952 AD and the western one, still accessible only by boat, was dedicated to Vishnu by **Udayadityavarman II** in the late 11th century.

MEKONG. Stretching over 4,200 kilometers, the Mekong is the fourth longest river in Asia. From its source in **China**, it flows southward through **Laos**, **Thailand**, Cambodia and **Vietnam** before emptying into the South China Sea. Much of the upper Mekong is impassable due to the many rapids, rocks and the rapid rush of water flowing out of the mountains. As the river flows southward and downward on terrain closer to seas level, the current slows and the bed widens making the middle Mekong, roughly the stretch which forms the frontier between Laos and Thailand, into a valuable channel of communication. The Mekong drops toward sea level at a falls just north of Kratié town and divides at the point where it joins the Tonlé-Bassac Rivers at **Phnom Penh**, thus forming the famous "four arms" (*quatre-bras*) creating one of the most unique ecological systems in the world. The rush of water produced by the annual monsoon rains in the mountains far to the north results in the reversal of the river flow into the enormous natural reservoir known as the **Tonlé Sap** (Great Lake). Over the centuries a wide variety of freshwater fish have spawned and feed on the green, submerged vegetation of the "inundated forest". They are then caught during the dry season several months later. The fertile, alluvial sediment deposited over the length of the river banks during the annual rainy season is crucial to Cambodian agriculture. But in recent years, declining water levels linked to upstream dams in China and Laos, plus deforestation and excessive fishing, place the economy of central Cambodia (and the Vietnamese delta) in jeopardy.

In 1995 and in recognition of the need for better management and development of the resources of the river, the four lower basin Mekong countries established the intergovernmental Mekong River Commission. In an effort to maximize the impact of international assistance, the commission produced a Basin Development Plan in February 2002 in which it prioritizes projects of cross-border importance. It also renewed appeals to Burma and China to support a basin-wide planning framework.

MEN CHHUM (1910-). Born on 15 February 1910 at Phsar Krom, **Pursat**, he was an inspector of primary schools and a member of the **Sangkum** elected to the **National Assembly** in 1962 in **Takeo**. He was appointed secretary of state for national education, youth and fine arts; secretary of state for the interior and religion in 1964, assistant secretary of state for religion 1964-1965 but was not reelected to the Assembly in 1966 when he stood in Koh Trap, **Kandal**. Among many others who had held high posts in the Sangkum, he joined the **Socio-Republican Party** when it became the party in power. He was elected to the Assembly of the **Khmer Republic** in September 1972.

MEN SAMAN (1953-). A native of **Kratié**, she joined the **Communist Party of Kampuchea** in the early 1970s and was a political commissar in the Armed Forces of the **National United Front of Kampuchea.** Assigned to "duties" in **Vietnam** in 1976, she returned to **Phnom Penh** in 1979 where she was in charge of setting up the Ministry of Defense in the Vietnamese promoted **People's Republic of Kampuchea (PRK)**. Concurrently deputy chair of the Women's Association of **United Front for the National Salvation of Kampuchea**, she was, upon her election to the party central committee in 1982, the highest ranking female cadre of the **People's Revolutionary Party of Kampuchea (PRPK)**. In October 1985 she was elected to the party's political bureau. Among her party posts she was director of the central committee's education and propaganda commission, 1984-1986 and then head of its organization bureau, 1985-1990. Also a deputy in the PRK **National Assembly** representing

Battambang, 1981-1993, she was reelected on the **Cambodian People's Party** list in **Svay Rieng** in both1993 and 1998.

MENH NAKRY (1910-). Born in **Kampong Thom,** he studied at the Pali school and while still a monk he worked at the **Buddhist Institute** and joined the **Democrat Party.** In 1946 he was elected to the Constituent Assembly and, in 1947, to the **National Assembly** representing Samrong Thom, **Kandal.** Elected again in 1951 for Chbar Ampeou, he was by this time editor of the **Democrat Party** newspaper *Pracheathipatay* and judged "an extremist" in French intelligence reports because of his contacts with the **Khmer Issarak.** A Democrat to the end, he ran and lost in the 1955 elections.

MEY MANN (1921-). Born on 10 May 1921 in **Prey Veng,** he was awarded a government scholarship to study construction engineering in France 1949-1953 and met Saloth Sar **(Pol Pot)** on the month long boat trip to Europe. Mey Mann then joined the Marxist Circle that met in **Keng Vannsak's** apartment, along with Sar, **Ieng Sary** and many other future leaders of **Democratic Kampuchea (DK).** Once back in **Phnom Penh** in 1954 Mey Mann and Saloth Sar supported the **Democrat Party** and, along with **Keng Vannsak** and Prince **Norodom Phurissara,** they took control of the party steering committee. Mann also spent some weeks underground with Saloth Sar in a **Viet Minh** base camp in Prey Veng in 1953 where the **Khmer People's Revolutionary Party (KPRP)** secretary **Tou Samouth** lived. He was among the many defeated candidates for the Democrats in the 1955 **National Assembly** elections but found work as an inspector for the Ministry of Public Works, taught math at **Kambuboth** where he was principal in the early 1960s and did clandestine propaganda work for the KPRP, the **Workers' Party of Kampuchea** after September 1960. He claims to have opposed the party's push toward armed struggle from 1963, the year Pol Pot became secretary, and was among those accused of being a "deviationist" in 1973 when, still residing in Phnom Penh, he urged the **Communist Party of Kampuchea** to negotiate with **Lon Nol.**

Having no formal role in the revolutionary DK regime of 1975-1979, he nevertheless agreed in May 1980 to be vice-president of the DK Red Cross upon his arrival at the DK holding center known as Site 8. He also took charge of education there, 1985-1992. Repatriated to Phnom Penh by the United Nations High Commissioner for Refugees (UNHCR), he worked as a translator for the **United Nations Transitional Authority in Cambodia (UNTAC)** in 1992-1993 and held a series of short term jobs in Phnom Penh after the departure of UNTAC. In 1997-1998 he headed the UNHCR office in **Pailin** where he organized short courses on human rights principles for local schoolteachers, former soldiers and municipal officials

MEY PHO (?-1975). He was a clerk in the Sala Lukhun in Phnom Penh in 1945 and was one of the seven officials who stormed into the royal palace on 9 August to try to get King **Norodom Sihanouk** to give more power to **Son Ngoc Thanh**. Escaping from jail in December 1945, he was a member of the first **Khmer Issarak** committee formed by **Poc Khun** in 1946 and joined the **Indochina Communist Party** while fighting in the **Dangrek range** in 1949. Two years later he was director of the information service of the Issarak Central Office in Kampot. He was "regrouped" with **Viet Minh** fighters to Hanoi in 1954. Mey Pho was a member of the overseas branch of the **Communist Party of Kampuchea (CPK)** and returned to Cambodia to work with the **National United Front of Kampuchea (FUNK)** in 1970. In September 1975, he was arrested at the celebrations of the 24th anniversary of the CPK which he had helped to found in 1951. He was executed soon afterward.

MEY SICHAN (c1936-1975). A career soldier, he went to **Lycée Sisowath** and then the Royal Military Academy. He was a brigadier general in the Republican Armed Forces and was one of their leading spokesmen. On 17 April 1975, as head of the 3rd Bureau of the army general staff, he organized a surrender and was on radio urging Republican soldiers to surrender when his broadcast was interrupted by communist guerrillas who made a chilling announcement that they had won the war. He was executed soon after the "Polpotists" began the evacuation of Phnom Penh.

MICHE, JEAN-CLAUDE (1805-1873). A French missionary, Miche joined the Missions Étrangères and arrived in Cochinchina in 1836. In 1839 he was posted to **Battambang**, then under Thai control. In 1848 and alarmed by news of the persecution of Catholics in Vietnam, Miche went to **Phnom Penh** where he received permission from his friend and confidente King **Ang Duang** to establish a Christian community at Ponhea Lu. Miche then became Vicar Apostolic in Cambodia where he lived until 1864. Because of his influence Miche was King **Norodom**'s intermediary in arranging a French protectorate. The eponym for École Miche in Phnom Penh, he died on 1 December 1873 in Saigon.

MINING. Cambodia has few exploitable mineral resources with small deposits of iron and gold not being commercially viable. Deposits of gemstones, principally sapphires and rubies in the northwest, near **Pailin**, were thoroughly exploited by Thai and Cambodian entrepreneurs after 1989 when Vietnamese troops withdrew from Cambodia and the region was occupied by the National Army of Democratic Kampuchea. Off-shore deposits of petroleum and natural gas have not been verified, and Cambodian claims to them would be subject to counterclaims from **Thailand** and **Vietnam**. Small deposits of coal, iron and gold are not commercially exploitable, while deposits of bauxite, particularly in the northeast, remain to be examined.

MINORITY POPULATIONS. There are approximately 20 non-Khmer ethnic groups in Cambodia representing less than five percent of the total population. The size of the **Chinese** and **Vietnamese** minorities is unknown as many long-term residents who speak Khmer appear to identify themselves as Khmer. The only available official estimates, from 1995, estimate the number of Chinese as 47180 and Vietnamese as 95,597. The former is traditionally urban and the latter is divided between those in Phnom Penh, rubber plantation workers along the Cambodian-Vietnamese border regions and fishermen. The **Cham** minority is believed to be the largest, numbering 203,881 in 1995. The **Khmer Loeu** groups identified in official reports include the Lao (19,819), **Kuy** (14,186), Jarai (11,549) and also the **Pear**. The total ethnic minority population was estimated at 370,463.

MISSIONARIES IN CAMBODIA. *See* CATHOLICISM.

MOHANIKAY. The largest and oldest of the two monastic orders in Theravada **Buddhism**, the other being the Thammayut which is centered in the royal court. Before 1975, approximately 85 percent of Cambodia's monks belonged to the Mohanikay *sangha* or clerical hierarchy with both orders traditionally in receipt of recognition and patronage from the royal court and the government. Buddhist monks were disrobed and Buddhism was proscribed in the **Pol Pot** years. When religious freedoms were restored in 1979, only the Mohanikay order was permitted to reform, and initially, only men aged 60 or older were allowed to become monks. In 1993, at Prince **Norodom Sihanouk**'s request, the Thammayut order was also restored.

MOK MARETH (1948-). He studied at Toulouse University, France, earning a doctorate in biology and was detained in a special camp in Kampong Cham province after his return to **Democratic Kampuchea** from late 1976 until 1979 when he found work in the newly formed **People's Republic of Kampuchea (PRK)** municipality of **Phnom Penh**. Deputy chairman of the Revolutionary People's Committee (deputy governor) from August 1981-1989, he was deputy minister of agriculture, 1989-1993. He was the **Cambodian People's Party (CPP)** choice for minister of the environment in 1993, but was appointed secretary of state in environment in November, becoming minister in October 1994. He was elected to the **National Assembly** on the CPP list in **Takeo** in July 1998 and was reappointed minister of environment in the **Hun Sen** government formed in November 1998.

MOLINAKA (MOUVEMENT DE LIBERATION NATIONALE DU

**KAMPUCHEA NATIONAL LIBERATION MOVEMENT OF KAM-
PUCHEA).** Formed from disparate armed groups on the Thai-Cambodian
border in August 1979 by **Kong Sileah** and **Nhem Sophon**, it was the
first military resistance group to swear fealty to Prince **Norodom Sihanouk**.
Backed by Cambodian émigrés, mainly from France, it fought the
Vietnamese army of occupation along the Thai-Cambodian border and
was the basis for the **FUNCINPEC** army established in 1981.

MOLINAKA NAKATAOR-SOU (Kampuchean Freedom Fighter Party).
A political party formed in 1992 and arising from **Molinaka**, its president
was **Prum Neakaareach**. A **FUNCINPEC** splinter party, it called for
territorial expansion and proposed developing **Sihanoukville** into a second
Hong Kong. It won one seat in the 1993 elections, in **Kampong Cham**,
but, plagued by internal dissent, it had dissolved by 1998.

MOM CHIM HUY (1939-). A native of **Takeo** and a former teacher, he
worked in the Ministry of Education of the **Khmer Republic**, survived
the **Democratic Kampuchea** regime as one of the **"new people"** and
then worked in the **People's Republic of Kampuchea** education system
from 1979. Named deputy minister of education 1989-1993, he was elected
to the **National Assembly** on the **Cambodian People's Party (CPP)** list
in **Kandal** in both 1993 and 1998 and is a CPP member of the 11-member
Permanent Standing Committee of the 1998 National Assembly.

MONDOLKIRI. This province, formed in 1960 and legally established in
December 1961, is located in the eastern highlands. It shares boundaries
with **Vietnam** and with **Kratié, Stung Treng** and **Ratanakiri**, covering
14,288 square kilometers. In the March 1998 **census** its population was
32,392, or 0.3 percent of the national total. The density of the population
is accordingly 2 per square kilometer only, the lowest in Cambodia. Low
settlement density also affects availability and access to schools. Only
32.8 percent of the people above the age of seven years were deemed
literate with literacy being higher in urban than rural districts (52.5 percent
compared to 27.2 percent). In 2001 the province was the site of a refugee
camp established by the United Nations High Commissioner for Refugees
for asylum seekers from the central highlands in Vietnam following
suppression of uprisings protesting land grabbing.

MONINEATH, Queen. *See* SIHANOUK, MONIQUE, PRINCESS.

MONIRETH, Prince. *See* SISOWATH MONIRETH, PRINCE.

MONIVONG, Prince. *See* SISOWATH MONIVONG, KING.

MONTAGNARDS. The French term for the mountain peoples in the
highland areas along the northeastern Cambodian-Vietnamese border.

They are today often identified as individual communities, e.g. Tampuon, Jarai, Steang or Kroeng among other. Some have separatist elements, and many once supported the *Front Uni pour la lutte des Races Opprimées*.

MONTEIRO, KENTHAO DE (1924-). Born on 19 November 1924 at Tani, Phnom Kong, **Kampot**, Kenthao was the son of **Pitou de Monteiro**. He studied in Paris and Strasbourg from 1946-1954 then became a barrister at the Sala Outor. A member of **Sangkum**, Kenthao was a member of the National Assembly for the seat of Chrey Loas, **Kandal**, 1958-1962, and held the same seat from 1962 until his retirement on 15 March 1966. Kenthao married Samphan Lonteine and they had two daughters. During the Khmer Republic, the family established strong links with the Republic of China, and moved to Taiwan.

MONTEIRO, KOL DE (1844-c1905). The son of Ros de Monteiro, a **Portuguese** traveler who came to Phnom Penh in the early 19th century and accompanied Father Bouillevaux when the missionary visited Angkor in 1850. Ros was also the man whom King **Ang Duang** sent to Singapore to try to persuade the British to come to Cambodia's defense, but instead King **Norodom** was forced to turn to France. Kol was sent to Singapore at the age of 11 to study English, and also studied astronomy. He appears to have been fluent in French and English, as well as Khmer. From 1858 when he returned to Cambodia, he worked as an interpreter in the king's service and though from 1861 he held diverse posts, he continued to be Norodom's personal interpreter and secretary. When King Norodom was asked by the French to sign the 1884 Convention, Kol, upon hearing the terms, is reported to have cried "Sire, this is not a convention that is proposed to Your Majesty, this is an abdication." Later during the meeting, the French managed to remove Kol under guard claiming that he had mistranslated some of the exchanges between them and the King. Later returning to high office, he was associated with the treasury 1886-1895, and he was appointed acting minister of the navy. In 1898 the Council of Ministers wanted him to become a minister but by then some at court believed Kol had become a "willing ally" of the **French Résident Supérieur**. It was King Norodom who finally decided he did not want Kol appointed as minister claiming that he was not sufficiently qualified.

MONTEIRO, PITOU DE (1897-1965). The son of **Kol de Monteiro**, Pitou was born on 18 March 1897 in **Phnom Penh** spending most of his life in government employ. After studying at the Cambodian School of Administration, he was the first president of the Court of Appeal and was minister of justice, minister of national education and youth, and later worked in the Prime Minister's Office and as Councilor of the Kingdom. In 1960 he was nominated as an alternate member of the Royal High

Council. On 20 July 1922 he had married Oum Sem Khaou and they had two children: Chichunh and **Kenthao**. Pitou died on 7 December 1965.

MOSQUES. There were believed to be some 113 mosques in the country before 1975 serving perhaps more than half a million people. Most were for the **Cham** Muslims who may have numbered 600,000 in 1970 but there were also South Asian and Malay Muslims in **Phnom Penh** and **Battambang**. Currently there are only 20 mosques, the result of deaths in the **Pol Pot** era, emigration and the decline in the numbers of Muslims.

MOUHOT, HENRI (1826-1861). French naturalist, explorer and writer who visited Cambodia in 1859-1860. After extended exploration of northeastern Cambodia, where he gathered specimens of plants, animals and insects, he spent three weeks at **Angkor Wat** in early 1860, taking copious notes, before continuing north on an expedition to Laos. He died there of fever on 10 November 1861, near Luang Prabang. His notes on Angkor, gathered posthumously into a lavishly illustrated book, made a deep impression in Europe, and stimulated French interest in Cambodia.

MOURA, JEAN (1827-1885). A French scholar and administrator as well as a naval officer, he was appointed Representative of the Navy in Phnom Penh, 1868-1879. He traveled widely in the countryside learning the Khmer language and afterward produced his *Le Royaume du Cambodge* (1883), a two-volume work indispensable for scholars of Cambodian history. He also compiled a Cambodian-French dictionary. Moura died in Toulouse on 17 May 1885.

MOVIES. *See* FILMS.

MU SOKHUA (1954-). Minister of women's and veterans affairs. A member of the Steering Committee of **FUNCINPEC**, she lived in the **United States** from the mid 1970s, completing higher degrees at San Francisco State (B.A., Psychology) and the University of California, Berkeley (M.A., Social Work). Between 1981-1986 Sokhua was Education and Social Services Coordinator for the **United Nations** Border Relief Operation. Returning to **Phnom Penh** in 1989, she founded the first Cambodian NGO, *Khemara*, in 1991, and was its director until 1995. Between 1995-1998 she was **advisor** to First Prime Minister **Norodom Ranariddh** on women's affairs. Elected to the **National Assembly** in 1998 in **Battambang**, she was appointed minister in the new Ministry of Women's and Veteran's Affairs established in law on 18 September 1999.

MY SAMEDY (1925-). Born in **Battambang**, he studied at Lycée Sisowath from 1942-1946, and at the Royal School of Medicine from 1946- 1950. After that he worked in radiology at the **Preah Keth Mealea Hospital** in 1950-1952. He became assistant medical director of the Battambang provincial hospital 1952-1955. For the next three years he studied x-ray and physiotherapy technologies in Japan then headed the radiology department at Preah Keth Mealea Hospital, while at the same time teaching at the new Faculty of Medicine. In 1966 he went to France for the first of several brief study visits linked to further training in radiology in French hospitals. He was clinical professor and medical head of radiology and physiotherapy services at the Khmer-Soviet Hospital from 1970-1975. In **Phnom Penh** throughout the final days of the **Khmer Republic**, My Samedi was among a group of 30,000 people evacuated to an area of **Kampong Thom** province inhabited mostly by **Kuy** who were "**old people**," and, though "**new people**" were generally resented as an economic and political burden, Samedi was permitted to practice traditional herbal medicine, 1975-1979.

In early 1979 he went to Phnom Penh and joined the **United Front for the National Salvation of Kampuchea (UFNSK)**. Reassuming a central role in the health sector, he became secretary-general of the **People's Republic of Kampuchea (PRK)** Red Cross on 16 May 1979 retaining this post until the legal demise of the PRK and of the successor **State of Cambodia** in October 1991. He also became dean of the Faculty of Medicine, Pharmacy and Dentistry in 1980, chairman of Phnom Penh committee of the UFNSK in 1981 when it was renamed **United Front for the Construction and Defense of Kampuchea** and a member of the PRK **National Assembly** being elected in Phnom Penh in May 1981 when, with 150,424 votes, he was not far behind **Heng Samrin** who had 155,405 or **Pen Sovan** who received 155,222. A frequent visitor to Europe in the 1980s, in his official Red Cross role, he was the first PRK citizen to be permitted to make a private visit to the **United States** in 1989. He was the seventh candidate on the **Cambodian People's Party** list for Phnom Penh in the elections in May 1993, and was not elected. In 1994 he became vice-president of the Cambodian Red Cross.

-N-

NAGARAVATTA ("**Angkor Wat**"). The first Khmer-language newspaper, 1936-1942, 1945, was edited by **Pach Chhoeun, Sim Var** and **Son Ngoc Thanh**. A weekly, its circulation was 4,000 to 5,000 copies. By providing news and commentary for the small, indigenous intelligentsia, including the politically aware **Mohanikay** Buddhist *sangha*, the paper played a central role in the creation of a modern national identity. **Pann Yung, Khieu Chum, Bunchhan Mol, Chuon Nath, Huot Tat, Hem Chieu, Nuon Duong,** Ngo Hong, Pang Khat, Ouk Chea, Sau Hay and Hy Heng were closely associated with the paper and wrote for it. They advocated or requested massive improvements in the national health and education services as well as the creation of an administrative corps of Khmers, and they also advocated the gradual removal of Vietnamese clerks and officers in the service of the Protectorate. The newspaper was censored by the French on several occasions in 1941-1942 and ceased publication following Pach Chhoeun's arrest in the demonstration on 20 July 1942. He resurrected it briefly in 1945 after the Japanese takeover on 9 March 1945.

NATIONAL ANTHEM. "Nokoreach" (royal city), composed by **Chuon Nath** in the 1940s, is the national anthem. It was first used after independence and until the *coup d'état* of 18 March 1970. It was replaced during the **Khmer Republic** and **Democratic Kampuchea** periods by specially composed and not very memorable songs. It was then revived as as anthem in February 1990, at the request of **Norodom Sihanouk**, when the **Coalition Government of Democratic Kampuchea** became the **National Government of Cambodia** and resumed using the pre-1970 flag and anthem. It was officially restored as the national anthem in the **constitution** promulgated in 1993. The hymn makes several references to Cambodia's Angkorean past.

NATIONAL ARMY FOR AN INDEPENDENT KAMPUCHEA/*Armée Nationale pour un Kampuchea Indépendant* **(ANKI).** Under the general command of Prince **Norodom Ranariddh**, this was the name of the military wing of **FUNCINPEC**, 1990-1992. **Toan Chhay** was Chief of Staff. While the **Coalition Government of Democratic Kampuchea** functioned, it was known as the **Armée Nationale Sihanoukienne**.

NATIONAL ASSEMBLY. The first democratic assembly in Cambodia was elected in September 1946 under the terms of a Franco-Khmer *modus vivendi* agreement signed earlier in the year. Officially this was not a representative body but a Constituent Assembly dedicated to drafting a constitution, promulgated in 1947. The first National Assembly was elected on 21 December 1947, lasting until it was dissolved on 19 September 1949. The second National Assembly was elected on 9 September 1951 and lasted until it was dissolved on 13 January 1953. The third National Assembly was elected on 11 September 1955, but it was dismissed in 1958 to make way for another, elected on 23 March 1958. The fifth National Assembly was elected on 10 June 1962 and completed its term on 20 July 1966. The sixth National Assembly was elected on 30 July 1966. As its term was for five years only, in 1970 it had its mandate extended by one year starting 23 November 1970 and lasting until 17 October 1971. After the promulgation of the **constitution** of the **Khmer Republic** on 10 May 1972, a new National Assembly was elected and functioned from 14 September 1972 until 12 April 1975. An Assembly of People's Representatives chaired by **Nuon Chea** was elected on 20 March 1976 in **Democratic**

Kampuchea but most of the work of this assembly was done by its permanent committee, also chaired by Nuon Chea. A second communist assembly was elected during the **People's Republic of Kampuchea** on 1 May 1981. **Chea Sim** was elected chairman of this assembly on 27 June 1981. Cambodia's second Constituent Assembly was elected under **United Nations** supervision and control on 23-28 May 1993, finishing its work on 21 September 1993 and becoming a National Assembly on 24 September 1993 when the new constitution was promulgated. Chea Sim was re-elected chairman. The current National Assembly, elected 26 July 1998, is chaired by Prince **Norodom Ranariddh**. The constitution stipulates that the Assembly shall be convened at least twice each year, that each session shall last at least three months and all meeting, will be public. Bills may be introduced by either the prime minister or the elected deputies. Those adopted are passed to the **Senate** for approval or for returning with proposals for modification.

NATIONAL BANK OF CAMBODIA. Originally organized at short notice in December 1954 by **Son Sann,** it was reestablished in 1980 by the **People's Republic of Kampuchea** authorities as the People's National Bank of Kampuchea. Within four years it had established thirty branches throughout the country and reestablished the *riel* as a national currency of exchange. Being responsible for managing the national debt as well as the money function, the governor and deputy governor of the Bank have ministerial rank and usually attend meetings of the Council of Ministers.

NATIONAL FRONT FOR THE LIBERATION OF SOUTH VIETNAM (NFL). Officially founded in December 1960 in South **Vietnam** with support from the Workers' Party of Vietnam, this front was organized in the late 1950s by veterans of the anticolonial **Viet Minh** movement and other Vietnamese in the Republic of Vietnam who rejected the repressive policies of the Ngo Dinh Diem regime. The armed forces of the NFL, pejoratively referred to as the **Viet Cong**, operated along the Cambodia-South Vietnam border, and had an extensive supply network inside Cambodia along the **Ho Chi Minh Trail**. In June 1967, and in order to preserve friendly relations with Prince **Norodom Sihanouk**, the Front proclaimed its respect for Cambodia's territorial integrity and its recognition of the existing borders between the two countries. It created a multiparty **Provisional Revolutionary Government of South Vietnam (PRG)** in 1969 after peace talks had commenced in Paris. The PRG was nominally in power for a few months after the communist military victory on 30 April 1975. In peacetime it was merged into the (ex-Viet Minh) multiparty Fatherland Front together with other mass organizations.

NATIONAL RECOVERY PARTY (*kanapac damkoeung prajajat*). This political party was founded by **Yèm Sambaur** in April 1950 soon after he lost the premiership and in expectation of an election campaign to follow. Encouragement to form the party came from King **Norodom Sihanouk** and the result was a political crisis that led to the suspension of the **National Assembly**. The original members of the party were those accused with Yèm Sambaur of betraying the **Democrat Party** leadership. Aiming to succeed where other "right-wing" parties had failed, a Steering Committee consisted of **Kosal**, **Ray Lamouth**, **Lam Ken** and **Phlek Phirun**. The party symbol was the monkey god, Hanuman, superimposed on a map of Cambodia with the legend "Reawakening of National Sentiment," and the symbols of the moon and five stars. The party motto was "Race, Religion, King." The party newspaper, directed by Thach Thuon and edited by Uch Chho, was called *Hanuman*, with a circulation of 2,000. A French-language newspaper, *Redressement National*, also operated at the same time. The party supported the monarchy and urged a regrouping of the nation to overcome the problems then facing it. It encouraged **Khmer Issaraks** to rally to the government and believed that all civil servants should fulfil the wishes of the king. On the economic front, it supported nationalization of the energy companies, transport and banks, as well as strict government controls and encouragement to certain sectors of the economy.

   The party successfully recruited many anti-Democrats and civil servants, but when Yèm Sambaur lost his position as prime minister, the party began to lose support. Lam Ken left for France after political disagreements, and Ray Lomuth, who became a minister in June 1950, left the party after disagreements with Yèm Sambaur. Yèm Sambaur turned to rallied Issaraks and persuaded **Dap Chhuon** to rally to the government. He was also in contact with Prince **Norodom Chantaraingsey**. By September 1950 the National Recovery Party was seen as the opposition to the **Sisowath Monipong** government and constantly demanded fresh elections for the **National Assembly**. Eventually elections were scheduled for September 1951, and during the campaign, **Mao Chay** left the party to form the **Victorious Northeastern Khmer Party**. This new party gained the support of Dap Chhuon, and the National Recovery Party drew the full fire of the Democrats. It was completely defeated in the 1951 National Assembly elections, with even Yèm Sambaur losing his seat. Party support declined rapidly with increased defections. By 1954 most members had joined with or sided with the **Victorious Northeastern Khmer Party** or the **Khmer Renewal Party**. In 1955 most of those remaining resigned from the party and joined the Sangkum. A small rump fought the 1955

National Assembly elections with miserable results. The party disappeared soon afterward.

NATIONAL UNION PARTY (*kanapac ruomcheat khemara*). Political party established by **Khim Tith** and **Leng Saem** in September 1947 to get support from older officials and bureaucrats unhappy with the **Democrat Party** ascendancy. They urged "moral union of all Cambodians to defend the motherland," and their party emblem was the four-faced Buddha symbolizing humanity, good works, health and impartiality. Boun Pa was secretary of the party, but beyond the leadership there was no grass-roots support structure.

In 1947 the party competed for 17 of the 75 seats in the **National Assembly** elections, winning only 0.4 percent of the vote. However, they won 8 of the 24 seats in the High Council elections in January 1948. Since then the leaders formed the Syndicalist Association of Cambodian Officials (ASPAC) to combat the influence of Democrats in the bureaucracy. Khim Tit, **Chan Nak** and Leng Saem all worked on the commission to revise the interim constitution. The party leadership published *La Verité* from 1949, a newspaper which was supposed to be nonpartisan but which nevertheless supported the Unionists. In the 1949-1951 constitutional crisis, the party favored the recall of the National Assembly, or the convening of some kind of national assembly chosen "by some means" other than further elections. They were obliged to participate in September 1951, and were defeated. Most National Union members readily deserted their party in 1955 in order to join Sangkum and the party closed down.

NATIONAL UNITED FRONT OF KAMPUCHEA (FUNK: Front Uni National du Kampuchea). A national resistance movement founded in May 1970 to fight the **Lon Nol** government and ostensibly to return Prince **Norodom Sihanouk** to power. Influenced from the outset by the underground **Communist Party of Kampuchea (CPK)** led by **Pol Pot**, the Front supported the **Royal Government of National Union of Kampuchea**, Sihanouk's government in exile by competing with the **Khmer Republic** authorities for control of local *khum* (township) and *srok* (district) administrations. The Front organized the People's Armed Forces for National Liberation, assisted by the **National Front for Liberation of South Vietnam** armed forces. While the army of the Front was under CPK control from its origins, Sihanouk and his followers controlled the GRUNK and FUNK central committee until 1973 when a reshuffling of portfolios and a larger role for "the interior" resulted in the communists gaining the upper hand by 1974. For approximately one year from 17 April 1975, the day of victory, and in the absence of any substantial administration in evacuated **Phnom Penh**, the CPK Standing Committee and the High Command of its army bypassed the GRUNK and local Front committees as it prepared the framework for **Democratic Kampuchea** promulgated on 5 January 1976.

NAY VALENTIN (1918-1975). Born on 7 February 1918 at **Kampong Cham**, the son of **Khuon Nay**, Valentin attended the National School of Administration and served as provincial official at **Kampong Thom**. He was secretary to the Cambodian Embassy in Thailand, before becoming assistant chief of the economic mission to China and director of the textile factory in Kampong Cham. He was ambassador to Hanoi and then ambassador to China in 1970. Nay Valentin was the man who personally informed Prince **Norodom Sihanouk** of his deposition in March 1970. When he handed the official communiqué to the prince, Sihanouk tore it up and fired Valentin who returned to Phnom Penh. In 1972 he was ambassador to Australia. He was killed in Cambodia, probably in 1975.

NEAK TA **("ancestor people").** This is the generic term for the ancestral spirits, and spirits of places or inanimate objects, that constitute perhaps the most important component of Khmer animism. *Neak ta* are thought to offer protection to the places where they are found and to people living there or passing through. Some are embodied in Angkorean statuary, others in featureless rocks, and still others inhabit trees or other objects. Often reverence for a *neak ta* will spring up in a region where a violent accident or a murder has taken place. The cults honoring the *neak ta* do not follow set liturgies or procedures. The idea that places are guarded or protected by ancestral spirits is shared by many people on the mainland of Southeast Asia and, in prerevolutionary days, China.

NEAL PHLENG (1900-1964). Born in **Battambang**, Neal Phleng studied medicine in Cambodia and in France. A qualified doctor, practising in **Phnom Penh**, in October 1945 he was director of the hygiene service. He was minister of health from 1949-1951 and minister of foreign affairs from March until October 1951. A prominent member of the **Liberal Party**, he was a candidate in the 1951 National Assembly elections in Kanduok, **Kandal**, and ran again, and again without success, in the 1952 High Council elections in Phnom Penh. In November 1953 Neal Phleng was appointed minister of public works and telecommunications, a portfolio he held for six months, being reappointed from January until September 1955. In 1953 he served in the National Consultative Assembly. It was primarily due to his influence that the Liberals refused, in 1955, to support the **Sangkum**, experiencing a humiliating defeat and disappearance as a result. From 1960 until his death, he headed the medical service of the *Chemins de Fer Royaux du Cambodge*. A brother, Neal Smoeuk, was a member of the **Progressive Democratic Party** who was elected to the High Council in 1955 to represent the technical branch of the civil service.

NETH LAING SAY (1924-1946). Born in **Phnom Penh**, Neth Laing Say was an interpreter and translator, and in August 1945, he was secretary to the Japanese army commander, Kubota, who was in charge of imperial affairs in the capital. On the night of 9 August, with six other officials, he stormed into the royal palace to attempt to impose an independent government. King **Norodom Sihanouk** recognized their "National Committee" and ordered the arrest of all cabinet ministers except **Son Ngoc Thanh** who became president of the Council of Ministers. All seven were later arrested and Neth Laing Say was accused of organizing the coup along with **Hem Savang**. Sentenced to 15 years of hard labor, he escaped in December 1945 from the Phnom Penh Central Prison, making for Thailand. There he joined the first **Khmer Issarak (KI)** Committee based in Bangkok. He next turned up in **Battambang** in June 1946 at a joint Issarak-**Viet Minh (VM)** meeting where he was named a political commissar in a new joint KI-VM command. Only a few months later in October 1946 he was killed in an ambush in **Kampong Speu** province. In a gesture of friendship and solidarity, the **Democrat Party** government of December 1947 granted Laing Say a posthumous pardon.

"NEW PEOPLE." An epithet for the people evacuated from **Phnom Penh** and other **Khmer Republic**-controlled towns after the communist victory on 17 April 1975. The "new people" coming into the liberated zones were also collected identified as "April 17 people," which indicated that they were behind the front lines on the enemy side during the 1970-1975 war. Most (though not all) new people were treated as "candidate" members of the agricultural cooperatives into which they were evacuated. In practice being a "candidate" member rather than a full member of the cooperative meant reduced food rations and menial work assignments. Discrimination against new people by the **"base people"** who were seen by the new people to be **"old people"** broke down toward 1978 when the revolutionary morale of the former was sapped by violent purges and the mutually endured hardships in **Democratic Kampuchea**.

NEWSPAPERS. A predominately subsistence economy combined with low rates of national literacy ensured that it was not until 1936 that the first Cambodian newspaper and also the first Khmer-language newspaper was produced. *Nagaravatta*, edited by **Pach Chhoeun**, **Sim Var** and **Son Ngoc Thanh** appear until 1942 when it was suspended and banned in the wake of the July 1942 demonstration. The major French-language paper during this period was *Cambodge,* a semiofficial newspaper that reported general news stories as well as excerpted material from the official government record, the *Journal Officiel du Cambodge*. Though *Cambodge* was originally published in a bilingual format, it was later divided into French and Khmer-language editions. By 1949 only the French-language edition was being published; it was briefly renamed *Angkor* in 1956, but reverted to *Cambodge* during the 1960s. In 1970 the same paper was renamed *Le Républicain*. Under this name it continued to appear until the fall of the **Khmer Republic** in April 1975.

With the formation of political parties in the late colonial era, a myriad of party newspapers, most of them short-lived, were produced. The **Liberal Party** maintained two papers, *Flambeau Khmer* and *Sereipheap* ("Freedom"), with the **Democrat Party** publishing *Le Démocrate* in French and *Pracheathipatay* ("The Democrat") in Khmer. The **Khmer Renewal Party** published *Khemara* ("Renewal") and the **National Union** promoted *La Vérité* ("Truth") which was officially nonpartisan and which lasted into the 1960s, by which time the party has disappeared. Both this paper and *Cambodge* helped to promote the independent weekly news magazine *Réalités Cambodgiennes* which first appeared in tabloid form in the late 1950s. The **National Recovery Party** published two papers, *Hanuman* in Khmer, after the warrior monkey of the same name, and *Redressement National* in French, while the **Party of the People** published *Samleng Khmer* ("The Khmer Voice").

Adding to the political mix, **Son Ngoc Thanh**, after he returned from forced exile in France in 1951 established *Khmer Krauk* ("Khmers, Awake!") which collapsed in March 1952 when he and **Ea Sichau** fled to the jungle. The 1950s produced several other new papers with clear political standpoints such as *Pracheachon* ("The People"), run by the pro-Viet Minh veterans of the **Khmer Issarak** days who had formed a **Krom Pracheachon**, a "people's group" (or "team") to field candidates in the 1955 elections. This paper appeared until 1960. Other progressive newspapers secretly promoted by the underground **Khmer People's Revolutionary Party**, on a commercial basis, included the Khmer-language *Mittapheap* ("Fraternity") and *Ekapheap* ("Unity") and the French-language *L'Observateur* ("Observer"). **Sam Sary** briefly produced a party newspaper in Bangkok, *Reastrthipatay* ("Democratic People"), just before the **Bangkok Plot** was exposed and almost certainly with foreign funding.

The 1950s produced two major French-language newspapers which each drew large revenue from advertisements. *La Liberté* provided an establishment viewpoint, while *Le Dépêche du Cambodge* ("The Cambodian Dispatch"), founded in 1957, offered more liberal and occasionally critical views. It was edited by **Chau Seng** with **Sim Var**, the publisher, occasionally lending a more conservative hand. The success of

"The Dispatch" and Prince **Norodom Sihanouk**'s nationalization of banking and insurance in 1963 prompted **Douc Rasy** together with other conservative deputies from the **National Assembly** to create the French-language *Phnom Penh Presse*.

There were also a number of Khmer-language papers during the 1960s. *Socheavator* ("The Good Life" or "Good Living") had the highest circulation of any daily newspaper in the country. It specialized in government scandal, gossip, crime and events in the Vietnam War. *Meatophum* ("Motherland") also engaged in populist muckraking and was, as was *Socheavator*, to a lesser extent, denounced by Prince **Norodom Sihanouk** as procommunist.

The mid-1960s saw a commercial and political clash between the many newspaper editors. Chau Seng ousted Sim Var from *Le Dépêche du Cambodge* and refounded his newspaper as *La Nouvelle Dépêche* ("The New Dispatch"). Prince Sihanouk became a regular contributor to the newspaper. From this period Sim Var turned his attention to *Khmer Ekkaraj* ("Khmer Independent"), a Khmer-language paper which, together with *Nokor Thom* ("Capital City," run by Sim Var's nephew, **Soth Polin**), dominated the Khmer-language press until late 1972.

Throughout the 1950s and 1960s, until 1967, there were also Chinese-language and Vietnamese-language newspapers for these language communities. The Chinese community supported five dailies at one time, while the equally large, but less affluent Vietnamese community had three major papers. Although popular within their respective communities, none of these had any influence within the population at large.

A 1951 law allowed anybody the right to publish and print a newspaper in any language and freedom of the press was reconfirmed in law in 1957 by another legislative act. Nevertheless, in 1967 noting the response of Chinese students to the Cultural Revolution in **China**, Prince Sihanouk banned all Chinese-language newspapers. In September 1967 all privately owned newspapers were banned. State-owned or controlled papers and magazines continued to appear, under tighter control with *Kampuchea* (in Khmer) and *Cambodge* being the major dailies.

Lon Nol was faced with civil war soon after the overthrow of Sihanouk, and it was not until August 1970 that he was able to allow freedom of the press. This was followed by a massive publishing frenzy with up to 20 daily newspapers. Funded by advertising and politicians from many different backgrounds (**In Tam**, **Lon Non**, Prince **Sisowath Sovannareth**, **Ung Mung**, etc), some were reputable newspapers, while others were scandal sheets purveying the worst form of gossip, and not infrequently, it was said, for the purpose of blackmail. *Khmer Ekkaraj* ("Khmer Independent") and *Koh Santepheap* ("Island of Peace") tended to be the most widely read, with *Nokor Thom* often containing the most lurid gossip. The French-language *Le Courrier Phnompenois* ("Phnom Penh Mail") was heavily subsidized by massive daily purchases by embassies, and there was also a short-lived *Phnom Penh Times*, published in English.

The publishing flurry reached a peak in 1972 with the presidential elections and then the founding of various registered political parties. In March 1973, following the assassination attempt on Lon Nol, a state of emergency was proclaimed and most of the papers were closed down. Few reopened, and when *Nokor Thom* accused Prince **Sisowath Sirik Matak** of the murder of Education Minister **Keo Sang Kim**, the editor was forced to flee into exile, ending up in California.

There were no newspapers and not much state publishing under the communist **Democratic Kampuchea** regime. A glossy month magazine, **Democratic Kampuchea**, was produced for display on poster boards, and for limited circulation abroad in French and English translations. The magazine appears to have been produced on the same press as *Kambuja*. The **Communist Party of Kampuchea** published a theoretical journal entitled *Tung Padevat* ("Revolutionary Flags") on a monthly basis from late 1972 until early 1979, but it was distributed only to party members.

The newspaper industry did not emerge again until 1979. Under the **People's Republic of Kampuchea**, the *Agence Khmère de Presse* was reestablished as the S.P.K., initials for for *Sarpordarmean Kampuchea* (Cambodian News Agency) in January and in the same month, the **United Front for the National Salvation of Kampuchea** published the weekly *Kampuchea*. By December 1979 these were joined by *Kangtoap Padewat* (Revolutionary Army). The Phnom Penh party committee of the **People's Revolutionary Party of Kampuchea (PRPK)** launched another weekly paper in 1981 entitle *Phnom Penh* and in October 1985 following the Fifth Party Congress of the PRPK, *Pracheachon* reappeared on a twice weekly basis being deemed for the first time an official party newspaper. In the wake of the **United Nations** interregnum, the private press has been restored. Some of these were based on earlier papers such as *Khmer Ekkaraj* and *Koh Santepheap*. The largest daily, *Rasmei Kampuchea*, was initially printed in Bangkok, being financed in part by Thai investors. With more than 40 staff, largely recruited from the official PRK and its successor **State of Cambodia** S.P.K. newsagency, it is reputed to sell 23,000 copies daily. Some of the larger of the smaller Khmer-language newspapers are *Damneung Pel Preuk* ("Morning News"), *Uddomgatikhmer* ("Khmer Ideal"), *Kamlang Thmei* ("New Force") and *Samleng Yuvachon Khmer* ("Voice of Khmer Youth"). Among the most successful of the new foreign-language newspapers are the twice-monthly, English-language, *Phnom Penh Post,* founded in 1992 and still edited and published by Michael

Hayes. *The Cambodia Daily* published by Bernard Krishner, is the only English-language daily. It carries local news as well as international agency stories with a Japanese-language supplement. A "Weekly Review" of the Daily is also available for overseas subscribers and carries the Cambodian news only. The principal French-language paper, *Cambodge Soir*, is published twice weekly. The current press law provides much freedom to the press, but international watchdog agencies such as Reporters Without Frontiers and Human Rights Watch regularly issued reports detailing abuses of press freedom in the 1990s. In the new millennium, Cambodia's newspapers are far from an effective "third estate."

NEY PENA (1948-). Born in **Svay Rieng**, he was a secondary school teacher in his home province and then in **Preah Vihear**. During the period of **Democratic Kampuchea**, he was in the countryside. He joined the **People's Revolutionary Party of Kampuchea (PRPK)** and was appointed president of the People's Committee in Preah Vihear province from March 1983 to March 1986, secretary of the PRPK provisional party committee in Preah Vihear province, April 1985, and first deputy minister of the interior in October 1985. Within the national party, by October 1984 he was elected as an alternate member of the Central Committee, and as a full member in February 1985 and then elected to the Political Bureau at the Fifth Party Congress of October 1985. He was appointed minister of the interior in March 1986, replacing **Khang Sarin**. In January 1989 he was in turn replaced by **Sin Song**, and became chairman of the PRPK Central Committee Propaganda and Education Commission, a post held until September 1990, when he was replaced by **Dith Munty**. He was then appointed deputy chairman of the PRPK Central Committee Control Commission. In June 1993 he was elected to the Constituent Assembly in **Kampot**, and in October 1993 when the **National Assembly** was formed, he became a member of its Commission for the Interior, National Defense and Anticorruption. In 1998 he was reelected to the National Assembly.

NGINN NIPPHA (1917-). The older brother of **Nginn Thappana**, Nginn Nippha was educated in **Phnom Penh**, Hanoi and France, where he attended a Jesuit school. In Hanoi he met and became friends with many men who later became leading communists in North Vietnam. He studied law, economics, finance and history and then was trained by the French in administrative matters, mainly legal, in Phnom Penh, Hanoi and Saigon. A jurist and a judge, he was one of the coauthors of the 1947 **constitution**, and a magistrate by 1949. He joined the **Khmer Renewal Party** and served on their Steering Committee in charge of party publications. In 1951 he ran for the **National Assembly** without success but as a distinguished jurist he was a member of Cambodia's delegation at the

1954 Geneva Conference.

Fluent in several regional languages, including Thai, Lao, Vietnamese and Mandarin, Nginn Nippha also headed the Department of Tourism. He was appointed under secretary of state and royal delegate for information, in charge of information and popular education in the **Penn Nouth** governments from January until November 1953. He was then general secretary of the royal palace, first secretary of the **National Bank of Cambodia**, general secretary of the Council of the Presidency, and first president-director-general of the *Caisse Nationale d'Équipement* ("National Development Bank"). In September 1966 he was a member of the Cambodian delegation negotiating with the **National Front for the Liberation of South Vietnam**. As a banker, in 1970 he participated in the International Monetary Fund and World Bank meetings in Washington. In June 1972 he was appointed deputy governor of the National Bank of Cambodia, replacing **Yem Samrong**. In 1974 he held the rank of general in the Armed Forces of **Khmer Republic**.

NGINN THAPPANA. The younger brother of **Nginn Nippha**, he was a career soldier in the Cambodian army and close colleague of **Lon Non**. He served as minister of state in charge of the interior, security, religion, veterans and tourism in the second **Son Ngoc Thanh** government from March to October 1972, during which period he was accused of having taken part in the rigging of the 1972 presidential elections. He was nevertheless reappointed to the cabinet by **Hang Thun Hak** as minister of state in charge of national defense from October 1972 to April 1973. Following this he was minister of state for public works and transport in the first **In Tam** government, May to October 1973 and third deputy prime minister responsible for national defense and coordination of the departments of information, public health, veterans and war victims in the second In Tam government from October until December 1973. He was promoted to second deputy prime minister and minister of national defense, veterans affairs and war victims in the first **Long Boret** government from December 1973 until June 1974 and was reappointed to the second Long Boret government with the additional portfolios of invalids, widows and orphans of war, public works and telecommunications which he held from June 1974 until March 1975.

NGO HOU (1907/8-). Born in **Battambang**, son of Ngo Yi, he was from a Vietnamese background. He was educated at **Lycée Sisowath** and the Hanoi Medical School, then returned to Phnom Penh where he was director at the Ministry of Health. He soon became a close confidant of Prince **Norodom Sihanouk**, mostly by becoming his favorite medical advisor and by cementing his friendship with business interests. In 1948 he was a founder of the Khmer Aero Club and Cambo-dia's first pilot. In 1951 he was involved in the accidental death of In Chan, a provincial official who was killed when Ngo Hou's airplane hit him. In August 1954, having already been given the rank of colonel, he became minister for national defense and public health, a portfolio he held until January 1955. In January 1958 he was appointed minister of public health, a post he held for four months.

By 1966, and though lacking in military training, Ngo Hou headed the Cambodian Air Force. He had been promoted to major general in August 1965 and was a lieutenant general by the time he accompanied Prince Sihanouk to Hanoi on the death of Ho Chi Minh in 1969. He was with Sihanouk on 18 March 1970 and following the Prince's overthrow, was among those in the royal entourage who was forbidden to return to the country. Sentenced to death *in absentia* for high treason in August 1970, his property was confiscated. He was subsequently appointed **Royal Government of National Union of Kampuchea (GRUNK)** minister of public health, religious and social affairs and was a member of the Central Committee of the **National United Front of Kampuchea (FUNK)**. Ngo Hou retired from active political life in the 1980s, but was among the first to be appointed High Councilor to the Throne in 1994. Ngo Hou's brother, Ngo Hong (1901-1974), was a member of the **High Council of the Kingdom** and was among those who voted to overthrow Prince **Norodom Sihanouk** in 1970.

NGO PIN (1941-). Born on 5 January 1941, and from a Sino-Khmer family, Pin was an engineer in the Ministry of Public Works, having been trained in the United States. He married Princess **Sisowath Aryavady** also known as Chamroeun Vong and they were in Phnom Penh in 1970 when on 17 September 1970 he was made a commander in the **Lon Nol** army. Soon after this the couple moved to Beijing, giving their support to the **Royal Government of National Union of Kampuchea** headed by Prince **Norodom Sihanouk**. Returning to Cambodia in 1975 Pin worked in the **Democratic Kampuchea (DK)** Foreign Ministry under **Ieng Sary**, principally as an English language teacher. He also worked occasionally as an interpreter for **Pol Pot** who in 1978 gave a widely broadcast film interview to Yugoslav journalists. Posted to the DK Embassy in Beijing in 1978, Chamroeun Vong remained behind in the ministry, becoming the principal English-language interpreter for **Khieu Samphan** after 1979. She quietly left the DK movement in 1984 and with their children moved to France. By 1987 Ngo Pin was posted to the DK office in Paris after which he, too, left the movement. He is now a member of **FUNCINPEC** and a secretary of state for Water Resources and Meteorology.

NGOR HAING (1947-1996). Born in Samrong Yong, **Takeo**, the son of Ngor Kea, from a Chinese family who owned a saw mill, Haing studied medicine at **Phnom Penh** from 1969-1975, working in military hospitals from 1971-1975. During the period of **Democratic Kampuchea** he worked in the countryside and often feared for his life, but managed to hide his middle-class background. His wife, Chang My Huoy, was among those who died from the extreme hardships. In 1979 he escaped to the Thai-Cambodian border and was in the refugee camp of Nong Chan, and then **Khao-I-Dang** where he worked as a doctor. In August 1980 he settled in the **United States**, living in Los Angeles. In 1984 he starred as **Dith Pran** in Roland Joffé's *The Killing Fields*, obtaining a Golden Globe as well as an Oscar for the best supporting male actor in a film. He wrote *A Cambodian Odyssey*, which was published in London in 1988, and traveled widely helping to publicize the human rights dilemmas facing Cambodia. In 1993 he portrayed a tormented Vietnamese father in Oliver Stone's film *Heaven and Earth*. He was robbed and murdered in a street attack on 25 February 1996, in Los Angeles.

NGUON CHEAN (1932-1975). Born on 13 February 1932, a onetime supporter of **Hu Nim**'s people's movement, he headed the secretariat of the High Council of Planning and National Defense in 1967. In June 1971 Chean was appointed to the **constitutional drafting committee** representing the Ministry of Social Action, Work and Employment. An inspector for pacification, he joined the **Socio-Republican Party** in 1972 and was elected to the **National Assembly** of the **Khmer Republic** in Preah Bat Chean Chum, **Takeo**. He was secretary of state for labor and social action in the last **Long Boret** government, March to April 1975.

NGUON CHHAY KRY (1920-). Born on 19 May 1920 at Kampong Thmar, **Kampong Thom**, the son of Hou Nguon and Mme (née Dith Sath), he studied at the Royal School of Administration. Deputy-governor of **Prey Veng, Siem Reap**, the Municipality of **Phnom Penh**, and then governor of **Pursat**, Nguon Chhay Kry became assistant head of the national police. In 1963-1964 he was director of railways and in September 1966 he was a member of the government delegation negotiating with the **National Front for the Liberation of South Vietnam**. In May 1967 he was appointed minister for public works and telecommunications, a post he held until August 1969. On 9 September 1968 Chhay Kry was elected president of the conference on the financing of the Prek Thnot Dam and three days later served as temporary minister of foreign affairs. In 1970 he was appointed general secretary at the Ministry of Foreign Affairs, a post he still held in 1972.

NGUON NHEL (1942-). Born in Baray, **Kampong Thom**, Nhel was a secondary school teacher working in the education department in Kampong Thom province, 1970-1975, and spent the period of **Democratic Kampuchea** in the countryside. In May 1980 he became president of the People's Committee of Kampong Thom, holding that position until September 1985. He was then appointed secretary to the **People's Revolutionary Party of Kampuchea (PRPK)** in **Phnom Penh**, holding that post until August 1990. A member of the Central Committee of the PRPK from October 1985, he was acting director general of Hévéaculture and in April 1989 was appointed to the politburo of the PRPK. In August 1990 Nhel became minister of agriculture and was elected **Cambodian People's Party** deputy for Kampong Thom in June 1993. He was elected as vice-president of the **National Assembly** Commission for Public Works, Transport, Communications, Posts, Industry, Energy, Mines and Trade in October 1993. In 1998 he was reelected to the National Assembly.

NHEAN KROEUN (1911-). Born on 15 June 1911 in **Battambang**, the son of Nhean and Mme (née Hong San), Kroeun completed his secondary education in Cambodia and then joined the Department of Waters and Forests. He rose to become director of the service of waters, forests and hunting in 1960, taking over from **Khieu Vann**; and was appointed secretary of state for agriculture and peasant affairs from October 1955 to January 1956. A prominent resident of the city of Kampong Thom, he became the president of the **Sangkum** Committee for the town and was also president of the Association for the Development of Teaching and the local cooperative. In the **Khmer Republic**, he joined the **Socio-Republican Party** and was elected to the **National Assembly** in September 1972 representing Srayau, **Kampong Thom**.

NHEIM SOKPHAL (1921-1976). Born on 14 June 1921 in **Phnom Penh**, the son of Ngo Nheim and Mme (née Pann Ken; sister of **Pann Yung**), he studied in France 1946-1949. A fully certified pharmacist, Sokphal returned to Phnom Penh to establish a pharmacy. After serving as secretary of state for public health, he was nominated by the **Sangkum** for a seat in the **National Assembly** to represent Phnom Penh, 1958-1962; and in the next Assembly, **Kampong Speu**, 1962-1966. Pann Ken, Sokphal's wife taught at École Sutharot. Through his mother, he was a first cousin of Kim Kosal, **Chau Sen Cocsal** and **Koun Wick**. His son, Sotheary, works at the *Bibliothèque Nationale* in Paris.

NHEK BUN CHHAY (1956-). Born in Ta Ong, Svay Chek, **Banteay Meanchey** which is not far from the frontier with **Thailand**, Bunchhay escaped from the **Democratic Kampuchea** authorities in January 1976 as their military and administrative control expanded throughout the country. On the Thai-Cambodian border he formed an anticommunist *Khmer Sar* (White Khmers) guerrilla group which a few years later became the basis for **Molinaka**. His autobiography describes in detail the problems facing the resistance in the border camps as well as his friendship with Prince **Norodom Ranariddh**. By August 1983 he was the deputy commander for technical operations in the *Armée Nationale Sihanoukienne* and was still on Ranariddh's side when, in July 1997, Second Prime Minister **Hun Sen** ordered his military forces to arrest or to assassinate the Prince as well as **FUNCINPEC** military leaders, including himself, **Chau Sambath** and **Krouch Yoeurn**. Though surrounded and wounded at his base near Pochentong airfield, Bunchhay escaped and succeeded in reestablishing a Royalist resistance zone and military base at **O'Smach**. In 1999 by which time Ranariddh had formed a second coalition with Hun Sen, he and **Serey Kosal** were pardoned for their momentary resumption of armed struggle and appointed to the **Senate**, Nhek Bun Chhay, as second vice-president. He is married to Sam Sopheap and they have two children.

NHEK PHONN (1910-197?). Born on 10 February 1910 in **Phnom Penh**, the son of Pick Nhiek and Mme (née Ing Saret), Phonn was a younger brother of **Nhiek Tioulong**. In 1953 he served in the National Consultative Assembly; and in 1955, as a candidate for the **Sangkum**, he was elected to the **National Assembly** for Kampong Chen, **Kampong Thom**. Afterward he served as Councilor of the Kingdom. A businessman, he ran Nhek Phonn & Co., was vice-president of the Chamber of Commerce and Agriculture and an **advisor** to the **National Bank of Cambodia**. Elected in 1966 to the National Assembly for Taing Krassaing, **Kampong Thom**, he was appointed secretary of state for trade in the first **Lon Nol** government.

NHEM SOPHON (1937-1983). Born at Kampong Svay, **Kampong Thom**, he joined the army in the 1950s and was a colonel in the paratroopers at the fall of the **Khmer Republic** in April 1975. Captured by the communists, he worked at a farm feeding pigs until his escape in 1976. Making his way to the border of **Thailand**, he joined **Kong Sileah** in the founding of **Molinaka** in August 1979, at that time the only guerrilla group to swear fealty to Sihanouk. He died of fever on 3 August 1983 while on a military mission.

NHIEK TIOULONG (1908-1996). Prime minister in 1962. The son of a provincial governor, Nhiek Tioulong was born 23 August 1908 in **Phnom Penh**, and attended **Collège Sisowath**, Phnom Penh, and Lycée Chasseloup Laubat, Saigon. On his return to Cambodia he studied at the French-run Cambodian School of Administration and then joined the government service. In 1931 he was assistant secretary of the Council of Ministers and assistant governor of **Prey Veng**. By 1937 he was governor of **Pursat** and in 1941 governor of **Kampong Cham** where the **French Résident** of the day, Monsieur E. Höffel, became a close friend and political confidante. During this period Tioulong established many private business connections which he maintained for the rest of his life. With the Japanese *coup de force* in March 1945 he was appointed governor of Phnom Penh.

With the Japanese-inspired declaration of independence for Cambodia in March 1945, Tioulong joined the new government and served as minister of education under **Son Ngoc Thanh**. However when the French returned in October 1945, Tioulong endorsed the French return and was appointed governor of **Battambang** and **Siem Reap**. In August 1946 he led the Cambodian delegation to the Dalat Conference; and in the following year, 1947, Tioulong and his friend and ally, **Lon Nol**, founded the **Khmer Renewal Party**, for which Tioulong boasted that he would win every seat at stake in Battambang. He became chief of staff of the Royal Cambodian Army in 1949, with the rank of colonel, and then served as minister of finance, and then of information in 1951, this series of appointments confirming his close rapport with the French, many Democrats and King **Norodom Sihanouk**. He was appointed royal delegate for information in July 1952. In July 1953 Tioulong was appointed minister of public works and communications; and in April 1954 became minister of public defense, in which period he hastily reorganized the army to meet the threatened **Viet Minh** invasion. He subsequently quarreled with King Sihanouk and, after heading the Cambodian military delegation to the Geneva Conference, he was appointed high commissioner in Paris where he remained until Prince **Sisowath Monipong** was appointed to that post in February 1955 and Tioulong was appointed ambassador to Japan. In 1956 and 1957 he was a delegate to the United Nations General Assembly; and in April 1958 became deputy prime minister, with the portfolios of economic planning and communications. He was appointed ambassador to the Soviet Union from 1957, concurrently ambassador to Czechoslovakia from 1959 and minister to Poland. Although nominated for another tour as ambassador to Japan, he instead returned to Cambodia in October 1960.

On 23 February 1962 Tioulong was appointed president of the Council of Ministers, ad interim. In 1963 he was president of the Council of Administration and president-director-general of the *Société Khmère des Distilleries* ("Khmer Distilleries Company"), as well as vice-president of the **High Council of the Throne** and Royal Delegate to **Kirirom** and **Bokor**. In 1965 he was president of **Royal Air Cambodge** and in 1968 was appointed governor of **Kirirom** (later renamed Tioulongville after him). It was during the Vietnam War that Tioulong's business acumen, and penchant for rent-seeking, came to the fore. He allowed and facilitated huge amounts of materiel to be brought from **Sihanoukville** to **Viet Cong** bases along the Cambodian-Vietnamese border. Initial acquiescence was followed by actively encouraging such supplies, and retaining the profits. At the time it was said that the Vietnamese agreed to 10 percent of the goods being given to the Cambodian army in payment for services rendered. The Vietnamese communists were thereby able to circumvent the **Ho Chi Minh Trail**, now being heavily bombed, and a few Cambodians who were aware of the deals at the time believe Tioulong is to be blamed for helping the communists defeat the **United States** and South Vietnam. Accusations of corruption and venality against him in this period were widespread, as were reports of him partying for weeks at a time.

In 1969 Tioulong resigned as commander-in-chief of the army and left Phnom Penh for France where he planned a quiet and luxurious retirement. His plans were disrupted in 1970 by the overthrow of his close friend, Prince **Norodom Sihanouk**, who turned to him for assistance with preparations for what was to become the **Kampuchean Royal Government of National Union (GRUNK)**. Once the GRUNK was launched, however, Tioulong kept a low profile, being among the tainted courtiers. He re-emerged as a political force when, after the Vietnamese invasion, exiles in Paris sought his assistance in establishing a political movement in support of the once-again exiled Prince Sihanouk. This resulted in the creation of the *Front Uni National pour un Cambodge Indépendent, Neutre, Pacifique et Coopératif* (**FUNCINPEC**) in 1981. Tioulong was prominent in émigré circles during the 1980s and was a patron of the cultural association and publishing house known as *Cedorek*. Appointed as a personal **advisor** by the king and to the **Constitutional Council**, his last known interview criticizes the government for obstruction the formation and operation of the Council. He married twice. With his first wife, he had one daughter, Regine. His second wife, Mme Puoat, was the mother of four daughters: Vissakha (who first married Prince Sisowath Dussadey, then married Mr Barbology); Rémy; Kethy, (who first married Prince **Norodom Chakrapong**, then married Patrice Farras); and **Saumara** (married **Sam Rainsy**). Nhiek Tioulong died 9 June 1996.

NIN SAPHON (1948-). Born in **Takeo**, she has a baccalaureate and was a teacher in **Phnom Penh** from 1970-1975. After the creation of the **People's Republic of Kampuchea (PRK)**, she was appointed vice-president of the Women's Association of Takeo province. She was assistant chief of administration in Takeo province from 1981 and also represented Takeo in the PRK **National Assembly** from August 1983 until May 1993. In May 1993 she was elected to the Constituent Assembly on the **Cambodian People's Party** list in Takeo, and elected deputy chair of the Assembly's

Commission on the Protection of Human Rights and Complaints in October 1993. Nin Saphon was reelected to the National Assembly in 1998, and is now secretary for the above Commission.

1916 AFFAIR. This was a series of popular demonstrations in Cambodia against taxes levied throughout **French Indochina** by the French colonialists as a means of defraying the costs of World War I. Over several months, as many as 100,000 peasants, in a series of large delegations, marched peacefully to Phnom Penh, presenting petitions to King **Sisowath**, who gave them personal reassurances, although the taxes were not repealed. The affair indicated to the French that the Khmers could mobilize *en masse*, but also that the king was able to dispel discontent.

NON-COMMUNIST RESISTANCE (NCR). This was the name chosen by **Son Sann**'s **Khmer People's National Liberation Armed Forces (KPNLAF)** and Prince **Norodom Sihanouk**'s **FUNCINPEC** armed forces in the run-up to the Paris International Conference on Cambodia in 1991, to distinguish them from the Communists' National Army of Democratic Kampuchea (NADK), with whom they were formally allied and recognized as a coalition government by the **United Nations**. The NCR received assistance from Thailand and China, which also assisted the NADK, and "non-lethal" aid from the United States, Singapore and other countries.

NON SUON alias **Chey Suon (1927-1976).** Recruited into the **Khmer People's Revolutionary Party (KPRP)** after joining the **Viet Minh**-sponsored *Khmer Issarak* in the late 1940s, he was the leader of the **Pracheachon** ("The People") Group organized in 1955 by communist veterans of the struggle for independence. He was among the group's candidates in the **National Assembly** who endured extensive harassment and ultimately, humiliating defeat at the polls. Afterward he was prominent in political circles in **Phnom Penh** for his outspoken comments and criticisms at the National Congresses of the people regularly convened by the **Sangkum** movement led by Prince **Norodom Sihanouk**. In turn he was frequently singled out in the prince's speeches of the late 1950s as one of the nation's leading "Reds," indeed one of the first of those to whom the prince attached the epithet *Khmer Rouge*. In early 1962 he was among the 15 members of the Pracheachon Group arrested by the security police for "subversive" activities in the run-up to the 1962 National Assembly elections. Initially sentenced to death his sentence was later commuted to life imprisonment. Non Suon was among the several hundred political prisoners released from jail in early 1970 soon after the *coup d'état* of 18 March. He fled the capital almost immediately to rejoin communist forces allied with the **National United Front of Kampuchea**. Though regarded as a Vietnamese-trained and oriented member of the

Communist Party of Kampuchea (CPK), formerly the KPRP, he was not among the first of the Viet Minh-era resistance fighters to be purged by the CPK in the 1970-1975 period. On 4 May 1975 he was recalled to Phnom Penh and placed in charge of finance and on 30 July 1975, by which time a decision had been made against the issuing of a new currency, he was asked to assume responsibility for setting up the revolutionary Ministry of Agriculture. He was detained in early October 1976, among the first of many high-level party cadres to be arrested and purged for suspected sabotage and counter revolutionary activities in the weeks and months to follow. In his answers to interrogators and torturers at **Tuol Sleng**, Non Chey protested his total loyalty to the party stating, "I believed in and respected the Party without qualification because for my entire life the Party had taken care of, nurtured and educated me politically, ideologically and organizationally and . . . [as my benefactor] it was imperative that I serve the Party and be absolutely determined to trod the path of the Party's line and to do whatever the Party might ask."

NONG KIMNY (1912-?). He studied in Saigon, joined the colonial administration in 1932 and held various provincial governorships. In 1941 he was appointed first private secretary, then director of the cabinet to King **Norodom Sihanouk**. Kimny was appointed secretary-general to the government from March until August 1945 and was wounded in August 1945 when army officers entered the royal palace to support **Son Ngoc Thanh**. From late 1945 until 1948 he was in France and served in the French diplomatic service from 1948 as first secretary at the French Embassy in Bangkok. In 1951 Nong Kimny was appointed minister to the **United States** and ambassador in 1952. He was vice-president of the Council of Ministers and minister of foreign affairs from April to September 1956. He then returned to Washington as ambassador. In 1970 Kimny was ambassador to India and **Thailand**, spending most of his time in the latter country. In 1972 he was ambassador to Malaysia. He married Tea Chhoan Huoy. Nong Kimny was a keen tennis player, despite the loss of one arm. He died in Paris in the late 1970s.

NOP BOPHAN (1923-1959). Born in **Kampong Speu**, he was a member of the clandestine **Khmer People's Revolutionary Party** and of its electoral arm, the **Pracheachon** ("The People") Group and one of the Pracheachon's candidates in the 1955 **National Assembly** elections in Kampong Taches, **Kampong Chhnang**. Managing editor and publisher of the newspaper, *Pracheachon*, he was attacked outside a police station on 10 October 1959 and died of injuries sustained two days later. His death is often cited as an example of official intolerance of freedoms of speech and of the press in the early years after independence. *See also* NEWSPAPERS.

NOP LEAN (1946-). Born on 19 October 1946 at Ta Buon, Koh Andet, **Takeo**, Nop Lean was a secondary school teacher and taught in **Kampot** and Takeo before being posted to **Phnom Penh**. In October 1980 he joined **Molinaka** and was a member of the administrative committee of Site B; he became a member of the National Council of **FUNCINPEC** in February 1992. In 1993 Nop Lean was appointed vice-president of the FUNCINPEC electoral committee for Takeo, being elected on 10 June 1993. In October 1993 he was appointed a member of the Commission for the Interior, National Defense and Anticorruption.

NORODOM, King (1834-1904). He was born in February 1834 at Mongkolborei, a Cambodian province controlled at the time by **Thailand**, while his father, Prince **Ang Duang**, served as governor. At his father's coronation in 1848, Prince Norodom was sent as a hostage to the Thai court, returning to Cambodia a decade later when he quarreled with his father and alienated members of the Muslim minority who staged a rebellion against him after Duang's death. At the suggestion of a French missionary, **Jean-Claude Miche**, Norodom signed a treaty of friendship with **France** in 1863, ushering in nearly a century of French protection. He underestimated French ambitions. In 1884 the French governor of **Cochinchina**, Charles Thomson, forced him to sign a series of concessions that gave administrative power in Cambodia to France. The clause abolishing slavery alienated the elite, and an anti-French rebellion soon broke out, perhaps with Norodom's encouragement. His younger brother, Prince **Sisowath**, allied himself with the French in putting down the revolt. By the 1890s Sisowath had gained French assurances that he would succeed his brother, whom the French bypassed in governing the kingdom. Norodom's last years were tinged with bitterness, ill health, and his growing hostility to France. King Norodom died of facial cancer on 24 April 1904. He was cremated in January 1906.

Norodom had 44 wives and 60 children. His eldest son was Prince Norodom Hassakan (1858-1888, whose non-royal descendants include the **Buor** and **Engly** families). Other sons included Prince Norodom Mayura (1862-1918) who was jailed by the French, Prince **Aruna Yukanthor** (1860-1934), Prince Duong Chakr (1861-1897, grandfather of Prince **Norodom Montana**), Prince Norodom Phanouvong (1871-1934, father of Prince **Norodom Phurissara**), Prince Norodom Sutharot (1872-1945, father of King **Norodom Suramarit**), Prince Norodom Sathavong (1875-1918, minister of the interior 1912-1918, father of Prince **Norodom Norindeth**), and Prince Norodom Chanthalekha (1891-1971, father of Prince **Norodom Chantaraingsey**).

NORODOM ARUN RASMEY, Princess (1955-). Born on 2 October 1955, the daughter of Prince **Norodom Sihanouk**, she married Prince **Sisowath Sirirath** and they had three children. They went into exile in the United States. In early 1991 she was married a second time to **Keo Puth Rasmey** in Beijing who is, by royal appointment, Cambodia's ambassador to Malaysia.

NORODOM BOPHA DEVI, Princess (1943-). Born on 8 January 1943, the eldest child of King **Norodom Sihanouk** and his first wife Phat Kanhol, she was a member of the Cambodian traditional ballet and married four times. Her first husband was Prince Norodom Norinractevong (1935-1970), son of Prince **Norodom Norindeth**, whom she married on 5 February 1959. They were divorced a few weeks later. She then married her cousin, Prince Sisowath Monichivan (1922-), and they had two children: Princess Monikossoma, born on 11 April 1960 and Princess Kalyane Tévi, born on 30 July 1961 (married Armand Gerbie). Bopha Devi and Monichivan were divorced in 1962. Her third husband was Bruno Forsinetti, son of the Italian Consul, and they had one daughter, Princess Chansita, born in 1965. Her fourth husband was Prince **Sisowath Chivan Monirak** whom she married in 1967. They had two sons: Prince Chivannaridh, born on 28 August 1967 and Prince Weakchiravuth, born on 1 May 1973. Remaining in **Phnom Penh** until February 1972, she left Cambodia and eventually moved to France where she taught classical Cambodian dancing. She and her new companion, **Khek Vandy**, moved to Phnom Penh where they lived throughout the 1990s. She was deputy minister of information and culture under Hun Sen in 1992-1993. Evacuated from the country in July 1997 following the Hun Sen Coup, Bopha Devi returned soon afterward, and in 1998 she became minister of culture.

NORODOM BOTUM BOPHA, Princess (1951-1976). The 10th child of King **Norodom Sihanouk**, she married Prince **Sisowath Chivan Monirak** in 1963 then married Prince Sisowath Doussady on 17 April 1967 at **Chamkar Mon**. After divorcing him, she married **So Photra**, an air force officer who was involved in a failed assassination attempt on Lon Nol in 1973. So Photra escaped in his airplane, and Princess Botum Bopha was sentenced to a long term of imprisonment. She was released later that year and went to live with her husband in Yugoslavia. In 1975 the couple, and her four children, returned to Cambodia and disappeared after April 1976.

NORODOM CHAKRAPONG, Prince (1945-). Among the most politically dynamic aristocrats of recent times, Chakrapong was born 21 October 1945, the fifth child and second son of King **Norodom Sihanouk**. He studied in France with his brother, **Ranariddh**, and returned to Cambodia in the 1960s. Graduating as the youngest air force officer of the 6th promotion, Chakrapong lived in Phnom Penh until 1973 when he left for Beijing. In 1975 he chose not to return to Cambodia and settled in France where he ran a Cambodian restaurant with his four wives. He became a general in the **Armée Nationale Sihanoukienne (ANS)** and was commander of the Royal Guard. In March 1985, following the death of **King Men**, Chakrapong was appointed deputy chief of staff. After disagreements with his half brother, Prince **Norodom Ranariddh**, he defected to the **People's Republic of Kampuchea** and was appointed minister for civil aviation and, visiting Hanoi on a goodwill mission in May 1992. In 1993, following the failure of the **Cambodian People's Party** to win the election, he organized a secession movement in the southeastern provinces bordering Vietnam. It collapsed and Prince Chakrapong left for Malaysia. He later returned to Phnom Penh but in 1994 was implicated in another coup attempt being forced to flee the country again. He later publicly announced his retirement from politics. A wife, *Neak Mneang* Dy Yath was elected to the National Assembly in 1998. In 2000 he launched his own private airline, Royal Phnom Penh Airways, a $2 million venture employing 200 people, including six foreigners, operating on mostly domestic routes and flying three times weekly between Phnom Penh and Bangkok.

NORODOM CHANTARAINGSEY, Prince (1924-1975). The youngest son of Prince Norodom Chanthalekha, he was born in **Phnom Penh**, attended École François Baudouin in Phnom Penh and married Princess Sisowath Samanvoraphong. A keen supporter of Cambodian independence, in 1945 he joined the Cambodian Volunteer Corps, known as the **Greenshirts**, recruited by the Japanese to fight the French. Soon afterward he joined **Poc Khun** who had formed the **Khmer Issarak** in Thailand. On 7 August 1945, along with **Dap Chhuon**, Chantaraingsey led the 300 Issaraks who captured Siem Reap. By April 1948 he had established himself in **Pursat** and **Kampong Speu**. In 1951 he was reported to have had about 500 men under arms in Kampong Speu. Cautious about **Yèm Sambaur's** attempts to rally Issaraks to the government, it was not until 20 February 1954 that he did rally to the king. Imprisoned for three years on a spurious charge of lèse majesté, he spent his time in prison writing romantic novels which were later well received.

Joining the Royal Cambodian Army, Chantaraingsey served with some distinction. By January 1970 he was director of the Bokor Casino. During the 1970-1975 war he commanded the 13th Infantry Brigade in Kampong Speu and was widely respected by his troops and the population. In fact he sold much of his property in **Phnom Penh** to ensure his troops were paid on time. Disputes with **Lon Non** led to moves to arrest him but his popularity was always his best protection, and he renounced his name, "Norodom," and his royal rank. A brigadier general from 1972-1975, he refused to surrender on 17 April 1975. Apparently he and his wife were living in the hills in Battambang when she was captured by patrolling **Democratic Kampuchea** soldiers who believed her to be an escapee from a nearby village. Unfortunately she was later recognized, and Chantaraingsey was killed in a desperate effort to save his wife.

NORODOM KANTOL, Prince (1920-1977). Prime minister from 1962-1964. Kantol was born on 15 September 1920 in **Phnom Penh**, the son of Prince Singhara. He attended **Collège Sisowath** and Lycée Chasseloup Laubat. He entered the Cambodian Administration in 1944 becoming the first assistant-governor of the Phnom Penh municipality. Moving to work in the Ministry of Finance, Kantol left the civil service in 1947 to study for a diploma in agricultural engineering at the Faculty of Sciences at the University of Nancy, France, returning to Cambodia in 1952 and becoming assistant-chief of the agricultural services. Kantol married Chuop Samon and they had eight children.

In 1953 Kantol became the first secretary at the Cambodian Embassy in Washington and was then promoted to envoy extraordinary and minister plenipotentiary in Tokyo. He was a member of the High Council of the Kingdom (president 1961-1962) and prime minister from 6 October 1962 until 21 October 1966, having the additional portfolios of interior and religion from May 1965. A member of the High Court of Justice, Kantol was president of **Sangkum**, vice-president of the **High Council of the Throne** and president of the **Royal Khmer Socialist Youth**. Kantol was arrested in 1973 when **Lon Nol** accused members of the royal family of inciting one of their number to bomb the presidential palace in which Lon Nol was nearly killed. However Kantol was soon released by the Republican authorities but did not survive the **Democratic Kampuchea (DK) period,** being arrested and executed by the DK authorities in 1977. His widow was living in Phnom Penh in 1989 with some of her children.

NORODOM MONTANA, Prince (1902-1975). Born on 18 March 1902 in Phnom Penh, son of Prince Monthonthanay and grandson of Prince Duong Chakr, Montana attended the Royal School of Administration and became a secretary in the French civil service before entering the Cambodian administration. He was minister of religion, becoming minister of the economy from March to August 1945, and minister of agriculture from August to October 1945. He founded the **Progressive Democratic Party** in April 1946. His party failed to win any seats in the **National Assembly**.

However Montana was elected in 1948 to the High Council of the Kingdom for **Kandal/Kampong Speu,** and he served in the National Consultative Assembly. He was minister for public training, sports and youth from November 1953 to April 1954, minister of religion, social action and labor briefly in April 1954 and minister of public health, social action and labor from April to July 1954. As minister of education from January to September 1955, he was defeated in the 1955 High Council of the Kingdom elections but contested the 1959 High Council elections for Kampong Speu, **Kampong Chhnang** and **Pursat** and was finally appointed governor of **Kampot,** then Kampong Speu. President of the Royal Council from 1963 until at least 1967, Montana married several times. With his first wife, Princess Norodom Pombacya, they had a son, Prince Pheanureak. By his wife, Chhang Sangvann, he had four children. By his other wives he had eight more children.

NORODOM NARADIPO, Prince (1946-1976). Born on 10 February 1946, the son of King **Norodom Sihanouk,** he was educated in **Phnom Penh** and in Beijing. On 17 November 1963 Sihanouk designated Naradipo as his successor. Naradipo spoke Chinese and was editor of the government's Chinese-language newspaper in **Phnom Penh.** Arrested by **Lon Nol,** he was jailed and when he was released in 1973, he went to China. Returning to Phnom Penh, he was killed by the **Democratic Kampuchea** authorities in 1976. In the late 1990s a man claiming to be Naradipo appeared in Phnom Penh but was denounced as fraudulent by Sihanouk.

NORODOM NORINDETH, Prince (1906-1975). The founder of the **Liberal Party,** Norindeth was the son of Prince Norodom Sathavong and grandson of both King **Norodom** and King **Sisowath.** Norindeth studied in France and in 1932 was the Cambodian delegate to the **French Résident.** From 1933 until 1943 he was second secretary to the Council of Ministers and in 1942-1943 was head of the youth movement of Cambodia, 1941-1943, and a member of the High Council for Youth in Indochina, 1942-1943. A member of the Royal Council, in 1946 he founded the Constitutionalist Party, soon renamed the Liberal Party, the first political party to be formed in Cambodia. It was actively supported by the French, campaigned to keep contacts with France and urged a mutually agreeable settlement to the issue of independence. Devastated when his party failed to make a good showing in the elections for the Constituent Assembly in 1946, Norindeth contested the 1947 National Assembly elections for Phnom Penh (2nd district) but failed to win it. In 1949 he fled from Cambodia to France after being implicated in the murder of the leader of the **Democrat Party, Ieu Koeus.** He returned to Phnom Penh in August 1951, still head of what was becoming an increasingly authoritarian Liberal

Party, but left it to support **Sangkum**. He was Cambodian ambassador to Yugoslavia from 1961-1963, ambassador to Burma in 1964 and to Australia from 1965. He married *neak monéang* Neal Line, daughter of **Neal Phleng**, and they had four children. His eldest son, Prince Norinractevong, married Princess **Norodom Bopha Devi**, eldest daughter of King **Norodom Sihanouk**.

NORODOM NORINDRAPONG, Prince (1954-). Born on 18 September 1954 in Phnom Penh, the 13th and youngest son of King **Norodom Sihanouk**, and the younger son of Princess **Monique**, he studied in Prague with his older brother, Prince **Sihamoni**, then went to Moscow where he completed his education. Returning to Cambodia, he was active in **Democratic Kampuchea** known as Comrade Rin. He was saved from execution due to the direct intervention of Chinese leader Mao Zédong and because of his ideological support for the Democratic Kampuchea revolution. His political loyalties led to considerable friction with his father. Norindrapong married Sinoun, and they had two children: Princess Simonarine, "Nanique," and Princess Moniouk. The family live predominantly in Beijing.

NORODOM PHURISSARA, Prince (1919-1976). Born on 13 October 1919 in Phnom Penh, the son of Prince Norodom Phanouvong and grandson of King **Norodom I**, he was in the Administrative Service and was one of the left-wing group within the **Democrat Party** who seized control of it in 1954, Phurissara being its secretary-general from 1953-1954. He graduated in law from the Faculty of Law and Economic Sciences, Royal University, Phnom Penh, in October 1958 and was under-secretary of state for the interior from January 1961 to August 1962, secretary of state for the interior and religion from October 1962 to December 1964, and minister of foreign affairs from November 1966 to March 1970. Fired by **Lon Nol** in 1970, he was held under house arrest. He married Princess Sisowath Darameth 'Pot' (1913-1970) and they had one daughter. After his wife's death, Prince Phurissara married *monéang* Phlus, and they had two sons. In January 1972 Phurissara, Phlus and the children left Phnom Penh to join the **National United Front of Kampuchea (FUNK)**, northwest of the capital. He was president of the FUNK committee in Phnom Penh and minister without portfolio from 1973-1975. In October 1975 Phurissara accompanied **Ieng Sary** to Thailand and was last seen by Prince **Norodom Sihanouk** in April 1976. He was killed at Phnom Praset later that year.

NORODOM PREYSOPHON, Prince (1954-). Born on 18 November 1954, son of King **Norodom Suramarit** and his wife *khun tep* Kanha Sophea Kim-An Yeap, brother of Prince **Norodom Sirivudh** and Princess

Norodom Vichara, and half brother of Prince **Norodom Sihanouk**, he married, in 1979, Princess Sisowath Vinayika, and they had two children: Prince Preyaro and Princess Verina.

NORODOM RANARIDDH, Prince (1944-). First prime minister 1993-1997. Ranariddh was born on 2 January 1944 in Phnom Penh, the second son of King **Norodom Sihanouk** by his first wife *neak monéang* Phat Kanhol. He was educated in Phnom Penh and in France. In Cambodia he was editor of *Le Courier Khmer* and delegate to the 1968 United Nations General Assembly. He married **Eng Marie** on 14 September 1968 in Phnom Penh. Prince Ranariddh then went to law school in Aix-en-Provence, France, where he studied for his doctorate in civil law, specialising in maritime law from January 1969, graduating in 1976. In December 1970 he was arrested after captured **National United Front of Kampuchea** guerrillas claimed that they had been paid and supplied by him. Although they gave patently false testimony, Ranariddh was put on trial and was jailed for involvement in various Royalist plots.

He became professor of political science and law at the University of Aix-en-Provence, living in France during the late 1970s. Assuming an active political role for the first time, he became his father's personal representative in Cambodia and Thailand in July 1983 and was appointed commander-in-chief and chief of staff of the **Armée Nationale Sihanoukienne** in February 1986. He then became president of **FUNCINPEC**, one of the three partners in the **Coalition Government of Democratic Kampuchea**, and was appointed to the **Supreme National Council** in 1990-1993. In the transitional government he was copresident and cominister for defence and the interior. He was elected as a deputy for Phnom Penh in the Constituent Assembly in May 1993 and was subsequently appointed prime minister of Cambodia—his FUNCINPEC party having won 45 percent of the vote (making it the largest party both in terms of votes and seats in the Assembly). The title *Samdech krom Preah Norodom Ranariddh* was conferred later that year. During his period as first prime minister, Prince Ranariddh gradually established an international profile, but suffered greatly from accusations that he resembled his father and deferred to him on too many occasions.

Prince Ranariddh's term as prime minister is recognized as one of quiet postwar consolidation and normalization of Cambodia's relations with the world. Tourism in Cambodia resumed and foreign investors began to supply much-needed foreign capital. The economy grew, and the prevalence of foreign companies for the first time began to impinge on all aspects of Cambodian business life. However, on a government level, he was steadily rendered powerless in the face of wide abuses of power by people associated with the rival **Cambodian People's Party (CPP)** as well as his own. Though he attempted in some periods to introduce modern regulations he never succeeded in realising the democratic hopes that were vested in him. The government, largely still controlled by the CPP, failed to clamp down on corruption, illegal logging in the countryside, drug-trafficking or the growing industry linked to the trafficking of women and children.

Disagreements between Ranariddh and **Hun Sen**, especially in relation to negotiations with the **Party of Democratic Kampuchea**, which continued to promote a low-intensity war in the countryside, continued to destabilize the government. In July 1997 while in France, Ranariddh was overthrown in a coup organized by Hun Sen during which many of his leading supporters were murdered and others fled overseas. Although he dedicated himself to fighting his way back to power, due to international pressure and lack of regional support, the prince was forced to reach some form of reconciliation with Hun Sen. In Paris Ranariddh oversaw the publication of his book *Droit public cambodgien*. Returning to Phnom Penh in 1998, he contested the July elections but was defeated by Hun Sen amid allegations of widespread electoral fraud. Ranariddh himself was elected to the National Assembly for **Kampong Cham** and was subsequently appointed the president of the **Senate**.

Prince Ranariddh and Princess Marie have three children: Prince Chakravuth, born on 13 February 1970 in Phnom Penh; Prince Sihariddh, born on 23 June 1972 in Phnom Penh and Princess Rattana Devi, born on 18 June 1974 in Aix-en-Provence.

NORODOM SIHAMONI, Prince (1953-). Born on 14 May 1953 in Phnom Penh, the son of King **Norodom Sihanouk** and his wife Princess **Monique.** He was educated at the Prague Lycée then studied at the Conservatorium of Prague, gaining the first prize in classical dance in 1971. In 1975 he gained a diploma from the Academy of Musical Art in Prague and wrote a thesis on Cambodian Fine Arts. He then studied cinematography in the Democratic People's Republic of Korea. From 1981 he was a teacher in classical dance at the Conservatorium Marius Petipa and the Conservatorium Gabriel Fauré in Paris. In 1984 he became director of the Ballet Deva and, in 1990, director of the film company Kherma. From February 1992 until November 1993 he was the permanent representative of the **Supreme National Council** at the United Nations, and in November 1993 was appointed Cambodian ambassador to the United Nations Educational, Scientific and Cultural Organization. Prince Sihamoni has become King Sihanouk's semiacknowledged heir in recent years, the succession reportedly supported by **Hun Sen** and the several members of the **Cambodian People's Party** who currently hold a majority in the Royal Council.

NORODOM SIHANOUK (1922-). King 1941-1955, 1993-. Born on 31 October 1922 in Phnom Penh, Sihanouk, the most important and enduring figure in 20th century Cambodian politics. He was the only child of Prince **Norodom Suramarit** and Princess **Sisowath Kossamak**. Both his paternal grandparents were children of King **Norodom**, and his maternal grandfather was King **Monivong**, son of King **Sisowath**. In fact, Prince **Norodom Sihanouk** was in the interesting position of all four of his great-grandparents being either sons or, in one instance, a grandson, of King **Ang Duang**. Sihanouk began his education at Lycée François Baudouin and **Lycée Sisowath**, both in Phnom Penh then attended Lycée Chasseloup-Laubat in Saigon.

On 25 April 1941, following the death of his grandfather, King **Monivong**, Sihanouk was summoned back to Phnom Penh by Admiral **Jean Decoux**, the French governor-general who appointed him king. Some of his earlier moves, with the advice of two of his uncles, Prince **Sisowath Monireth** and Prince **Sisowath Monipong**, were to modernise and reform the country. **Thiounn**, minister at the palace for 39 years, was sent into retirement, and there was a brief attempt to modernize the language by using a western-style script—a reform that was rapidly abandoned.

It was in late 1941 that Sihanouk took his first wife, *phat* Kanhol, and they had two children: Princess **Norodom Bopha Devi**, born on 8 January 1943 and Prince **Norodom Ranariddh**, born on 2 January 1944. In 1942 King Sihanouk took his second wife, his aunt, Princess Sisowath Pongsamoni, with whom he remained until 1951. They had seven children: Prince **Norodom Yuvaneath**, born on 17 October 1943; Prince Norodom Ravivongs, born on 8 November 1944; Prince **Norodom Chakrapong**, born on 21 October 1945; Princess Norodom Soriya Roeunsey, born on 6 April 1947; Princess Kanthi Bopha, born in 1948; Prince Norodom Khemanourak, born on 26 September 1949 and Princess **Norodom Botum Bopha**, born on 18 January 1951.

On 9 March 1945, when the Japanese rounded up and jailed the French, King Sihanouk was induced to declare independence which took place on 18 March. What followed was a short-lived Kingdom of Kampuchea, in which Sihanouk's uncles advised him to retain a relatively low profile. However, on 6 August 1945, a crowd of some 30,000 assembled outside the royal palace to demonstrate against the French—the Japanese being about to lose the Pacific War. To preempt the return of the French, on 9 August some national guardsmen rushed the palace and captured most of the cabinet ministers. Sihanouk escaped leaving Monireth to confront the intruders, but the young king still had to make an immediate decision which was to appoint **Son Ngoc Thanh**, a supporter of the coup, as prime minister.

When the French did return to Cambodia, Sihanouk appointed Prince Monireth as prime minister and, withdrawing from politics, remained aloof from day-to-day developments. In 1946 Sihanouk took his third wife, Princess Thavet Norleak, but they had no children. His fourth wife was Princess Sisowath Monikessan, and they had one son: Prince **Norodom Naradipo**, born on 10 February 1946, and later designated as Sihanouk's successor. His fifth wife was *mâm* Manivan Phanivong from Laos, and they had two children: Princess Norodom Suchata, born on 10 March 1953 and Princess **Norodom Arun Rasmey**, born on 2 October 1955. His sixth wife was **Monique Izzi**, daughter of François Izzi, a Frenchman of Italian descent, and his wife Pomme Peang. They had two children: Prince **Norodom Sihamoni**, born on 14 May 1953 and Prince **Norodom Norin-drapong**, born on 18 September 1954. After his marriage to Monique, Sihanouk began to be less restless, and the two shared the rest of their life together.

Although Sihanouk was president of the Council of Ministers from 2-31 May 1950 and again from 16 June 1952 until 23 January 1953, the king later said that it was the death of his daughter, Princess Kanthi Bopha (who died 14 December 1952 of leukaemia), that caused him to embark on a political career. He wrote that her death reminded him of his own mortality, and he therefore gave up the life of a "playboy" prince to become a politician. However, his real entry into the political scene had come some months earlier, when in June 1952 he had supported the movement of troops into Phnom Penh to dismiss the **Huy Kanthoul** government. But it might well have been the death of his daughter that hastened his urge for independence.

Anxious to gain independence for Cambodia, and equally keen on not allowing the **Democrat Party**, which dominated Cambodian politics, to achieve their demands for the French to leave, the king decided to embark on his Royal Crusade for Independence—a mixture of genuine enthusiasm, bravado, press leaks, overseas excursions and threats to arm the population. As a result, the French agreed to grant Cambodia independence on 9 November 1953. Sihanouk was later to compare this action to other countries in Southeast Asia where independence was achieved at a heavy price in lives. In return for this, the French were allowed to maintain their financial interests in the country. Sihanouk was briefly prime minister again from 7-17 April 1954. With the **Geneva Conference** on Indochina in 1954, the amended Cambodian Constitution precluded a king from also taking an active role in politics, and Sihanouk abdicated as king on 2

March 1955. Then, after returning from the **Bandung Conference** in April, he set about establishing his political movement the *Sangkum Reastr Niyum* ("Popular Socialist Community") which defeated all the political parties in the 1955 National Assembly elections. Sihanouk then served as president of the Council of Ministers from 3 October 1955 to 4 January 1956, again from 29 February 1956 to 24 March 1956, from 15 September to 15 October 1956, from December 1956 to 7 July 1957, and again from 10 July 1958 to 12 April 1960.

During this period, Sangkum dominated the Cambodian political scene and Sihanouk traveled around the country many times each month opening new schools, hospitals and agricultural projects. He "resurrected" several royal festivals, some of which had not existed beforehand and took on the role of being a God-King—the man who brought Cambodia prosperity. And certainly Cambodia basked in this new prosperity—the massive impetus that Sihanouk gave to education and the huge increase in the number of schools and the literacy rates led to a burgeoning civil service and well-paid and prosperous government sector. Even though many government employees were inefficient, or in some cases corrupt, most of the country was content and at peace with itself.

Following the death of his father in April 1960, a referendum was held in which Sihanouk won an overwhelming majority of votes cast, becoming head of state from 14 June 1960 until his overthrow on 18 March 1970. Officially he was prime minister only once more, from 17 November 1961 until 29 July 1962. During the late 1950s and the 1960s Sihanouk was the editor of numerous books, newspapers and magazines. He directed **films** and took an active part in the running of the country known by the affectionate title, *Samdech Euv* ("Great or Supreme Father") His speeches were published and distributed—yet he became a victim of his own success. By the mid-1960s the civil service was no longer able to absorb the multitude of graduates keen on white collar jobs, and the economy began to stagnate.

However, Sihanouk's main task during this period was not dealing with the economy of the country, but with matters of state—especially the growing war in Vietnam and how he could extricate Cambodia from the conflict which was rapidly affecting the whole region. It is now well-known that he made a deal with the Vietnamese communists whom he felt would certainly win the war against South Vietnam. In return for turning a blind eye to support for the National Front for the Liberation of South Vietnam, and supplies going through the country (Cambodia was still neutral), after the conclusion of the war, Vietnam would respect Cambodia's borders and sovereignty. The overthrow of Ngo Dinh Diem in 1963, and his subsequent assassination, made Sihanouk wary of the

Americans and led to the reducing of diplomatic ties in 1963 and the closure of the U.S. Embassy in 1965. It was at this point that Sihanouk designated Prince Naradipo as his successor. Stressed and increasingly ill, Sihanouk found relief in filmdirecting.

Sihanouk therefore decided to go to France for a rest and health cure. Meanwhile events in Cambodia led to opposition leaders, especially Prince **Sisowath Sirik Matak** and **Lon Nol**, deciding to go ahead with a plan to overthrow him. On 18 March 1970, while in Moscow, he was dismissed as head of state by the National Assembly and High Council of the Kingdom which had met in joint closed session. The prince went to Beijing where, owing to his personal friendship with **Zhou Enlai**, the Chinese premier, the Chinese government offered him support to fight his way back to power. Sihanouk broadcast an appeal to arms later that month and became president of the **Royal Government of National Union of Kampuchea (GRUNK)** from 1970 until 1975 when the Khmer Republic (which had been declared in October 1970) finally fell after its military defeat. During that time Sihanouk spent much of his time in Beijing, but also his international prestige managed to get many countries to support his government-in-exile. In March 1973 he briefly returned to Cambodia and was filmed at **Angkor Wat**.

In 1975 Sihanouk was prevented from immediately returning to Cambodia and although nominal head of state from 25 April 1975, even after his return on 10 September 1975, he was never allowed to wield any power. In fact, for much of the period he was kept under house arrest. The prince was forced into retirement in 1976, escaping from Phnom Penh with the withdrawing **Democratic Kampuchea (DK)** forces in January 1979. Apparently the Vietnamese had hoped to capture him, but even with the speed of their advance during their three-week war against the DK forces, they were unable so to do.

Resurfacing in Beijing, Sihanouk urged that the **United Nations** should not recognize the new government of **Heng Samrin**. He then went to live in Pyongyang, guest of another of his friends, Kim Il Sung. Several groups of exiles were established to support him—notably **Molinaka**. On 21 March 1981 he established the United National Front for an Independent, Neutral, Peaceful and Cooperative Cambodia (**FUNCINPEC**) which became his political movement. In July 1982 they formally joined in alliance with the ex-**Pol Pot** communists who has taken the name **Party of Democratic Kampuchea** and the **Khmer People's National Liberation Front**, led by **Son Sann**. FUNCINPEC armed forces, the **Armée Nationale Sihanoukienne (ANS)** fought a guerrilla war against the Vietnamese-backed **Hun Sen** government and Sihanouk, as president of the **Coalition Government for Democratic Kampuchea**, lent the exiles massive international prestige.

With the **Paris International Peace Agreement** in 1991, Sihanouk returned to Cambodia on 14 November. However, his attempt to become an unelected president was stymied by the agreement which called for national elections and a constitution. In October 1992 Sihanouk left Phnom Penh, pleading illness, and was only coaxed back to his country by the **United Nations Transitional Authority in Cambodia** in May 1993, on the eve of the elections. When they were over, he became chief of state of the interim government. At that point, the constituent assembly unanimously declared the March 1970 coup d'état against him null and void and reinstated Cambodia's 1970 national flag and national anthem. After a second absence, Sihanouk returned home in September 1993 to promulgate the constitution, which reinstated him, on 24 September, as Cambodia's king, a position he had last occupied in 1955. At that time, his wife, née Monique Izzi, was given the title of Queen Monineath. However the prince returned soon afterward to Beijing, where he continued to receive medical treatment for a prostate condition before coming to Cambodia briefly in 1994. While in exile, he bombarded the fledgling Cambodian government with contradictory messages and admitted to some journalists that he was interested in regaining genuine power.

In early 1995 the prince returned to Phnom Penh for a somewhat longer stay. He seemed to have lost some of his vigor: whether this reflected genuine physical ills, his distress at Cambodian politics or both is impossible to determine. In 1996 he moved to Beijing for health treatment for his increasingly serious cancer. Following Hun Sen's coup in July 1997, Sihanouk prevaricated, but returned to Cambodia, landing at Siem Reap and not meeting with Hun Sen. He later acquiesced in the overthrow of his son, Prince Ranariddh—the succession speculation centering on Prince Norodom Sihamoni. In recent years, plagued by ill health, Sihanouk has reduced public appearances considerably and spends most of his time in China.

Sihanouk's life has been retold countless times, and four major autobiographical books have been published so far: *Sovenirs doux et amers* (Bitter-Sweet Memories) which covers his life until 1970; *My War with the CIA* which covers his "war' with the United States from the 1950s until 1973; *War and Hope*, and *Prisoner of the Khmer Rouge* which covers his life until 1980. The subject of an opera, he has continued to direct films, produced in North Korea, and then again in Cambodia.

NORODOM SIRIVUDH, Prince (1951-). Born on 8 June 1951, son of Prince (later King) **Norodom Suramarit** and his last wife, Kim-An Yeap, he is half brother of King **Norodom Sihanouk**. He married Keo Kosey, his cousin, and they had a son, Prince Siririth. He married, secondly, Christine Alfsen, and they had three children. Sirivudh lived in Paris in the 1970s and then New York. From 1982-1988 he was a member of the **Coalition Government of Democratic Kampuchea** delegation to the **United Nations**, and from 1988-1992 was working in the **FUNCINPEC** offices in Thailand. He moved to Cambodia where he became general-secretary of FUNCINPEC-Kampuchea, and he was in charge of the party office in Phnom Penh from 1992-1993. He was minister for social security and humanitarian aid, and was elected as a FUNCINPEC deputy for **Kampong Cham**, June 1993. After the elections, he was promoted to vice prime minister and minister for foreign affairs and international cooperation. He resigned from the government on 23 October 1994 in solidarity with **Sam Rainsy** (who had resigned three days previously). In 1995 he was involved in a scandal during which he was apparently recorded making a telephone call in which he made remarks about the possible death of **Hun Sen**. Hun Sen immediately sent guards to arrest him, and Sirivudh, still foreign minister, was held under house arrest while the **National Assembly** revoked his immunity from prosecution. The crisis ended after the king's intervention, with Sirivudh being permitted to leave the country for exile in France, all the while insisting upon his innocence. His seat in the Assembly remained vacant until the 1998 elections. During those elections, his house in Phnom Penh was used as the headquarters for the **Sam Rainsy Party**. Allowed to return from exile in 2000, he became once again general secretary of FUNCINPEC in 2001.

NORODOM SURAMARIT (1896-1960). King 1955-1960. The second child of Prince Norodom Sutharot, Prince Suramarit was born on 6 March 1896 in **Phnom Penh**. He was educated at Collège Sisowath, Phnom Penh, and Lycée Chasseloup-Laubat, Saigon. After returning from South Vietnam he entered the Colonial Administration in 1918, and soon afterward became Aide de Camp to his father. He married Princess **Sisowath Kossamak Nearireath** in 1920 in Phnom Penh and they had one son, Prince **Norodom Sihanouk**, born in 1922. Following the succession of his father-in-law to the throne in 1927, he embarked on a career in the government. Promoted to chancellor at the royal palace in 1929, minister of marine in March 1929, he later held portfolios of trade and agriculture. Prince Suramarit later married Princess Sisowath Duong Mathuret, and his third wife was Khun Tep Kanha Sophea Kim-An Yeap, daughter of **Kim An**, a provincial chief. Suramarit and Yeap had three children: Princess **Norodom Vichara**, born in 1946; Prince **Norodom Sirivudh**, born in 1951 and Prince **Norodom Preyasophon**, born in 1954.

Although he was working under the French, Suramarit was a passionate nationalist, a friend of **Pach Chhoeun**, an early nationalist leader and support from Suramarit enabled **Son Ngoc Thanh** to establish *Nagaravatta*, the first Khmer-language newspaper. The prince was sent to France just before World War II to settle difficulties with the Colonial Ministry, and in 1941 he resigned his ministerial post and became chairman of the Council of Regency for his son who had succeeded to the throne, whereupon he assumed the title Samdech Preah Borum Reachea Beida. Prince Suramarit acceded to the throne with the abdication of his son, Sihanouk, becoming king on 2 March 1955. He was crowned on 5 March 1956, and during his reign gained much prestige for the royal family by remaining aloof from inter-factional disputes within the government and retaining the dignity of the office. He died on 3 April 1960 and was cremated in Phnom Penh with his funeral lasting from 20-27 August 1960.

NORODOM VICHARA, Princess (1946-). Born on 17 August 1946, she was the daughter of **Norodom Suramarit**, half sister of **Norodom Sihanouk** and full sister of Prince **Norodom Sirivudh**. Her first husband was Tep Samana, son of **Tep Phan**, and her second husband was Yves Dumont whom she married in 1983. A member of **FUNCINPEC**, she was elected to the National Assembly for **Siem Reap** in 1998.

NORODOM YUVANEATH, Prince (1943-). Born on 17 October 1943, the eldest son of King **Norodom Sihanouk** and Princess Sisowath Pongsamoni, Yuvaneath has never been acknowledged as his father's heir. His civil functions were restricted to nonpolitical events such as the 1959 World Scout Jamboree when he represented Cambodia. He married *neang* Pheup and they had a daughter, Chhavarangsi. With his second wife, Tea Kim Yin, they had four children: Prince Yuveakdury, Prince Ravouth, Princess Pekina and Princess Yuveadevi. Leaving Phnom Penh on 13 March 1970, he officially joined the **Royal Government of National Union of Kampuchea** but did not return to his country after the defeat of the **Khmer Republic** of **Lon Nol** in 1975. Instead he worked in a Hong Kong factory then as a waiter in a local restaurant. From 1980 until 1994 he lived in Rhode Island and worked for a company making surgical implements. In 1993 he was appointed to the **Throne Council**.

NOU BENG (1935-). Born in 1935 in **Ratanakiri**, from the Lao minority, Beng joined the **Khmer Issarak** in 1952 and in 1954 was sent to Hanoi where he studied medicine and sanitary hygiene. He joined the **National United Front of Kampuchea** in 1971 but broke with the **Communist Party of Kampuchea** in 1974, returning to Vietnam. In December 1978 he rallied to the **United Front for the National Salvation of Kampuchea** and in April 1980 was appointed **People's Revolutionary Party of**

Kampuchea (PRPK) member in charge of health, then minister of health and social affairs in February 1981. From May 1981 until May 1993 he represented Ratanikiri in the National Assembly. Vice-president of the National Assembly, he was president of the Commission for Culture and Social Action. In January 1987 he was appointed vice-president of the PRPK for **Kratié** and was president of the People's Committee of Kratié province. Nou Beng was third candidate on the **Cambodian People's Party** list in Kratié in May 1993 and was not elected. On 18 December 1993 he was appointed governor of Kratié province.

NOU, KASSIE né **Neou Chantha**. Born in Oudong, he was a translator for the British Broadcasting Corporation. His wife and children were killed during the **Democratic Kampuchea (DK)** period but he managed to survive, although he was held at the DK prison camp at Kach Roteh. On 8 June 1979 he was one of the 45,000 refugees who escaped into Thailand at Preah Vihear. The secretary-general of the Association of Cambodian Survivors, he owned a gas station in Washington, D.C., and lived at Falls Church, Virginia. An opponent of the **People's Republic of Kampuchea**, he was an interpreter for the United Nations in Cambodia 1992-1993 and established the Cambodian Institute of Human Rights in September 1993. He was vice-chairman of the National Election Commis-sion in 1998 resigning before the formal announcement of **Hun Sen**'s victory.

NOU NEOU, Mme. A keen Buddhist, she was a night club performer who also owned a Phnom Penh bookshop. Neou was elected to the National Assembly for Preah Molou, **Pursat**, in July 1966, and in October was appointed under-secretary of state for tourism by Lon Nol. In 1969 Neou was a member of the National Committee for Khmer-German Friendship and in 1970 married **Lam Ken**, a prominent veterinary surgeon, later brigadier general. In October 1970 she founded and was leader of the Patriotic Women's Youth Commandos. Nearly two years later she founded the **Women's Party** to contest the September 1972 legislative elections, but support failed to materialize, and her party withdrew its members' candidacy.

NOU SAING KHAN or **Nu Sangkhan**. In 1971 he was appointed advisor to Lon Nol for maritime resources. He joined **FUNCINPEC** and was fourth on the party list for Siem Reap in 1993. Although not elected at the time, on 25 June 1995, he took the seat vacated by **Sam Rainsy** who was expelled from the National Assembly. Saing Khan was appointed vice-minister for transport in 1993 and was under-secretary of state of public works and transport from 1994. He is now a Secretary of State for Urbanization and Construction.

NOUTH NARANG. He gained a degree in literature then studied tourism from 1972-1975 he was studying at the École Pratique des Hautes Études, Paris. During the 1980s he was director of the **Centre de Documentation et de Recherche sur la Civilisation Khmère (CEDOREK)** and in 1992 joined the **Cambodian People's Party**. He was appointed minister of culture and fine arts in 1993-1994. He was co-author, with Michel Butor, of *Angkor silencieux*.

NUON CHEA né **Lau Ben Kon (1927-)**. "Brother Number Two" within the **Communist Party of Kampuchea (CPK)**, he was born in **Battambang** of Sino-Khmer parents. His mother was a cook for the royal family when they visited Battambang, and during **World War II**, when Battambang came under Thai control, Chea pursued secondary studies in Bangkok under the patronage of his sister's brother-in-law, **Sieu Heng** who later became secretary of the protocommunist **Khmer People's Revolutionary Party (KPRP)**. At Thammasat University, Chea joined the **Communist Party of Thailand**. He transferred his allegiance to the **Indochina Communist Party (ICP)** in 1947 or 1948. When in 1951 the party was divided into three national branches, the Cambodian party, the KPRP, elected his former patron, Sieu Heng, as secretary. Both men subsequently traveled to Hanoi for brief periods of political training, 1952-1954.

He returned to Phnom Penh in 1954 and worked closely with Saloth Sar (**Pol Pot**), also by this time back from France and a member of the KPRP. At a party congress held in Phnom Penh in September 1960, following Sieu Heng's devastating defection to the government, the party was reorganized as the **Workers' Party of Kampuchea** and **Tou Samouth** became the its first secretary. Nuon Chea was given the second position. When Samouth disappeared in 1962, however, Saloth Sar became acting secretary in Chea's place, after rumors had been spread that Chea was still in contact with Sieu Heng. When Sar fled to the *maquis* in 1963, Nuon Chea remained in Phnom Penh and worked there in secret with Vorn Vet until 1967 when **Norodom Sihanouk** crushed the **Samlaut Uprising** in which Chea may have been tangentially involved. From then on, he remained at Saloth Sar's side, as "Brother Number Two," charged with training and organizational matters. In 1975, following the victory of the **National United Front of Kampuchea**, under communist control by 1975, Chea, continued to be in charge of internal party organization, propaganda and training. In the **Democratic Kampuchea** (DK) period he sometimes served as acting prime minister and was never far from Pol Pot's side.

Nuon Chea remained important in the party (ostensibly dissolved in 1981) after the defeat and collapse of the DK regime and presided over occasional study sessions for cadre, held at bases in Thailand. Rumors in 1995 suggested that he was in poor health, but both he and **Khieu Samphan** appeared fit in December 1998 when they surrendered to the government and traveled to Phnom Penh to meet with **Hun Sen** in 1998. Among those likely to be prosecuted if an international tribune is established for the purpose of investigating war crimes and crimes against humanity in 1975-1978, he lives in quiet retirement near **Pailin.**

NUON DUONG (1908-). Variously described as having been born in either **Kratié** or **Phnom Penh**, he studied at the Pali School and was a member of the Tripitaka Commission at the Buddhist Institute. He later became a bicycle salesman in Phnom Penh and was an organizer of the July 1942 demonstration. Arrested by the French, Duong was sentenced to death by a court martial in Saigon, but the sentence was commuted to life imprisonment with hard labor. Released in March 1945, he returned to Phnom Penh and started work on *Nagaravatta*. With the arrest of **Son Ngoc Thanh**, he fled to Cochinchina then to Thailand where he was vice-president of the Committee for the Liberation of the Khmer People. Head of information of the committee, he later became their treasurer in Thailand. From May 1952 he was working for Son Ngoc Thanh in Surin. Returning to **Phnom Penh**, he joined the Democrat Party and contested the 1955 National Assembly elections for Kratié. After the election, he appears to have retired from politics.

NUON KHOEUN (1944-1977). A prominent nationalist writer of the early 1970s, Nuon Khoeun was born at Angkor, Siem Reap district of **Siem Reap** province. His unwed mother had settled there voluntarily because she wanted the child that was the cause of her separation from her father's household. Khoeun's father, a cross-border trader or trafficker during the occupation years, visited only rarely as he was growing up. He had married after the war and had other children. His parents were reunited only briefly when his father became a widower. Educated at the local temple school, in 1957-1961 he attended Lycée Siem Reap, earning his Baccalaureate and from 1963-1968, he studied at the Faculty of Pedagogy, University of Phnom Penh earning a *Licence* in history in 1968. A teacher from 1965, he taught at Collège Ang Tasom but was assigned to a lycée in Kampong Cham city in 1968-69. Startled by the economic impact of informal trading along the frontier with Vietnam and "the corruption that touched everyone"—people were "horribly shocked" by the state casino and the involvement of the Royal family—he published, under pseudonyms, a series of highly critical articles in the national press. In December 1969 two articles, lightly revised and expanded, appeared as a Khmer language book entitled *March to West*. It covered imagery arousing fears of the decline of the Khmer nation into historical oblivion as a result of the inexorable rise of the Vietnamese. The first edition sold out immediately, partly the result of the Republic of Vietnam embassy buying copies to destroy. A second larger edition published in 1970 fanned anti-Vietnamese sentiments already aroused by the coup promoters. The South Vietnamese Embassy sought to ban the book, removed from shelves in Phnom Penh shops only after after substantial numbers had been sold. Pro-Sihanouk protestors descended on Lycée Siem Reap after 18 March 1970, demanding Nuon Khuoen, who had fled in fear of his life to the capital.

From 1970-1973, Nuon Khuon was a part-time history lecturer at the Faculty of Arts, Phnom Penh University. In 1972, on his first only trip overseas, he represented Cambodia at the international conference of Francophones held in Dakar, Senegal, visiting Paris on the way back to Phnom Penh. Writing mostly for *Khmer Ekareach* or *Nokor Thom,* his political commentaries betrayed deep disillusionment with the **Khmer Republic**, described first as an "unfinished" revolution and then as "lost." Elected leader of the national teacher's union in 1972, he disappeared from Phnom Penh on 17 March 1973, together with **Tourn Sok Phallar**, both eluding their surveillance officers and momentarily concealing their defection to the **National United Front of Kampuchea (FUNK)** by spreading rumours of his arrest in the wake of a crackdown against striking schoolteachers.

Assigned to a base in **Kratié** where he worked in the underground information ministry, Khoeun returned to Phnom Penh after 1975, to work in the Ministry of Information headed by **Hu Nim**. Among the first of the non-communist FUNK intellectuals to fall under suspicion, he was taken to **S-21** on 21 October 1976 where he appears to have refused to confess to any wrongdoing. He was sent to his death on 12 May 1977.

NUON NINARA (1935-). Born on 15 May 1935 at Koh Sautin, **Kampong Cham**, Ninara served in the army and rallied to the **National United Front of Kampuchea (FUNK)** in 1970. He worked on sabotage activities before being posted to FUNK-controlled territory. He spent the period of 1975-1979 in the countryside and in 1980 became a refugee on the Thai-Cambodian border. On 11 October 1980 he joined **Molinaka** at Nong Chan and became an administrative officer at Site B. In February 1992 he was appointed to the National Council of **FUNCINPEC** and was elected as a deputy for Kampong Cham on 10 June 1993. In October 1993 he was appointed to the Commission for the Interior, National Defense and Anti-corruption.

NUON PAET. A commander in the National Army of **Democratic Kampuchea**, it was he who held the three European hostages taken during a train robbery in 1994. After quietly surrendering to the Royal Government in 1995, together with a small group of former National Army of Democratic Kampuchea fighters and their families, he lived under government protection until just after the 1998 elections. He was then arrested and jailed by the **Hun Sen** government, then anxious to improve relations with the West. He was brought to trial in mid-1999, convicted of murder and kidnapping and sentenced to life imprisonment. His associate and deputy at the time, **Chhouk Rin,** testified against him.

-O-

O'SMACH. A township in **Battambang** province, on the Cambodian-Thai border, it was the center of a border dispute in December 1965 when two Cambodians, an army officer and a police officer, were both killed. It rose to prominence in August 1997 as the last part of Cambodian territory where **FUNCINPEC** soldiers held out against those loyal to **Hun Sen.**

L'OBSERVATEUR **("The Observer").** A French-language newspaper published and edited by **Khieu Samphan** from 22 September 1959 to 12 August 1960, it appeared twice-weekly for a total of 90 issues. Initially tolerated by Prince **Norodom Sihanouk,** *L'Observateur* promoted a modernist culture and ideological standpoints deeply hostile to monarchy, paternalism and dependence. Its editorials and features focused on topics ranging from the neglect and scorn of the poor in Cambodian society, the Cold War, Indian films (criticized for fantastic themes) and the solar system, features on science often taking aim at "feudalist" superstitions, including astrology. *L'Observateur* sought in these ways to reform the political culture of the Sihanouk state. In opposition to prevailing elite views, it denied that Cambodia was uniquely blessed by nature and often argued that hierarchies of inequality were destructive of social order and were neither natural nor desirable. When the paper generated a buzz inside Francophone intellectual circles, Prince Sihanouk denounced it as "communist" grouping it with the Khmer-language **newspapers,** *Pracheachon, Mittapheap* and *Ekapheap* and indeed many clandestine communists, for example, **Son Sen**, wrote for *L'Observateur* using pen names.

As a French-educated intellectual, Khieu Samphan enjoyed greater status within political society than many other editors and publishers, notably **Nop Bophan,** and for a time, he seemed less vulnerable to the personal harassment and abuse suffered by others. But when he wrote editorials in their defense or in defense of freedom of the press, he, too, was assaulted, beaten and stripped naked by agents of **Kou Roun** on a busy Phnom Penh street in July 1960. The ensuing furore in the rest of the press unnerved the prince. He judged the newspaper reading public to be taking sides with the "reds," his rage made all the deeper by the succession crisis surrounding the unexpected death of King **Norodom Suramarit** and the seizure of power by Kong Lê in a neutralist, military coup in Vientiane. All progressive newspapers, including *L'Observateur*, were proscribed in August 1960. Some 30 reporters, typesetters and editors, including Khieu Samphan, were jailed without charge for several weeks. *L'Observateur* never reappeared.

OC-EO. Archaeological site in southern Vietnam, linked by scholars to "**Funan**" and excavated by the **École Française d'Extrême-Orient** over three months in 1944. The site covered an area of 450 hectares and consisted of a landmass enclosed by canals. Excavations revealed foundations in stone and brick for impressively large structures while shards, beads and jewelry uncovered at the site revealed its prosperity and its occupancy at the beginning of the Christian era by people in contact, over great distances, with India and the Roman Empire. Other artifacts from Oc-Eo are datable as late as the sixth century AD. It has been suggested that the site was one of many port cities that sprang up in the region at this time to deal with trade between the Indian subcontinent and China.

ODDAR MEANCHEY. This province was first created in 1965, with its capital at Samrong. At its creation the province had a population of 28,000, occupying some 7,666 square kilometers. It disappeared as a discrete **administrative division** under the Pol Pot regime and was part of a province named Siem Reap-Oddar Meanchey in the **People's Republic of Kampuchea**. Between 1993-1999 parts of it were incorporated into **Banteay Meanchey** and **Siem Reap** provinces. It was reestablished on 27 April 1999, receiving a governor and an annual budget of 99 million riels. In the view of the authorities in Phnom Penh, creation of the province permitted closer control of cross-border trading and communications at **O'Smach**, a royalist military stronghold after the July 1997 **coup d'état**. Now a casino town, there are about 700 gamblers per day visiting O'Smach Resort and Royal Hill Resort, and secondary economic activities, including a sex trade, have emerged. The March 1998 census reports it has a population of 68,279, with 32.7 percent being residents of urban areas, more than twice the national average of 15.7.

OEUR HUNLY (1946-). Born on 16 March 1946 at Kohdach, Mok Kampoul, Kandal, his older sister married Chan Phâl, a **Khmer Issarak** commander in Kandal. He attended Lycée Tuol Kork and **Lycée Sisowath** then worked in the administration of Pochentong International Airport, Phnom Penh. In 1974 he came to Melbourne, Australia to study and was second-in-charge of the Cambodian Information Office in Canberra, along with **Keat Sokun** and **Theam Bun Srun**. Hunly was appointed the second representative of Prince **Norodom Sihanouk** in Australia in 1987 and was an active member of **FUNCINPEC** and also the Australian Liberal Party. In 1997 he returned to Cambodia and in the 1998 elections was the sixth reserve on the FUNCINPEC party list for Kandal.

OEUR TRALUCH. He was a member of the **Liberal Party** and was elected in the 1951 National Assembly elections for Kampong Trabek, **Prey Veng**. In 1953 he served in the National Consultative Assembly and in 1966, as a member of Sangkum, was elected to the National Assembly for Cham, Prey Veng. One of the most vociferous critics of the **Viet Cong** and North Vietnamese presence in Cambodia in 1969-1970, he led many of the National Assembly debates on the issue which led to the overthrow of Sihanouk. His wife, Ker Saksithan, worked at the **Preah Keth Mealea Hospital**.

OFFICE 100. The code name for the Vietnamese military encampment in eastern Cambodia which served as a refuge for Saloth Sar (**Pol Pot**) and other high ranking Cambodian Communists in 1963-1965; the camp moved back and forth across the frontier in response to U.S. and South Vietnamese military pressures. In later years, Pol Pot and his colleagues were reluctant to discuss the years they spent in Office 100 which marked the lowest ebb of their political fortunes.

OFFICE 870. The code name for the closely guarded encampment in Trat province, eastern Thailand which served as **Pol Pot**'s headquarters in the late 1980s (see **"870"**). The camp was located just inside Thailand, some 20 kilometers east of Trat city. **Khmer Rouge** political and military cadre visited the camp on a regular basis to receive politico-military briefings lasting several days from Pol Pot and his immediate colleagues.

OK NALL (1926-c1975). Born on 12 July 1926 in **Svay Rieng**, he graduated in law from the Royal University of Phnom Penh in October 1953 and was attached to the Prime Minister's Office in 1958. In 1966 he was appointed governor of Kratié, and by 1969 he was a director of the Bureau of Information—it has been alleged that he was an Australian agent, but evidence is at best skimpy. By June 1970 he was editor of *Le Courier Phnompenhois*. During the Khmer Republic, he was appointed to the committee to oversee the June 1972 presidential elections. Even though at the time he proclaimed **Lon Nol** the winner, he later wrote to **Keo Ann** telling him that he had won. This evidence was used by Keo Ann to establish his Government of Free Cambodia based in France.

OK SAKUN (1932-). Born on 26 December 1932 in **Pursat** province, he attended **Lycée Sisowath** before gaining a government scholarship to study engineering in France. He failed his entrance examination to the École Centrale and was recalled to **Phnom Penh** where he worked for the national railways. It was he who likely arranged the venue for the Congress of the **Khmer People's Revolutionary Party** in 1960 which resulted in the party's reorganization. In 1963 he was among those named by Prince **Norodom Sihanouk** on the "list of 34" suspected communists whom the prince invited to form a cabinet, as they "knew how China worked." Fearing **Workers' Party of Kampuchea** organizational activities secrets had been uncovered, **Ieng Sary, Son Sen** and Saloth Sar (**Pol Pot**) disappeared into the countryside while Ok Sakun and his French wife returned to France. In 1970 he helped to organize the **National United Front of Kampuchea** among Cambodians in France and was appointed the Front's Central Committee and head of its Paris office which became the unofficial, de facto diplomatic mission of Sihanouk's **Royal Government of National Unon of Kampuchea (GRUNK)**. He returned to Cambodian in December 1975 together with most other FUNK and GRUNK representatives and diplomatic personnel, being assigned after brief periods of reeducation to the Foreign Minister of **Democratic Kampuchea**. After 1979 he returned to France having been appointed representative of Cambodia attached to the United Nations Educational, Scientific and Cultural Organization, an appointment later renewed by the **Coalition Government of Democratic Kampuchea**, a position held from 1982 until November 1993. Partly in this capacity, and partly as a supporter of the **Party of Democratic Kampu-chea,** he observed the first talks between Sihanouk and **Hun Sen** at Fère-en-Tardennois, France, representing **Khieu Samphan,** foreign minister of the CGDK, on 7-8 November 1988. He retired in 1993 and lives in France.

"OLD PEOPLE." This phrase was used to designate those who lived in the liberated zones controlled by the **National United Front of Kampuchea (FUNK)** before the Communist victory of 17 April 1975. *See also* BASE PEOPLE; "NEW PEOPLE."

ONG THONG HOEUNG (1945-). Born on 7 August 1945 at Chrung Romeas, Koh Thom, Kandal, he studied political economy at Vincennes, University of Paris VII from 1969-1976, joining the **National United Front of Kampuchea** soon after it was established in 1970. By 1974 he was first secretary in the diplomatic mission in Paris of the **Royal Government of National Union** in charge of relations with the European Community. Summoned by to **Democratic Kampuchea** in 1976, he was assigned to reeducation classes and then sent to a "special camp" in the red earth area of **Kampong Cham** where he remained interned. Shifted to Boeung Trabek rehabilitation center in **Phnom Penh** in 1978, he was evacuated from Phnom Penh just in advance of the Vietnamese occupation of the capital but later slipped away from the retreating **Democratic Kampuchea** authorities to return to the capital where he was employed as an archivist at **Tuol Sleng,** from June to October 1979. He then sought refugee in **Khao-I-Dang**, later Phanat Nikhon, holding centers in **Thailand.** Resettled in Belgium in 1982, he edited the influential political magazine *Perspectives* in the late 1980s. Since the mid-1990s, he has supported first the **Khmer Nation Party**, since 1998, the **Sam Rainsy Party**, being leader of the branch in Belgium. Since 2000 he has been managing director of the Belgium human rights magazine *Monde des Droits de l'Homme* ("World of Human Rights").

OP KIM ANG (1923-1975). One of the hardline Republicans who overthrew **Norodom Sihanouk** in 1970, Op Kim Ang was born on 1 January 1923 at Kanchrieach, **Prey Veng**. He graduated from the Royal School of Administration and was governor of **Stung Treng** from 1955-1956, Prey Veng from 1956-1958 and **Kampong Cham** from 1958-1960. After that he served as president of the Ministries of the Interior and National Defense. In 1962 Op Kim Ang was elected to the National Assembly for Prey Veng, and then served as minister for national defense in the first **Lon Nol** government. He left office with Lon Nol in April 1967, returning in August 1969 as third deputy prime minister in charge of finance and planning, and the coordination of economic and financial affairs. In March 1970 Op Kim Ang was one of the leading members of the plot that resulted in Sihanouk's deposition on 18 March, and he was appointed as minister of the interior, security and religious affairs in July 1970. In March 1972 his younger brother, Op Kim Aun, was involved in a series of actions which led up to the **Koy Pech Incident** in which Koy Pech, a student, took refuge in the university buildings in a protest against the Lon Nol government.

Op Kim Ang was a prominent member of the **Republican Party** of Prince **Sisowath Sirik Matak** when it was founded in 1972, being elected to its 10-man Central Committee on 23 July. However, the party boycotted the legislative and **senate** elections in September. However in an attempt to reconcile Lon Nol with the Republicans, in 1973 Op Kim Ang was appointed advisor to Lon Nol. In October he became second vice-prime minister in charge of public works and coordination of Departments of Community Development, Labor, Public Well-being, Postal Services, Telecommunications and Tourism. In December when **In Tam** resigned as prime minister, Op Kim Ang was first vice-prime minister and minister of public works under **Long Boret**. After the departure of **Saukham Khoy** with the Americans on 11 April 1975, Op Kim Ang was co-opted as a representative of the Republican Party on the Supreme Committee of **Sak**

Suthsakhan. He remained in Phnom Penh until the fall of the Republic, and was killed soon after being captured 17 April 1975. His son went to France and became editor of *Moul Khmer*, a newsletter published by **Sim Var**.

OPERATION BREAKFAST. This was the code word for the secret **United States** bombing of Cambodia which started on 18 March 1969. It involved the bombing of the Prey Veng/South Vietnam border area, west and northwest of Tay Ninh where the **Viet Cong** had established sanctuaries which they believed the Americans would not attack. Kept secret from the American public, Operation Breakfast ceased in April 1970, following the overthrow of Prince **Norodom Sihanouk** by **Lon Nol**. Whether or not the Americans received Sihanouk's genuine assent to the bombing is not known. An *impromptu* remark made by Sihanouk to the American emissary Chester Bowles in 1968 indicated he would not object to U.S. assaults on Vietnamese sanctuaries and this was later cited by Henry Kissinger to justify both the bombings and U.S. secrecy. The United States and Cambodia resumed diplomatic relations, broken in 1965, while the secret campaign was in full swing.

OPERATIONS CHENLA I and II. These were military operations launched by **Lon Nol**'s army against Vietnamese armed forces in 1970 and 1971. The objective was to free communications between **Phnom Penh** and Kampong Thom city. Both operations were supported by the **United States** to divert pressure on U.S. forces in **Vietnam**, and both were marred by faulty planning and cavalier execution. Lon Nol's troops were pinned down along main roads and suffered heavy casualties. Chenla II collapsed in December 1971 when Vietnamese troops, with support from some Khmer forces, dispersed the Phnom Penh columns causing a disorderly retreat of Republican forces, who abandoned their weapons and vehicles en route. Chenla II was the last offensive operation mounted by the Khmer Republic. *See also* BARAY.

OPERATION EAGLE-PULL. On 10 April 1975, when it became clear that **Phnom Penh** would fall to the **Khmer Rouge** in a matter of days, an evacuation of American personnel, Cambodian government officials and third-country nationals was organized for 11 April. However, although **Saukham Khoy**, the acting president, and **Long Botta** did join the evacuation, the rest of the cabinet refused to leave. The evacuation of 276 people on 11 April was the first **United States** evacuation from any country since the communist victory in mainland China in 1949.

OPERATION FREEDOM DEAL. This was the **United States** bombing campaign against Cambodian targets initiated in 1973 following the refusal of the **Royal Government of National Union of Kampuchea** to enter into a cease-fire with the **Lon Nol** regime. During the campaign, which began in February and lasted until August 1973, U.S. planes dropped half a million tons of bombs onto Cambodian soil, more than three times the amount dropped on Japan in the closing months of World War II. Casualties, certainly high, were never fully assessed. The main advantage of the bombing, from the U.S. point of view, was that it delayed the fall of **Phnom Penh**. That the casualties were inflicted on a country with which America was not at war and where no American lives were endangered was never seriously debated in U.S. government circles, but popular opposition to the campaign led to the bombing being halted, under U.S. Congressional pressure, in August 1973.

OPERATION SAMMAKI ("Solidarity"). A Cambodian military operation commanded by Prince **Norodom Sihanouk** in early 1953 to demonstrate the offensive capacities of the Cambodian army no longer under French control. The zone, in **Battambang**, chosen for the operation had been used by communist resistance forces, most of whom had left the area before the operation took place. After several weeks of desultory operations, seven "enemies" were killed and five prisoners captured. **Lon Nol**, acting for the first time in a military capacity, handled publicity for the operation— praising Sihanouk's military skills.

OUDONG. The royal capital of Cambodia from 1602 until 1811 and again from 1847 to 1866, before its transfer to Phnom Penh (40 kilometers to the south) under the French protectorate in 1866. The ashes of many of Cambodia's kings are buried on the slopes of a small hill rising above the plain. Oudong was fought over and bombarded in the 1970-1975 war, and many of its handsome 19th century Buddhist temples were destroyed. However, many of the stupas which hold the ashes of the kings have survived such as those of King **Chey Chetta II**, King **Ang Duang** and King **Sisowath Monivong**.

OUKTHOL, ANDRÉ (1947-1980). A student in Lyon in the early 1970s, he had been a supporter of the **National United Front of Kampuchea** **(FUNK)** but moved to support **Lon Nol** after fighting between students in Paris culminating in the Cambodia House incidents in January 1973. Later, claiming to be Prince Soriavong (son of Prince **Norodom Kantol**), he reemerged on the Thai-Cambodian border as head of his own provisional government. Nicknamed the "mad prince," he was killed in January 1980 in an interfactional dispute on the border.

OUK THOUTCH (1894-19). Born in **Phnom Penh**, he was educated at **Lycée Sisowath**. He was a secretary in the administrative services and was *chauvraysrok* in **Siem Reap** and **Svay Rieng**. Appointed chef de cabinet at the Ministry of Agriculture, he was minister of religion in 1947 and secretary-general of the office of the prime minister in 1950-1951. Thoutch, the father of **Thonn Ouk**, was appointed to the National Consultative Council in 1953 and contested the 1955 **High Council of the Kingdom** elections for civil servants (administration). He was president of the High Council in March 1953 and contested the 1959 High Council elections for the government administration. His wife died on 17 February 1964.

OUM CHHEANG NGUON (1905-   ). Born on 1 July 1905 in **Kampong Cham**, the son of Oum Mok and Mme (née Ea Hak Sea), he was the younger brother of **Oum Chheangsun**. Chheang Nguon entered the government service in 1925 and soon rose to the position of governor of Kampong Thom and later of **Stung Treng**, **Siem Reap**, and assistant mayor of Phnom Penh. He served in the French colonial forces in **World War II**. In 1949 he was chief of the King's Civil List and in 1951 was appointed first secretary of the Cambodian Legation at Bangkok. He was director of the Bureau of Economic and Financial Affairs to the president of the Council of Ministers and represented Cambodia at the Economic Commission for Asia and the Far East. Later Oum Chheang Nguon served as advisor to the High Commission in Paris, councilor then chargé to the Embassy in Tokyo and ambassador to Laos. He had married Ea Neang in 1924 and they had eleven children.

OUM CHHEANGSUN (1900-   ). Prime minister in 1951 and 1956. Born on 1 June 1900 at **Kampong Cham**, son of Oum Mok and Mme (née Ea Hak Sea), Chheangsun was the brother of **Oum Chheang Nguon**. After completing his schooling, he became an instructor in the educational system and later was appointed as inspector of secondary education in 1941. By 1945 he was chief of the education service. In 1947 he helped **Khim Tith** form the **National Union** and was elected to the High Council of the Kingdom in 1948 to represent civil servants (technical branch). He was also on the Royal Council and was president in 1950. On 3 March 1951 he was appointed prime minister, beginning his second administration on 14 May. He was in charge of organizing the September 1951 elections to the **National Assembly**, ending his term on 12 October. He contested the elections to the **High Council** in 1952. In June he accepted the post of director of the Prime Minister's Office. In 1955 Oum Chheangsun joined the **Sangkum** and was elected to the 1955 National Assembly for Mien, Kampong Cham, and served briefly as president of Sangkum as well as president of the National Assembly. He was prime minister again from 5 January to 29 February 1956. In 1958 he was named ambassador to

Vietnam. He contested the 1959 High Council elections for the technical branch of the civil service. Oum Chheangsun married Nginn Leang.

OUM MANNORINE (1924-). The half brother of Queen Monineath (Princess **Monique Sihanouk**), he was the mainstay of the Royalist regime in Phnom Penh in the late 1960s. Mannorine was the son of Oum Phankeo, a colonel in the French colonial army, and his second wife, Mme Pomme Peang. They had five children, Mannorine, being born on 4 March 1924 in Phnom Penh. The second son, Oum Vinavuth was an army officer killed by the **Khmer Issarak** in 1948, and the youngest child, Oum Sophanith married Ieu Pannakar, son of **Ieu Koeus**.

A career soldier, Oum Mannorine was a member of the **Greenshirts** in 1945 and then served in the army and was a major in the department of surface defense, becoming under-secretary of state for surface defense in the **Son Sann** government from 1 May 1967 to 30 January 1968. He was responsible for quelling the **Samlaut Uprising** and was secretary of state for surface defense from 31 January 1968 until 13 August 1969. When **Lon Nol** became prime minister for the second time, in 1969, Oum Mannorine, now a lieutenant colonel, remained in charge of surface defense until his forced resignation on 17 March 1970. Just prior to his resignation, he had been involved in several attempts to prevent the overthrow of Prince **Norodom Sihanouk**. Indeed, he had managed to forestall the plan to topple the Prince on 16 March and had attempted to have Lon Nol arrested that evening. Oum Mannorine was held under house arrest by Lon Nol until 20 June 1973 when he was released and flew to China on 5 November 1973. There he learned Chinese, before moving to France where he became a restauranteur.

He returned to Phnom Penh and was received by **Heng Samrin** in March 1992 and was later appointed chef de cabinet to King Norodom Sihanouk and made a general. In 1993 he was appointed royal ambassador to the Democratic People's Republic of Korea. Oum Mannorie married Kep Sonn, a teacher, on 1 January 1949, and they had six children. The fourth, Manola, married Peter Schier, a German sinologist who has published several studies of Cambodian politics.

OUM SAM (1911-). Born at Chak Angre, **Kandal**, he graduated from the Cambodian School of Administration and after being a magistrate in **Phnom Penh** and **Takeo**, Sam became a judge. A member of the **Victorious Northeastern Khmer Party**, he was elected to the National Assembly in 1951 for **Siem Reap** town, their safest seat. From June 1952 until January 1953 he was secretary of state for public health and social action. In 1953 he served in the National Consultative Assembly. In 1958 he was elected to the National Assembly for **Kampot** town.

-P-

PACH CHHOEUN (1896-1971). Journalist, librarian and patriot. Born in **Phnom Penh**, Pach Chhoeun enlisted as an interpreter in the French colonial army in **World War I** and served in Flanders. Trained as an archivist in Hanoi in the 1920s, he returned to Phnom Penh and was in the French colonial administration until 1925 when he resigned to work in business, being employed in commercial houses and banks in 1927-1936. During this time he was director of the *Nagaravatta* newspaper of **Son Ngoc Thanh**. From 1936-1942 he lived in north Vietnam, returning to Phnom Penh where he was involved in the July 1942 demonstration against the French. Arrested, he was sentenced to death, commuted to hard labor for life on the prison island of **Poulo Condore** until he was released in March 1945. Back in Phnom Penh, he took up a position as minister of the national economy and recovery from August to October 1945, fleeing Phnom Penh with the return of the French and working with the **Viet Minh**. He surrendered to the French in May 1946 and was imprisoned by the French and exiled to **Cochinchina**, and then to France from 1947-1950.

He returned in November 1950, after the French president pardoned him. He campaigned on behalf of the Democrat Party in 1951 and became director of the Royal Library in Phnom Penh. He was appointed minister of state in charge of information in the **Huy Kanthoul** government from October 1951 to June 1952. After that he retired from politics and worked in his own business, mainly involved in running a garage in Phnom Penh. Chhoeun became curator of the National Library in the late 1950s after the eclipse of the Democrats and the imposition of Sihanouk's personal rule and never reentered political life. He had married Douc Ok, eldest sister of **Douc Rasy**, and they had a son, Mondet Chhoeun, an accomplished musician who died of wounds while serving in the army of the **Khmer Republic**, 2 August 1970. His father never recovered from the news and died 18 October 1971.

PAILIN. A municipality with the legal status of a province established in 1997. Previously part of **Battambang** province, and located on the Thai border, Pailin is the smallest of Cambodia's 24 provinces and municipalities. The March 1998 **census** report puts its population at 22,906. By the time of the February 2002 commune elections, this had nearly doubled to 41,958. The city is famous historically for its sapphire mines, exploited since colonial times by a small Shan-Burmese minority known as the *kola* people, for its fruit orchards and for the large coffee plantation established there in the 1960s. In the **Khmer Republic**, the city was the center of a province called Sangkum Meanchey. In 1989, after the withdrawal of Vietnamese troops from Cambodia, it was attacked and occupied by the National Army of **Democratic Kampuchea (DK)**. The DK authorities began, with Thai technological assistance, to exploit the gem mines, as well as forests in the region, on a industrial scale, briefly earning tens of millions of dollars with which to cushion the end of Chinese aid to the movement in 1991. The principal headquarters for the **Party of Democratic Kampuchea** remained in the region following the withdrawal of the faction from the peace process in Cambodia in 1992 and until 1993 when the town was briefly recaptured by government troops, forcing **Pol Pot** and others to shift their base of operations to **Anlong Veng**. In 1996 a policy dispute divided the National Army of Democratic Kampuchea divisions based in Pailin from the Pol Pot leadership causing the Pailin group, under the leadership of the former DK Foreign Minister **Ieng Sary**, to defect to the **Hun Sen-Norodom Ranariddh** government. Pailin was briefly a semiautonomous zone under the control of Sary's Democratic National Union Movement (DNUM). During the 1998 elections it was the only constituency in which ballot counting was not organized by the **Hun Sen** government's National Election Commission, and as the DNUM is not an electoral party, the **Sam Rainsy Party** won the **National Assembly** seat with 51 percent of the vote. The **Cambodian People's Party** bounced back in the February 2002 local elections, winning 36 of the 44 council seats in the city's eight *khum* ("communes").

PAL SAN (1915-). Born in **Phnom Penh**, he worked in the Ministry of Agriculture and joined **Sangkum**. In 1955 he was elected to the National Assembly for Svaypor, **Battambang**. In June 1971 Pal San was appointed to the **constitutional drafting committee** representing the mutual help association of employees of the land registry. Joining **Molinaka**, he was later a member of **FUNCINPEC**. In December 1993 he was appointed first deputy governor of **Koh Kong** province.

PAN SOTHI (1936-1975). He studied at the University of Missouri, gaining a science degree and returned to **Phnom Penh** where he was appointed lecturer at the School of Mines returning the **United States** to earn a doctorate in psychology and statistics. A supporter of **Lon Nol**, he was appointed to represent former students from the United States on the **constitutional drafting committee** in June 1971. From May 1971 until March 1972 he was minister of education and cultural affairs. In 1972 Pan Sothi joined the **Socio-Republican Party** and was elected to the **National Assembly** of the Khmer Republic for Svaypor, **Battambang**. He was elected to head the Assembly Committee for Foreign Affairs and was minister of education and parliamentary relations under **Long Boret** from June 1974, with the additional position of deputy prime minister of the Khmer Republic until 12 April 1975. Although variously reported as having been evacuated on **Operation Eagle-Pull**, Pan Sothi remained in Phnom Penh and was captured at Vat Katt, after attempting to leave the capital on 17 April. He is presumed to have been killed soon afterward.

PANH RITHY (1964-). Born in **Phnom Penh**, he spent the period of Democratic Kampuchea in the countryside and escaped as a refugee in 1979 to the Mairut camp in Thailand. In 1980 he moved to France where he studied at the IDHEC. A film maker, he produced *Site 2* (1989) and *Cambodge: entre guerre et paix* (1991). His film *Les gens de la Rizière* was selected for showing at the Cannes film festival in 1994.

PANN YUNG (1880-1954). Born at Triton, **Cochinchina**, a cousin of **Chau Sen Cocsal**, Pann Yung was a longtime friend of the family of **Son Sann**, also from *Kampuchea Krom*. He served as governor of **Pursat**, **Svay Rieng** and **Kampong Speu**. Additional links to business and professional circles were assured through the marriage of his sister, Pann Ken, to **Nheim Sokphal**. In the 1930s, he collaborated with **Son Ngoc Thanh**, **Pach Chhoeun** and **Sim Var** on *Nagaravatta*. In September 1945 he was among those forced to flee to Thailand after having earlier failed to secure Thai support for Cambodian independence. In February 1946 he was president of the first Committee of the **Khmer Issarak**. He returned to Cambodia in April 1946 and joined the **Democrat Party**. Yung was president of the Cambodian delegation to the Assembly of the French Union in 1951 but was defeated when he contested the National Assembly seat of Kampong Luong, **Kandal**, as an independent. Soon afterward he rejoined the Democrats and was appointed as Cambodian councilor to the French Union, moving to live in Paris. Pann Yung died 27 November 1954.

PARIS INTERNATIONAL CONFERENCE ON CAMBODIA. Convened in October 1991, this conference was to ratify decisions hammered out over the previous year among the permanent five representatives on the **United Nations** Security Council, as well as other interested parties. The conference called for an end to the civil war in Cambodia and set in place the UN protectorate over Cambodia, later known as the **United Nations Transitional Authority in Cambodia**, that was in effect in 1992-1993, pending national elections. The conference ostensibly ended the Cold War-oriented patronage by great powers of contending Cambodian factions, and thus returned Cambodia to the world of Southeast Asia from which it had been isolated by over 20 years.

PARIS PEACE AGREEMENT. *See* PARIS INTERNATIONAL CONFERENCE ON CAMBODIA.

PARTY OF DEMOCRATIC KAMPUCHEA (PDK). This was name taken by the political arm of the overturned **Democratic Kampuchea** regime from 1981 when their discredited **Communist Party of Kampuchea** was dissolved, until 1994 when **Khieu Samphan** announced the existence of the provisional government of a new party of national unity and well-being.

PARTY OF THE PEOPLE (*kanapac reastr*). The name of this party employs the term for the "king's subjects" in its reference to "the people." It was founded in May 1950 by a breakaway **Democrat Party** group led by **Sam Nhean**. An immensely charismatic figure, Nhean was able to steer it through major political problems. The party program advocated a "good neighbor" policy with the rest of Southeast Asia, effectively an early appeal to neutralism in the face of the challenge to French power posed by the insurgent **Viet Minh**. It established a cell and cadre structure in villages managed mostly by Sam Nhean's son, **Sam Sary**. A paternalist concern to protect the people was conveyed in the party emblem, a wreath of rice. **Mey Nosey**, a former member of the **Progressive Democrat Party** was the publisher of the party newspaper which was called *Samleng Khmer* ("Voice of the Khmer"). It failed to win any seats in the 1951 **National Assembly** elections, being swept aside by the landslide victory of the Democrat Party. It disappeared in 1955 when most members joined the **Sangkum**.

PAU CONFERENCE. This meeting on a series of technical matters arising from the **Franco-Cambodian Treaty** produced a series of agreements which relaxed France's colonial controls over Cambodia and also the Associated States of Vietnam and Laos. They were signed at Pau in France on 27 November 1950. Their aim was to move French Indochina gradually toward independence under French guidance and protection and thereby to lend more nationalist credibility and loyalty to **Bao Dai**, in particular, but also to King **Norodom Sihanouk**. The Cambodian delegation was led by Prince **Sisowath Monipong** and chaired by **Sum Hieng**. It included **Au Chheun, Chan Nak, Chau Sen Cocsal, Chuop Samloth, Lam Ken** and Prince **Sisowath Sirik Matak**.

PAVIE, AUGUSTE JEAN MARIE (1847-1925). A French explorer, author and administrator, as a young man, Pavie supervised the installation of telegraph lines connecting **Phnom Penh** with **Cochinchina** and **Thailand**. Surveying missions for the lines took him to remote parts of Indochina not previously visited by Europeans, and the reports of these expeditions provide valuable information about Cambodia at this time. Pavie also published translations of Cambodian folk tales. In the 1880s and 1890s, he was involved in French efforts to gain suzerainty over Laos.

PEAR (PORR) MINORITY. A Mon-Khmer speaking group inhabiting hilly areas of Pursat, Battambang and Kampong Thom, largely assimilated in recent years into Cambodian society. In the 19th century, the Pear were active in collecting wild cardamom that was presented annually as tribute to the Thai court.

PECH CHEANG. A native of **Kampong Cham**, he was a teacher initially recruited to the communist revolutionary cause by **Koy Thuon**, one of his teachers at Lycée Sihanouk, Kampong Cham, in 1960. Working underground from the mid-1960s, he was briefly imprisoned in 1966 for agitating among monks and rubber plantation workers and jailed for a second time in 1967 when he was apprehended in the act of procuring weapons for the planned communist uprising in 1968. He was released under the general amnesty for political prisoners in 1970. He led military forces in **Kampong Thom** and **Siem Reap** during the 1970-1975 war and was briefly chairman of the National Bank, working under **Non Suon** in 1975. He was then assigned to the foreign ministry headed by **Ieng Sary**. He was appointed ambassador of **Democratic Kampuchea** to **China** in 1976 and was safely out of the country when Koy Thuon's network was purged. He continued to serve as the **Coalition Government of Democratic Kampuchea** ambassador in Beijing after 1982 and until 1993. He was a member of the stillborn provisional government of national unity and well-being announced by **Khieu Samphan** on 10 July 1994, remaining with the DK movement until his departure from **Anlong Veng** for **Pailin** in 1997 or 1998.

PEN NAVUT (1934-1990). A teacher, in 1962 he was at the Collège Svay Rieng. Navut was vice-chairman of the **People's Republic of Kampuchea (PRK)**-USSR Friendship Association from December 1979 and assistant to the education minister from April 1980. Navut was minister of education in the PRK from June 1981, and also a member of the Central Committee of the **People's Revolutionary Party of Kampuchea** which was established in that year. He died 12 March 1990 in a Phnom Penh hospital.

PEN PAN NHA (1941-). Born at Kampong Seim, **Kampong Cham**, he was trained as a veterinarian and was head of the veterinary department of the **Phnom Penh** municipality before 1975—spending the period of **Democratic Kampuchea** in the countryside. In August 1982 he was appointed assistant editor of *Kampuchea*, becoming editor in the following month. In April 1986 he became assistant editor of *Pracheachon*. He served as vice-minister of agriculture from October 1988 until June 1993. Elected deputy for **Prey Veng**, he was vice-president of the Commission for Economics, Planning, Investment, Agriculture, Rural Development and the Environment from October 1993. He was reelected to the National Assembly in 1998.

PEN SOVAN (1936-). Prime minister in 1981. Born on 15 April 1936 at Chan Tep, Tram Kak, **Takeo**, he joined the **Khmer Issarak** as a boy of 15. During the early 1950s he served in the guard corps of Ek Choeun (**Ta Mok**), who was born close to his native village. In 1954 he was among those "regrouped" in Vietnam. He was believed to have graduated from the military training school for senior officers. In 1970, still in Hanoi, he rallied to **National United Front of Kampuchea (FUNK)** and worked on FUNK Radio with Ieng Sary and Ieng Thirith until February 1971. Once back in Cambodia Pen Sovan came into conflict with Pol Pot and Ieng Sary in 1973 and fled to Vietnam in January 1974.

Pen Sovan was one of the founders of the **United Front for the National Salvation of Kampuchea** in 1978 and became the secretary-general in 1979 as well as the first secretary of the **People's Revolutionary Party of Kampuchea**. From May until December 1981 he represented Phnom Penh in the **National Assembly** and became vice-president to the Council of State, prime minister and minister of defense. In November 1981 he criticized the continued Vietnamese presence in Cambodia and was dismissed on 5 December and imprisoned in Vietnam for ten years. In 1988 he was placed under house arrest in Hanoi. At that time the **People's Republic of Kampuchea** declared that he had been suffering from a mental illness for 10 years, and he was held in custody in Phnom Penh. Freed by the Vietnamese, he established his new home in Takeo on 25 January 1992 later forming a new political party which has failed to attract much support. Although he was initially thought to have been killed during the July 1997 *coup de force* mounted by Hun Sen against Prince **Norodom Ranariddh**, he had succeeded in going into hiding managing to escape Phnom Penh only in August, flying to Kuala Lumpur and temporary political exile. He later returned to Cambodia and his memoirs were published in the United States in 2002. He is now the president of the National Sustaining Party of Cambodia which was founded in 1998.

PEN YUTH (1932-1975). He joined the **Pracheachon** in 1955 before the elections in which he contested the National Assembly seat of Chhouk, **Kampot**. Director of the Pracheachon newspaper, *The Nation*, from 24 June to 25 October 1955 (39 issues), he was arrested on 24 October for opposing the **United States**-Cambodian military agreement. Soon afterward he decided to leave political activism and eventually joined the Cambodian army. A supporter of **Hang Thun Hak**, he also became associated with Lon Non. In 1972, as a major in the army, he founded the new **Pracheachon Party**, funded by **Lon Non**, to contest the legislative elections in September 1972. He contested the seat of **Kampot** without success. He is believed to have been killed in April 1975, soon after the fall of the Khmer Republic.

PENGPAS YUKANTHOR, Princess (1892-1969). Born on 28 July 1892 in Phnom Penh, she was the daughter of Prince **Aruna Yukanthor** and sister of Princess **Pinpeang Yukanthor**. She went to school in Saigon and became a teacher at the Malika Primary School founded by her mother. President of the association of women of the French Union, she was minister of national education, sports and youth from June 1952 until January 1953, minister charged with public instruction and fine arts until July 1953, and minister of state in charge of public health until November 1953. She died 29 October 1969 in Phnom Penh.

PENH THUOK. *See* VORN VET.

PENN NOUTH (1906-1985). Prime minister 10 times between 1948 and 1976. Born on 1 April 1906 in Phnom Penh, he was educated in **Phnom Penh** and at the Cambodian School of Administration. He was a clerk in the French colonial service before transferring to the Cambodian administration. Secretary to the **French Résident** in Phnom Penh, he was appointed *anouc montrey* in 1935 and then held some posts as district head. In 1938 he went to France as an appointee of the Cambodians to work in their Ministry of Overseas in Paris. On his return to Phnom Penh before the outbreak of World War II, he joined the Ministry of Interior and Religion then became head of the office at the Ministry of the Palace, Finances and Fine Arts. In 1945 when Cambodian Independence was initially proclaimed, he was chief clerk in the Ministry of Finance. As such he was vice-minister of finance until 15 October 1945. From then until February 1946 he assumed control in **Kampong Cham**. In February 1946 Penn Nouth became mayor of Phnom Penh, and as a keen supporter of the **Democrat Party**, was secretary of state charged with Phnom Penh in the Prince **Sisowath Youtévong** government from December 1946 to July 1947. He was a member of the Cambodian delegation to the Dalat Conference in 1946.

In the 1947 National Assembly elections Penn Nouth was elected for Koh Sautin, **Kampong Cham**. Penn Nouth was minister of state from July 1947 to February 1948, and advisor to the government from February to August 1948. He then became prime minister and minister for the interior and for information from 15 August 1948 to 21 January 1949. Under **Yèm Sambaur**, he took part in the negotiations for the Franco-

Cambodian Treaty of 8 November 1949. When King Sihanouk took over from Yèm Sambaur in May 1950, Penn Nouth was briefly, for five days, minister of state, charged with national defense. Close to King **Norodom Sihanouk**, he was one of the two official private advisors to the throne.

Penn Nouth returned as prime minister, royal delegate, and minister of sports and youth from 24 January until 29 July 1953 and was reappointed prime minister, royal delegate for the direction of the government, minister of finance, sports, youth and education from 29 July until 22 November 1953, presiding over the Proclamation of Independence celebrations. In the turmoil of the 1950s cabinet reshuffles, Penn Nouth was prime minister and minister of the economy and finance from 7 to 17 April 1954, prime minister until 31 July 1954; reappointed as prime minister on 1 August and carrying through his fifth (officially, or sixth in practice) government until 26 August. His next government lasted from 27 August 1954 to 25 January 1955, and he was prime minister again from 21 January until 10 April 1958, also holding the portfolio of foreign affairs. Much admired by King **Norodom Suramarit**, he was raised to the dignity of *Samdech* and also dean of the Royal Council until its dissolution in 1960. At this point Penn Nouth left the Phnom Penh political scene to take up an appointment as ambassador to Paris. He returned as prime minister and minister of the interior and religion, 28 January to 16 November 1961. On 17 November he took the additional portfolio of religion in a government nominally led by Prince **Norodom Sihanouk**, a position he held until 12 February 1962. Ill health forced him to retire from politics. However, following the resignation of **Lon Nol** in April 1967, Penn Nouth was brought back to the government as an advisor. On 31 January 1968 he was appointed prime minister, a position he held through two major reshuffles, until 13 August 1969 when Lon Nol was returned to lead the government.

By this time Penn Nouth was a close confidante and aide to Prince Sihanouk and one of his most trusted advisors. He was overseas at the overthrow of Sihanouk in 1970 and assisted the prince with his planning in the early days against Lon Nol. Penn Nouth was deputy head of the delegation to the Summit Conference of the Indochinese Peoples on 24-25 April 1970, held near the Lao-Vietnamese-Chinese border region, and became prime minister in the **Royal Government of National Union of Kampuchea (GRUNK)**. In August 1970 he was sentenced to death in absentia for high treason. Also a member of the Central Committee of **National United Front of Kampuchea (FUNK)** and president of the Political Bureau of the Central Committee, he was active organizing GRUNK political activities, remaining the figurehead head of the administration. In September 1975 he returned to Phnom Penh with

Sihanouk and survived the FUNK purges. He was again a nominal prime minister until 1976. However, without any real power, he went to live in France in 1979, where he died on 18 May 1985—a luncheon in his honor was held by Prince Sihanouk in Beijing on 27 July 1985. He had several sons, including **Penn Thol**, Penn Thula and Penn Nhach, onetime governor of Kandal Province. These three sons joined the **Khmer People's National Liberation Front**.

PENN THOL (1934-). Born on 6 February 1934 in Phnom Penh, son of **Penn Nouth**, he studied in France and gained a diploma from the École Supérieure de Commerce in Toulouse in 1957. He then worked at the National Bank for Trade and Industry in Paris in 1958. Returning to Phnom Penh, Penn Thol joined the Ministry of Foreign Affairs in May 1959 and in October 1959 was trade attaché at the Cambodian Embassy in Tokyo, a post which he held until 1964 when the embassy was closed. He was general-secretary at the Chamber of Commerce, Industry and Agriculture 1965-1967, secretary of state for the economy from September 1967 to January 1968, secretary-general to the office of Prince **Norodom Sihanouk** 1968-1969 and to the Cabinet Office in 1969. After the overthrow of Sihanouk, Penn Thol was inspector general of the Ministry of Trade 1970-1971 and secretary general of the Chamber of Commerce, Industry and Agriculture from 1972-1975.

Penn Thol spent the years of **Democratic Kampuchea** in the countryside and then worked as a peasant in the north of Cambodia 1979-1980, becoming a refugee in France in May 1980. From October 1982 to October 1983 he was head of the **Khmer People's National Liberation Front (KPNLF)** Bureau of Information in Tokyo, KPNLF assistant to the Khmer Nationalist Movement in Tokyo from November 1983 to December 1988 and was head of the office of **Son Sann**. In November 1991 he was appointed to the secretariat of the **Supreme National Council**, and was a member of the Steering Committee of the **Buddhist Liberal Democratic Party** and second vice-president of the party from May 1992. In May 1993 he was elected deputy for **Kampong Speu** and became vice-president of the Commission for Foreign Affairs, International Cooperation, Information and Media, October 1993.

PEOPLE'S PARTY (or GROUP). *See* PRACHEACHON.

PEOPLE'S PARTY OF KAMPUCHEA. *See* CAMBODIAN PEOPLE'S PARTY (CPP).

PEOPLE'S REPRESENTATIVE ASSEMBLY OF KAMPUCHEA (PRAK). Elected on 20 March 1976, reportedly by limited franchise, this assembly of 250 included 50 representatives of workers, 150 representatives of peasants and 50 representatives of the National Army of Democratic Kampuchea. The workers representatives were elected in sectoral constituencies to represent Phnom Penh factory workers, railway workers, transport workers, dock workers, provincial factories, plantation workers, miners, fishermen and electricity workers. Peasants' representatives were elected in geographical constituencies corresponding to **Democratic Kampuchea (DK)** zones and special regions. The DK assembly was the first and only assembly to award seats to the military. The changes in representational format are less significant than they may appear, however, because the PRAK was convened for brief periods, only once or twice a year. Like other communist legislative bodies of the period, it met mostly for the purpose of lending its formal approval to policies devised in practice by the Standing Committee of the ruling **Communist Party of Kampuchea.** *See also* ADMINISTRATIVE DIVISIONS.

PEOPLE'S REPUBLIC OF KAMPUCHEA (PRK). This was the name given to the state by the Vietnamese-installed Cambodian government in 1979. This communist formulation was abandoned in 1989, when efforts were being made to entice Prince **Norodom Sihanouk** to return to the country and to accept a leading role in the government, in accordance with the "national reconciliation" formula then promoted by the Mikhail Gorbachev. The country's new name, until 1993, was **State of Cambodia (SOC).**

PEOPLE'S REVOLUTIONARY PARTY OF KAMPUCHEA (PRPK). This was the name given to the new Communist Party formed in **Phnom Penh** in 1981 by the Vietnamese-backed dissidents and defectors from the **Communist Party of Kampuchea** who, with the support of the Vietnamese army, overturned the **Democratic Kampuchea** regime and established the **People's Republic of Kampuchea.** The new party was led by **Pen Sovan** and in rapid succession **Chan Si, Heng Samrin, Chea Sim** and **Hun Sen.** Its name echoes that of the ethnic people's party founded in 1951, the **Khmer People's Revolutionary Party (KPRP)** to which historical links are claimed to establish a direct line of revolutionary descent from the **Indochinese Communist Party.** The KPRP changed its name to **Cambodian People's Party (CPP)** and ceased to be a cadre-based, vanguard party in October 1991 when a special congress abandoned Marxism-Leninism and embraced "multiparty" electoral democracy. The change was deemed necessary in the run up to the **Paris International Conference on Cambodia** a week later where the CPP agreed to United Nations-organized, liberal elections.

PEOPLE'S SOCIALIST COMMUNITY. *See* SANGKUM REASTR NIYUM.

PEOU LIDA. *See* SISOWATH SOUTÉVONG, PRINCESS.

PEPPER. This was an important export in pre-1970 Cambodia. Pepper was cultivated primarily by Chinese farmers in the province of Kampot and its quality—especially of the white variety—was highly regarded by the French, who traditionally imported most of the crop. Production declined sharply with the insecurity of the 1970s and 1980s.

PHENG PHAN Y. He was appointed director of the quartermasters stores for the Royal Army in 1958 and in 1970, as colonel, was head of the Royal Army Staff Headquarters. He was one of the key Sihanoukists left in control of the country when Prince **Norodom Sihanouk** went to France. Involved in the **Oum Mannorine** attempt to wrest power from **Lon Nol** on the evening of 16 March, he was arrested and held under arrest on a boat in the Mekong until 1973 when he was released.

PHI TACH (1953-). Born on 9 October 1953 in **Prey Veng**, he studied law in **Phnom Penh** 1973-1975. During the period of **Democratic Kampuchea**, he was in the countryside. Joining the **People's Republic of Kampuchea** government in 1979 he was in their first promotion of their diplomatic corps of their Ministry of Foreign Affairs in 1980. From 1979 he headed the Soviet Union and the Eastern Europe section of the Foreign Ministry. In 1984 he was appointed ambassador to East Germany and in 1986 appointed ambassador to Albania. From then until 1993 he worked in the Foreign Ministry in Phnom Penh but clearly disillusioned with the government. After a year of further training at the École Nationale d'Administration in Paris, he became deputy director of the **Institute of Democracy**. By February 2000 he had joined the **Sam Rainsy Party** and managed the party office.

PHILASTRE, PAUL LOUIS-FÉLIX (1837-1902). Born in Brussels, Philastre was a naval lieutenant and came to **Cochinchina** in 1861. In 1876 he was appointed representative in **Phnom Penh** and held the position until an appointment in Hue in 1879. He codified Vietnamese law some of which was later adapted to Cambodia; a street in Phnom Penh was later named after him.

PHILATELY. Modern-style postal services were established by the French who issued the first postage stamp (for "Indo-Chine") in 1889. In 1907 stamps ranging from 20c to 75c showed a "Cambodian," with the rest showing Annamites, Lao and Muong. The first stamps showing **Angkor Wat** were issued in 1927, with King **Sisowath Monivong** featuring on stamps issued in 1936. King **Norodom Sihanouk** appears on stamps in 1942. Following the **Pau Conference**, stamps were no longer issued centrally by the colonial authorities but by the Cambodian government.

Commemorative issues depicted temples, royal festivals, membership of international organizations and wildlife. Although the **Khmer Republic** was proclaimed in October 1970, stamps bearing the name "Cambodia" which commemorated the death of Chuon Nath were published in 1971. Postal services continued, in a haphazard form, until April 1975. Although five pictorial stickers from **Democratic Kampuchea** were circulated in early 1978 it seems likely that these were propaganda labels not stamps. The **People's Republic of Kampuchea (PRK)** resumed issuing stamps on 10 April 1980 soon after the reintroduction of the riel—although some stamps from the Khmer Republic were overprinted for use in 1979. PRK stamps were printed in Havana, Cuba, and continued to be used during the **State of Cambodia** and **Kingdom of Cambodia** periods. In recent years, newly printed national stamps series have featured colorful psittacines, protected animals and national temples. Stamps were issued in 1995 to honor **Queen Norodom Monineath Sihanouk** and the 100th Anniversary of the Postes & Telegraphes of Phnom Penh. Throughout the 1990s, many stamps were issued to commemorate the anniversaries of the United Nations and its agencies as well as the Olympic Games.

PHIMAI. This was a 12th century Cambodian Buddhist temple in northeastern Thailand, 72 kilometers from Korat. It was dedicated in 1108, the second year of the reign of King **Dharanindravarman I**. The temple, which consists of a central tower and accessory buildings, was restored by French archaeologists in the 1950s. It was probably the principal temple in the tributary city of Bimapura, mentioned in other inscriptions, of which no other traces have survived.

PHLEK CHHAT (1922-). Born on 16 February 1922 at Sauthnikom, Siem Reap, he attended **Lycée Sisowath** and also Lycée Louis le Grand. A civil engineer, he trained at the École Nationale des Ponts et Chausées in Paris, returning to Cambodia where he joined the Ministry of Public Works. Heavily involved in the building of the port of **Sihanoukville**, he then took part in the construction of the railway from Phnom Penh to the port. In 1958 he was appointed general manager of the Cambodia Electric Co. By 1963 he was chief engineer in the Public Works Department and director-general of planning, with the rank of secretary of state. He was Minister of industry in the **Norodom Kantol** government 1965-1966 and, in 1969, president of the National Committee for Khmer-Filipino friendship. **Lon Nol** appointed Chhat chairman of the Mekong Committee in August 1970, and minister of state in charge of planning, foreign aid and development from March to October 1972. He was married and had four children.

PHLEK PHIRUN (1914-1975). Born on 11 May 1914 at Svaypor, **Battambang**, son of Chhith Phlek and Mme (née Phlong Kauv), Phlek Phuon was the brother-in-law of **Ung Krapumphka**. He joined the French colonial services as a clerk, became secretary to the **French Résident** in 1933 and rose to the position of assistant chief of service of Waters and Forests in **Kampot** by 1948. He was minister of agriculture in 1949 and again in 1951. Originally a member of the **Democrat Party**, he broke away and became a member of **Yèm Sambaur's National Recovery Party**. In 1962 he was elected to the National Assembly representing Takeo and was elected to the 1966 National Assembly representing Prante Preah, Battambang. He married Choul Baytang and they had four sons and seven daughters (one daughter, Chhoeunera, married Zoubeida Abdoul Carime, a prominent Phnom Penh businessman). In 1966 Phirun was minister of public works and telecommunications in the first Lon Nol government returning to that position in the second **Lon Nol** government from 1970-1971. Phlek Phuon was appointed president of Cambodia House in Paris in 1970 but only held the position briefly being appointed advisor to the Lon Nol government 1970-1973. His wife was under secretary of state for labor and social welfare in the **Hang Thun Hak** government, October 1972 to April 1973. He was in Phnom Penh in April 1975 and one of those who took refuge in the French Embassy. He was expelled from the Embassy with **Sisowath Sirik Matak** and **Ung Bun Hor** on 20 April 1975 and is presumed to have been killed later that day. His wife had been the first vice-president of the administrative council of the Cambodian Red Cross in the 1960s and was vice-chairman of the Kampuchean Red Cross from October 1979 and secretary-general of the National Assembly from July 1981, being a member for a Phnom Penh constituency.

PHNOM BAKHENG. This is a small hill (65 meters high) in the Angkor region, selected by King **Yasovarman I** (r 889-910) as the site for his five-terraced temple mountain, or Yasodharagiri, where a lingam bearing the king's name was consecrated in 907. The hill, representing **Mount Meru**, as all temple-mountains did, stood at the center of Yasovarman's walled and moated capital of **Yasodharapura**, an area estimated at approximately 1,500 hectares. One hundred and eight towers—the number is significant in Hindu iconography—were grouped on seven levels around the central tower.

PHNOM KULEN. This is a range of hills some 40 kilometers north of the Angkor complex, famed since Angkorean times as a refuge for hermits and contemplative monks. The hills contain many vestiges of Angkorean architecture, including some datable to the reign of **Jayavarman II** in the ninth century. Indeed, Phnom Kulen is believed to be the place where

Jayavarman II declared "independence" in AD 802. Historians also believe that the region was the site of a pre-Angkorean ceramics industry.

PHNOM PENH. The capital city, it was founded, according to legend, in the 15th century by a pious woman whose name was Penh and who saw a Buddha image floating in the river, pulled it to shore and built a shrine (*Wat Phnom*) to house it. Some not necessarily reliable **chronicle histories** attribute the city's founding to the semilegendary Cambodian king **Ponhea Yat.** The city's location, at the confluence of the **Mekong** and Tonlé Sap-Bassac Rivers, made it an important port by the 17th century, certainly in the eyes of European traders who began to use it then. However, when the local Mekong Delta came under Vietnamese administration toward the end of that century, access to the ocean was blocked and Phnom Penh became less prosperous. During the 18th and 19th centuries, Cambodia's royal capital lay to the north at **Oudong**, but the French shifted the capital of their new protectorate of Cambodia back to Phnom Penh in 1866, stressing the importance of river transport in establishing commercial links with their new holdings in **Cochinchina**. By 1953, when independence was gained, it was inhabited by approximately 500,000 people. This number swelled to two million in the early 1970s, when refugees fleeing the war sought asylum there. The residents of Phnom Penh and of all provincial towns were evacuated to rural collectives by the **Pol Pot** revolutionaries in April 1975 and for the whole of the **Democratic Kampuchea** period Phnom Penh was largely empty, although some industrial areas and government buildings were used. Urban life was restored during the Vietnamese occupation and by 1990 it was inhabited by around a million people, some of these being casual or seasonal workers. In legal and administrative terms, Phnom Penh is one of four muncipalities in Cambodia, each of these being administratively equal to a province. The city has seven districts: Chamkar Mon, Don Penh, Prampi Mekkakra, Tuol Kork, Dangkao, Mean Chey and Russei Keo and a total population of 999,804 in the March 1998 **census**. The economically active workforce was 423,747 of which 45.3 percent (191,924) were women. The census also reported that the number of "migrants" within the enumerated population, those who had a previous residence outside of the municipality, was 73.4 percent of the city's residents. Female migrants most often relocated for "family reasons" while male migrants most often relocated "in search of employment." Even in the capital city, according to the census, firewood or charcoal was the principal source of energy used in the majority of households with liquid petroleum gas being used in only one quarter of households. Arrested development and rustification is also evident in the streets, three quarters being unpaved dirt roads. In 2002 the city's governor,

Chea Sophara, banned heavy trucks and other heavily loaded vehicles from using the capital's rapidly disintegrating paved roads. The city lacks the resources and equipment for maintenance or repair.

Voting patterns in the capital city reveal the absence of a national political consensus. In the 1998 **National Assembly** elections, the **Cambodian People's Party (CPP)** won seven seats; the **FUNCINPEC,** eight seats and the **Sam Rainsy Party (SRP)**, three seats. In the 2002 *khum* ("commune") elections, 652 seats on 76 commune councils were contested by the same three parties with the CPP winning 350 (55.2 percent), FUNCINPEC, 66 (10.1 percent) and SRP, 236 (36.2 percent). These figures indicate that the Royalist Party faces life or death challenges in the next round of the National Assembly constitutionally set for 2003.

PHNOM PENH POST. An English-language **newspaper**, published every two weeks, the *Post* established in 1992 it is a major independent source of news and information about Cambodia. The publisher and editor in chief, Michael Hayes, and Kathleen O'Keefe, managing director, both citizens of the **United States**, have steadily upheld conventional professional standards of reporting and integrity and especially in moments of crisis. Cambodians working for small opposition newspapers in the Khmer medium believe press freedom is assured only because the foreign-owned *Post* stands in the way of repression.

PHO PROEUNG (1903-c1975). Prime minister 1960-1961. Born on 12 August 1903 in **Kampong Cham** into a prominent Brahmin family, Pho Proeung served in local government, rising to the position of governor of **Kampot** in 1947. He was secretary of national defense in the second **Yèm Sambaur** government from September 1949 until May 1950, minister of religion and information from April until July 1954 and minister for national education and fine arts from August 1954 until January 1955. In 1955 he joined **Sangkum** and was briefly president of the movement. He then served as minister for labor and social action, and of religion from April until July 1958 and was prime minister from April 1960 until January 1961. He was also, from early 1959, a member of the Royal Council, an organization that lasted until King **Norodom Suramarit**'s death. For many years Pho Proeung had been director of the Royal School of Administration, and also ultimate head of the various Cambodian secret services in the early 1960s. In 1958 he was elected to the **National Assembly** representing Koki, **Kandal,** and on 6 April 1960 was a minister in the Regency Council. In 1962 he left for Paris and was ambassador to France. However, by 1963 he had returned to Phnom Penh and was appointed director of the Khmer-language news magazine *Neak Cheat Niyum* following the massive losses in sales made by his predecessor **Ung Hong Sath**. He withdrew from active politics soon afterward. From April 1971 until 1973 he was appointed advisor to **Lon Nol**. Pho Proeung had married Mey San, who died on 11 December 1947, aged 48, leaving several children. His second wife came from Koh Sautin, Prey Veng.

PHOUK CHHAY (1939-1977). A native of Samrong district in Takeo, Phouk Chhay's family was very poor and left him for long periods in local temples in the care of Buddhist monks. He started school late, in 1949, but having joined other pupils in a pro-**Son Ngoc Thanh** and proindependence demonstration, he was expelled in 1950. He then managed to win a scholarship to Collège Preah Raj Samphear, **Kampot**, where he studied from 1952-1956, and then, again with a scholarship, to the prestigious Lycée Descartes in Phnom Penh, 1956-1958. In 1959 he registered in the Faculty of Law and Economics of the Royal University in **Phnom Penh** where he studied law and became good friends with **Uch Ven** who was then secretary of the library of the faculty. Having no support from his family, Phouk Chhay worked in several private schools as a teacher, one job in 1961-1962 being at **Chamroeun Vichea** as Uch Ven was chairman of the school board. One of his teachers at the Faculty of Law was Hou Youn who appears to have introduced him to **Chau Seng** who invited him to write for *La Dépêche du Cambodge* ("The Dispatch of Cambodia"). In 1963 he married, and as his wife came from a wealthy family with connections to radicals of the Khmer Issarak period, he was able to give more time to his studies and to his political interests.

Although attracted by modern progressive ideas of "revolution" and change, and also concerned about the growing and neglected needs of students in the 1960s, he was among the promoters and organizers of the **Assemblée Générale des Étudiants Khmers (AGEK)**, Cambodia's first major student movement or union formed finally in 1964. Though he had completed his degree in April 1963, he was elected chair of the AGEK and **Tourn Sok Phallar**, who represented engineering students, was elected secretary-general. Under his leadership AGEK grew from a few hundred students to about 3,000. Phouk Chhay also participated in other intellectual and professional organizations in the 1960s as a result of his growing network of personal and professional contacts. Among the clandestine communists he came to know and admire were **Koy Thuon**, who had been a teacher of Tourn Sok Phallar's, and **Tiv Ol**. In late 1967 he was arrested and momentarily faced a trial and death sentence for sedition in the crackdown ordered by Prince **Norodom Sihanouk** against pro-Chinese groups, especially the Cambodia-China Friendship Association led by **Hu Nim** and himself. There are no reports of any trial. Phouk Chhay was incarcerated with other political prisoners including **Non Suon**.

Among those pardoned and released in the general amnesty granted to political prisoners in 1970 by **Lon Nol**, Phouk Chhay did not immediately join the liberated zones of the **National Union Front of Kampuchea (FUNK)** because it was headed by Sihanouk. He wrote an article for *New Cambodge*, a news magazine that had replaced *Kampuja*, criticizing Sihanouk's agricultural policies. After a few months, however, he had no illusions about the counterrevolutionary orientation of the emerging **Khmer Republic**. He then joined Non Suon, and others he had met in prison, in the Southwest Zone, which included his native province, and served as a political commissar of the FUNK armed forces of the Zone. He was assigned to Pochentong Airport after the seizure of Phnom Penh in 1975 then attached to the Central Committee office, but Phouk Chhay rapidly fell under suspicion in 1976 when purges of cadres associated with "liberal" anti-Sihanoukist activities of the 1960s began. Some of his associates claimed in their forced confessions that Phouk Chhay, like his erstwhile mentor Hou Youn, believed the Khmer peasantry would never accept the total abolition of private property because peasants "loved whatever belonged to them as much as their own lives." His interrogators also clearly believed, with great irony in view of the poverty into which he had been born, and with immense remoteness from the courage and intelligence he displayed in the service of the revolution, that he had been seduced to the privileged circles in which he had lived in the capital. He was arrested in early 1977 and taken to **Tuol Sleng** from where, on 6 July 1977, he was sent to his execution.

PHU QUOC. This large and sparsely populated island is located just south of the coastal towns of **Kampot** and **Kep**. Because it was south of the **Brevié** line, it was administered by **Cochinchina** and is today administered by **Vietnam**. In the absence of a legally established maritime boundary, resolution of competing claims to Phu Quoc depend on resolution of other competing claims to offshore rights advanced by Vietnam, **Thailand**, **Malaysia** as well as Cambodia.

PHUM. A word of Sanskrit origin which in literal terms refers to a settled "land" or territory. In modern *Khmer* language, it refers to a rural hamlet and is often translated as "village."

PHUNG TON (1926-1976). Prominent Academic. Born on 1 January 1926 in **Phnom Penh**, the son of Phuong Phuong, *mekhum* of Prey Sor, Kandal and Mme (née Pleng Tan), he went to school in Phnom Penh and in 1947 went to Paris to study law at the Faculty of Law. He remained there for seven years and wrote a doctoral thesis, *La Crise Cambodgienne* (The Cambodian Crisis), which was accepted at the University of Paris in 1954. Phung Ton joined the **Democrat Party** and contested the 1955 National

Assembly elections for Svaypor, **Battambang**. He then entered academia and in 1964 was rector of the Royal University of Phnom Penh, teaching public law. Associated with **Hou Youn**, he was a member of the committee to support His Majesty's Neutrality Policy in the 1960s, but gradually moved to support for **Lon Nol** and the Americans. In 1970 he was appointed general inspector in charge of the committee for drafting the **constitution**. This process resulted in the controversy surrounding the dismissal of **Keo Ann**. Appointed advisor to Lon Nol in 1973, Phung Ton then left for France where he was living at the time of the fall of the Khmer Republic in April 1975. At the end of 1975 he led a party of some 300 Cambodian students who returned to Phnom Penh. Arrested by the **Democratic Kampuchea** authorities, he was taken to **Tuol Sleng** on 12 December 1976 and killed soon afterward. *See also* CHHOUK MENG MAO.

PHY THIEN LAY (1922-1975). Born on 16 May 1922 at Sras Chik, **Battambang**, son of Phy and Mme (née Hieu), he studied in Battambang and at **Lycée Sisowath**. He gained a diploma from the Royal School of Administration and entered the judicial services. He was secretary to the **French Résident** at **Kandal** in 1940, being a magistrate in Battambang in 1947. He married Ieam Chanmouly, and they had one son, Nundrith. He became active in **Sangkum** and was selected (and elected) as deputy for Preanet Preah, Battambang, in 1958 and again in 1962. From June 1959 until April 1960 he was under secretary of state for national education. In October 1962, he was appointed secretary of state of justice, remaining until December 1964, and in 1963 was president of the Juridical and Constitutional Commission of the **National Assembly**. One of the few deputies to be reelected in 1966, he represented Svaypor, Battambang, until the Assembly was finally closed down in 1971. A devout Buddhist, Phy Thien Lay represented the **Chuon Nath** Association on the **constitutional drafting committee** in June 1971, and remained in Phnom Penh until the fall of the Republic in April 1975. He was captured by soldiers of the **National United Front of Kampuchea** at Vat Katt while leaving Phnom Penh on 17 April 1975, and is presumed to have been killed later that day.

PIBUN SONGGRAM, Luang (1897-1964). Prime minister of Thailand from 1938-1945, 1948-1957. A French-trained officer in the Thai army, he became defense minister in 1934 and prime minister four years later. Pibun led the Thai agitation against French Indochina during the late 1930s, leading to the Franco-Thai War in 1940 when Thailand seized the provinces of **Battambang** and **Siem Reap**, managing to get Japanese acceptance for this in their "independent" arbitration. He then entered into a treaty with Japan and declared war on the Allies. Forced from office on 2 August 1945, he returned to prominence following the death of King Ananda Mahidol in June 1946. Pibun was prime minister from 9 April 1948 until his overthrow in a military coup by Field Marshal Sarit Thanarat in 1957. It was during his term in office that Thailand contested possession of **Preah Vihear** temple.

PIN YATHAY (1943-). Born in **Oudong**, the son of Chhor and Mme (née Loan), he was educated in **Phnom Penh** and won a scholarship to Montreal University where he studied engineering. He returned to Cambodia in 1965 and worked as an engineer at the Ministry of Public Works. He married Khem Thary and their son, Sudath, was born in 1967. Thary died in 1969 and Yathay married her sister. They had two children: Navath, born in 1971 and Staud, born in 1973. A supporter of **Lon Nol**, Pin Yathay was appointed director of the Department of New Works and Equipment in the Ministry of Public Works. In September 1970 he was gazetted lieutenant colonel. He became director of the Oudong Meanchey Association, organizing the visit of **Lon Nol** to that area in January 1975. He also served on the committee of coordination with **Lon Non**. Being evacuated from Phnom Penh in April 1975, he escaped from Cambodia and lived in exile in France. His experience of life in **Democratic Kampuchea** is related in *L'utopie meurtrière* (Murderous Utopia), published in Paris in 1979 and in London in 1987, under the title *Stay Alive, My Son*. Yathay's brother, Pin Lean Thoeun, a gem dealer, who lived in Melbourne, Australia, was murdered on 4 December 1997.

PINPEANG YUKANTHOR, Princess (1894-1966). Born on 26 December 1894 in **Phnom Penh**, she was the daughter of Prince **Aruna Yukanthor** and sister of Princess **Pengpas Yukanthor**. She became a teacher in Phnom Penh then taught at the Malika School. In 1912 Pinpeang became headmistress of the Pavie school then started teaching at Collège Norodom. In March 1945 she was promoted to director of public education, and president of the Association of Women of the French Union. From 1948 until 1958 she was a member of the Cambodian delegation to the Assembly of the French Union, becoming vice-president of the Assembly. President of the council of administration of the Finance Society of Cambodia and the Plantations Society of **Kratié**, she died on 26 December 1966 in Paris and her body was brought back for cremation in Phnom Penh.

PISETH PILICA née Ouk Eab Pily (1965-1999). She was a film star and ballet dancer who had been born in **Phnom Penh**, the daughter of Ouk Eab, a schoolteacher who taught French, and Meng Mony. She had two sisters but her parents and one sister died under the **Democratic Kampuchea** regime. She was evacuated to **Pursat** province to live with an uncle named Sao Piseth whose name she took, becoming Sao Piseth Pily. She returned to Phnom Penh in 1979 when the **People's Republic of Kampuchea (PRK)** was established and from 1980 studied traditional dance at the newly reopened Faculty of Fine Arts. After graduating in 1988, she worked in the arts and performances section of the PRK Ministry of Culture and Fine Arts. At this time, she began to act in films taking the stage name Piseth Pilica. She was best known for her role in the 1988 film *Sramol Anthaka* ("Shadow of Darkness") which depicted the suffering in the **Pol Pot** era. She was also a star of the traditional Royal Ballet and received much critical acclaim and personal pride for her "perfectly correct, original" standard of performance ensuring Cambodia's first prize award at the Ramayana Festival held in Bangkok in 1997. By this time she also taught dance and drama at the Faculty of Fine Arts and lent support to women's groups advocating improved training and employment opportunities for women. Piseth Pilica was shot by a hired gunman in a crowded street in Phnom Penh on 6 July 1999. She died in the hospital seven days later. No one has been summoned nor charged. In a large display of public grief, more than 10,000 people, many of them women, attended Pilica's cremation, ceremonies which were held on the grounds of the Faculty where she taught. Princess **Norodom Bopha Devi**, minister of culture and fine arts, was among the speakers who paid tribute to her achievements. *See also* FILMS.

POC (1833-   ). Born in Battambang, the son of a high official, Poc's first appointment was in the Royal Customs at **Kampot**, where his elder brother worked as the chief official. Poc then became a Buddhist monk and afterward became one of King **Norodom**'s pages. He fought against **Si Votha**, working with the French to suppress the uprising. In 1889 he was appointed minister of the navy, a position he held for the next six years. He became minister of the palace in 1898 and was appointed minister of justice in the following year, despite Norodom's opposition to his promotion. Indeed Jean Hess argued that Norodom claimed that Poc should have been sent to jail for corruption rather than end up in control of justice. Poc's son was Poc Duch. He became assistant to the minister of justice in 1902. Head of palace protocol, Duch married Long and they had three children: **Poc Khun**, Poc Hell and Poc Loun (married Bunchhan Mongkhun).

POC DOEUSKOMAR (1933-1971). The son of Poc Thuon, and grandson of **Poc Khun**, Doeuskomar was educated in Paris and returned to Phnom Penh where he joined the foreign service. He was posted to Australia in 1959 as third secretary, his uncle being the ambassador. Back in Phnom Penh, he became the manager of the National Credit Bank. Fearing arrest by Prince **Norodom Sihanouk**, he fled to the jungle in **Kampong Cham** with **Uch Ven** on 29 July 1968. Staying underground in **Kampot**, he later joined the communists operating near Kirirom. In April 1970 he was named vice-minister of foreign affairs in the **Kampuchean Royal Government of National Union (GRUNK)** and was in the Central Committee of the **National United Front of Kampuchea (FUNK)**. Although he is noted as a signatory on a November 1972 declaration issued from the "liberated zone," and appears in some photographs dating from "this period," it seems that he died of illness in 1971. Doeuskomar's sister, Poc Mona, was a member of the GRUNK mission to Paris in 1974 and was minister-counselor in the Cambodian delegation to the United Nations in Geneva in 1992.

POC KHUN (1904-   ). The son of Poc Duch, he married Chhan On, sister of Khuang Aphaiwong, prime minister of Thailand, and they had three children: Poc Vane (married Prince **Sisowath Monireth**), **Poc Thieun** and Poc Thuon (father of **Poc Doeuskomar**, Poc Yanine and Poc Mona). He was the founder of the **Khmer Issarak** on 18 December 1940 in Bangkok. Poc Khun's brother Poc Hell married Thiounn Yung, daughter of **Thiounn**. Poc Hell contested the 1952 High Council elections for the judiciary and was appointed to the National Consultative Council in the following year. In 1955 he was a member of the **Democrat Party**.

POC THIEUN (1916-1987). Born on 25 March 1916 in Phnom Penh, son of **Poc Hell**, he attended **Lycée Sisowath** and joined the civil service. Private secretary to the king, and later chief clerk in the Ministry of Justice, he was minister for national education in 1951. He was also active in the **Khmer Renewal Party** of **Lon Nol** and **Nhiek Tioulong**. In 1961 he was appointed minister to Australia, later being recalled after a diplomatic dispute. In 1971 he was ambassador to South Korea. He married, 16 January 1938, Soriya Tho, and they had two children. Living in Denver, Colorado, he died in July 1987.

POL POT né **Saloth Sar (1925-1998).** Prime minister 1976-1979. Born in January 1925, according to his own account, or on 25 May 1928 according to Ministry of Education records of the late 1940s, Saloth Sar's grandfather was Phen, a reasonably prosperous farmer in Kampong Thom who owned between 20 to 40 hectares of land. Phen had at least two children, Neak Chey and Phen Saloth. Chey, a daughter, married Chhim Long, a secretary to the local **French Résident** and their daughter, Meak eventually joined the **royal ballet** and became a minor wife of King **Monivong** (they had a son, Prince Kossorak). Phen Saloth married Sok Neam, and they had nine children (two of whom were possibly adopted): Loth Saroeung; Loth

Suong, born in 1911; Saloth Seng; Saloth Nhep; Saloth San; **Saloth Chhay**, born in 1926; Saloth Sar; and one additional daughter and son. Two of the family had contacts with the royal palace: Loth Saroeung, a daughter, was in the royal ballet and was a minor concubine of King Monivong; and Loth Suong worked at the royal palace and married **Chea Samay**, a ballet teacher. They had a son, Pen Thuol.

At an early age Saloth Sar went to stay with his brother, Loth Suong, at the palace. Except for six months as a Buddhist novice in the 1930s, he was educated entirely in the French language medium–at École Miche 1937-1942; and then at Collège Preah Sihanouk in Kampong Cham (1942-1947) where he learned to play the violin and also played soccer with **Lon Non**. After leaving Kampong Cham, he attended a technical school in Phnom Penh 1947-1949. While in the capital he met **Ieng Sary**, already active in the anti-colonial movement. The two became close friends. Both supported the Democrat Party which won the 1947 elections. In 1949 Saloth Sar was given a government scholarship to study in France; Ieng Sary receiving one in the following year. Saloth Sar registered for courses in radio-electricity in Paris, but he failed to attend classes regularly and earned no diplomas or degree. In France he met two of the Khieu sisters, **Khieu Ponnary** and **Khieu Thirith**, who married Ieng Sary. Saloth Sar married Khieu Ponnary after his return to Phnom Penh, on Bastille Day in July 1956.

The time in Paris was crucial to his political development. In 1952 he became a member of the French Communist party and joined a Cambodian Marxist study group organized by **Keng Vannsak** as well as Ieng Sary. His scholarship was withdrawn not long afterward in the summer of 1952 for academic reasons, forcing him to return to Cambodia in early 1953. By the middle of 1953 he had slipped underground to join a **Khmer People's Revolutionary Party (KPRP)** unit based on the Vietnamese border and under **Viet Minh** protection. While many KPRP members were evacuated to northern Vietnam following the Geneva Conference of 1954, Sar returned to Phnom Penh, where he campaigned for the Democrat Party in the 1955 elections and worked clandestinely with **Nuon Chea**, **Vorn Veth** and others to preserve the underground KPRP. After the **Sangkum** candidates won nearly every seat in the 1955 parliamentary election, Sar lost interest in electoral politics. In 1956 he began teaching geography, history and civics at a private high school in Phnom Penh all the while serving as the principal secretary for the underground KPRP secretary, **Tou Samouth**. In 1960, when the Workers' Party of Kampuchea was secretly formed, Sar was elected to its Central Committee. Following Tou Samouth's disappearance two years later, Sar was elected secretary of the party's permanent committee (in 1963), while Nuon Chea, who was deputy secretary of the party was momentarily acting secretary. That Tou Samouth had been murdered by Sihanouk's police may have been confirmed only in 1965 by overseas parties.

In 1963, increasingly nervous about Sihanouk's police and the inclusion of his name on the list of 34 prominent leftists published that year, Sar fled Phnom Penh living for two under renewed Vietnamese protection in "Office 100," in Ratanakiri province. He traveled to communist Vietnam and China for fourteen months in 1965-1966. While in China, he received military training as well as a positive view of the Cultural Revolution but in Vietnam he was offended by the patronizing and domineering manner of Le Duan, secretary of the Vietnamese Workers' Party. In 1966 Sar secretly changed the name of his party to the **Communist Party of Kampuchea (CPK),** thereby signaling his independence from Hanoi but without informing the Vietnamese. In early 1968, after the abortive **Samlaut Uprising**, and most likely with the knowledge and support of the Vietnamese party, the CPK launched an armed struggle against Sihanouk.

The overthrow of Prince **Norodom Sihanouk** on 18 March 1970, long anticipated by the CPK, brought to an end Cambodia's neutrality in the Vietnam war and forced the Prince who refused to accept the verdict of the coup, to enter into a broad political and military alliance with the CPK. With diplomatic backing from China and massive military support from the People's Army of Vietnam, the CPK armed struggle became a bitter civil war. Over the ensuing five years, membership in the CPK may have reached 50,000, rising from approximately 2-3,000 members in 1969. Saloth Sar refused to participate in a cease-fire agreement reached by the Vietnamese with the USA in early 1973. This led to saturation bombings of much of eastern Cambodia by the US Air Force during the first nine months of the year, a development which likely resulted in over 10,000 deaths. It also deepened the resolve Saloth Sar and most of the party leadership to carry on with a revolution that would be wholly independent from Vietnam's and leave the party in exclusive possession of state power. In January 1975 the CPK laid siege to Phnom Penh, ending all road and river transport to the capital and eventually forcing President Lon Nol and most leaders of the Khmer Republic into exile. Within hours after entering the city on 17 April 1975, its inhabitants were instructed to evacuate, allegedly for their own security, and it was said, temporarily, to rural collectives.

Saloth Sar and much of the party's central committee entered Phnom Penh without fanfare a week later. Continuing to identify themselves only as the revolutionary "organization" (*angkar*), the communists proceeded to abolish all currencies of exchange and to establish skeletal ministries for agriculture, industry, foreign affairs, information, social welfare and culture as the framework for a totally planned economy and society. The country was renamed Democratic Kampuchea and identified as a worker-peasant state constitution in a new constitution promulgated in 1976. Following elections for an "assembly of representatives of the people" in which the franchise may have been limited to **base people**, a new government was formed. "Pol Pot"–a pseudonym for Saloth Sar, was named as prime minister. Fearing assassination and perhaps in imitation of Stalin also, Pol Pot ran Democratic Kampuchea from hiding, changing his residence several times a week. Foreign observers were unable to identify him as Saloth Sar until he visited China in September 1977. It was on this occasion that he also revealed the existence of the CPK.

By the middle of 1977 heavy fighting, almost certainly instigated by the Khmer, had broken out between Cambodia and Vietnam. Pol Pot was convinced that Vietnamese-trained or influenced traitors within his own party and counter-revolutionary "saboteurs" or agents in the hire of the US Central Intelligence Agency or the Russian KGB were responsible for production failures as well as the failure of his army to defeat the Vietnamese "aggressors." Over 20,000 party members were arrested, interrogated and eventually sent to their deaths, most ending up at the party security headquarters known as S-21 (and later as "Tuol Sleng"). For this massive purge, there were never any regrets. Driven from power in January 1979, Pol Pot consistently denied that as many as one or two million people may have perished under his regime. On a few occasions he claimed had naively "trusted too many people" and that his naiveté had allow enemy agents to wreak havoc giving rise to some "thousands" of deaths only. The communist **United Front for the National Salvation of Kampuchea** organized with backing from Vietnam and installed in power in Phnom Penh in January 1979 would later put the death toll at 3.7 million. Pol Pot and Ieng Sary were convicted in absentia of "genocide" in a hastily organized show trial held in August 1979.

From 1979 until 1983 the dislodged but not wholly defeated Democratic Kampuchea army waged guerrilla war against new Vietnamese-backed **People's Republic of Kampuchea (PRK)**. **Khieu Samphan** replaced Pol Pot as the nominal leader of the Democratic Kampuchea government in a cabinet reshuffle in December 1979. The CPK was formally dissolved in 1981. With the country's independence called into question by Vietnam's military occupation, the DK resistance was quickly joined by two non-communist movements, the **KPNLF** of **Son Sann** and the royalist **FUNCINPEC**. A nationalist alliance among so many old enemies being out of the question, the three agreed to a loose **Coalition Government of Democratic Kampuchea (CGDK)**. This restructured government succeeded in; gaining diplomatic recognition from the United Nations which also called for the withdrawal of all "foreign" forces from Cambodia. Pol Pot announced his official "retirement" from politics at the age of 60 in 1985. His retreat from public view, determined in part by ill health, coupled with the unilateral withdrawal of all Vietnamese "volunteers" in 1989, led to a cease-fire and the convening, in 1991, of the **Paris International Conference on Cambodia**.

At the conference in Paris, the Democratic Kampuchea negotiators led by Khieu Samphan and **Son Sen** who had argued in support of the negotiated settlement within the **Party of Democratic Kampuchea (PDK)** insisted Pol Pot was no longer politically active. However Pol Pot, **Ta Mok** and a younger generation of army leaders subsequently refused to comply fully with the arrangements for the disarming and cantonment of the belligerent armies and also ensured that the PDK would boycott the 1993 elections. About this time he established his final major base at **Anlong Veng** and actively communicated with subordinates with the military code number "99." Defectors in this period consistently praised Pol Pot for his genteel and compassionate manner which combined with his historical stature, allowed him to retain leading control over the movement almost to the end.

In 1996 and greatly weakened by defections and loss of income, the permanent committee of the PDK ordered the renationalization of all private property, including bicycles and garden tools, in zones under its control. NADK divisions based in Pailin and Phnom Malai whose families had prospered as a result of economic liberalisation and trade with Thailand, refused to comply and with the support of Ieng Sary formally laid down their arms and surrender to the government. In June 1997, and to forestall his likely defection to Pailin and Phnom Penh, Pol Pot ordered the execution of his longterm comrade in arms, and former DK Defence Minister Son Sen together with his wife and their children. For this he was pursued to the Thai frontier by **Ta Mok** who subsequently arrested him and put him on trial in the presence of foreign journalists. Pol Pot, appearing frail and downcast, sat through the proceedings visually unmoved. On 25 July 1997 he was judged guilty of treason and of the murder of Son Sen and sentenced to life imprisonment. He later gave an exclusive interview to Nate Thayer of the Hong Kong based *Far Eastern Economic Review* expressing no regrets.

Pol Pot married Khieu Ponnary in 1956, but they had no children. Though theirs was a marriage of much warmth, intellectual as well as emotional, throughout the 1950s and 1960s, the two drifted apart during the war years of the 1970s. This coincided with Khieu Ponnary suffering bouts of mental illness. About 1984, and with Ponnary's consent, it is said, Pol Pot married **Mea Som**, and they had a daughter. Unconfirmed reports suggested that the couple may have had a son in 1991.

Still in detention Pol Pot died on 15 April 1998 near Anlong Veng. Thai military specialists and some reporters who had known him were allowed to examine and photograph the body which was hastily cremated. Mea Som later revealed that Pol Pot lived out his final days in fear of betrayal by comrades who may have decided to turn him over to international authorities for prosecution. Although Pol Pot was certainly in ill-health the circumstances surrounding his terminal cardiac arrest remain mysterious. In 2001 his cremation site and some of his former houses in Anlong Veng were being developed as tourist sites.

POLICE. Prior to independence in 1953, the Cambodian police force was controlled by the French and divided between the *gendarmerie* (who were involved in combating banditry in rural areas) and the *Sûreté* which dealt with criminal investigation (including tracking down political activists). The police force was transformed, after independence, into the Royal Khmer Police which was divided into four sections: the National Police (based on the *Sûreté*, but also dealing with price controls and immigration), the Phnom Penh Municipal Police, the Town Police (which operated in provincial capitals and other towns) and the Surface Defense Forces (originally formed as a territorial defense force). The latter organization included the Provincial Guard and the Chivapol, a part-time militia group originally raised in 1954 to prevent an expected Viet Minh invasion of the country. In the period leading up to his overthrow in March 1970, Prince Norodom Sihanouk put the Phnom Penh Municipal Police under the control of Buor Horl, and he placed Surface Defense under his brother-in-law **Oum Mannorine**. Other prominent policemen included **Kou Roun** and **Lon Non**.

In May 1970 the police force was reorganized with both the Town Police and the Surface Defense Forces merged into the army. At the same time the Phnom Penh Municipal Police was disbanded and most of its members transferred to the National Police. However it was restricted essentially to dealing with petty crime and also economic espionage. Responsibility for the maintenance of order as well as traffic control was handed over to the army's military police corps, although in December 1971 the police were, once again, given the task of dealing with political dissent.

During the period of Democratic Kampuchea the security apparatus, controlled by **Son Sen**, was involved in matters of national security and suspected cases of foreign espionage. Petty crime was dealt with at the village level.

From the installation of the People's Republic of Kampuchea in 1979, the police became closely associated with the ruling **People's Revolutionary Party of Kampuchea**. It was used to stifle dissent and during the run-up to the United Nations-sponsored elections in 1993, retained its reputation for very heavy-handed treatment of political opponents. With widespread crime throughout Cambodia, the police seem able to locate petty criminals, who are often dealt with in a summary fashion. Their inability to locate those responsible for political crimes, remains a major problem for the present government.

PONHEA YAT, King (1397-1467). A semilegendary Cambodian monarch, he is credited with abandoning Angkor "because it was too close to **Ayudhya**," according to the Cambodian chronicles, and founding **Phnom Penh** soon afterward, in 1437.

POPULATION. At the time of the February 2002 commune elections, the total population was estimated at 11,774,097 of which almost 53 percent were 18 years or more and therefore entitled to register to vote. The 1998 **census** estimates the annual rate of population growth at 2.49 percent and the density of population per square kilometer at 64. The population is also young, as there have been two recent baby booms, one in the early 1980s following the food crisis of 1979-1981 and another after the end of the civil war in 1991. In the 1998 census, children aged 0-14 years made up 42.8 percent of the population, the economically active 15-64 age band, 53.7 percent and the elderly, those 65 and older, merely 3.5 percent.

The civil war (1970-1975), the ensuing collectivization under the revolutionary **Democratic Kampuchea** regime, and resumed resistance and civil warfare (1979-1991) have altered the demographic balance of the population. Conservative estimates are evident in the 1998 census results. For example, the total number of 20-24 year olds counted was noticeably small indicating low birthrates and high infant mortality in the 1977-1981 period. The sex ratio is most unbalanced for the 40-44 age bracket, those who were born in the peaceful, postcolonial years of 1954-1958. This confirms the high male battlefield death rates in the 1970s and 1980s. The percentage of female-headed households was fixed at 25.7 percent in 1998. The large majority of the female heads of household, 62.1 percent, are over the age of 40, many regarded as "widows," the Khmer term being used in reference to widowed women and abandoned wives or mothers or women separated by mutual agreement from their husbands. The mean age at the time of first marriage is 24.2 years for men and 22.5 for women, figures slightly lower than in neighboring Vietnam and Thailand. *See also* EDUCATION.

PORTUGUESE IN CAMBODIA. The earliest records of Portuguese missionaries and adventurers in Cambodia are from the 16th century, soon after the establishment of the Portuguese foothold in Malacca. Descendants of Portuguese remained in Cambodia, often as artillery experts. Their descendants in some cases became members of the elite. Some Portuguese words e.g. *riel*—"royal," a unit of currency—and *kradas* from *carta,* paper, testify to a Portuguese presence. Portuguese families in Cambodia include that of Joseph Delopez and **Kol de Monteiro**.

POUKOMBO (1820-1867). A 19th century Cambodian monk, he led followers into rebellion in 1865-1867 against the French and King **Norodom**, claiming to be a royal prince. His royal pedigree was dubious (an actual Prince Poukombo having died in infancy) but he was able to attract hundreds of adherents and for a time threatened the French protectorate. He was ambushed and beheaded by a pro-Norodom crowd in **Kampong Thom** at the end of 1867. In the 1970s, under the Khmer Republic, his antiroyal, anticolonial stance transformed him briefly into a national hero. In the 1980s a major street in **Phnom Penh** was given his name.

POULO CONDORE. Island in the South China sea used in the French period, and by the South Vietnamese government between 1954 and 1975, as a penal colony. Several Cambodian patriots including **Hem Chieu** and **Pach Chhoeun** were imprisoned there in the 1940s when they came into contact with the Vietnamese Communists imprisoned there.

PRACHEACHON (People's Party/Group). Formed in 1955 following the Geneva Conference of 1954, and known alternatively as the People's Party or the People's Group (Krom Pracheachon), this was the electoral wing of the underground **Khmer People's Revolutionary Party (KPRP)**. It allowed communists and their nationalist sympathizers to participate in the democratic process of national reunification envisaged by the Conference. It was registered by **Keo Meas** and its aim was "to unite the whole Khmer people in the national community without distinction of race (majority and minority), class, party or religion, in order to fight the imperialists and their servants, to defend peace, consolidate independence, achieve democracy and raise the standard of living of the people." The party symbol was a plow. Saloth Sar **(Pol Pot)**, recently back from France, was a propagandist for the movement, which gained 29,503 votes (4 percent) in the election and lost all 35 seats that it contested. In 1976, under **Pol Pot**, several prominent former members of the movement, suspected of plotting against him, including **Non Suon**, **Chou Chet** and Keo Meas, were arrested, tortured and executed.

PRASAT KRAVANH (Cardamon temple). A small Cambodian temple at Angkor, dedicated to Vishnu, built in the reign of **Isanavarman II** in AD 921, under nonroyal patronage. The format of the temple with five towers placed in a line is unusual, and the handsome carvings in brick inside the monument are unique in Cambodian art.

PREAH KETH MEALEA HOSPITAL. Established in 1891, until 1955 it was the only hospital of any size in Phnom Penh. It remained in operation until 1975 when it was evacuated on 17 April, as portrayed in the film, *The Killing Fields*.

PREAH KHAN. Cambodian Buddhist temple complex, covering several hundred hectares, constructed at Angkor under **Jayavarman VII** (r c1178-c1220). The main temple was dedicated to Jayavarman VII's father, and the Buddha image in his honor was dedicated there in 1191. Scholars believe that the temple complex housed thousands of servants and devotees. An inscription indicates that over 100,000 people were mobilized to provide food for the temple on a regular basis. In the 1990s, the temple complex was restored under the auspices of the United Nations Educational, Scientific and Cultural Organization and the World Monuments Fund.

PREAH KO ("Sacred Cow"). Cambodian temple in the Roluos complex, dedicated in AD 879 by King **Indravarman I** to honor his immediate ancestors. The temple consists of six brick towers with richly carved lintels, and its inscriptions indicate that its religious orientation was Shivite.

PREAH KO PREAH KAEV ("Sacred cow [and] sacred jewel"). A popular Cambodian legend that relates the picaresque adventures of two creatures probably representing, respectively, the Hindu and Theravada components of Cambodian culture. In an earlier form, the legend relates that two statues, one of a cow and the other a Buddha image, contained sacred documents (*kbuon*).

PREAH VIHEAR. The province which borders **Thailand** and **Laos,** is named after the 11th century temple of **Preah Vihear**. The provincial capital, a city of approximately 22,000 people, is Tbeng Meanchey. Located on a plateau astride the **Dangrek** Range, most of the province is heavily forested and inhospitable to agricultural activity. With a population of 119,261 in the March 1998 **census** dispersed over 13,251 square kilometers, it has one of the lowest population densities in the country, at 9 people per square kilometer.

PREAH VIHEAR (Khao Prah Viharn). A temple dramatically positioned on a promontory of the **Dangrek** Range on the border with Thailand. It was built in the early 11th century under King **Suryavarman I** and today it is accessible only with difficulty from the Cambodian side of the cliffs. In the 1950s Thai army troops occupied the site, claiming it as part of their national heritage, and only abandoned it after Cambodia mounted a challenge to the Thai claims in the International Court of Justice which in 1962 passed judgement in favor of Cambodia. Neglected by both countries for most of the 1960s, 1970s and 1980s, the temple was opened to limited forms of tourism via joint Thai-Cambodian agreements in the 1990s. By late 2001 Cambodia rejected these agreements and the site is currently closed.

PREAP IN (1938-1964). Born in Kampong Trach, **Kampot**, the son of farmers, Preap In studied at the Collège Technique in Phnom Penh and then joined the **Khmer Serei** of **Son Ngoc Thanh**, based in South Vietnam. A nephew of **In Tam**, he believed that he was offered an amnesty to return to Cambodia. However, he was arrested, subjected to a public trial in front of Prince **Norodom Sihanouk** and sentenced to death. A film of his execution was shown in cinemas throughout Cambodia and, in hindsight, was seen by many as the beginning of the decline of Sihanouk's prestige as head of state.

PREY VENG. A province with a capital city of the same name. The rectangular shaped province borders **Kampong Cham** to the north, **Svay Rieng** to the east, **Kandal** to the west and **Vietnam** to the south. It covers 4,883 square kilometers, and its population in the March 1998 **census** was 946,042. Part of the old Eastern Zone of **Democratic Kampuchea**, wartime deaths were high as revealed by the larger than usual number of female-headed households, 60,585 or 31.2 percent of all households in the province. A rich agricultural province in the **Mekong** Delta, the density of settlement of the population on the land is high: 194 people per square kilometer, compared to the national average of 64. The province also houses some pre-Angkorean ruins, notably near the town of **Ba Phnom**, believed by some scholars to have been an important center, and possibly the capital, in of ancient **Funan**.

PROGRESSIVE DEMOCRATIC PARTY (*kanapac chamroeun cheat khmer*). Founded by Prince **Norodom Montana** in April 1946, it initially drew support from King **Norodom Sihanouk**. The party was centrally run with the party symbol being an arrow passing through three wings, all on a white background. The party advocated an increase in public health, education (more schools, scholarships in France) and public works, and sought to encourage French technicians to work in Cambodia. It believed in the creation of a Cambodian army and compulsory national service. The first Executive Committee of the party consisted of Prince

Montana (president), Neal Smoeuk (brother of **Neal Phleng**), **Au Chheun**, **Chea Chinkoc**, Mey Nosey, Sam Thieu, Ponn Vu Thanh and Ly Kim Khouth (members). The party did disastrously in the 1946 elections and again in the 1947 National Assembly elections. However, it managed to get three members elected to the High Council in January 1948: Prince Montana, Mey Nosey and Au Chheun, although the latter soon resigned from the party and the High Council and Mey Nosey joined **Sam Nhean**'s **Party of the People** in June 1950. Chea Chinkoc was the first party member to become a minister. During the **Yèm Sambaur** premiership, the Progressive Democratic Party called for elections and also the introduction of proportional representation which would have allowed smaller parties to obtain a share of power. **Oum Chheang Nguon** was secretary-general of the party at this time, but, in spite of his energetic efforts and those of other royalists on its behalf, it was defeated again in the 1951 elections and ceased to play any role in political life after that.

PROM SENG (1920-). Born on 8 January 1920 at Chhoeuteal, **Svay Rieng**, the son of a village mayor, he was a member of the police in **Battambang**, joining the Ministry of Agriculture in 1948. A member of the **Khmer Renewal Party**, he contested the 1947 National Assembly elections for Koh Sautin, **Kampong Cham**. He joined Sangkum and contested the by-election for Preah Mlou, **Pursat**, in May 1960. A wealthy farmer, he was elected to the National Assembly for Battambang in 1962-1966, and re-elected in 1966 for the seat of Kuak Khmaum, Battambang. He was under-secretary of state for social affairs and labor in the first **Lon Nol** government in 1966-1967. Prom Seng was a member of the National Assembly in 1970 when it deposed Prince **Norodom Sihanouk** as head of state. He was appointed assistant to the president of the council of ministers in charge of public instruction in 1970. In 1973 he was appointed an advisor to Lon Nol.

PROM THOS (1927-c1986). Born on 5 January 1927 at Lovea, **Siem Reap**, the son of Prom Rath and Mme (née Ouk Nok) he attended **Lycée Sisowath** and was given a government scholarship to study radio-electricity in France from 1947-1953. On his return, he was a member of **Sangkum** and was elected to the National Assembly in 1958 for Banteay Meas, **Kampot**. He was president of the Parliamentary Information and Press Commission 1958-1959. Reelected in 1962, he was the center of some anti-**Norodom Sihanouk** intrigue having been approached by the U.S. Central Intelligence Agency who were interested in knowing where **Lon Nol** stood vis-à-vis Sihanouk. He was secretary of state of trade in the second Lon Nol government, March to July 1970, and minister of industry in the third Lon Nol government, July 1970 to May 1971. In 1973 he was appointed advisor to Lon Nol and later left for exile in Paris. His sister married **Ung Hong Sath**.

PROTECTORATE OF CAMBODIA (Protectorat du Cambodge). This was the official name of Cambodia during the French colonial period from 1863-1954. The protectorate was established at the request of King **Norodom**, who responded willingly enough to French pressure, soon after the French established their colony known as **Cochinchina** in southern Vietnam.

PROVISIONAL REVOLUTIONARY GOVERNMENT OF SOUTH VIETNAM (PRG). Formed in May 1969 and including many prominent non-communist intellectuals, the PRG was the political arm of the **National Front for the Liberation of South Vietnam (NFL)**. Officially a neutralist revolutionary government, it was immediately accorded diplomatic recognition from Phnom Penh where the NFL had maintained a diplomatic office since June 1967. The PRG Embassy, as it was by 1970, was attacked on 11 March in the course of demonstrations against the Vietnamese communist use of Cambodian territory and in the run up to the overthrow of Norodom Sihanouk in March 1970.

PRUM NEAKAREACH. Styled "King of the Dragons," he was president of the **Molinaka Nakataor-Sou** (Khmer for Freedom Party) which contested the 1993 elections. The party won only one seat in the Constituent Assembly.

PUK SOUM (1926-). Born in Krabau, Kanchai Meas, **Prey Veng**, he joined the communists in 1956, taking over from *Achar* Nuon as a leader of the movement in Prey Veng. In 1973-1975 he was head of the Patriotic Monks' Association and from 1975-1978 was head of the agricultural collective at Tuol Khleang, Dauntey. Joining the **United Front for the National Salvation for Cambodia**, he was head of the Prey Veng provincial religious affairs unit.

PUNG PENG CHENG (1916-2001). Born in **Phnom Penh**, he was educated in Cambodia and became a school inspector in 1939, rising to the position of under-secretary of state for national education and secretary of state for information in 1958. From 1960-1970 he was secretary-general to the **High Council of the Throne**. In 1971 he went to Beijing with his wife and he was director of the Office of Prince **Norodom Sihanouk** from 1971-1975. Deciding not to return to Phnom Penh in 1975, he worked for the United Nations Educational, Scientific and Cultural Organization for three years and was appointed Prince Sihanouk's private advisor from 1979-1988. In 1989 he returned to Phnom Penh to support **Hun Sen** and worked on a commission to revise the **constitution**. From July 1989 until

June 1993 he was attached to the cabinet office. In 1991 Pung Peng Cheng was believed to have been about to form an opposition party but this never eventuated and in 1993 he was nominated by the king to the **Constitutional Council**. His daughter, Kek Galabru, married a French diplomat. Pung Peng Cheng died on 10 November 2001.

PUNG PENG CHENG, Mme. *See* TONG SIV ENG.

PURGES IN DEMOCRATIC KAMPUCHEA. The **Communist Party of Kampuchea (CPK)** quietly resorted to purges of its ranks from as early as 1971. The first victims were the 1954 **Khmer People's Revolutionary Party** "regroupees". Many had returned to Cambodia in 1970 expecting to play prominent roles in the armed struggle but found they were often not trusted by those who had remained "inside" the Cambodia and the underground party. By 1973-74 nearly all had been demoted, or arrested and executed, or had fled for their own security to Vietnam. Purges in the last years of the 1970-75 civil war were directed by the leadership of the Special Zone near Phnom Penh. By 1976 a special CPK security facility, know as **S-21** (Salaor Office 21) had been established in the former Tuol Svay Prey high school in southern Phnom Penh. By this time the attention of the purge apparatus shifted to former KPRP cadres who had remained behind in 1954, namely the old Pracheachon party group, including **Keo Meas**, **Non Suon** and **Mey Pho**. Purges in the first half of 1977 swept through the ranks of educated cadre, blamed for failures in implementing the poorly conceived Four Year Plan, especially in the north and northwest. Purges later in the year concentrated on people suspected of links with **Vietnam**. In 1978, as fighting with Vietnam continued, the largest purges targeted cadre and soldiers in the eastern part of the country, where Vietnamese military attacks had been effective. The last wave of purges, toward the end of 1978, were of party members associated with industrial developments, because Pol Pot feared that they would mobilize factory workers to rise against him, backed by the Vietnamese. The Pol Pot regime interpreted anything that went wrong in the Democratic Kampuchea era as the work of traitors, and since different things went wrong at different times, traitors included children, as well as men and women. The number of people executed by the regime between 1975 and the end of 1978 has been estimated conservatively at 100,000. While the exact numbers who lost their lives from purges will never be known, documents left at S-21, now the Museum of Tuol Sleng and only one of the network of party prisons, indicate 16,000 party members were killed there.

PURSAT. A Cambodian province, bordering **Battambang** and **Kampong Chhnang**, it covers 12,693 square kilometers, and its population is estimated at 213,000. Much of the province is heavily forested and relatively inaccessible. Because of its low population, it was chosen by Democratic Kampuchea as a province where "**new people**" evacuated from Phnom Penh could clear land and produce several crops of rice a year. In fact, the areas in the province where evacuees worked were among the least productive and most malarial in Cambodia, and thousands of new people died of disease, malnutrition, and overwork.

PUTH CHHAY (1917-1954). Born in **Kandal** province, he was convicted of several felonies and jailed in 1942 and again in 1946. On both occasions he escaped and by 1950 was leading a group of **Khmer Issarak**—carrying a reward of 100,000 piastres on his head. In 1953 he rallied to the government in exchange for a commission in the Royal Army. He was killed by the Viet Minh during **Operation Sammaki**. *See also* KEM SREY.

-R-

RAILWAYS. The first railway to be built in Cambodia was a 385-kilometer line which connected Phnom Penh to Poipet (from where there was a connection to the State Railway of Siam). It was built in two sections— the first from **Phnom Penh** to Mongkolborey was constructed by the Compagnie des Chemis de Fer du Sud de l'Indochine 1930-1932; this line was purchased by the Chemin de Fer Non Concédés de l'Indochine in 1936. The leg from Mongkolborey to Poipet was finished in 1939-1940.

In July 1952 the entire Cambodian railway network was formed into the Chemins de Fer du Cambodge, and work on a further line from the capital to **Sihanoukville**, via **Kampot**, started in 1960. It was opened in stages in 1969, the final stretch on 20 December. The railway ceased to function during the Khmer Republic, and in mid-1978 Democratic Kampuchea announced that it was building a new line from Samrong to **Kampong Speu** following a study undertaken by Chinese engineers. This did not eventuate, but the railway network reopened again in 1982. The line through **Battambang** was regularly attacked. Still fairly hazardous, only the southwestern line from Phnom Penh to **Kep** and **Sihanoukville** still operates.

RAJENDRAVARMAN II. King of Cambodia 944-968, Rajendravarman was a nephew of **Yasovarman I** who usurped the throne and reestablished the Cambodian capital at Angkor after it had been transferred by **Jayavarman IV** to the region of Koh Ker. Rajendravarman carried out an aggressive foreign policy, expanded his kingdom to the west and set up a provincial form of administration. Under his reign, the royal temples of Pre Rup, a classical temple-mountain, and the Eastern Mebon were built, and also the smaller, gem-like temple known as **Banteai Srey**, 30 kilometers north of **Angkor**.

RAMAYANA. *See* REAMKER.

RATANAKIRI. In the far northeast, Ratanakiri is a tri-border province and a demographic crossroads, its shared boundaries with **Laos** and **Vietnam,** being almost the same length as those shared with **Mondolkiri** province to the south and **Stung Treng** province to the west. The province covers 10,782 square kilometers, with a population of 94,243 in the March 1998 **census**, estimated to have increased to 100,130 by February 2002. Many who live here belong to the non-Hinduized ethnic **minority populations**, known as **montagnards** in **French Indochina** or as *Khmer loeu* ("upper Khmer")*,* among the dominant, lowland **Khmer.** By the late 1960s Prince **Norodom Sihanouk** attempted, partly for reasons of national security, to develop the economy and to settle lowland Khmer in the province. The Central Committee office of the **Communist Party of Kampuchea** was located there, the Cambodian leg of the **Ho Chi Minh** trail passed through and the **Front Uni Pour La Lutte des Races Opprimées (FULRO)** was active across the border in the highlands of Vietnam.

RAY BUC. The son of Ray Orn and Mme (née Srey Phor), he was the older brother of **Ray Lamouth**. Buc served as provincial administrator in **Prey Veng** but was removed for corruption. In 1945 he joined the **Khmer Issarak** in Thailand, but rallied to the government at Sisophon in January 1947. An independent, he contested the 1951 National Assembly elections for Phniet, **Battambang,** and then returned to the government service and became chief clerk at the **Buddhist Institute.** He was also president of the Association of Friends of the Pali School.

RAY LAMOUTH (1905-c1975). Born on 7 July 1905 at Sisophon, **Battambang,** the son of Ray Orn and Mme (née Srey Phor), Lamouth was the younger brother of **Ray Buc.** Ray Lamouth was secretary in the postal services and in March 1945 was director-inspector of the posts, telephones and telegraphs. A member of the **Democrat Party**, he took part in anti-French demonstrations in 1946-1947 and was elected to the 1947 National Assembly for Kampong Chhnang town. He was elected secretary of the Assembly and was minister of trade in 1949 and of economic affairs from June until December 1950. He was then minister of religion. Briefly a member of the **National Recovery Party** of **Yèm Sambaur,** he established the Independent Party and contested the 1951 National Assembly elections for Kampong Chhnang town. He then joined **Sangkum** and was elected to the 1958 National Assembly for Kampong

Chhnang and the 1962 National Assembly representing Kampong Cham. Lamouth was president of the Public Works and Telecommunications Commission and also the Budget Commission 1958-1959. In June 1971 he was appointed to the **constitutional drafting committee** as a representative of the Association of Friends of Buddhist High Schools. Lamouth was minister of state attached to the Prime Minister's Office for national reconciliation under **In Tam** from May until December 1973. Lamouth married Phang Sowat and they had eight children.

RÉALITÉS CAMBODGIENNES. A French-language weekly magazine, published in Phnom Penh, it flourished in the Sihanouk era. Neocolonial in orientation, the paper strongly supported the government of **Norodom Sihanouk**. In 1970 the anti-Sihanouk parliamentarian and journalist **Douc Rasy** was appointed editor, and though he was dismissed for taking the side of foot soldiers in a salary dispute within the army, the magazine continued to appear and to support the **Khmer Republic** until March 1975.

REAM CHOUENG PREY (1545-1596). King of Cambodia. A minor prince, he usurped the throne following the Siamese sacking of **Longvaek** in 1594. Using locally raised troops, he defeated a small Thai army of occupation and proclaimed himself king in 1595, only to be assassinated by the European adventurers **Diego Veloso** and Blas Ruiz a year later.

REAMEA THIPODEI (Chan). King of Cambodia 1620-1659. The youngest son of King **Chey Chetta** who seized the throne from his uncle in a coup d'état, aided by Cambodian Muslim troops. Soon afterward, the king converted to Islam. In the late 1640s he had to deal with European pressures to open trading facilities in Phnom Penh. He was overthrown by forces loyal to his uncle, aided by Vietnamese troops, in 1658. Taken to Vietnam in an iron cage, he was released soon afterward and, if the chronicles are to be believed, died in exile.

REAMKER **("The Glory of Rama").** An epic poem, composed in the 16th or 17th century, based on the ancient Indian epic the Ramayana. The surviving text relates only a portion of the Indian tale, and its poetic form suggests that it was intended to be recited to accompany dancers rather than to be read as a whole. The poem relates the story of an Indian prince, Rama, and his wife Sita, models of aristocratic virtue and Buddhist behavior, who are separated by ill fortune and eventually reunited, after much travel, many hardships and a series of adventures. Incidents from the poem appear in the bas-reliefs at **Angkor Wat**, in wall paintings on many Cambodian Buddhist temples, and they were reenacted by the royally sponsored dance-troupe in Phnom Penh. The tale was immensely popular in colonial and postcolonial times, and its major figures were important in Cambodian folklore.

REASTR NIYUM. This was the political party formed in 1998 by **Ung Huot**, then first prime minister, to contest the elections of that year. Although two **FUNCINPEC** deputies, Om Radsady and Ros Chheng joined, the party was heavily based on personal friends of relatives of its leader and failed to win any seats in the elections. By the end of 2001 Ung Huot was negotiating a return to FUNCINPEC.

RED CROSS. This was established in Cambodia during the rule of Prince **Norodom Sihanouk,** and the honorary president was Princess Monique Sihanouk (now Queen **Monineath**). From 1970-1975 it was funded directly by the government. It did operate, on a small scale, during **Democratic Kampuchea**, and supplied much aid to the border refugee camps from 1979 until 1989.

RED KHMER *See* KHMER ROUGE.

REPUBLICAN PARTY. Founded on 15 June 1972, it had its roots in the Independent Republican Association of **Tep Khunnah**. Prince **Sisowath Sirik Matak** was elected secretary-general and the party drew its support from Sino-Khmer businessmen as well as some important military figures such as Pok Saman and **Thong Van Fan Muong**. Its members also included **Op Kim Ang, Trinh Hoanh** and Seng Bun Korn, president of the Inadana Jati Bank. At the first party congress on 23 July 1971 the party adopted the symbol of a male and female head, representing the family. The party boycotted the **National Assembly** elections in September 1972. In 1973 the Republican Party agreed to allow ministers to join the Cabinet, but these ministers refused to answer questions in the National Assembly which they considered illegal.

REVOLUTIONARY ORGANIZATION. *See* ANGKAR PADEVAT.

RICE. The principal item in Cambodia's diet and the main crop grown by Cambodian farmers for several thousand years. There are over a hundred varieties of edible rice cultivated in the country. Some mature faster than others, and some strains are preferred in drier and wetter regions. Because so little agricultural research has been carried out in Cambodia and because the agricultural sector of the economy is starved of government funds, the quality of Cambodian rice has remained uneven, and Cambodian rice is not yet competitive with the rice of other Southeast Asian countries on the international market. *See also* AGRICULTURE.

RIEL. The Cambodian unit of currency. It was introduced at independence replacing the piastre which had been used under the French protectorate.

RONG PHLAMKESAN, also **Rong Them Ea Chramhaysone** or **Phlam Kaysan (1932-)**. Born in **Koh Kong** from an ethnic Thai background, he rallied to the **National United Front of Kampuchea (FUNK)** in 1970, but after disagreements with **Pol Pot** rebelled against the communist leadership along with **Say Phuthang**. He did not emerge on the political scene until 1979 when he was political commissar for Koh Kong. From May 1981 he was a member of the Central Committee of the **Kampuchean People's Revolutionary Party**, then the **Cambodian People's Party (CPP)**. In February 1983 he was secretary to the party for Koh Kong representing the province in the National Assembly until May 1993. In June 1993 he was elected as CPP deputy for Koh Kong, but resigned his seat to become governor of the province in December 1993. In 1999 he was appointed to the Senate by the CPP.

ROS CHANTRABOT (1945-). A teacher of French and philosophy in Cambodia, he worked on *Le Courier Phnompenois* newspaper, founding *Basli Angkor* ("Light of Angkor"). A keen student activist, he was a confidante of **Lon Non**, and in June 1971 Chantrabot represented the Republican Association on the **constitutional drafting committee**. Soon afterward he went to France where he wrote a thesis on the Khmer Republic at the École des Hautes Études en Sciences Sociales. Lon Non, in France in 1974, assisted him with the thesis, and as a result it provides a closer insight into the Republic than most other works. The thesis was completed in 1978 and published in Paris in 1993.

ROS CHETHOR (1932-c1975). Born on 13 May 1932 at **Phnom Penh**, son of Ros Thong, court clerk at **Kampong Thom**, and Mme (née Poum Sen), he graduated from **Lycée Sisowath**, and, winning a scholarship for studies in France, he registered at the École Supérieure des Beaux Arts 1950, but became ill, spent most of the next two years in a sanatorium and returned to Cambodia in 1953. On returning to Phnom Penh he was a teacher and then technical advisor to *Kampuja* magazine and managing director of Neak Cheat Niyum Press. He rallied to **National United Front of Kampuchea** in February 1971 and was a signatory of the **Declaration of Patriotic Intellectuals** in September 1971. In 1974 he was vice-minister of foreign affairs in the **Royal Government of National Union of Kampuchea**.

ROS SAMAY. After serving in the **Democratic Kampuchea** army, he left and became deputy commander-in-chief of the armed forces and also secretary general of the Vietnamese-established **United Front for the National Salvation of Kampuchea (UFNSK)** in December 1978. A member of the UFNSK Central Committee, he was minister in charge of special affairs, religious affairs, Buddhism, drafting of the constitution and economic relations with foreign countries from December 1979 and minister of special affairs from April 1980. He was also chairman of Kampuchea's World Peace Council and chairman of the religious movement.

ROS SARET (?-1976). He worked at the Land Registry Office at the Ministry of Agriculture and was a member of the **Khmer Renewal Party**. He contested the 1947 National Assembly elections for Sampong Chey, **Kampong Cham** and the 1951 National Assembly elections for Prek Dambaung, **Kandal**. During the 1950s he continued to work at the Central Land Registry. In 1971 he was appointed to the **constitutional drafting committee** for the Association for the Accumulation of Merits. In 1972, a member of the **Socio-Republican Party**, he was elected to the **Senate** of the Khmer Republic. He was captured on 7 November 1975 and taken to **Tuol Sleng** where he was executed on 20 May 1976.

ROS SRENG (1939-). The head of the **People's Revolutionary Party of Kampuchea (PRPK)** for **Pursat** province in May 1979, he represented the province in the National Assembly from May 1981 until May 1993. A member of the Central Committee of the KPRP from April 1989, he was party secretary in Pursat and governor of the province 1992-1993. The first on the **Cambodian People's Party** list for Pursat in the May 1993 elections, he was elected but resigned taking part in the Prince **Norodom Chakrapong** secessionist ploy. In December 1993 he was appointed governor of Pursat. In 1999 he was appointed to the Senate by the CPP. *See also* REASTR NIYUM.

ROYAL AIR CAMBODGE (RAC). Cambodia's national airline was first established as a joint venture in 1956 with 40 percent French ownership. As Royal Air Cambodge it began operating normal international and domestic flights in June 1964. By 1969 it had three aircraft, primarily serving on national routes. Following the overthrow of Sihanouk in 1970, the company was renamed Air Cambodge, and then Cambodia Airways International, which continued in operation until April 1975. With assistance from the **Soviet Union** and **Vietnam**, the company was resurrected by the **People's Republic of Kampuchea** in the 1980s as Kampuchea Airways. After the war and the reestablishment of constitutional monarchy, a reorganized joint state-private company resumed trading in 1994 under the name Royal Air Cambodge, the private investment and managerial assistance coming from Malaysia. RAC flew from Phnom Penh to Bangkok, Kuala Lumpur, Singapore, Ho Chi Minh City, Guangzhou and Hong Kong leasing some of its aircraft. This company closed on 16 October 2001 unable to finance cumulative debts of more than 30 million U.S. dollars. A sharp slump in income after 11 September

2001 was partly to blame. The State Secretariat for Civil Aviation (which holds $11 million of the bad debt) has since negotiated a rescue package with Hainan Airlines of **China**. The new company, formed in April 2002, will operate under the name Cambodia Air using at least two Boeing jets leased from Hainan. Two new international routes are to be added to RAC's existing schedules: Phnom Penh-Hainan-Beijing plus Phnom Penh-Tokyo. Hainan Air will hold a 49 percent stake in Cambodia Air and has agreed to manage the new company and to retain and retrain most of RAC's 230 employees. It refuses any responsibility for the failed company's debts. The State Secretariat for Civil Aviation will hold a 41 percent stake in Cambodia Air and CTG, the remaining 10 percent.

ROYAL BALLET. Dance is arguably the most important of the performing arts in Cambodia. The Royal Ballet in Cambodia traces its origins to the **Angkor** period. The dancers, according to tradition, were captured by the Siamese in 1432 and taken to Ayudhya. They later returned to Cambodia and until the twentieth century, court dancers lived a secluded life in the grounds of the palace, performing for Kings, and serving also as consorts. The keeping of classical dancers who in their art invoked images of celestial power was a custom reproduced in provincial towns by some of the more important governors. In the late colonial period when resources for maintaining a large royal troupe ran out, the French colonial administration made some dancers into professional teachers and civil servants, a measure contributing to the popularization and commercialization of the art form. In the first reign of King **Norodom Sihanouk**, dancers were permitted to live outside of the palace grounds and to marry. In the 1960s, Sihanouk's eldest daughter, Princess **Norodom Bopha Devi**, currently minister of culture and fine arts, was the undisputed star of the Royal Ballet. Lacking royal patronage after 1970, the ballet gradually split up, and the multiple styles and positions of classical court were revived only slowly in the 1980s and 1990s. *See also* PISETH PILICA.

ROYAL CHRONICLES. *See* CHRONICLE HISTORIES.

ROYAL CRUSADE FOR INDEPENDENCE. This was the name given to the campaign carried out by **Norodom Sihanouk** in 1952-1953, following his bold dissolution of the **Democrat Party**-controlled **National Assembly**. In a major international tour, Sihanouk vigorously pleaded Cambodia's case for independence. Although the unwelcome publicity embarrassed the French, royal pleading for Cambodia's immediate independence fell on deaf ears in Paris. Traveling next to the **United States**, the Prince was informed that neither the U.S. nor the United Nations could intervene. Disappointed and angered, he returned to Cambodia via **Thailand**, going to **Battambang**, not to **Phnom Penh**. From there, he appealed for a mass uprising in support of a peasant march on Phnom Penh. Khmer soldiers in the French colonial army defected in significant numbers and some **Khmer Issarak** militants also rallied to the royal cause. French officials, alarmed by the growing size of the movement as the royal march on the capital took form, decided abruptly to concede independence thereby allowing the king to return to the capital in triumph. This grant of independence was confirmed at the Geneva Conference in 1954, further strengthening the king's political position. The Royal Crusade rapidly entered national mythology as Sihanouk laid claim to the title "father of independence," arranged the submission or surrender of the remaining noncommunist Issarak fighters and the political marginalization of all others who were deemed "Khmer-Viet Minh." Expressed in other terms, the Royal Crusade was an astonishing act of political usurpation, dispossessing the French and the Democrats of their power and the Issarak, of their nationalist credentials.

ROYAL GOVERNMENT OF NATIONAL UNION OF KAMPUCHEA (Gouvernement Royal d'Union Nationale du Kampuchea: GRUNK). This was the government-in-exile headed by Prince **Norodom Sihanouk** between 1970 and 1975. In 1973 and 1974 GRUNK came close to achieving recognition by the United Nations at the expense of the **Lon Nol** government in power in the capital **Phnom Penh**. It was dismantled in 1976 when the government of **Democratic Kampuchea** was established in Phnom Penh.

ROYAL HOTEL (HOTEL LE ROYAL). Built in 1928-1929, it was originally run by the government of Indochina. On 1 September 1951 the hotel was handed over to the Cambodian government, and in April 1952 the Société Cambodgienne d'Hotellerie et de Tourisme (SOCHOT) was established to take charge of it and other hotels. As one of the most prestigious hotels in Cambodia, it had 42 staff in 1941 (30 percent being Cambodian) and 135 in 1965 (85 percent Cambodian). It reopened in the 1980s as the Royal Phnom Penh Hotel or *Le Phnom*, in brief. Purchased and renovated in the 1990s by Raffles International, Le Royal today has 208 rooms and suites, a ballroom, a health spa and a swimming pool as well as a business center. The hotel features centrally in the award-winning film, *The Killing Fields*, as many journalists resided there in the 1970-1975 period but, as Phnom Penh was not accessible in the early 1980s, the hotel scenes were not filmed there.

ROYAL KHMER SOCIALIST YOUTH (Jeunesse Socialiste Royale Khmère: JSRK). A youth organization, similar to the Boy Scout

Movement, but associated with **Sangkum**, it was founded in 1957 and within a year had a membership of 219,000. By 1965 it was semi-compulsory for boys and girls to join, and its membership stood at 846,000. Established on 5 September 1959, although the idea was first raised in a 1957 government statute, it was sponsored by Queen **Sisowath Kossamak**, with its president Prince **Norodom Sihanouk** determining policies with the aid of 10 other officers. Financial control was exercised by the Council of Ministers, and there is an executive director, assisted by the general commissariat. Each JSRK branch is organized into team, group, company and sector. Following the deposing of Sihanouk in 1970, the movement was absorbed into the Salvation Youth. With the onset of war, interest flagged, and it was gradually marginalized.

RUBBER. Rubber latex was an important source of foreign exchange during the 1950s and 1960s, and while production of latex continued on a diminished scale throughout the 1970s and 1980s, by the 1990s most tree stock was old and production fell steadily in year-to-year terms. Exports also fell from an officially recorded 11,227 tons in 1992 to an estimated 2,000 tons in 1997, some of the decline reflecting illegal sales organized by plantation workers and managers. Established by the French in eastern Cambodia in the 1920s, alongside similar holdings in Vietnam, Cambodia's plantations covered 30 hectares in 1956 and 58 hectares by 1966, producing 49,000 tonnes of latex in 1966. Rubber accounted for 32 percent of the kingdom's export earnings in 1965. The plantations were severely damaged by bombardment and defoliants in the fighting in the 1970s but were restored haphazardly under Pol Pot and somewhat more systematically by the Vietnamese-installed regime that followed. Efforts by the government to lease the plantations to French and Malaysian firms have been unsuccessful and are opposed. From the investor's perspective, returns on investments would be only slowly realized while the opposition of plantation workers and leading politicians in the **Cambodian People's Party (CPP)** adds political risks to the economic ones.

-S-

S-21. *See* TUOL SLENG.

SAK SUTHSAKHAN (1928-1994). Head of state from 12-17 April 1975. Born on 8 February 1928 in **Battambang**, he attended École Doudart de Lagrée and was briefly involved in the **Greenshirts** in 1945. He then proceeded into the army, being in the first graduation from the Royal Military Academy, Cambodia, and attending the École d'Instruction d'Infanterie et Coetquidam, France, in 1948 and the École d'Instruction de Genie at Angers in 1949. Returning to Cambodia in 1950, Sak Suthsakhan was commander of the 2nd Battalion and commander of the **Siem Reap** autonomous sector. In 1952 he was head of the 4th Bureau of National Defence and also attended the École d'état-major France (1952) and the École Supéeure de Guerre (1955).

In 1954 Sak Suthsakhan, aide-de-camp to the chief of the general staff, represented Cambodia in the delegation to the **Geneva Conference**. In October 1956 he was appointed secretary of state for national defense, apparently the youngest defense minister in the world at that time. He remained as minister of national defense, also with responsibility for information in the eighth **Norodom Sihanouk** government. From 1958 until 1962 Sak Suthsakhan was commander of the 2nd military region, returning to the cabinet in November 1961 as under-secretary of state for the interior, for Royal Police and national defense until the end of 1965.

Sak Suthsakhan was appointed as assistant to the tactical chief of the general staff in 1966 and was believed to have been actively involved in the overthrow of Sihanouk in March 1970, after which he was appointed to the general staff. In 1971 he led a mission to the **United States** and, although he served briefly as minister of state in charge of national defense in 1972, he soon returned overseas as a "roving" ambassador with his main aim to win diplomatic support for the Khmer Republic and to lobby for it at the United Nations. Although not involved in party politics during the Khmer Republic, in 1972 he was seen as leaning toward the **Republican Party**, before eventually linking himself with **Lon Nol's Socio-Republican Party** by mid-1973. In 1974 Sak Suthsakhan returned to Cambodia, but was back at the United Nations soon afterward with the rank of lieutenant general. It was not until February 1975 that he returned to Phnom Penh and was appointed commander-in-chief on 12 March 1975. On 21 March he was appointed vice-prime minister and minister of national defence. On 12 April, following the departure of **Saukham Khoy**, Sak Suthsakhan assumed the position of head of state (as supreme commander) of the Khmer Republic. By this time the military situation was desperate and Phnom Penh fell on 17 April 1975, Sak Suthsakhan leaving the city by helicopter with **Thach Reng** moments ahead of the the **National United Front of Kampuchea** forces storming the Olympic Stadium from where his helicopter had taken off. His account of the fall of the Khmer Republic, *The Khmer Republic at War and its Final Collapse*, was published by the U.S. Army Center of Military History, Washington, D.C., in 1980.

Sak Suthsakhan settled in the United States but soon afterward joined **Son Sann** to form the Khmer People's National Liberation Armed Forces (KPNLAF), a merger of various factions along the Thai-Cambodian border.

He then was one of the major forces in the establishment of the **Khmer People's National Liberation Front (KPNLF)**, remaining in command of its army. In 1982 he rose to the four-man Steering Committee and was involved in the takeover of the KPNLF in 1986. Ousted and then restored, relations with Son Sann were never the same again. Sak Suthsakhan formed the **Liberal Democratic Party** and contested the 1993 elections in Cambodia. However he failed to win a seat in the new parliament, and some of its members joined other political movements.

Married with four children, Sak Suthsakhan's wife, Evelyn, a teacher, had worked on *Kampuja* under Sihanouk and then with the Association of Cambodian Women. One of his sons, Sak Sireyvath, was in the National Gendarmerie when he fell in battle in August 1972. Sak Suthsakhan, himself, rallied to the newly elected coalition government in 1993 and died after a heart attack on 29 April 1994.

SALOTH CHHAY (1926-1975). Son of Phen Saloth and Mme (née Sok Nem), and brother of Saloth Sar (**Pol Pot**), he was a member of the left-wing group within the **Democrat Party** who seized control of the party in 1954, but left to join the **Pracheachon** Party and was director of *Sammaki* newspaper. Arrested in July 1955 for opposing the Cambodian-U.S. military agreement, he was released and was on **Hou Youn**'s committee to support His Majesty's Neutrality Policy. He later became a newspaper journalist and in 1971-1972 was the editor of *Prayojan Khmer*, a daily newspaper funded by Lon Non. He was a founder of the **Pracheachon** Party of Penn Yuth, which was supported by Lon Non as a method of gaining an opposition party to stand in the September 1972 legislative elections. He stood for the seat of Phnom Penh but failed to be elected. He died on the evacuation of Phnom Penh in April 1975.

SALOTH SAR. *See* POL POT.

SAM BITH. Formerly the commander of the elite Division 405 of the National Army of Democratic Kampuchea, Bith was the superior officer to whom **Nuon Paet** reported when three Westerners were taken hostage during a train robbery on 26 July 1994. Thirteen Cambodians died in the attack while the three Western hostages, Jean-Michel Braquet from France; Mark Slater from the UK and David Wilson from Australia were killed about six weeks later when they were deemed of "no further use." Transcripts of radio communications released at Nuon Paet's July 1999 trial revealed Paet had discussed recommendations to "destroy" the hostages with Bith before the three were killed. The recommendations allegedly came from **Pol Pot**. Bith surrendered to the Royal Government following the 1996 defection of **Ieng Sary**. In exchange for advising the government in its dealings with remaining **Democratic Kampuchea** forces in **Anlong Veng**, he was made a major general in the Royal Cambodian Armed Forces. His immunity from prosecution was lifted at the time of Nuon Paet's trial. He was then charged with murder, kidnapping and other criminal offences in January 2000 but failed to respond to a municipal court summons. In July 2001 Bith was suspended from duty when the Ministry of Defense began an investigation into his 1994 actions. He moved to Sdao, near **Battambang**.

SAM KANITHA (1951-). Born on 2 August 1951 in **Phnom Penh**, she studied science and taught political science and biology in secondary schools. A **FUNCINPEC** agent during the 1980s, she was elected a FUNCINPEC deputy in May 1993. In October 1993 she was secretary of the National Assembly's Commission on Human Rights and Reception of Complaints. In 1999 she was appointed to the **Senate**. She is married with three children.

SAM NHEAN (1890-1963). Educated at various Buddhist Schools, Sam Nhean served in the Cambodian administration from 1912-1946. A member of the **Democrat Party**, he rapidly grew to prominence with his oratorical skills. In 1946 he was elected to the Constituent Assembly; and in 1947 he was elected to the National Assembly representing Sampong Chey, **Kampong Cham** and was then elected vice-president of the National Assembly. In 1949 after allegations against him over fishing permits, he demanded the lifting of his own parliamentary immunity to contest charges, none of which stuck. As a result he grew disenchanted with the Democrat Party and left to form his own *Gana Reastre* or **Party of the People**. He contested the 1951 National Assembly elections for Prek Thmey, Kandal; the by-election for Cham, **Prey Veng** and the 1952 High Council elections for the representative for farmers and husbandmen. From 1951 until 1955 he edited *Cambodian Voice*.

   One of the founders of **Sangkum**, Sam Nhean was political advisor to their weekly magazine, *Sangkum Reastr Niyum*. In February 1956 Sam Nhean was a member of the Cambodian Goodwill Mission to Communist **China** and in July 1956 led the Cambodian Journalists' Delegation to North Vietnam. In 1957 he was appointed secretary-general of the **Royal Khmer Socialist Youth**. He married and had at least two children: **Sam Sary** and Sam Dulnet.

SAM RAINSY (1949-). Born on 10 March 1949 in Phnom Penh, son of **Sam Sary**, he attended schools in Paris and London and then Lycée Descartes and Lycée **Sisowath** in Phnom Penh. Leaving Cambodia for France when he was 16, he studied at Lycée Janson de Sailly and gained a diploma from the Institute of Political Studies in Paris in 1971, and then gained a diploma in economic sciences and accountancy in 1979 and an MBA from INSEAD Business School at Fontainebleau in 1980. He worked in several different banks in Paris and joined the Paribas group in 1988 before running his own accountancy practise in Paris. In 1989 he was appointed as representative of Prince **Norodom Ranariddh** in Europe and was Director of the **FUNCINPEC** bulletin *Vimean Ekreach*, published in Paris—he had been a founding member of FUNCINPEC in 1981. In 1971 he married **Tioulong Saumara**, daughter of **Nhiek Tioulong**; they had three children. They returned to Cambodia in June 1992.

On his return, Sam Rainsy, a member of the Supreme National Council, 1992-1993, became minister of economics and finance then was elected **FUNCINPEC** deputy for Siem Reap in June 1993. He was appointed, by King **Sihanouk**, as minister of state and minister of the economy and finances in the government. At the end of that year he was designated finance minister of the year by *Asiamoney* magazine, published in Hong Kong but resigned from his government positions following a vote of no confidence in the National Assembly, 20 October 1994. In December 1994 Prince Norodom Ranariddh, first prime minister, made a joke about his impending death, and on 13 May 1995 he was expelled from FUNCINPEC and then from the National Assembly. Sam Rainsy immediately put together plans for establishing a political party and his **Khmer Nation Party** (*Cheat Khmer*) was formed in late 1995, after Rainsy toured expatriate Cambodian communities to rally support.

On 30 March 1997, while Sam Rainsy was holding a rally outside the National Assembly, assassins whom the FBI later concluded were connected to the government, threw hand grenades into the crowd—some 20 people were killed. Soon afterward Rainsy, having trouble registering his Khmer Nation Party in Phnom Penh, left Cambodia and toured expatriate communities speaking to large crowds. On his return in the run-up to the 1998 elections, he renamed his party the **Sam Rainsy Party**. In the elections, in spite of massive intimidation aimed directly against his supporters, his party came third, after the **Cambodian People's Party** and FUNCINPEC. Sam Rainsy was elected to the National Assembly for Kampong Cham, and in November 1998 he became the leader of the opposition in the National Assembly.

SAM RAINSY PARTY. This political party, formed from the **Khmer Nation Party**, is the official opposition in the Cambodian National Assembly. Led by **Sam Rainsy** it supports liberal democracy and Western-style capitalism using a lighted candle as its symbol. It has campaigned on the platforms of raising the wages of textile workers by free collective bargaining and also establishing a system which allows for the full accountability of the police. During the 1998 elections it won an absolute majority of the votes in the one area (**Pailin**) where vote-counting was not conducted by the **Cambodian People's Party (CPP)** and was pronounced to have come third in the election by the CPP-dominated electoral officials. In the commune elections of 2002, the party won 1,354 council seats, 12 percent of the total 11,259 and control of 13 councils, six of these being in **Phnom Penh**.

SAM SARY (1917-c1961). Born on 6 March 1917 in Kampong Speu Province, son of **Sam Nhean**, he attended **Lycée Sisowath** and in 1939 joined the judicial service to train to become a magistrate. He was successively a juge d'instruction and avocat general. In 1945 he was appointed chief of political affairs and police then director of control of direct taxes, Phnom Penh. Interrupting his career, he went to Paris 1946-1950 to continue his education. He studied law at the University of Paris, and also studied at the Centre for Higher Administrative Studies in Paris. His friendship with the young king is on display in his book *La Grande Figure de Norodom Sihanouk* (published by the royal palace in 1955).

Sary was a member of the Cambodian delegation to the **Geneva Conference** in 1954 and was later instrumental in forming Sihanouk's political movement, the **Sangkum**. He visited the United States in 1956 and impressed officials there with his anticommunist stance. He became Cambodian ambassador to London in 1957 and was brought home in disgrace after he had physically abused a female member of his staff, and she complained to the police. Cut off from Sihanouk's patronage, Sary sought support for a change in the national political regime. He founded an antiroyalist political party, the Democratic People's Party (*kanapac reastrethipatay)*, naming another prominent opposition personality, **Chau Bory**, as vice-president, and using its newspaper to agitate against Sihanouk. He received clandestine funding from Thai and South Vietnamese officials. One of the conspirators in the **Bangkok Plot** of 1959, he disappeared from view afterward, almost certainly killed by agents under contract to **Lon Nol**. His nephew, Siv Vuthay, was executed for treason in 1960. In Em (1913-2001), his wife, and her son, **Sam Rainsy**, moved to Paris in the mid-1960s.

SAMBOR PREY KUK. An archaeological site in **Kampong Thom** province, about 19 kilometers north of the provincial capital, the site contains several pre-Angkorean temples in brick dating from the first half of the seventh century AD, which probably graced the vanished pre-Angkorean city of **Isanapura**.

SAMDECH EUV (**"prince papa"**). The affectionate title by which **Norodom Sihanouk** was widely known in the 1960s, in 1969, shortly before he was overthrown, Sihanouk appeared under this heading in the Phnom Penh telephone directory. The title reappeared after 1991 when Sihanouk returned to Cambodia.

SAMLAUT UPRISING. Communist-inspired insurgency against the Cambodian government that broke out in southern **Battambang** in early 1967 and was brutally repressed. The uprising was ignited by heavy-handed rice requisitions ordered by Prince **Norodom Sihanouk** and carried out by the Cambodian army under **Lon Nol**. The requisitions were intended to make up the shortfall of surplus rice being exported clandestinely to Vietnamese communist troops fighting in **Vietnam**. The Samlaut area had a long history of insurgency and local radicals were active in stirring up resistance. Cambodia's communist leaders at this stage were faraway in the northeast and played no role in the uprising, although they hastened to stop it, via an emissary sent from Phnom Penh, once it had failed. Prince Norodom Sihanouk assumed incorrectly that the uprising had been supported by his allies, the Vietnamese communists, and by the close of the year his policies became more anticommunist.

SAMRONG SEN. An archaeological site in **Kampong Thom** province, it was excavated haphazardly in the 1870s and more systematically in the 1920s. Excavations indicated that the site had been inhabited for at least a thousand years, up to AD 500. Numerous stone and bronze tools found on the site provided a rough framework for scholars in the colonial era as they mapped Cambodia's prehistory.

SAN THAT (1945-1975). A student activist, he was one of the group that organized the demonstrations outside the National Assembly on 16 March in the lead-up to the overthrow of Prince **Norodom Sihanouk**. In 1972 he was one of the major protagonists in what became the Koy Pech incident. A secondary school teacher, he joined the **Socio-Republican Party** and was elected to the **National Assembly** of the Khmer Republic in September 1972 for the seat of Peam Oknha Ong, Vihear Suor. In April 1975 San That was evacuated to **Battambang** and died or was killed soon afterward.

SAN YUN (1905-1974). Prime minister 1956-1957. Born on 15 June 1905, the son of Kan San and Mme (née Kong Hang), he was educated at **Collège Sisowath**. He joined the administrative services in 1923 as secretary to the royal household. From May until August 1945 he became permanent secretary to the cabinet and from August 1945 until December 1946 was secretary-general of the government and director of the Royal Printing Press. He was governor of **Takeo** province from June 1948 to December 1949, governor of Phnom Penh from December 1949 to December 1953 and governor of Kampong Cham province from December 1953 to October

1955. San Yun served as minister of the interior and surface defense, October 1955 to January 1956 and was then appointed prime minister from October 1956 until 2 January 1957, also holding the portfolios of interior, foreign affairs, national defense and sanitation. On 3 January 1957 he was reappointed prime minister and was minister of foreign affairs, economic and financial affairs, national defense and the interior. He lost this position on 8 April after losing a vote of confidence on an economic policy. From January until April 1958 San Yun was minister of state for the national economy and planning under **Penn Nouth**. He was then appointed director-general of the royal palace, a post he kept until 1960; but was reappointed to that position after the 1962 elections. In the interim he was president of Sangkum. From 1963 until 1967 he was political director of *Réalités Cambodgiennes*, the Phnom Penh weekly news magazine. At the time of the overthrow of Prince **Norodom Sihanouk** in 1970, San Yun was secretary-general of Sangkum, but soon resigned from that position and went into political retirement. San Yun had married a daughter of Pho Proeung and had six children. He died on 3 March 1974.

SANGHA. A Pali word used to describe a Theravada Buddhist clerical hierarchy headed by the Sangharaja. It is also used more generally when referring to the monastic population of a country, like Cambodia, where Buddhism is practiced.

SANGKUM REASTR NIYUM (Peoples' Socialist Community). The nationally oriented political movement founded by Prince **Norodom Sihanouk** soon after he abdicated the throne in 1955. A requirement for recruits was that they abjure membership in other political parties. The intended effect was to abolish those parties. Unsurprisingly, in a tumultuous campaign, Sangkum candidates captured over 80 percent of the vote and all 91 seats in the 1955 elections called for by the Geneva Conference. Over the next few years, Sihanouk chose the term "Buddhist socialism" to describe the eclectic practices of the movement, which he altered from time to time. Although he had envisaged it originally as a quasi-independent force, the movement soon became identified with the prince, and was subservient to his control. Handpicked Sangkum candidates took all the seats in elections in 1958 and 1962. Some were known communists, most were centrists and a few were conservatives. The political intention of the movement was to stamp out open debate. The movement's official organ was the weekly, bilingual French-Khmer language journal *Neak Cheat Niyum* ("The Nationalist"). In its 15-year existence, The Sangkum was closely identified with the Prince, and soon after he was overthrown in 1970—by a National Assembly composed entirely of Sangkum members—the movement was formally abolished. It was never revived, although in 1993 the **Cambodian Peoples' Party**, courting favor with Sihanouk, claimed erroneously to be the heir of the Sangkum. Later in the 1998 elections **Ung Huot**, then first prime minister, called his party **Reastr Niyum**.

SANSKRIT. Ancient Indian language, used in pre-15th century Cambodia for inscriptions in verse found in Hindu and Mahayana Buddhist temples. The quality of the Sanskrit varied from time to time and place to place. With the advent of Theravada Buddhism, and its use of Pali, knowledge of Sanskrit disappeared.

SAO PHIM also **So Vanna (?-1978).** Little is known of his origins, but as a young man, in the early 1950s he was active in the **Khmer Issarak** in the late 1940s and joined the **Indochina Communist Party** in 1950 in eastern Cambodia. With other communists, he was evacuated to northern Vietnam in 1954, returning home in 1956. In 1960 he joined the Central Committee of the newly constituted **Workers' Party of Kampuchea**, fleeing to the *maquis* in the eastern part of the country in 1963. He spent the next few years in areas under Vietnamese communist control, often living alongside the secretary of the **Communist Party of Kampuchea**, Saloth Sar (**Pol Pot**). He also retained his territorial strength in the east during the civil war. In 1976, under Democratic Kampuchea, he remained on the Central Committee and served as party secretary for the Eastern zone of the country. Widely popular in eastern Cambodia, Sao Phim was suspected as early as 1976 of having pro-Vietnamese leanings. He finally fell out of favor with Pol Pot in 1978 following successful Vietnamese incursions. As cadre and soldiers from the zone were systematically purged, Sao Phim sought advice from Phnom Penh and when he failed to receive it, knowing he would be purged himself, he committed suicide.

SAO SAROEUN. The **Kampuchean People's Revolutionary Party** secretary for Sangke, **Battambang**, from August 1987, he was sixth candidate on the **Cambodian People's Party** list for **Kampong Chhnang** and was not elected. In December 1993 he was appointed second vice-governor of Kampong Chhnang.

SAR HOR. When captain in the Cambodian army, he was a member of the delegation to the **Geneva Conference** in 1954 along with Lon Nol. Resigning as governor of **Kampong Speu** in August 1970, he was promoted from colonel to brigadier general. He was a senior officer in the Republican army in the early 1970s, as deputy governor of Kampong Speu; but as commander of military region V, he was blamed with mishandling the Angkor Chey operation. Hor was, however, promoted to deputy chief of staff, and in October 1972 was appointed minister of state charged with the interior. He was minister of state for veterans affairs in the first **In Tam** government from May to December 1973.

SAR KHENG (1951-). Born on 15 January 1951 in Ang Daung Satt village, Karboa, Kanchea Meas, **Prey Veng**, from a peasant family, Sar Kheng is a brother-in-law of **Chea Sim**. He rallied to **National United Front of Kampuchea (FUNK)** in 1970 and became secretary to the Kraboa Commune and vice-president of the National Association for Youth in Kanchea Meas from 1970-1972. He was in charge of printing the FUNK magazine *Ponleu Bopea* 1973-1975 and became a local party leader in the early years of Democratic Kampuchea. Indeed in 1976 he was **Communist Party of Kampuchea (CPK)** permanent secretary for the Northeast Zone. In 1977 he fled to Vietnam and rallied to the **United Front for the National Salvation of Kampuchea** in 1978. In April 1980 he became the personal secretary to Pen Sovan, and in March 1982 was appointed director of the cabinet assisting the Central Committee of the **People's Revolutionary Party of Kampuchea (PRPK)** and a member of the Central Committee in his own right in November 1984. He then served as director of the office of the Central Committee, January 1989. He helped Hun Sen turn the PRPK into the **Cambodian People's Party (CPP)** in 1989 and became vice-prime minister and minister of the interior in 1992. In June 1993 he was elected as CPP deputy for Battambang; and was then appointed as deputy-prime minister and cominister of the interior and public security in the Royal Cambodian Government. Taking an active part in the July 1997 coup, he is widely recognized as a possible alternative to Hun Sen as leader of the party and of the government. In 1998 he was reelected to the National Assembly and was reappointed as deputy prime minister.

SAR KIM KHOY (1926-). Born on 2 March 1926 at Prom Treang, **Siem Reap**, the son of a businessman, he attended **Lycée Sisowath**, and was given a government scholarship to study in France 1947-1953. On his return he worked at the Customs and Excise Department. Khoy was nominated by **Sangkum** to contest the seat of Phniet, **Battambang**, in the 1958 National Assembly elections and duly elected. He was president of the Parliamentary Finance Commission 1958-1959. In June 1959 he was appointed secretary of state for the interior and parliamentary relations, being under-secretary of state for the same portfolio from April 1960 to January 1961. In June 1971 he represented the Ministry of Finance on the **constitutional drafting committee**.

SAR KIM LOMOUTH (1930-). A French-trained economist, he was a member of the **Democrat Party** from 1946-1955 and teacher at **Lycée Sisowath**. Lomouth was an inspector of the railways and then he studied law at the Faculty of Law and Economic Sciences, **Phnom Penh**, graduating in March 1964. From 1964 until 1975 he was the manager of the Inadana Jati Bank, Phnom Penh, and was a clandestine member of the **Communist Party of Kampuchea**. In the 1975-79 government of **Democratic Kampuchea (DK)** he was the vice-president of the foreign trade bank and also secretary of state for supply and transportation. In December 1979 he was appointed minister of finance in the reshuffled DK government led by **Khieu Samphan**. In this capacity he led the DK delegation to Singapore for a meeting of governors of Southeast Asian central banks. Although he remained loyal to the DK movement throughout the **United Nations Transitional Authority in Cambodia** period, in February 1995 he defected through Thailand.

SARIN CHHAK. (1922-1979). Born on 2 January 1922 in Phnom Penh, son of Sarin and Mme (née Sann), he graduated from the Royal School of Administration and initially worked in local government, including the Municipality of Phnom Penh. He was already a senior administrator in the Ministry of Foreign Affairs in his 40s when he earned a *licence* in law from the Faculty of Law, University of Phnom Penh, and a doctorate in political science from the Faculty of Law, University of Paris. His well-researched thesis on the haphazard colonial demarcation of Cambodia's eastern frontier with Vietnam was published in Paris in 1966 (see bibliography). While a student in Paris, he served concurrently as the Director of Cambodia House (*Maison du Cambodge*) and Cambodia's Permanent Representative to UNESCO. Because of his specialist legal knowledge, Sarin Chhak was invited in 1966 to join the delegation negotiating with the National Front for the Liberation of South Vietnam for recognition of Cambodia's "existing" frontiers. In 1967 he was appointed ambassador to Algeria. Still in Cairo on 18 March 1970, Sarin gave his support among the first to the deposed Prince **Norodom Sihanouk** and to the **National United Front of Kampuchea (FUNK)** and attended the Summit Conference of Indochinese Peoples on 24-25 April 1970 in China. He was minister of foreign affairs in the **Royal Government of National Union of Kampuchea (GRUNK)** from April 1970 until 19 July 1975, as well as a member of the Central Committee of the FUNK and the front's Political Bureau. (In August 1970 a court in the **Khmer Republic** sentenced him to death *in absentia* for these alleged acts of high treason.) It was Sarin Chhak who accompanied **Thiounn Prasith** to Pyongyang to persuade Prince **Norodom Sihanouk** to return to Phnom Penh after the 17 April 1975 victory, and in late August 1975 he accompanied the delegation led by **Ieng Sary** that went to Lima, Peru. After returning to Cambodia with Sihanouk in September 1975, he was sent to a series of reeducation camps before being given a minor post in Ieng Sary's Foreign Ministry in late March 1976. As purges within the **Democratic Kampuchea** ministries gathered pace, he was incarcerated at Boeng Trabek reeducation center in March 1977 along with most other "old society" ambassadors and intellectuals who returned from abroad. Rehabilitated and back in the Foreign Ministry in November 1978, he disappeared from view soon after the Vietnamese army occupied Phnom Penh on 7 January 1979. He was married to Koy Vansinn. On 16 October 2001, three of their four children, naturalized citizens of France, completed legal proceedings officially declaring the two of them and their older brother to be deceased.

SATH HASSAVY (DE MONTEIRO) (1926-). Born in **Phnom Penh**, he was a member of the **Khmer Labor Party** and contested the 1955 National Assembly elections for Koh Thom, **Kandal**. In 1959 he was implicated in the **Sam Sary** plots against Prince **Norodom Sihanouk**. During the first years of the Khmer Republic he was secretary-general of the Veterans' Association, editor of *Le Courier Phnompenhois* and joined the **Socio-Republican Party**. In September 1972 he was elected to the National Assembly of the Khmer Republic of Samrong, Oddar Meanchey. From June 1974 until March 1975 he was under-secretary of state for the Prime Minister's Office in charge of press, documentation and public relations.

SATHA. King of Cambodia 1579-1596. His reign was marked by his rivalry with his brother, Srey Soryiyopor, who defeated a Thai invasion in 1588. Following the successful Thai attack of 1592, Satha fled to the Lao city of Stung Treng, where he died in 1596. Earlier in his reign, he visited **Angkor Wat**, supposedly while hunting, and partially restored the temple.

SAUKHAM KHOY (1915-1996). Acting president, 1-12 April 1975. A career soldier, he was governor of **Kampong Cham** 1950-1951 and in August 1965 was promoted to major general. His first move into politics was in 1966 when he was appointed to the *contre-gouvernement*, the "shadow cabinet" to **Lon Nol**, with responsibility for national defense. He remained there in some form or another until 1970 and took no part in the moves against Prince **Norodom Sihanouk** in March 1970. Khoy joined the **Socio-Republican Party** in 1972 and was one of the army representatives on the **Senate** in September 1972, being elected president of the Senate at its first session on 4 October. Popular, honest and respected, he had spent most of the civil war 1970-1975 on the battlefield. In 1975 he was drawn back to Phnom Penh politics, and after the departure of Lon Nol on 1 April 1975, Saukham Khoy became interim president. His tenure was terminated when he joined the American evacuation of Phnom Penh on 12 April, when he left for Thailand. He then moved to ·the **United**

States where he retired from politics. In 1986 he was living in Houston, Texas.

SAVANG VONG. *See* KRUOCH SAVANG.

SAY BORY (1940-). Born on 29 January 1940, he studied at the Royal School of Administration and gained an economics degree. Bory was deputy-governor of Siem Reap in 1966-1969, in 1971 he represented the Alliance for Peace on the **constitutional drafting committee**. After earning a doctorate in law in Paris in 1974 he worked in the Mayor's Office, Paris 1981-1982. A leading figure in the **Khmer People's National Liberation Front**, he was their principal legal advisor and was later employed as a consultant to the **United Nations Transitional Authority in Cambodia** on constitutional matters. In October 1993 he was a professor of constitutional law in Phnom Penh. He was minister and then secretary of state in charge of National Assembly liaison, 1993-1995 when he also founded the Cambodian Bar Association (October 1995). He is one of the King's appointees to the **Constitutional Council**.

SAY CHHUM (1945-). Born in Koh Sautin, **Kampong Cham**, he was a secondary school teacher, being held by the **National United Front of Kampuchea** in 1970-1975. In October 1985 he was elected to the Central Committee of the **People's Revolutionary Party of Kampuchea (PRPK)** and provincial secretary for Kampong Speu. He was then minister of agriculture March 1986 to August 1990 and vice-president of the Council of Ministers. A member of the politburo of the PRPK and then the **Cambodian People's Party**, he was first deputy prime minister in the **Hun Sen** government 1992-1993. Elected to the Constituent Assembly for **Kampong Speu**, he was a member of the Commission for the Interior, National Defense and Anticorruption. He was reelected to the National Assembly in 1998.

SAY PHUTHANG (1925-). Born on 17 July 1925 at Koh Kong, he is from the ethnic Thai minority. Among the members of the Khmer People's Party of Cambodia who decided to go to Vietnam in 1954 he attended a Communist Party school and military academy in Hanoi. Rallying to the **National United Front of Kampuchea (FUNK)** in 1970, he broke with Pol Pot in 1974, and returned from Vietnam in 1979 as one of the most senior leaders of the communist defectors from the **Communist Party of Kampuchea**. From April 1980 until October 1985 he was president of the organizational committee of the Central Committee of newly-formed **People's Revolutionary Party of Kampuchea (PRPK)** and a member, later vice-president of the Council of State 1981-1993. A deputy for Phnom Penh in the National Assembly 1981-1993, he was a member of the

Politburo of the PRPK and then the Cambodian People's Party. He was elected to the Constituent Assembly for **Kandal** but resigned his seat and in December was appointed to the **Throne Council**.

SDACH TRANH (**"regional kings"**). In precolonial Cambodia, the *sdach tranh* were five high ranking officials with administrative responsibilities for distinct "territories" or *dei*. In the 19th century, these were located at Thboung Khmum, **Ba Phnom**, Treang, **Pursat** and Kampong Svay. It is not clear if the officials were hereditary, appointed by the king, or both. References to *sdach tranh* do not appear in any Angkor texts, and the institution did not survive the colonial era.

SEAT CHHE alias **Tum (1932-1977)**. Born at Chhieu Khmau, Koh Thom, **Kandal**, he was the son of Sou Seat and Mme (née Eap Eang Ly). Attending the Pali School of Bottum Vaddey, **Phnom Penh**, he became a monk. During his last years of study 1953-1954, he became interested in politics and taught at **Chamroeun Vichea School** where he met **Ieng Sary, Uch Ven** and other radicals, secret communists and Marxist intellectuals. A supporter of the **Democrat Party** in 1955, he helped in the production of their newspaper and also contributed to the **Pracheachon** newspaper. In 1963 while he was still teaching at Chamroeun Vichea, Saloth Sar (**Pol Pot**), just before he left Phnom Penh, gave him the party archives to keep in his house 1959-1962, and in 1963 he fled to the jungle. Active in the 1970-1975 civil war, soon after the proclamation of **Democratic Kampuchea**, he was among the intellectuals who fell under suspicion. Arrested on 29 April 1977, he was taken to **Tuol Sleng** and executed soon afterward.

SECOND INDOCHINA WAR. *See* INDOCHINA WARS.

SEK SAMIET. The district leader in **Koh Kong**, and then governor of the province in 1967, he was appointed governor of **Battambang** in 1968, remaining in that position (with a few intermissions when he was dismissed for corruption, before being reappointed) until 17 April 1975. During his tenure the Republican military campaigns in Battambang were marked by incompetence and allegations of widespread corruption—Sek Samiet was regularly accused of selling ammunition to the enemy forces in the Sihanoukist, communist and Vietnamese-organized **National United Front of Kampuchea**. Appointed major general, he was a close supporter of **Lon Nol** delivering him a massive number of votes in the 1972 elections. He escaped to **Thailand** on 17 April and spent several years along the Thai-Cambodian border trying to rally some resistance to **Democratic Kampuchea**. His wife was Meas Rommany, daughter of Meas Duy, and they had several children. He is now a **Cambodian People's Party** member of the Senate.

SENATE. Established in September 1972 by the **Khmer Republic** to serve as an Upper House (replacing the **High Council of the Kingdom**), it consisted of twenty-four elected members, eight Senators nominated by the civil service and a further eight nominated by the Armed Forces. All the forty senators from 1972-1975 were members of the **Socio-Republican Party.** In 1999 the Senate was reestablished with thirty-two members nominated by the **Cambodian People's Party (CPP)**, twenty by **FUNCIN-PEC**, seven by the **Sam Rainsy Party,** and two by the King. **Chea Sim**, nominee of the CPP is the chairman of the Senate, Prince **Sisowath Chivan Monirak** is the first vice-chairman and General **Nhek Bun Chhay** is the second vice-chairman.

SENG SUNTHAY (?-1970). A professional soldier, in 1959 he was appointed director of army communications, replacing Houl Khoun who was posted to Paris. Remaining in that position for the next 11 years, he was a close confidante of Prince **Sisowath Sirik Matak**. Heavily involved in the overthrow of Prince **Norodom Sihanouk** in 1970, he was found dead in a hotel on 20 March 1970 along with a colleague. At first appearance it looked as though the two had shot each other, but it is more likely that both were murdered. One rumor was that Seng Sunthay had been given orders to shoot Prince Sihanouk if he returned to Phnom Penh in March 1970—either way it does appear that he was murdered by pro-Sihanouk officers. His widow, Yip My Yong, and their children remained in Phnom Penh where his two sons still live in impoverished circumstances.

SEREI KOSAL (1953-). Born on 12 October 1953 at Psar Leu, Bakan, **Pursat**, he gained a degree in civil engineering from the University of Phnom Penh in 1974 and began work as a teacher at Lycée Bang Kak, Phnom Penh, 1974-1975. During the period of **Democratic Kampuchea** he helped in a resistance group *Neak Sa* ("White Dragon") in Pursat. Uncovered in 1978, many of the members fled to **Thailand**. There, in 1979, Serei Kosal helped found, with **Chan Bory**, *Sereikar Cheat* ("National Liberation") in Oddar Meanchey. Kosal was appointed lieutenant colonel in **Armée Nationale Sihanoukienne** but was captured in 1989 on a mission in Banteay Meanchey. Held in prison in Vietnam until 1990, he was released and returned to Thmar Dou where he became brigadier general of the **National Army for an Independent Kampuchea**. When Soeung Kiri, president of the **FUNCINPEC** electoral committee for **Battambang** was assassinated, Serei Kosal became acting president. Elected to the Constituent Assembly in May 1993 in Battambang, he resigned to become first deputy governor of of the province in December 1993. One of the targets of the July 1997 **Hun Sen** coup, he managed to escape from Phnom Penh to **O'Smach**, from where he helped **Nhek Bun**

Chhay to organize armed resistance. He returned to Phnom Penh in 1999 as an **advisor** to Prince **Norodom Ranariddh** and was appointed by FUNCINPEC to the **Senate**.

SEUY KEO. An early northeastern region communist dissident in the **Communist Party of Kampuchea**, it was he and **Bou Thang** who led the mutiny in Voeunsai in 1974 when **Pol Pot** began purging Vietnamese-trained revolutionaries. In 1979 as the new **People's Republic of Kampuchea** began to organize an army, he was its first chief of general staff. By 1989 he was deputy minister of defense and in 1999, after nomination by the **Cambodian People's Party**, he was appointed to the **Senate**.

SIEM REAP. A province with a capital city of the same name, it is located on the northern shore of the **Tonlé Sap**, the heartland of the ancient Angkorean empire. Sharing boundaries with the provinces of **Battambang, Banteay Meanchey, Oddar Meanchey, Preah Vihear and Kampong Thom**, it covers 10,897 square kilometers. The March 1998 **census** put its population at 696,164. Population density, at 68 per square kilometer, is just above the national average of 64. The province was annexed by Siam in 1794 and was restored to Khmer sovereign control, only after pressure from France, in 1907. Much of it, this time excluding **Angkor Wat**, was again annexed by Thailand 1941-1946. The *srok* ("district") of Siem Reap which contains the provincial capital had a population of 119,528 (1998). To facilitate international tourism, Siem Reap city has the only international airport outside of Phnom Penh. The **Cambodian People's Party** won 515 (77 percent) of the 668 seats in the local commune elections of 2002.

SIEN AN (c1930-1977). Briefly a classmate of **Ieng** Sary at **Lycee Sisowath** Sien An studied engineering in France and returned to Cambodia in 1953 where he immediately joined the armed struggle against the colonialists and the underground **Khmer People's Revolutionary Party (KPRP)**. Attached as an interpreter to the Polish delegation in the **International Control Commission** after 1954, he was among those publicly denounced as communist by Prince **Norodom Sihanouk** in 1963 and forced to flee underground. By 1968 he had been assigned to party work in **Vietnam**. An early supporter of the **National United Front of Kampuchea (FUNK)**, Prince **Norodom Sihanouk** appointed him to the FUNK Central Committee in April 1970 and as he was already working in Hanoi, appointed Royal Government of National Union Ambassador to North Vietnam. He was sentenced to death *in absentia* for high treason by a high court in the Khmer Republic in August 1970. His wife, Prum Sieng, was sentenced to 20 years hard labor *in absentia* in August 1970. In December 1975 he was recalled to Phnom Penh, along with all other FUNK and GRUNK diplomatic personnel, put through a brief period of "re-education" and assigned to B-1, the new foreign ministry headed by Ieng Sary. He and Prum Sieng were caught up in the **purges in Democratic Kampuchea** being arrested on 29 December 1976 and sent to **Tuol Sleng** where he was executed in 1977.

SIENG LEPREASS (1941-). Born on 29 March 1941 at Prek Tameak, **Kandal**, he studied English literature at the University of Southern California from 1962-1966 and was a presenter then producer for Voice of America from 1968-1979. At the request of the U.S. State Department, he moved to the Thai-Cambodian border to help distribute U.S. aid to the refugees from 1979-1987. A member of the **Khmer People's National Liberation Front (KPNLF)**, he was also a member of the delegation of the **Coalition Government of Democratic Kampuchea** to the United Nations with the rank of ambas-sador and KPNLF delegate to the peace talks 1987-1991. He was a reserve KPNLF member of the **Supreme National Council** 1992-1993, worked at the Ministry of Information from 1993 and was the secretary-general of the Khmer New Generation, created by **Ieng Mouly** in August 1993.

SIEU HENG (c1922-1975). Secretary of the **Khmer People's Revolutionary Party (KPRP)** 1951-1958, Heng's parents, from Kampuchea Krom, had settled in **Battambang** in the 1930s. During World War II, when the province was annexed by **Thailand**, Sieu Heng joined the **Khmer Issarak** guerrilla movement and in 1946 the **Indochina Communist Party**, inspiring his wife's nephew, later known as **Nuon Chea**, then a student in Bangkok, to join him. In the First Indochina War (1946-1954) he was prominent in the resistance, and his fluency in Vietnamese was an advantage. Evacuated to Vietnam in 1954, he returned to Cambodia two years later. By 1958 he was demoralised by dwindling support for the KPRP, he defected to the government and quietly returned to Battambang. He remained there throughout the 1960s and the civil war 1970-1975 but was assassinated along with other alleged 'traitors' immediately after the war, allegedly on the orders of Nuon Chea, then deputy secretary of the **Communist Party of Kampuchea**.

SIHANOUK, MONINEATH Queen (1936-). Born on 18 June 1936, she was the daughter of François Izzi, a Frenchman of Italian extraction working in the construction business in Phnom Penh and his wife Mme Pomme Peang (previously the wife of Oum and mother of **Oum Mannorine**). When François Izzi went back to France in 1939 for military service, Monique, her birth name, and her sister Nanette (who married Prince

Sisowath Methavi) were looked after by Prince **Sisowath Sirik Matak**. Monique studied at Lycée Descartes and met **Norodom Sihanouk**, whom she married on 5 March 1955; they had already had two sons, Prince **Norodom Sihamoni**, born in 1953 and Prince **Norodom Norindrapong**, born in 1954.

Monique has always remained out of mainstream politics, and has been a loyal supporter of her husband. She was active in the Cambodian **Red Cross** from 1960 (honorary president from March 1961) until March 1970 when her husband was overthrown. At that time supporters of **Lon Nol** criticized her for corruption, accusing her of selling land to the Vietnamese but never proffered any real evidence. She was sentenced in absentia to hard labor for life in a show-trial organized in Phnom Penh in August 1970. A member of the Central Committee of the **Royal Government of National Union of Kampuchea (GRUNK)** from 1973, she returned to Phnom Penh with her husband in September 1975 and lived with him until their evacuation in January 1979—living together in exile in Beijing and Pyongyang. On 10 November 1993 she was proclaimed Queen Norodom Monique of Cambodia, styled Her Majesty Queen Norodom Monineath Sihanouk of Cambodia. During all her years in political life, she has declined all requests for interviews.

SIHANOUK TRAIL. This was the name given by journalists to the Cambodian portion of the so-called **Ho Chi Minh trail**, a network of roads running south from North Vietnam, used to supply Vietnamese communists during the Vietnam War. It was also sometimes used to describe the alternative route used by the North Vietnamese, from **Sihanoukville** to the border.

SIHANOUKVILLE (Kampong Som). One of the nation's four municipalities and the site of the country's only deep-water port, it was developed under the aegis of a French aid program in the 1950s and linked to Phnom Penh by a friendship highway built with aid from the **United States**. Prior to the establishment of the port, it was a village of some 40 families but by 1960 it had a population of 3,293 people. The March 1998 **census** reported the population at 155,690, on a territory of only 870 square kilometers. Historically known as Kampong Som, and then Sihanoukville as it developed, the name of Kampong Som was restored by the **Lon Nol** coup group in 1970. It was renamed Sihanoukville for a second time in 1992. The municipality has three *srok* ("districts"), 22 *khum* ("subdistrict" or "commune") and 85 *phum* ("villages" or "hamlets"). The **Cambodian People's Party (CPP)** won 93 (64.6 percent) of the 144 contested commune council seats, **FUNCINPEC**, 31 (21.5 percent) and the **Sam Rainsy Party**, 20 (13.9 percent).

SIM KA (1948-). A supporter of the communists when he was a student in the late 1960s, he joined the **Communist Party of Kampuchea (CPK)** in 1972 but defected from **Pol Pot** in 1978 to join the **United Front for the National Salvation of Kampuchea (UFNSK)**. He was president of the UFNSK People's Committee in **Kampong Cham** 1979-1981 and elected to the Central Committee of the **People's Revolutionary Party of Kampuchea (PRPK)** at its first congress in May 1981. From October 1985 he was a member of the control commission of the Central Committee of the PRPK and vice-president from June 1988. An alternate member of the politburo from April 1990, he was secretary to the PRPK committee for Phnom Penh in August 1990. In the 1993 elections he was second on the **Cambodian People's Party (CPP)** list for Phnom Penh but resigned before the results were formally declared.

SIM SOM (c1928-1990). A senior Communist personality, he militated on bhalf of the communist movement at the National Institute of Pedagogy in the 1960s being forced to flee to the jungle following the publication of the "list of 34" suspected communists in 1963. He was a signatory to the 1971 **Declaration of Patriotic Intellectuals** and clearly a member of the **Communist Party of Kampuchea (CPK)** by this year. In the **Democratic Kampuchea** period he was ambassador to the Democratic People's Republic of Korea, retaining that position until the 1980s. Posted to the Thai-Cambodian border, he was Chairman of the CPK Committee of the Rear Base Area and responsible for looking after some 150,000 civilian supporters and dependents of the National Army of Democratic Kampuchea who lived at Phnom Malai. He died suddenly on 25 April 1990 after being struck by a falling tree during a rainstorm.

SIM VAR (1906-1989). Prime minister 1957-1958. Born in **Kampong Cham** province, Sim Var was secretary-interpreter in Phnom Penh courts; and then worked with **Son Ngoc Thanh** in his *Nagaravatta* newspaper. During this period he was keen to explain his political ideas to the people, and politicize the population of **Phnom Penh**, which he hardly ever left. He worked in the forestry department and was involved in the July 1942 demonstrations against the French. A close friend of Prince **Norodom Sihanouk**'s father, Prince (later King) **Norodom Suramarit**, in 1945 he became Thanh's chief clerk on the latter's return from Japan. Sihanouk was later to accuse him of collaborating with the French before the war— but the opposite is more accurate.

In February 1947 Sim Var was arrested after having been implicated in the **Black Star Affair**, when some Cambodians were alleged to have been involved in an anti-French cult. Much of the evidence does appear to have been fabricated, but Sim Var still spent eight months in prison in

Saigon being released in November. A keen member of the **Democrat Party**, he was the vice-president of the Constituent Assembly, before becoming delegate to the French Union from July 1948 until 1951. In June 1951, as he was to do in 1972, he returned from abroad to contest the Cambodian National Assembly elections for **Kampong Cham** city as a Democrat candidate. Of the three other delegates to the French Union who returned, two other Democrats were elected, with the independent being defeated. However, Sim Var failed to gain his seat.

When in 1954 the Democrat Party was taken over by Prince **Norodom Phurissara**, and other left-leaning activists such as **Keng Vannsak,** many of the older Democrats (including Sim Var) resigned. He denounced the new Democrat leadership as communist and went as far as opposing any Democrat representation in the 1955 caretaker government of **Leng Ngeth**. Following his resignation from the Democrats, Sim Var was a founding member, and first secretary-general of **Sangkum**, and was prime minister from February 1956, and prime minister and foreign minister from 26 July 1957 until 8 January 1958. After **Ek Yi Oun**'s six-day government (and Penn Nouth returning for 11 weeks), Sim Var returned as prime minister and minister for national defense from 29 April to 22 June 1958— one of the few periods when **Lon Nol** did not hold the defense portfolio. He was voted out of office by the National Assembly and was appointed ambassador to **Japan** in January 1958. It was there that he met his second wife, Yoko. He was withdrawn in 1964 when the embassy in Tokyo was closed on grounds of economy. He then returned to Phnom Penh and became political director of *La Dépêche du Cambodge* 1963-1966. In 1966 he was elected to represent Phnom Penh in the National Assembly. Sim Var denounced the Khmer-American Military Aid Agreement, and along with his son-in-law, **Soth Polin**, editor of *Nokor Thom* ("Great City"), he dominated Cambodian news media until 1974. He was also vice-prime minister and coordinator of social affairs, education, anticorruption and youth in October 1966.

After the overthrow of Sihanouk, Sim Var started producing a sumptuous art magazine, *Nokor Khmer*, which was published in English and French. As one of the main supporters of the Khmer Republic, he soon found himself sidelined, and was sent back to Tokyo as ambassador in June 1971, still remaining in control of his main organ, *Khmer Ekkaraj* ("Khmer Independent"), the major Khmer-language daily newspaper. In 1972 Sim Var took soundings about standing in the presidential elections against Lon Nol. However, even though he was nominated for the June 1972 presidential elections, he was disqualified due to the fact that his wife was a foreigner. Sim Var withdrew from politics soon after this and settled in France. In exile Sim Var published *Moul Khmer*, the newsletter of the Mouvement pour le Soutien de la Liberté Khmère, and was associated with the establishment of the Khmer People's National Liberation Front. He died in Paris on 21 April 1989.

SIN SEN (1944-). Born in Prey Veng, nephew of **Chea Sim**, he assisted his uncle from 1970-1978 and was gazetted major general in January 1989. He was appointed vice-minister of the interior from January 1989 to April 1992 then vice-minister of security from April 1992 to June 1993. Appointed to the **Supreme National Council** in 1991, he was the subject of some of the **United Nations** investigations into political assassinations. The fifth **Cambodian People's Party (CPP)** candidate for Phnom Penh, he was not elected. Deputy minister of security and then under-secretary of state for the interior from November 1993, he was appointed secretary of state for the interior, 4 July 1994. However, he was accused of being involved in the coup attempt on 2 July. Resigning from the CPP on 29 August 1994, he was sentenced to 18 years in jail on 28 October.

SIN SONG (1947-). Born in 1947 in **Prey Veng** province, from a peasant family, he was active in the **Khmer Issarak** and rapidly became a supporter and aide to **Chea Sim** 1970-1977. In 1977 as the purges within the **Communist Party of Kampuchea (CPK)** gathered pace he fled to Vietnam. There he was quickly recruited into the Vietnamese sponsored **United Front for the National Salvation of Kampuchea** and the new **People's Revolutionary Party of Kampuchea (PRPK)**. From May 1981 until June 1993 Sin Song was a member of the National Assembly for **Kampong Cham**. In May 1981 he was appointed deputy-minister of the interior and in August 1988 was minister of the interior and national security, a post he eventually relinquished in April 1992. He was promoted to general in January 1989, elected to member of the Central Committee of the PRPK in April 1989 and member of the **Supreme National Council** from 10 September 1990 until 12 February 1992. From April 1992 until June 1993 he was minister for National Security and was accused by the **United Nations Transitional Authority in Cambodia** and others as the instigator of criminal irregularities in the 1993 election campaign, some of resulted in deaths. This led to pressure from the **United Nations** and his eventual sacking. In May 1993 he was elected as a **Cambodian People's Party (CPP)** member for Prey Veng, but resigned protesting against the election results. In June 1993 he was involved in the attempted secession and fled to Vietnam on 15 June, later returning to Prey Veng.

Sin Song was accused of intriguing against the government in the coup attempt on 2 July 1994 and was imprisoned the following day. However, he escaped on 4 September 1994, but had been expelled from the CPP on 29 August 1994. On 28 October 1994 Sin Song was condemned to 20 years imprisonment by a military tribunal and was arrested 5 November in Bangkok. Thailand refused to extradite him to Cambodia. His children go to school in Melbourne, Australia.

SISOWATH, Collège/Lycée. A coeducational secondary school in Phnom Penh, it was Cambodia's first and for many years its only lycée, founded as a Collège in 1911 (and refounded as a Lycée in 1934). Classes were taught in French even after independence, and its former pupils (who formed an Alumni Association), played a prominent role in the early phases of Cambodian nationalism, and many of them, including **Khieu Samphan**, **Hu Nim** and **Ieng Sary**, later became prominent in the Communist movement. **Son Ngoc Thanh** (who did not attend the school) was the first to see the influence of the Alumni Association. Its office-holders have included **Chheam Van**, **Douc Rasy** and **Huy Kanthoul**. During the Khmer Republic it was renamed Lycée Phnom Daun Penh.

SISOWATH (1840-1927). King of Cambodia 1904-1927. Son of **Ang Duang**, and half brother of King **Norodom** and father of King **Sisowath Monivong**. Sisowath was born on 7 September 1840 in **Battambang**, a protégé of the Thai court. He was educated in Bangkok and returned to Cambodia in the 1860s after Norodom had been crowned king by the French. Eager to become king himself, Sisowath curried favor with the French and in the late 1860s raised an army to defeat the rebel pretender **Poukombo**, and his own half brother, Prince **Sivotha**. In the anti-French rebellion of 1883-1884, which may have had Norodom's clandestine support, Sisowath again took the French side and probably received word that he would succeed his brother when the time came.

When Norodom died, Sisowath became king and was crowned on 28 April 1906. Later that year he paid a state visit to France and in the following year welcomed the return of Battambang and **Siem Reap** to Cambodia from Thailand. For the remainder of his reign he presided affably over Cambodia's gradual emergence into the modern world, without managing to play a leading part in the process himself. Political life was dominated by **Thiounn** and his dealings with the French. Sisowath supported the French during World War I and is best remembered for his establishing of **Collège Sisowath** which was the foremost secondary school in the country until 1975.

King Sisowath had at least 19 wives. His eldest son was Prince Sisowath Wothavong (1858-1904, father of Prince **Sisowath Watchayavong**). He was also the father of Prince **Sisowath Essaravong** (1858-1907); Prince Sisowath Nophkao (1861-c1930, grandfather of Prince **Sisowath Poracsi** and Prince **Sisowath Sovannareth**); Prince Sisowath Monivong (1875-

1941); and Prince Sisowath Sopuphanouvong (1888-1955, minister for war during the 1930s). When King Sisowath died on 9 August 1927 in Phnom Penh, he was succeeded by his son Monivong.

SISOWATH AYRAVADY, Princess (1942-). Also known as Sisowath Chamroeun Vong, she was born on 27 January 1942, the third child of Prince Indravong. She was also the step daughter of **Norodom Phurissara** who married her mother in the early 1970s in the liberated zone of the **National United Front of Kampuchea (FUNK)**. In her schooldays she was tutored by **Ieng Sary**. She married **Ngo Pin** and together they lived in Beijing, both working in the Foreign Ministry of the **Royal Government of National Union of Kampuchea**. For much of the **Democratic Kampuchea** period, following brief periods of reeducation in the countryside, she lived in **Phnom Penh**, working in the Foreign Ministry. From 1979 until 1984 she worked as the English language translator for **Khieu Samphan**. She moved to France with her children in 1985.

SISOWATH CHIVAN MONIRAK, Prince (1936-). Born on 1 February 1936, son of King **Sisowath Monivong**, he married Phon Vonsin and they had one daughter, Princess Munirasy. He married a second time to Princess **Norodom Botum Bopha**, daughter of Prince **Norodom Sihanouk**; and married a third time to Princess **Norodom Bopha Devi**, eldest daughter of Norodom Sihanouk. With his third wife, he had two sons: Prince Chivannaridh and Prince Weakchiravuth. A captain in the Cambodian Royal Army in the 1960s, he then went to France and by 1990 was living in Los Angeles. He was inspector of fraud for the department of social security in California. Returning to Phnom Penh, he was appointed president of Kampuchea Airlines on 4 July 1994, which became **Royal Air Cambodge** on 2 January 1995. He resigned from his position on 28 April 1995. In 1999 he was nominated by **FUNCINPEC** as first vice-president of the **Senate**.

SISOWATH DUONGCHIVIN, Prince (1933-1975). The 15th child of King **Monivong**, he attended **Lycée Sisowath** and the Royal School of Administration. Joining the Ministry of Agriculture he was promoted to governor of **Kampot** in March 1970, retaining that position until November 1971. Chief of the directorate of the civil service in March 1972, in May 1973 he became minister of agriculture. He married Princess Santa, daughter of Prince **Sisowath Sirik Matak** and they had five children. It was long rumored that Prince Sirik Matak wanted to restore some form of monarchy during the Khmer Republic, and much evidence points to Duongchivin as being his candidate. Duongchivin was captured at Vat Katt while trying to leave Phnom Penh on 17 April 1975; he was killed later that day. His widow is a member of the National Assembly.

SISOWATH ESSARO, Prince (1920-   ). Born on 2 May 1920 in Phnom Penh, son of Prince Sisowath Rathary and *neak monéang* Troeung Yoeun, he was a brother of Prince **Sisowath Sirik Matak** and Prince **Sisowath Methavi**. Essaro graduated from the School of Administration in 1941 and the School of Physical Education at Phanthiet. He joined the **Democrat Party** in 1946 and worked in the Defense Ministry where he was chief clerk in October 1947. He then joined the **Khmer Renewal Party** of **Lon Nol** and in 1951 was chief clerk in the Ministry of Interior and was appointed chief of the Phnom Penh municipal police on 11 July 1952. He served as under-secretary for the president of the council, in charge of sport, youth and junior education from July until November 1953, under-secretary for education with the same portfolios until April 1954 and minister of education and information in April 1954. Essaro then entered the army receiving the rank of lieutenant colonel. He was reappointed minister of education and information from April to July 1954 and Royal Delegate for Sports.

Posted to Paris, he was the Cambodian ambassador to the United Nations Educational, Scientific and Cultural Organization and director-general of the Cambodia House at Cité University, Paris, until August 1970. He was close to his brother, Sirik Matak, and when Sihanouk threatened to kill cabinet ministers and deputies in March 1970, it was Essaro who taped the outburst and sent the tape to those in Phnom Penh eager for the overthrow of Sihanouk. He was involved in support for the Khmer Republic during the disturbances among the Cambodian students in Paris in 1973. He married Princess Wathanary, and they had three children: Princess Vinayika, Princess Theravady, and Prince Tesso.

SISOWATH ESSARAVONG, Prince (1858-1907). The sixth child of King Sisowath, he was one of the major property owners in Cambodia, being named, in 1906, as a possible heir to his father. He married 10 times. With his third wife, Keth, he had a son, Prince Rathary (1878-1946; father of Princes **Sisowath Sirik Matak, Essaro** and **Methavi**).

SISOWATH KOSSAMAK (1904-1975). Queen and regent 1960-1970. Born on 9 April 1904 in Phnom Penh, she was the daughter of King **Monivong** and his main wife, Princess Norodom Kanviman Norleak. After a sheltered childhood in Phnom Penh, she married Prince **Norodom Suramarit** and they lived quietly until 1941 when their only child, Prince **Norodom Sihanouk**, was proclaimed king. Following Sihanouk's unexpected abdication in 1955, Kossamak became queen, and Suramarit king. For the next few years Kossamak exercised a restraining influence on her son. When Sihanouk became chief of state following Suramarit's death in 1960, the Queen's political influence declined, although she remained the

"Supreme Guardian of the Throne" as a ceremonial monarch and embodiment of the monarchy until the proclamation of the Khmer Republic in October 1970.

Queen Kossamak was a patron of the **Royal Ballet** and retained an aloof distance from the political scene. A dispute over her business activities, when *Newsweek* magazine insulted her, led to the suspension of diplomatic relations with the **United States** in 1965. In 1970, when her son was deposed by the National Assembly and High Council of the Kingdom, she was one of the few major Royalist figures who did not express any surprise at these actions. She was stripped of her titles with the proclamation of the **Khmer Republic** on 9 October 1970. Remaining in Phnom Penh until 1973, she maintained the royal palace during the first three years of the Republic and was then sent, along with many other members of the royal family, to Beijing, where they remained until 1975 where she died on 27 April.

SISOWATH METHAVI, Prince (c1917-1976). Born in Phnom Penh, son of Prince Sisowath Rathary and *neak monéang* Troeung Yoeun, he was brother of Prince **Sisowath Sirik Matak** and Prince **Sisowath Essaro**. Methavi attended the Cambodian Military School and studied briefly in France. On his return he was commissioned as a captain in the army in December 1954 and was appointed as the military attaché to Paris in August 1966. Methavi was president and director-general of **Air Cambodge** and acted as unofficial banker for members of the royal family. Methavi's main connection came through his wife, Nanette Izzi, sister of **Monique Sihanouk**. They had six children: **Sisowath Thomico**; Sisowath Tackavit; Sisowath Amrindo; Sisowath Chittara; Sisowath Suthary and Sisowath Sophana.

Methavi was in the Cambodian delegation to Hanoi for Ho Chi Minh's funeral, returning to receive the rank of colonel. He became ambassador to East Germany on 13 March 1970 but was fired on 18 March by the **Lon Nol** government. Never active in politics, he declared his support for the **Royal Government of National Union of Kampuchea (GRUNK)** on 18 November 1970 and served as chef de cabinet for Prince **Norodom Sihanouk** for the duration of the GRUNK. Methavi and Nanette returned to Phnom Penh in 1976 and they were both killed soon afterward.

SISOWATH MONICHEAT, Prince (1922-). The son of King **Sisowath Monivong**, he was a member of the **Progressive Democratic Party** and contested the 1947 National Assembly elections for Kampong Chhnang town. As a member of the **Khmer Labor Party** he contested the 1955 National Assembly elections for Kandok, Kandal. He married twice and had two children.

SISOWATH MONIPONG, Prince (1912-1956). Prime minister 1950-1951. Born on 20 August 1912 in Phnom Penh, son of King **Monivong** and his primary wife Princess Kanviman, Monipong went to Nice High School 1927-1930 along with his brother Monireth, returned to Cambodia for a year in a Buddhist monastery then returned to France and studied at St. Cyr and the School of Aviation. He served with the French air force in the Battle for France in 1940, returning to Cambodia soon after the surrender of France. He was assistant secretary-general to the royal palace from 1940, minister of foreign affairs and education from October 1945 to December 1946 and represented Cambodia at the signing of the 1949 Treaty recognizing Cambodia as an Associated State in the French Union. He was prime minister and minister of the interior and information from 1 June to 31 December 1950 and again with the additional portfolios of health, labor and social action from 1 January to 2 March 1951.

Prince Monipong married Andrée Lambert and they had a son, Prince Sisowath Samyl Monipong. He married for a second time to Ros Chhomya and had three children: Princess Moniraingsy, Prince Monisisowath and Princess Pongsiriya. He married a third time to Son Sunnary and they had two children: Princess **Sisowath Southevong** ("Mme Peou Lida") and Princess Pongneari (who married a son of **Son Sann**). With his fourth wife, Chan Sorey, Monipong had five more children: Prince Duong Daravong, Princess Phuong Nara, Prince Tikou, Princess Dahila and Princess Marie-José. He also had another daughter, Princess Sisowath Soveth (who married **Khuon Nay**).

An unprepossessing man, he was able to get a far deeper insight into the events in Phnom Penh during this period than many other members of the royal family. He was appointed counselor to the government in 1952, a post specially created for him. Monipong was appointed Cambodian High Commissioner to France in March 1955. He died at the High Commissioner's residence in Paris on 31 August 1956 of a heart attack.

Prince Monipong's eldest son, Prince Samyl Monipong, was the military attaché at the Cambodian Embassy in Paris. He married Princess Norodom Daravadey and they had two children: Prince Ravivaddhana Monipong, an historian, and Princess Ubbolvadey. They live in Paris.

SISOWATH MONIRETH, Prince (1909-1975). Prime minister 1945-1946. Born on 25 November 1909 in **Phnom Penh**, Monireth was the eldest son of King **Monivong** and his primary wife Princess Kanviman. He attended Nice High School in 1927-1930, and studied political science, before returning to Cambodia in 1934 to be appointed secretary-general of the royal palace. He held various other court appointments until he enlisted in the French Foreign Legion on 2 December 1939. Commissioned as a sublieutenant, he took part in the Battle for France in May-June 1940 and was mentioned in dispatches. Monireth then returned to Cambodia, where the French governor-general decided against putting him on the throne nominating Prince **Norodom Sihanouk** as King Monivong's successor. Monireth then took up the responsibility of being an advisor to his nephew, and on the return of the French in late 1945, he became prime minister from 17 October 1945 to 14 December 1946. He was then chief of the general staff of the Royal Cambodian Army, promoted to general then appointed as Cambodian representative in Paris. He presented his credentials as High Commissioner in January 1953 and in July 1954 returned to Phnom Penh on leave. Monireth, appointed "Second Personage of the Kingdom," represented Sihanouk at the coronation of Queen Elizabeth II in London. He resigned as High Commissioner in February 1955 (his brother Monipong taking over). During the late 1940s and 1950s, he shared his nephew's contempt for party politics and was frequently called on for special tasks, but was never given the position for which he was best trained, minister of defense, because some feared his competence and suspected his ambitions. After King Suramarit's death, Monireth served on the Regency Council that named Sihanouk chief of state. In 1964 he wrote his unpublished memoirs, critical of Sihanouk and other Cambodian figures.

Originally supporting the **Khmer Renewal Party**, he went into semi-retirement in 1955-1960, being minister of state charged with national defense and general sanitation from September to October 1956, and he was appointed to the Regency Council, 6 April 1960, becoming grand councillor to the throne, president of the **High Council of the Throne** and was promoted to military councillor to the head of state, with the rank of general (4 stars) on 31 October 1963. He was an inspector general in the army in 1960. Briefly a Buddhist monk, Monireth was also a poet. In 1967 he returned to politics as president of the High Council of the Throne and delegate of the head of state to the Army High Command. He married *neak monéang* Poc Vane, daughter of Poc Hell, and they had four children: Prince **Sisowath Rethnara**; Prince Rakmoni, a soldier; Prince Monisowath and Prince Pongmoni, a soldier. Monireth and his wife also adopted Vanareth, a relative of the Poc family. Monireth kept a low profile during the Khmer Republic, refusing to give interviews to the press which he felt would inflame the situation, especially as Republican fever gripped many branches of the government. He wrote his memoirs, which have survived but which remain unpublished. On 17 April 1975 he was refused admission to the French Embassy and calmly joined the exodus from Phnom Penh. He was alive as late as September 1975.

SISOWATH MONIVONG (1875-1941). King of Cambodia 1927-1941, Monivong was the sixth son of Prince **Sisowath**, half brother of the then-reigning Cambodian king, **Norodom**. Born on 27 December 1875, he attended the École Coloniale in Paris and gained a commission in the French army, serving briefly in Algeria before returning home to act as private secretary for his father, whom he succeeded as king in 1927. His 14-year reign was relatively uneventful, and the king suffered more than his father had from constraints placed on him by the French. Monivong was an enthusiastic patron of the **Royal Ballet**, an accomplished poet and a pious Buddhist, presiding over the formation of the Buddhist Institute in 1930 and sponsoring a new edition of the Cambodian royal chronicles. During his reign, the Cambodian economy expanded with the establishment of rubber plantations, the construction of a railway from Phnom Penh to the Thai border and the completion of a network of paved roads throughout the kingdom. In the 1930s, a better educated group of Cambodians began entering the civil service and Cambodian provincial governors were given wider responsibilities. King Monivong became embittered following the Franco-Siamese war of 1940-1941 when **Battambang** and much of **Siem Reap** (but not the Angkorean monuments) reverted to Thai control. He died at **Bokor** on 24 April 1941 having refused to meet any French officials for several months. His primary wife was Princess Kanviman, daughter of Prince Norodom Hassakan. Some of his 25 children include: Princess (later Queen) **Sisowath Kossamak** (1904-1975); Prince **Sisowath Monireth** (1909-1975); Prince **Sisowath Monipong** (1912-1956); Princess Sisowath Thavet (married **Khuon Nay**); Prince **Sisowath Rathasa** (1918-1971); Prince **Sisowath Monicheat** (1922-); Prince Sisowath Monichivan (1932-), married Princes **Norodom Bopha Devi**; Prince **Sisowath Duongchivin** (1933-1975) and Prince **Sisowath Chivanmonirak** (1936-).

SISOWATH PORACSI, Prince (1921-). The son of Prince Sisowath Popanath (and great-grandson of King **Sisowath**), Poracsi was a member of **Sangkum**. Elected to the **National Assembly** in 1958 and again in 1962, he was secretary of state for the economy (agriculture) in 1961, for social action from November 1961 to August 1962.

SISOWATH RATHASA, Prince (c1918-1971). A son of **King Monivong** he was a customs officer and joined **Sangkum** in 1966, contesting the National Assembly elections for Chreylas, **Kandal**, and the 1967 by-election for Prek Ambel (Saang), Kandal. He contested the 1968 High Council elections and represented the Dockers' Association at the July 1967 National Congress. Well-known for palace contacts which enabled him to secure government contracts for his friends, he was assassinated on 21 December 1971 while planning to leave **Phnom Penh.**

SISOWATH RETHNARA, Prince (1933-1975). The eldest son of Prince **Sisowath Monireth,** he graduated from the Royal School of Administration and worked in the Foreign Ministry until 1970 when he moved to the Ministry of Justice for work in the Committee for Liaison and Coordination of Labor established in September 1970. He married Princess Sisowath Pongsiriya and both were killed by the Communists in 1975.

SISOWATH SIRIK MATAK, Prince (1914-1975). Acting prime minister 1971-1972. Born on 22 January 1914 at Phnom Penh, the son of Prince Sisowath Rathary and *neak monéang* Troeung Yoeun, he was the older brother of Prince **Sisowath Methavi** and Prince **Sisowath Essaro.** He went to Lycée Chasseloup-Laubat from 1928-1934, becoming a Mandarin in 1930 and graduating from the National School of Administration in 1938. Sirik Matak entered the provincial government and was promoted to Anouc Montrey 1st Class in 1947. In 1946 he had been an early member of the **Democrat Party,** secretly directing the party committee in **Kampong Cham,** but left it to join the **Khmer Renewal Party.** His next promotion came as governor of **Pursat** in 1948-1949 then Vorac Montrey 2nd class in April 1949. Later that year he was appointed major in the Royal Cambodian Armed Forces and was on the personal military staff of the king. He then served as assistant chief of staff and head of army intelligence. In August 1949 he was appointed as military commander of the **Siem Reap** autonomous zone but quarreled with **Dap Chhuon** leading to the Prince being recalled in November. He was demobilized when the king's personal military staff was disbanded in May 1950 and appointed to take charge of administration in the Ministry of the Interior.

Prince Sirik Matak accompanied Prince **Sisowath Monipong** to the **Pau Conference** in 1950 and became director of the Prime Minister's Office. He married Princess Keathneari, daughter of Prince Norodom Ketsara, and they had five children: Princess Cheriya (married Sien Dy); Princess Santa (married Prince **Sisowath Duongchivin**); Prince Olary; Prince Lichavi and Prince **Sirirath.** By another wife, a commoner, he had another daughter, Kanika.

A longtime minister, Sirik Matak was secretary of state for defense from June 1952 to January 1953; minister of defense, posts and telecommunications from January to July 1953; minister of defense from January to September 1955, again from January to September 1956, with the additional portfolio of education from March to April 1956, and minister of defense, information and tourism from July 1957 to January 1958.

At this point Sirik Matak left cabinet politics and was chief inspector of the kingdom's affairs in 1958 and Cambodian delegate to the United Nations Educational, Scientific and Cultural Organization. From 1962-1964 he was appointed ambassador to China and Mongolia, based in Beijing. After returning to Phnom Penh, he was minister of state for education from late 1964 until 1966, also holding the position as head of the **Royal Khmer Socialist Youth**. From 1966-1969 he was ambassador to **Japan** and the Philippines, resident in Tokyo, returning to Phnom Penh and being appointed deputy prime minister on 14 August 1969. The prince actively built up links with the Cambodian business community who became his major supporters over the next few years. He led a delegation to East Germany, returning in October 1969. As a brigadier general in the Royal Cambodian Armed Forces, he was the major coordinator of the plan to overthrow his cousin, Prince **Norodom Sihanouk**, in March 1970. Following the overthrow, he became first vice-prime minister in charge of the interior, coordination, religious affairs, order, security, surface defense and national education, renouncing his royal title on 9 October 1970 with the proclamation of the Khmer Republic.

Although loyal to, and a friend of **Lon Nol**, events in 1970 meant that Sirik Matak and Lon Nol started moving apart. Sirik Matak tried to prevent the massacres of the Vietnamese in early 1970 and tried to build up the morale of the Cambodian Army, its strength sapped by the corruption of some generals. With Lon Nol's heart attack in February 1971, it was clear that firm leadership from Sirik Matak might save the Khmer Republic. In May 1971 he was delegated prime minister and minister of defense, a post he held until 11 March 1972, when he was briefly prime minister in his own right. However he soon came under attack by **Keo Ann**, and student protests against him resulted in his resignation on 13 March. Appointed advisor to Lon Nol "with the rank of prime minister" in May 1972, he began to feel the pressure to form a political party. On 15 June the Independent Republican Association, run by **Tep Khunnah**, became the **Republican Party**. On 23 July at the Party's first Congress, Sirik Matak was elected secretary-general; the party refused to take part in the elections of September 1972. An advisor to Lon Nol from 21 March 1973, he was one of the members of the High Political Council who desperately attempted to cobble together a coalition of major political forces in Phnom Penh.

Gradually sidelined, Sirik Matak withdrew from politics. He bravely refused an American offer of evacuation on 11 April 1975, his note of regret, condemning the Americans, being widely published. With the fall of the Republic, he took refuge in the Calmette Hospital then the French

Embassy where he was secreted away by diplomats. Asked by them to leave on 21 April 1975, he walked calmly to his captors and was taken to the **Cercle Sportif**, just outside Phnom Penh, where he was beheaded.

SISOWATH SIRIRATH, Prince (1950-). Born in **Phnom Penh**, son of Prince **Sisowath Sirik Matak**, he won a scholarship at Lycée Descartes in 1959. He married Princess **Norodom Arun Rasmey**, daughter of Prince **Norodom Sihanouk**, in 1961. They went into exile in the **United States** just before the fall of the **Khmer Republic** and were divorced in 1988. In 1983 Sirirath received accreditation as a member of the Permanent Delegation of **Democratic Kampuchea (DK)** at the **United Nations** representing the royalist **Molinaka**, and later **FUNCINPEC** in the **Coalition Government of Democratic Kampuchea**. In 1992 he replaced **Thiounn Prasith** as the National Government of Cambodia representative there. A member of the National Council of **FUNCINPEC**, Prince Sirirath was elected to the Constituent Assembly in **Kampong Cham** province in June 1993. Although provisionally designated for a top civil service job in the provisional government of June 1993, he was not included in the government formed in October and later resigned from the National Assembly on 5 July 1994 to become ambassador to the **United States**. He was also confirmed as the Royal Government of Cambodia's permanent representative at the **United Nations**. During the July 1997 coup instigated by **Hun Sen**, Prince Sirirath was the only overseas ambassador to come out publicly in favor of Prince **Norodom Ranariddh**. In 1998 he was elected once again to the National Assembly for **Battambang** and named co-minister of national defense in the 1998 government.

SISOWATH SIRIVUDH PANHARA, Prince. Son of Princess Sisowath Samanvoraphong, and her husband, a commoner, Panhara was later raised to a royal rank by King **Norodom Sihanouk**. A supporter of the Khmer Republic, Panhara lived in Paris in the early 1970s and was among those arrested and imprisoned after Cambodia House incidents (and convicted by a French Court of the murder of a Cambodian supporter of **National United Front of Kampuchea**). He was later released and became active in **FUNCINPEC**. Returning to Cambodia in 1991, he worked in the office of Prince **Norodom Ranariddh**. Panhara was appointed under-secretary of state for culture and fine arts on 1 November 1993 then secretary of state for culture and fine arts on 20 October 1994, a post in which he was reconfirmed in 1998.

SISOWATH SOUTHEVONG, Princess also **Peou Lida (1945-1994).** Born on 17 September 1945, the daughter of Prince **Sisowath Monipong**, she married Peang Sorin in 1968. She later married Suy Hean then Dr. Peou.

Evacuated from Phnom Penh with her family in April 1975, she lived in **Battambang** where her husband, a medical doctor, was killed on 21 August 1976 and three of her children perished. After the Vietnamese invasion, she supported the **People's Republic of Kampuchea (PRK)** and was elected to the PRK National Assembly for **Takeo**. She was also deputy-chairwoman of the United National Front for Salvation and Defense of the Kampuchea. She died of cancer in October 1994.

SISOWATH SOVANNARETH, Prince (1919-1977). Born on 3 December 1919 in Phnom Penh, the grandson of King **Sisowath**, he was an inspector of education in Kandal in the late 1950s. Elected to the National Assembly in 1962 for Kandal, and reelected in 1966, he was also a newspaper editor. Taking advantage of a scandal involving **Ung Mung**, Prince Sovannareth used the opportunity to campaign against corruption. On 4 April 1972 he was very badly injured in a grenade attack, probably organized by Ung Mung. After a miraculous survival he died five years later in **Democratic Kampuchea**. He was the adoptive father of **Keat Sokun**.

SISOWATH THOMICO. The eldest son of Prince **Sisowath Methavi**, he renounced his royal title in 1970 (the designation was honorific anyway) and supported the Khmer Republic. He later moved to Paris where he became a member of the **Khmer People's National Liberation Front**. An article he wrote criticizing his uncle, Prince **Norodom Sihanouk**, in 1987 provoked a huge outcry.

SISOWATH WATCHAYAVONG, Prince (1891-1972). Prime minister 1947-1948. Born on 13 September 1891 in **Phnom Penh**, the fourth child of Prince Sisowath Wothavong, Watchayavong grew up in Phnom Penh and attended the École des Sciences Politiques, joining the **Democrat Party** in 1946. He was minister of justice from December 1946 until July 1947 and prime minister, as well as minister of justice, following the death of Prince **Sisowath Youtévong** from 25 July 1947 to 20 February 1948. The prince became a magistrate in 1951 and in 1953 served in the National Consultative Assembly. He was appointed to the High Council of the Kingdom in 1967. Prince Watchayavong married many times and had at least 25 children including Prince Sisowath Phanurath and Prince Sisowath Vuthin, both active in politics. He lived in Phnom Penh until his death on 30 January 1972.

SISOWATH YOUTÉVONG, Prince (1913-1947). Prime minister 1946-1947. Born in Oudong, Prince Youtévong was the son of Prince Chamraenvongs and Princess Sisowath Yubhipan. He studied at Collège Sisowath and then Lycée Chasseloup Laubat in Saigon before going to France where he studied and worked for the next 15 years. He was a foundation scholar at St. Louis, received his *licence* from the Faculty of Sciences at Montpellier in 1938 and earned a doctorate in physical sciences in 1941. Later he was awarded a certificate in investigative astronomy. While in France, Youtévong married Dominique Lavergne, and was a member of the French Socialist Party. He, **Chhean Vam** and others discussed the possibility of forming a democratic party in Cambodia while many of the 1940s generation were still students in France.

When Prince Youtévong returned to Phnom Penh in mid-1946 (by first-hand accounts), the **Democrat Party** had been established and he became its president and leading spokesman. After the September elections for the Consultative Assembly, he became the first president of that assembly and, from 15 December 1946, was prime minister and minister of the interior. One of the primary authors of the new Constitution, he fell ill with malaria after a retreat at **Kep** and, though taken to the hospital, he was exhausted from overwork and chronic tuberculosis and succumbed. He died on 18 July 1947 at **Preah Keth Mealea Hospital** and was cremated the following day in Phnom Penh. With the terrifying effects of the **Black Star Affair** still in mind, many Democrat Party faithful believed French doctors had given their leader poisonous injections.

SI VOTHA (1841-1891). Cambodian dissident prince and half brother of **Norodom** and **Sisowath**, Si Votha opposed the French protectorate and led a rebellion against French control in 1877. He also took part in the more widespread revolt of 1883-1884. The prince retained a following in the sparsely populated northern part of the kingdom and never rallied to the government.

SLAT PEOU also **Soriya Chhapchhit (1929-1960).** He worked in the Cambodian embassies in **Thailand**, India and the **United States**, returning to Phnom Penh to work in the Ministry of Foreign Affairs. A member of **Sangkum**, he was elected to the 1958 National Assembly for **Siem Reap** town. He was arrested by Prince **Norodom Sihanouk** and executed in February 1960 for complicity in the **Dap Chhuon** plot.

SLAVERY. Although unpaid workers bound to particular masters for life were a feature of precolonial Cambodia (and much of precolonial Southeast Asia) the English term "slave" cannot be fitted precisely to the social categories of unpaid, bonded servants. These "slaves," as they were termed by visitors such as **Zhou Daguan**, were involved in the construction of many of the temples in Cambodia, as well as in agricultural and household duties. During the sacking of **Angkor** in 1432, the Thais enslaved all the population they captured, and these were taken to the Thai capital of Ayudhya where they were sold. Cambodian delegates to the Franco-

Cambodian talks of 1946 initially resisted French proposals to outlaw debt bondage in the national constitution.

SO CHY (1944-). Born on 14 February 1944 at Kampong Tralach, **Kampong Chhnang**, he was a captain in the Royal Army. With the rank of lieutenant-colonel he served in the Republican Army from 1970-1975. Spending the period of **Democratic Kampuchea** in the countryside, he joined **Molinaka** in July 1979. Director of the military training camp called **Kong Sileah** after one of the founders of **Molinaka**, he was involved in armed operations in **Battambang, Siem Reap** and **Kampong Cham**. Captured by the Vietnamese in 1980, he was quickly freed by **Khan Savoeun** and became brigadier general in the **National Army for an Independent Kampuchea**. A member of the **FUNCINPEC** National Council in February 1992, he was vice-president of their electoral committee for **Kampong Thom** in 1993. Elected as a deputy for Kampong Thom, he was a member of the Commission on Legislation.

SO KHUN (1949-). Born in **Kandal**, he was an agronomist working in the irrigation department. Head of the office of the Ministry of Agriculture 1970-1975, he spent the period of **Democratic Kampuchea** in the countryside. In September 1981 he was appointed director of the hydrology department, and was deputy minister of agriculture from February 1986 to April 1992. A member of the Mekong Committee, he was minister of transport, posts and telecommunications from April 1992 to June 1993. In June 1993 he became a deputy for Takeo and was minister of transport, then secretary of state for posts and telecommunications, and in 1994 minister of posts and telecommunications. In 1998 he was reelected to the National Assembly.

SO NEM (1924-c1976). Born on 12 March 1924 in **Phnom Penh**, he was a secondary school teacher and then head of the office of national education. He was, for a time, director of the *Agence Khmère de Presse* and was elected to the **National Assembly** for Speu, Kampong Cham, in 1958 and re-elected in 1962. From 1959-1960 he was secretary of state for religion and was secretary of state for trade from 1964-1965. Identified as one of the country's leading progressives in the "affair of the 34" in 1963, he was president of the Cambodia-China Friendship Association banned by Prince **Norodom Sihanouk** in October 1967 when his name was also summarily removed from the mast head of the Princes "Bulletin du Contre-Gouvernement". He was secretary of state for trade from May to October 1966, **Sangkum** delegate to the Socialist Alliance meeting in Yugoslavia in June 1966, general secretary of the shadow cabinet and in September 1966 a member of the delegation negotiating border issues with the

National Front for the Liberation of South Vietnam. So Nem was minister for public health from May to September 1967, being abruptly dismissed in October. He observed events in March 1970 from the sidelines, perhaps communicating with the underground **Communist Party of Kampuchea (CPK)**. In June 1971 he represented the National Bank of Cambodia on the **constitutional drafting committee created by the Khmer Republic**. He defected to the **National United Front of Kampuchea** in early 1972, and disappeared from public view. He is believed by many to have been among those intellectuals knowledgeable about economics who, in 1975, criticized the CPK method of socialist construction without a currency of exchange.

SO PHOTRA (c1942-1976). He was an air force captain and in 1971 married Princess **Norodom Botum Bopha**, daughter of King **Norodom Sihanouk**. On 18 March 1973 he was the pilot who bombed the **Chamkar Mon** in an assassination attempt on **Lon Nol**, the so-called "So Photra Incident." He flew into territory held by the **National United Front of Kampuchea** and then flew to Hainan. Moving to Beijing and to Yugoslavia, he returned to Phnom Penh after April 1975 and was executed by the Communists.

SOCIO-REPUBLICAN PARTY. Formed in June 1972 from the Socio-Republican Association, this party was essentially the political movement of **Lon Nol**. Its main factions at the start were those which supported Keam Reth (traditional Republicans) and the adherents of **Keng Vannsak** (members of the former Democrat Party). Later the factions were known as Dangkor and **Dangrek**—the former being the supporters of **Lon Non**, and the latter focusing around **Son Ngoc Thanh** and also **Hang Thun Hak**. The party was anticommunist, and anti-Sihanouk—its three principal values were declared to be "republicanism, social responsibility and nationalism," with "all power emanating from the people." Although it did draw on some of the elements of the **Khmer Renewal Party**, it adopted **Angkor Wat** as its party symbol. As most elections were uncontested, it swept the polls in the September 1972 legislative and **senate** elections, dominating the government until April 1975.

SOK AN (1950-). Born in **Takeo**, he was a graduate of the Royal School of Administration. In May 1982 he was appointed director of the office of the Ministry of Foreign Affairs and in February 1983 was secretary-general of the Committee of Defense and Peace. In April 1985 Sok An was appointed to head the administration in the Foreign Ministry. Seven months later he was appointed ambassador to New Delhi (India being the only noncommunist country to recognize the **People's Republic of Kampuchea**). Returning to Phnom Penh, Sok An became deputy minister of foreign affairs, taking an important part in the formulation of the **State of Cambodia** foreign policy and assisting **Hun Sen** in the peace negotiations during this period. He was deputy minister of the interior in 1992 and headed the office of the Central Committee of the **Cambodian People's Party** in 1990-1993. In 1993 he was elected as a deputy for Takeo and was minister at the cabinet office in 1995. In 1998 he was reelected to the National Assembly and appointed minister of state.

SOK CHENDA SOPHEA (1956-). Born on 27 April 1956 in Phnom Penh, Chenda Sophea attended Lycée Descartes and a school in Vientiane, Laos. Residing in France in the 1980s, he studied at Aix en Provence and ran a tourism and hotel agency. He returned to Phnom Penh in January 1993, declaring his support for **FUNCINPEC**. Following the elections, he was under-secretary of state for tourism in 1993-1995. He was general-secretary of the Cambodian Development Council (CDC) in November 1999 when Cambodia deported a foreign-born, Internet pornographer. He stated that while Cambodia welcomed most forms of foreign investment, the CDC was not interested in promoting sex tourism.

SOK CHHONG (1918-c1995). Born in **Battambang**, he was a member of the secret police under **Son Ngoc Thanh** in 1945 and was also a founder of the **Democrat Party** in the following year. Sok Chong was elected to the 1947 National Assembly representing Triel, **Kampong Thom** Province. He gave up his seat to become one of the Democrat nominees to the Assembly of the French Union until 1951 when he returned, in June, to contest the National Assembly elections, and was reelected again for the seat of Triel. He was minister for the national economy (agriculture, husbandry, industry and trade) in the **Huy Kanthoul** government from October 1951 to June 1952. When King **Norodom Sihanouk** decided to seize the initiative away from the Democrat Party, Sok Chong was arrested on the night 13 January 1953 and held in jail. However, he remained in the Democrat Party until 1955 then temporarily left politics to study law at the Faculty of Law and Economic Sciences at Phnom Penh University, graduating in 1961. He then worked in the Waters and Forests Administration. In April 1962, on the resignation of Dy Sath, Sok Chong was appointed minister of trade. In May 1971 he was appointed second deputy president of the Council of Ministers, responsible for finance and the coordination of economic and financial affairs, a post he held until March 1972. In May 1973 he emerged as a possible compromise prime minister, but **Lon Nol** finally appointed **In Tam**. Sok Chong went into exile in the United States.

SOK THUOK, also known as Penh Thuok. *See* VORN VETH.

SOLIDARITY GROUPS *See KROM SAMMAKI.*

SOM KIM SUOR (1949-). Born in Choeng Prey, **Kampong Cham**, she studied agriculture through lower secondary at Chamcar Daung. During the **Democratic Kampuchea** period she endured very heavy manual work in the countryside and joined the **People's Republic of Kampuchea (PRK)** being appointed deputy director-general of the "Voice of the Kampuchea People" Radio in 1979. She was elected in May 1981 to the PRK National Assembly representing **Kampot** and retained her seat until May 1993. A member of the Central Committee of the **People's Revolutionary Party of Kampuchea (PRPK)** and then the **Cambodian People's Party**, she was editor of the daily official PRPK *Pracheachon* newspaper from September 1985. She was also president of the Association of Journalists of Kampuchea during the final years of the PRK and the **State of Cambodia**. In 1993 and in 1998 she was reelected to the National Assembly.

SOM SAM AL (1930-1972). Born on 20 September 1930 in **Kampong Cham**, the son of Khim Phinn, prison governor in Kampong Cham, Som Sam Al was educated at Collège Preah Sihanouk where he was a friend of **Lon Non**. He also studied at **Lycée Sisowath** and Collège Technique, before going to France to study cinematography from 1949-1954. He became the manager of Films Meanchey, the first movie film company in Phnom Penh in 1960. He was killed, along with his family, by Vietnamese soldiers allied to the **National United Front of Kampuchea**. *See also* FILMS.

SON CHHAY né **Chhay Hoc Sun (1956-).** Born on 1 January 1956 in Siem Reap, he attended Wat Damnak Primary School and Lycée Siem Reap before graduating B.A. and M.Sc. from Flinders University, South Australia, and also receiving a diploma of education from nearby Adelaide University. He taught at schools in South Australia where he was a member and convenor of the Senior Secondary Assessment Board. Son Chhay was also vice-president of the Cambodia-Australia Association from 1981-1986 and a **Khmer People's National Liberation Front (KPNLF)** representative in Australia from 1989. Returning to Phnom Penh in preparation for the 1993 elections, he was appointed head of the **Buddhist Liberal Democratic Party (BLDP)** Finance Department. Elected to the Constituent Assembly for Siem Reap, he was secretary for the Commission on Education, Religious Issues, Culture and Tourism. Following the **Hun Sen** coup in July 1997, he sought refuge in Adelaide. The first of the BLDP members of parliament to return after the coup, he joined the **Sam Rainsy Party** and was their candidate for Siem Reap province. He is married with three children.

SON NGOC MINH also *Achar* **Mean (c1915-1972).** One of the first Cambodians to join the Vietnamese communists in their anti-colonial armed struggle, Son Ngoc Minh was born in **Kampong Chhnang** of Khmer-Vietnamese parents. Following the usual pattern in the 1920s and 1930s, he was educated in Buddhist schools and was an ordained Buddhist monk when he fled **Phnom Penh** following the 1942 demonstration. In 1945 he joined the **Indochina Communist Party**, alongside another former monk, **Tou Samouth**, and adopted a pseudonym implying that he was a relative of **Son Ngoc Thanh**, then under house arrest in France. Following the **Geneva Conference**, Son Ngoc Minh regrouped with other **Khmer People's Revolutionary Party (KPRP)** in Vietnam where he and Tou Samouth were acknowledged leaders of the clandestine expatriate Cambodian Communists. He joined the Central Committee of the **Workers' Party of Kampuchea (WPK)** in absentia in 1960 and welcomed Saloth Sar (**Pol Pot**) when he visited Hanoi in 1965. Minh died in a hospital in Beijing in December 1972. The **People's Republic of Kampuchea** honored him as a patriot and communist. His portrait appeared on 100 riel banknotes, and naming one of Phnom Penh's principal avenues after him.

SON NGOC THANH (1908-1977). Born in Travinh, Cochinchina, his parents being **Khmer Krom** landowners, his father was Son Neo, a Cambodian; and his mother was Thai Thi Bi, from a Chinese-Vietnamese family. Thanh's brother, Son Ngoc Nguyen later became a senator in South Vietnam. Son Ngoc Thanh was educated at a high school in Saigon and then won a French government scholarship to study in France. He went to Montpellier, where he took his baccalaureate in philosophy, gained a teaching diploma and studied law for a year in Paris. In 1933 he returned to Indochina and moved to Phnom Penh working in the National Library. He joined the Alumni Association of **Collège Sisowath** (Lycée Sisowath), founded in 1935, although he never attended the school. After a brief period in north **Vietnam** in 1936 he returned to Cambodia and was a magistrate at **Pursat** and a public prosecutor in Phnom Penh, before becoming secretary and then deputy director of the **Buddhist Institute**.

In Phnom Penh he turned his activities to politics and along with **Sim Var** and **Pach Chhoeun** established *Nagaravatta*, the first Khmer-language newspaper. The newspaper appears to have been funded by Prince **Norodom Suramarit** and was not anti-French, but anticolonial. It advocated moderate reforms to allow greater Cambodian participation in commerce, greater educational opportunities and equal treatment before the law for Cambodians and the French. In 1938 he founded Yuvasala, a youth organization to promote fraternal relations with Vietnam, and favored the teaching of Vietnamese in Cambodian schools. Thanh at this period viewed **Thailand** as a greater predator than **Vietnam**. Public protests against the French reached a peak in 1942 when **Hem Chieu** and others, notably **Bunchhan Mul** and **Pach Chhoeun**, led a demonstration against the French. By now **Norodom Sihanouk** was king and there were many Japanese soldiers in Phnom Penh and indeed throughout French Indochina. Son Ngoc Thanh was residing with a Japanese officer fearful of arrest by the French and was not present at the demonstration. The French broke up the rally, a riot ensued and Thanh was forced to go into hiding.

Son Ngoc Thanh was condemned to death in absentia, and escaped from Phnom Penh to live in **Japan** for the next three years. Meanwhile the Japanese gradually lost their grip on much of Southeast Asia which they had conquered in 1941-1942. With the French in Indochina supporting the Vichy government, the Japanese seized control of Indochina forcing Prince **Norodom Sihanouk** in Cambodia and **Bao Dai** in Vietnam to declare their country's independence. Sihanouk declared independence and established the first "independent" government of Cambodia. Pach Chhoeun and Bunchhan Mul returned to Phnom Penh, and it was not until May 1945 that Son Ngoc Thanh returned to Cambodia. He was appointed foreign minister, but following a demonstration in August 1945 became prime minister on 14 August. Soon afterward the French returned to Cambodia and the British who accompanied the French arrested Thanh on 16 October. He was taken to Saigon and sentenced to 20 years in jail. This was later commuted to house arrest in France.

The next six years of Thanh's life was spent at Poitiers, France, where he completed a law degree. Throughout this period the French granted limited autonomy to Cambodia, but still retained much control over the country. In October 1951 Thanh returned to Phnom Penh and was greeted at the airport by thousands of supporters. In March 1952 he left Phnom Penh and joined the **Khmer Issarak** guerrillas to fight the French. He appealed to students to join him and **Hang Thun Hak**, **Ieu Yang** and **Um Sim** were among those who went into the jungle to join his noncommunist Cambodian nationalist movement, the Issaraks. From that time until 1970 Thanh spent his time working against the French and then against the Sihanouk government. He was supported by the governments of Thailand, South Vietnam and the United States which allowed him to have limited access to arms, but also allowed him to use radio transmitters to broadcast against Sihanouk. Increasingly the battle between him and Sihanouk assumed more of a personal nature. On 30 September 1959 Thanh was sentenced to death by Cambodian courts for consorting with Thailand, South Vietnam and "elements at the **United States** Embassy in Phnom

Penh" in treasonous activities. For most of the 1960s Son Ngoc Thanh provided only "annoyance" value to Sihanouk, his supporters in the jungles in Thailand and South Vietnam being small. However when there were moves to depose Sihanouk in the late 1960s Son Ngoc Thanh and his brother, Son Ngoc Nguyen, became involved in dealing with Prince **Sisowath Sirik Matak** and then **Lon Nol**. Soon after the overthrow of Sihanouk, Thanh returned to Phnom Penh where his death sentence was "invalidated" by a military tribunal.

During the early 1970s Son Ngoc Thanh's supporters and those of Lon Nol joined together to form the **Socio-Republican Party**, the former being known as the **Dangrek** faction (after the mountain range where Thanh had lived during some of his years in exile) and Lon Nol's (and **Lon Non**'s) supporters became the Dangkor faction. In 1972 following Sirik Matak's resignation, Thanh became prime minister of the Khmer Republic. He survived an assassination attempt on 21 August 1972 when a parked car exploded alongside his motorcade while Thanh was traveling to the Foreign Ministry. During this period Lon Nol was elected president of the Khmer Republic. At this point the Khmer Republic was eager to negotiate with Sihanouk for a cease-fire or end to the civil war and having Thanh as prime minister made it harder to bargain with the Sihanoukists. Thus Thanh resigned and Hang Thun Hak became prime minister. After this Thanh gradually faded out of mainstream politics and went to live in South Vietnam in 1973. He was living there when the communists took control of both Cambodia and South Vietnam in 1975. Although it was believed by many that he had an understanding with several North Vietnamese Communist leaders, it appears clear that he probably died on 8 July 1977 in a Vietnamese prison camp.

SON PHUOC THO (1920-   ). Born on 5 May 1920 in Travinh, South Vietnam, he was a businessman, member of the **Democrat Party**, and was elected to the **National Assembly** in 1951 for the seat of Taing Kraing, **Kampong Cham**. In 1953 he served in the National Consultative Assembly; and was elected to the National Assembly again in 1962 for Kampong Cham. Secretary of state for cultural affairs from September to October 1956, he was secretary of state for cultural and media affairs from October 1956 to January 1957, secretary of state for budgeting from January to April 1957 and secretary of state for planning from August to October 1962. Associated with Marxist politicians such as **Hou Youn**, he was named in 1963 as a likely communist, resulting in him having much of his journalistic career destroyed. He was director of *Meatophum* newspaper from about 1956 until 1969.

SON SANN (1911-2000). Prime minister 1967-1968. Born on 5 October 1911 in **Phnom Penh**, the son of Son Sach, he was from a family of eminent Khmer Krom who settled in Cambodia to take up a post under Prince Sisowath Souphanouvong, then minister for war. Son Sann studied in Phnom Penh before going to Paris where he graduated from the École des Hautes Études Commerciales in 1933. He also studied briefly in London where he learned English. Returning to Cambodia, he joined the civil service in 1935, serving in the provinces of **Prey Veng** and then **Battambang** where he was in charge of trade and other activities. Cambodia was then embroiled in the Franco-Thai War of 1940, and following its conclusion, Son Sann was a member of an economic mission to Tokyo in 1941—Japan having negotiated the peace settlement that ended that war.

Son Sann was an early supporter of the **Democrat Party**, becoming a member of its Steering Committee. He served as vice-president of the Council of Ministers and minister of finance in the **Sisowath Youtévong** government from December 1946 to August 1947. With the death of Youtévong, Son Sann remained as vice-president of the Council of Ministers (deputy prime minister) until February 1948 and was vice-president of the council and minister for economic affairs, finance and planning from February to August 1948. In January 1948 Son Sann was elevated to Chevalier of the Legion of Honour and was vice-president of the Council of Ministers and minister for economic and financial affairs from August 1948 to January 1949. During that time he represented Cambodia at several overseas conferences.

Following the rise of the right wing under **Yèm Sambaur**, Son Sann became foreign minister from June 1950 to March 1951. He contested the seat of Phnom Penh (6th quarter) in the 1951 elections, a seat previously held by **Ieu Koeus**. He was easily elected, but after the dismissal of the **Huy Kanthoul** government in 1952, and the "crushing" of the Democrat Party, Son Sann resigned from leadership of the party. He only reentered politics as a member of Sangkum and was appointed minister of finance from January to April 1958. He later served in several governments as vice-president of the Council of Ministers, and minister of foreign affairs from July 1958 to April 1960, minister of state for finance and the national economy from January to November 1961, minister of state for finance and national economy from November 1961 to February 1962 and minister of finance and national economy, February to August 1962. Sonn Sann served as director of the National Bank of Cambodia from 1964-1968 (his signature appearing on Cambodian banknotes), becoming prime minister on 1 May 1967, after the resignation of **Lon Nol**. He was succeeded by **Penn Nouth** on 31 January 1969. Following the overthrow of Prince

Norodom Sihanouk in March 1970 Son Sann was placed under house arrest and later left Cambodia for France. By June 1970 he was in Beijing actively promoting a plan which urged reconciliation between Sihanouk and Lon Nol. This continued after the proclamation of the **Khmer Republic** in October 1970, and by late 1971 he had much support from prominent politicians and diplomats in Phnom Penh, Beijing and Paris. However the move was condemned by the Chinese Premier **Zhou Enlai** in March 1972 and followed by Lon Nol elevating himself to president of the Khmer Republic in the following month. Nevertheless Son Sann continued to try to negotiate a peace settlement until 1974 when he was forced to leave Phnom Penh after threats against his life by army officers close to Lon Non.

In Paris in April 1975 Son Sann was asked to lead the Association of Overseas Cambodians and eventually became president of the General Association of Khmers Overseas. By 1978 plans were afoot to launch the **Khmer People's National Liberation Front (KPNLF)** to serve as a front for groups along the Thai-Cambodian border and elsewhere who were united in their opposition to the Communists. This was well under way when the Vietnamese invaded Cambodia establishing the People's Republic of Kampuchea. The **Khmer People's National Liberation Armed Forces (KPNLAF)** was launched in 1979 and with its its political wing, the KPNLF soon became the major noncommunist force along the Thai-Cambodian border and within the Cambodian communities overseas. The KPNLAF later joined with the **Armée Nationale Sihanoukienne** to form the **Non-Communist Resistance**. These two, along with the National Army of Democratic Kampuchea, joined to form the **Coalition Government for Democratic Kampuchea** in 1982. Son Sann, a devout Buddhist, married Nema Machhwa, and they had seven children: **Son Soubert**, Son Monir and Eveline (married Dr. **Chhay Hancheng**), as well as three more sons and a daughter. A brother, Son Qui, was a prominent ear, nose and throat surgeon in Phnom Penh.

SON SEN (1930-1997). Born on 12 June 1930 in Huong Hoa, Travinh, south Vietnam, his father, Son Ng was a farmer and Son Sen went to **Phnom Penh** in 1946 to complete his schooling at the École Normale. There he supported the student wing of the newly emerging **Democrat Party** which militated for independence from the French. Rewarded by the Democrats in 1950, he was sent to Paris on a scholarship to study education. In Paris, Son Sen, along with a small group of like-minded individuals, became active in the Marxist circle of students. He completed his undergraduate degree in literature, but failed the entrance examination to the École Normale Supérieure. Son Sen joined the French Communist Party; but when the Democrat party lost its grip on government in Phnom Penh, he lost his scholarship.

On his return, Son Sen took up a teaching position at a government primary school before moving to **Lycée Sisowath**. There he met and later married **Yun Yat**, another teacher, and was soon promoted to director of studies at the National Pedagogical Institute in Phnom Penh where he was able to utilize his abilities to persuade politically aware teachers to join secret procommunist organizations. In 1958 Son Sen joined **Sangkum** but only four years later was dismissed from the Institute for *lèse majesté*. Son Sen was co-opted onto the Central Committee of the Workers' Party of Kampuchea in the following year. After the disappearance of **Tou Samouth** and the "affair of the 34," Son Sen fled from the capital together with Saloth Sar (**Pol Pot**), Ieng Sary and others. He organized salt flat workers and peasants in the provinces of Kampot, Takeo and Kampong Speu, and succeeded in provoking anti-government struggles in 1967-1968. These failed to bring down the first **Lon Nol** cabinet but in 1970 he announced his support of Prince **Norodom Sihanouk** and was appointed Chief of Staff, People's Armed Forces for the National Liberation of Kampuchea, the fledgling army of the **National United Front of Kampuchea (FUNK)** being based in the Northeast Zone of the country. When the FUNK army seized Phnom Penh in 1975, Son Sen took personal charge of the evacuation of the city. From August 1975 Son Sen was the deputy prime minister and minister of defense in **Democratic Kampuchea**.

In the Pol Pot period, Son Sen controlled the party security apparatus centered on S-21 which "dealt with" cadres suspected of having committed treason and other serious offenses against the revolution or its policies or against the CPK government. His involvement in these operations is beyond any doubt, but his was not the guiding hand in the **purges in Democratic Kampuchea**. By late 1978 some of the confessions of S-21 inmates, extracted under torture, implicated Son Sen in some "traitorous" activities notably in the mysterious death of the British academic **Malcolm Caldwell** on 24 December 1978. He escaped arrest, however, for only days later the Vietnamese invaded Cambodia and captured Phnom Penh in January 1979 forcing the DK authorities to flee to the Thai-Cambodian border.

Once on the run, the Khmer Rouge leadership suspended their self-destructive purges, and Son Sen escaped arrest and almost certain death. Hiding in the jungles along the Thai-Cambodian border, Son Sen, bespectacled and always distinguished in appearance, was frequently spotted by journalists seeking interviews with Pol Pot. He was re-appointed deputy prime minister and minster of defense in the new DK government formed by **Khieu Samphan** in December 1979 but his primary duties were military. By 1982 the ex-communist **Party of Democratic**

Kampuchea (PDK), the Royalist FUNCINPEC and the predominently republican KPNLF, had formed the **Coalition Government of Democratic Kampuchea (CGDK).** Son Sen's role in presiding over the Defense Committee of the CGDK made him an important go-between the military and civilian components of the nationalist, but otherwise, unlikely allies. Following the Jakarta and then the Paris Peace Talks, Son Sen returned to the spotlight as a member of the **Supreme National Council (SNC)** which represented and protected the country's sovereign independence until elections for a lawful government were held under United Nations' auspices. In hindsight, Son Sen was perhaps more determined than most in the PDK to ensure that the Khmer Rouge were reintegrated into national politics and participate in the elections. However in May 1992 when younger military officers began to challenge his leadership and when the SNC failed to acquire administrative powers in Phnom Penh he was relieved of his positions.

When the PDK abandoned its office in Phnom Penh in early 1993, low intensity warfare resumed in opposition to the UN electoral process and against the emergent alliance between the royalist FUNCINPEC and Hun Sen's Cambodian People's Party. Although identified as a minister in the Provisional Government of National Unity and Well-Being headed by Khieu Samphan in 1994, Son Sen exercised little power or authority in this role. He failed in 1996 to persuade once loyal military commanders at Pailin and Phnom Malai to respect orders from the High Command and Pol Pot to renationalize private household property and watched from the sidelines as his lifelong associate Ieng Sary led a breakaway movement. Son Sen and his wife remained in Anlong Veng with Pol Pot but in 1997 when Pol Pot may have been negotiating secretly with representatives of FUNCINPEC, and Son Sen was trying to organize a separate peace with Second Prime Minister Hun Sen he, his wife and their children were brutally murdered on 10 June 1997, allegedly on the orders of Pol Pot. The PDK army, led by **Ta Mok,** mutinied, disrupting all secret talks, arresting Pol Pot and triggering the July 1997 coup in Phnom Penh. A full historical accounting of Son Sen's role in the final years of the DK movement has yet to appear.

SON SOUBERT (1942-   ). Born on 20 June 1942 in **Phnom Penh,** son of **Son Sann,** Soubert attended Malika School, Phnom Penh, and completed his secondary education at St. Louis de Gonzagues, a Jesuit institute in Paris on 1954-1961. He then studied arts at the University of Paris (Sorbonne), obtaining a Higher Diploma in Archaeology from the École de Louvre. He completed his Diploma in Higher Studies in 1968 then studied in Rome, the **United States, Japan** and **Australia,** before joining the **École Française d'Extrême-Orient** at Pondicherry in India 1971-1973. This wide knowledge of foreign countries provided him with a broad international perspective, something that was to help him in years to come.

With the fall of the **Khmer Republic**, Son Soubert returned to Pondicherry, where he worked at the French Institute of Indology in 1975-1979. For the next four years he was manager of a food business in Nice, France, where he was active working with Cambodian refugees. With his father, he was one of the founders of the **Khmer People's National Liberation Front (KPNLF)** in 1979, and President of the KPNLF Red Cross. In 1984 he was working with his father, then prime minister of the **Coalition Government for Democratic Kampuchea**, and by 1986 was a member of the Executive Committee of the KPNLF, in charge of foreign affairs. He represented the KPNLF at the **Paris International Conference on Cambodia** in 1989 then was appointed vice-president of the KPNLF in charge of foreign affairs in September 1991.

Son Soubert was a member of several technical committees attached to the **Supreme National Council**, largely in charge of humanitarian issues. In May 1992 he was the second member, and secretary-general of the **Buddhist Liberal Democratic Party (BLDP)**. In June 1993 he was elected as a BLDP deputy for **Battambang**, then became second vice-president of the National Assembly in October 1993, and later second vice-president of the Assembly's permanent committee. He was also first vice-president of the Commission for Parliamentary Procedures.

SONGSAKD KITCHPANICH. *See* KITCHPANICH SONGSAKD.

SONN MAM (1888-1966). Born on 29 October 1888 in **Phnom Penh**, son of Mam and Mme (née Suon) and cousin of **Tip Mam**, he was a widely respected medical doctor. Mam obtained a local medical degree in 1911 and in 1917 went to France where he obtained a French medical degree. He spent many years in France studying psychiatry; in fact in 1927 he became a French citizen. In 1940 Sonn Mam founded the Psychiatric Hospital at Takhmau, **Kandal**, of which he remained director until the week before his death. He was minister for health from February to August 1948 and minister for foreign affairs, public works and communications in May 1950, under-secretary of state for health, labor and social action, January to March 1951 and vice-president of the Council of Ministers, minister of health, labor and social action, May to October 1951. Sonn Mam contested the seat of Prey Svay, **Svay Rieng** province, on behalf of the **National Recovery Party** in the 1951 National Assembly elections. He was minister for health and foreign affairs in the **Huy Kanthoul** government, October 1951 to June 1952 then retired from politics and continued to run the Takhmau Psychiatric Hospital, as well as being professor of the Royal School of Medicine. His first wife, Iem Tes, with whom he had five children including **Sonn Voeunsai**, died on 27 September 1949, aged 59. He married his second wife Chhit Sophy on 8 August 1955. Dr. Sonn Mam died on 22 January 1966.

SONN VOEUNSAI (1911-). Born in Phnom Penh, the son of **Sonn Mam** and Mme (née Iem Tes), he studied at **Lycée Sisowath** and in Saigon, then traveled to Paris in 1931. He graduated with a degree in engineering from the École Centrale des Arts et Manufactures in Paris in 1939. He then became a reserve officer in the French army and served in the campaigns against the Germans 1939-1940. He was made chief engineer of public works in March 1945. He became vice-minister of national defense under Prince **Sisowath Monireth** in 1945, spent some time in Washington and was a delegate to the Dalat Conference. He was minister of national defense under Prince **Sisowath Youtévong** in December 1946 and under Prince **Sisowath Watchayavong** in July 1947; and minister for national economy and public works from August 1948 until January 1949, minister of national defense 7 May 1950 to 2 March 1951, and minister of public works, March to May 1951. He then resigned and was the Cambodian delegate to the Economic Commission for Asia and the Far East (ECAFE). He returned to the cabinet as minister for the interior and national defense in the **Huy Kanthoul** government, October 1951 to June 1952. He was appointed director-general of the railways, which became one of the best-managed department of the Cambodian administration. He resigned from the **Democrat Party** when the left wing took control of the party executive but did not join **Sangkum** until 1959. He visited Australia in the ECAFE in that year. After a long period out of active politics, he was ambassador to Paris in 1968, and appointed as the **Lon Nol** government's ambassador to Washington in June 1970. Sonn Voeunsai married a daughter of Leng Saem.

SORIAVONG, Prince. *See* OUKTHOL, ANDRÉ.

SOS MAN (1902-c1973). A **Cham** elder, he joined the **Indochina Communist Party** of **Ho Chi Minh** in 1950 and served as deputy head of the Workers' Committee in **Kampong Cham** province. From July 1953 until April 1954 he studied at the Tay Nguyen guerrilla warfare school in the central highlands of Vietnam and was appointed major. He then lived in Hanoi and studied Marxism-Leninism there and in Moscow and Beijing. Returning to Cambodia in 1970, he joined the **Communist Party of Kampuchea (CPK)** Eastern Zone Committee and established the Eastern Zone Islamic Movement which he ran with his son, **Mat Ly**. In 1971 he was identified as a spokesman for Muslims within the **National United Front of Kampuchea**.

SOTH POLIN (1943-). The nephew of **Sim Var**, and longtime journalist and aggressive critic of **Norodom Sihanouk**, Soth Polin was editor of *Nokor Thom* ("Great City") newspaper during the Khmer Republic. In 1970 his newspaper was one of the major scandal sheets concentrating its energies on criticising Queen **Monique Sihanouk**. Supporting Sim Var's abortive attempt at the presidency in 1972, in 1974 *Nokor Thom* contained a major article by Soth Polin which accused Prince **Sisowath Sirik Matak** of the murder of **Keo Sang Kim**, the education minister, and **Thach Chia**. The accusation was unsubstantiated and almost certainly inaccurate. On the day the newspaper hit the streets, Soth Polin fled Phnom Penh. He moved to Long Beach, California, and is the author of a number of books.

SOU PHIRIN. Vice-president of the People's Committee and member of the Standing Committee of the **People's Revolutionary Party of Kampuchea (PRPK)** in **Takeo** in September 1990, he rose to president of the People's Committee for Takeo, and along with all other provincial party leader of the time had his title changed to "governor" in 1992. Elected to the Constituent Assembly for Takeo in the May 1993 elections, he resigned his seat before the proclamation of results and was appointed pronvincial governor of Takeo, 18 December 1993. In March 1999 he was appointed governor of **Kampong Chhnang** province.

SOUK SAM ENG (1956-). Born in Sangkum Thmei, **Preah Vihear**, or in **Kampong Thom** province where his parents were garden (*chamcar*) farmers, he was forced to do heavy manual work during the **Pol Pot** years. In the **People's Republic of Kampuchea** elections of May 1981 he was elected to the National Assembly in Preah Vihear where he had been involved in the creation of local people's revolutionary (i.e. party) committees. He then represented the province from February 1986 until May 1993; was president of the People's Committee for Preah Vihear from 1981 to March 1986, and secretary of the **People's Revolutionary Party of Kampuchea (PRPK)** from August 1986 until 1992. In 1991 Souk Sam Eng was elected to the Central Committee of the **Cambodian People's Party** and in 1992, as with all other province level party secretaries, redesignated "governor" of Preah Vihear. Elected to the Constituent Assembly for Preah Vihear in 1993, he was a member of the Commission for Economics and Planning. He was reelected to the National Assembly in 1998 but Preap Tann replaced him as governor of Preah Vihear in March 1999.

SOUTH-EAST ASIA TREATY ORGANIZATION (SEATO), 1954-1977. Organized by the United States in 1954 in the aftermath of the French defeat in Indochina, SEATO was the principal instrument of U.S. cold war containment policy in the Southeast Asian region in the 1950s and 1960s.

Signatories to the treaty, also known as the Manila Pact, included America's principal European allies of the time, **France**, the **United Kingdom**, **Australia** and New Zealand and in Asia, **Thailand**, the Philippines and Pakistan. Unlike the North Atlantic Treaty Organization, member states were not automatically obliged to mount a mutual defense if any one of them was attacked: they were obliged to consult, only. The Treaty formally extended an "umbrella of protection" over the three newly independent countries of Vietnam, Laos and Cambodia who were forbidden to enter into foreign military alliances by the terms of the **Geneva Agreements** of 1954. Fears that **Norodom Sihanouk** would ignore these provisions and enter into a postcolonial defense alliance with the USA were rife among Cambodian nationalists and communists in the 1950s but the prince formally rejected the SEATO offer of protection when he announced his foreign policy of neutrality in 1955 and never wavered from this position. SEATO articles were invoked when the United States sent military advisors and then soldiers into South Vietnam in the 1960s, with most treaty states, supplying small military forces to support the US war effort there. The communist military victories of 1975 and the emergence of détente in Europe rendered this treaty organization obselete. It was formally disbanded on 30 June 1977.

SREI REACHEA. A semilegendary King of Cambodia (r 1469-1492), son of King **Ponhea Yat**, crowned in 1469, most of his 23-year reign, if the chronicles depicting it are to be believed, was taken up with wars against Siam (**Thailand**) and with putting down dynastic rivals.

SREI THOMREACHEA. King of Cambodia 1627-1635. His reign was marked by serious rivalries with his uncle, the prince regent. Srei Thomreachea was killed in the course of a rebellion led by his uncle. The king enjoyed a high scholarly reputation.

SREY SAMAN (1924-). Born on 10 Nov 1924 in **Kampot**, the son of Srey Chum and Mme (née Kim Koy), he studied at the Royal Khmer Military School and in Paris. A professional soldier, he worked in the Ministry of National Defense. In September 1966 he was a member of the Cambodian delegation negotiating with the **National Front for the Liberation of South Vietnam**. He was a colonel in 1968 and also chief of staff of national defense. In 1974 he became a major general in the Republican Army. Saman married Prak Ny in 1959 and they had six children.

SROK. Khmer language term usually translated as "district," a subdivision of the province (*khet*). In colloquial Khmer speech, the word also denotes "land" (or *pays* in French) as in the phrase *srok khmer,* literally "land of the Khmer," or Cambodia. *See also* ADMINISTRATIVE DIVISIONS.

STATE OF CAMBODIA (SOC) *ro't Kampuchea.* The name chosen by the Vietnamese-installed regime in Phnom Penh in 1989, to supersede the **People's Republic of Kampuchea (PRK)**, the name taken by the government when it assumed office in January 1979. The removal of the communist reference to a "people's republic" allowed for the possible restoration of the monarchy. The SOC administration governed in Phnom Penh through the national elections of 1993, when the country's official name became the Kingdom of Cambodia (*Kampuchea* in Khmer).

STUNG TRENG. Cambodian province with a provincial capital of the same name. The province covers 11,209 square kilometers and borders **Ratanakiri, Kratié, Mondolkiri, Preah Vihear, Kampong Thom** and **Laos.** According to the March 1998 **census**, the population was only 81,074 making it one of the smallest, twentieth in population size, of the country's 24 provinces and municipalities. Curiously the National Election Commission reported that its population had fallen to 75,393 in 2002, and assuming both figures are broadly accurate, this suggests there has been very high outward migration into Laos or other parts of Cambodia. The **Mekong** flows rapidly through the mountains and plateau regions of this province but is not easily navigable and its waters have not been widely tamed either for agriculture or for hydropower, most lighting coming from kerosene lamps according to the report of the census.

SUM CHHUM (1924-   ). Born on 6 July 1924 at Khbal Kas, Kiensvay, **Kandal**, son of Nou Sum, farmer, and Mme (née Ouk Oum), he attended **Lycée Sisowath** and was awarded a government scholarship to study agronomy in France from 1947-1953. He was an agricultural engineer and was involved in research in tropical agronomy. Rector of Phnom Penh Technical University, he was a member of the **Socio-Republican Party** Central Committee. From October 1972 until April 1973 Chhum was minister of planning and national development. From May until October he was minister of information in the **In Tam** government and from October until December 1973 was minister for veterans' affairs. His wife was Ung Pochheang, and they had three children.

SUM HIENG (1898-c1965). Born in Triton, South Vietnam, he was a career civil servant and was minister of the interior in the **Son Ngoc Thanh** government from August to October 1945. Minister of religion, religious affairs and fine arts from October 1945 to December 1946, he contested the 1948 High Council elections for **Pursat** and **Kampong Chhnang**. Hieng was vice-president of the Council of Ministers and minister of planning in the **Yèm Sambaur** government from February to September 1949, holding the same position in the brief **Ieu Koeus** provisional government then in the second Yèm Sambaur government from September 1949 to May 1950. He was the chairman of the Cambodian delegation to the **Pau Conference** in 1950. In 1958 he was Cambodian representative in Saigon.

SUM MANIT (1930-). Born on 1 January 1930 at Anlong Romiet, Kandal Stung, **Kandal**, he attended **Lycée Sisowath** and then Lycée Chasseloup Laubat in Saigon. In 1955 he graduated from the Royal School of Administration. Joining the diplomatic service, he worked in the Office of the Minorities and in 1959 was appointed to the Cambodian High Commission in Saigon. Further postings included chargé d'affaires in Rangoon in 1960, second (then first) secretary in Belgrade, chargé d'affaires in Bangkok in 1970, councillor in Singapore in 1971-1973 and minister-councillor in Tokyo in 1974-1975. In France as a refugee after 1975, he worked for Citroen. He was appointed deputy minister to the cabinet office then secretary of state in the Royal Government during the 1990s.

SUON KASET, Mme née **Su Sokhomaly.** She was a teacher at the Khmer-English School in Phnom Penh, her pupils including **Lim Hong**. She married Suon Kaset, an inspector of waters and forests in the Ministry of Agriculture and worked as the chief editor of *Kampuja*, a glossy social and arts magazine published by Prince **Norodom Sihanouk**. Supporting the overthrow of Sihanouk in 1970, Mme Suon Kaset joined the staff of Prince **Sisowath Sirik Matak**, for whom she had a great admiration. She worked for him during his period as acting prime minister 1971-1972 then worked for Henry Kamm, reporter for *The New York Times*. Leaving Phnom Penh in March 1975, she moved to Paris and worked for *The New York Times* there. From 1975-1978 Mme Suon Kaset was one of the supporters of **Son Sann** in the moves that eventually led to the founding of the **Khmer People's National Liberation Front (KPNLF)** in 1979. Respected for her knowledge, her passion to help the refugees on the Thai-Cambodian border during the 1980s and her anticommunist ideals, she was a staunch opponent of corruption in the border refugee camps. Suon Kaset worked at the office of the KPNLF in Ramintra (Bangkok). Remaining loyal to Son Sann, she was a founding member of the **Buddhist Liberal Democratic Party**.

SUONG SIKOEUN. An active member of the **National United Front of Kampuchea**, he lived in China from 1970-1974 returning to Cambodia where, during the period of **Democratic Kampuchea**, he worked in the foreign ministry under **Ieng Sary**. Returning to China in 1979-1980 and again from 1990-1992, he was interviewed just before President Jiang

Zemin's November 2000 visit to Cambodia. Sikoeun dismissed criticisms of China's support of the **Pol Pot** regime. China's advice to the **Democratic Kampuchea (DK)** leadership had been generally sound, and moderate, he claimed, but it passed unheeded. His wife, Laurence Picq, a French citizen, also worked under Ieng Sary from 1975-1979. Her account of her life in the DK foreign ministry, the only book-length treatment by somebody close to the DK leadership, *Beyond the Horizon,* was published in Paris in 1984 and in New York in 1989.

SUPREME NATIONAL COUNCIL (SNC). This was the body conceived and formed at the **Jakarta Informal Meeting (JIM)** of 1990 in conjunction with proposals for the establishment of a temporary **United Nations** "authority" to administer Cambodia for an interim period. Cambodia could not be placed in trusteeship because it was a fully sovereign nation-state and a signatory of the UN charter. The SNC thus formally enshrined and protected national sovereignty while the **United Nations Transitional Authority in Cambodia (UNTAC)** assumed administrative control, monitored the cease-fire and prepared national, self-determining elections. In theory, the SNC shared power with UNTAC; in practice, both the SNC and UNTAC struggled to control or administer the country during 1991-1993 neither being fully sovereign nor comfortable with shared sovereignty. The SNC formula nevertheless overcame the 1989 **Paris International Conference** failure to form an all-party interim government and cleared the way for the Paris agreements of 1991.

The SNC consisted of six members appointed by the Phnom Penh-based **State of Cambodia** and two members each from the three political parties in the Beijing-based **Coalition Government of Democratic Kampuchea (CGDK).** Prince **Norodom Sihanouk,** taking one of the FUNCINPEC seats, chaired the SNC. His commitment and loyalty to the process gradually subsided when UNTAC imposed an election law which had not been agreed to by the SNC, when the **Party of Democratic Kampuchea (PDK)** attempted to expand its governmental role and the disarmament process failed. Disputes over judicial proceedings against individuals detained for human rights violations finally led to the prince's boycott of SNC deliberations in late 1992 and early 1993. The SNC was summarily and unilaterally dissolved by the Cambodian side following the national elections in May 1993 and a "provisional" Royal Government gradually assumed administrative control outside of the Paris framework for transition.

SURYAVARMAN I. King of Cambodia 1002-1050. A Buddhist, he came to the throne by absorbing several small kingdoms that had developed in eastern Cambodia in the late 10th century. In 1011, his followers swore loyalty to him in an oath preserved in an inscription in the temple now known as the royal palace at **Angkor**. Suryavarman presided over the construction of the Western Baray and extended Angkorean jurisdiction into northeastern Thailand and southern Cambodia. During his reign several new urban centers *(pura)* were noted in inscriptions, which also testify to his patronage of public works throughout the region.

SURYAVARMAN II. King of Cambodia 1113-1150. A king most renowned in modern times for presiding over the construction of **Angkor Wat**, the massive temple dedicated to the Hindu deity Vishnu around AD 1130 that probably also served, eventually, as Suryavarman's tomb. He was the first monarch in nearly a century to govern a more or less unified kingdom. He was also the first Angkorean king to establish formal diplomatic relations with China.

SUY SEM (1947-). Born in Bakan, **Pursat**, he studied law in **Phnom Penh** and was a civil servant employed in the Ministry of Labor and Social Welfare 1970-1975. During the **Democratic Kampuchea** years he was evacuated to the countryside then joined the **People's Republic of Kampuchea (PRK)** administration. In 1991 he was deputy minister of planning and was appointed to the Central Committee of the **Cambodian People's Party (CPP)** in 1992. In January 1993 he became minister of labor and social action and in May 1993 was elected to the National Assembly on the CPP list in Pursat. In 1994 he became secretary of state for social welfare, labor and veterans' affairs. He was reelected to the National Assembly in 1998.

SVAY RIENG. A province that geographically protrudes into **Vietnam**, north of the Mekong Delta with a provincial capital of the same name. Settled for centuries, this province has relatively poor or overworked agricultural soils and has long been a center of trade, including smuggling, to and from Vietnam. The province was of strategic importance during the **Second Indochina War** because of its proximity to Saigon. It was secretly bombed by the **United States** from 1968 and was a center of anti-Vietnamese and anti-Sihanouk demonstrations in March 1970 as well as an area of contact between early *Khmer Issarak* and **Viet Minh** groups and the communist revolutionary movements in the two countries. In the March 1998 **census**, the population of the province was 478,252 and of the two districts incorporating the city, 150,778. By February 2002, the population of the province had grown to 505,350. Support for the ex-communist **Communist People's Party (CPP)** was high in the commune elections. The CPP won 71.5 percent of the votes, 367 seats of the total of 516.

SVAY SO (1913-). Born in **Takeo**, he was a clerk in the French colonial administration before entering the Cambodian civil service in 1938. An outspoken nationalist, he was elected a **Democrat Party** deputy for Chrey Las, **Kandal**, in 1947. Minister of finance from February to August 1949, he was secretary-general of the American Aid Committee. In 1951 he was elected to the National Assembly for Kampong Luong, Kandal, but was arrested for his anti-French and anti-Royalist activities in January 1953 when he was president of the National Assembly. Very deeply opposed to the armed struggle and to the **Son Ngoc Thanh** and **Son Ngoc Minh** ideological tendencies within the nationalist movement, he remained with the **Democrat Party** after 1954, working with the executive committee led by **Keng Vannsak** and **Norodom Phurissara** during the 1955 election campaign. He was a candidate for the party in a Phnom Penh constituency but was defeated at the polls. In June 1971 he was appointed to the **constitutional drafting committee** representing the mutual aid association of retired civil servants.

-T-

TA KEO (temple-mountain). Sivaite sandstone temple, built in the late 10th or early 11th century under King **Rajendravarman**. It is unusual in that it has only minimal surface decoration, much of which appears to have been left unfinished.

TA MAING. *See* LOEUNG SINAK.

TA MOK né **Oung Chhoeun**, also known as **Chhit Chhoeun (1925-   ).** The military strongman in the final years of the **Pol Pot** movement, Mok was born in Pra Keap, near Trapeang Thom Tbong, in the Tramkak district in the western part of **Takeo** province. His grandfather, Oung, married a Chinese from **Kampot**—and their son, Oung Preak (Mok's father) was a monk at the local pagoda for some 20 years before he married, went into farming and the timber business and raised a family of seven—Mok, the firstborn being followed by two brothers and then four sisters. He attended the local pagoda at Trapeang Thom Tbong, and after entering the monkhood left for Phnom Penh to study at the Pali school near Wat Langka achieving the primary Pali School leaving certificate and honorific recognition as a teacher of Pali sometime in the 1940s. He had joined the **Khmer Issarak** armed struggle by 1949, became a full member of the Indochinese Communist Party in 1950 and in 1951, when the ICP was replaced by national revolutionary parties, saw his membership transferred to the **Khmer People's Revolutionary Party**.

Returning to Takeo in 1954 Ta (*Grandfather)* Mok started his own family and worked with his father, earning his living mostly by logging in the forest and selling processed timber. Though he was responsible for party organizational work in the south throughout the 1950s, he may not have met Saloth Sar (**Pol Pot**) until after the disappearance of **Tou Samouth** to whom he would have reported. It is significant that Mok went underground in 1963 at the same time as Saloth Sar, **Ieng Sary** and **Son Sen** even though his name did not appear on the on list of 34 suspected communists published in Phnom Penh in March 1963. At a secret and extraordinary **Communist Party of Kampuchea (CPK)** Special Assembly held in the same year he was appointed to the Central Committee, an indication of his support for a new armed struggle and for the stepped up armed propaganda work of the CPK. In 1968, following the death of the secretary of the CPK Southwest Zone, Ta Mok was appointed to that position.

Once back in Takeo, and especially after the overthrow of **Norodom Sihanouk** on 18 March 1970, Mok was responsible for raising a regional army. His daughter Khum, was, by this time, married to Khe Muth, CPK secretary for the Tramkak region. All four sons, two daughters, and three other sons-in-law, as well as two brothers-in-law, were also office holders in the Takeo CPK. As a strong and tightly knit family group, they managed to take political and military control of much of the Southwest Zone (essentially Takeo, Kampot and Kandal provinces) long before the Khmer Rouge victory in 1975. In 1973 they created the first, model agricultural collectives in which all produce and private possessions were held in communal stores and granaries under the control of the CPK/FUNK village committees. Part of the evolving communist system in the Southwest was an "interrogation" (and execution) center under Ta Mok's control at Krang Kra, in which 477 people, some scarcely teenagers, were executed. This center was part of a nationwide network of wartime party prisons which, after 1975, were superseded by or subordinated to *Santebal 21*, known as **S.21**. A man of quiet demeanor who unlike Pol Pot possessed no commanding presence or charisma, he, his sons and sons-in-law were, from 1976, centrally involving in the carrying out of the **purges in Democratic Kampuchea**.

The Vietnamese invasion of Cambodia in December 1978 forced Ta Mok to flee Takeo for the Thai-Cambodian border. In the absence of Son Sen who had assumed field command in the East Zone, he was named deputy commander in chief and chief of staff of the National Army of Democratic Kampuchea. Not a commander to draw attention to himself or to avoid the battlefield, Ta Mok lost a leg in the ensuing war against the Vietnamese army of occupation and the **People's Republic of Kampuchea** armed forces. Apart from his military activities, Mok was instrumental in financing the war effort as aid from China and the **ASEAN** countries first declined and then, from 1989, ceased altogether. He was heavily involved in massive logging operations along the Thai-Cambodian border once the Party of Democratic Kampuchea (PDK) succeeded in auctioning off large concessions to Thai entrepeneurs. His troops also collected taxes and other huge sums from Thai and other foreign gem miners and jewelry merchants who sought mining concessions near **Pailin**, a town located on the northwest end of the Cardomom range in Battambang province which is not far from the Thai border. Allegedly banked in Thailand and partly invested in Thai companies, including possibly a petrol station in Surin province which served as a depot for the NADK, the funds were rapidly depleted after 1993. Based at **Anlong Veng** in June 1997 when Pol Pot ordered the summary execution of Son Sen, Mok pursued and captured Pol Pot as he attempted to flee into Thailand and quietly presided over the people's tribunal organized to purge and sentence Pol Pot in July 1997. In March 1999 he was captured and imprisoned in Phnom Penh. Legal proceedings against him have been stalled by the absence of appropriate laws and any court of jurisdiction. As of 2002, he has not been formally charged.

TA PROHM. Cambodian temple complex, consecrated in 1186 by **Jayavarman VII**. Probably the first of the many Buddhist temples constructed by this monarch, **Ta Prohm** was left unrestored by French archaeologists to show visitors the decay into which Angkorean ruins had fallen when rediscovered by the French in the 19th century.

TAKEO. A province with a capital bearing the same name. Bordering **Kandal, Kampot** and **Kampong Speu** provinces, Takeo covers 3,818 square kilometers and in the March 1998 **census** had a population of 790,168. Located on a plain on the coast and initially settled in pre-Angkorean ruins, the agricultural regions are heavily, and perhaps overly, populated in view of current technologies and the carrying capacity of the land. The province was a major recruiting ground for the **Communist Party of Kampuchea** in the late 1960s and early 1970s when indebted peasants began to lose control over their produce, their lands and livelihoods. As the center of the Southwest Zone in **Democratic Kampuchea**, Takeo was controlled by **Ta Mok**. The sixth largest of Cambodia's province, in population terms, it had grown to 815,200 people by the time of the February 2002 commune elections, heavily dominated by the **Cambodian People's Party** led by **Hun Sen**.

TAN BUN SUOR (1937-). He studied engineering at the University of Nancy, gaining his doctorate in 1964. He returned to Cambodia as lecturer at the University of Phnom Penh from 1964-1969, dean of the science faculty from 1969-1970 and Professor from 1970. Moving to Paris, he was involved in pro-Republican movements, heading his own movement, the Movement of Khmer Democrats and was a founding member of the **Liberal Democratic Party**. In May 2001 he held the information portfolio in the Sam Rainsy Party shadow cabinet.

TAN KIM HUON (1924-). Born on 22 February 1924 at Mongkolborey, the son of Tan Cheav and Mme (née Ean Lam), Tan Kim Huon studied mathematics at Hanoi and then worked as a teacher assistant at **Lycée Sisowath**. In 1946 he went to France to study at the Lycée Louis Le Grand for his eventual entry into the Institute of Agronomy, which he attended from 1948-1950. He then proceeded to the National School of Waters and Forests at Nancy then the Technical Center for Tropical Wood at Nogent-sur-Marne. He returned to Cambodia in April 1953 receiving a series of civil service posts in the Ministry of Agriculture linked to his technical expertise. He returned to academic work on a more or less full-time basis when he was appointed rector of the Royal University of Agriculture from September 1969 until 1971. In June 1970 he was chairman of the Foreign Affairs Committee of the National Assembly. He represented the Ministry of Agriculture on the **constitutional drafting committee** of June 1971. From 1971 he was also chairman of the Committee for the Protection of Cultural Properties. His participation in party politics began in 1966 when he was elected to the National Assembly in Preah Vihear province. He was elected unopposed, a rival candidate having dropped out before election day. A critic of the first Lon Nol government formed after these elections, he was editor-in-chief of the official opposition "Bulletin de Contre-Gouvernement" from October 1967 to April 1968. In early 1972 he joined the **Socio-Republican Party** and was re-elected to the National Assembly in September 1972 in Serei Reath, a precinct of Phnom Penh.

TAN NADY also known as Nady Tan. A pilot, trained at the Air Academy at Tours, France, in 1965, he worked at the air base at Clermont-Ferrand in 1967. In 1973 he was awarded a diploma in management and leadership from the United States Air University, Maxwell, Alabama. During the remaining years of the civil war, 1973-1975, he was involved in air defense work at **Kampong Chhnang** and **Battambang**, moving to the **United States** as a refugee in 1976. He worked for the Indochinese Cultural and Service Center 1976-1982 and was executive director of the International Refugee Center in Oregon 1982-1993. In 1989 Tan Nady earned an M.A. in public administration from Oregon University and in 1993 moved back to Cambodia. He worked in the personal secretariat of Prince **Norodom Ranariddh** and for **FUNCINPEC** in the 1993 election campaign and was appointed secretary-general for the cabinet government in May 1994. From early 1997 he was among the first in the top leadership circles of FUNCINPEC to express his personal dissatisfaction with Ranariddh's leadership of both government and party. Already associated with a FUNCINPEC splinter group at the time of the July 1997 coup, he was appointed minister of tourism in September 1997, replacing the self-exiled Ranariddh loyalist **Veng Sereivuth**. In 1998 he became Deputy President of the **Reastr Niyum (RN)** party founded by **Ung Huot**. He was among the RN members who quietly returned to the FUNCINPEC in 2000.

TAN PA (1892-1971). Born in **Phnom Penh**, son of Tan Kheng Long and Mme (née Ly Ou), he was an entrepreneur, forester and importer-exporter, best known for constructing the road from Battambang to Phnom Penh. During the late 1950s he was reputedly one of the richest men in the country and ran a network of companies. In 1910 he married Ly Siou Beo and they had nine children. Of his daughters, Wat Tho married Ong Poxay, and Wat Eng married Ong Po Koun. He died on 17 January 1971.

TAN UK NAM IENG (1920-). Born on 3 May 1920 near Sisophon, **Battambang**, the son of Tan Uk and Mme (née Niou), he attended **Lycée Sisowath** and the Royal School of Administration then studied abroad. After some time in the civil service, in 1956 he was promoted to head of the office of the minister of information; transferring in the following year to the Interior Ministry. In 1958 he was head of the prison services and in the following year was inspector of municipal affairs. In 1966 he was comfortably elected as deputy to represent **Phnom Penh**, 3ème in the National Assembly elections—a result, marred as it was, best remembered for one of the lowest turnouts in Cambodia's history. In November 1970 he narrowly defeated **Ung Mung** for the vice-presidency of the National Assembly. After 1975 he moved to Montrouge, France.

TANG SAROEUN (1925-c1995). Among the communist veterans of the anti-colonial **Khmer Issarak** movement, Tang Saroeun was born in Phnom Penh where his parents owned enough land to do some farming. He joined the armed struggle in 1950 in Kampong Cham, immediately receiving training as a military intelligence officer, and sometime between 1951-1954, he also joined the **Khmer People's Revolutionary Party (KPRP)**. In 1954 he was ordered by his party "to fulfill duties and undertake studies abroad," according to an official biography, In other words he was regrouped with the **Viet Minh** soldiers then serving in Cambodia and along with 1-1,500 other Cambodian guerrilla fighters, evacuated with them to points north of the newly established demilitarized zone (DMZ). At first he was a worker in a match factory but was sent in 1957 to Phu Tho for political studies, then to Vinh Phuc in 1958 for further courses and finally attached to a mine in Tinh Tuc until 1962. After attending the

Dong Trieu School for Workers and Peasants and being trained as a clerk and administrator, he worked, from 1966-1970, for the external relations department of the Workers' Party of Vietnam, reporting to Xuan Thuy. It was he who organized the return in late 1970 of around 1,000 Cambodian "regroupees" from Vietnam in support of the effort to build an effective **National United Front of Kampuchea (FUNK)**. He returned himself in a party that numbered about 120 as they began their long march down the Ho Chi Minh trail into northeastern Cambodia. No more than 63-68 of them arrived, he claimed in an interview in 1978. The regroupees were dispersed around the country, Saroeun becoming a district party secretary, and a member of the **Communist Party of Kampuchea (CPK)** province committee in Kampong Cham. When CPK purges against regroupees began in 1973, he was demoted and shifted into an administrative post in the provincial health service. In 1974 after many of his relatives were killed he slipped across the border to Vietnam.

Among the promoters of the **United Front for the National Salvation of Kampuchea (UFNSK)**, he was named minister of trade in the **People's Republic of Kampuchea (PRK)** from 1979 to 1981, being replaced by Chan Phin in that year, and was minister for economic and cultural cooperation with foreign countries, 1985-1988 when the ministry was disbanded. He was then trade minister until 1990. Accused of corrupt practices as the economy was liberalized, he was abruptly fired and retired in September 1990 as a result of labor protests in which some workers were killed.

TEA BANH (1945-). Born on 5 November 1945 at **Koh Kong**, from an ethnic Thai family, in 1962 he joined the **Communist Party of Kampuchea**, and during the civil war from 1970-1975 was a member of **National United Front of Kampuchea (FUNK)**. However in April 1974 he broke with Saloth Sar (**Pol Pot**) and formed a guerrilla group opposing him from 1947-1949. Tea Banh was one of the first 14 founding members of the **United Front for the National Salvation of Kampuchea** in December 1978 and was appointed as president of the Military Committee of Koh Kong province in 1979. He took the lead in the formation of the People's Revolutionary Armed Forces of Kampuchea in January 1980 and was assistant chief to the commander-in-chief, in August 1980. He was elected in May 1981 to the National Assembly of the **People's Republic of Kampuchea**, and represented **Kampong Thom** there and in the **State of Cambodia** National Assembly until May 1993. In September 1982 Tea Banh became vice-minister for defense, in charge of aviation, and a member of the Central Committee of the **People's Revolutionary Party of Kampuchea (PRPK)** in 1985; and minister of communications, transport and post. He was promoted to vice-president of the Council of Ministers in November 1987 with the extra portfolio of defense in August 1988. In January 1989 he was a three-star general and was a member of the **Supreme National Council** from 1990-1993, being elected as a **Cambodian People's Party** representative for **Siem Reap** in the Constituent Assembly, May 1993. Vice-minister of defense, in 1993 he was appointed cominister of national defense. He was reelected to the National Assembly in 1998 and appointed once again as cominister of defense with the administrative rank of minister of state.

TEAP BAEN (1930-c1999). An army officer, he was promoted to brigadier general in the Republican army in 1974 and in 1975 managed to escape to the border, eventually being resettled in the United States. Briefly associated with **Molinaka**, he was named commander-in-chief and chief-of-staff of the **Armée Nationale Sihanoukienne (ANS)** by In Tam in September 1981, holding this post until February 1986. It was as a result of his efforts and long experience both a soldier serving under Prince **Norodom Sihanouk,** and then **Lon Nol** (and then Sihanouk again), that a Joint Military Command between the **Khmer People's National Liberation Armed Forces (KPNLAF)** and the ANS was established. Baen lost his post when he retired after being accused of embezzling funds set aside for refugee relief work. Returning to Phnom Penh in the 1990s after many years in Surin, Thailand, he was appointed to the Royal Council. He married Phay Cheolim, daughter of Phay Luon, onetime governor of Svay Rieng.

TELEVISION. The Cambodian television service (Télévision Royale Khmère) started on 7 February 1966. Controlled by the minister of information it broadcast news and also drama. From October 1970 until April 1975 it was known as the Television of the Khmer Republic and gained a reputation for political comment when **Koy Pech** appeared on an interview criticizing **Lon Nol.** Reestablished by the **People's Republic of Kampuchea,** the first station was Cambodian Television (now National Television of Cambodia) which opened on 3 December 1983. Khmer TV (Channel 9) was established in 1992 and is privately owned, and Apsara TV (Channel 11) was founded in April 1996 being owned by the Apsara Media Group. Bayon Radio and Television (originally Bayon Radio) started transmitting in January 1998. The other television station is Phnom Penh TV (Channel 3).

TENG BUNMA né **Khaou Tengma (1941-).** Born on 3 September 1941 in **Kampong Cham,** he grew up in **Battambang** and then at Skoun, near **Kampong Cham.** He rose to prominence with the instability along the

Thai-Cambodian border in the 1970s and 1980s. Much of Teng Bunma's money no doubt comes from the rise in property prices in Bangkok—he certainly invested heavily in land there; and he has vigorously denied any involvement in narcotics. Close to some of the **Cambodian People's Party** leadership, although he did manage to visit the United States as an economic advisor to **Chea Sim**; any return visit has been ruled out because the U.S. government has banned him under Section 212 of the nationality act. In Phnom Penh he is president of the Chamber of Commerce and has never hidden his support for Hun Sen, openly admitting the role he played in the 1997 Coup. He is married and has one son.

TEP CHHIEU KENG (1930-1975). Born on 3 September 1930 at Prek Kak, Kampong Cham, the son of Tep Cheng and Mme (née Sarinn), he studied cinematography in Paris. In 1960 he was appointed director of **Agence Khmère de Presse** and was secretary of state for information from August 1969 until July 1970; in January 1970 he was director of *Réalités Cambodgiennes*. At the fall of the **Khmer Republic**, he was detained by revolutionary soldiers and was, as of early May 1975, being held for interrogation at the Monorom Hotel in Phnom Penh. It is presumed that he was executed later that month. His wife was Pou Sayon.

TEP HEN. He was a representative of the Kampuchean Committee for Defense of the Peace in the 36th Session of the **United Nations** Commission for Human Rights, Geneva in March 1980. Joining the **People's Republic of Kampuchea (PRK)** Foreign Ministry, he was head of the USSR and the Eastern European department. In November 1985 he was PRK ambassador to Vietnam and in 1995 was appointed ambassador to Cuba being replaced by Chhim Prong in 1999.

TEP IM, SOTHA PAUL (1934-1975). Born on 6 January 1934, Tep Im was the son of a teacher and the grandson of a court official. After studying at the Catholic Institute in Paris and the Institut des Hautes Études, also in Paris, he returned to Cambodia and was appointed as vicar at **Battambang**—in 1966 he was only one of four Cambodians who had been ordained into the Roman Catholic Church. He gained his doctorate from the Gregorian University, Rome, his thesis being on the first Catholic missionaries who worked in Cambodia in the 16th and 17th centuries. In 1971 he was appointed as bishop and apostolic prefect of Battambang. During the Khmer Republic he worked hard to translate the Bible into Cambodian, but was captured by the Communists at the fall of Battambang and killed late in April 1975.

TEP KHUNNAH (1934-1997). Born on 24 August 1934 in Prey Chraing, Kanchai Mea, **Prey Veng**, son of Tep Chum, *chauvraysrok* of Kanchai

Mea, Tep Khunnah was from a family of 14 children. His father was a member of the 1946 Constituent Assembly, and Khunnah went to **Lycée Sisowath** and won a government scholarship to study at Montpellier, France, in 1955. In 1963 he was Vespa Director of The East Asiatic Company Ltd, the Danish trading conglomerate. By 1969 he was president and director-general of SONAPNEU, the government tire manufacturing company. In 1971 he was a founder of the Independent Republican Association, which in 1972 became the **Republican Party**, led by **Sisowath Sirik Matak**. From 1972 until its banning in 1973 he published *Bulletin of Excerpts*, which contained English-language summaries from the Khmer language press, which was widely used by the foreign community and foreign journalists in Phnom Penh. He survived an assassination attempt on 25 March 1973, when the pillion passenger of a motorcyclist placed a handgrenade on his jeep as he was driving near the Korean Embassy, an attack probably ordered by Brigadier General **Lon Non**. By May 1973 he had left for France, and there met, and is believed to have fought with, Lon Non in a Paris night-club. He moved to Quebec in 1974. One of his sisters married Tim Carney, U.S. diplomat based in Phnom Penh and Bangkok from the 1970s.

TEP KHUNNAL (1950-). Son of Mr. Tep and Mme Tep (née **Khieu Thirath**), and a nephew by marriage of **Pol Pot** and **Ieng Sary**, he studied civil engineering at the University of Phnom Penh and from late 1974 until 1977, at the University of Toulouse. Returning to **Democratic Kampuchea** in the same year, he was among the first group of reeducated intellectuals to be rehabilitated in 1978. He worked with **Thiounn Mumm** and 16 others attached to the Ministry of Culture and Information to establish an Institute of Technological Studies. In 1980 he was attached to the UN Mission of **Democratic Kampuchea (DK)** in New York where he worked with **Thiounn Prasith**, the DK ambassador to the **United Nations** from 1980-1993. He was a senior member of delegations representing the **Party of Democratic Kampuchea (PDK)** at the peace conferences convened in Paris (1989), Jakarta (1990) and Paris (1991) and worked in Phnom Penh with **Khieu Samphan** in the PDK delegation attached to the **Supreme National Council**, 1992-1993. In June 1994 he was a member of the delegation to the Round Table talks organized by King **Norodom Sihanouk** in North Korea which failed to persuade the PDK to abandon its armed struggle. Later the same year, he was named a minister in the newly formed provisional government of national solidarity and well-being led by Khieu Samphan. A close friend of **Son Sen**, he was alienated from the **Democratic Kampuchea** cause and **Pol Pot**'s leadership when in 1997 Pol Pot ordered the murder of his mentor. Tep Khunnal was among those who arranged the trial of Pol Pot for treason and murder in July 1997 and who allowed the journalist Nate Thayer to film part of the trial and, later, to interview Pol Pot before his death in April 1998. He married **Mea Som**, Pol Pot's widow, later the same year.

TEP NANNORY (1949-). Born on 27 July 1949 at Lauri, Treang, **Takeo**, he studied in France and taught history and geography in **Kampot**. During 1979-1982 he was an official in the Phnom Penh municipality, then went to Thailand and joined **Molinaka** in Nong Chan in 1982. Administration director at Nong Ek in 1983, he was head of the police among the Sihanoukist refugees in the Site B refugee camp 1984-1985. In February 1993 Nannory was a member of the **FUNCINPEC** National Council. In the following year he served as president of the FUNCINPEC electoral committee for Takeo. Elected as deputy for Takeo, he resigned his parliamentary mandate in July 1994, having been named as governor of **Prey Veng** on 18 December 1993. In 1998 he was elected to the National Assembly for Prey Veng.

TEP PHAN (1905-c1985). Born on 10 September 1905 at Kandal Stung, **Kandal**, he was governor of **Kampong Thom**, secretary of state for the interior 1948-1949, governor of **Battambang** and minister of trade and industry in 1951. Phan led the Cambodian delegation to the **Geneva Conference** in 1954, on his return served as minister of national defense and as minister of the interior and foreign affairs, August 1954 to January 1955, chief of staff for surface defense and deputy-governor of the National Bank. He was governor of Phnom Penh in 1960 at which time he was an alternate member of the Royal Council. In July 1970 he was appointed advisor to Lon Nol. Tep Phan married Tan Saoyouth and they had eleven children.

TEP VONG (1931-). A Buddhist monk, in the 1981 National Assembly elections he was elected as a deputy for **Siem Reap**, becoming vice-president of the National Assembly in July 1981. A monk superior in July 1988, Tep Vong became superior of the Mohanikay Order in 1992 and, *ex officio*, member of the **Throne Council** from 24 September 1993.

TET OFFENSIVE. A military action initiated by Vietnamese Communist forces in late January February 1972 in an attempt to ignite a general uprising in southern Vietnam that would, it was hoped, drive American forces from Vietnam. In Cambodia, the offensive coincided with the start of armed struggle by the **Communist Party of Kampuchea**, a move probably taken on Vietnamese advice. After the offensive, in which South Vietnamese communist casualties were high, North Vietnamese troops replaced those southern Vietnam in Cambodia who had been allowed to install themselves in the country by **Norodom Sihanouk** as early as 1965. Friction soon developed between these new arrivals and local people.

THACH CHAN (1922-   ). Born on 8 May 1922 at Travinh, South **Vietnam**, the son of Thach Xuone, an army officer, and Mme (née Suin), he was head of the office of the Ministry of Agriculture and a planter running a rubber plantation at Tapao for the government. In 1962 he was elected to the **National Assembly** for Kauk Prich, **Takeo** and was reelected in 1966. In 1972 he joined the **Socio-Republican Party** and was elected to the National Assembly of the Khmer Republic in September. He managed to arrange, through negotiations, the defection of 700 Communists in March 1974. Thach Chan married Khoun Mak Ly and they had five children.

THACH CHIA (1938-1974). From a **Khmer Krom** background, he was minister of national welfare and culture in the **Son Ngoc Thanh** government in 1972 and minister of labor and social welfare in the **Hang Thun Hak** government from 1972-1973. A close confidante of **Keo Sang Kim**, the two were taken hostage by demonstrating students on 4 June 1974 and held on the grounds of a high school. The two were then killed by a mysterious, but clearly professional assassin. Almost 20 years later, in the early 1990s, a defector from the **Party of Democratic Kampuchea** claimed the killings had been ordered and carried out by his party. The aim was to deepen the conflicts dividing the **Khmer Republic** authorities from the students and to alienate more students from the regime.

THACH RENG (1933-2002). Born on 15 February 1933 in **Phnom Penh**, from a Khmer Krom family, he served as a cadet in the Royal Cambodian Armed Forces in 1955 studied in France from 1957-1960 and in the **United States** in 1961. Returning to Phnom Penh, he studied law at the University of Phnom Penh from 1962-1969, while still serving in the army. Associated with **Lon Nol**, he assisted in saving Phnom Penh from the **National United Front of Kampuchea (FUNK)-Viet Cong** attacks in 1970 and was promoted to brigadier general, in charge of the commandoes 1971-1972; he was then assistant director for security 1972-1975, in charge of the Special Forces. He escaped from Phnom Penh in the same helicopter as **Sak Suthsakhan** on 17 April 1975 and moved to the United States where he lived until 1982. In July 1982 he joined the **Khmer People's National Liberation Front (KPNLF)** and became assistant to the commander of the **Khmer People's National Liberation Armed Forces** from 1982-1984 and member of the military committee of the KPNLF—opposing too close contact with the **Armée Nationale Sihanoukienne (ANS)**. In charge of the KPNLF mission to France 1984-1992, he was advisor to Son Sann from 1986. During this period he also studied at the Institute of Political

Studies in Paris. Returning to Phnom Penh on 3 February 1992, he was responsible for the election campaign of the **Buddhist Liberal Democratic Party (BLDP)** from 1992-1993 and was the third candidate for his party for Phnom Penh, failing to be elected in May 1993. He was minister for rural development but left politics for a career in business soon afterward. In 1997 Thach Reng was appointed to the **National Assembly** to fill a posting left vacant by the death of a BLDP-**Son Sann** Party colleague. He was the only member of the party to remain in Cambodia after the July 1997 Coup when Hun Sen ousted Prince **Norodom Ranariddh**, and Thach Reng was the only member of the assembly to vote against the deposition. He died on 15 August 2002 in Phnom Penh.

THACH SARY (1925-1975). Born in Travinh, South **Vietnam**, he was a secretary in the office of the Japanese official, Kubota in 1945 and was one of the officials who stormed into the royal palace on 9 August to try to get King Sihanouk to give more power to **Son Ngoc Thanh**. The others included two of his brothers, **Thach Thuon** and Thach Nhoung. Released from jail in December 1947, four years later he was elected deputy secretary of **Sam Nhean**'s **Party of the People**. He joined the armed forces and served in the 1950s and 1960s and then under **Lon Nol** became a brigadier general and chief of the Quartermaster's Corps. He was executed after the fall of the Republic in April 1975.

THACH TOAN (1935-). A qualified doctor, he served in the army and in 1970 was director of Khmers Abroad, heading the Assembly Committee for Health, Social Affairs, Labor and Employment. He was minister of labor, social action, refugees and community development in the first **Long Boret** government, December 1973 to June 1974 and minister of labor and social action in the last **Long Boret** government from January 1974 to March 1975.

THAILAND. Cambodia's post-Ankorean history has been shaped to a large extent by its relations with its neighbor to the west, beginning with the kingdom of Ayudhya (1350-1767) and continuing under subsequent Thai rulers. In the post-Angkorean era, cultural and linguistic traffic between the two countries blended Khmer and Thai elements so thoroughly that modern scholars often have difficulty in distinguishing them. Thai interest in Cambodia quickened in the 16th century, when European commercial pressures on Ayudhya encouraged its kings to seek exportable goods farther afield and when successive Khmer monarchs, emboldened by successful Burmese attacks on Ayudhya, led their expeditionary armies into Siam. Thai suzerainty over the Khmer court was firmly established at the end of the 16th century, when a Thai army destroyed the Khmer royal capital of

Lovek. Over the next two hundred years, Khmer kings and ambitious princes formed alliances with the Thai or the Vietnamese to gain or stay in power.

When the Chakri dynasty came to power in Thailand in 1782, the Khmer kingdom had been devastated by armies invading from east and west. In 1794 the Thai king placed a young protégé, **Ang Eng**, on the Cambodian throne. At the same time, the Thai assumed control over the provinces of **Battambang** and **Siem Reap**, only relinquishing them to Cambodia under French pressure in 1907.

In 1940 the Thai launched military attacks on Cambodia and Laos in an effort to regain areas they had given up earlier in the century to the French. Under the terms of a peace treaty brokered by Japan, Battambang and Siem Reap came back under Thai control from 1941 to 1946, when Thailand reluctantly relinquished the provinces to France. In the 1950s Thai policy toward Cambodia was keyed to Cold War priorities. In this context, Prince **Norodom Sihanouk**'s neutral policies were suspected as communist, and successive Thai governments worked to undermine the Prince's rule. Diplomatic relations were broken in 1961. However, following the overthrow of Sihanouk, the Thai offered only token assistance to the pro-American regime that replaced him and made peace quickly with the Communists after their victory in 1975. The Vietnamese invasion of 1979 promoted a nationalist and military alliance between the two neighboring states and throughout the 1980s, the armed forces under **Pol Pot** were given unofficial use of rear base areas along, and sometimes, inside the Thai border. With the withdrawal of Vietnamese forces in 1989, continuing Thai support for the armies and parties embraced by the **Coalition Government of Democratic Kampuchea** acquired a commercial dimension as Thai entrepreneurs began exploiting timber reserves and gemstone across the border. After the United Nations sponsored elections of 1993 and the partial restoration of the Khmer monarchy, Thailand extended full diplomatic recognition to the authorities in **Phnom Penh**, thereby depriving the declining DK movement of resources or political legitimacy. At the same time, elements in the Thai military continued to treat northwestern Cambodia as an exploitable, open frontier region rather than a portion of a sovereign, independent state. This two track approach in foreign policy corresponded to a similar reorientation of Chinese foreign policy in the region.

THAMMAYUT. Reformist order of Thai and Cambodian Buddhism, founded by the Thai King Rama IV (Mongkut) and favored by the Khmer court for the next hundred years. In the 1960s approximately 15 percent of all monks belonged to the Thammayut sect; the vast majority belonged to the unreformed Mahanikay. Both monastic orders were dismantled after 17 April 1975 and only the Mahanikay was allowed to function after the Vietnamese invasion in 1979. In 1993, however, at King **Norodom Sihanouk**'s request, the Thammayut order was restored.

THEAM BUN SRUN. He studied at the Royal School of Administration, being in the 4th promotion. He then entered the diplomatic service. In 1975 he was chargé d'affaires at the Embassy of the Khmer Republic in Canberra, Australia, being granted political asylum after the fall of the Republic. He lived in Canberra and during the 1980s was the representative of Prince **Norodom Sihanouk** in Australia and also manager of the Cambodian Information Office in Canberra. He studied at the Australian National University; his masters' thesis was *Cambodia in the Mid-Nineteenth Century: A quest for survival 1840-1863* (1981). He returned to **Phnom Penh** and was appointed governor of **Sihanoukville** in 1993.

THIOUM MUONG (1906/8-). Born in **Phnom Penh**, he worked in the Ministry of Interior and Religion from 1933-1942 and was associated with the **Nagaravatta** newspaper. Fearing arrest after the 1942 Buddhist protest, he fled to **Battambang** province, then under Thai occupation. He was stripped of his Cambodian citizenship in February 1943 but returned to Phnom Penh in August 1945 and participated in the 9 August 1945 coup. Son Ngoc Thanh made him commander of the 500-man "Cambodian Voluntary Force" known as the **Greenshirts**. After the return of the French he supported the **Democrat Party** and was elected to the National Assembly in 1951 for **Kampong Chhnang** town. He failed in his bid for reelection for that seat in 1955.

THIOUNN (1864-1946). A high-ranking Cambodian palace official of uncertain social origins, he played an influential role and amassed a large fortune under three successive Cambodian kings. Rapidly making im himself indispensable to the French, he held the office of minister of the palace from 1898 until 1941. During that period he was undoubtedly the most powerful man in the country and through close patronage links and marriages, was closely related to the Poc and Bunchhan families. In the 1930s, as minister of the palace, he supervised the writing of the definitive edition of the Cambodian royal chronicle. However when **Norodom Sihanouk** was crowned in 1941, Thiounn was eased out of office by the French. He married Kom and they had three children including Thiounn In, head of the veterinary services in Phnom Penh and a longtime member of **Sangkum**. Thiounn died in September 1946.

THIOUNN MUMM (1925-). Prominent Marxist intellectual and revolutionary. Born on 8 December 1925 in **Phnom Penh**, son of Thiounn

Hol and Mme (née Moly), grandson of **Thiounn**, and brother of **Thiounn Thioeun, Thiounn Thioum, Thiounn Prasith** and Thiounn Chum (Mme **Chhean Vam**), he was educated in Phnom Penh and at the University of Hanoi. Mumm traveled to France on a French government scholarship in 1946 and soon distinguished himself in the field of applied science, earning several degrees, and became was the first and only Cambodian to graduate from the prestigious École Polytechnique in Paris. In 1951 he joined the **Communist Party of France** and was one of the key figures in the Marxist discussion group in Paris that drew many Khmer students, including Saloth Sar (**Pol Pot**) into the French party. In August 1951 he took part in an international youth congress in East Berlin. He returned home briefly in 1954-1955, assisted the **Democrat Party**, was elected to their executive committee in February 1955, but due to his contacts with **Son Ngoc Thanh**, he fled to Paris when threatened by arrest. He remained in France until 1970, acting as a "godfather" for Cambodian students, encouraging them in their studies and drawing many into the world of politics.

In 1970, he traveled to Beijing where he and **Sarin Chhak** drafted the political program for the **National United Front of Kampuchea (FUNK)** and aided Prince **Norodom Sihanouk** in the creation of the **Royal Government of National Union of Kampuchea**. As a result of his renewed collaboration with the Prince, he was among those sentenced to death *in absentia* for high treason in August 1970. Mumm was a prominent spokesman for the revolutionary nationalist cause in the early 1970s, but was given little to do under **Democratic Kampuchea** apart from presiding over a small Science and Technology Institute in Phnom Penh 1976-1978. In December 1979 he was appointed minister of science. Bearing mind that this was a cabinet formed in wartime and sometimes on the run, this was not much of a job at all. In 1982, after an official visit to other countries, he slipped away to France where he continues to live in exile.

THIOUNN PRASITH (1930-). Born on 3 February 1930 in Phnom Penh, son of Thiounn Hol and Mme (née Moly), he was brother of **Thiounn Thoieun, Thiounn Thioum, Thiounn Mumm** and Thiounn Chum (Mme **Chhean Vam**). By his own admission, he was less than the best student in the family and his studies were also interrupted and disrupted by wartime relocations. He attended **Lycée Sisowath**, 1935-1941, but a transfer to Lycée Chasseloup-Laubat in Saigon for the final years of study for the baccalaureate was cut short when he was forcibly repatriated to Phnom Penh in April 1945 by the Japanese occupation administration. He then completed his baccalaureate at Lycée Sisowath in 1949. In Paris 1949-1955 he initially studied dentistry and pharmacy but in 1951 he joined the Marxist study circle and after two years of dedicated anti-colonial militancy, he joined the **Communist Party of France** in 1953. Returning to Cambodia in December 1955, Prasith worked for the royal railroads (*Chemins de Fer Royaux du Cambodge*), and was secretary of the secret **Khmer People's Revolutionary Party (PRPK)** branch organized by railroad workers who included **Ok Sakun**. This branch hosted the party congress convened in Phnom Penh in September 1960 at which the PRPK ceased to be an ethnic Khmer people's party and declared itself the **Communist Party of Kampuchea**. Alarmed by security reports about communist "agitation" Sihanouk's security police arrests scores of journalists working for *L'Observateur* and other campaigning newspapers, jailing them without charge for several weeks, and transferred Thiounn Prasith into a new post in the Ministry of Public Works. Identified as a communist in the "affair of the 34" in 1963, and sharing the same fears as Saloth Sar (**Pol Pot**), **Son Sen**, **Ieng Sary** and others who fled to the jungle, he abruptly returned to France. Though among those sentenced to death *in absentia* for high treason in August 1970: Prasith was not politically active again until July 1970 when he traveled to Hanoi and Beijing. In 1970-75 he frequently represented the **National United Front of Kampuchea (FUNK)** at international meetings, and from 1976, worked in the Ministry of Foreign Affairs of **Democratic Kampuchea (DK)**, heading the Asia Department. After 1979 he was appointed DK ambassador to the **United Nations**, a post held until 1992. Granted political asylum by the United States, he continues to live in New York.

THIOUNN THIOEUN (1920-). Born on 17 December 1920 in Phnom Penh, he was son of Thiounn Hol and Mme (née Moly). Brother of **Thiounn Thioum, Thiounn Munn, Thiounn Prasith** and Thiounn Thieum (Mme **Chhean Vam**). After completing high school in Hanoi 1942-1945, Thiounn Thioeun studied medicine at the Faculty of Medicine, University of Paris, receiving his MD in 1951. Politically aware from his school days, he was a supporter of Son Ngoc Thanh in the late 1940s but was a active supporter of the communist movement by the early 1950's. A practicing as well as teaching doctor, he was dean of the Faculty of Medicine and Medical Director of the Khmero-Soviet Friendship Hospital in the 1960s. He abandoned his posts in 1970, slipping into the jungle before formally declaring his allegiance to the **National United Front of Kampuchea (FUNK)** on 14 February 1971. He was appointed **Kampuchean Royal Government of National Union (GRUNK)** minister of health, and was a signatory to the 1971 **Declaration of Patriotic Intellectuals**. Reappointed minister of health in Democratic Kampuchea, 1975-1979, and from 1979-1982, he headed the Health and Social Welfare Committee of the **Coalition Government of Democratic Kampuchea** from 1982. In July 1994 he was appointed special advisor to the prime minister for health and hygiene in the Provisional Government of National Unity and Well-being formed by the declining DK movement in 1994. He was among the intellectuals who left **Anlong Veng** in 1997-98.

THIOUNN THIOUM (1924-). Born on 25 May 1924 in Phnom Penh, son of Thiounn Hol and Mme (née Moly), he was brother of **Thiounn Thoeunn, Thiounn Mumm, Thiounn Prasith** and Thiounn Chum (Mme **Chhean Vam**). He studied in Hanoi 1942-1945 and gained a doctorate in law in Paris—his thesis being *Le pouvoir monarchique au Cambodge*. Returning to Cambodia in 1952 he became a law professor at the University of Phnom Penh and a director of several companies including Société d'import-export Tridara and S.A. Les Huileries Khmères, 1956-1975. During the initial period of **Democratic Kampuchea** he lived and worked in the countryside. However, in August 1978 he was summoned to Phnom Penh and appointed secretary of state for finance for the purpose of restoring a banking system and an economy with a currency of exchange—at a time when the government was preparing itself for an onslaught from Vietnam. Evacuated from Phnom Penh in January 1979 he was promoted to minister for economy and finances in the December 1979 DK government headed by **Khieu Samphan**. Never a partisan for the revolution, or a politician, Thiounn Thioum was quickly demoralized by the wartime situation slipping away to France in mid-1984.

"THIRD FORCE" (1972). This was the name given to a plan to form a coalition government and army between moderate members of the **National United Front of Kampuchea** (FUNK), such as **Ker Meas**, and disillusioned members of the Khmer Republic, such as **Cheng Heng** and **Norodom Kantol**. It was championed by France, especially the French ambassador to Beijing, Étienne Manac'h. Denounced by **Zhou Enlai** in March 1972, the plan came to naught. However it was used by the Khmer Rouge to purge some moderates, such as **Huot Sambath**, from their government in 1976-1977.

THIRD INDOCHINA WAR. *See* INDOCHINA WARS.

THOEK KROEUN VUTHA. Deputy secretary of the provincial **People's Revolutionary Party of Kampuchea** (PRPK) committee, and president of the people's Committee of **Kratié** in the late 1980's, he succeeded Nhem Heng as provincial party secretary and was elected to the PRPK Central Committee in March 1989. As a result of a decision to abandon collective leadership at province level and to restore the pre-communist gubernatorial system, Thoek Kroeun Vutha became governor of Kratié in 1992. Elected in May 1993 to the National Assembly on the **Cambodian**

People's Party (CPP) list for Kratié, he resigned almost immediately, allowing another CPP candidate to hold the seat. He was replaced as governor by a **FUNCINPEC** appointee in early 1994. In December 1998 he was appointed deputy secretary of state in the Ministry of Environment.

THONG KHON (1951-). Known to have been deputy chairman of the People's Revolutionary Party Committee of Phnom Penh municipality in January 1984, he was chairman of the committee, deputy secretary of the municipal **People's Revolutionary Party of Kampuchea (PRPK)** and an alternate member of the PRPK Central Committee in June 1985. Frequently identified as "mayor" of Phnom Penh after 1985, he represented the capital in the National Assembly from February 1988 until May 1993. From August 1990 until June 1993 he was deputy minister of information and culture, and on 1 November 1993 was appointed deputy-secretary of state for tourism. On 20 October 1994 he was promoted to secretary of state for tourism. Elected to the National Assembly in 1998 for Kampong Thom he was re-appointed secretary of state for tourism in the Hun Sen government.

THONG VAN FAN MUONG. He was colonel and commander of the 1st military region in March 1970 when he, together with **Nginn Thappana**, took charge of demobilizing **Khmer Serei** forces, some in U.S. commanded Civilian Defense Irregular Groups in South Vietnam, and integrating them into the national army. He was ambassador-designate to Australia in July 1972 but did not take up the position. He was a member of the Supreme Committee of **Sak Suthsakhan** from 12-17 April 1975 which failed in the 11th hour to arrange a peaceful surrender. He married Princess Norodom Rotsaray, a daughter of Prince **Norodom Montana**.

THONN OUK (1917-). Born in October 1917 in **Phnom Penh**, the son of Ouk Thouch, he graduated from **Lycée Sisowath** and then studied law in Paris, returning to Cambodia on 15 June 1946. He was chief clerk in the Prime Minister's Office; and in 1948 became secretary of state for information. One of the founders of the **Democrat Party**, and a close friend and classmate of Prince **Sisowath Youtévong**, he was elected to the National Assembly in 1947 for Phnom Penh, being re-elected in 1951. In September 1951 he was appointed as delegate to the Assembly of the French Union. One of the liberal ministers in the government of **Huy Kanthoul**, he was among the Democrats who abandoned politics after 1955, refusing to joining the **Sangkum**. He was later president of the national oil company. In the 1980s, he lent support to the KPNLF, and was a member of the eight-man Provisional Central Committee for the Salvation of the KPNLF formed in 1985. He married Var Saoreac, daughter of **Var Kamel**. In the 1980s Ouk was living in Paris.

THOR PENG LEAT (1935-). Born in Baray, **Kampong Thom**, he studied at the Faculty of Law and Economic Sciences in **Phnom Penh**, and taught at the Royal School of Administration. In June 1971 he was a member of the **constitutional drafting committee** and in 1973 was an advisor to Lon Nol. Evacuated to the countryside 1975-1979, he was later able to settle in France where he worked for Air France. Returning to Phnom Penh in 1992 he became an economic advisor to **Hun Sen** and in 1993 was elected to the Constituent Assembly for Phnom Penh. He was vice-president of the Commission for the Assembly, but resigned his seat to become governor of the National Bank of Cambodia in July 1994.

"THREE GHOSTS." This was the epithet used in 1970 to refer to the three missing parliamentarians, **Hou Youn, Khieu Samphan** and **Hu Nim** who disappeared in 1967. The numerous assassinations, arbitrary arrests and disappearances of suspected communists and student activists, led many to presume the three were dead. A few, including **Khim Tith,** claimed to have seen evidence of their demise. After the 1970 coup, **Norodom Sihanouk** gave each of them a portfolio in his **Royal Government of National Union of Kampuchea (GRUNK)** even though he wondered if **"Lon Nol** had not succeeded in assassinating them." The prince asked **Ieng Sary** upon his arrival in Beijing in 1971 to produce photographs. Thus prompted, and to derail the idea that GRUNK was a fiction created by exiled royalists forced to employ "ghosts" in their cause, photographs of the three were circulated in the last months of 1971 to prove they were still alive.

"THREE TONS PER HECTARE." One of the exhorting slogans adopted under **Democratic Kampuchea** to indicate the amount of paddy that was to be harvested, on average, from each hectare of cultivated land throughout the country. The plan target was far in excess of the nation's prewar average which was about one ton a hectare. Like many Democratic Kampuchea slogans, the phrase itself seems to have been derived, without acknowledgment, from China, and specifically from an agricultural campaign launched in China in 1973. *See also* RICE.

THRONE COUNCIL (Council of the Throne). This body was formed in line with Article 13 of the constitution of September 1993 amended in 1999 states that within seven days of the death of the king, a new monarch shall be chosen by a Throne Council. The Council includes the prime minister, the president and vice-presidents of the **Senate** and of the **National Assembly** and the heads of the Mohanikay and Thammayut orders.

THUN BUNLY (1950-1996). A political activist and journalist, Thun Bunly was murdered in a motor drive-by shooting on the morning of 18 May

1996. At the time of his death, he published and wrote for the leading opposition newspaper *Udom Kate Khmae* ("Khmer Ideal."). He had been many times summoned to ministries (interior or information) and cautioned about the "inability to guarantee his security" in relation to articles appearing in his paper or about willfully publishing information judged "defamatory." He had also endured prejudicial court proceedings, convictions, large fines and brief imprisonment, all viewed at the time as part of a broad campaign to curb freedom of the press. His killer, believed to have been a security guard for a senior regime personality, has never been brought to justice. Both national and international human rights agencies viewed the killing as an attempt not only to repress media criticism but to demoralize supporters of the **Khmer Nation Party** led by **Sam Rainsy**. Thun Bunly was among the cofounders of the party and a member of its Central Committee at the time of his death. During a brief tour of France in February 1996, Bunly pleaded for national reconciliation which was fully inclusive, embracing even "outlawed" parties and for a concomitant reduction in the role and power of the "pro-Vietnamese" party of **Hun Sen**.

THUN SARAY (1951-). Born on 3 December 1951 in Au Raing Euv, **Kampong Cham**, he gained a degree in economics. Imprisoned from April 1975 until February 1976, he was sent into the countryside. From 1980-90, he was deputy director of the Institute of Sociology, directed by **Vandy Kaon**. He was jailed a second time, together with **Ung Phan**, from May 1990 until October 1991 when they and others attempted to form an opposition Liberal Socialist Democratic Party. A founding member and president of ADHOC (Association of Human Rights of Cambodia) from 1992, he is the author of, *Histoire des monnaies au Cambodge* [History of Cambodian currency], published in Phnom Penh in 1988.

TIM DONG (1924-). Born on 26 February 1924 at Khbal Koh, **Kandal**, son of Pen Tim and Mme (née Em Vann), he attended the École Normale in Phnom Penh and in Paris from 1949-1952. He continued his studies in Europe and Asia. He was director of "War Psychology of the Royal Cambodian Army," and was editor of the magazine *Cambodge Militaire*. He also took part in missions against the **Viet Minh** in the 1950s. Tim Dong became secretary of state for information and tourism from July 1957 to January 1958, secretary of state for information from April 1958 to February 1959 and for information and tourism from February to June 1959 and again from October 1962 to December 1964. Royal delegate to the municipality of **Kep** in 1963, he was elected to the 1958 National Assembly for Rokakong, Kandal, and was president of the Kandal Red Cross and director of the Tourism Department in 1964-1967. Tim Dong was governor of Kandal in early 1970, one of the key Sihanoukists left in position when Prince **Norodom Sihanouk** went overseas in January. As a result he was a part of **Oum Mannorine**'s countercoup to capture **Lon Nol**, but when this failed, on 16 March, he himself was arrested and jailed. He was released in 1973 and flown to Beijing. He then retired from politics.

TIM KENN (1907-1973). Born in **Takeo**, the older brother of **Tim Nguon**, he was a secretary in the French colonial service and in March 1945 was appointed chief clerk in the Interior Ministry. A member of the **Khmer Renewal Party**, he contested the 1947 National Assembly elections for Samrong Thom, **Kandal**. He was minister of public works and communications, 1950-1951 and minister of national education in March 1951. Director of the Royal School of Administration, he became an inspector of labor. In 1968 he contested the High Council elections. He was killed in a rocket attack on Phnom Penh in 1973.

TIM NGUON (1920-1975). Born on 20 June 1920 in **Takeo**, he completed his secondary schooling and joined the civil service in December 1941. Appointed first assistant to the governor of the provinces of **Prey Veng**, **Kampong Cham** and **Kandal**, he was also several times *chauvraysrok* (District Head) in the Province of Kampong Cham. Tim Nguon helped oversee the return of **Siem Reap** and **Battambang** to Cambodia in 1946. After his service in regional administrations, in 1947 he was chief clerk in the Ministry of National Defense when he became a founding member of the **Khmer Renewal Party** established by **Lon Nol** and **Nhiek Tioulong**. By 1950 he was assistant to the governor of Kandal province, but left for France in July to pursue academic studies. He returned in 1951 and contested the National Assembly elections for Chrey Vien, Kampong Cham. He was appointed head of the Ministry of Foreign Affairs on 11 July 1953. In 1954 he was governor of Prey Veng and concurrently commander of Prey Veng and **Svay Rieng** military subsector, with the rank of lieutenant colonel. He then became governor of Kampong Cham, minister of the interior then minister for national defense and national security.

In 1966 Tim Nguon was appointed ambassador to Australia. However, after less than a year there, he became embroiled in a controversy in which students in Australia tried to send money to offices of the **Provisional Revolutionary Government for South Vietnam**. He was expelled from Australia in November 1967 and on his return became governor of **Battambang**. He became minister of finance in the third **Lon Nol** government from 2 July 1970 until 5 May 1971, serving as minister of state for the Prime Minister's Office from May 1971 until 12 March 1972. After this Tim Nguon tried to mediate between Lon Nol and Prince **Sisowath Sirik Matak** and was even considered as a successor to Sirik

Matak when he resigned as prime minister on 15 March 1972. He was appointed ambassador to Thailand in mid-1972 and died of a heart attack on 8 March 1975 at St. Louis Hospital, Bangkok. Tim Nguon was married to Se Koun Than, they had seven children.

TIOULONG, SAUMARA (1950-). Born on 9 July 1950 in **Phnom Penh**, daughter of **Nhiek Tioulong**, by his first wife, she grew up in Paris, Tokyo and Moscow from 1954-1959. She then studied law at the University of Paris, 1971 earning a diploma in economics and finance from the École des Hautes Études Politiques in Paris in 1974. She remained in Paris during the 1970s and 1980s and obtained a second diploma from the European Institute of Administration in 1980 and a third in financial analysis in Paris in 1988. She married **Sam Rainsy**, and they have three children. From 1976-1982 she worked in investments with the Banque Indosuez, Paris, and was head of the department when she left in 1982 to work as a director of the Bank Robert Fleming 1983-1988 and then with Mobilière Conseil, still in Paris 1989-1991. She returned to Cambodia with her husband in 1992 and in the following year became deputy governor of the National Bank of Cambodia. A major political figure in her own right, she retained her post after the dismissal of her husband in 1995 and in 1998 was elected as a **Sam Rainsy Party (SRP)** candidate to the National Assembly for **Phnom Penh**. Since 1992 she has held the foreign affairs and international portfolio in the SRP shadow cabinet. *See also* WOMEN IN CAMBODIA.

TIP MAM, Mme née **Ieam Saorim.** The daughter of Ros Ieam and Mme (née Keo Chanlak), in 1953 she married Tip Mam. A medical doctor, she had studied anatomy in Paris and on her return to Cambodia worked as director of the Biology Institute of Cambodia. She was secretary of state for public health and social action from 1965 to 1966, minister of planning in the first **Lon Nol** government from 1966-1967 and minister of social action and labor from 1967-1969. During the Khmer Republic, she bore a grudge against Prince **Sisowath Sirik Matak** for refusing to allow her go abroad with her severely injured son. Her husband was a brigadier general in the Republican army by 1974, and they had two children.

TIV OL (1933-1977). Born in December 1933 in Kor, **Kampong Cham**, he was a nationalist activist from the early 1950s who was initially attracted by the ideas of **Son Ngoc Thanh**. He gradually fell under the influence of Mey Phat and **Uch Ven** who introduced him to **Son Sen** who sponsored him when he joined the **Communist Party of Kampuchea (CPK)** in 1958. He taught part time at different times at Lycée **Chamraoen Vicchea** and **Kambuboth.** He taught literature at Lycée Preah Sihanouk, Kampong Cham from 1955-1960, when, to keep him away from students, he was transferred to a desk job in the Ministry of Education. He was active in the teachers association of the 1960s and a promoter of the progressive but non-communist **Assemblée Générale des étudiants Khmères (AGEK)** but lost contact with some party comrades after 1963 when Son Sen left Phnom Penh. He in his turn fled Phnom Penh in October 1967, fearing arrest and imprisonment as a result of the suppression of the Cambodia-China Friendship Association. He worked for the revolution in the North Zone from 1968-1973 and was then transferred to the office of the Central Committee of the CPK in Ratanakiri to work with **Pol Pot**. In the final years of the civil war, 1970-1975, Tiv Ol worked in the Ministry of Propaganda headed by **Hu Nim** and after April 1975, he worked in this ministry until September. He had health problems during this period and was subjected to political reeducation and reassigned to the Central Committee office. He was arrested there on 6 June 1977, after many other urban intellectuals had implicated him in antiimperialist activities in the 1960s, activities judged pro-CIA by the CPK leadership. He was taken to **Tuol Sleng** and executed after mid-September.

TMENH CHEY ("Tmenh the Victorious"). A comic and widely popular figure of Cambodian, Lao and Thai folk literature; a poor young man noted for his ability to outguess and outmaneuver the rich and powerful, by resorting to such tactics as false naiveté and plays on words. His antics, like those of the African American *Brer Rabbit*, were pleasing to ordinary people in Southeast Asia, accustomed to acting as subjects, subordinates and underdogs.

TOAN CHHAY. Educated at Collège Siem Reap in 1959, he moved to **Phnom Penh** to continue his studies becoming a dentist. He served in the employ of army of the **Khmer Republic**, 1970-1974 but left angered by the corruption. After 17 April 1975 he rebelled against the communists having succeeded in mobilizing 1,800 followers in the Khleang Moeung movement. These were some of the first members of the **Khmer People's National Liberation Armed Forces (KPNLAF)**. Joining **FUNCINPEC** in 1981, he received some training in the United States, worked his way through the ranks of the *Armée National Sihanoukienne* and was made a general and then chief of staff in the **National Army for an Independent Kampuchea**. He was deputy minister of the interior and public security in 1993, becoming governor of **Siem Reap** in December 1993. Involved in a series of incidents in Siem Reap town, and having rebelled against Prince **Norodom Ranariddh**'s leadership of FUNCINPEC in early 1997, he was one of the potential candidates for the post of first prime minister after the prince was ousted in July but was appointed minister for agriculture instead, replacing Tao Seng Hour who had fled into exile.

TOL LAH (1944-). A 1964 graduate of the Faculty of Pedagogy who taught high school physics, he immigrated to USA in 1975. Returning to the Thai-Cambodian border in the early 1980s, he joined **FUNCINPEC**, and was a lieutenant general in the National Army for an Independent Cambodia at the end of the war. He was appointed minister of higher and technical education in 1993, secretary general of the National Assembly in November 1993, and minister of education, youth and sport from October 1994. A Ranariddh loyalist Tol Lah abandoned both posts following the ousting of Prince **Norodom Ranariddh** from the premiership in July 1997, being replaced as minister of education by Than Sina. In 1998, and running again for FUNCINPEC, he was elected to the National Assembly for **Phnom Penh**. Subsequently he was appointed minister of education, youth and sports and second deputy prime minister. Tol Lah lost both posts following the ousting of Prince **Norodom Ranariddh** from the premiership in July 1997 but in 1998, following the formation of a second FUNCINPEC-**Cambodian People's Party** coalition, he was reappointed. In mid-2001 after organizing several internationally funded primary school projects in remote regions, he was one of the two Royalist ministers openly criticized for mismanagement of ministerial affairs by Prime Minister **Hun Sen**, who takes pride in his personal patronage of the school system. *See also* UK VITHOUN.

TONG SIV ENG also **Pung Peng Siv Eng (1919-2001).** One of the most prominent women politicians of postcolonial Cambodia, Siv Eng was the first woman ever to be elected to the National Assembly in 1958. Born on 31 October 1919 in Koh Sautin, Kampong Cham, she was a primary school teacher and principal who trained in colonial era schools in both Phnom Penh and Saigon. She married **Pung Peng Cheng** in 1939. Immediately after her election to the Assembly, she was named head of its Health Commission. In 1960 she joined the government for the first time as state secretary for labor and public welfare. Reelected to the Assembly in 1962 and again in 1966, she was named minister of public health, social affairs and labor in the first **Lon Nol** government from October 1966 to April 1967. At the National Assembly on 18 March 1970 she was among three deputies who in a free vote might have voted to allow Prince **Norodom Sihanouk** to retain his post as head of state. But under the threat of gunmen posted in the gallery and outside the parliament building, she voted with the majority, the vote to depose then being deemed unanimous. She and **Pung Peng Cheng** quietly left Cambodia in 1971, and both officially joined the **National United Front of Kampuchea** **(FUNK)** in Paris in early 1972. They returned to Cambodia in 1989 after a private meeting with Prime Minister **Hun Sen** who gave each of them senior advisory roles in the State Council of the **State of Cambodia**, 1989-1993. One of Siv Eng's two daughters Pung Chhiv Kek Galabru founded Licadho, a Cambodian Non-Governmental Organization (NGO), in 1992.

TONLÉ SAP. The lake and river in Cambodia, technically composed of water backing up in the rainy season from the Mekong and other rivers, covers 3,000 square kilometers during the dry season, swelling to 7,500 square kilometers in the wet season. Its depth ranges from 2.2 meters to 10 meters and it is the center of Cambodia's fishing industry which provides about 60 percent of all fish consumed in the country.

TOU SAMOUTH also *Achar* **Sok (c1922-1962).** A prominent **Khmer Krom** nationalist turned communist, Tou Samouth was born in Vietnam but sent to Cambodia for his upper primary and secondary schooling by his Khmer parents.Samouth spent several years as a Buddhist monk in **Phnom Penh**, where he was affiliated with the Buddhist Institute. Following the monks' demonstration of 1942, he fled to the countryside and by 1947 had become active in the anti-French resistance. Evacuated to north Vietnam in the early 1950s, Samouth returned to Cambodia in 1955 and took charge of urban work for the **Khmer People's Revolutionary Party (KPRP).** His personal secretary at this stage was Saloth Sar (**Pol Pot**). When the KPRP was formally upgraded to the **Communist Party of Kampuchea** in 1960, Samouth became secretary of its Central Committee. In 1962 he was betrayed and captured by the police and taken to **Lon Nol**'s house where he was tortured for a week. He refused to name his colleagues and was killed at Stung Meanchey pagoda. He was replaced as secretary of the permanent standing committee of the party by Saloth Sar, who was subsequently elected secretary of the KPRP Central Committee. In 1979, Tou Samouth was honored by **People's Republic of Kampuchea**, as were many other veterans of the early communist movement, many having lost their lives in the **purges in Democratic Kampuchea**. A major avenue in Phnom Penh was named after him.

TOUCH KIM (1921-). Born on 5 January 1921 in **Kampot**, the son of Chrun Touch and Mme (née Ouk Khout), he studied at the Faculty of Law, **Phnom Penh**, and then at Lyon. Gaining his doctorate in France, he was secretary of state for labor, social action and reform in 1956; secretary of state for the Prime Minister's Office and for coordination, research and reform from 1956-1957, economic affairs from January to April 1957; public works and telecommunications from April to July 1957, public works, telecommunications and public health from 1957 to 1958, minister of finance from April to July 1958, minister for economic and financial affairs from July 1958 to February 1959; and again in the same portfolio from April 1960 to January 1961. He was a protégé of **Son Sann** and was governor of the National Bank 1969-1970. He married Sakeal Nabo and they had five children.

TOURN SOK PHALLAR (c1941-1977). A nephew of Tourn Lang, a member of the National assembly from 1962-1966, Sok Phallar was a graduate of the Khmero-Soviet Technical School, Tourn Sok Phallar was an engineer in the Ministry of Public Works and secretary-general of the national students' union known as the Assemblée Nationale des Étudiants Khmères led by **Phouk Chhay**. Although he was successfully recruited into the underground communist movement in the 1960s, the party never succeeded in seizing control of the student's movement. Tourn Sok Phallar was briefly imprisoned by the authorities in 1966-1967 after being caught in the act of distributing anti-Sihanouk leaflets. While in prison he met some of the many communist political prisoners jailed between 1962-1966 but by the time of his release, the students' movement, deemed to have strayed from the official party position of supporting Sihanouk, and essentially Sihanouk's anti-imperialism, received no more communiques nor advice. Though a quiet supporter of the **National United Front of Kampuchea** from the time of its formation in 1970, Phallar remained in Phnom Penh and represented the Ministry of Public Works on the **constitutional drafting committee** in June 1971. After the violent suppression of the national teachers protests in February and March 1973, he slipped out of Phnom Penh together with **Nuon Khoeun**. In 1975 he was assigned to the Ministry of Public Works headed by Toch Phoeun. Caught up in the **Communist Party of Kampuchea** purge of former urban intellectuals which began in late 1976, he was arrested in early 1977, taken to **Tuol Sleng** where he was forced to confess to treasonous activities against the party and then executed.

TRIBHUVANADITYAVARMAN. King of Cambodia 1165-1177, a high-ranking official about whom little is known, who seized power from **Yasovarman II** in a coup d'état and was replaced in turn by **Jayavarman VII** following a **Cham** invasion of Angkor. His palace may have occupied the site of Jayavarman VII's temple of **Preah Khan**.

TRIBUTARY SYSTEM. A system of foreign relations, perfected by China and adapted for use by the Thai and Vietnamese courts in their relations with Cambodia in the early 19th century. Under the system, gifts from the Cambodian monarch were dispatched on a regular basis to Hue and Bangkok, in exchange for diplomatic recognition. It is likely that tributary missions offered opportunities for trade and for delegates to gather political intelligence, as well as to express relative rankings between patron and client states. As far as Cambodia was concerned, the system peaked in the mid-19th century and fell into disuse with the arrival of the French.

TRINH HOANH (1924-1975). Born on 9 September 1924 at Trapeang, Russey, **Kampong Thom**, the son of Trinh Bac, Hoanh was educated at the École de Formation des Instituteurs and became headmaster of a small government school, rising to director of schools from 1943-1952. In 1950 he entered politics joining the **Khmer Renewal Party**. He contested the 1951 National Assembly elections for Taing Kraing, Kampong Cham, and the subsequent by-election in 1952. After his defeats he receded from the political scene until the formation of **Sangkum** which he joined on its creation. Trinh Hoanh was elected to the 1955 National Assembly for Mohaleap, **Kampong Cham**, and then for Koh Sautin in 1958. In 1962 he represented Siem Reap town, being re-elected in 1966. A prominent newspaper columnist, Trinh Hoanh was under-secretary of state for religion from May 1965 to October 1966. When **Lon Nol** was appointed prime minister following the 1966 National Assembly elections, Trinh Hoanh joined the shadow cabinet as minister responsible for anti-corruption and judicial control from 4 November 1966 until 1969.

Later accused of being involved in the plotting that led to the overthrow of **Norodom Sihanouk** in 1970, Trinh Hoanh was appointed Minister of Information, but was dismissed from the cabinet in July 1970 for what was seen as his failure to explain the overthrow of Sihanouk to the world at large. He was secretary-general of Sangkum, keeping the party together during the early years of the Khmer Republic. In June 1971 he was a government advisor on the **constitutional drafting committee**. From 1972 Trinh Hoanh became a leading figure in Prince **Sisowath Sirik Matak**'s **Republican Party**, being elected to its 10-man Central Committee at the first Party Congress on 23 July 1972. In 1973 he was president of the **Chuon Nath** Association. His last cabinet post was as minister for information and tourism in the first **Long Boret** government from December 1973 until June 1974. He remained in **Phnom Penh** at the fall of the Khmer Republic and was killed by the communist soldiers when they captured the capital on 17 April 1975.

TRUONG MEALY (1941-). Born on 28 January 1941 in Truong Khanh, Soctrang, south Vietnam, and orphaned at the age of eight, two years later he was recruited into the **Viet Minh** as an agent collecting information in the Mekong Delta and Saigon. He gained his baccalaureate in Saigon in 1960 and then moved to Phnom Penh where he continued his studies. In 1970 he went to Sydney to study for his diploma in Teaching English as a Foreign Language (TEFL) then studied humanities at the University of Paris. He remained in Paris as a teacher and on 27 April 1975 was a founding member, with **Son Sann**, of the General Association of

Cambodian Residents, a civic and cultural association. Truong Mealy became a founding member of the Cambodian Buddhist Association, based in Paris, and also the Khmer-Lao-Vietnamese Association for Human Rights. He wrote several textbooks on natural science during this period. In the mid-1980s he moved to Bangkok and was in charge of humanitarian aid and social affairs in the **FUNCINPEC** office. In 1991 he was appointed to work in the office of Prince **Norodom Sihanouk**, where he remained for the next three years, based in Pyongyang, Beijing and finally Phnom Penh. On 3 August 1994 he accepted the appointment as Cambodian ambassador to Japan. He retired in 1999 and was replaced by **Ing Kieth**. Honorary President of the Association for the Protection of Khmer Cultural Heritage, Truong Mealy's most recent work, *Conquer Our Destiny* was published in Japan.

TUM TAEV. This was a Cambodian narrative poem composed in 1915 by a Buddhist monk, Som (1852-1932), drawing on materials from oral tradition and royal chronicles. The poem, set in precolonial times, unflinchingly describes the corruption, brittleness and authoritarianism of traditional society. In the period of Prince **Norodom Sihanouk**, journalistic references to the poem were occasionally taken as coded attacks on Sihanouk's regime, but the poem remained on school curricula and influenced many modern Khmer writers.

TUOL SLENG (S-21). This museum is located on the site of the **Democratic Kampuchea**-era **Communist Party of Cambodia (CPK)** security and interrogation center in southern Phnom Penh in which returned intellectuals, CPK cardes, factory workers, ministerial personnel and others suspected of wrongdoing or sabotage were held. Occupying what had been the Lycée Ponhea Yat from the Sihanouk era, as well as several hectares surrounding the school, it was opened toward the end of 1975, at first being located in the Phnom Penh suburb of Takhmau. Between then and the Vietnamese invasion of January 1979, at least 15,000 detainees were brought to Tuol Sleng where they were interrogated, tortured and condemned to death. Some were killed on the spot, but most were trucked outside the city for execution. Only half a dozen prisoners survived when the facility was discovered in January 1979 following the Vietnamese occupation of Phnom Penh. Approximately 4,000 confession texts, covering over 100,000 pages, as well as many administrative documents and 6,000 photographic negatives from Tuol Sleng survived. They attest to a three-year reign of terror and reveal the fantastic fears of massive anti-party conspiracies at the very top of the CPK. In late 1979, benefiting from East German advice, Tuol Sleng was transformed into a national genocide museum. In the early 1990s, the archives were microfilmed under the auspices of the Cambodian Ministry of Culture and Cornell University.

TY BORASY also **Bo Rasy (1939-)**. Senator. A graduate of Lycée **Sisowath**, Ty Borasy taught history at Lycée Yukanthor before becoming general-secretary of the Khmer-Soviet Friendship Technical Institute. From 1965-1975 she was principal of Lycée Neary (Phnom Penh). She was evacuated to the countryside in 1975 and it is believed that her husband, Song Leng, a former director of the Inadana Jati Bank, perished during the **Democratic Kampuchea** era. In 1979, she was among the many women recruited to work in the new **People's Republic of Kampuchea** state apparatus. She became deputy-director of the Information Bureau of the Ministry of Foreign Affairs, a post held until 1982 when she was promoted to director of the Asia-Australia department of the Ministry. From 1984-1990 she was deputy minister of foreign affairs and then State of Cambodia ambassador to Moscow with accreditation to several Eastern European countries, Mongolia and the Saharan Arab Republic. Among her political duties, she was vice-president of the Cambodia-Mongolia Friendship Association. Between 1995-1998 she was the personal advisor to **Hun Sen** for women's affairs. She was appointed to the **Senate** by the **Cambodian People's Party** in 1999.

-U-

U SAY (1926-). Army Officer. Born on 11 May 1926 at Kampong Trabek, Prey Veng, the son of Yung U and Mme (née Sath), he joined the Cambodian army and gained diplomas from the National Military School and from the Higher School of Quartermaster Services in Paris. He was a director of administrative services of the Royal Army and was lieutenant colonel and was head of the military officer in the Ministry of National Defense by 1963. In 1968 he was promoted to full colonel and was appointed chief of the general staff. He was minister of state for national defense in the **In Tam** government, May to October 1973. By 1974 he was a major general in army of the **Khmer Republic**. U Say married Denise Leprest and they had three children.

UCH KIM AN (1943-). Born on 1 January 1943 in Kratié, he attended Lycée Sihanouk, **Kampong Cham**, and then Lycée Descartes from 1953-1961. This was followed by study at the Technical College of Sydney, Australia, from 1962-1963, the University of Adelaide from 1963-1965, the Faculty of Pedagogy, Phnom Penh from 1965-1967 and the Faculty of Law and Economic Sciences from 1969-1972. A teacher of English, he worked in the diplomatic section of the National School of Administration in 1972-1974. Uch Kim An married a daughter of Princess Amaravaddey (who had previously been married to Keo Kimsan, who was the sister of Keo Kosey, the wife of Prince **Norodom Sirivudh**) and they had two children. Uch Kim An married, secondly, Sothia. She was able to escape to France, while he remained in Democratic Kampuchea, working in the countryside until 1979. Recruited to the new **People's Republic of Kampuchea** he was deputy director of the international organizations department of the Ministry of Foreign Affairs and in November 1988 became director of the political department. In 1991 he was appointed vice-minister to the office of the Council of Ministers and advisor to the prime minister. In 1993 he was briefly deputy became vice-minister of foreign affairs in the provisional colatition government but was appointed secretary of state for foreign affairs instead. In 1998 he was reappointed to this cabinet post.

UCH VEN (1931-c1973). Born on 11 May 1931 in **Kampot**, he attended the École Normale, living at the house of Svay Sok who worked in the royal palace. He then studied at Montpellier, France 1949-1953 and participated in the Marxist study circle in Paris. Back in Phnom Penh he completed a *licence* in law in 1957, taught at the École Normale and at **Chamroeun Vichea** and was Secretary of the Buddhist University. The writer of commentaries for many of the newspapers of the day, he replaced his friend **Chau Seng** as managing director of *La Dépêche* between 1959-1961 while Seng worked in France. A member of the clandestine **Khmer People's Revolutionary Party** and, from 1960, the **Communist Party of Kampuchea (CPK),** he was one of a small number of cadres responsible for liason with leaders in the party's central committee, specifically **Nuon Chea, Vorn Veth** and **Son Sen**. Also a member of the **Sangkum**, he was elected to the 1958 **National Assembly** for Snuol, Kratié. Later appointed as director of the Inadana Jati (National Credit) Bank, he fled Phnom Penh in July 1968 for the security of the underground following the arrest of **Chau Sau**, managing director of the bank in a political crisis linked to the launching of the CPK armed struggle against Sihanouk, the opening of US-North Vietnamese peace talks in Paris, the resignation of Prime Minister **Son Sann**, and an influx of about 20,000 **Khmer Krom** refugees seeking temporary protection after the Tet Offensive in South Vietnam. Uch Ven married Son Thi Catha, and they left Phnom Penh with **Poc Doeuskomar**. Ven died of illness, or possibly by his own hand, sometime in 1972 or 1973.

UDAYADITYAVARMAN I. King of Cambodia, 1002-1010. Very likely a usurper, he may have ruled briefly at Angkor but for most of his reign, he was in Koh Ker, the capital first constructed by **Jayavarman V.** An inscription about him has been found there and other evidence attests to a rival reigning at Angkor.

UDAYADITYAVARMAN II. King of Cambodia 1050-1066. Reputedly a strong ruler, he succeeded Suryavarman I and supervised the construction, in the 1060s, of the temple-mountain known as the **Baphuon**. Inscriptions refer to several rebellions in Udayadityavarman's reign, instigated by military leaders. One found at Sdok Kak Thom provides copious information on the *devaraja* cult, the Shaivite foundation ritual introduced by **Jayavarman II** and observed for over two centuries at Angkor. It is likely that Utyadityavarman supervised the construction of a moated wall around Angkor, of roughly the same dimensions as the one built in the late 12th century by **Jayavarman VII**. The temple of West Mebon was also constructed during his reign.

UK VITHOUN. A judge, he was in charge of introducing a system of justice for children from 1970-1975. From 1975-1982 he lived in France where he was director of litigation and earned a doctorate in law (in 1981). A member of **FUNCINPEC**, he was appointed under-secretary of state for justice in November 1993, and on 20 July 1994 he was promoted to secretary of state for justice and a member of the Government Committee for Jurisprudence. On 21 August 2001, as a result of criticisms from prime minister **Hun Sen,** he was censured by the Assembly and removed from his post and the cabinet. **Tol Lah,** another FUNCINPEC minister sometimes singled out for criticism by the prime minister, has retained his post.

UM (1821-c1898). Born in **Pursat** province, at the age of 16 he entered the service of Prince **Ang Duang** accompanying the future king to Bangkok. He then fought with Ang Duang and the Siamese against the Vietnamese, with the result that when Ang Duang became King, Um was appointed director of the royal pages. In 1861 he was named as assistant to the minister of war, and in 1868 he became minister of war. He later served as minister of justice and in 1888 he was appointed *akkamohasena* (prime minister), holding that position during the Yukanthor Affair when Prince **Aruna Yukanthor** heavily criticized Um whom he claimed had joined forces with corrupt French officials in exploitation and removing honest officials from their posts. Thus it appears that during the 1890s Um left his service to the royal family to serve the interests of the French.

UM SAMUTH (1928-). Born on 25 February 1928 in **Svay Rieng**, son of Um Chim, driver with the Ministry of Public Works, and Mme (née Chap Sok), he studied at **Lycée Sisowath** and then went to Paris to study from 1949-1955. Returning to Phnom Penh, he was dean of the Faculty of Art and Architecture in the late 1960s. Um Samuth was secretary of state for culture in the **Hang Thun Hak** government from October 1972 to April 1973, retaining the portfolio in the **In Tam** governments in 1973, and in the first **Long Boret** government, December 1973 until June 1974. His younger brother Colonel, later Brigadier Um Savuth, led the **Khmer Republic** army to defeat in **Operation Chenla I**. Savuth was ineffective and half paralysed as a result of his own bravado having been injured when he had ordered a subordinate to shoot a live cat off his head—a prank that resulted in some of his head being blown away. He was killed in a road accident during the night of 4 November 1972. Savuth was a cousin of the wife of **Jean Fernandez**.

UM SIM (1932-). Born on 29 May 1932 at Chihe, **Kampong Cham**, he was at Lycée Descartes as well as Lycée Sisowath, participating in the student strike of 1949 organized by **Keng Vannsak, Ieng Sary** and others in response to the **Democrat Party** call for independence from France. He then studied in the **United States** earning a B.A. and an M.A. in Electrical Engineering (telecommunications) from the University of Illinois in 1959 and 1962 respectively. In 1965 he was appointed head of the postal and telecommunications training school at the Royal Technical University and was Dean of the School of Electronics from 1965. Although he was not a politician, he was among the many English-speaking, US-educated professionals who were recruited into senior positions in the government and the armed forces from 1970, serving as minister of telecommunications in the third **Lon Nol** government from July 1970 to May 1971. In 1972 he became director of the office at the Ministry of Foreign Affairs, and then was the Khmer Republic's roving ambassador and last ambassador to Washington. In April 1975 when the **Khmer Republic** faced defeat, he attacked the **United States** and its foreign policy in Cambodia by telling the US government "you have taken advantage of us". In 1985 he was living in Melbourne, Florida.

UN NOENG (1942-). Born in Sandan, **Kampong Thom**, he studied at the Faculty of Pedagogy, University of Phnom Penh until 1962 and then worked as a school teacher in **Siem Reap**. From 1967 he undertook further studies, including practice teaching and became a secondary school teacher in Phnom Penh. He spent the period of **Democratic Kampuchea** in the countryside and in May 1981 was appointed chief of the people's revolutionary committee for the district of Baraty, Kompong Thom. From May 1981 until May 1993 he was a member of the **National Assembly** representing Kampong Thom and in February 1988 was appointed secretary of the **People's Revolutionary Party of Kampuchea (PRPK)** in Baray district. In 1992 Un Noeng was appointed vice-governor of Kampong Thom and in May 1993 was elected to the National Assembly as **Cambodian People's Party (CPP)** deputy for Kampong Thom. In October 1993 Noeng was appointed secretary of the Commission for

Foreign Affairs, International Cooperation, Information and the Media. In 1998 he was reelected to the National Assembly.

UN TRAMUCH (1936-). Born on 5 February 1925 at Phnom Srok, **Battambang**, Tramuch was the son of Chuon Un and Mme (née Kossum Dara). He was elected to the National Assembly in 1962 representing **Kampot** and in 1966 easily won the election for the seat of Bavel, Battambang. He was minister of agriculture in the third **Lon Nol** government from July 1970 to May 1971, minister of general mobilization under **Son Ngoc Thanh** from March to October 1972 and was advisor to Lon Nol in charge of the Phnom Penh municipality from March 1973. He married Ong Smil and they had two children.

UNG BUN ANG (1949-). Accountant and financial advisor. Born on 31 December 1949 in **Battambang**, eldest son of Ung Khun Meng, he attended Lycée Preah Harirak Rama, Phnom Penh. In 1970, after Prince **Norodom Sihanouk** was deposed, he won a Colombo Plan scholarship to study economics in Australia. Graduating with a B.Ec. and later an M.B.A. from University of Queensland, his professional career has focused on accounting and financial planning. He was appointed justice of the peace 1983 by Queensland state government, and has been prominent and extensively involved in the Khmer community in Australia after the influx of Khmer refugees, especially in Melbourne where he resides. In 1986 Ung Bun Ang began to publish the very first computerized Khmer magazine, *Neak Noam Sar* ("The Courier"), in Australia critical of political, social, and economic development in Cambodia. He was a visiting lecturer in Khmer History and Culture at the Royal Melbourne Institute of Technology from 1994 to 1996.

After **Sam Rainsy** was eventually expelled from the National Assembly in 1995 and decided to set up his own political party, Ung Bun Ang played the most significant role in setting up the party's network in Australia. Since 1996 he has been president of the **Sam Rainsy Party** (formerly Khmer Nation Party) Australia New Zealand. Ung Bun Ang was reunited in 1980 with his family from refugee camps including his brother, Ung Bun Heang, a cartoonist for *Nokor Thom*, who wrote of his experiences under Pol Pot regime in *The Murderous Revolution* published in 1985.

UNG BUN HOR (1930-1975). Born on 10 February 1930 at Tani, **Kampot**, son of Ung Peng An. He was elected to the National Assembly in a by-election for Koki, **Kandal**, in 1960, in spite of some question over validation of his victory. However, in 1962 he was reelected (unopposed) to represent Kandal, being defeated in 1966. He then joined the Royal Government as a sports delegate 1968-1969, before being posted overseas. He was ambassador to Cuba at the time of the overthrow of **Norodom**

Sihanouk and was ejected from the country by the Cuban government because of his support for Lon Nol. In fact, he and his wife were summarily expelled and deported so quickly that they were not even given time to pack their personal possessions. On his return to Cambodia he became director of receipts in the Finance Ministry. He joined the **Socio-Republican Party** and was elected to the **National Assembly** of the Khmer Republic in September 1972, representing Takhmau, Kandal. On 23 September 1974, two days after the return of **Lon Non** to Cambodia, he was elected president of the National Assembly and was the Socio-Republican Party's member in the Supreme Committee that ruled Cambodia from 12-17 April 1975. He still held that position when the Republic collapsed in April 1975. Ung Bun Hor's wife and children had moved to France, but he had remained in Phnom Penh. On 17 April he took refuge in the French Embassy, but was ejected on 19 April. He was killed soon after being led away.

UNG HONG SATH (1920-1977/78). Born on 25 December 1920 at Rolea Peir, **Kampong Chhnang**, the son of Ung Hout and Mme (née Nong Samary), he attended **Lycée Sisowath** and studied radio-television in France. Hong Sath was a school headmaster and then was appointed director of the National Radio after having served briefly as technical inspector of Radio Télévision Française. He was a member of the **Party of the People** and contested the 1951 National Assembly elections for Chhoeur Tom, Pursat. Moving to support **Sangkum**, he was elected to the **National Assembly** in 1958 for Phnom Kong, **Kampot** and was reelected in 1962. From 1964 until 1967 he was the editor of *Neak Cheat Niyum* ("The Nationalist"), a Sangkum news magazine. In 1967 he was appointed president of the National Committee for Aid and Assistance to Veterans and in 1968 was second vice-president of the Council of Ministers in charge of the interior and religious affairs. He was second deputy prime minister in the second **Lon Nol** government of 1969-1970. A prominent member of Sihanouk's *contre-gouvernment* (shadow cabinet) since 1967, Ung Hong Sath resigned from the government in December 1969 in protest against a National Congress decision to adopt liberal reforms of the economy with aid from international financial institutions. He was among the Sihanoukists detained during the dramatic events of February-March 1970. He opposed the ensuring war, attempting together with other prominent old regime personalities to defend a neutralist or **"third force"** standpoint as political life polarized. His patriotism and loyal to Sihanouk were initially recognized by the **Democratic Kampuchea** authorities but by late 1976 when it was clear that the Prince would not actively contribute to the consolidation of the communist revolutionary state, his historic allies were detained and executed. He married Prom Kim Lanh, the sister of **Prom Thos**, and they had four children.

UNG HUOT (1945-). First prime minister 1997-1998. Born on 1 January 1945 at Chak Angre, Kandal Stung, **Kandal**, Ung Huot's father died while he was a teenager. He studied at **Lycée Sisowath** then studied commerce at **Phnom Penh** University, majoring in accounting and finance. He began work as a manager of the accounting department of the Khmer Distilleries (SKD) in Phnom Penh. In 1971 he won a scholarship to Australia and studied business administration at the University of Melbourne. He was president of the Khmer Students in Victoria Committee. It was in Melbourne that he met Yvonne Kong, and her son Chak "Jon-Jon," and they were married soon afterward. In 1974 he graduated with an M.B.A., and then completed a diploma of Education at Melbourne State College. In 1975 he refused to return to Cambodia when his studies were finished, and remained as a refugee, later gaining Australian citizenship. In 1976 he was recruited by the Australian government to assist in migrant resettlement. He was also recruited by Telecom Australia (now Telstra), the Australian telecommunications conglomerate that later installed a new telecommunications system in Cambodia. He worked for White Pages and later as product manager and marketing manager.

Living in Vermont, in the far-eastern suburbs of Melbourne, in 1978 he founded, and became president of, the Khmer Community of Victoria, the Cambodian association closely linked to **FUNCINPEC**. In 1981 he was elected president of FUNCINPEC in Australia, hosting visits by both Prince **Norodom Sihanouk** in February-March 1985 and later Prince **Norodom Ranariddh**. He later joined Prince Ranariddh's staff. In 1991 with the political settlement, he returned to Phnom Penh and soon took over public relations for FUNCINPEC. He was a delegate to the Pattaya II and Paris International Conference on Cambodia in October 1991, a member of the Steering Committee for FUNCINPEC and the National Council of FUNCINPEC from February 1992, and director of the party's campaign strategy in 1993. Elected for Kandal province, he was appointed Minister of Posts and Telecommunications in the Cambodian government. In 1993 he was appointed minister of education, youth and sports, and was vice-chairman of the Cambodian Olympic Committee.

On 28 October 1994, following the removal of Prince **Norodom Sirivudh**, he became minister of foreign affairs and international cooperation; being denounced by the Khmer Rouge as a "whipped dog of Australia." His rise to the prime ministership was equally dramatic and came following the overthrow of Prince Norodom Ranariddh in the July 1997 coup. During the coup itself, he was in Paris, but returned to Phnom

Penh, via Singapore, and took up his new position which had been offered to him by Hun Sen with alacrity. In the run-up to the 1998 elections he formed his own party, **Reastr Niyum** which failed to win any seats in the 1998 elections which he had proclaimed as "free and fair." Moving to Hawthorn, Australia, in 1999 he tried to rejoin FUNCINPEC but the party committee refused to readmit him.

UNG HY (1884-1964). *Akkamohasena* (prime minister) 1945. Ung Hy served in the colonial administration under the French. On 12 March 1945 he became the minister of finance and in essence the head of the first government of the **Kingdom of Kampuchea** which took office after King **Norodom Sihanouk** declared independence at the behest of the Japanese. He remained as *Akkamohasena* until 13 August and continued on as minister of finance under **Son Ngoc Thanh**, finally relinquishing office on 16 October 1945. Three of his daughters married leading officials who were to hold high office in the Khmer Republic: **Cheng Heng**, **Iat Bountheng** and Yèm Monirath, onetime Governor of Battambang. He also had five sons. Ung Hy remained an influential figure behind the scenes in Phnom Penh during the 1950s, and "spiritual father" of **Penn Nouth**. In November 1960 he was feted in Beijing. He died on 16 October 1964. He was survived by at least two brothers: Ung Hou, who died 7 February 1972, aged 71; and Ung Nhach who was governor of **Kampot** in 1973 and brigadier general in the Republican Army in 1974.

UNG KRAPUMPHKA. Son of Ung Chroun and Mme (née Keng Yoc Liem), he was under-secretary of state for public works and telecommunications from January 1958 and became the rector at the Royal Technical University in the late 1960s. He was minister of public works and agricultural engineering in the third **Lon Nol** government, July 1970 to May 1971. He married Phlek Metary, sister of **Phlek Phirun** and daughter of Ouk Phlech.

UNG MUNG (1933-1975). Born on 16 June 1933 at Rumduol, **Svay Rieng**, Mung was the son of Ung Tun, and he grew up in **Phnom Penh**. He was elected to the National Assembly for **Kampong Speu** in 1962 and reelected for the seat of Kraing Ampil, Kampong Speu, in 1966. Ung Mung was implicated in a scandal unveiled by Prince **Sisowath Sovannareth** in which a schoolgirl, Chhun Kim Yin, committed suicide on 2 December 1967, after the politician ended his affair with her. Secretary of state for tourism in the second **Lon Nol** government from 1969-1970, on 16 March 1970, he was one of the deputies who led the debate which was supposed to bring down Prince **Norodom Sihanouk**—but it failed, only for the prince to be finally overthrown two days later. In November 1970 he was narrowly defeated by **Tan Uk Nam Ieng** for the vice-presidency of the National

Assembly and became an advisor to Lon Nol. During the **Khmer Republic** he was a notorious figure in the **National Assembly** and once, after he had denounced **Hoeur Lay Inn**, he was physically attacked by his adversary being saved from serious injury by his personal bodyguards who intervened. He is presumed to have been killed in 1975 at the end of the war. His wife, née Yos Maliel, was a politician in her own right. Educated at **Lycée Sisowath** where her father taught, she was secretary of state for tourism, 1967-1969. In 1971 she attempted to sue *Nokor Thom* newspaper for libel in response to criticism of her performance at the department of tourism. She lived in exile in Paris.

UNG PHAN. A Communist Party of Kampuchea (CPK) administrator who worked in the Eastern Zone after 1975, he fled to Vietnam with **Hun Sen** on 20 June 1977 out of fear of imminent arrest. He became head of the office of **Heng Samrin** from 1979-1981, was minister attached to the Prime Minister's Office in June 1981 and director of the Prime Minister's Office in 1985. He was minister of communications, transport, post and telecommunications from August 1989 until June 1990 and also a member of the Central Committee of **People's Revolutionary Party of Kampuchea (PRPK)** in April 1989. He represented Prey Veng in the **People's Republic of Kampuchea** National Assembly, February to August 1990, but arrested and jailed in May 1990, when he, **Thun Saray** and others attempted to form the Liberal Democratic Socialist Party. In July 1990 he was expelled from the PRPK being released from prison in October 1991 under the terms of a general amnesty for all political prisoners agreed in Paris. In January 1992 he created the Free Democrats' Party and on 29 January was victim of an assassination attempt allegedly perpetrated by people connected to the **Cambodian People's Party (CPP)**. In June 1992 he joined **FUNCINPEC** and was appointed advisor to Prince **Norodom Ranariddh**. Elected to the Executive Committee of the party in March 1993, Ung Phan was elected a FUNCINPEC deputy for Svay Rieng in May 1993. He was minister of state in the Royal Government of Cambodia in 1995. In the same year he was the man with whom Prince **Norodom Sirivudh** was allegedly chatting—the tape of this telephone conversation resulting in the prince being exiled from the country and sentenced to a jail term for threatening the life of **Hun Sen**. Having already alienated many in FUNCINPEC Ung Phan formed, in April 1997, a breakaway section of the party which attracted preliminary recognition from Hun Sen and the CPP. Ung Phan replaced Veng Sereivuth as the tourism minister following the ousting of First Prime Minister Prince Norodom Ranariddh. The reformation of a FUNCINPEC-CPP coalition government in 1998 left him with no political role.

UNG SAMY. A nephew of **Chea Sim**, he commanded the **People's Republic of Kampuchea** armed forces in **Battambang** province in October 1986. In March 1987 he was appointed **People's Revolutionary Party of Kampuchea (PRPK)** secretary for Battambang province. In April 1989 he became a member of the PRPK Central Committee and, following the 1993 elections, he was appointed as governor of Battambang, officially confirmed on 18 December 1993. He was accused, during the United Nations period, of involvement in arbitrary arrests and also the deaths of political opponents in Battambang during the election campaign. He was appointed Governor of Pursat on 12 March 1999.

UNITED FRONT FOR THE NATIONAL CONSTRUCTION AND DEFENSE OF KAMPUCHEA (UFCDK). The principal mass organization of the **People's Revolutionary Party of Kampuchea (PRPK)**, the name of this body is sometimes translated as the Solidarity Front for the Construction and Defense of the Kampuchean Motherland. Formed in December 1981 it superseded the **United Front for the National Salvation of Kampuchea** which was deemed to have completed its primary task of seizing of power from the **Pol Pot** government. According to the constitution of the **People's Republic of Kampuchea**, the aims and objections of the new Front are to mobilize the people to carry out the policies of the ruling PRPK and of the state, to strengthen steadily the worker-peasant alliance and to encourage progressive and patriotic outlooks at all levels of society and in all ethnic and religious communities. The last Honorary Presidium of seven people, elected in 1989, was headed by **Heng Samrin**. The National Council (80 people) was chaired by **Chea Sim**. Leading members of the Council, especially those heading the three principal mass organizations embraced by the Front, namely **Mat Ly** of the **Federation of Trade Unions of Kampuchea**, Sam Sundoeun of the **Association of Revolutionary Youth of Kampuchea** and **Mean Saman** and **Chhouk Chhim** of the **Association of Revolutionary Women of Kampuchea** were often involved in representing the government, the party and the country at international meetings or in negotiating exchange and cooperation agreements. The Solidarity Front disappeared in 1991 when the PRPK was dissolved, its headquarters, the Sihanouk era foreign ministry, being leased to entrepreneurs who opened a hotel.

UNITED FRONT FOR THE NATIONAL SALVATION OF KAMPU-CHEA/"*RENAKSE SAMAKKI SANGKROH CHEAT KAMPUCHEA*" (UFNSK). Formally created at a clandestine "congress" of 200 held 2-3 December 1978 near Snuol, the UFNSK was the vehicle for the national uprising against the **Pol Pot** government and his **Democratic Kampuchea** regime. The congress elected a Central Committee of 14 led by **Heng Samrin** and **Chea Sim**. The remaining 12 were: **Ros Samay**, **Mat Ly**, Bu

Mi, **Hun Sen**, **Mean Saman**, Mme Meas Samnang, Neou Samon, Long Sim, Hem Samin, Mne **Chey Kanh Nha**, **Chan Vèn** and Prach Sun. Among its first decisions, the Central Committee agreed to found an official news agency, named *Saporamean Kampuchea* or S.P.K. in brief, and a radio station which was named "Voice of the Kampuchean People." The congress also published a declaration in which the "reactionary Pol Pot-**Ieng Sary** gang and their families" are accused of establishing a "dictatorial, militarist and fascist regime, unmatched in history for its ferocity." The regime is attacked for "razing" towns and for evacuating millions of people from urban communities to the countryside where everyone had been put at risk and many forced to die "slowly through hard labor." The "Pol Pot-Ieng Sary gang" were further attacked for usurping the leadership of the revolutionary movement, for trampling all traditions underfoot and of seeking to serve "the strategic aims of great-nation expansion of the Chinese authorities." The "historic mission" of the UFNSK was to promote regime change, to secure the rights of the Cambodian people to life and basic freedoms, to divise and to implement "genuinely" socialist economic policies and to abolish the "reactionary" culture of the dictatorship by developing national education, doing away with compulsory marriage and discrimination against ethnic minorities and foreigners and by punishing the "die-hard reactionary chieftains who have committed bloody crimes against the people." The meeting was also a call to arms for by the end of the month the **Vietnamese invasion** was underway. As far as the communist defectors from the **Communist Party of Kampuchea** and the leaders of the Communist Party of Vietnam were concerned, there was an organizational need to create a front organization so as to enable very badly divided and militarily weak groups and strata within Cambodian society to unite with each other and with Vietnamese "volunteers" for the sole negative purpose of removing Pol Pot from power. For further developmental purpose the Salvation Front was transformed into the **United Front for the Construction and Defense of the Kampuchea** in 1981.

UNITED KINGDOM. Although the first contacts with Cambodia were through the East India Company which established a factory in the 1650s, it was in the 1850s that some Cambodians thought that it might be a good idea to conclude a treaty with the British to stop Vietnamese and Thai incursions. Eventually they signed a treaty with France. Many tens of thousands of British tourists visited Angkor in the 1950s and 1960s; and the United Kingdom supported, initially at any rate, the Khmer Republic. As one of the five permanent members of the **United Nations** Security Council, British support for the Paris Peace Agreement in 1991 was regarded as vital to its success as all other members of the permanent five had special relations with one or more parties to the conflict.

UNITED NATIONS BORDER RELIEF OPERATION (UNBRO). In the 1980-1981 food crisis arising from the Vietnamese invasion, massive population migrations and the collapse of the **Democratic Kampuchea** system of production collectives, international relief agencies set up relief operations at strategic points along the border with **Thailand**. Initially, UNICEF was the lead agency during the emergency but in 1982 UNBRO was set up so as to monitor and to coordinate the distribution of food and other forms of relief aid to the holding centers that were administered by the three resistance parties. The World Food Program was the lead agency. UNBRO also facilitated the work undertaken by Embassies in the interviewing and processing of applications by Cambodians for resettlement in third countries and worked with the Thai army in devising programs of aid to "affected villagers" in Thailand.

UNITED NATIONS TRANSITIONAL AUTHORITY IN CAMBODIA (UNTAC). Administrative body established by the Paris Peace Agreements of 1991 to prepare Cambodia for general elections. By the middle of 1992, over 22,000 UN personnel, half of them military forces, had arrived in Cambodia. They departed rapidly following the promulgation of the new Cambodian constitution in September 1993. Despite the swift, severe economic dislocations resulting from such a large, and predominently affluent group of foreigners, and serious shortcomings in relation to the framework decisions reached in Paris—especially the failure to disarm and to regroup the warring party armies in accordance with the Paris agreements and the failure to foster an environment free of fear and intimidation for the May elections—the UNTAC interregnum be deemed a partial success. Cambodia emerged from the 1993 elections with a government recognized as legal and legitimate by most other nation states thus bringing to an end more than 10 years of diplomatic isolation. The armed struggle for power mounted by the **Party of Democratic Kampuchea** was steadily eclipsed by battle fatigue, and by the massive UN program of reconstruction and development, the restoration of free public schooling and a free press; the emergence of civil and human rights organizations and renewed economic optimism. Apart from the gross organizational and individual negligeance that contributed to the current HIV/AIDS pandemic, UNTAC's shortcomings, though serious, do not account for continuing economic and political instability.

UNITED STATES. From its recognition of Cambodia on 7 February 1950, and the early 1990s, U.S. policy toward Cambodia tended to reflect its foreign policy ambitions in other parts of Indochina, and was strongly influenced by the exigencies of the Cold War. In the late 1950s Prince **Norodom Sihanouk**'s neutralist foreign policy, seen as pro-communist, alarmed hard liners in the U.S. government. It has been clearly established that US government agencies were involved in plots to overthrow the prince, hatched in Bangkok and Saigon, in 1959. However, from 1955 until 1963 the United States also gave substantial military and economic assistance estimated at $83.7 million. Relations chilled in 1963 when Sihanouk rejected American military aid claiming, among other things, that it was insufficient. In 1964 he refused to accredit a new U.S. ambassador, and diplomatic relations were suspended in May 1965. Over the next three years, Sihanouk's tacit diplomatic alliance with the communist revolutionary forces fighting the American and the South Vietnamese put him in the line of fire. After the US secured the Prince's private and personal consent to bomb Vietnamese sanctuaries in Cambodia, the **Communist Party of Kampuchea**, most likely acting with the consent of and advice of the party in Hanoi, lauched a national armed uprising against the Prince. On 2 July 1969, Sihanouk partially abandoned the anti-American imperialism element in his foreign policy of "neutrality" and renewed relations with the United States.

Through its South Vietnamese allies and contacts within the **Khmer Krom** community, the United States army may have encouraged the anti-communist and ultra-nationalist personalities around **Lon Nol** to plot against Prince Sihanouk. The US Army in Vietnam appeared not to notice the transfer of troops in the Civilian Defense Irregular Groups into Cambodia while Washington quickly acknowledged the anti-communist outlook of new government when it was formed in 1970. A month-long US "incursion" into Cambodia had the effect of driving Vietnamese communist troops based in sanctuaries along the frontier and now allied to the new **National United Front of Kampuchea** deeper into the country and the ill-conceived and poorly executed Cambodian offensives against the Vietnamese that followed severely weakened the Cambodian army. As the war intensified, the US ambassador, Emory Swank, was frequently overruled by military advisors. His even more hard-line successor, John Gunther Dean, inheriting an insolveable situation, evacuated Phnom Penh with his staff in April 1975, only days and hours before the CPK forces seized it.

U.S. efforts to establish diplomatic relations with the Pol Pot regime were rebuffed, but following the Vietnamese invasion of 1979 the United States, Thailand and the rest of the ASEAN countries rejected the application of the **People's Republic of Kampuchea** for Cambodia's seat in the **United Nations** General Assembly, Thus Cambodia's seat continued to be occupied by **Democratic Kampuchea** as it was Cambodia's only lawful government, The **United States** turned a blind eye to China's decision to arm all nationalist parties will to mount a war against the Vietnamese presence in Cambodia, but did provide "non-lethal" aid and food aid to the non-communist resistance and to the civilians living in border holding centers. Successful arms reductions negotiations with the Russians and the collapse of communist regimes in Europe, brought an abrupt end to the Cold War "proxy war" in Cambodia, In January 1990 and led by the United States, the Perm Five nations in the **United Nations** Security Council began monthly and bimonthly deliberations with each and with the waring Cambodian parties, slowly establishing the framework for the Paris agreements of 1991. The United States reestablished diplomatic relations with Cambodia not long after the departure of UNTAC and pledged over $40 million in development aid.

On balance, US policy toward Cambodia since its withdrawal from Vietnam in 1975 has reflected its strategic aims and interests in the global arena. The current US commitment to promoting democratization and human rights ensures that Cambodia will continue to receive priority in some US aid programs. In 1989, as indicated in the entry on the **economy**, the garment industry received privileged access to US markets subject to continuing progress in the development of labor relations.

UNITED STATES BOMBING OF CAMBODIA. *See* OPERATION BREAKFAST; OPERATION FREEDOM DEAL; UNITED STATES.

-V-

VAN PINY (1940-1977). One of the fouding members of the **Assemblée Générale des Étudiants Khmers,** Van Piny was a graduate of the diplomacy section of the Royal School of Administration and studied law at the Royal University graduating in May 1965. A private secretary to Prince **Norodom Sihanouk** and assistant director of protocol, he was appointed cultural counselor at the Cambodian Embassy in Paris. On 31 July 1970 Piny rallied to Prince Sihanouk and joined him in Beijing. He was a member of the Central Committee of the **National United Front of Kampuchea** and in 1973 was named **Royal Government of National Union of Kampuchea** second vice-minister of foreign affairs. He returned to Phnom Penh in September 1975, and was among the diplomats sent to "the base" for a brief period of re-education and revolutionary "strengthening" and arrived at the Ministry of Foreign Affairs in April 1976 suffering from.being forbidden to wear his glasses and poor food rations. Neither a communist nor a royalist Viny was among the intellectuals who did not always agree with **Ieng Sary** with whom he had worked in Beijing and who was foreign minister. He was arrested and taken to **Tuol Sleng** on 20

November 1977, accused of being a French spy, along with **Sarin Chhak** with whom he had worked amicably, and sent to his death in early 1978.

VANDY KAONN (1942-). A 1966 graduate of the Faculty of Pedagogy, he taught French and English at Prey Nop College in **Kampot** for two years before being recalled to Phnom Penh to take up a post as a writer for the official state newspaper, *Cambodge*. He became deputy director of the government press agency, **Agence Khmère de Presse (AKP)**, at the same time. In 1969, when he was responsible for political affairs in the Ministry of National Education secretariat, he was one of the founders and editor-in-chief of *Le courrier phnompenhois*. During the **Khmer Republic** years, he taught philosophy in Phnom Penh high schools while continuing to work for AKP, becoming its chief writer in 1970. He also wrote for several other Khmer language papers or magazines, notably *Chadomuk, Mohachon* and *Khmerathibotey* and was managing director and publisher of the major French-language daily, *Le Républicain*. He went to France in 1972 to begin research for a doctorate in sociology but owing to difficulties with his scholarship, he returned to Phnom Penh in 1973. Between 1975-1979, he worked in the countryside, successfully disguising his intellectual background. After 1979 he was one of the most prominent, noncommunists to become associated with the **People's Republic of Kampuchea (PRK)**. Secretary-general of the Kampuchea-Vietnam Friendship Association from September 1979 until August 1989, he became deputy secretary-general of the United Front for the National Salvation of Kampchea/United Front for the Construction and Defense of Kampuchea in May 1981. He also won a seat in the National Assembly in May 1981 representing **Battambang**, a post held until August 1989. From June 1981 to August 1989, he one of the seven members of the Council of State of the PRK, a body headed by **Heng Samrin**. In 1982 he was appointed president of the Legal Commission of the PRK National Assembly and was the founder and director of the Institute of Sociology in Phnom Penh. **Thun Saray** was his deputy. He courageously raised the issue of Corruption in the PRK until he finally, quietly, left the service of the regime in August 1989, remaining in France during a mission there. He has written two books, *Cambodge: 1940-1991 ou la politique sans les Cambodgiens* (1993) and *Cambodge: La Nuit Sera Longue* (1996). He is currently completing his doctorate at the University of Nice Sophia Astipolis.

VANN MOLYVANN (1926-). Architect. A nephew of **Penn Nouth**, Vann Molyvann was born on 23 November 1926 at Ream, **Kampot**, son of Vann, an officer in the French Sûreté, and Mme (née Peak), and studied architecture at the École Nationale Supérieure des Beaux Arts in Paris, 1946-1955. He also studied at the Architectural Association of London, and during his time in Paris he was the president of the Khmer Students' Association. Returning to **Phnom Penh**, he worked as an architect and was appointed in charge of the Administration of Civil Construction with responsibility for the control of the urban sprawl of Phnom Penh. He designed many of the major public works projects in Phnom Penh—the Independence Monument, the **Chamkar Mon** and the Olympic Stadium, the latter of which was built by his friend **Khaou Chuly**. In 1962 he was appointed secretary of state for public works and telecommunications and in 1967 was minister of national education. In 1969 he was minister of national education and fine arts. During the **Lon Nol** period, he remained in Phnom Penh and in September 1970 he was appointed to the rank of colonel, but in the mid-1970s he left for Paris where he lived throughout the 1980s. In 1991-1992 Vann Molyvann worked for the United Nations Educational, Scientific and Cultural Organization in Laos and in 1993 he joined the **Cambodian People's Party** of **Hun Sen**—moving back to his old villa in Phnom Penh. He was appointed minister of state in charge of culture, fine arts and urbanization in the Provisional National Government of Cambodia then held the same position in the Royal Government of Cambodia from 1993. In the late 1990s until his retirement in 2001 he headed the Apsara Authority, a zoning and planning body responsible for overseeing the protection and development of the Angkor region. Molyvann married Trudy Amberg in 1961 and they have three children.

VANN SUN HENG (1944-　). Born in Sithor Kandal, **Prey Veng**, a professor at the Faculty of Arts, Phnom Penh University, he spent the period of 1975-1979 in the countryside. In September 1980 he was appointed assistant director-general of the *Voice of the Cambodian People* (radio station) and exactly a year later was promoted to director-general. He was then appointed as assistant then director-general of the Radio-TV of the **People's Republic of Kampuchea** and then the **State of Cambodia**. In May 1993 he was elected to the National Assembly on a **Cambodian People's Party** list in Prey Veng and was a member of the Commission on Education, Religious Issues, Culture and Tourism. He was reelected in 1998. In the current Assembly he is a member of the Commission on Legislation.

VAR HUOT (1935-　). Born on 30 December 1935 in **Kampong Cham** province, he graduated from the Faculty of Law, **Phnom Penh** in 1956 and in 1960 he was appointed as principal collector and administrative director of the Customs Department. After a study of economic and commercial sciences in Phnom Penh and in Paris, in 1969 he studied at the École Nationale des Douanes at Neuilly-sur-Seine, France, returning to Phnom Penh as the deputy secretary of state in charge of the Narcotic

Bureau. In 1971 he studied at the Police and Narcotics School in Washington D.C., and in 1973 studied in Wellington, New Zealand. During the period of **Democratic Kampuchea**, he was a refugee in Paris 1975-1990. Joining the **Cambodian People's Party (CPP)**, in 1992 he was appointed an advisor to Hun Sen, and was minister of trade in the Provisional National Government of Cambodia and then in the Royal Government. He lost the trade portfolio to **Cham Prasith** in a cabinet reshuffle approved by the National Assembly on 20 October 1994 and was posted to London. From 31 January 1995 until 1999 he was ambassador to the United States. He is married to Ny Saudy.

VAR KAMEL (1898-1966). Born on 16 November 1898 in **Phnom Penh**, son of Nhonh Var and Mme (née Chim), he studied in Phnom Penh, Hanoi and **France**. In France he attended Lycée Mignet in Aix-en-Provence then studied at the School of Law and Administration in Phnom Penh, joining the Colonial Administration in 1923. Rising rapidly, he held several provincial governorships. In 1943 he was inspector of administrative affairs, and was minister of religion, religious education and fine arts in the government of the Kingdom of Kampuchea from 12 March to 13 August 1945. Var Kamel held the same portfolio under **Son Ngoc Thanh** until October 1945 then served as minister of national economy from October 1945 to December 1946. He then became governor of Phnom Penh and inspector of political and administrative affairs in the Ministry of Interior in 1949. Although in 1951 he was nominated as minister to Bangkok, he did not proceed, accepting instead the post of secretary-general of the Ministry of Foreign Affairs. He returned to the Ministery of Interior in June 1952. By 1963 he was Ambassador to India. He married and had four children, one of whom was Kamel Saoreac who married **Thonn Ouk**. Var Kamel died on 29 May 1966.

VELOSO, DIEGO (c1550-1599). A Portuguese adventurer, he reached Cambodia in about 1582 and endeared himself to King **Satha** (r 1579-1596) who adopted him as a son and arranged a marriage to one of his cousins. Veloso was joined by a Spanish adventurer, Blas Ruiz, who arrived in Cambodia in 1593. In the following year, Sattha dispatched Veloso to Manila with a royal letter asking for Spanish help against the Siamese, promising privileges for Catholic missionaries in return. However by the time the message reached Manila King Satha had been overthrown.

VENG KHUON (1923-). An ethnic Brao, Veng Khuon was born in 1923 in **Stung Treng** province. Recruited into the **Khmer Issarak** resistance by 1951, he was among the first members of the **Khmer People's Revolutionary Party (KPRP)** created in that year. He appears to have returned to his home and family in 1954 when many other KPRP members were evacuated from Cambodia with **Viet Minh** soldiers and "regrouped" in North Vietnam. In 1974 he supported the breakaway movement of many highland **Communist Party of Kampuchea** cadres in the Northeast military zone and on 20 March, fled for his life to Vietnam. After 7 January 1979 he became chairman of the **Preah Vihear** province people's committee and secretary of the provisional committee of the **People's Revolutionary Party of Kampuchea** in the province. In May 1981 he was replaced in both posts by **Ney Pena** and was elected to the **National Assembly** of the **People's Republic of Kampuchea** holding the seat for Preah Vihear. By 1985 he was secretary of the PRPK provincial committee in his native province. Replaced by Som Sopha, his deputy secretary, in 1988, he appears to have retired from public life by 1991. *See also* SEUY KEO.

VENG SEREIVUTH (1960-). Born in **Prey Veng** he survived the dangers and hardships of **Democratic Kampuchea** but feeling the country after 1979 he was resettled in New Zealand. In 1988-1989 he worked at the **FUNCINPEC** office in Bangkok and from 1989-1991 in the private secretariat of Prince **Norodom Ranariddh**. Returning to **Phnom Penh** at the end of 1991, he was part of the FUNCINPEC team attached to the secretariat of the **Supreme National Council**. In May 1993 he was elected to the constituent assembly to represent Prey Veng and in June he was appointed to the cabinet office in the Provisional National Government of Cambodia and also minister of tourism in the Royal Government in 1995. A member of the FUNCINPEC steering committee and a Ranariddh loyalist in 1997, he was replaced at the Ministry of Tourism by **Ung Phan** in September 1997. In 1998 he was reelected to the **National Assembly** in Prey Veng and reappointed minister of tourism in the new coalition government.

VICTORIOUS NORTHEASTERN KHMER PARTY (*kanapac Khmer Eisan Meanchey*). A political party founded in February 1951 by **Mao Chay** after a personality clash with **Yèm Sambaur**. The party relied heavily on support from **Dap Chhuon** and used, as its symbol, the two crossed national flags with the constitution on a platform above them. It never published a prgram but its campaign focused on the need to make all Khmers aware of the grandeur of their heritage, and the importance of serving the monarchy. In 1955 it dissolved to allow its members to join the **Sangkum**.

VIET CONG. An acronym and pejorative based on a contraction of the Vietnamese language phrase for Vietnamese communist (*Viet Nam Cong San*). From the mid 1950s the South Vietnamese press and U.S. aid officials used "Viet Cong" in reference to all suspected or known communists, and broadly as a substitute for **Viet Minh** and as a slur against any individual associated with the communist side in the anticolonial war. Ngo Dinh Diem followed by **United States** officials began by the 1960s to distinguish between "invaders" from North Vietam and southern insurgents. Viet Cong soon became a synonym for the "communist terrorists" as in Malaya and the term applied more specifically to the armed guerrillas operating under the control of the **National Front for the Liberation of South Vietnam (NFL)** and who in 1969 prepared for coming to power by creating their **Provisional Revolutionary Government of South Vietnam**. Many NFL soldiers used sanctuaries in Cambodia or purchased their supplies and took delivery of their arms there. The United States launched secret bombing campaigns such as Operation Menu and **Operation Breakfast** in order to root out and destroy "Viet Cong" supply routes.

VIET MINH. An acronym formed from the Vietnamese-language term for National League for Independence (*Viet Nam Doc Lap Dong Minh Hoi*). The League was an all-party front organization of the **Indochina Communist Party**. It was founded in 1941 as an organization for galvanizing political and military opposition to the Japanese occupation in pursuit of national independence. Following the seizure of power in Hanoi in August 1945 it became the vehicle for armed struggle against French colonialism from 1946-1954. The Viet Minh army, led by General Vo Nguyen Giap, assisted the **Khmer Issarak** in Cambodia, recruiting about 3,000 Cambodians to the communist cause by 1954. After 1954, the Viet Minh organization in the communist Democratic Republic of Vietnam was reorganzied for peacetime purposes and renamed the Fatherland Front.

VIETNAM. Much Cambodian history and key elements in modern Khmer nationalism are related to hostile encounters with kingdoms to the east. In the Angkorean period, the Kingdom of Champa, located in what is now central Vietnam posed a serious military threat to the survival of the Khmer state and civilization, Cham armies succeeding in sacking Angkor in the 12th century. The conquest of Champa by the expansionist Lê Dynasty in the 15th century eliminated this threat but cleared the way in turn for the southward expansion of Vietnamese population settlements into the **Mekong** Delta, then an integral part of the Khmer Kingdom. The transformation of the fishing village of Prey Nokor into the commercial city that became Saigon was completed under French colonial auspices, the French chosing to ignore dynastic frontiers when fixing the territorial boundaries of their colony of **Cochinchina.** Tensions over border demarcation, periodic irredentist claims to the lost provinces of **Kampuchea Krom** and the sovereign isolation of **Khmer Krom** citizens of Vietnam from their ethnic homeland, must be counted among the enduring legacies of European intervention in local international relations.

Since independence, and as a matter of national security, Cambodian ruling elites have attempted to distance themselves or to remain neutral in civil conflicts dividing the Vietnamese nation. Cambodia granted de jure diplomatic recognition to the Democratic Republic of Vietnam in 1967 and allowed the **Provisional Revolutionary Government of South Vietnam** to open an official mission in 1969. This retreat from neutrality came about partly because the Saigon authorities and the **United States** had refused to acknowledge the territorial integrity of Cambodia within its existing frontiers, that is, those of the late 1960s (and arguably now). That **Norodom Sihanouk** believed the communist revolutionaries would eventually succeed in expelling the Americans from Vietnam was also a factor. After 18 March 1970 the Vietnamese communists became his allies, committing "volunteer" forces to the Cambodian battlefield. In 1979, and eventhough thoroughly alienated from the failed **Democratic Kampuchea** regime, Sihanouk, once again supported by China, refused to work with the Vietnamese-imposed, **Heng Samrin** authorities. Throughout the 1980s Vietnam opposed a role for the United Nations in a settlement of the political conflicts unleashed by its 1978-79 invasion, relenting in 1991 only as the communist party power collapsed in the Soviet Union. With both Vietnam and Cambodia joining ASEAN not long afterward, many bilateral tensions eased, as each government was forcefully obliged by the new regional context, to concentrate on neglected problems of development and of international cooperation.

VIETNAMESE INVASION OF 1978-79. Fearing a coordinated two-front assault from **Democratic Kampuchea** in the south and the People's Republic of China in the north, Vietnam lauched a 14-division, 200,000 man offensive against **Pol Pot** on 24 December 1978, capturing Phnom Penh on 7 January 1979. The invasion followed the breakdown of negotiations between the two communist revolutionary regimes and almost two years of low-intensity conflict. The invasion was facilitated by a small number of defectors from the **Communist Party of Kampuchea**, led by **Heng Samrin** and **Chea Sim** who organized the **United Front for the National Salvation of Kampuchea (UFNSK)** three weeks earlier. The Vietnamese and their UFNSK supporters nevertheless failed to strike a decisive blow against the National Army of Democratic Kampuchea (NADK). The **third Indochina war** commenced when the regrouped NADK formed a national alliance with the new armies formed under the banner of the **Khmer People's National Liberation Front** and FUNCINPEC to resist the Vietnamese occupation.

VIETNAMESE MINORITY. Although ethnic Vietnamese began settling in Cambodia from the 18th century, the number of settlers increased sharply in the French colonial era. Large numbers of Vietnamese workers were brought into Cambodia in the early 20th century to work in the newly established **rubber** plantations and to service construction, transport and commercial activities. Vietnamese also took a dominant share of lower echelon posts in the administrative services of the protectorate, being more adept at passing the necessary entrance examination than were Khmer (or in the case of Laos, Lao) applicants. Since the last century, Vietnamese river boat dwellers have been prominent in the commercial fishing sector on the **Tonlé Sap** while Vietnamese farmers are most numerous in eastern provinces bordering Vietnam. Intermarriage with ethnic Khmers has been rare. This is due to a historically conditioned political view of Vietnamese immigrants as the advance guard for invading Vietnamese armies. It is also partly because the Khmer are endogamous and expect foreigners to assimilate, especially to embrace Buddhism. In colonial times and until the 1970s most Vietnamese residents of Cambodia were Roman Catholics.

By the late 1960s the Vietnamese minority is believed to have numbered approximately 600,000 people. Under Lon Nol, Vietnamese inhabitants were harassed, hundreds were assassinated, and close to 200,000 were evacuated or deported to South Vietnam. Most of the remaining long-term residents were repatriated or deported to Vietnam in 1975-1976, in the months immediately following the **Khmer Rouge** seizure of **Phnom Penh**. Large numbers returned during the 1980s when the **People's Republic of Kampuchea (PRK)** encouraged their return, viewing them as a valuable political bulwark against the return of the Khmer Rouge to power. By special decrees in 1982 and 1983, the PRK authorities allowed all former Vietnamese residents as well as their friends and relatives from Vietnam to resettle in Cambodia and many were incorporated into village solidarity groups. In an oblique reference to local Khmer hostility to Vietnamese resettlement and immigration, the PRK decrees called for special "educational" efforts to be made in regions where the Vietnamese settled. Vietnamese fisher families regularly suffered violent and inhumane assaults from Khmer Rouge forces or unknown vigilante groups.

The arrival of the **United Nations Transitional Authority in Cambodia** in 1992 triggered a construction boom in Phnom Penh and coincided with economic liberalization and rising unemployment in Vietnam, both phenomena inadvertently precipitating a major wave of economic migrants from southern Vietnamese cities. Many of these workers, whose arrival reignited Khmer nationalist fears, proved to be temporary migrants while many of those who settled, took Khmer wives and integrated themselves into local communities. By March 1995 when the Ministry of Interior issued provisional estimates of the size of national minority populations, ethnic Vietnamese numbered 95,597 only, much less than the 1- to 2-million total often discussed in the early 1990s. The general population census of 1998 asked respondents to identify their "mother tongue," but the tabular results from this question have yet to be published. The enumerated size of minority populations, especially of Vietnamese, **Cham** and Chinese is a sensitive issue in view of ongoing national debates over the nature and modalities of possible criminal trials for **genocide**, war crimes or crimes against humanity.

VORN VETH né **PENH THUOK** also known as **Sok** and as **Sok Thuok** **(1931-1978).** The most senior member of the **Communist Party of Kampuchea (CPK)** to be purged in the **Democratic Kampuchea (DK)** era, Sok completed primary school in the town of Siem Reap and in 1952 graduated from Lycée Battambang. Sent to Phnom Penh to attend college, he lived with his aunt and her husband who were supports of the **Son Ngoc Thanh** wing of the **Democrat Party**. In June 1953 he slipped out of the capital to Slap Leng, near Kampong Speu, in order to join **Savang Vong**'s band of **Khmer Issarak** and met **Meas Samay**. By November both had decided Savang Vong was a "pirate" and part of a pro-French "network." They ran away but were caught and imprisoned for more than three months until March 1954. Once back in Phnom Penh Sok briefed Democrat Party personalities, including Ping Say, about his life as a freedom fight, brief though it was. He was then advised of how he could make contact with the Vietnamese backed Issarak forces. With Sok Khnol, he left Phnom Penh a second time and after a month, they arrived in Santey in the East (military) Zone. There he met Saloth Sar (**Pol Pot**) and about nine other intellectuals, as well as the **Khmer People's Revolutionary Party (KPRP)** leader **Tou Samouth**. Back in Phnom Penh toward the end of October Sok became a teacher at **Chamroeun Vichhea** and was inducted into the KPRP, sponsored by Saloth Sar in December 1954. In 1955 he also joined the **Sangkum** so as to encourage and protect Sihanouk's anti-US stance of neutrality and all while building underground networks for the communist movement. In 1959 he joined the party committee for Phnom Penh; in 1960 he attended the party congress which tranformed the KPRP into the **Workers' Party of Kampuchea** and after 1966 into the **Communist Party of Kampuchea (CPK)**. In 1963 having remained behind in Phnom Penh while Saloth Sar, **Ieng Sary, Son Sen**, and others fled, he was elected to the central committee of the party.

From 1964-1968, Sok Thuok, as he was then known, attempted with other underground party members to guide and direct popular movements in the capital, dismayed at some moments at the bourgeois, anti-royalis outlook of many and at others, by the breadth and depth of the governmen repression of worker and student activism. He joined the armed struggle in 1969 only, initially going to the Southwest zone which was led and dominated by veterans of the Issarak period. During the civil war, Sok worked from 1972 in the Special Zone being made responsible for the education and training of intellectuals who rallied to the cause of the CPK backed **National United Front of Kampuchea** (FUNK). After April 1975 and officially after the formation of the first government of **Democratic Kampuchea** in 1976, Penh Thuok using the pseudonym Vorn Veth was named deputy prime minister responsible for the economy. Known to have supported the intensifying purge process in its early stages, by 1978 with his secretary for agriculture, **Non Suon,** and the secretary for industry, Mey Prang and many other friends and comrades from the urban struggle of the 1960s having perished, he was sent to **Tuol Sleng** on 2 November, being accused of liberal, bourgeois cultural orientations, for favoring the recall of old society technicians to assist ailing factories, for example, and of spying for the American CIA. He was reportedly summoned by sponsor, Pol Pot, at the time of his arrest and dealt a blow that broke his leg. Vorn Veth was executed soon afterward.

VYADHAPURA. A pre-Angkorean Cambodian kingdom, contemporary with **Isanapura**, it was probably located in the vicinity of present-day Prey Veng. **Jayavarman II** celebrated his independence from "Java" in a ceremony at Vyadhapura, recorded in a subsequent inscription.

-W-

WAT OUNALOM. The headquarters of the Mohanikay Buddhist *sangha* in Phnom Penh, this temple community was first established in 1443. The **Buddhist Institute,** which located there before 1975, has been reestablished since 1989 on the second floor of the main building.

WOMEN IN CAMBODIA. Although women play an indispensible role in social and economic life, and constituted nearly 52 percent of the total population on census day 1998, recognition, enhancement and protection of women's rights has been slow. Feminine figures feature centrally in Khmer literature and folklore, often as models of proper behavior (eg Rama's consort, Sita) and often as victims of male mischief or foolishness. They also highlight the importance of women in the family, in agricultural rituals and work and in marketing and handicrafts, suggesting also that they are guardians of traditional morality and national well-being. Buddhist festivals in pre-revolutionary Cambodia were organized largely by women and so were other village-based religious festivals and ceremonies that punctuated the agricultural year. At the same time, women had no voice in the political process, and no feminist movement developed in pre-revolutionary Cambodia. During his first reign **Norodom Sihanouk** encouraged a handful of well-educated or socially prominent women to pursue political careers, and all women 20 years or older received the right to vote.

During the early **Khmer Republic** years some young women joined the armed forces for the first time but it was only under Pol Pot that large numbers of women from rural and lowly backgrounds saw their traditional roles in the family, the army, production and party politics radically changed and expanded. The historical impact of the revolution was nevertheless negative and not least because, as Karl Marx once insisted, equality in misery is worthless. Elitest traditions of political control were also preserved in **Democratic Kampuchea**. Several wives, all well-qualified were high-ranking figures in the party, with two, namely **Khieu Thirith** and **Yun Yat**, receiving ministerial posts. There is little evidence that women who were powerful in the communist movement succeeded in exercising their administrative powers independently of their husbands or in support of the interests of women.

The political subordination and victimization of women was finally recognized but also exploited by the **People's Republic of Kampuchea** authorities who, for a while, gave preference to women job applicants who had been widowed by the purges, hardships and civil warfare that raged throughout the 1970s. In the 1980s even if they were fortunate enough to possess a small bit of agricultural land, more women needed to secure work outside of the home in order to have some cash income. A women's coalition for peace, national reconciliation and free elections emerged as early as 1992, quickly taking up the issue of mine clearance as central to the stabilization of household budgets (for women who were disabled were abandoned and children who were injured were cared for by their mothers). Women also organized against the growing problem of domestic violence and in support of major legal reform ensuring greater sexual equality in rights to divorce. A centre devoted to raising public awareness of "women's voices" led by the mid 1990s to the studies of women and the representation of women in the media. Compared to these many areas of advance, efforts to promote equality between the sexes in party politics have faltered as the principal parties have either rejected proposals to reserve up to 30 percent of available nominations for the **National Assembly** or insufficient numbers of interested, capable women have come forward. Only five of the 122 deputies elected in 1998 were women. Yet, in 2002, Prime Minister **Hun Sen** reportedly complained to the king that chaos would ensue if as many as 20 women like Princess **Norodom Vichara**, chair of the Assembly's Commission on Foreign

Affairs, International Cooperation, Propaganda and Information and **Tioulong Saumura** won election to the Assembly. The King told him not to worry as finding 18 more would take a long time.

WOMEN'S PARTY. The first women's party was created by **Nou Neou** in August 1972. It nominated some women candidates for the **Khmer Republic** elections in September 1972, but the party withdrew its candidates before the polling. In the postwar 1993 and 1998 elections other women's parties, including the Party of Neang Neak Cambodian Women, the Cambodian Women's Party, Women's Party for the National Salvation of Cambodia and the Women and Nation's Rule of Law Party have fielded a small number of candidates. Women who were successful in the 1998 Assembly elections and the 2002 local elections represent the three main parties: **FUNCINPEC**, the **Cambodian People's Party** and the **Sam Rainsy Party**.

WORKERS' PARTY OF KAMPUCHEA (WPK). This was the name taken by the **Khmer People's Revolutionary Party (KPRP)** in 1960 at the secret Congress organized in the railroad station of **Phnom Penh** in September 1960. The WPK placed the Cambodian revolutionary organization on an equal footing with the Workers' Party of Vietnam, a move apparently supported by Vietnam at the time, in an attempt to rescue and support the faltering party. **Tou Samouth** was elected secretary at the Congress, as the KPRP secretary **Sieu Heng** had defected to the government. The survival of the party was called into question for a second time in 1962 when Samouth was assassinated.

WORLD WAR I. During the war thousands of Cambodians served in France. These included **Khim Tith** and **Pach Chhoeun**. On their return veterans were forbidden from organizing social gatherings and any suggestion of an occasional reunion was actively discouraged by the French. A monument in Phnom Penh commemorated their service and included the names of those who died—it was among the monuments torn down by the communists in 1975.

WORLD WAR II. Although Cambodia was never a theatre of war between 1939 and 1945, two incidents related to the larger conflict had important repercussions on its later history. The first was the **Franco-Siamese War** of 1940-1941, which forced the French, under Japanese pressure (called "mediation"), to yield the provinces of **Battambang** and most of **Siem Reap** to the Thai. The second was the Japanese *coup de force* of 9 March 1945 when they sequestered French officials throughout Indochina and informed local leaders, including King **Norodom Sihanouk**, that their countries had gained independence. The five months that ensued before the French returned to Indochina in force in October 1945 gave many young Cambodians, Lao and Vietnamese a valuable foretaste of independence.

During World War II some Australian and British prisoners were held in prisoner-of-war camps in Cambodia, mainly en route to Saigon. Cambodia was also subject to a United States bombing raid in 1943 aimed at disrupting Japanese naval operations in the region but causing collateral civilian deaths. Fearing the worst many families in Phnom Penh sent their children to live with relatives in the countryside and the episode was a central feature in a famous Khmer language novel.

-Y-

Y PHANDARA (1949-). Born on 19 September 1949 in **Phnom Penh**, he studied at **Lycée Sisowath** until 1968 and then in Paris from July 1972 until 1978. He joined the **National United Front of Kampuchea (FUNK)** in September 1972 and returned to Cambodia in February 1978, where he was held at Boeung Trabek reeducation camp in Phnom Penh. By November 1979 he was a refugee in **Khao-I-Dang** holding center just across the frontier in Thailand from where he secured passage back to France. He wrote *Retour à Phnom Penh*, an autobiographical account of his experiences and treatment, which was published in 1982. Returning to Phnom Penh again in 1992, he established the Cambodge-Renaissance Party and contested the May 1993 elections for a seat in Phnom Penh, but was not successful.

Y TUY (1927-). Born on 12 September 1927 at **Kampot**, the son of Y Neang and Mme (née Lonh Chreth), he attended **Lycée Sisowath** and married Penn Thansi; they had seven children. Y Tuy studied at the École Nationale de l'Administration in Paris earning a diploma. He then returned to Cambodia and was a *chauvraysrok*, *phouchhouykhet* then secretary-general of the Council of Ministers and later secretary-general to the prime minister. In March 1958 he was elected to the National Assembly representing Kandol Chrum, **Kampong Cham** and from April to July 1958 Y Tuy was deputy secretary of state for the interior and territorial defense. He resigned from the Assembly in 1960 to accept another government post. In 1962, following fresh elections, he was appointed governor of Kampong Thom, Kampong Cham and governor of Phnom Penh from 1968-1969. He was among the supporters of Prince **Norodom Sihanouk** placed under house arrest on 16-17 March 1970.

YANG SEM (1945-). A refugee in the United States in the 1970s, he joined **Molinaka** and then **FUNCINPEC** in the 1980s. After having agreed to have his name placed on the FUNCINPEC list in **Kratié** in preparation for the Constituent Assembly elections of May 1993, he decided to join the **Cambodian People's Party**. It was too late to change any of the party lists and he was elected. Nevertheless, he was not seated in the Assembly as he had by his own volition given up membership of the party that had nominated him. The decision to hand the seat to the next candidate on the FUNCINPEC list was supported by Assembly leaders from both CPP and FUNCINPEC out of concern to discourage elected deputies from willfully changing parties.

YASODHARAPURA. Name given by King **Yasovarman I** at the end of the ninth century to the newly delineated urban complex now known as Angkor, with its center at Phnom Bakheng, Yasovarman's temple-mountain.

YASOVARMAN I. King of Cambodia 889-910. Founder of **Yasodharapura** (Angkor) and the first Cambodian king to place his capital in the Angkor region. Succeeding his father, **Indravarman I**, he gained power following a protracted civil war. Yasovarman was a powerful monarch, whose empire extended from southern Laos to southern Cambodia and westward into Chantaburi province of present-day Thailand. After building the temple of Lolei at Roluos, he established a new capital, Yasodharapura, centered around the temple-mountain of Phnom Bakheng. The eastern Baray was dug during his reign. The walls surrounding the new city, which can still be traced today, indicate that Yasodharapura was 16 square kilometers in size, larger than any medieval European city.

YASOVARMAN II. King of Cambodia 1150-1165. He succeeded **Suryavarman II**, but does not seem to have been a close relation. During his reign, the temples of Banteai Samre, Thommanon and Chau Say Tevoda were completed, and it is likely that some of the Roluos temples were restored—perhaps because Yasovarman II traced his lineage to that region. So much temple construction suggests a protracted period of peace. On his return from a military campaign to the west, Yasovarman appears to have been overthrown in a coup d'état.

YÈM SAMBAUR (1913-1989). Prime minister 1949-1950. Born on 2 February 1913 at Sisophon, **Battambang**, son of Yèm, a judge, he attended **Collège Sisowath**, completed his baccaleareate in 1935 in Hanoi and then studied for a few years at a French university. In 1939 he was a judge of instruction and president of **Kampong Cham** court. Sambaur married Has Boungar, daughter of Has Boun, a rich landowner, and they had a daughter, Yèm Dararath (married Im Chhayrith). In 1946 he joined the newly formed **Democrat Party** and was a candidate for the party in the 1947 National Assembly elections for Peani, **Kampong Chhnang**. Once in the Assembly he became leader of the parliamentary party, becoming one of its most accomplished debaters. However, after a dispute with other leaders of the party, he left and in 1948 formed his **National Recovery Party**. The party was expected to win the following elections and, as the Assembly was suspended, Yèm Sambaur managed to be appointed prime minister on 12 February 1949, holding that position until 2 May 1950. During that period he negotiated the Franco-Cambodian Treaty of 1949 which awarded limited independence to Cambodia.

However the Treaty and Yèm Sambaur's rapport with the Court and the French aroused controversy, especially among pro-Issarak nationalists within the Democrat Party and among students who demonstrated in favor of total independence. In the September 1951 elections, rather than gaining power, the National Recovery Party suffered a humiliating defeat winning only 7.1 percent of the vote and no seats, a turn of events that severely dented his pride. His arrest in 1952, in connection with the assassination of **Ieu Koeus** two years earlier, became the immediate cause of the dismissal of the Democrat government of **Huy Kanthoul**. During this stage he was rumored to have formed a close friendship with Princess (later Queen) **Sisowath Kossamak**. With the realignment of political forces against the Democrats in the mid-1950s Yèm Sambaur became a major force in the **Sangkum**. In November 1953 he was appointed minister of national economy in the **Chan Nak** government, becoming minister of finance in the **Norodom Sihanouk** government in April 1954, under **Penn Nouth** in April to July 1954 and minister of the budget, trade and industry from August 1954 until January 1955. **Leng Ngeth** appointed him minister of national economy during 1955. In 1954 he had been a member of the Cambodian Mission to Paris to discuss and agree on the detailed aspects of decolonization. He was then politically marginalized for nearly 15 years becoming a keeper of the national archives in the National Library.

Yèm Sambaur opposed Sihanouk in the late 1960s and was minister for justice in the second Lon Nol government. He organized some of the early protests against the Vietnamese in **Svay Rieng** and, following the attacks on the embassies in March 1970, was sent, with Prince **Norodom Kantol**, to explain the situation to Prince Norodom Sihanouk. They, however, never left the country as the prince refused to see them. After the overthrow of Sihanouk, Yèm Sambaur took control of foreign affairs He put the new government's case to the Jakarta Conference in Indonesia on 16-17 May 1970, but to little avail. In July 1970 he was reappointed minister of state in charge of justice. In March 1972 Yèm Sambaur was offered the prime ministership, but with no real power, by Lon Nol, and he declined, leading to the appointment of **Son Ngoc Thanh**. Keeping hi portfolio, Sambaur was now the second most senior person in the cabinet. In May Yèm Sambaur's friend and ally **Huy Mong** stood for the presidency, but withdrew under pressure from Lon Non. His next political move was to form the **National Union** in August-September 1972, but this again collapsed. In October he was replaced by **Chhan Sokhon** as minister of state in charge of justice. Effectively rebuffed as well as defeated, he decided to abandon party politics. During the last years of the Khmer Republic, Yèm Sambaur was honorary consul for the Republic of Haiti. He left Phnom Penh in early 1975 and lived in exile in Paris where he died.

YÈM SARONG (1923-). Born on 24 July 1923 at Kampong Svay, Sisophon, son of Yèm and Mme (née Ream Sok). He studied mathematics at **Lycée Sisowath** and in Hanoi then taught briefly at Lycée Sisowath before winning a government scholarship to study in France in 1946. A supporter of the **Democrat Party**, government records on scholarship students reveal that while in France he registered for some "unauthorized" courses in political science and that he did not pursue the degree at Hautes Études Commerciales for which the scholarship had been awarded. He returned to Phnom Penh in January 1953 with a diploma in statistics. In 1968 Yèm Sarong was minister of finance, and in 1968-1969 he was director-general of the Banque Khmère pour le Commerce. Ambassador to Switzerland from 1972-75, he settled in Grenoble. Sarong married Marie Thérèse Pochard and they had four children.

YIM SOKHA alias **Chan Rattana (1962-2002).** Party activist and editor in chief of the newspaper *Samleng Youveakchon Khmer* ("Voice of Khmer Youth"). A medical doctor by training, Chan Rattana was prominent among a group of student supporters of the **FUNCINPEC** party in the 1993 elections but, by April 1994, he and other former student activists, disappointed by the ex-communist-royalist coalition government, established "Voice of Khmer Youth" a biweekly, opposition newspaper. Very rapidly, its promoters received threats to their lives, often anonymous, believed to have emanated from official security agencies. The first publisher and manager, Nonn Chan, was shot and killed in broad daylight in September 1994. In January 1995 the Ministry of Information issued a suspension order following publication of a brochure entitled "Only the King can save Cambodia: Cambodians want peace." Articles in the paper portrayed first prime minister Prince **Norodom Ranariddh** as weak and manipulated by the second prime minister **Hun Sen.** In February 1995 Chan Rattana was sentenced to one year in prison and fined five million riels for "disinformation" and "defamation." He was declared a prisoner of conscience by Amnesty International upon his imprisonment in June 1996. A founder-member of the Khmer Nation Party, today known as the **Sam**

Rainsy Party (SRP), Yim Sokha is head of the party's finances. In 1998 he was one of 15 SRP candidates elected to the National Assembly. He was killed in a car crash in 2002.

YISALES YASYA (?-1976). A Cham Muslim, he worked in the Ministry of Religious Affairs, and was a member of the Sangkum. He competed without success in the 1966 National Assembly elections for the predominantly Cham region of Krek, Kampong Cham. Elected in September 1972, he was a senator of the Khmer Republic until 1975. Recognized by the Communists in early 1976, he was imprisoned at Tuol Sleng and executed on 2 May 1976.

YIT SRONN (1891-1972). He worked in the French colonial service, transferring to the Cambodian administration. He was governor of Kampong Thom, Kandal and then Kampong Cham. Although appointed minister of the interior in the Chhean Vam government from February to August 1948, the King refused to allow him to control the national police and awarded this responsibility to Yèm Sambaur. Yit Sronn was minister of religion and fine arts from August 1948 to January 1949. In 1953 he served in the National Consultative Assembly. Yit Sronn married Kim and they had five children. He died on 8 September 1972 and was cremated at the Langka Pagoda, Phnom Penh. His eldest son, Yit Kim Seng, a medical doctor, was minister of health in the government of the People's Republic of Kampuchea from June 1981 until August 1990.

YOS SON (1941-   ). The head of the People's Republic of Kampuchea Ministry of Foreign Affairs department dealing with the North and South America and Western Europe, in 1984 he was promoted to head of the press section at the ministry. He was appointed minister of education in August 1990. A prominent member of the Cambodian People's Party, he was elected to the National Assembly in 1998 for Kampong Cham becoming a member of the Commission on Foreign Affairs, International Cooperation, Propaganda and Information.

YOTHEA. A Khmer language term, derived from Sanskrit, and meaning "soldier" or "combatant"; this word was revived under Democratic Kampuchea as a means of according greater recognition to soldiers as a distinctive group of workers. DK propaganda sometimes characterized the state as a "worker, peasant, soldier" state.

YOU HOCKRY. He gained a diploma from the National School of Administration; and was a civil servant in Kampong Cham before 1975. In the late 1970s and early 1980s he lived in the United States, returning to Phnom Penh in 1992 to become director of the Office of the President of FUNCINPEC. He was elected to the Constituent Assembly for Kampong

Cham in May 1993; and was deputy minister of the interior, 1993-1995. In 1998 he was reelected to the National Assembly and appointed cominister of the interior with the rank of minister of state. In 2002 FUNCINPEC sought to replace him with **Khan Savoeun** but failed.

YUKANTHOR AFFAIR. See ARUNA YUKANTHOR, Prince.

YUN YAT (1934-1997). The wife of **Son Sen,** she was a teacher at **Lycée Sisowath** where like **Khieu Ponnary** she was known as a feminist and socialist. She remained at her post in 1963 when her husband left Phnom Penh joining him in 1965. After the adoption of the **Democratic Kampuchea (DK)** constitution in 1976, she was named minister of culture, education and schooling in the first DK government being one of only nine ministers. As culture minister, she was responsible for the state publishing house but as schooling was limited and there were only a few official groups engaged in the performing arts, it is not clear how the ministry may have functioned. In 1977 she received the Ministry of Information and Propaganda portfolio after the arrest and purge of **Hu Nim** becoming minister of propaganda and education. She was thus responsible for offical DK radio broadcasts. As the purges extended into the highest ranks of the party, statements made by **Kang Keck Ieu** confirm she and her husband narrowly escaped being purged in 1978. On 15 December 1979, in the wake of Vietnam's invasion, she was named minister of culture and education in the second DK government led by **Khieu Samphan** She remained with the DK movement and underground until June 1997 when she was murdered together with her husband and children upon the orders of **Pol Pot.**

YUON. Khmer language word of uncertain etymology, probably derived from Sanskrit *yavana* ("barbarians"), used widely in everyday conversation in reference to "Vietnamese". Although it was not judged derogatory before the 1960s and was used as a colloquial designation for Vietnamese in the Thai as well as Khmer languages, the word was deemed pejorative by the **Communist Party of Kampuchea** whose spokesmen then deliberately employed it as a term of abuse. The term is now widely seen by Vietnamese and others, including many Khmers, to be derogatory and insulting. It is used in political speech at present both in a customary, old fashioned careless manner and also, more worrying, to indicate nationalist superiority and ethnic hostility.

YUTH PHOU THANG. He was from the ethnic Thai minority in Cambodia and in February 1987 was appointed secretary of the **People's Revolutionary Party of Kampuchea (PRPK)** in **Prey Veng.** In July 1990 he was promoted to the Central Committee of the PRPK. In the 1993 elections, he was the second candidate on the **Cambodian People's Party** list in Prey Veng, and although he was elected, he resigned his seat lending his support to the secessionist movement promoted by **Norodom Chakrapong**. On 20 December 1993 he was appointed first vice-governor of Prey Veng. On 12 March 1999 he was promoted to governor of the economically important province of **Koh Kong**.

-Z-

ZHENLA ("Chenla"). This was the name given in contemporary Chinese accounts to pre-ninth century Khmer kingdoms or settlements which periodically sent tribute to the Chinese court. Archaeological evidence suggests that from the fourth to the early eighth century there was a steady development of architectural skills and artistic styles that led logically to the refined forms at **Angkor**. The kingdoms known collectively as Zhenla were located in the Mekong Basin, and cities from the period have been located near present-day cities of Kampong Thom and Siem Reap.

ZHOU DAGUAN (CHOU TA KUAN). A 13th-century Chinese emissary, he visited **Angkor** 1296-1297 as part of a delegation sent by the newly installed Mongol monarchs. Zhou left an invaluable account of what he saw. He was favorably impressed by the grandeur of Angkor and recorded incisive, sometime unflattering, details about religious practices, local customs and social structure.

ZHOU ENLAI (1898-1976). A Chinese Communist leader, minister and politician, whose interest in Cambodian affairs dated from the **Geneva Conference** of 1954, when Zhou was **China**'s foreign minister. In this capacity he participated in the **Bandung Conference** in Indonesia in 1955 and befriended **Norodom Sihanouk** there. For the next 20 years Zhou cultivated the prince and was rewarded with Sihanouk's unfailing sensitivity to Chinese foreign policy concerns. Zhou was instrumental in persuading the Prince to form the **Royal Government of National Union of Kampuchea** and the **National United Front of Kampuchea** in 1940. His is also the hand behind the "Sihanouk card." China protected and used Prince as a means of exercising indirect leverage and influence in Cambodian affairs, and indeed, throughout Southeast Asia. In his turn Sihanouk enjoyed greater independence and leverage in his relations with leaders of the **Communist Party of Kampuchea (CPK)** as a result of his independent and personal friendships with Zhou and with Kim Il Sung. After Zhou's death in 1976, CPK leaders were more freely able to isolate the prince from state affairs and placed him under house arrest.

Bibliography

Introductory Essay

Until the 1980s most scholarly articles and books on Cambodia were written in French, and only a few of these were translated into English. Today there is a growing literature in the English language, some of it produced by expatriate Cambodians living in Australia, Europe or North America. Growing international and regional interest in Cambodia also ensures that many Khmer- or French-language texts written in Cambodia are quickly issued in English translation while, in Thailand and Singapore, many 19th and 20th century French-language classics are being translated and reissued in English.

The most extensive bibliography published to date is *Cambodia* (Oxford: Clio, 1998) by Helen Jarvis. The only other major bibliography, by Zaleha Tanby, appeared in 1982. Since then, two revolutionary regimes have collapsed, constitutional monarchy has been restored and Cambodia has joined ASEAN. There was renewed civic and scholarly engagement with each transition and each successive phase of "opening" up contributed to the proliferation of personal memoirs of the recent past. This bibliography is not exhaustive. Rather, it seeks to indicate the range of sources available in key subject areas. It includes the most accessible studies available as well as a limited number of recent doctoral dissertations. Technical manuals, including language and science texts and business dictionaries, have been omitted.

Contents

1. GENERAL

Bibliographies

Burns, R.D., and Milton Leitenberg. *The Wars in Vietnam, Cambodia and Laos, 1945-1982*. Santa Barbara, Calif.: Clio, 1984.

Jarvis, Helen. *Cambodia*. Oxford: Clio, 1998.

Keyes, Charles F. *Southeast Asian Research Tools: Cambodia*. Honolulu: University of Hawaii Press, 1979.

Long Seam and Y.P. Dementiev. "Bibliographie en langue russe sur le Cambodge (1956-1979)" [Bibliography of Russian-language works on Cambodia], *Bulletin de l'École Française d'Extrême-Orient* Vol. 68 (1980), p. 289-311.

Rodriguez, Ines. "Selected, annotated English language bibliography of the Kampuchean Revolution 1970-1979." *Southeast Asian Research Materials Newsletter* No. 18 (May 1981), p. 1-26.

Tamby, Zaleha. *Cambodia: A Bibliography*. Singapore: Institute of Southeast Asian Studies, 1982.

Dictionaries

Aymonier, Étienne. *Dictionnaire Français-Cambodgien* [French-Cambodian dictionary]. Saigon: Imprimerie Nationale, 1874.

Daniel, Alain. *Dictionnaire pratique Cambodgien-Français* [Practical Cambodian-French dictionary]. Paris: Institut de l'Asie du Sud-est, 1985.

Guesdon, Joseph. *Dictionnaire Cambodgien-Français* [Cambodian-French dictionary]. Paris: Plon, 1930, 2 vols.

Headley, R.K., et al. *Cambodian-English Dictionary*. Forest Grove, Oreg.: Catholic University of America Press, 1977, 2 vols.

Hoang Hoc. *Tu Dien Viet-Khome* [Vietnamese-Khmer dictionary]. Hanoi: Nha Xuat Ban Khoa Hoc Xa Hoi, 1977, 2 vols.

Huffman, Franklin, and Im Proum. *English-Khmer dictionary*. New Haven, Conn.: Yale University Press, 1977.

Institut Bouddhique. *Vacananukram Khmaer: Dictionnaire Cambodgien* [Khmer dictionary]. 5th Edition. Phnom Penh: Institut Bouddhique, Vol. 1, 1967; Vol. 2, 1968. Reprinted in Paris: Institut de l'Asie du Sud-Est, n.d. (c1985).

Jacob, Judith. *A Concise Cambodian-English Dictionary*. London: Oxford University Press, 1974.

Jenner, Philip, and Saveros Pou. *A Lexicon of Khmer Morphology*. Honolulu: University of Hawaii Press, 1982.

Pou, Saveros. *An Old Khmer-French-English Dictionary*, Paris: CEDORECK, 1992.

Smyth, David, and Tran Kien. *Tuttle Practical Cambodian Dictionary, English-Cambodian, Cambodian-English*, Rutland, Vt.: Charles E. Tuttle, 1995.

Tep Yok, Ly Vuong, and Thao Kun. *Petit Dictionnaire Français-Cambodgien* [Concise French-Cambodian dictionary]. Phnom Penh: Librarie Phnom-Penh, 1962.

Ung Tea Seam, and Neil ffrench Blake. *Phonetic English-Khmer Dictionary*, Bangkok: Seam & Blake Dictionaries, 1991.

Archives

Arfanis, Peter, and Jarvis, Helen. "Archives in Cambodia: Neglected Institutions." *Archives and Manuscripts* (Sydney) Vol. 21/2, p. 252-62.

Deane, John F. "The preservation of books and manuscripts in Cambodia." *American Archivist* Vol. 53 (April 1990), p. 282-97.

Giese, Diana, and Jarvis, Helen. "Cultural reconstruction in Cambodia and Vietnam." *National Library of Australia News* (July 1995), p. 9-12.

Jarvis, Helen. "The National Library of Cambodia: Surviving for Seventy Years." *Libraries and Culture* Vol. 30/4 (1995), p. 391-408.

General Surveys

Curtis, Grant. *Cambodia: A Country Profile*. Stockholm: Swedish International Development Authority, 1990.

Great Britain. Naval Intelligence Division. *Indochina*. London: Naval Intelligence Division, 1943.

Mabbett, Ian, and Chandler, David. *The Khmers*. Oxford: Blackwell, 1995.

Morizon, René. *Monographie du Cambodge* [Monograph on Cambodia]. Hanoi: Imprimerie d'Extrême Orient, 1931.

Ross, Russell R. *Cambodia: A Country Study*. Washington D.C.: U.S. Government Printing Office, 1990.

Steinberg, David J. *Cambodia: Its People, Its Society, Its Culture*. New Haven, Conn.: HRAF Press, 1959.

Travel and Guide-Books

A 1930s guide to Saigon, Phnom Penh and Angkor, Bangkok: Asia Books, 1992.

Bowden, David. *Cambodia*. Crows Nest NSW: Little Hills Press, 1996.

Dannaud, J.-P. *Cambodge*. Saigon, n.p. 1956.

Eliot, Joshua, and John Colet. *Cambodia*. London: Footprint Guide, 2000.

Madrolle, C. *Indochine du Sud: Cambodge, Cochinchine* [Southern Indochina: Cambodia, Cochinchina]. Paris: Hachette, 1926.

Madrolle, C. *To Angkor: The Madrolle Guides*. Paris: Société des éditions géographiques, maritimes et coloniales, 1939.

Népote, Jacques. *Indochine*. Geneva: Guide Artou, Olizane, 1990.

Neveu, Roland. *Phnom Penh and Cambodia*. Bangkok: Great Little Guide, 1993.

Philpotts, Robert. *A Guide to Phnom Penh*. London: Blackwater, 1993.

Ray, Nick. *Cambodia*. Oakland: Lonely Planet, 2000.

Smith, G.V. *A Shell Guide to Cambodia,* Phnom Penh: Shell Oil Co., 1966.

Vietnam et Angkor [Vietnam and Angkor]. Paris: Guides Jika, 1991.

Zepp, Raymond. *Cambodia Less Travelled*. Phnom Penh: Bert's Books, 1997.

Zepp, Raymond. *A Field Guide to Siem Reap Pagodas*. Siem Reap: KEAP 2000.

2. ECONOMIC

Economy and Population

Cambodia, Kingdom of. *Report on the Cambodia Socio-Economic Survey 1997*. Phnom Penh: National Institute of Statistics, Ministry of Planning, 1998.

Delvert, Jean. "L'economie Cambodgienne et son évolution actuelle" [The Cambodian economy and current trends]. *Tiers Monde* No. 4 (Jan-June 1963), p. 193-212.

Dumont, René. "Projet de rapport sur les possibilités de développement de l'économie agraire Khmère au départ des 'reformes économiques." Phnom Penh: FAO, 1994.

Ea Méng-Try. "Kampuchea: A country adrift." *Population and Development Review* Vol. 7, No 2 (1981) p. 209-228.

Emerson, Bridget. *A Legacy of Conflict: Trauma as an Obstacle to Poverty Alleviation in Rural Cambodia*. Phnom Penh: International Development Research Center, 1997.

General Population Census of Cambodia 1998: Final Census Results. Phnom Penh: National Institute of Statistics, Ministry of Planning, 1999.

Hughes, Caroline. *The political economy of the Cambodian transition*. London: Curzon Press, 2002.

Keat Chhon. *45 Months at the Ministry of Economy and Finance*. Phnom Penh: Cambodian Institute for Cooperation and Peace, 1998.

Kleinpeter, Roger. *Le Cambodge foncier* [Land in Cambodia]. Paris: Ducet Montchrestien, 1937.

Lelart, Michel. "La monnaie et l'économie Cambodgienne 1955-1970" [Cambodian money and economy]. *Mondes en développement* No. 28

(1979) p. 691-715.

Migozzi, Jacques. *Cambodge: Faits et Problèmes de Population.* Paris: Editions du CNRS, 1973.

Phouk Chhay. "The social and economic heritage of the old regime." *New Cambodge* No. 1 (May 1970), p. 50-52.

Prescott, Nicholas, and Menno Pradhan. *A Poverty Profile of Cambodia.* Washington, D.C.: World Bank Discussion Paper No. 373, 1997.

Prud'homme, Remy. *L'Economie du Cambodge* [The Cambodian economy]. Paris: Presses Universitaires de France, 1969.

République Khmère. *Annuaire Statistique 1969* [Statistical yearbook, 1969]. Phnom Penh: L'institut national de la statistique et des recherches économique, Commissariat Général au Plan, n.d. (1971).

Robequain, Charles, *The Economic Development of French Indochina.* London: Oxford University Press, 1944.

Royal Government of Cambodia. *Interim Poverty Reduction Strategy of Cambodia.* Phnom Penh: Ministry of Planning, 2000.

Royaume du Cambodge. *Annuaire statistique rétrospectif du Cambodge (1937-1957)* [Retrospective statistical yearbook of Cambodia, 1937-1957]. Phnom Penh: Ministère du Plan, 1958.

Summers, Laura. "The sources of economic grievance in Sihanouk's Cambodia." *Southeast Asian Journal of Social Science* Vol. 14, No. 1 (1986), p. 16-34.

Agriculture

Challard, Jean-Pierre. "The Jute Culture." *Kambuja* No. 53 (15 Aug 1969), p. 90-94; No. 54 (Sept 1969), p. 108-12.

"La culture du poivre" [Pepper Cultivation]. *Kambuja* No. 14 (15 May 1966), p. 50-57.

Delvert, Jean. *Le paysan Cambodgien* [The Cambodian Peasant]. Paris: Mouton, 1961.

Gourou, Pierre. *Land Utilization in French Indo-China.* Washington D.C.: Institute of Pacific Relations, 1945.

Hanks, Lucien M. *Rice and Man: Agricultural Ecology in Southeast Asia.* Chicago: Aldine, 1972.

Hellei, A. "L'agriculture du Cambodge et les problèmes du paysan khmer, de 1962 à 1974" [Cambodian Agriculture and Problems of the Khmer Peasant from 1962 to 1974]. *Mondes en développement* No. 29 (1979), p. 750-66.

Hellei, A. "L'influence des précipitations sur le rendement du paddy" [The impact of rainfall on paddy yield]. Phnom Penh, *Etude Statistique*, No. 1 de l'INSERE, 1970.

Heng Long. "Industry of rubber." *Kambuja* No. 6 (15 Sept 1965), p. 44-49.

Murshid, K.A.S. *Food Security in an Asian Transitional Economy: The Cambodian Experience*. Phnom Penh: Cambodia Development Resource Institute, 1998.

Rozemuller, H. B. *Overview of Rice Millers Associations in North West Cambodia*. Phnom Penh: Center for Advance Study, 1998.

Srey Kheng. "Pharmaceutical industry in Cambodia." *Kambuja* No. 26 (15 May 1967), p. 98-104.

Srey Thon. "L'élévage au Cambodge" [Animal Husbandry in Cambodia]. *Kambuja* No. 11 (15 Feb 1966), p. 67-71.

Tichit, Lucien. *L'agriculture au Cambodge* [Agriculture in Cambodia]. Paris: Agence de cooperation culturelle et technique, 1981.

"The Vine in Cambodia." *Kambuja* No. 30 (15 June 1967), p. 71-75.

Nonagricultural Industries

Even, Loic. "Ceramics making in Cambodia." *Kambuja* No. 33 (15 Dec 1967), pB-H.

Fujiwara, Hiroshi. *Khmer Ceramics from the Kamratan Collection in the Southeast Asian Ceramics Museaum*. Kyoto: Oxford University Press, 1990.

Green, Gill. "The Cambodian Weaving Tradition: Little known weaving and loom artefacts," *Arts of Asia*, Vol. 27, No. 5 (1997), p. 78-90.

Keat Chhon. "Rapport sur les Perspectives de Développement Industriel" [Report on Industrial Development], *Le Sangkum* No. 49 (1969) p. 52-59.

Michon, Michel-Maurice. *Souvenirs d'un Monde Disparu: Les Plantations de Caoutchouc (Viet-Nam, Cambodge 1956-1972)* [Memories of a Lost World: The Rubber Plantations of Vietnam, Cambodia 1956-1972]. Paris: la pensée universelle, 1987.

"The National Tyre Company." *Kambuja* No. 43 (15 Oct 1968), p. 48-51.

Rooney, Dawn F. *Khmer Ceramics*. Singapore: Oxford University Press, 1984.

Sithirith, M. *Fishing Conflict in Battambang*. Phnom Penh: NGO Forum on Cambodia, 2000.

Srey Keng. "The Khmer Oxygen and Acetylene Company." *Kambuja* No. 25 (15 April 1967), p. 67-74.

Touch Kim, and Charles Meyer. "The Industrialization of Cambodia by the Sangkum Reastr Niyum." *Kambuja* No. 43 (15 Oct 1968), p. 28-111.

Yean Ly Seng. "L'industrie du papier" [The Paper Industry]. *Kambuja* No. 15 (15 June 1966), p. 56-62.

Development

Cambodia Development Resource Institute. www.cdri.org.kh.

Chim Charya, Srun Pithou, So Sovannarith, John McAndrew, Nguon Sokunthea, Pon Dorina, and Robin Biddulph. *Learning from Rural Development Programmes in Cambodia*. Phnom Penh: Cambodia Development Resource Institute, 1998.

Council for Development of Cambodia. www.cambodia.investment.gov.kh.

Hu Nim. *Les Services Publics Économiques au Cambodge* [Public Economic Services in Cambodia]. Thesis, submitted for the doctorate in public law, Faculty of Law and Economics, Royal University, 1965.

Keat Chhon. "Rapport sur la gestion des enterprises d'état" [Report on the management of state enterprises] *Le Sangkum* No. 31 (1968), p. 35-41.

Keat Chhon, and Aun Pon Moniroth. *Cambodia's Economic Development*. London: ASEAN Academic Press, 1999.

Keat Chhon, and core staff of the Council for the Development of Cambodia. *Evolving the Long-Term Vision for the Rehabilitation and Development of Cambodia,* bilingual English and Khmer. Phnom Penh: Cambodian Institute for Cooperation and Peace, 1998.

Khieu Samphan. *Cambodia's Economy and Industrial Development,* translated and with an introduction by Laura Summers. Ithaca, N.Y.: Cornell University Southeast Asia Program Data Paper 111, 1979.

Muscat, Robert, and Stromseth, Jonathan. *Cambodia: Post-settlement Reconstruction and Development*. New York: Columbia University Press, 1989.

Népote, Jacques, and de Vienne, Marie-Sybille. *Cambodge; laboratoire d'une crise: Bilan economique et prospective* [Cambodia: Laboratory of a Crisis: Economic Balance Sheet and Prospects]. Paris: CHEAM, 1994.

NGO Forum. www.bigpond.com.kh.

Per Ronnas. *From Emergency Relief to Development Assistance: How can Sweden Best Help Cambodia?* Stockholm: SIDA, 1995.

Tith Huon. *Problème de l'assainississement dans la fonction publique Cambodgienne* [The task of cleaning up corrupt practice in the Cambodian civil service]. Thèsis pour la doctorate en Sciences Administratives; Paris, II, 1976.

HISTORICAL

General Surveys

Chandler, David P. *A History of Cambodia*. 3rd edition, Boulder, Colo.: Westview Press 2000.

Chandler, David P. *The Tragedy of Cambodian History: Politics, War and Revolution since 1945*. New Haven, Conn.: Yale University Press, 1991.

Delvert, Jean. *Le Cambodge* [Cambodia]. Paris: Presses Universitaires de France, 1983.

Herz, Martin F. *A Short History of Cambodia from the Early Days of Angkor to the Present.* London: Stevens & Sons, 1958.

Igout, Michael. *Phnom Penh: Then and Now.* Bangkok: White Lotus, 1993.

Jennar, Raoul M. *Les Clés du Cambodge: faits et chiffres; repères historiques; Profils Cambodgiens; Cartes.* Paris: Maisonneuve & Larose, 1995.

Kiernan, Ben, and Boua Chanthou (eds). *Peasants and Politics in Kampuchea, 1942-1981.* London: Zed Press 1982.

Norodom Sihanouk. *Souvenirs doux et amers* [Bitter-sweet memories]. Paris: Hachette, 1981.

Pham Viet Trung, Nguyen Xuan Ky, and Do Van Nhung. *Lich su campuchia* [Cambodian history]. Hanoi: Nha Xuat Ban Bai Hoc Va Trung Ho Chuyen Nghiep, 1982.

Thion, Serge. *Watching Cambodia.* Bangkok: White Lotus, 1993.

Werly, Richard, *Eternal Phnom Penh: Contemporary Portrait of a Timeless City.* Hong Kong: Fortune Image Ltd, 1995.

Archaeology and Prehistory

Bayard, Donn. "The roots of Indo-Chinese civilization recent developments in the pre-history of Southeast Asia." *Pacific Affairs* Vol. 53/1 (Spring 1980), p. 89-114.

Higham, Charles. *The Archaeology of Mainland Southeast Asia.* Cambridge: University Press, 1989.

Levy, Paul. *Recherches prehistoriques dans la region de Mlu Prei* [Studies of prehistory in the Mlu Prei region]. Hanoi: EFEO, 1943.

Malleret, Louis. *L'archéologie du delta du Mekong* [Archeology in the Mekong delta]. Paris: EFEO, 1959-63, 7 vols.

Mourer, C., and R. Mourer. "Prehistoric research in Cambodia." *Asian Perspectives* Vol. 14 (1973), p. 35-42.

Mourer, R. "Lang Spean and the Prehistory of Cambodia" in Bartstra, G.-J. et al. (eds). *Modern Quarternary Research in Southeast Asia.* Rotterdam: Balkerna, 1975, p. 29-56.

Saurin, E. "Le paleolithique du Cambodge oriental" [Paleography in eastern Cambodia]. *Asian Perspectives* Vol. 9 (1966), p. 96-110.

Early History and Angkor Period

Aeusrivinge, Nidhi. "The *Devaraja* Cult and Khmer Kingship at Angkor." In Kenneth Hall and John Whitmore (eds.). *Explorations in Early Southeast Asian History.* Ann Arbor: University of Michigan Center of South and Southeast Asian Studies, 1976, p. 107-48.

Auboyer, Jeannine. *Angkor.* Barcelona: Poligrafa, 1971.

Aymonier, Étienne. *Le Cambodge.* Paris: Leroux, 1901, 3 vols.

Aymonier, Étienne. *Khmer Heritage in the Old Siamese Provinces of Cambodia, with Special Emphasis on Temples, Inscriptions and Etymology.* Translated by Walter Tips. Bangkok: White Lotus 1999. [Volume 2 of *Le Cambodge.*]

Barth, A., and A. Bergaigne. *Inscriptions sancsrites du Cambodge* [Sanskrit inscriptions in Cambodia]. Paris: Imprimerie Nationale, 1885-93, 2 vols.

Bhattacharya, K. *Les religions brahmaniques dans l'ancien Cambodge* [Brahmin religion in old Cambodia]. Paris: EFEO, 1961.

Boisselier, Jean. *La statuaire khmère et son evolution* [Khmer statuary and its development]. Saigon: EFEO, 1955, 2 vols.

Boisselier, Jean. *Le Cambodge.* Paris: Bocard, 1966.

Brand, Michael. *The Age of Angkor.* Canberra: Australian National Gallery, 1992.

Bongert, Yvonne. "Note sur l'escalvage en droit khmer ancien." *Etudes d'histoire du droit privé offertes à Pierre Petot.* Paris: Librairie Générale de Droit et de Jurisprudence, Montchrestien, Jurisprudence, 1959, p. 7-26.

Briggs, Lawrence P. *The Ancient Khmer Empire.* Philadelphia: American Philosophical Society, 1951; Bangkok: White Lotus 1999.

Briggs, Lawrence P. "Siamese attacks on Angkor before 1430." *Far Eastern Quarterly* Vol. 8/1 (1948), p. 3-33.

Chakravarti, Adhir. *Royal Succession in Ancient Cambodia.* Calcutta: Asiatic Society, 1982.

Chakravarti, Adhir. *The Sdok Kak Thom Inscription.* Calcutta: Sanskrit College, 1978.

Chou Ta Kuan. *The customs of Cambodia.* Bangkok: Social Science Association Press 1987; Bangkok: The Siam Society 1993.

Coedès, Georges. *Angkor: An introduction.* New York: Oxford University Press, 1962.

Coedès, Georges. *Articles sur le pays Khmer* [Articles on the land of the Khmer]. Paris: EFEO, 1988-92, 2 vols.

Coedès, Georges. *The Indianized States of Southeast Asia.* Honolulu: East-West Center, 1968.

Coedès, Georges (ed). *Inscriptions du Cambodge* [Inscriptions from Cambodia]. Paris & Hanoi: L'École Française d'Extrême-Orient, 1937-66, 8 vols.

Coedès, Georges, and Dupont, P. "L'inscription du Sdok Kak Thom" [The Sdok Kak Thom inscription]. *Bulletin d'École Française d'Extrême-Orient* Vol. 43 (1942-43), p. 57-134.

Cohen, Joan Lebold. *Angkor: Monuments of the God Kings*. London: Thames & Hudson, 1975.

Condominas, Georges (ed). *Disciplines croisées: Hommage à Bernard Philippe Groslier* [Interdisciplinary essays in honour of B.P. Groslier]. Paris: Editions de l'École des hautes etudes en sciences sociales, 1992.

Dagens, Bruno. *Angkor: La forêt de pierre* [Angkor: Forest of stone]. Paris: Gallimard, 1989.

Das, R. *Art traditions in Cambodia*. Calcutta: Mukhopadhay, 1974.

Dumarcay, Jacques, and Pascal Royere. *Cambodian Architecture: Eighth to Thirteenth Century*. Leiden: Brill Academic, 2001.

Felten, Wolfgang, and M. Lerner. *Thai and Cambodian Sculpture from the 6th to the 14th Century*. London: P Wilson, 1994.

Finot, Louis, et al. *Le temple d'Angkor Wat*. Paris: EFEO, 1927-32, 7 vols.

Fournereau, L. *Les ruines d'Angkor* [The ruins of Angkor]. Paris: Leroux, 1890.

Freeman, Michael, and Roger Warner. *Angkor: The Hidden Glories*. Boston: Houghton, Mifflin Co., 1990.

Ginsberg, Allen. *Angkor Wat*. London: Fulcrum Press, 1968.

Giteau, Madeleine. *Khmer Sculpture and the Angkor Civilization*. London: Thames & Hudson, 1965.

Groslier, Bernard-Philippe. "Our knowledge of Khmer civilization: A reappraisal." *Journal of the Siam Society* Vol. 53 (1960), p. 1-28.

Groslier, Bernard-Philippe. *Angkor: Art and Civilization*. New York: Praeger, 1966.

Groslier, Bernard-Philippe, and Dumarcay, J. *Le Bayon*. Paris: EFEO, 1973, 2 vols.

Groslier, Georges. *A l'ombre d'Angkor* [In the shadow of Angkor]. Paris: Challamel, 1916.

Groslier, Georges. *Recherches sur les Cambodgiens* [Research on Cambodians]. Paris: Challamel, 1921.

Hall, Kenneth R. "Khmer Commercial Development and Foreign Contacts under Suryavarman I." *Journal of Economic and Social History of the Orient* Vol. 18/3 (Oct 1975), p. 318-36.

Higham, Charles. *The Archaeology of Mainland Southeast Asia*. Cambridge: Cambridge University Press, 1989.

Higham, Charles. *The Civilsation of Angkor*. London: Weidenfeld & Nicolson, 2001.

Jacob, Judith. "Pre-Angkor Cambodia: Evidence from the Inscriptions Concerning the Common People and Their Environment." In R.B. Smith and W. Watson (eds.). *Early Southeast Asia*. Oxford: Oxford University Press, 1979, p. 406-26.

Jacob, Judith. "The Ecology of Angkor: Evidence from the Khmer Inscriptions". In P.A. Stott (ed.). *Nature and Man in Southeast Asia.* London: School of Oriental and African Studies, 1979.

Jacques, Claude. "Le pays Khmer avant Angkor" [The land of the Khmer before Angkor]. *Journal des savants* (Jan-Sept 1986), p. 59-83.

Jacques, Claude. "Sources on Economic Activities in Khmer and Cham Lands." In David G. Marr and A.C. Milner (eds). *Southeast Asia in the Ninth to Fourteenth centuries.* Singapore: ISEAS, 1986, p. 327-34.

Jacques, Claude. *Angkor.* Cologne: Könemann, 1990.

Jacques, Claude. *Angkor: Cities and Temples.* London: Thames & Hudson, 2000.

Jacques, Claude, and Michael Freeman. *Ancient Angkor.* London: Thames & Hudson, 1999.

Jelen, Janos, and G. Hegyl. *Angkor and the Khmers: Brutality and Grace.* Budapest: Hegyi & Partners, 1990.

Jenner, Philip. *A Chrestomathy of Pre-Angkorean Inscriptions.* Honolulu: University of Hawaii Press, 1980, 3 vols.

Jenner, Philip. *A Chronological Inventory of the Inscriptions of Cambodia.* Honolulu: University of Hawaii Center for Asian & Pacific Studies, 1980.

Jessup, Helen, and Thierry Zephir. *Sculpture of Angkor and Ancient Cambodia: Millennium of Glory.* Washington D.C.: National Gallery of Art, 1997.

Kirsch, Thomas A. "Kinship, genealogical claims and social integration in ancient Khmer society: an interpretation," in C.D. Cowan and O.W. Wolters (eds.). *Southeast Asian History and Historiography: Essays Presented to D.G.E.Hall.* Ithaca, N.Y.: Cornell University Press, 1976, p. 190-201.

Krasa, Miloslav. *The Temples of Angkor.* London: A Wingate, 1963.

Kulke, Hermann. *The Devaraja Cult.* Ithaca, N.Y.: Cornell University Southeast Asia Program Data Paper 108, 1978.

Lajonquiere, Lunet de. *Inventaire descriptif des monuments du Cambodge* [Descriptive inventory of the monuments of Cambodia]. Paris: Maisonneuve, 1902-11, 2 vols.

Leclère, Adhémard. *Histoire du Cambodge* [History of Cambodia]. Paris: Librairie Guenther, 1914.

Lee, Sherman. *Ancient Cambodian sculpture.* New York: New York Graphic Society, 1969.

Ly Kim Long. *An Outline of Cambodian Architecture.* Varanashi, India: Prakashan, 1967.

Mabbett, Ian. "Devaraja." *Journal of Southeast Asian History* Vol. 10/2 (1969), p. 202-23.

Mabbett, Ian. "Kingship at Angkor." *Journal of the Siam Society* Vol. 66/2 (July 1978), p. 1-58.

Mabbett, Ian. "*Varnas* in Angkor and the Indian caste system." *Journal of Asian Studies* Vol. 36 (1977), p. 429-42.

Majumdar, R.C. *Inscriptions of Kambuja.* Calcutta, Asiatic Society, 1953.

Mannika, Eleanor. *Angkor Wat: Time, Space and Kingship.* Honolulu: University of Hawaii Press, 2000.

Moore, W.Robert. "Angkor, Jewel of the Jungle." *National Geographic* Vol. 117 (1960), p. 516-69.

Mus, Paul. "Angkor in the time of Jayavarman VII." *Indian Art and Letters* Vol. 11/2 (1937), p. 65-75.

Myrdal, Jan, and Gun Kessle. *Angkor: An essay in Art and Imperialism.* New York: Pantheon, 1970.

Nouth Narang. *Angkor silencieux* [Silent Angkor]. Paris: Sous le vent, 1988.

Parmentier, Henri et al. *A Guide to the Temple of Banteay Srei at Angkor.* Bangkok: White Lotus, 2000.

Pym, Christopher. *The Ancient Civilization of Angkor.* New York: Mentor Books, 1968.

Quaritch Wales, H. *Angkor and Rome: A Historical Comparison.* London: B.Quaritch, 1965.

Ricklefs, Merle C. "Land and law in the epigraphy of tenth century Cambodia." *Journal of Asian Studies* Vol. 26 (1967), p. 411-20.

Rooney, Dawn. *Angkor: An Introduction to the Temples.* Bangkok: Asia Books, 1994.

Roveda, Vittorio. *Khmer Mythology.* London: Weatherhill, 1997.

Sahai, Sachchidanand. "Territorial administration in Ancient Cambodia." *Southeast Asian Review* Vol. 2 (1977), p. 35-50.

Sharan, Mahesh K. *Political History of Ancient Cambodia, from 1st Century A.D. to 15th Century A.D.* New Delhi: Vishwavidya, 1986.

Sharan, Mahesh K. *Select Cambodian inscriptions.* Delhi: S.N. Publ, 1981.

Sharan, Mahesh K. *Studies in Sanscrit Inscriptions of Ancient Cambodia.* New Delhi: Abhinav, 1974.

Steirlin, H. *Angkor.* Fribourg: Office du Livre, 1970.

Stencel, R., and Eleanor Moron. "Astronomy and Cosmology at Angkor Wat." *Science* Vol. 293 (1978), p. 281-87.

Vickery, Michael. *Society, Economics and Politics in Pre-Angkor Cambodia.* Tokyo: Toyo Bunko, 1998.

Vickery, Michael. "Some remarks on early state formation in Cambodia." In David G. Marr and A.C. Milner (eds.). *Southeast Asia in the ninth to fourteenth centuries,* Singapore: ISEAS 1986, p. 95-115.

Vickery, Michael. "The reign of Suryavarman I and royal factionalism at Angkor." *Journal of Southeast Asian Studies* Vol. 16/2 (1985), p. 227-45.

White, Peter T. "Ancient glory in stone." *National Geographic* Vol. 161/5 (May 1982), p. 552-89.

Wolters, Oliver W. "Jayavarman II's military power: the territorial foundation of the Angkor Empire." *Journal of the Royal Asiatic Society* (1973), p. 21-30.

Wolters, Oliver W. "Northwestern Cambodia in the seventh century." *Bulletin of SOAS* Vol. 37 (1974), p. 355-84.

Yung, Peter. *The Khmers in Ancient Chinese Annals.* Oxford: University Press, 2000.

Early Modern History

Bassett, David K. "The trade of the English East India Company in Cambodia 1651-1656." *Journal of the Royal Asiatic Society* (1962), p. 35-62.

Bernard, Henri. "Angkor, la capitale religieuse du Cambodge et sa decouverte par les Japonais aux 16e-17e siècle" [Angkor, the religious capital of Cambodia, and its discovery by the Japanese in the 16th-17th centuries]. *Monumenta Nipponica* Vol. 3 (1940), p. 637-42.

Bouillevaux, C.E. *Voyage dans l'Indochine (1848-1856)* [Voyage in Indochina 1848-56]. Paris: Palme, 1858.

Boxer, C.R. "Spaniards in Cambodia." *History Today* Vol. 21 (April 1971), p. 280-87.

Briggs, Lawrence Palmer. *The Ancient Khmer Empire.* Philadelphia: American Philosophical Society, 1951.

Briggs, Lawrence Palmer. "Spanish intervention in Cambodia." *T'oung Pao* Vol. 39 (1949), p. 132-60.

Buch, W.J.M. "La compagnie des Indes et l'Indochine" [The Indies and Indochina Company]. *Bulletin de l'École Française d'Extrême-Orient* Vol. 36 (1936), p. 97-196.

Cabaton, A. *Brève et véridique relation des évènements du Cambodge par Gabriel Quiroga de San Antonio* [A brief and true account of Cambodia by Gabriel Quiroga de San Antonio]. Paris: E. Leroux, 1914.

Cabaton, A. *Les Hollandais au Cambodge au XVIIe siècle* [The Dutch in 17th-century Cambodia]. Paris: E. Leroux, 1914.

Chandler, David P. "An anti-Vietnamese rebellion in early nineteenth century Cambodia: Pre-colonial Imperialism and a pre-nationalist response." *Journal of Southeast Asian Studies* Vol. 6/1 (March 1975), p. 16-24.

Chandler, David P. *Facing the Cambodian Past.* Chiang Mai: Silkworm Books, 1996.

Ebihara, May. "Societal organization in sixteenth and seventeenth century Cambodia." *Journal of Southeast Asian Studies* Vol. 15/2 (Sept 1984), p. 280-95.

Giboulot, F. Laurent. "Marine Française et interventions exterieures, 1815-1870" [The French navy and overseas interventions, 1815-70]. *Revue Historique des Armées* No. 1 (1992), p. 108-14.

Giteau, Madeleine. *L'iconographie du Cambodge post-Angkorien* [Post-Angkorean iconography in Cambodia]. Paris: EFEO, 1975.

Groslier, Bernard-Philipe. *Angkor et le Cambodge au XVIe siècle après les sources portugaises et espagnoles* [Angkor and Cambodia in the 16th century from Portuguese and Spanish sources]. Paris: Presses Universitaires de France, 1958.

Hamilton, Alexander. *A New Voyage to the East Indies*, edited by Ian Morson, and Justin J. Corfield. Lampeter: Edwin Mellen, 2002.

Khin Sok. *Le Cambodge entre le Siam et le Vietnam de 1775 à 1868* [Cambodia between Siam and Vietnam, 1775-1868]. Paris: EFEO, 1991.

Khin Sok. "Les Chroniques Royales Khmères" [The Cambodian Royal Chronicles]. *Mon-Khmer Studies* Vol. 6 (1977), p. 191-215.

Khin Sok. *Chroniques Royales du Cambodge, de Bana Yat à la prise de Lanvaek (de 1417 à 1595)* [Cambodian Royal Chronicles from Bana Yat to the fall of Lovek, 1417 to 1595]. Paris: EFEO, 1988.

Khin Sok. "Quelques documents Khmers relatifs aux relations entre le Cambodge et l'Annam en 1843" [Some Khmer documents related to the relations between Cambodia and Annam in 1843]. *Bulletin de l'École Française d'Extrême-Orient* Vol. 74 (1985), p. 403-23.

Mak Phoeun. *Histoire du Cambodge: De la fin du XVIe siècle au debut du XVIIIe* [History of Cambodia from the end of the 16th century to the start of the 18th century]. Paris: EFEO 1995.

Mak Phoeun. *Chroniques Royales du Cambodge (de 1594 à 1677)* [Cambodian Royal Chronicles 1584-1677]. Paris: EFEO, 1981.

Mak Phoeun. *Chroniques Royales du Cambodge, des origines légendaires jusqu'à Paramaraja 1er* [Cambodian Royal Chronicales, from legendary origins up to Paramaraja I]. Paris: l'EFEO, 1984.

Mak Phoeun, and Po Dharma. "La première intervention militaire Vietnamienne au Cambodge en 1658-1659" [The first Vietnamese military intervention in Cambodia 1658-59]. *Bulletin de l'École Française d'Extrême-Orient* Vol. 73 (1984), p. 285-318.

Mak Phoeun, and Po Dharma. "La deuxième intervention militaire Vietnamienne au Cambodge (1673-1679)" [The second military intervention of the Vietnamese in Cambodia 1673-79]. *Bulletin de l'École Française d'Extrême-Orient* Vol. 77 (1988), p. 229-61.

Muller, H.P.N. *De Oost-Indische compagnie in Camboja en Laos* [The (Dutch) East India Company in Cambodia and Laos]. The Hague: Martinus Nijhoff, 1917.

Piat, Martine (transl.). "Chroniques Royales Khmer," *Bulletin de la Société des Etudes Indochinois* Vol. 49 (1974), p. 1-144 & 859-93.

Pou, Saveros. *Guirlande de chhbab*. Paris: CEDORECK, 1988, 2 vols.

Pym, Christopher (ed.). *Henry Mouhot's Diary*. Kuala Lumpur: Oxford University Press, 1966.

Souty, François J.L. "Des Nederlandais en Indochine au XVIIe siècle: Essai sur l'echange, les mesures de la valeur et les prix relatifs (1610-1680)" [The Dutch in Indochina in the 17th century: Exchange, measures of value, and relative prices, 1610-80]. *Revue Française d'Histoire d'Outre-Mer* Vol. 78/2 (1991), p. 177-206.

Sullivan, Michael. "The discovery of Angkor." *History Today* Vol. 10 (March 1960), p. 169-79.

Teixeira, Manuel. "Os Missionarios Portugueses em Camboja e no Siao" [Portuguese missionaries in Cambodia and Siam]. *Boletim Ecclesiastico da Diocese de Macao* Vol. 59 (1961) & Vol. 61 (1963).

Tomé Pires. *Suma Oriental...* London: Hakluyt Society, 1944.

Vickery, Michael T. *Cambodia after Angkor: The Chronicular Evidence for the 14th and 16th Centuries*. PhD Thesis, Yale University. Ann Arbor: University Microfilms, 1977, 2 vols.

Wolters, O.W. "The Khmer kings at Basan (1371-1373)." *Asia Major* Vol. 12/1 (1966), p. 44-89.

Woodside, Alexander. "Medieval Vietnam and Cambodia: A comparative comment." *Journal of Southeast Asian Studies* Vol. 15 (1984), p. 315-19.

Colonial Period, 1863-1953

Brodrick, Alan. *Little Vehicle: Cambodia and Laos*. London: Hutchinson, 1949.

Boun Chan Mul. *Kuk Noyobay* [Political Prison]. Phnom Penh: Apsara Press 1971.

Chandler, David P. "The assassination of *résident* Bardez (1925): A premonition of revolt in colonial Cambodia." *Journal of the Siam Society* Vol. 70/1-2 (1982), p. 35-49.

Chandler, David P. "The Kingdom of Kampuchea, March-October 1945: Japanese sponsored independence in Cambodia in World War II." *Journal of Southeast Asian Studies* Vol. 17/1 (March 1986), p. 80-93.

Collard, Paul. *Cambodge et les Cambodgiens: Metamorphose du royaume Khmer* [Cambodia and the Cambodians]. Paris: Société d'editions Geographiques, Maritimes et Coloniales, 1925.

d'Alzon, Claude Hesse. *La présence militaire Français en Indochine 1940-1945* [The French military presence in Indochina 1940-1945]. Vincennes: Publ du Service Historique de l'Armée de Terre, 1988.

Delaporte, Louis. *Voyage au Cambodge* [Voyage to Cambodia]. Paris: Ch. Delagrave, 1880.

Edwards, Penny. *Cambodge: The Cultivation of a Nation 1860-1945*. PhD Thesis, Monash University, 1999.

Engelbert, Thomas. "The enemy needed: The Cochin China issue and Cambodian factional struggles 1949-50." *South East Asia Research* Vol. 6/1 (1998).

Flood, Thadeus. "The 1940 Franco-Thai border dispute and Phibun Songkhram's commitment to Japan." *Journal of Southeast Asian History* Vol. 10/2 (Sept. 1969), p. 307-15.

Forest, Alain. *Le Cambodge et la colonisation Française: Histoire d'une colonisation sans heurts, 1897-1920* [Cambodia and French colonization: the history of colonization without friction 1897-1920]. Paris: L'Harmattan, 1980.

Franck, Harry A. *East of Siam: Ramblings in the Five Divisions of French Indo-China*. London: T. Fisher Unwin, 1939.

Garnier, Francis. *Voyage en Indochine* [Voyage in Indochina]. Paris: Hachette, 1885.

Hervey, Harry. *Travels in Indo-China*. London: Duckworth, 1927.

Hess, Jean. *L'affaire Yukhantor* [The Yukanthor affair]. Paris: Félix Julien, 1900.

King, D.O. "Travels in Siam and Cambodia." *Journal of the Royal Geographical Society* Vol. 30 (1860), p. 177-82.

Lamant, Pierre L. "L'affaire Duong Chakr" [The Duong Chakr affair]. *Revue Française d'Histoire d'Outre-Mer* Vol. 67/1-2 (1980), p. 123-50.

Lamant, Pierre. "Les partis politiques et les mouvements de resistance Khmer vus par les services de renseignements Français (1945-1952)" [Political parties and Khmer resistance movements as viewed by the French intelligence services]. *Guerres mondiales et conflits contemporains* Vol. 148 (1987), p. 79-96.

Lamant, Pierre. *L'affaire Yukhantor* [The Yukanthor affair]. Paris: Societe Française d'Histoire d'Outre-Mer, 1989.

Lamb, Alastair. "British Missions to Cochinchina 1778-1822." *Journal of the Malayan Branch of the Royal Asiatic Society* Vol. 44/3-4 (1961).

Lancaster, Donald. *The Emancipation of French Indo-China*. Oxford: Oxford University Press, 1961.

Langlois, Walter. *André Malraux: The Indochina Adventure*. London: Pall Mall Press, 1966.

Leclère, Adhémard. "Histoire de Kampot, et de la rébellion de cette province en 1885-1887" [History of Kampot and the rebellion in that province 1885-87]. *Revue Indochinoise* No. 60-61 (30 June & 15 July 1907), p. 828-41 & 933-52.

Lewis, Norman. *A dragon Apparent: Travels in Indo-China*. London: Jonathan Cape, 1951.

Loti, Pierre. *A Pilgrimage to Angkor*. Chiang Mai: Silkworm Books, 1996.

Manley, David. "The battle of Koh Chang: January 14th, 1941." *The Journal: The Society of Twentieth Century Wargamers* No. 28 (Autumn-Winter 1997).

Mouhot, Henri. *Travels in the Central Parts of Indo-China During the Years 1856, 1859 and 1860*. London: John Murray, 1864; *Travels in Siam, Cambodia and Laos 1858-1860*. Singapore: Oxford University Press 1992.

Moura, Jean. *La royaume du Cambodge* [The Kingdom of Cambodia]. Paris: Leroux, 1883, 2 vols.

Olivier, Robert. *Le Protectorat Français au Cambodge* [The French Protectorate of Cambodia]. PhD Thesis, Université de Paris 1969.

Osborne, Milton E. "King-making in Cambodia: From Sisowath to Sihanouk." *Journal of Southeast Asian Studies* Vol. 4 (1973), p. 169-85.

Osborne, Milton E. "Peasant politics in Cambodia: The 1916 Affair." *Modern Asian Studies* Vol. 12/2 (1978), p. 217-43.

Osborne, Milton E. *River Road to China*. London: Allen & Unwin 1975; Sydney: Allen & Unwin 1997.

Osborne, Milton E. *The French Presence in Cochinchina and Cambodia*. Ithaca, N.Y.: Cornell University Press, 1969.

Paloczi-Horvath, George. "Thailand's war with Vichy France." *History Today* Vol. 45/3 (March 1995), p. 32-39.

Preschez, Philippe. *Essai sur la démocratie au Cambodge*. Paris: Fondation Nationale des Sciences Politiques, 1961.

Reddi, V.M. *A History of the Cambodian Independence Movement*. Tirupati: Sri Venkateswara University, 1970.

Seton, Grace Thompson. *Poison Arrows*. London: Travel Book Club, 1938.

Sitwell, Osbert. *Escape with Me! An Oriental Sketch-Book*. London: Macmillan, 1949.

Taboulet, G. (ed.). *La geste française en Indochine* [French action in Indochina]. Paris: Adrien Maisonneuve, 1955, 2 vols.

Tauch Chhuong. *Battambang during the Time of the Lord Governor*. Translated by Hin Sithan, Carol Mortland, and Judy Ledgerwood. Honolulu: East-West Center, 1994.

Thompson, Virginia. *French Indo-China*. New York: Macmillan, 1937.

Thornton, Phillip T. *Albert Sarraut, a Metropolitan in the Colonies: Indochina 1911-1919*. PhD Thesis, University of Hawaii, 1980.
Tully, John. *Cambodia under the Tricolour: King Sisowath and the "Mission Civilisatrice" 1904-1927*. Clayton, Vic.: Monash University, 1995.

Independent Cambodia 1954-1975

Anson, Robert S. *War News: A Young Reporter in Indochina*. New York: Simon & Schuster, 1989.
Armstrong, John P. *Sihanouk Speaks*. New York: Walker, 1964.
Bowden, Tim. *One Crowded Hour: Neil Davis, Combat Cameraman 1934-1985*. Sydney: Collins, 1987.
Burchett, Wilfred. *Mekong Upstream: A Visit to Laos and Cambodia*. Hanoi: Red River Publishing House, 1957.
Burchett, Wilfred. *Second Indochina War: Cambodia and Laos Today*. London: Lorrimer Publishing, 1970.
Caldwell, Malcolm, and Lek Hor Tan. *Cambodia in the Southeast Asia War*. New York: Monthly Review Press, 1975.
Carr, Earl A. *The Origins and the Precipitating Factors of the Khmer Revolution, 1945-1975*. PhD Thesis, Southern Illinois University, 1977; Ann Arbor: University Microfilms, 1978.
Chandler, David P., Ben Kiernan, and Lim Muy Hong. *The Early Phases of Liberation in Northwestern Cambodia: Conversations with Peang Sophi*. Clayton, Vic.: Monash University Centre of Southeast Asian Studies Working Paper, 1976.
Conboy, Kenneth, and Kenneth Bowra. *The War in Cambodia 1970-75*. London: Osprey, 1989.
Corfield, Justin J. *Khmers Stand Up! A History of the Cambodian Government 1970-1975*. Clayton, Vic.: Monash University, 1994.
Davidson, Jim. *Indo-China: Signposts in the Storm*. Longman: Singapore, 1979.
Deac, Wilfred P., and Summers, Harry. *Road to the Killing Fields: The Cambodian War of 1970-1975*. College Station: Texas A&M University Press, 1997.
Dommen, Arthur J. *The Indochinese Experience of the French and the Americans: Nationalism and Communism in Cambodia, Laos and Vietnam*. Bloomington: Indiana University Press, 2001.
Downie, Sue. *Down Highway One: Journeys through Vietnam and Cambodia*. St. Leonards, NSW: Allen & Unwin, 1993.
Fillieux, Claude. *Merveilleux Cambdodge* [Marvellous Cambodia]. Paris: Société continentale d'editions modernes illustrees, 1962.

Frieson, Kate. *The Impact of Revolution on Cambodian Peasants, 1970-1975.* PhD Thesis, Monash University. Ann Arbor: University Microfilms, 1992.

Gauthier, Victor. "Pioneer city: Kirirom," *Kambuja* No. 10 (15 Jan 1966), p. 48-64.

Girling, J.L.S. "Crisis and conflict in Cambodia," *Orbis* Vol. 14/2 (Summer 1970), p. 349-65.

Grant, Jonathan S. et al. (eds.) *Cambodia: The Widening War in Indochina.* New York: Washington Square Press, 1971.

Hanna, John Clark. "Mystery of the SS *Columbia Eagle* hijacking," *Vietnam* (Feb 2001), p. 44-48 & 64.

Heckman, Charles W. *The Phnom Penh Airlift: Confessions of a Pig Pilot in the early 1970s.* Jefferson, N.C.: McFarland 1990.

Isaacs, Arnold R. *Without Honor: Defeat in Vietnam and Cambodia.* Baltimore, Maryland: Johns Hopkins University Press 1983.

Kiernan, Ben. *The Samlaut Rebellion and Its Aftermath 1967-1970.* Clayton, Vic.: Monash University, 1975, 2 vols.

Kirk, Donald. *Wider War: The struggle for Cambodia, Thailand and Laos.* New York, Praeger, 1971.

Kosut, Hal. *Cambodia and the Vietnam War.* New York: Facts on File, 1971.

Lacouture, Jean (with Norodom Sihanouk). *Indochine vue de Pékin.* Paris: Seuil, 1971.

Leifer, Michael. "Peace and war in Cambodia." *Southeast Asia* Vol. 1 (1971), p. 59-73.

Littaye-Suon, Edouard. "Les causes profondes de la chute de la monarchie au Cambodge" [The actual causes of the fall of the Cambodian monarchy]. *Le Republicain* (18 March 1973), p. 1 & A-K.

Mack, Andrew. "America's role in the destruction of Kampuchea." *Politics* [Australia] Vol. 16/1 (1981), p. 135-45.

Meyer, Charles. *Derrière le sourire khmer* [Behind the Khmer smile]. Paris: Plon, 1971.

Neveu, Roland. *Cambodia: The Years of Turmoil 1973-1999, Witness to War, Misery and Hope.* Bangkok: Asia Horizon Books, 2000.

Norodom Sihanouk. *La monarchie cambodgienne et la croisade royale pour l'independence* [The Cambodian monarchy and the Royal Crusade for Independence]. Phnom Penh: Reasmey, 1961.

Norodom Sihanouk. *Principaux discours, messages, déclarations et allocutions de son altesse royale le Prince Norodom Sihanouk en 1962* [The principal speeches, messages, statements and pronouncements of H.R.H. Prince Norodom Sihanouk in 1962]. Phnom Penh: Ministère de l'information, 1963.

Norodom Sihanouk. *Recueil d'editoriaux du Prince Norodom Sihanouk parus dans la revue Kambuja du no. 22 – 33 de l'année 1967* [Editorials by Prince Norodom Sihanouk from the magazine *Kambuja*, No. 22-33 of 1967]. Phnom Penh: Ministère de l'information, 1969.

Norodom Sihanouk, and Wilfred Burchett. *My War with the CIA.* Harmondsworth: Penguin Books, 1971. Reprinted with revisions 1974.

Nuon Khoeun. "A look at the local press." *New Cambodge* No. 1 (May 1970), p. 53-54.

Osborne, Milton. *Before Kampuchea: Preludes to Tragedy.* London: Allen & Unwin, 1979.

Osborne, Milton. *Sihanouk: Prince of Light, Prince of Darkness.* Honolulu, University of Hawaii Press, 1994.

Partridge, Larry. *Flying tigers over Cambodia: An American Pilot's Memoirs of the 1975 Phnom Penh airlift.* Jefferson, N.C.: McFarland 2001.

Pike, Douglas. "Cambodia's War." *Southeast Asian Perspectives* (March 1971), p. 1-48.

Pomonti, J.-C., and Serge Thion. *La crise cambodgienne: Des courtisans aux partisans* [The Cambodian crisis: From sycophants to partisans]. Paris: Gallimard 1971.

Poole, Peter A. *Cambodia's Quest for Survival.* New York: American Asian Educational Exchange, 1969.

Pratt, Colin. *Killing the Khmer.* Surrey Hills North, Vic.: Sea Tiger Marine, 2000.

Preschez, Philippe. *Essai sur la démocratie au Cambodge* [Essay on democracy in Cambodia]. Paris: C.E.R.I. 1961.

Pym, Christopher. *Mistapim in Cambodia.* London: Hodder & Stoughton, 1959.

Pym, Christopher. *The Road to Angkor.* London: Robert Hale, 1959.

Quinn, Kenneth. "Political change in wartime: The Khmer Krahom revolution in southern Cambodia." *Naval War College Review* Vol. 28 (1976), p. 3-31.

Ros Chantrabot. *Le République Khmère et l'Asie du Sud-Est* [The Khmer Republic in Southeast Asia]. Thesis for the École des Hautes Etudes en Sciences Sociales, Paris 1976. Published as *La République Khmère 1970-1975.* Paris: l'Harmattan, 1993.

Sak Sutsakhan. *The Khmer Republic at War and the Final Collapse.* Washington D.C.: U.S. Army Center of Military History, 1980.

Scott, Peter. *Lost crusade: America's Secret Cambodian Mercenaries.* Annapolis, Md: Naval Institute Press 1998.

Shaw, John Martin. *The United States Army in the 1970 Cambodian Incursion (Military).* PhD Thesis, University of Kentucky 1995.

Shawcross, William. *Sideshow: Nixon, Kissinger and the Destruction of Cambodia*. New York: Simon & Schuster, 1979.

Simon, Sheldon. *War and Politics in Cambodia: A Communications Analysis*. Durham, N.C.: Duke University Press, 1974.

Swain, Jon. *River of Time*. London: Heinemann, 1995.

Tully, John A. *"Certain and inevitable misfortune": War and Politics in Lon Nol's Cambodia, March 1970 - December 1971*, MA Thesis, Monash University, Australia, 1990.

von Marschall, Walther Baron. *The War in Cambodia: Its Causes and Military Development and the Political History of the Khmer Republic 1970-1975*, Royal College of Defence Studies 1975 Course Thesis.

Wood, Richard. *Call Sign Rustic: The Secret Air War over Cambodia*. Washington D.C.: Smithsonian Institution Press, 2002.

Democratic Kampuchea 1975-1979

Ablin, David, and Marlowe Hood (eds.). *The Cambodian Agony*. Armonk, N.Y.: M.E. Sharpe, 1987.

Barnett, Anthony; Chanthou Boua and Ben Kiernan. "Bureaucracy of death: Documents from inside Pol Pot's torture machine." *New Statesman* (1 June 1980), p. 669-76.

Barron, John, and Anthony Paul. *Murder in a Gentle Land: The Untold Story of Communist Genocide in Cambodia*. New York: Crowell, 1977.

Becker, Elizabeth. *When the War was Over: The Voices of Cambodia's Revolution and Its People*. New York, Simon & Schuster, 1986.

Burgler, R.A. *The Eye of the Pineapple: Revolutionary Intellectuals and Terror in Democratic Kampuchea*. Saarbrucken: Breitenbach 1990.

Caldwell, Malcolm. *Malcolm Caldwell's Southeast Asia*. Edited by Bob Hering and Ernst Utrecht. Townsville, Qld.: James Cook University, 1979.

Carney, Timothy. *Communist Party Power in Cambodia: Documents and Discussion*. Ithaca, N.Y.: Cornell University Press, 1977.

Chandler, David P., and Ben Kiernan (eds.). *Revolution and its aftermath in Kampuchea: Eight Essays*. New Haven, Conn.: Yale University Press, 1983.

Chandler, David P.; Ben Kiernan and Chanthou Boua (eds.). *Pol Pot Plans for the Future: Confidential Leadership Documents from Democratic Kampuchea, 1976-1977*. New Haven, Conn.: Yale University Press, 1988.

Chomsky, Noam, and Edward Hermann. *After the Cataclysm*. London: South End Press, 1979.

Debre, François. *Cambodge: La revolution dans le forêt* [Cambodia: the revolution in the forest]. Paris: Flammarion, 1976.

Democratic Kampuchea, Ministry of Foreign Affairs. *Black paper: facts and evidences of the acts of aggression and annexation of Vietnam against Kampuchea*. Phnom Penh: Department of Press & Information, 1978.

Etcheson, Craig, *The Rise and Demise of Democratic Kampuchea*. Boulder, Colo.: Westview Press, 1984.

Fein, Helen. "Revolutionary and anti-revolutionary genocides: A comparison of state murders in Democratic Kampuchea, 1975 to 1979, and in Indonesia, 1965 to 1966." *Comparative Studies in Society and History* Vol. 35/4 (1993), p. 796-823.

Hamel, Bernard. *De sang et de larmes* [Of blood and tears]. Paris: Albin Michel, 1977.

Hamel, Bernard (ed.). *Temoignages sur le genocide au Cambodge* [Accounts of the genocide in Cambodia]. Paris: S.P.L., 1976.

Hildebrand, George, and Gareth Porter. *Cambodia: Starvation and Revolution*. New York: Monthly Review Press, 1976.

Honda Katuiti. *Journey to Cambodia*. Tokyo: n.p. 1981.

Jackson, Karl D. (ed.). *Cambodia 1975-1978: Rendezvous with Death*. Princeton, N.J.: Princeton University Press, 1989.

Kiernan, Ben. *Cambodia: The Eastern Zone Massacres*. New York: Columbia University Press, 1988.

Kiernan, Ben. *The Pol Pot Regime: Politics, Racism and Genocide*. New Haven, Conn.: Yale University Press, 1996.

Kiljunen, Kimmo (ed.). *Kampuchea: Decade of Genocide — Report of a Finnish Inquiry Commission*. London: Zed Books, 1984.

Lacouture, Jean. *Survive le peuple cambodgien* [May the Cambodian people survive]. Paris: Seuil, 1978.

Locard, Henri. *Les slogans d'Angkar* [The slogans of Angkar]. Phnom Penh: University of Phnom Penh: 1994.

Locard, Henri. *Prisonnier de l'Angkar* [Prisoner of Angkar]. Paris: Fayard, 1993.

Martin, Marie-Alexandrine. "L'industrie dans le Kampuchea Democratique" [Industry in Democratic Kampuchea]. *Etudes rurales* (Jan-Sept 1983), p. 77-110.

Max, Pierre. *Le Cambodge de Silence* [The Cambodia of silence]. Paris: n.p, 1976.

McCormack, Gavan. "The Kampuchean Revolution 1975-1978: The problem of knowing the truth." *Journal of Contemporary Asia* Vol. 1/2 (1981), p. 75-118.

Morris, Stephen J. *Why Vietnam invaded Cambodia: Political Culture and the Causes of the War*. Stanford: Stanford University Press 1999.

Newman, Robert S. *Brahmin and Mandarin: A Comparison of the Cambodian and Vietnamese Revolutions.* Clayton, Vic.: Monash University Centre of Southeast Asian Studies, 1978.

Norodom Sihanouk. *Prisonnier des khmers rouges* [Prisoner of the Khmer Rouge]. Paris: Hachette, 1986.

Norodom Sihanouk. *War and Hope: The Case for Cambodia.* New York: Pantheon Books, 1980.

Picq, Laurence. "Le Cambodge sous les Khmers Rouges" [Cambodia under the Red Khmer]. *Mondes et Cultures* Vol. 45/3 (1985), p. 463-71.

Ponchaud, François. *Cambodia: Year Zero.* New York: Holt, Rinehart & Winston, 1977.

Ross, Robert. *The Indo-China Tangle 1975-1979.* New York: Columbia University Press, 1988.

Rowan, Roy. *The Four Days of Mayaguez.* New York: W.W. Norton & Company, 1975.

Sliwinski, Marek. *La génocide khmer rouge: Une analyse démographique* [The Khmer Rouge genocide: A demographic analysis]. Paris: L'Harmattan, 1995.

Smith, Frank, *Interpretive accounts of the Khmer Rouge Years: Personal experience in Cambodian Peasant World View.* Madison: University of Wisconsin Press, 1989.

Steinbach, J. *Phnom Penh Liberée* [Phnom Penh liberated]. Paris: Editions sociales, 1976.

Thion, Serge, and Kiernan, Ben. *Khmers rouges!* Paris: Albin Michel, 1981.

Um, Khatarya. *Brotherhood of the Pure: Nationalism and Communism in Cambodia.* PhD Thesis, University of California. Ann Arbor: University Microfilms, 1991.

Vickery, Michael. *Cambodia, 1975-1982.* London: South End Press, 1984.

Vickery, Michael. "How many died in Pol Pot's Kampuchea?" *Bulletin of Concerned Asian Scholars* Vol. 20 (1988), p. 70-73.

Welaratna, Usha (ed). *Beyond the Killing Fields: Voices of Nine Cambodian Survivors in America.* Stanford: Stanford University Press, 1993.

Willmott, W.E. "Analytical errors of the Cambodian Communist Party." *Pacific Affairs* Vol. 54/2 (Summer 1981), p. 209-27.

Y Phandara. *Retour a Phnom Penh: Le Cambodge du génocide à la colonisation* [Return to Phnom Penh: Cambodia from genocide to colonisation]. Paris: Editions AM Metaille, 1982.

Political Developments since 1979

Amnesty International. *Kampuchea Political Imprisonment and Torture* London: Amnesty International, 1987.

Ashley, David. *Pol Pot, Peasants and Peace: Continuity and Change in Khmer Rouge Political Thinking 1985-1991.* Bangkok: Chulalongkorn University, 1991.

Bartu, Peter. *The Fifth Factor: The United Nations Interest in Cambodia 1991-1993.* PhD Thesis, Monash University 1998.

Bekaert, Jacques. *Kampuchea Diary, 1983-1986.* Bangkok: D.D. Books, 1987.

Brown, Frederick Z. *Rebuilding Cambodia,* Washington, D.C.: Johns Hopkins University, 1992.

Burchett, Wilfred. *The China-Cambodia-Vietnam Triangle,* Chicago: Vanguard Press, 1981.

Carney, Timothy. "Heng Samrin's armed forces and the military balance in Cambodia." *International Journal of Politics* Vol. 16/3 (1986), p. 150-85.

Carney, Timothy. "Kampuchea in 1981: Fragile stalemate." *Asian Survey* Vol. 22/1 (1982), p. 78-87.

Carney, Timothy. "Kampuchea in 1982: Political and military escalation." *Asian Survey* Vol. 23/1 (1983), p. 73-83.

Chanda, Nayan. "Cambodia in 1986: Beginning to tire." *Asian Survey* Vol. 27/1 (1987), p. 115-24.

Chanda, Nayan. "Cambodia in 1987: Sihanouk on center stage." *Asian Survey* Vol. 28/1 (1988), p. 105-15.

Chanda, Nayan. "Civil War in Cambodia?" *Foreign Policy* Vol. 76 (Fall 1989), p. 26-43.

Chanda, Nayan. *Brother Enemy: The War after the War.* New York: Harcourt Brace, 1986.

Corrèze, Françoise. *Choses vues au Cambodge* [Things seen in Cambodia]. Paris: Editeurs français reunies, 1980.

DeNike, Howard J.; John Quigley and Kenneth J. Robinson (eds.). *Genocide in Cambodia: Documents from the Trial of Pol Pot and Ieng Sary.* Philadelphia: University of Pennsylvania Press, 2000.

Elliott, David (ed.). *The Third Indo-China Conflict,* Boulder, Colo.: Westview Press, 1981.

Evans, Grant, and Kelvin Rowley. *Red Brotherhood at War: Vietnam, Cambodia and Laos since 1975.* London: Verso, 1984; rev. ed. 1990.

Frings, Viviane. *Allied and equal: The Kampuchean People's Revolutionary Party's Historiography and its Relations with Vietnam (1979-1991).* Clayton, Vic.: Monash University, 1994.

Frings, Viviane. *The failure of Agricultural Collectivization in the Peoples' Republic of Kampuchea.* Clayton, Vic.: Monash University, 1993.

Gilboa, Amit. *Off the Rails in Phnom Penh.* Bangkok: Asia Books, 1998.

Gunn, Geoffrey C., and Jefferson Lee. *Cambodia Watching Down Under.* Bangkok: Institute of Asian Studies, Chulalongkorn University, 1991.

Haas, Michael. *Cambodia, Pol Pot, and the United States: The Faustian Pact.* New York: Praeger, 1991.

Haas, Michael. *Genocide by Proxy: Cambodian Pawn on a Superpower Chessboard.* New York: Praeger, 1991.

Hamel, Bernard. *Sihanouk et le drame Cambodgien* [Sihanouk and the Cambodian "problem"]. Paris: l'Harmattan, 1992.

Heder, Stephen. *Kampuchean occupation and resistance.* Bangkok: Chulalongkorn University, 1980.

Heder, Stephen. "Cambodia's armed struggle: The origins of an independent revolution." *Bulletin of Concerned Asian Scholars* Vol. 10 (1978), p. 2-23.

Heder, Steve, and Judy Ledgerwood (eds.). *Propaganda, Politics and Violence in Cambodia: Democratic Transition under United Nations Peacekeeping.* Armonk, N.Y.: M.E. Sharpe, 1996.

Heininger, Janet E. *Peacekeeping in Transition: The United Nations in Cambodia.* New York: Twentieth Century Fund Press, 1994.

Hervouet, Gérard. "The Cambodian Conflict: The Difficulties of Intervention and Compromise." *International Journal* Vol. 45/2 (1990), p. 258-91.

Hughes, Caroline. "Khmer land, Khmer soul: Sam Rainsy, populaism and the problem of seeing Cambodia." *South East Asia Research* Vol. 9/1 (2001), p. 45-71.

Jennar, Raoul. *Chroniques Cambodgiennes 1990-1994* [Cambodian Chronicles 1990-1994]. Paris: L'Harmattan, 1995.

Kiernan, Ben (ed.). *Genocide and democracy in Cambodia: The Khmer Rouge, the United Nations and the International Community.* New Haven, Conn.: Yale University Press, 1993.

Kiernan, Ben (ed.). *Democracy and Genocide in Cambodia.* New Haven, Conn.: Yale University Press, 1994.

Klintworth, Gary. *Vietnam's intervention in Cambodia in International Law.* Canberra: Australian Government Publishing Service, 1989.

Lechervy, Christian, and Richard Petris. *Les Cambodgiens face a eux-memes?* [Cambodians face themselves?]. Geneva: Fondation pour le progres de l'homme, 1993.

Livingston, Carol. *Gecko Tails: A Journey through Cambodia.* London: Weidenfeld & Nicolson, 1996.

Luccioli, Esmeralda. *Le mur de bambou: le Cambodge après Pol Pot* [The bamboo wall: Cambodia after Pol Pot]. Paris: Editions Regine Deforges 1988.

Martin, Marie-Alexandrine. *Vietnamised Cambodia: A Silent Ethnocide.* Singapore: Indochina Report, 1986.

Martin, Marie-Alexandrine. "Les progrès de la Vietnamisation du Cambodge" [The continuing vietnamization of Cambodia]. *Etudes* Vol. 364/2 (1986), p. 149-62.

Mason, Linda, and Roger Brown. *Rice, Rivalry and Politics: Managing Cambodian Relief.* Notre Dame, Ind.: Notre Dame University Press, 1983.

Mysliwiec, Eva. *Punishing the Poor: The International Isolation of Cambodia.* Oxford: OXFAM, 1988.

Peou, Sorpong. *Conflict Neutralization in the Cambodia War: From Battlefield to Ballot-Box.* Kuala Lumpur: Oxford University Press, 1997.

Peou, Sorpong. *Intervention and Change in Cambodia: Towards Democracy?.* St Martin's Press: New York, 2000.

Pilger, John, and Barnett, Anthony. *Aftermath: The struggle of Cambodia and Vietnam.* London: New Statesman Books, 1982.

Prior, Marie. *Shooting at the Moon: Cambodian Peaceworkers Tell Their Stories.* Canberra: M.P.A. Publishing, 1994.

Raszelenberg, Patrick, and Peter Schier. *The Cambodia Conflict: Search for a Settlement, 1979-1991: An Analytical Chronology.* Hamburg, Instituts fur Asienkunde, 1994.

Regaud, Nicolas. *Le Cambodge dans la tourmente: Le troisième conflit indochinois* [Tormented Cambodia: The third Indochina war]. Paris: L'Harmattan, 1992.

Roberts, David. *Political transition in Cambodia 1991-99: Power, Elitism and Democracy.* Richmond, U.K.: Curzon Press, 2000.

Selochan, Viberto, and Carlyle A. Thayer (eds). *Bringing Democracy to Cambodia.* Canberra: Australian Defence Studies Centre, 1996.

Shaplen, Robert. *Bitter Victory.* New York: Harper & Row, 1986.

Shawcross, William. *The Quality of Mercy: Cambodia, Holocaust and Modern Conscience.* London: Simon & Schuster 1985.

Smith, Hugh (ed.). *International Peace Keeping: Building on the Cambodian Experience.* Canberra: Australian Defense Studies Centre, 1994.

Vickery, Michael. "The Cambodian People's Party: Where does it come from, where is it going." *Southeast Asian Affairs 1994.* Singapore: I.S.E.A.S., 1994.

Vickery, Michael. *Kampuchea: Politics, Economics and Society.* London: Lynn Reinner 1986.

Vickery, Michael. "Notes on the political economy of the People's Republic of Kampuchea." *Journal of Contemporary Asia* Vol. 20 (1990), p. 435-64.

Zhou Mei. *Radio UNTAC of Cambodia: Winning Ears, Hearts and Minds.* Bangkok: White Lotus 1994.

Biographies and Autobiographies

Ashe, Var Hong. *From Phnom Penh to Paradise: Escape from Cambodia.* London: Hodder & Stoughton 1988.

Boun Sokha. *La massue d'Angkar* [The Angkar catastrophe]. Paris: Marcel Julien, 1979.

Chandler, David P. *Brother Number One: A Political Biography of Pol Pot.* Boulder, Col: Westview Press, 1992.

Criddle, Joan D., and Teeda Butt Mam. *To Destroy You is No Loss: The Odyssey of a Cambodian Family.* New York: Atlantic Monthly Press, 1987.

Eng Hoa. *Le vent sauvage* [The bitter wind]. Paris: Ramsay, 1984.

Hin Chamrithy. *When the Broken Glass Floats: Growing Up under the Khmer Rouge.* New York: W.W. Norton, 2000.

Ken Khun. *De la dictature des Khmer Rouges à l'occupation Vietnamienns, Cambodge 1975-1979* [From Red Khmer dictatorship to Vietnamese occupation]. Paris: L'Harmattan, 1994.

Kim Retsy; Jean-Pierre Hiegel and Colette Landrac. *La prison sans murs* [The Prison without walls]. Paris: Fayard, 1992.

May Someth, with James Fenton. *Cambodia Witness.* London: Faber, 1986.

Mehta, Harish C., and Julie B. Mehta. *Hun Sen: Strongman of Cambodia.* Singapore: Graham Brash, 1999.

Moeung Sonn, and Locard, Henri. *Prisonnier de l'Angkar* [Prisoner of Angkar]. Paris: Fayard, 1993.

Ngor, Haing, with Roger Warner. *Surviving the Killing Fields: The Cambodian Odyssey of Haing S. Ngor.* London: Chatto & Windus, 1987.

Norodom Sihanouk. *Prisonnier des Khmers Rouges* [Prisoner of the Khmer Rouge]. Paris: Hachette, 1986.

Picq, Laurence. *Beyond the Horizon.* New York: Hill and Wang, 1989. Originally published in French: *Au delà du ciel: Cinq ans chez les Khmers Rouges.* Paris: Bernard Barrault, 1984.

Pin Yathay. *Stay Alive My Son.* London: Bloomsbury, 1987. This is an abridged, revised version of *L'utopie meurtrière* [Deadly utopia]. Paris: Robert Laffont, 1980. Reissued, Brussels: Complexe, 1989.

Schanberg, Sydney. *The Death and Life of Dith Pran.* New York: Penguin, 1980.

Sheehy, Gail. *Spirit of Survival.* New York: William Morrow, 1986.

Sor Sisavang. *L'enfant de la rizière rouge* [The child of red ricefields]. Paris Fayard, 1990.

Stuart-Fox, Martin, and Ung Bunheang. *The Murderous Revolution: Life and Death in Pol Pot's Kampuchea.* Chippendale, N.S.W.: Alternative Publishing Company, 1985.

Szymusiak, Molyda. *The Stones Cry Out: A Cambodian Childhood.* New York: Hill and Wang, 1986.

Ung, Loung. *First They Killed My Father.* Sydney: HarperCollins, 2000.

Vandy Kaonn. *Le Cambodge 1940-1991: La politique sans les Cambodgiens* [Cambodia 1940-1991: Politics without Cambodians]. Paris: L'Harmattan, 1993.

Yu Tan Kim Pho, and Ida Simon-Barouch. *Le Cambodge des Khmer Rouges: Chronique de la vie quotidienne* [Red Khmer Cambodia: The course of everyday life]. Paris: L'Harmattan, 1990.

POLITICAL

Constitution and Law

Abrams, Floyd, and Diane Orentlicher. *Kampuchea after the Worst: A Report on Current Violations of Human Rights.* New York: Lawyers' Commitee for Human Rights, 1985.

Bongert, Yvonne. "'La monarchie Cambodgienne," *Recueils de la Société Jean Bodin pour l'histoire comparative des institutions* Vol. XX, 1ère partie. Bruxelles: Librairie Encyclopedique, 1970, p. 677-781.

Center for Advanced Study, *Democracy in Cambodia, A Survey of the Cambodian Electorate.* Phnom Penh: The Asia Foundation, 2001.

Chandler, David P. "The Constitution of Democratic Kampuchea (Cambodia): the semantics of revolutionary change." *Pacific Affairs* Vol. 49/3 (Fall 1976), p. 506-15.

Clairon, Marcel. *Notions essentielles du droit civil Khmer* [Basics of Khmer civil law]. Phnom Penh: EKLIP, 1963.

Collins, William A., et al. *Final Report: Baseline Survey of Voter Knowledge and Awareness.* Phnom Penh: Center for Advanced Study, 1998.

Council of Jurists. www.bigpond.com.kh/council of jurists.

Gour, C.-G. *Institutions constitutionelles et politiques du Cambodge* [Constitutional and political institutions in Cambodia]. Paris: Dalloz, 1965.

Hawk, David. "International human rights law and Democratic Kampuchea." *International Journmal of Politics* Vol. 16/3 (Fall 1986), p. 3-38.

Heder, Stephen with Brian D. Tittemore. *Seven Candidates for Prosecution: Accountability for the Crimes of the Khmer Rouge.* Washington, D.C.: War Crimes Research Office, American University, 2001.

Imbert, Jean. *Histoire des Institutions Khmères*. Phnom Penh: Annales de la Faculté de Droit, 1961.

Jennar, Raoul M. *The Cambodian Constitutions 1953-1993*. Bangkok: White Lotus, 1995. Originally published in French: *Les Constitutions du Cambodge, 1953-1993*. Paris: La documentation française, 1994.

Jennar, Raoul Marc. *Cambodge: Une presse sous pression*. Paris: Reporters sans frontières, 1997.

Kao Kim Hourn, and Norbert von Hofmann (eds.). *National Elections: Cambodia's Experiences & Expectations*. Phnom Penh: Cambodian Institute for Cooperation and Peace, 1998.

Laurent, Maurice. *L'armée au Cambodge et dans les pays en voie de développement du Sud-est asiatique* [The army in Cambodia and in the developing countries of Southeast Asia]. Paris: Presses Universitaires de France, 1968.

Lawyers' Committee for Human Rights. *Cambodia: The Justice System and Violations of Human Rights*. New York, Lawyers' Committee, 1992.

Leclère, Adhémard. *Les codes Cambodgiens* [Cambodian laws]. Paris: E. Leroux, 1898, 2 vols.

Leclère, Adhémard. *Recherches sur la legislation Cambodgienne* [Research in Cambodian laws]. Paris: A. Challamel, 1890.

Leclère, Adhémard. *Recherches sur le droit public des Cambodgiens* [Research on Cambodian public laws]. Paris: A.Challamel, 1894.

"Legal and Political Development in Cambodia." Special issue, *Cambodia Report* Vol. 3/1 (1997), p. 1-37. (Published by the Center for Advanced Study, Phnom Penh).

"Loi sur la nationalité, 9 octobre 1996" [Nationality law of 9 October 1996] *Annales de la faculté de droit et des sciences économiques de Phnom Penh*. Phnom Penh: Thevoda, 1997, p. 121-126.

Mehta, Harish C. *Cambodia Silenced: The Press Under Six Regimes*, Bangkok: White Lotus 1997.

Norodom Ranariddh, Prince. *Driot public cambodgien* [Cambodian Public Law]. Perpignan, France: Presses universitaires de Perpignan, 1998.

Ong Thong Hoeung, and Laura Summers. "The statute of the Communist Party of Kampuchea." In *The Party Statutes of the Communist World*, edited by William B. Simons and Stephen White. The Hague: Martinus Nijhoff, 1984. p. 235-259.

Shawcross, William. *The Quality of Mercy: Cambodia, Holocaust and Modern Conscience*. London: Andre Deutsch, 1989.

Sok Siphana, J.D. (ed). *Proceedings. International Conference on Cambodian Legal and Judicial Reform in the Context of Sustainable Development*. Phnom Penh: Council for the Development of Cambodia and the U.N.D.P., 1998.

Soth Polin, and Sim Kimsuy. "Kampuchea." In John A. Lent (ed.). *Newspapers in Asia: Contemporary Trends and Problems.* Hong Kong: Heinemann Asia, 1982.

Smith, Roger M. "Cambodia." *Governments and Politics of Southeast Asia.* Edited by George McT. Kahin. Ithaca, N.Y.: Cornell University Press, Second Edition, 1964. p. 595-679.

Yonekura, Yukiko. *The Emergence of Civil Society in Cambodia: Its Role in the Democratisation Process.* PhD Thesis, University of Sussex, 1999.

Communist Movements

Carney, Timothy. *Communist Party Power in Kampuchea (Cambodia). Documents and Discussion.* Ithaca, N.Y.: Cornell University, 1977.

Chandler, David P. "A revolution in full spate: Communist Party policy in Democratic Kampuchea, December 1976." *International Journal of Politics* Vol. 16/3 (1986), p. 131-49.

Chandler, David P. "Revising the Past in Democratic Kampuchea: When Was the Birthday of the Party?" *Pacific Affairs* Vol. 56/2 (1983), p. 288-300.

Chandler, David. *Voices from S-21: Terror and History in Pol Pot's Secret Prison.* Berkeley, Calif.: University of California Press, 1999.

Goscha, Christopher, and Thomas Engelbert. *Falling Out of Touch: A Study of Vietnamese Communist Policy towards an Emerging Cambodian Communist Movement 1930-1975.* Clayton, Vic.: Monash University, Centre of Southeast Asian Studies, 1995.

Heder, Stephen. *Pol Pot at Bay: People's War and the Breakdown of the 1991 Paris Agreement.* PhD Thesis, School of Oriental & African Studies, University of London, 1999.

Kiernan, Ben. *How Pol Pot Came to Power.* London: Verso, 1985.

Norodom Sihanouk. "Le communisme au Cambodge." *France Asie* Vol. 15, Nos. 144-145 (1958), p. 192-206 & 290-306.

Peschoux, Christophe. *Les nouveaux Khmers Rouges* [The "new" Khmer Rouge]. Paris: L'Harmattan, 1992.

Shinde, B.E. "Outline History of Kampuchean Communism 1930-78." *China Report* [India] Vol. 18/1 (1982), p. 11-47.

Summers, Laura. "The C.P.K.: Secret Vanguard of Pol Pot's Revolution: A Comment on Nuon Chea's Statement" and the text of "Statement of the Communist Party of Kampuchea to the Communist Workers' Party of Denmark, July 1978, by Nuon Chea." *Journal of Communist Studies* Vol. 3/1 (March 1987), p. 5-36.

Other Political and Social Movements

Abdul Gaffar Peang-Meth. "A study of the Khmer People's National Liberation Front and the Coalition Government of Democratic Kampuchea." *Contemporary Southeast Asia* Vol. 12/3 (1990), p. 172-85.

Birsens, Soriya J.M. "Refugié à Samlor Chnangn: Histoire d'un camp" [In refuge at Samlor Chnangn: The history of a camp]. *Etudes* Vol. 365/3 (1986), p. 163-74.

Corfield, Justin J. *A History of the Cambodian Non-Communist Resistance 1975-1983.* Clayton, Vic.: Monash University, 1991.

Dufresne, Jeffrey Robert. *Rebuilding Cambodia: Education, Political Warfare, and the Khmer People's National Liberation Front.* EdD Thesis, University of St. Thomas, St. Paul, Minnesota, 1993.

Etcheson, Craig. "The Khmer way of exile: Lessons from three Indo-Chinese Wars." *Journal of Political Science* Vol. 18 (1990), p. 94-123.

Fields, Rona M. "Life and death on a small island: Vietnamese and Cambodian refugees in Indonesia." *Migration World* Vol. 20/5 (1992), p. 16-20.

Golub, Stephen. *Seeking Shelter: Cambodians in Thailand.* New York: Lawyers Committee for Human Rights, 1986.

Hamel, Bernard. *Résistances en Indochina 1975-80.* Paris: IREP, 1980.

Hamel, Bernard. "Les Refugies Cambodgiens dans la Société Française" [The Cambodian refugees in French society]. *Mondes et Cultures* Vol. 46/3 (1986), p. 541-48.

Kiernan, Ben. "Khmer (Kampuchean)," in James Jupp (ed.). *The Australian People.* North Ryde, N.S.W.: Angus & Robertson 1988, p. 658-59.

Reynell, Josephine. *Political Pawns: Refugees on the Thai-Kampuchean Border.* Oxford: Oxford University Press, 1989.

Robinson, W. Courtland. *Double Vision: A History of Cambodian Refugees in Thailand.* Bangkok: Institute of Asian Studies, Chulalongkorn University, 1996.

Sutter, Valerie O'Connor. *The Indochina Refugee Issue and National Interests.* PhD Thesis, University of Virginia, 1985.

Tarr, Chou Meng. *Peasant Women in Northeastern Thailand: A Study of Class and Gender among the Ethnic Khmer Loeu in Buriram.* PhD Thesis, University of Queensland, St. Lucia, 1986.

Turkoly-Joczik, Robert L. "Cambodia's Khmer Serei movement." *Asian Affairs: An American Review* Vol. 15/1 (1988), p. 48-62.

Welaratna, Usha. *Beyond the Killing Fields: Voices of Nine Cambodian Survivors in America.* Stanford: Stanford University Press, 1993.

Foreign Policy and International Relations

Abdul Gaffar Peang-Meth. *Cambodia and the United Nations: Comparative Foreign Policies under Four Regimes.* PhD Thesis, University of Michigan, 1980.

Bitar, Mona K. "Bombs, plots and allies: Cambodia and the Western Powers, 1958-59." *Intelligence and National Security* Vol. 14/4 (1999), p. 149-80.

Boucher, Jean-Marie. *The Relationship between Cambodia and China 1954-1970.* PhD Thesis, London School of Economics, University of London 1978.

Brown, Frederick Z., and David G. Timberman (eds). *Cambodia and the International Community: The Quest for Peace, Development, and Democracy.* New York: Asia Society, 1998.

Chakraborti, Tridib. *India and Kampuchea.* Calcutta: Minerva, 1985.

Chang, Pao-Min. *Kampuchea between China and Vietnam.* Singapore: Singapore University Press, 1985.

Clymer, Kenton J. "The perils of neutrality: The break in U.S.-Cambodian relations, 1965." *Diplomatic History* Vol. 23/4 (1999), p. 609-31.

Doyle, Michael W. *UN Peacekeeping in Cambodia: UNTAC's Civil Mandate.* Boulder, Colo.: Lynne Rienner for the International Peace Academy, 1995.

Field, Michael. *The Prevailing Wind.* London: Methuen, 1967.

Han Suyin. "Why Cambodia rejected aid." *Eastern Horizon,* Hong Kong (Feb 1964), p. 10-15.

Hazen, Sebhat Merse. *Kampuchea: The Foreign Policy Behavior of External Powers: 1954-1982.* PhD Thesis, University of Southern California, 1983.

Heder, Stephen R. "The Kampuchean-Vietnamese Conflict." *The Third Indochinese Conflict.* Edited by David W.P. Elliott. Boulder, Colo.: Westview, 1981.

Hughes, Caroline Sian. *Human Rights in Cambodia: International Intervention and the National Response.* PhD Thesis, University of Hull, 1998.

Kamm, Henry. *Cambodia: Report from a Stricken Land.* New York: Arcade, 1998.

Kao Kim Hourn (ed.). *Cambodia in ASEAN.* Phnom Penh: Cambodian Institute for Cooperation and Peace, 1995.

Kesavan, K.V. "Japan's policy toward the Kampuchean question." *Asian Survey* Vol. 25/11 (1985), p. 1123-33.

Leifer, Michael. *Cambodia: The Search for Security.* New York: F.A. Praeger, 1967.

MacIntyre, Andrew J. "Interpreting Indonesian foreign policy: The case of Kampuchea, 1979-1986." *Asian Survey* Vol. 27/5 (1987), p. 515-34.

Marsot, Alain-Gérard. "China's aid to Cambodia." *Pacific Affairs* Vol. 42/2 (Summer 1969), p. 189-98.

Pouvatchy, Joseph R. "Cambodian-Vietnamese Relations." *Asian Survey* Vol. 26/4 (1986), p. 440-51.

Pradhan, P.C. *Foreign Policy of Kampuchea.* London: Sangam Books, 1987.

Regaud, Nicolas. *Le Cambodge dans la tourmente. Le troisième conflit Indochinois 1978-1991* [Cambodia in turmoil. The third Indochina conflict, 1978-1991]. Paris: L'Harmattan, 1992.

Sar Desai, D.R. *Indian Foreign Policy in Cambodia, Laos and Vietnam 1947-1964.* Berkeley: University of California Press, 1968.

Sarin Chhak. *Les frontières du Cambodge* [The borders of Cambodia]. Paris: Dalloz, 1966.

Shawcross, William. *Cambodia's New Deal, a Report.* Washington, D.C.: The Carnegie Endowment for International Peace, 1994.

Smith, R.B. "Cambodia in the context of Sino-Vietnamese relations." *Asian Affairs* Vol. 16/3 (1985), p. 273-87.

Smith, Roger M. *Cambodia's Foreign Policy.* Ithaca, N.Y.: Cornell University Press, 1965.

Summers, Laura. "Cambodia: The Prospects for a United Nations-controlled solution." *Asian Review,* Vol. 5 (1991), p. 43-71.

Thayer, Carlyle A. "Cambodia and Regional Stability: ASEAN and Constructive Engagement." Phnom Penh: The CICP Distinguished Lecture Series, No. 14, June 1998.

Theeravit, Khien. "Thai-Kampuchean relations: Problems and prospects." *Asian Survey* Vol. 22/6 (1982), p. 561-76.

Thompson, Robert. *No Exit from Vietnam.* New York: McKay, 1969.

Thu-huong Nguyen-vo. *Khmer-Viet Relations and the Third Indochina Conflict.* Jefferson, N.C.: McFarland & Company, 1992.

United Nations. *The United Nations in Cambodia, 1991-1995.* New York: United Nations Blue Book Series, Department of Public Information, 1995.

Williams, Maslyn. *The Land In Between: The Cambodian Dilemma.* New York: William Morrow, 1970.

Worthing, Peter M. "Strange bedfellows: China and Cambodia since 1949." *American Asian Review* Vol. 18/3 (2000), p. 53-76.

SOCIAL

Anthropology

Bennoun, Phillip; Robert Bennoun and Paula Kelly. *The Peoples from Indo-China.* Richmond, Vic.: Hodja, 1984.

Bit Seanglim. *The Warrior Heritage: A Psychological Perspective of Cambodian Trauma.* El Cerrito, Calif: Bit Seanglim, 1990. Reissued, Phnom Penh.

Boua, Chanthou. "Women in today's Cambodia." *New Left Review* No. 131 (1982), p. 44-61. Available in French translation as "La Femme dans la République Populaire du Kampuchea." *ASEMI* Vol. 13/1-4 (1982), p. 287-314.

Cambodia, Commission des Moeurs et Coutumes. *Ceremonies des douze mois. Fêtes annuelles des cambodgiens.* Phnom Penh: Portail, 1950.

Condominas, Georges. "Les cambodgiens." In *l'Ethnologie de l'Union Française.* Paris: 1953, vol. 2, p. 588-619.

Delvert, Jean. "La vie rurale au Cambodge" [Rural life in Cambodia]. *France-Asie* Vol. 15 (April 1958), p. 94-104.

Delvert, Jean. *Le paysan Cambodgien.* The Hague: Mouton, 1961.

Ebihara, May. "Beyond Suffering: The Recent History of a Cambodian Village." In Borje Ljunggren (ed.). *The Challenge of Reform in Indochina.* Cambridge, Mass.: Harvard University Press, 1993, p. 149-66.

Ebihara, May. "Khmer Village Women in Cambodia: A Happy Balance." In V. Matthiasson (ed.). *Many Sisters: Women in Cross Cultural Perspective.* New York: Free Press, 1974, p. 305-47.

Ebihara, May. "Return to a Khmer Village." *Cultural Survival Quarterly* No. 14 (1990), p. 67-70.

Ebihara, May. *Svay: A Khmer village in Cambodia,* PhD Thesis, Columbia University, 1968. Ann Arbor: University Microfilms, 1971.

Ebihara, May; Judy Ledgerwood and Carol Mortland (eds.). *Cambodian Culture since 1975: Homeland and Exile.* Ithaca, N.Y.: Cornell University Press, 1994.

Eisenbruch, Maurice. "The ritual space of patients and traditional healers in Cambodia." *Bulletin d'École Française d'Extrême-Orient* Vol. 79/2 (1992), p. 283-316.

France-Asie. "Presence du Cambodge" Special issue, November-December 1955.

Hinton, Alexander Laban. "Why did you kill? The Cambodian Genocide and the Dark Side of Face and Honor." *Journal of Asian Studies,* Vol. 57/1 (1998) p. 93-122.

Kalab, Milada. "Monastic Education, Social Mobility and Village Structure in Cambodia." In David Banks (ed.) *Changing Identities in Modern Southeast Asia.* The Hague: Mouton, 1976, p. 155-69.

Kalab, Milada. "Study of a Cambodian Village." *Geographical Journal* Vol. 134 (1968), p. 521-36.

Leclere, Adhemard. *Cambodge: Fêtes civiles et religieuses.* Paris: Imprimerie Nationale, 1916.

Leclere, Adhemard. *Les fêtes locales au Cambodge.* Paris: Leroux, 1914.

Ledgerwood, Judy. *Changing Khmer Conceptions of Gender: Women, Stories, and the Social Order.* PhD Thesis, Cornell University. Ann Arbor: University Microfilms, 1990.

Martel, Gabrielle. *Lovea, village des environs d'Angkor* [Lovea, village in the region of Angkor]. Paris: École Française d'Extrême-Orient, 1975.

Martin, Marie-Alexandrine. *Cambodia: A Shattered Society.* Translated by Mark W. McLeod. Berkeley and Los Angeles, University of California Press, 1994. First published in French: *Le Mal Cambodgien: Histoire d'une société traditionnnelle face à ses leaders politiques, 1946-1967.* Paris: Hachette, 1989.

Monod, Guillaume. *Le Cambodgien.* Paris: Larose, 1931.

Népote, Jacques. *Parenté et organization sociale dans le Cambodge moderne et contemporain.* Geneva: Etudes Orientales & CEDOREK, 1992.

Nou Ker, and Nou Nhieuk. "Kpuon Abah-Bibah ou le livre de mariage des Khmers." *Bulletin de l'École Française d'Extrême-Orient* Vol. 60 (1973), p. 243-328.

Olivier, Georges. *Les populations du Cambodge.* Paris: Librairie de l'Academie de Medecine, 1958.

Olivier, Georges. *Anthropologie des Cambodgiens.* Paris: EFEO, 1968.

Pich Sal. *Le mariage Cambodgien.* Phnom Penh: Université Bouddhique, 1962.

Poethig, Kathryn Aileen. *Ambivalent Moralities: Cambodian Americans and Dual Citizenship in Phnom Penh.* PhD Thesis, University of California, Berkeley. Ann Arbor: University Microfilms, 1997.

Porée Maspero, Evéline. *Ceremonies des douze mois.* Phnom Penh: Institut Bouddhique, 1960.

Porée Maspero, Evéline. *Ceremonies privées des Cambodgiens.* Phnom Penh: Institut Bouddhique, 1958.

Porée Maspero, Evéline. *Les rites agraires des Cambodgiens.* The Hague: Mouton, 1962-1967, 3 vols.

Porée, Guy, and Evéline Maspero. *Ceremonies des Douze mois.* Phnom Penh: Institut Bouddhique, 1950.

Porée, Guy, and Evéline Maspero. *Moeurs et coutumes des Cambodgiens.* Paris: Payot, 1938.

Porée Maspero, Evéline et al. *La vie du paysan Khmer* [Khmer peasant life]. Phnom Penh: Institut Bouddhique, 1969.

Thierry, Solange. "Contribution a une etude de la société Cambodgienne." *l'Ethnologie* (1964-65), p. 50-71.

Thierry, Solange. *Les Khmers* [The Khmers]. Paris: Seuil, 1964.

Utting Peter (ed.). *Between Hope and Insecurity: The Social Consequences of the Cambodian Peace Process.* Geneva: UNRISD, 1994.

Zimmerman, Cathy with the assistance of Sar Samen, Men Savorn, and Brad Adams. *Plates in a Basket Will Rattle: Domestic Violence in Cambodia.* Phnom Penh: Asia Foundation, 1994.

Royal Family

Corfield, Justin J. *The Royal Family of Cambodia.* Melbourne: Khmer Language & Culture Centre, 1993.

Dumarcay, Jacques. *The Palaces of South-East Asia.* Singapore: Oxford University Press, 1991.

Fuchs, Paul. *Fêtes et ceremonies royales au Cambodge d'hier* [Festivals and royal ceremonies in olden Cambodia]. Paris: l'Harmattan, 1991.

Jeldres, Julio, and Somkid Chaijitvanij. *The Royal Palaces of Phnom Penh and Cambodia Royal Life.* Bangkok: Post Books 1999.

Leclere, Adhémard. "La Cour d'un Roi du Cambodge" [The Court of the King of Cambodia]. *Bulletin de la Société d'Ethnographie de Paris* Vol. 1 (Oct 1913), p. 41-76.

Népote, Jacques. *Le Palais du roi Norodom I (1860-1973).* PhD Thesis, Université de Paris X-Nanterre, 1973.

Népote, Jacques, and Prince Ravivadhana Monipong. *État Present de la Maison Royale du Cambodge.* Paris: Institut de la Maison Royale du Cambodge, 1994.

Osborne, Milton E. "King-making in Cambodia: From Sisowath to Sihanouk." *Journal of Southeast Asian Studies* Vol. 4/2 (1973), p. 169-85.

www.norodomsihanouk.org

Cham and Muslim Communities

La Communauté Islamique au Kampuchéa [The Islamic Community of Kampuchea]. Phnom Penh: United Front for the Construction and Defense of the Fatherland of Kampuchea, 1983.

Kiernan, Ben. "Kampuchean Muslims: An uncertain future." *Journal* (Institute of Muslim Minority Affairs) Vol. 10/1 (1989), p. 28-40.

Kiernan, Ben. "Orphans of genocide: The Cham Muslims of Kampuchea under Pol Pot." *Bulletin of Concerned Asian Scholars* Vol. 20/4 (1988), p. 2-33; "Comments on Cham population figures" by Michael Vickery, *Bulletin of Concerned Asian Scholars* Vol. 22/1 (1989), p. 31-33; "The genocide in Cambodia 1975-79" by Ben Kiernan, *Bulletin of Concerned Asian Scholars* Vol. 22/2 (1990), p. 35-40.

Manguin, Pierre-Yves. "The introduction of Islam into Champa." *Journal of the Malaysian Branch of the Royal Asiatic Society* Vol. 58/1 (1985), p. 1-28.

Marrison, Geoffrey E. "The Chams and their literature." *Journal of the Malaysian Branch of the Royal Asiatic Society* Vol. 58/2 (1985), p. 45-70.

Po Dharma. "Notes sur les Cham du Cambodge" [Notes on the Chams of Cambodia]. *Seksa khmer* [Khmer Studies]. Nos. 3-4 (1981), p. 161-84.

Starner, Frances. "The Chams: Muslims the world forgot." *Asiaweek* (21 Nov 1980), p. 24-25.

Vu Can. "The community of surviving Muslims." *Vietnam Courier* No. 4 (1982).

Chinese

Clammer, John R. "French studies on the Chinese in Indochina: A bibliographical survey." *Journal of Southeast Asian Studies* Vol. 12/1 (March 1981), p. 15-25.

Frings, K. Viviane. "'The turbulent but commercially viable Chinese': A comparison of French and British Colonial policies towards the Chinese in Southeast Asia." *Itinerario* Vol. 19/1 (1995), p. 48-68.

Kiernan, Ben. "Kampuchea's ethnic Chinese under Pol Pot: A case study of systematic social discrimination." *Journal of Contemporary Asia* Vol. 16/1 (1986), p. 18-29.

Népote, Jacques. "Legitimacy, ethnicity and nationality in modern Cambodia: The Chinese minority and the cultural breaking up of the Cambodian society in the XIXe and XXe centuries." In *A Rothko Chapel Colloquium*, Houston, Texas, 1983.

Willmott, William E. *The Chinese in Cambodia.* Vancouver: University of British Columbia Press, 1967.

Willmott, William E. "The Chinese in Kampuchea." *Journal of Southeast Asian Studies* Vol. 12/1 (1981), p. 38-45.

Willmott, William E. "History and sociology of the Chinese in Cambodia prior to the French Protectorate." *Journal of Southeast Asian History* Vol. 7/1 (March 1966), p. 15-38.

Wilmott, William E. *The Political Structure of the Chinese Community in Cambodia.* London: Athlone Press, 1970.

Khmer Krom

Thach Bunroeun. *The Kampuchea-Krom Geopolitical Issue.* New York: The National Association of Khmer Kampuchea-Krom, 1986.

Khmer Loeu

Baradat, R. "Les Samre ou Pear, population primitive de l'ouest du Cambodge" [The Samre or Pear, a primitive people in the west of Cambodia]. *Bulletin de l'École Française d'Extrême-Orient* (1941), p. 1-150.

LeBar, Frank M.; Gerald C. Hickey, and John K. Musgrave (eds.). *Ethnic Groups of Mainland Southeast Asia.* New Haven, Conn.: Human Relations Area Files Press, 1964.

Vietnamese

Dassé, Martial. "Les Vietnamiens au Cambodge 1978-1988" [The Vietnamese in Cambodia, 1978-88]. *Etudes Polémologiques* No. 50 (1989), p. 173-82.

Forest, Alain. "Cambodgiens et Vietnamiens au Cambodge pendant le protectorat Français" [Cambodians and Vietnamese in Cambodia during the French Protectorate]. *Pluriel* No. 4 (1975), p. 3-23.

Khy Phanra. *La Communaute Vietnamienne au Cambodge a l'époque du Protectorat Française* [The Vietnamese Community in Cambodia during the French Protectorate]. Paris: Université de Paris III, 1974, 2 vols.

"Life is difficult for ethnic Vietnamese minority in Cambodia." *New York Times* (14 Nov 1971).

Pouvatchy, J. "Cambodian-Vietnamese relations." *Asian Survey* Vol. 26 (1981), p. 440-51.

Tarr, Chou Meng. "The Vietnamese minority in Cambodia." *Race & Class* Vol. 34/2 (1992), p. 33-47.

Education

Ayres, David M. *Anatomy of a Crisis: Education, Development and the State in Cambodia 1953-1998.* Honolulu: University of Hawaii Press 2000.

Bezançon, Pascale. "Louis Manipoud: Un reformateur colonial meconnu" [Louis Manipoud: a little-known colonial reformer]. *Revue Française d'Histoire d'Outre-Mer* Vol. 82/4 (1995), p. 455-87.

Clayton, Thomas. *Education and the politics of language: Hegemony and Pragmatism in Cambodia, 1979-1980.* Hong Kong: The University of Hong Kong Comparative Education Research Center, 2000.

Delvert, Jean. "L'oeuvre Française d'enseignement au Cambodge" [French work on education in Cambodia]. *France Asie* Vol. 115 (1956), p. 309-20.

Gautier, Victor. "The Royal Technical University." *Kambuja* No. 13 (15 April 1966), p. 98-111.

Ho Tong Lip. "The Royal University of Agricultural Sciences." *Kambuja* No. 22 (15 Jan 1966), p. 34-40.

Jordens, Justin. *A 1991 State of Cambodia Political Education Text*. Clayton, Vic.: Monash University Centre of Southeast Asian Studies, 1991.

"The new quarters of the Royal Military Academy inaugurated by Samdech." *Kambuja* No. 33 (15 Dec 1967), p. 126-27.

Parry, R.F. "The Pagoda Schools of Cambodia." *Oversea Education* Vol. 10/2 (Jan 1939), p. 57-67.

Phung Ton. "The national education under the Old Regime." *New Cambodge* No. 2 (June 1970), p. 38-40.

Phuong Ton, and Claude Szawarski. "The Royal University, Doyen of Cambodian Universities." *Kambuja* No. 10 (15 Jan 1966), p. 76-85.

Pring Key. "The University of Fine Arts." *New Cambodge* (Nov 1971), p. 34-53.

"The Royal Military Academy." *Kambuja* No. 33 (15 Dec 1967), p. 128-31.

"The Royal University of Kampong Cham." *Kambuja* No. 23 (15 Feb 1966), p. 42-52.

Sum Chum. "L'Université Populaire." *Kambuja* No. 16 (15 July 1966), p. 82-86.

"The Takeo-Kampot Royal University." *Kambuja* No. 43 (15 Oct 1968), p. 92-93.

United States. Department of Health, Education and Welfare. *Cambodian Education System 1960-1975*. Washington D.C.: U.S. Department of Health Education and Welfare, Office of Education, Refugee Task Force 1978.

Religion

Ang Choulean. *Les êtres surnaturels dans la religion populaire Khmère* [Supernatural beings in popular Khmer beliefs]. Paris: Editions CEDORECK, 1986.

Bizot, François. *Le don de soi-même. Recherches sur le Bouddhisme Khmer* [The gift of one's self. Research on Khmer Buddhism]. Paris: École Française d'Extrême-Orient, 1981.

Bizot, François. *Le figuier à cinq branches. Recherches sur le Bouddhisme Khmer* [The five-branched fig tree. Research on Khmer Buddhism]. Paris: École Française d'Extrême-Orient, 1976.

Cambodia, Ministry of Information. *Le Bouddhisme au Cambodge* [Buddhism in Cambodia]. Phnom Penh: Royal Government Press, 1962.

Ghosananda, Bhikkhu. *Step by Step*. Berkeley, Calif.: Parallax, 1992.

Khmer Buddhist Association, Rithisen. *Buddhism and the Future of Cambodia*. Rithisen: Khmer Buddhist Research Center, 1986.

Khy Phanara. "Les Origines du Caodaisme au Cambodge (1926-1940)" [The Origin of Caodaism in Cambodia 1926-1940]. *Mondes Asiatiques* Vol. 3 (Autumn 1975), p. 315-48.

Leclère, Adhémard. *Le Bouddhisme au Cambodge* [Buddhism in Cambodia]. Paris: Leroux, 1899.

Martini, F. "Organization du clergé Bouddhique au Cambodge" [The organization of the Buddhist clergy in Cambodia]. *France-Asie* (Nov-Dec 1955), p. 416-24.

San Sarin. "The Monastic Robes of our Buddhist Monks." *New Cambodge* No. 9 (Jan 1971), p. 50-73.

Yang Sam. *Khmer Buddhism and Politics from 1954 to 1984,* Newington, Conn.: Khmer Studies Institute, 1987.

Christianity

Buddhism and the Development of Khmer Society, Proceedings of the seminar held in Phnom Penh, 21-23 November 1994. Phnom Penh: Anlongvil, 1995.

Burke, Todd, and DeAnn. *Anointed for Burial: Cambodia's Like a Mighty Wind.* Plainfield, N.J.: Logos International, 1977.

Oats, William N. *I Could Cry for These People: An Australian Quaker Response to the Plight of the People of Cambodia.* North Hobart, Tas.: Quaker Service Australia, 1994.

Penfold, Helen. *Remember Cambodia.* Sevenoaks, Kent: O.M.F. Books, 1990.

Pianet, Jean. *Histoire de la mission du Cambodge* [History of the mission in Cambodia]. Hong Kong: n.p., 1929.

Ponchaud, François. *La cathedrale dans la riziere:450 ans d'histoire de l'Eglise au Cambodge* [The Cathedral in the ricefield: 450 years of church history in Cambodia]. Paris: Le Sarment Fayard, 1990.

Smith, Mrs. Gordon H. *Gongs in the Night: Reaching the Tribes of French Indo-China.* Grand Rapids, Michigan: Zondervan Publ., 1943.

Tuck, Patrick J.N. *French Catholic Missionaries and the Politics of Imperialism in Vietnam 1857-1914.* Liverpool: Liverpool University Press, 1987.

Linguistics

Antelme, Michel. A Study of Naming Systems from Ancient to Modern Cambodia. PhD Thesis, University of London, 2001.

Ehrman, Madeline. *Contemporary Cambodian: Grammatical Sketch.* Washington, D.C.: Foreign Service Institute, 1972.

Fabricius, Pierre. "Renaissance de la Langue Cambodgienne: Étude du language administratif." *Cambodge d'aujourd'hui*, No. 6 (Juin 1959) p. 19-25.

Huffman, Franklin E. *An Outline of Cambodian grammar.* PhD Thesis, Cornell University. Ann Arbor: University Microfilms, 1967.

Huffman, Franklin E. *Bibliography and Index of Mainland Southeast Asian Languages and Linguistics.* New Haven, Conn.: Yale University Press, 1986.

Jacob, Judith. *Cambodian Linguistics, Literature and History,* collected articles edited by David A. Smyth. London: School of Oriental & African Studies, University of London, 1993.

Jenner, Philip N., and Saveros Pou. *A Lexicon of Khmer Morphology.* Honolulu: University of Hawaii Press, 1982.

Pou, Saveros. "Lexicographie vieux Khmer" [Old Khmer lexicography]. *Seksa khmer* [Khmer Studies]. No. 7 (1984), p. 67-178.

Literature

Bernard Thierry, Solange. *Le Cambodge des contes* [Cambodia through folk tales]. Paris: L'Harmattan, 1986.

Carrison, Muriel Paskin with assistance from the Venerable Kong Chhean, translator. *Cambodian Folk-tales from the Gatiloke.* Rutland, Vermont: Charles Tuttle, 1987.

Chandler, David P. (transl.). *Favourite Stories from Cambodia.* Singapore: Heinemann, 1978.

Chandler, David P. (transl.). *The friends Who Tried to Empty the Sea: Eleven Cambodian Folk-Tales.* Clayton, Vic.: Monash University Centre of Southeast Asian Studies, 1976.

Chandler, David P. "Normative poems (*chhbab*) and pre-colonial Cambodian society." *Journal of Southeast Asian Studies* Vol. 15/2 (Sept 1984), p. 271-79.

Guesdon, J. "La litterature khmere et le Bouddhisme" [Khmer literature and Buddhism]. *Anthropos* Vol. 1 (1906), p. 91-109 & 228-295.

Jacob, Judith. *Reamker: The Cambodian Version of the Ramayana.* London: The Royal Asiatic Society 1986.

Keng Vannsak. "Quelques aspects de la littérature Khmère" [Aspects of Khmer literature]. *Annales de la Faculté des lettres et des sciences humaines de l'université royale,* 1967. p. 39-54.

Khing Hoc Dy. *Contribution à l'histoire de la littérature Khmère;* Vol. 1: *l'époque classique.* Paris: L'Harmattan, 1990; Vol. 2: *Ecrivains et expressions litteraires du Cambodge au XXeme siècle.* Paris: L'Harmattan, 1993. [A contribution to the history of Khmer literature, Vol. 1: The classical age; Vol. 2: Writers and literary expression in Cambodia in the 20th century]

Leclère, Adhémard. *Cambodge: Contes et legends* [Cambodia: tales and legends]. Paris: Bouillion, 1895.

Ledgerwood, Judith. *Changing Khmer Conceptions of Gender: Women, Stories and the Social Order.* PhD Thesis, Cornell University. Ann Arbor: University Microfilms, 1989.

Ma Lai Khem. "Khmer literature." *New Cambodge* No. 2 (June 1970), p. 68-70.

Milne, A.R. (transl.). *Mr. Basket Knife and other Khmer Folk-Tales.* London: George Allen and Unwin, 1972.

Népote, Jacques, and Khing Hoc Dy. "Literature and Society in Modern Cambodia." In Tham Seong Chee (ed.). *Essays on Literature and Society in Southeast Asia.* Singapore: Singapore University Press, 1981, p. 56-81.

Pou, Saveros. *Etudes sur le Ramakerti (XVIe-XVIIe siècles)* [Studies on the Ramayana (16th-17th centuries)]. Paris: EFEO, 1977.

Rim Kin. *Sophat ou les surprises du destin* [Sophat, or destiny's surprises]. Translated by Gérard Groussin. Paris: L'Harmattan, 1994.

Saddhatissa, H. "Pali Literature in Cambodia." *Journal of the Pali Text Society* (1981), p. 178-97.

Soth Polin. *L'anarchiste.* Paris: La Table Ronde, 1980.

Thompson, Ashley. "Oh Cambodia! Poems from the border." *New Literary History* Vol. 24/3 (Summer 1993), p. 519-44.

Vandy Kaonn. *Une reflexion sur la litterature Khmère* [A reflection on Khmer literature]. Phnom Penh: Institute of Sociology, 1981.

Arts, Music and Dance

Bocquet, Mario. *Les danseuses d'Angkor* [The dancers of Angkor]. Neuilly: Mario Bouquet, 1975.

Brandon, James. *Theatre in Southeast Asia,* Cambridge, Mass: Harvard University Press, 1967.

Boisselier, Jean. *Trends in Khmer Art.* Edited by Natasha Eilenberg and Melvin Elliott. Ithaca: Cornell University Southeast Asia Program Studies on Southeast Asia No. 6, 1989. Originally published in French, *Tendances de l'art Khmèr.* Paris: Publications du Musée Guimet/Presses Universitaires de France, 1956.

Cravath, Paul. *Earth in Flower: An Historical and Descriptive Study of the Classical Dance Drama in Cambodia.* PhD Thesis, University of Hawaii. Ann Arbor: University Microfilms, 1985.

Cuisinier, Jeanne. "The gestures in the Cambodian ballet: Their traditional and symbolic significance." *Indian Art and Letters* Vol. 1/2 (1927), p. 92-103.

Danielou, A. *La musique du Cambodge et du Laos* [The music of Cambodia and Laos]. Pondicheri: Institut français, 1957.

Ghosh, Amitav. "Dancing in Cambodia." *Granta* No. 44 (1993), p. 127-69.

Giteau, Madeleine. *Khmer Sculpture and the Angkor Civilization.* Diana Imber (transl.). London: Thames and Hudson, 1965.

Lafreniere, Bree. *Music through the Dark: A Tale of Survival in Cambodia.* Honolulu: University of Hawaii Press 2000.

Lee, Sherman E. *Ancient Cambodian Sculpture.* New York: The Asia Society Inc. 1969.

Marchal, Sappho. *Danses Cambodgiennes* [Cambodian Dances]. Paris: Macon, 1930.

Parmentier, Henri. *L'art Khmer primtif* [Primitive Khmer art]. Paris: EFEO, 1927; *L'art Khmer classique* [Classical Khmer art]. Paris: EFEO, 1939.

Pech Tum Kravel. *Sbek Thom: Khmer Shadow Theater.* Bilingual Khmer/ English. Ithaca, N.Y.: Cornell University Southeast Asia Program & UNESCO, 1995.

Phim Toni Samantha, and Ashley Thompson. *Dance in Cambodia.* Singapore: Oxford, 1999.

Prasidh Silpabanleng. "Thai music at the Court of Cambodia: A personal souvenir of Luang Pradit Phairoh's visit in 1930." *Journal of the Siam Society* Vol. 58/1 (1970), p. 121-24.

Sam Sam-ang. *Traditional Music of Cambodia.* Middletown, Conn.: Center for the Study of Khmer Culture, 1987.

Shapiro, Toni. *Dance and the Spirit of Cambodia.* PhD Thesis, Cornell University. Ann Arbor: University Microfilms, 1994.

Stock, Diana (ed.). *Khmer Ceramics 9th-14th Century.* Singapore: Southeast Asian Ceramic Society, 1981. Reprinted, Bangkok: White Lotus, 1981.

UNESCO-Phnom Penh. *Traditional Musical Instruments of Cambodia.* Phnom Penh: UNESCO, 1994.

Sports

Becker, Henri, and François Do. "The awakening of Khmer football." *Kambuja* No. 33 (15 Dec 1967), p. 164-65.

"Sports in Cambodia – Rapid Progress under direction of Head of State Prince Sihanouk." *Le Sangkum* No. 25 (1967) p. 100-102.

About the authors

Justin Corfield teaches History and International Studies at Geelong Grammar School, Australia.

Laura Summers teaches comparative politics and international relations in the Department of Politics and International Studies, University of Hull, England.